MERSEYSIDE

STREET ATLAS

THE ESSENTIAL CITY STREETFINDER

ISBN 09 202 2707

The maps in this Atlas are based upon the Ordnance Survey Maps with the sanction of the Controller of H.M. Stationery Office, with additions obtained from Local Authorities. The Ordnance Survey is not responsible for the accuracy of the National Grid on this Production.

The representation on these maps of a Road, Track or Footpath is no evidence of the existence of a right of way.

The contents of this publication are believed correct at the time of printing. Nevertheless the Publishers can accept no responsibility for errors or omissions or for changes in the details given.

GEOGRAPHIA

Geographia Ltd., 63 Fleet Street, London EC4Y 1PE
Telephone 01-353 2701/2

CONTENTS

Local Information Guide v

Local Government v

Hospitals v
Liverpool Health Authority v
St. Helens Health Authority vi
Southport and Formby Health Authority vi
South Sefton Health Authority vi
Wirral Health Authority vii
Special Psychiatric Hospitals vii

Secondary Education vii
Liverpool City Council vii
Metropolitan Borough of Knowsley viii
Metropolitan Borough of St. Helens ix
Metropolitan Borough of Sefton ix
Metropolitan Borough of Wirral x

Further Education xi

Travel Information xii
General xii
Air xii
Bus xii
Ferry xii
Rail xiii

Tourism xv
Tourist Information Centres xv
Art Galleries and Museums xv
Other Places of Interest xv

Leisure and Entertainment xvi
Theatres and Music Halls xvi
Cinemas xvi
Sports Centres and Swimming Pools xvii
Municipal Golf Courses xviii
Private Golf Clubs xviii
Football and Rugby Grounds xix
Race Courses xix

Key to Map Section xx

Map Section 2

Index 154

Each entry in this guide has a reference to enable the user to locate it in the map section. If, through lack of space, an entry does not appear on the map then the reference will direct the user to the street on which the entry is located.

Abbreviations used in this guide:

Cath. — Cathedral	Hosp. — Hospital	Sec. — Secondary
Coll. — College	Infirm. — Infirmary	Swim. — Swimming
Comp. — Comprehensive		

LOCAL GOVERNMENT

Merseyside Metropolitan County Council
P.O. Box 95
Metropolitan House
Old Hall Street
LIVERPOOL
Tel: 051-227-5234
p93 O32

Knowsley Metropolitan Borough Council
P.O. Box 17
Municipal Buildings
Hall Lane
KIRKBY
Tel: 051-548-6555
p43 V24

Liverpool Metropolitan City Council
Municipal Buildings
Dale Street
LIVERPOOL
Tel: 051-227-3911
p94 P32

St. Helens Metropolitan Borough Council
Town Hall
Corporation Street
ST. HELENS
Tel: 0744 24061
p63 GG27

Sefton Metropolitan Borough Council
Town Hall
Trinity Road
BOOTLE
Tel: 051-922-4040
p73 P28

Wirral Metropolitan Borough Council
Town Hall
Brighton Street
WALLASEY
Tel: 051-638-7070
p93 N31

HOSPITALS

LIVERPOOL HEALTH AUTHORITY

Alder Hey Children's Hospital
Eaton Road
Liverpool
Tel: 051-228-4811
p97 V31

Broad Green Hospital
Thomas Drive
Tel: 051-228-4878
p97 V32

Liverpool Dental Hosp.
Pembroke Place
Tel: 051-709-0141
p94 Q32

Liverpool Maternity Hospital
Oxford Street
Tel: 051-708-7282
p94 Q32

Mill Road Maternity Hospital
Mill Road
Tel: 051-263-2656
p95 R31

Mossley Hill Hospital
Park Avenue
Tel: 051-724-2335
p114 T35

Newsham General Hosp.
Belmont Road
Tel: 051-263-7381
p74 S30

Olive Mount Hospital
Old Mill Lane
Tel: 051-722-2261
p96 U33

Park Hospital
Orphan Drive
Tel: 051-263-9641
p74 S30

Princes Park Hospital
96 Upper Parliament Street
Tel: 051-709-7361
p94 Q33

Rathbone Hospital
Mill Lane
Tel: 051-722-6163
p96 U32

Royal Liverpool Children's Hospital
Telegraph Road (Heswall)
Tel: 051-342-6221
p134 G41

Royal Liverpool Children's Hospital
Myrtle Street
Tel: 051-709-0821
p94 Q33

Royal Liverpool Hospital
Prescot Street
Tel: 051-709-0141
p94 Q32

St. Paul's Eye Hospital
Old Hall Street
Tel: 051-236-6766
p93 O32

Sefton General Hospital
Smithdown Road
Tel: 051-733-4020
p113 S34

Sir Alfred Jones Memorial Hospital
Church Road
Tel: 051-427-5111
p131 V38

Women's Hospital
Catherine Street
Tel: 051-709-5461
p94 Q33

Windsor Day Hospital
40 Upper Parliament Street
Tel: 051-709-9061
p94 Q33

ST. HELENS & KNOWSLEY HEALTH AUTHORITY

Eccleston Hall Hospital
Holme Road
St. Helens
Tel: 0744-26232
p62 DD27

Newton Community Hospital
Bradlegh Road
Newton Le Willows
Tel: 092-52-22731
p84 NN28

Rainhill Hospital
Rainhill
Prescot
Tel: 051-426-6511
p80 EE30

St. Helens Hospital
Marshalls Cross Road
St. Helens
Tel: 0744-26633
p82 HH28

Whiston Hospital
Warrington Road
Whiston
Tel: 051-426-1600
p100 CC31

SOUTHPORT AND FORMBY HEALTH AUTHORITY

Christiana Hartley Maternity Hospital
Curzon Road
Southport
Tel: 0704-42901
p6 P6

Hesketh Park Hospital
Albert Road
Southport
Tel: 0704-34411
p6 P4

Southport General Infirm.
Scarisbrick New Road
Southport
Tel: 0704 42901
p6 P6

Southport Promenade Hospital
Leicester Street
Southport
Tel: 0704 34411
p5 O5

Sunnyside Hospital
Knowsley Road
Southport
Tel: 0704-34411
p6 P4

SOUTH SEFTON HEALTH AUTHORITY

Fazakerly Hospital
Lower Lane
Liverpool
Tel: 051-525-5980
p56 S25

Walton Hospital
Rice Lane
Liverpool
Tel: 051-525-3611
p55 Q27

Waterloo Hospital
Haigh Road
Liverpool
Tel: 051-928-5321
p39 N24

Arrowe Park Hospital
Arrowe Park Road
Upton
Tel: 051-678-5111
108 H36

Ashton House
76 Village Road
Oxton
Tel: 051-652-3143
110 L35

Clatterbridge Hospital
Bebington
Wirral
Tel: 051-334-4000
141 M40

Hoylake Cottage Hospital
Birkenhead Road
Hoylake
Tel: 051-632-3381
p88 C33

Priory Day Hospital
Upton Road
Bidston
Tel: 051-652-1486
p109 J34

St. Catherine's Hospital
Church Road
Birkenhead
Tel: 051-652-2281
p110 M35

Victoria Central Hospital
Mill Lane
Wallasey
Tel: 051-638-7000
p92 L31

SPECIAL PSYCHIATRIC HOSPITALS

Moss Side and Park Lane
Maghull
29 U20

SECONDARY EDUCATION

LIVERPOOL CITY COUNCIL

Aigburth Vale Comp.
Aigburth Vale
113 S36

Alsop Comp.
Queens Drive
74 R28

Anfield Comp.
Breckside Park
74 S30

Archbishop Beck (RC)
Cedar Road
56 R26

Archbishop Blanch
Sefton Park Road
113 R34

Breckfield Comp.
Hamilton Road
73 Q30

Broughton Hall (RC)
Yewtree Lane
76 W30

Campion (RC)
Prince Edwin Street
94 Q31

Cardinal Heenan (RC)
Honeysgreen Lane
p76 W30

Carr Lane Comp.
Carr Lane
p75 U28

Childwall Valley Comp.
Childwall Valley Road
p97 W33

Collegiate Comp.
Shaw Street
p94 Q31

De La Salle (RC) Comp.
Carr Lane East
p76 V28

Fazakerley Comp.
Sherwoods Lane
p57 T25

Gateacre Comp.
Grange Lane
p116 X34

Highfield Comp.
Queens Drive
p97 V32

Hillfoot Hey Comp.
School Lane
p132 X37

Holly Lodge Comp.
Queens Drive
p75 U30

Holt Comp.
Queens Drive
p97 V33

**Liverpool Institute
High (Boys)**
Mount Street
p94 Q33

**Liverpool Institute
High (Girls)**
p94 Q33

Netherley Comp.
Childwall Valley Road
p116 Y34

New Heys Comp.
Heath Road
p115 V36

Notre Dame (RC)
Everton Valley
p73 Q29

viii

Nugent (RC)
Overbury Street
p95 R33

Our Lady of Fatima (RC)
Margaret Street
p95 R31

Paddington Comp.
Mount Vernon Road
p95 R32

Pope John Paul (RC)
Alderwood Avenue
p133 Z39

Quarry Bank Comp.
Harthill Road
p115 V35

Queen Mary Comp.
Long Lane
p56 S27

St. Brigid's (RC)
Silvester Street
p73 P30

St. Francis Xavier (RC)
Beaconsfield Road
p115 W35

St. Hilda's High
Croxteth Drive
p113 S34

St. John Almond (RC)
Horrocks Avenue
p131 V38

St. John Bosco (RC)
Stonebridge Lane
p57 U27

St. Julies (RC)
Speke Road
p116 X36

St. Margarets' High
Aigburth Road
p114 T36

St. Marys (RC)
Ullet Road
p114 T34

Shorefields Comp.
Dingle Vale
p113 R35

Speke Comp.
Central Avenue
p132 Y39

Stanley Park Comp.
Priory Road
p74 R29

The Blue Coat
Church Road
p114 U34

The King David High
Childwall Road
p97 V33

West Derby Comp.
Quarry Road
p75 U30

Yew Tree Comp.
Fincham Road
p77 X30

METROPOLITAN BOROUGH OF KNOWSLEY

Brookfield Comp.
Bracknell Avenue
Kirkby
p58 V25

Cantril Comp.
Little Moss Hey
Stockbridge Village
p77 Y29

**Halewood Comp.
(Grange Wing)**
The Avenue
Halewood
p133 Z37

Hey Comp.
Seel road
Huyton
p99 Z32

Higher Side Comp.
Cumber lane
Whiston
p100 CC31

Page Moss Comp.
Weston Avenue
Huyton
p98 X31

Parkway Comp.
Stockbridge Lane
Huyton
p77 Y29

Prescot Comp.
Knowsley Park Lane
Prescot
p79 BB29

Roby Comp.
Rupert Road
Huyton
p98 Y31

Ruffwood Comp.
Roughwood Drive
Kirkby
p43 W23

**St. Augustine of
Canterbury (RC) Comp.**
Longview Drive
Huyton
p99 AA31

**St. Columba's (RC)
Comp.**
Knowsley Lane
Huyton
p78 Z30

St. Dominics (RC) Comp.
Lordens Road
Huyton
p77 X30

**St. Edmund Arrowsmith
(RC) Comp.**
Scotchbarn Lane
Whiston
p74 CC30

St. Gregory's (RC) Comp.
Bewley Drive
Kirkby
p43 W24

St. Kevin's (RC) Comp.
Roughwood Drive
Kirkby
p43 W23

St. Paul's (RC) Comp.
Wood Road
Halewood
p133 Z37

The Gonzaga (RC) Comp.
Wellcroft Road
Huyton
p77 Z31

METROPOLITAN BOROUGH OF ST. HELENS

Campion (RC) High
Stafford Road
St. Helens
p80 EE28

Central High
North Road
St. Helens
p63 GG27

Cowley High
Hard Lane
St. Helens
p62 EE26

Grange Park High
Broadway
p80 EE29

Haydock High
Clipsley Lane
Haydock
p65 LL26

Mount Carmel (RC) High
Prescot Road
St. Helens
p80 DD28

Notre Dame (RC) High
Mill Brow
Eccleston
p62 EE27

Parr High
Fleet Lane
St. Helens
p82 JJ28

Rainford High
Higher Lane
Rainford
p34 DD21

Rainhill High
Portico Lane
Prescot
p80 DD30

Rainhill High
Warrington Road
Rainhill
p102 FF32

Rivington High
Rivington Road
St. Helens
p62 EE27

St. Aelred's (RC) High
Birley Street
Newton-le-Willows
p67 OO27

St. Alban's (RC) High
Washway Lane
St. Helens
p63 GG26

St. Anselm's (RC) High
Boardmans Lane
St. Helens
p64 JJ26

St. Cuthbert's (RC) High
Berrys Lane
St. Helens
p82 JJ28

Selwyn Jones High
Ashton Road
Newton-le-Willows
p67 OO26

Sutton High
Elton Head Road
St. Helens
p81 GG30

West Park (RC) High
Alder Hey Road
Eccleston
p62 EE26

METROPOLITAN BOROUGH OF SEFTON

Ainsdale High
Sandringham Road
Southport
p12 M10

Birkdale High
Windy Harbour Road
Southport
p9 N9

Chesterfield High
Chesterfield Road
Crosby
p39 O23

Chesterfield High
(Annexe)
Haigh Road
Crosby
p39 N24

Christ the King (RC) High
Stamford Road
Southport
p9 O8

Countess of Derby High
Browns Lane
Litherland
p41 R23

Deyes High
Deyes Lane
Maghull
p28 S20

Formby High
Freshfield Road
Formby
p16 K15

Greenbank High
Hastings Road
Southport
p9 N8

Hillside High
Breeze Hill
Bootle
p55 Q27

Hillside High
Quarry Road
Bootle
p55 Q27

Holy Family (RC) High
Virgin's Lane
Thornton
p39 O22

King George V College
Scarisbrick New Road
Southport
p10 Q7

Litherland High
Sterrix Lane
Litherland
p40 P24

Maghull High
(Ormonde Wing)
Ormonde Drive
Maghull
p28 S21

x

Maghull High (Old Hall Wing)
Old Hall Road
Maghull
p28 S21

Manor High
Manor Road
Liverpool
p38 M22

Maricourt (RC) High
Hall Lane
Maghull
p28 S21

Meols Cop High
Meols Cop Road
Southport
p6 Q6

Range High
Stapleton Road
Formby
p19 J17

Sacred Heart (RC) High
Liverpool Road
Crosby
p39 N23

St. Ambrose Barlow (RC) High
Copy Lane
Litherland
p40 P23

St. Ambrose Barlow (RC) High (Annexe)
St. Nicholas Drive
p40 P23

St. Augustine's (RC) High
King Avenue
Bootle
p55 Q26

St. George of England (RC) High
Fernhill Road
Bootle
p55 P26

St. Wilfrid's (RC) High
Orrell Road
Litherland
p55 P25

Salesian (RC) High
Netherton Way
Litherland
p55 Q25

Stanley High
Fleetwood Road
Southport
p2 Q3

Warwick Bolam High
The Marian Way
Litherland
p40 Q23

Warwick Bolam High
Glovers Lane
Litherland
p40 Q23

METROPOLITAN BOROUGH OF WIRRAL

Bebington Sec. (Boys)
New Chester Road
New Ferry
p127 O38

Bebington Sec. (Girls)
Higher Bebington Road
Bebington
p127 N38

Birkenhead Institute High (Boys)
Tollemache Road
Birkenhead
p91 K33

Bishop Challoner (RC) High
Park Road West
Birkenhead
p91 K33

Bishop Challoner (Annexe)
Park Road South
Birkenhead
p110 L34

Bromborough Secondary
Acre Lane
Bromborough
p143 P41

Calday Grange Grammar (Boys)
Grammar School Lane
West Kirby
p106 C36

Eastham Secondary
Plymyard Avenue
Eastham
p148 P43

Hilbre Secondary
Frankby Road
West Kirby
p106 C35

Marian (RC) High
New Hey Road
Upton
p108 H35

Mosslands
Mosslands Drive
Wallasey
p91 K31

Oldershaw
Valkyrie Road
Wallasey
p71 L30

Oldershaw (Annexe)
Ormond Street
Wallasey
p71 L30

Oxley
Oxley Avenue
Leasowe
p90 H31

Park High (Upper)
Park Road South
Birkenhead
p110 L34

Park High (Lower)
Park Road North
Birkenhead
p91 K33

Pensby Secondary
Irby Road
Heswall
p123 F39

Plessington (RC) High (Upper)
Woodland Road
Rock Ferry
p127 N37

Plessington (Lower)
Old Chester Road
Bebington
p127 O37

Prenton High (Girls)
Hesketh Avenue
Rock Ferry
p110 M36

Ridgeway County High
Noctorum Avenue
Noctorum
p109 J35

Rock Ferry High (Boys)
Ravenswood Ave
Rock Ferry
p127 N37

St. Mary's (RC) College
Wallasey Village
Wallasey
p70 K30

St. Mary's (Annexe)
Leasowe Road
Wallasey
p91 J31

The Henry Meoles
Birket Avenue
Moreton
p90 H31

Weatherhead High (Girls)
Mount Pleasant Road
Wallasey
p71 L30

**West Kirby
Grammar (Girls)**
Graham Road
West Kirby
p105 B35

**West Kirby Grammar
(Annexe)**
Hoyle Road
Hoylake
p87 B33

Wirral Grammar (Boys)
Cross Lane
Bebington
p127 N39

Wirral Grammar (Girls)
Heath Road
Bebington
p127 N39

Woodchurch High
Carr Bridge Road
Woodchurch
p109 J35

FURTHER EDUCATION

University of Liverpool
Abercromby Square
Liverpool
p94 Q32

**LIVERPOOL
POLYTECHNIC:**
Main Address
Mount Pleasant
Liverpool
p94 Q32

Faculty of Art & Design
Hope Street
Liverpool
p94 Q33

Faculty of Engineering
Byrom Street
Liverpool
p94 P32

F. L. Calder Campus
Dowsefield Lane
Allerton
p115 W36

I. M. Marsh Campus
Barkhill Road
Aigburth
p114 T36

**Central Liverpool College
of Further Education**
Myrtle Street
Liverpool
p94 Q33

**Childwall Hall College
of Further Education**
Childwall Abbey Road
Childwall
p115 W34

**Colquitt Technical &
Nautical Catering College**
Colquitt Street
Liverpool
p94 Q33

**Kirkby College of
Further Education**
Cherryfield Drive
Kirkby
p43 V24

**LIVERPOOL INSTITUTE
OF HIGHER EDUCATION**
**Christ's & Notre
Dame College**
Woolton Road
Liverpool
p115 V34

St. Katharine's College
Stand Park Road
Liverpool
p115 V34

**Mabel Fletcher
Technical College**
Sandown Road
Liverpool
p96 T32

**Millbank College
of Commerce**
Bankfield Road
Liverpool
p75 T30

**Newton-le-Willows Coll.
of Further Education**
Crow Lane East
Newton-le-Willows
p66 NN27

**North-East Liverpool
Technical College**
Muirhead Avenue East
Liverpool
p75 U28

Old Swan Technical Coll.
Broad Green Road
Liverpool
p96 U31 .

Prescot College of Further Education
Warrington Road
Prescot
p79 CC30

Riversdale College of Technology
Riversdale Road
Aigburth
p130 T37

St. Helens College of Art & Design
Victoria Square
St. Helens
p63 GG27

St. Helens College of Technology
Water Street
St. Helens
p63 FF27

Southport College of Art & Technology
Mornington Road
Southport
p6 P5

Southport Coll. (Annexe)
Scarisbrick New Road
Southport
p6 P6

The City of Liverpool Coll. of Higher Education
Liverpool Road
Prescot
p78 AA30

The Hugh Baird College of Further Education
Balliol Road
Bootle
p73 P28

WIRRAL METROPOLITAN COLLEGE:
Birkenhead Site
Borough Road
Birkenhead
p110 M35

Carlett Park Site
Carlett Park
Eastham
p150 R41

Wallasey Site
Withens Lane
Wallasey
p71 L30

TRAVEL INFORMATION

GENERAL

Merseyside Passenger Transport Executive
Hatton Garden
Tel: 051-236-7676
p94 P32

'Merseytravel' Office
Williamson Square
p94 P32

AIR

Speke Airport
Tel: 051-494-0066
W39 131

BUS — TERMINALS

Bickerstaffe Street
St. Helens
p63 GG27

Cherryfield Drive
Kirkby
p43 W24

Chester Street
Birkenhead
p93 N33

Lord Street
Southport
p5 O5

Mann Island
Liverpool
p93 O32

Paradise Street
Liverpool
p94 P32

Pier Head
Liverpool
p93 O32

Skelhome Street
Liverpool
p94 O32

FERRY — TERMINALS

Brocklebank Dock
(Ferry to Dublin)
p72 O28

Langton Dock
(Ferry to Belfast)
p72 O28

Pier Head
(Ferries to Seacombe, Woodside & Isle of Man)
p93 O32

assenger Timetable & Fare enquiries Tel: 051-709-9696
'Talking Timetable' for services to London Tel: 051-708-6454
raveline—recorded information on significant changes:
    Tel: 051-246-8021 (Local)
    Tel: 051-246-8030 (Main Inter-City routes)

RAVEL CENTRES:

Castle Street
iverpool
94 P32

Lime Street Station
iverpool
94 Q32

STATIONS:

Aigburth
130 T37

Ainsdale
12 M10

Aintree
56 R25

Allerton
131 V37

Bank Hall
73 P29

Bebington
127 O38

Bidston
91 J32

Birkdale
9 O7

Birkenhead Central
111 N34

Birkenhead North
91 K32

Birkenhead Park
92 L33

Blundellsands & Crosby
38 M23

Bootle New Strand
54 O27

Bootle Oriel Road
72 O28

Broad Green
97 V32

Bromborough
143 P41

Bryn
51 NN22

Central
p94 P32

Cressington
p130 U37

Ditton
p135 DD38

Earlestown
p67 NN27

Eccleston Park
p80 DD30

Edge Hill
p95 S33

Fazakerley
p56 S25

Formby
p19 K16

Freshfield
p16 K14

Garston
p131 V38

Garswood
p50 LL23

Green Lane
p111 N35

Hall Road
p38 L22

Hamilton Square
p93 N33

Heswall
p140 J41

Hightown
p25 L19

Hillside
p9 N8

Hooton
p148 P44

Hough Green
p119 DD36

Hoylake
p105 B34

Hunts Cross
p132 Y37

Huyton
p99 Z32

James Street
p94 P32

Kirkby
p43 V23

Kirkdale
p73 P28

Leasowe
p90 G32

Lime Street
p94 Q32

Maghull
p29 T21

Manor Road
p88 C33

Meols
p88 D33

Meols Cop
p6 Q5

Moorfields
p94 P32

Moreton
p90 G32

Mossley Hill
p114 U35

Neston
p145 K45

New Brighton
p71 L29

Newton-le-Willows
p67 PP27

Old Roan
p41 R23

Orrell
p36 JJ19

Orrell Park
p56 R26

Pemberton
p37 LL19

Port Sunlight
p127 O39

Merseyside Rail Network

1 Birkenhead North
2 Birkenhead Park
3 Hamilton Square
4 Birkenhead Central
5 Moorfields
6 Lime Street
7 James Street
8 West Allerton

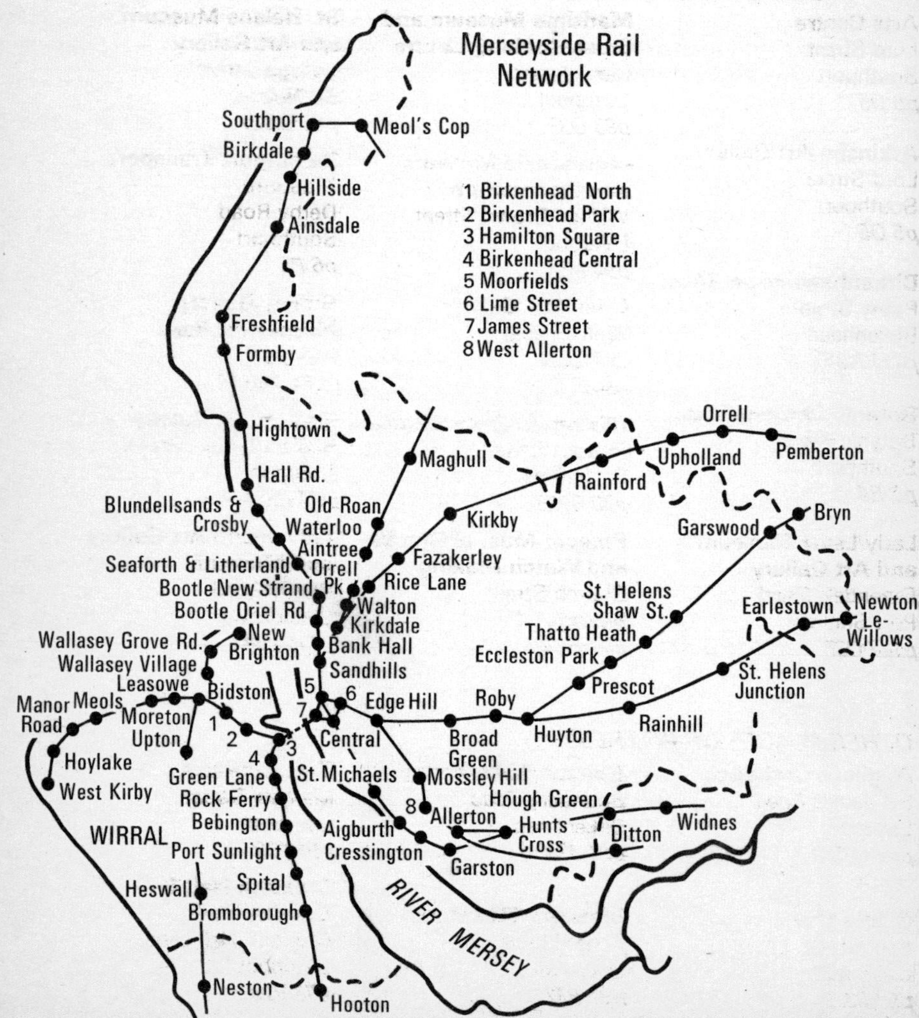

TOURISM

xv

TOURIST INFORMATION CENTRES

Liverpool and Merseyside
Merseyside Tourism
Lime Street
p94 Q32

Birkenhead
Central Library
Borough Road
p110 M34

Huyton
Municipal Buildings
Archway Road
p99 Z32

Kirkby
Municipal Buildings
Cherryfield Drive
p43 V24

New Brighton
Bathing Pool
Promenade
p71 L28

Southport
Cambridge Arcade
Lord Street
p5 O5

Wallasey
The Grange
Grove Road
p70 K30

ART GALLERIES AND MUSEUMS

Arts Centre
Lord Street
Southport
p5 O5

Atkinson Art Gallery
Lord Street
Southport
p5 O5

Birkenhead Priory Mus.
Priory Street
Birkenhead
p111 N34

Botanic Gardens Mus.
Botanic Road
Southport
p7 R4

**Lady Lever Museum
and Art Gallery**
Greendale Road
Port Sunlight
p127 O38

**Maritime Museum and
Brass Rubbing Centre**
Mann Island
Liverpool
p93 O32

**Merseyside Museum
and Planetarium**
William Brown Street
Liverpool
p94 P32

Open Eye Gallery
Whitechapel
Liverpool
p94 P32

Pilkington Glass Museum
Prescot Road
St. Helens
p80 EE28

**Prescot Mus. of Clocks
and Watch Making**
Church Street
Prescot
p79 BB30

**St. Helens Museum
and Art Gallery**
College Street
St. Helens
p63 GG27

**Steamport Transport
Museum**
Derby Road
Southport
p6 P5

Sudley Gallery
Mossley Hill Road
Liverpool
p114 T36

Walker Art Gallery
William Brown Street
Liverpool
p94 P32

**Williamson Art Gallery
and Museum**
Slatey Road
Birkenhead
p110 L34

OTHER PLACES OF INTEREST

Anglican Cathedral
St. James Road
Liverpool
p94 Q33

Beatle City
Seel Street
Liverpool
p94 P32

Bidston Observatory
Boundary Road
Birkenhead
p91 J33

Bluecoat Chambers
School Lane
Liverpool
p94 P32

Cavern Walks
Mathew Street
Liverpool
p94 P32

**Croxteth Hall &
Country Park**
Croxteth Hall Lane
Liverpool
p76 V28

n Festival Site
ulaneum Docks
erpool
113 R36

Knowsley Safari Park
Prescot By-pass
Prescot
p79 BB29

Leasowe Lighthouse
Leasowe
p89 F31

Liverpool Botanic Gardens
Calderstones Road
Liverpool
p115 V35

Liverpool Town Hall
Water Street
Liverpool
p94 P32

Metropolitan (RC) Cath.
Brownlow Hill
Liverpool
p94 Q32

Perch Rock Battery
Marine Parade
New Brighton
p71 L28

Royal Liver Building
Georges Pierhead
Liverpool
p93 O32

St. Georges Hall
Lime Street
Liverpool
p94 P32

St. John's Beacon
Houghton Street
Liverpool
p94 P32

Speke Hall
Speke
p151 W40

LEISURE AND ENTERTAINMENT

THEATRES AND MUSIC HALLS

Birkenhead Repertory
Grange Road West
Birkenhead
p110 M34

Empire
Lime Street
Liverpool
p94 Q32

Everyman
Hope Street
Liverpool
p94 Q32

Floral Pavilion
Virginia Road
New Brighton
p71 L28

Heswall Hall
Telegraph Road
Heswall
p139 G40

Hippodrome
Corporation Street
St. Helens
p63 GG27

Little Theatre
Hoghton Street
Southport
p5 O5

Neptune
Hanover Street
Liverpool
p94 P32

Philharmonic Hall
Hope Street
Liverpool
p94 Q33

Playhouse
Williamson Square
Liverpool
p94 P32

Royal Court
Roe Street
Liverpool
p94 P32

Southport Theatre & Floral Hall
Promenade
Southport
p5 O5

Theatre Royal
Corporation Street
St. Helens
p63 GG27

Woodchurch Leisure Centre
Carr Bridge Road
Woodchurch
p109 J35

CINEMAS

A.B.C.
Argyle Street
Birkenhead
p111 N34

A.B.C.
Bridge Street
St. Helens
p63 GG27

A.B.C.
Lime Street
Liverpool
p94 Q32

A.B.C.
Lord Street
Southport
p5 O5

Astra Entertainment Centre
Northway
Maghull
p28 S20

Carlton
Green Lane
Liverpool
p75 T30

Classic
Alderley Road
Hoylake
p87 B33

Classic
Allerton Road
Liverpool
p114 U35

Classic
Conway Street
Birkenhead
p92 L31

Classic
Crosby Road North
Crosby
p39 N24

Classic
Lord Street
Southport
p5 O5

Odeon
London Road
Liverpool
p94 Q32

Studios
Brownlow Hill
Liverpool
p94 Q32

Unit 4
King Street
Egremont
p94 M31

Woolton Picture House
Mason Street
Woolton
p116 X36

SPORTS CENTRES AND SWIMMING POOLS

Austin Rawlinson Pool
North Parade
Speke
p137 Z39

Balliol Swimming Baths
Balliol Road
Bootle
p73 P28

Bathing Pool (outdoor)
Kings Parade
New Brighton
p71 L28

Belle Vale Swimming Pool
Belle Vale Centre,
Liverpool
p116 Y34

Bootle Stadium
Maguire Avenue
Bootle
p55 Q27

Boundary Road Swimming Baths
Boundary Road
St. Helens
p63 FF27

Bridgefield Forum Leisure Centre
Cartbridge Lane
Halewood
p117 AA36

Burroughs Gardens Baths
Burroughs Gardens
Liverpool
p94 P31

Byrne Avenue Recreation Centre & Pool
Byrne Avenue
Rock Ferry
p111 N36

Concourse Sports Centre and Pool
Grange Road
West Kirby
p105 B35

Crosby Swimming Baths
Manners Road
Crosby
p38 L24

Everton Park Sports Centre
Buckingham Street
Everton
p73 Q30

Fernhill Sports Centre
Fernhill Road
Bootle
p55 Q27

Ford Recreation Centre
Ford Precinct
Birkenhead
p90 H30

Garston Recreation Centre and Pool
Speke Road
Liverpool
p131 V38

Grange Road West Sports Centre
Grange Road West
Birkenhead
p110 L34

Guinea Gap Baths and Recreation Centre
Riverview Road
Wallasey
p93 N31

Halewood Sports Centre
Barncroft Road
Halewood
p133 AA37

Harold Davies Baths
Prescot Road
Liverpool
p97 W31

Huyton Leisure Centre and Pool
Roby Road
Huyton
p98 Y32

Kirkby Sports Centre and Pool
Valley Road
Kirkby
p43 V24

Kirkby Swimming Pool
Hall Lane
Kirkby
p43 W24

Leasowe Recreation Centre and Pool
Twickenham Drive
Leasowe
p90 H31

Lister Drive Baths
Lister Drive
Liverpool
p96 T31

**Lodge Lane Sports
Centre and Pool**
Lodge Lane
Liverpool
p95 R33

Margaret Street Baths
Margaret Street
Liverpool
p95 R31

**Oval Sports Centre,
Pool and Ski Slope**
Old Chester Road
Bebington
p127 N37

Parr Swimming Baths
Recreation Street
St. Helens
p64 HH27

**Picton Sports Centre
and Pool**
Picton Road
Wavertree
p96 T33

Queens Drive Baths
Smithy Lane
Walton
p73 Q28

**Scotchbarn Swimming
Pool**
Scotchbarn Lane
Prescot
p79 CC30

Sea Bathing Lake
Marine Drive
Southport
p5 N5

**Selwyn Jones Swim.
Pool**
Ashton Road
Newton-le-Willows
p67 OO26

Stable Street Baths
Stable Street
Liverpool
p112 Q34

**Sutton High Sports
Centre**
Elton Head Road
Marshall's Cross
p81 GG30

Swimming Baths
Esplanade
Southport
p5 N5

Westminster Road Baths
Westminster Road
Kirkdale
p73 Q29

William Roberts Baths
Utting Avenue East
Norris Green
p75 T28

**Woodchurch Leisure
Centre and Sportsbarn**
Carr Bridge Road
Woodchurch
p109 J35

Woolton Baths
Quarry Street South
Woolton
p116 X36

MUNICIPAL GOLF COURSES

Allerton Park
Menlove Avenue
Liverpool
p115 W36

Arrowe Park
Arrowe Park Road
Woodchurch
p124 H37

Bootle
Dunnings Bridge Road
Litherland
p40 Q24

Bowring Park
Roby Road
Roby
p98 X32

Brackenwood
Bracken Lane
Bebington
p126 M39

Hoylake
Carr Lane
Hoylake
p105 B34

Liverpool
Ingoe Lane
Kirkby
p57 U25

Warren Park
Sea Road
Wallasey
p70 K29

Sherdley Park
Marshalls Cross Road
St. Helens
p81 GG29

Southport
Park Road
Southport
p6 P4

PRIVATE GOLF CLUBS

Bidston
Scoresby Road
Bidston
p90 H31

Bromborough
Roby Hall Road
Bromborough
p142 O42

Caldy
Links Hey Road
Caldy
p122 D38

Childwall
Naylors Road
Childwall
p99 Z33

Eastham Lodge
Ferry Road
Eastham
p150 R42

Formby
Victoria Road
Formby
p15 J14

Grange Park
Prescot Road
St. Helens
p80 DD28

Haydock Park
Newton Lane
Newton-le-Willows
p67 PP26

Hesketh
Cockle Dick's Lane
Southport
p6 Q4

Heswell
Cottage Lane
Heswell
p139 G42

Hillside
Hastings Road
Southport
p9 N8

Huyton & Prescot
The Fairway
Huyton
p99 AA31

Leasowe
Leasowe Road
Leasowe
p90 G31

Lee Park
King's Drive
Gateacre
p116 Y35

Prenton
Golf Links Road
Prenton
p126 L37

Royal Birkdale
Waterloo Road
Southport
p9 N8

Royal Liverpool
Meols Drive
Hoylake
p105 B34

Southport and Ainsdale
Bradshaws Lane
Ainsdale
p12 M10

Southport Oldlinks
Moss Lane
Southport
p7 R5

Wallasey
Bayswater Road
Wallasey
p70 J30

West Derby
Yew Tree Lane
West Derby
p76 W30

West Lancashire
Hall Road West
Crosby
p38 L22

Wirral Ladies
Bidston Road
Birkenhead
p109 K34

Woolton
School Lane
Woolton
p132 X37

FOOTBALL AND RUGBY GROUNDS

Everton FC
City Road
p73 Q28

Liverpool FC
Anfield Rd
p74 R29

St. Helens RFC
Knowsley Road
p62 EE27

RACE COURSES

Aintree
Liverpool
p41 S24

Haydock Park
Ashton in Makerfield
p52 OO24

KEY TO MAP PAGES

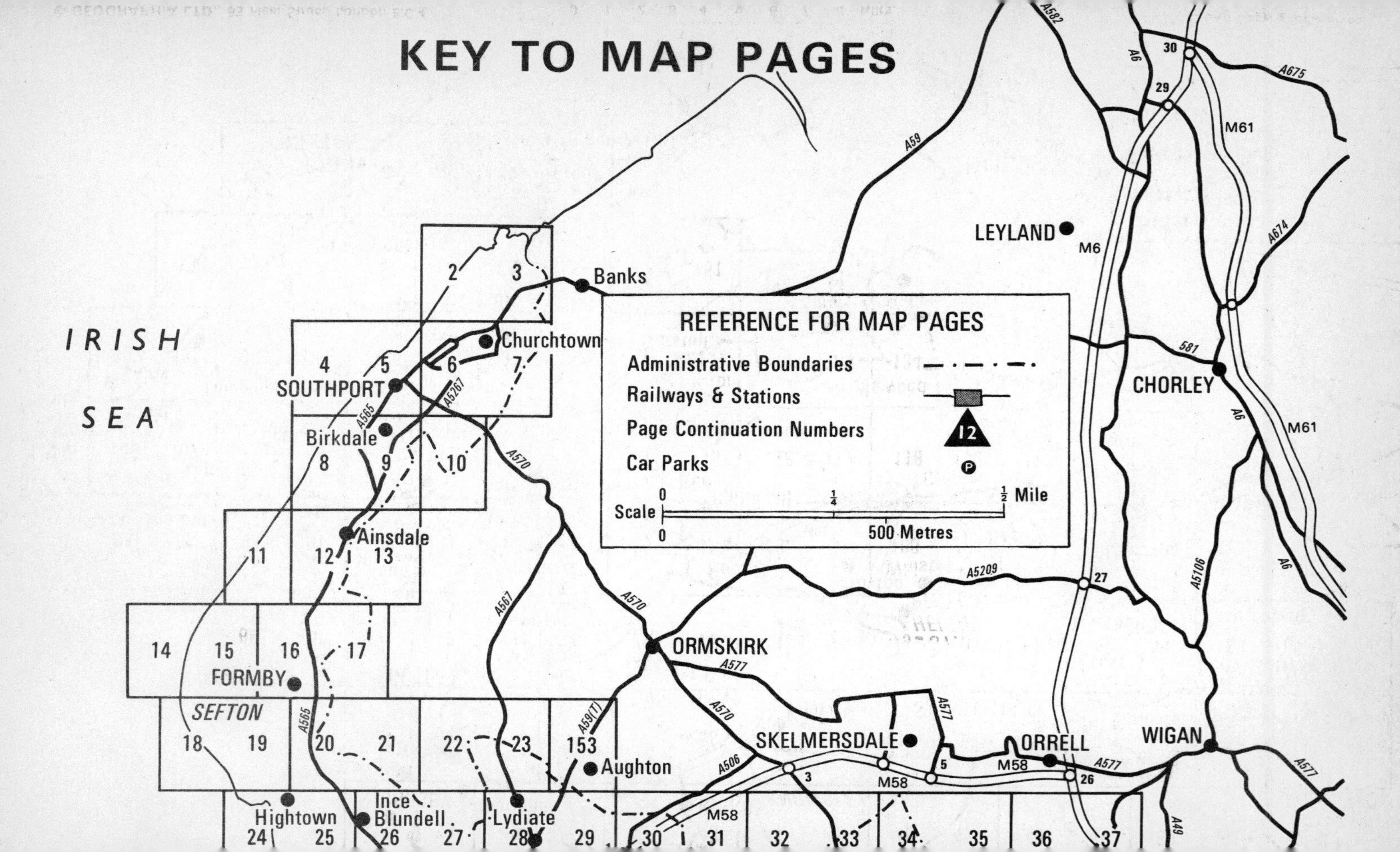

IRISH SEA

REFERENCE FOR MAP PAGES

Administrative Boundaries ─ ∙ ─ ∙ ─

Railways & Stations

Page Continuation Numbers **12**

Car Parks **P**

Scale

0 ¼ ½ Mile

0 500 Metres

Banks

Churchtown

SOUTHPORT

Birkdale

Ainsdale

FORMBY

SEFTON

Hightown

Ince Blundell

Lydiate

Aughton

ORMSKIRK

SKELMERSDALE

WIGAN

ORRELL

LEYLAND

CHORLEY

A565
A570
A567
A5267
A59
A582
A6
A675
A571
A49
A577
A5106
A570
A577
A5209
A570
A506
A459(T)

M6
M61
M58

2 3 4 5 6 7 8 9 10 11 12 13 14 15 16 17 18 19 20 21 22 23 24 25 26 27 28 29 30 31 32 33 34 35 36 37 153

501 27 26 5 3 30 29

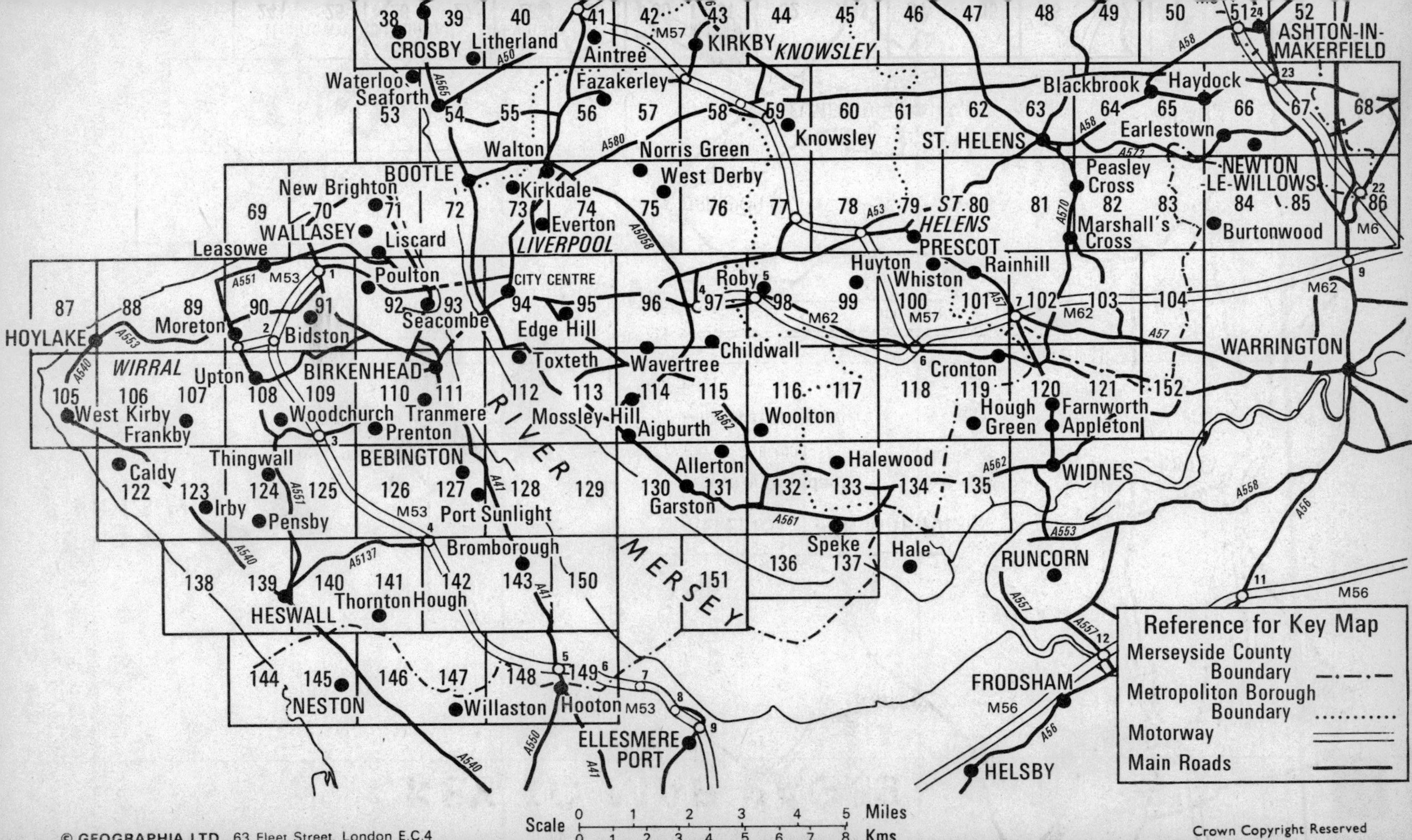

Reference for Key Map

Merseyside County Boundary
Metropoliton Borough Boundary
Motorway
Main Roads

Scale

Miles
Kms.

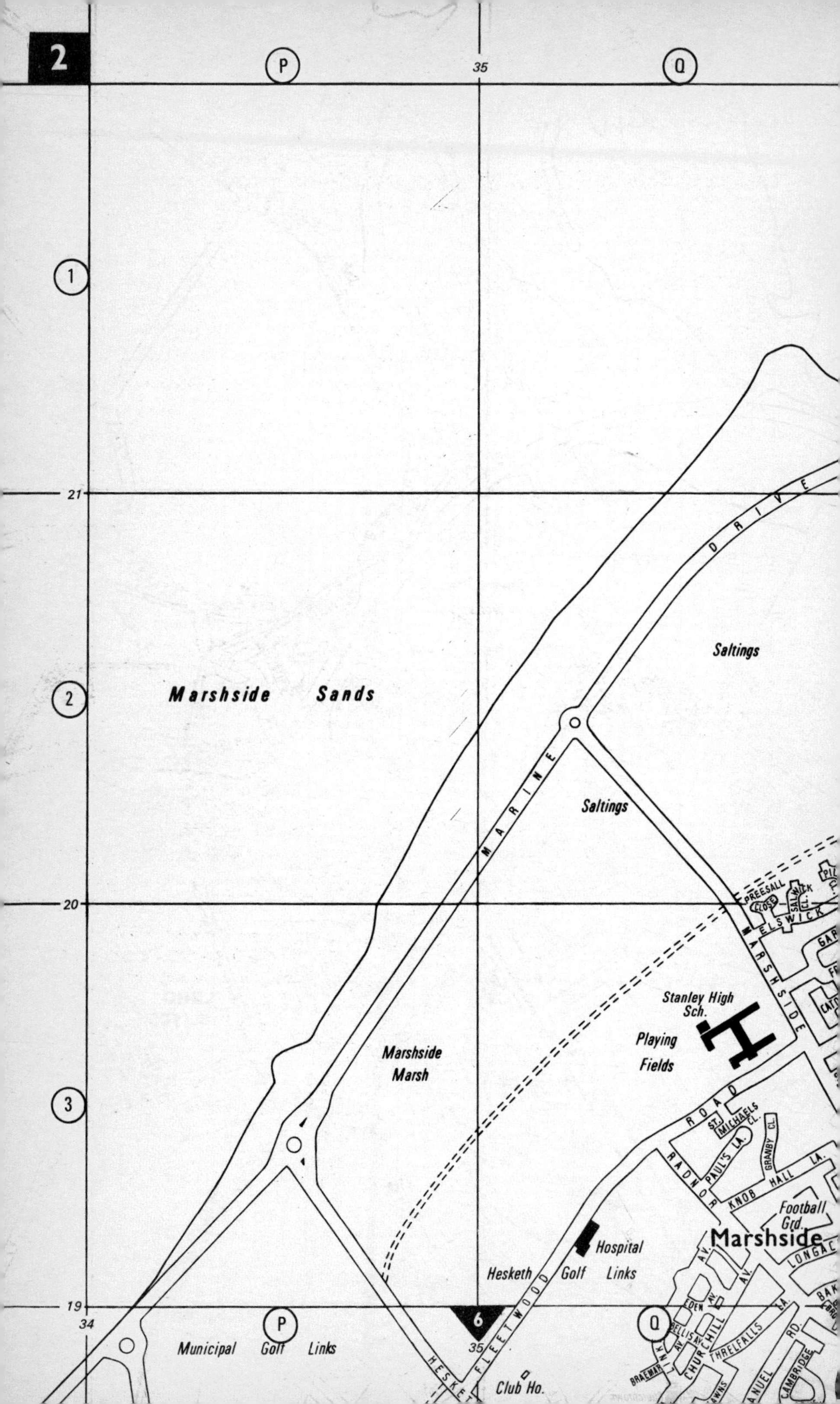
2
P
35
Q
1
21
2
3
20
19
34
Marshside Sands
Saltings
Saltings
MARINE DRIVE
Marshside Marsh
Stanley High Sch.
Playing Fields
MARSHSIDE
PREESALL
CLOSE
SALWICK CL.
ELSWICK
RADNOR ROAD
ST. MICHAELS CL.
PAUL'S LA.
GRANBY CL.
KNOB HALL LA.
Football Grd.
Marshside
Hospital
Hesketh Golf Links
FLEETWOOD
HESKETH
6
35
P
Q
Municipal Golf Links
Club Ho.
EDEN AV.
BELLIS AV.
CHURCHILL AV.
THRELFALLS LA.
BRAEMAR
LINK AV.
CAMBRIDGE
RD.

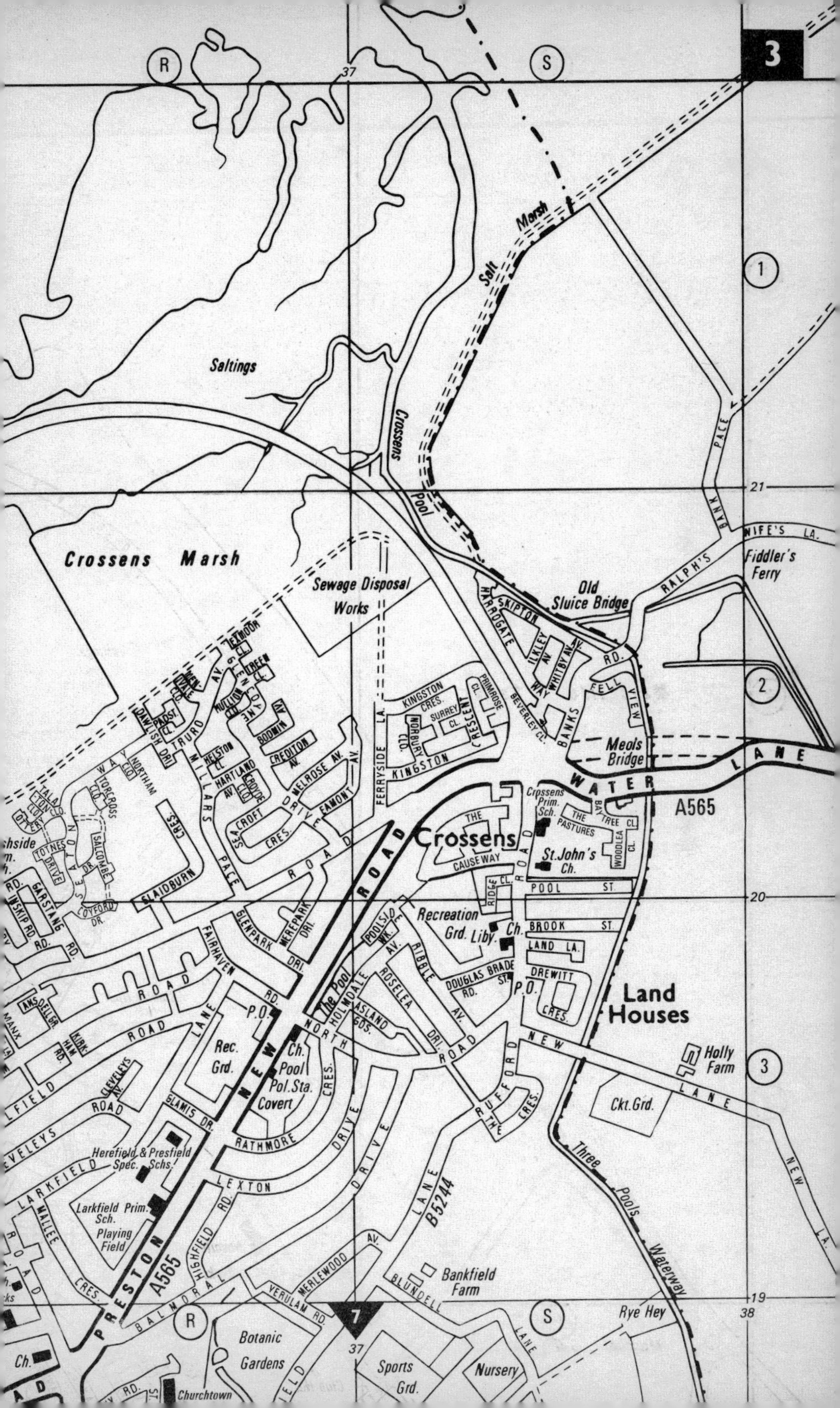
3
R
S
37
Saltings
Salt Marsh
Crossens Pool
Crossens Marsh
Sewage Disposal Works
Old Sluice Bridge
Fiddler's Ferry
WIFE'S LA.
RALPH'S
BANK PACE
21
1
2
3
20
19
38
Meols Bridge
WATER LANE
A565
Crossens
Crossens Prim. Sch.
St.John's Ch.
THE PASTURES
BAY TREE CL.
WOODLEA CL.
THE CAUSEWAY
POOL ST.
BROOK ST.
LAND LA.
DREWITT CRES.
Land Houses
Holly Farm
Ckt.Grd.
NEW LANE
NEW LA.
Three Pools Waterway
Rye Hey
Recreation Grd.
Liby.
Ch.
P.O.
DOUGLAS BRADE
RIBBLE AV.
ROSELEA DRI.
ROAD
RUFFORD
THE CRES.
KINGSTON CRES.
SURREY CL.
NORBURY CLO.
KINGSTON
CRESCENT
PRIMROSE CL.
FERRYSIDE LA.
HARROGATE
SKIPTON
ILKLEY AV.
WHITBY AV.
WAY
BEVERLEY CL.
BANKS RD.
FELL VIEW
EAMONT AV.
MELROSE AV.
DRIVE
SEA CROFT
THE CRES.
CREDITON AV.
BODMIN
HARTLAND AV.
HELSTON CL.
CROYDE
MILLARS PACE
ROAD
TRURO AV.
DAWLISH DRI.
PADST.
NORTHAM
WAY
SEATON
SALCOMBE
TORCROSS
TOTNES DRIVE
COYFORD DR.
SEA DR.
SLAIDBURN CRES.
GARSTANG RD.
INSKIP RD.
GLENPARK DRI.
MEREPARK DRI.
FAIRHAVEN RD.
ROAD
NEW ROAD
The Pool
POOLSIDE WK.
HOLMDALE AV.
ASLAND GDS.
NORTH ROAD
P.O.
Ch.
Pool
Pol.Sta.
Covert
Rec. Grd.
LANE
ROAD
KIRKHAM RD.
ANSDELL GR.
MANX
CLEVELEYS AV.
CLEVELEYS ROAD
GLAMIS DR.
RATHMORE
CRES.
DRIVE
DRIVE
LEXTON
Herefield & Presfield Spec. Schs.
LARKFIELD
Larkfield Prim. Sch.
Playing Field
MALLEE CRES.
ROAD
PRESTON NEW ROAD
A565
HIGHFIELD RD.
BALMORAL
LANE
B5244
MERLEWOOD AV.
VERULAM RD.
BLUNDELL
Bankfield Farm
7
Botanic Gardens
Sports Grd.
Nursery
Churchtown
Ch.

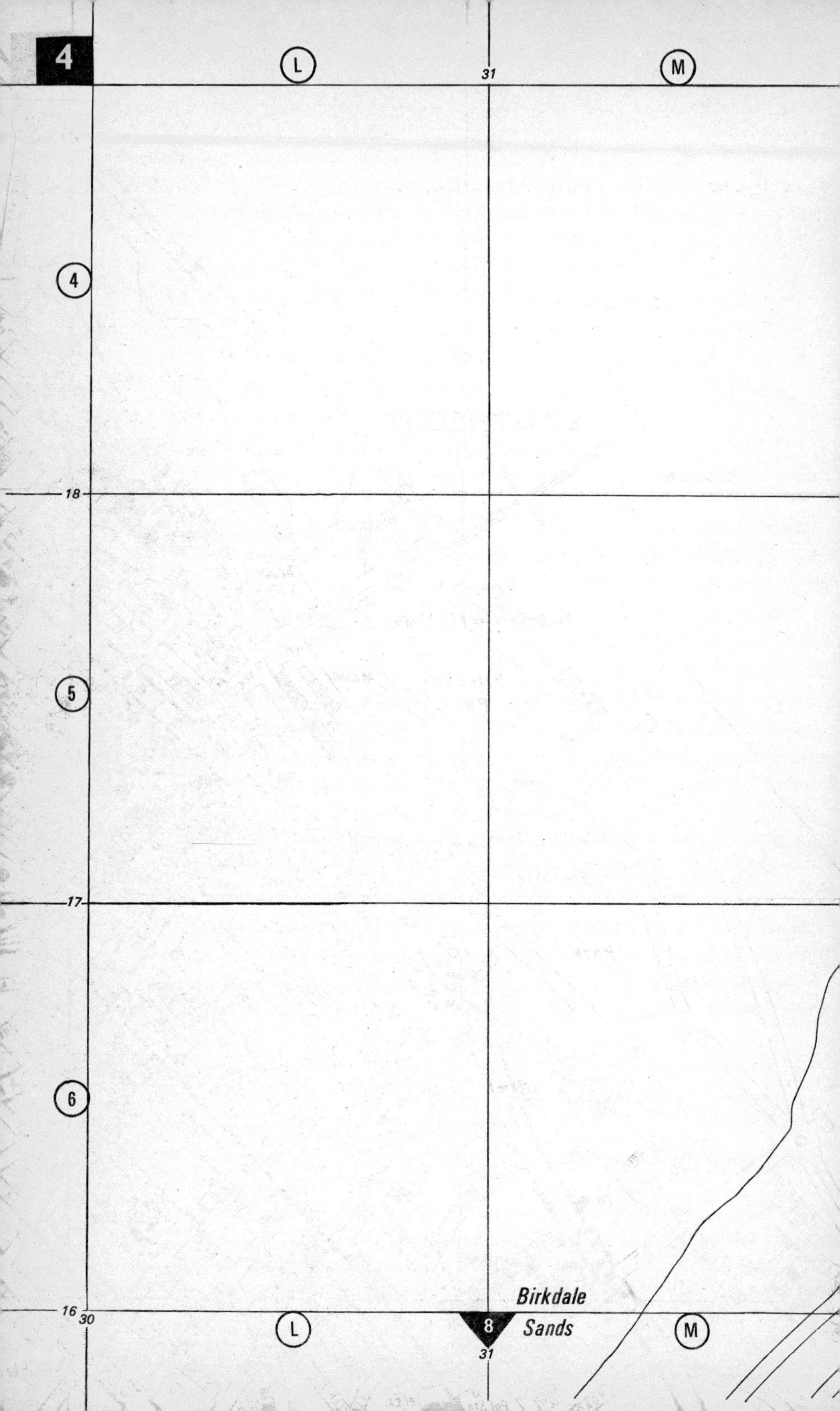

4

L

31

M

4

18

5

17

6

16 30

L

8 31

Birkdale
Sands

M

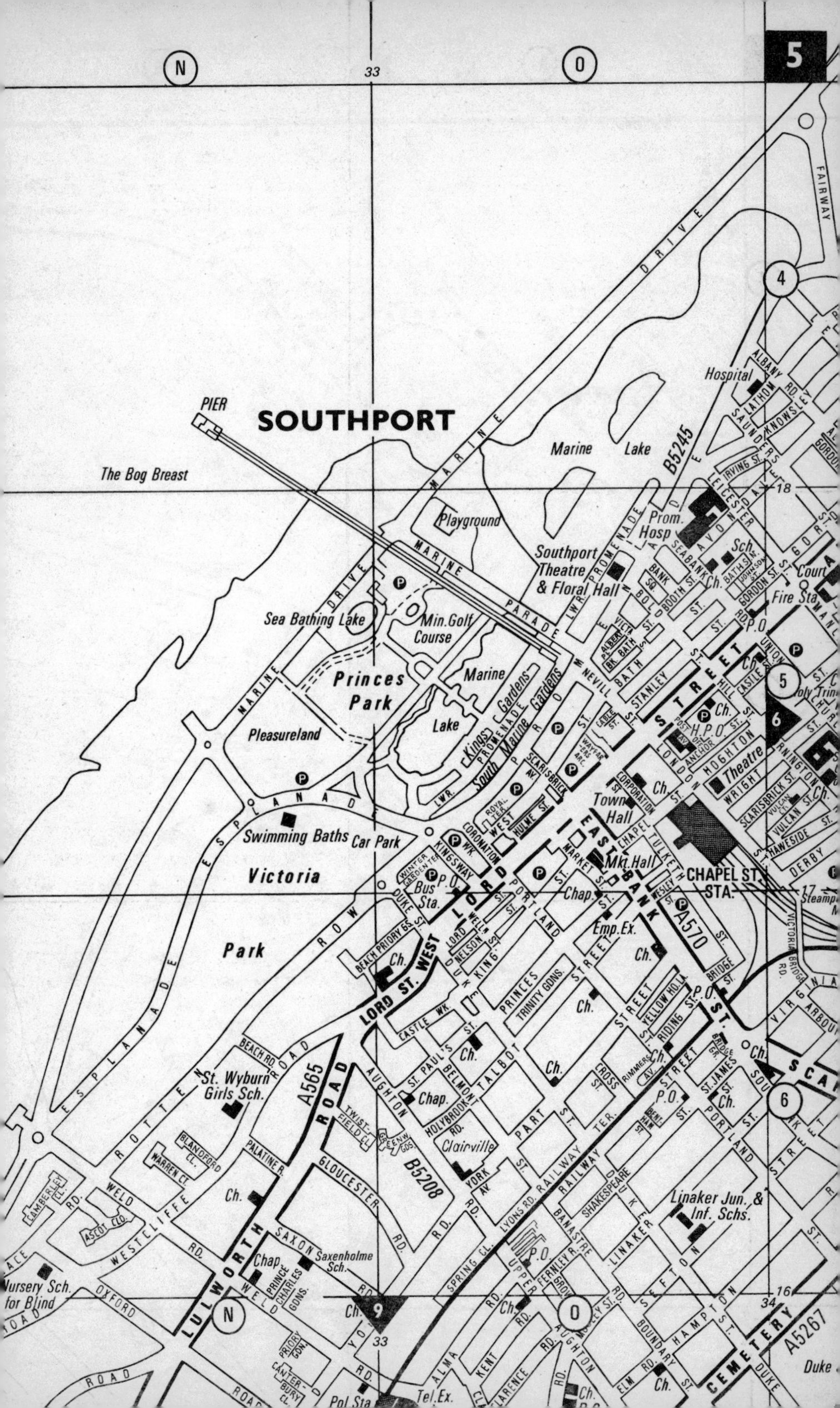
5
N
O
33
SOUTHPORT
PIER
The Bog Breast
MARINE DRIVE
Marine Lake
B5245
Playground
Prom. Hosp
Southport Theatre & Floral Hall
Hospital
MARINE PARADE
Sea Bathing Lake
Min. Golf Course
Princes Park
Marine Lake
Kings Gardens
South Marine Gardens
Pleasureland
ESPLANADE
Swimming Baths
Car Park
Victoria Park
LORD STREET
Town Hall
Mkt. Hall
CHAPEL ST. STA.
Theatre
Bus Sta.
LORD ST. WEST
A565
A570
ROTTEN ROAD
St. Wyburn Girls Sch.
B5208
Clairville
LULWORTH ROAD
Saxenholme Sch.
Linaker Jun. & Inf. Schs.
CEMETERY
A5267
Nursery Sch. for Blind
Pol. Sta
Tel. Ex.
Fire Sta.
Court
Emp. Ex.
H.P.O.
Steamport
4
6
9
16
17
18
34

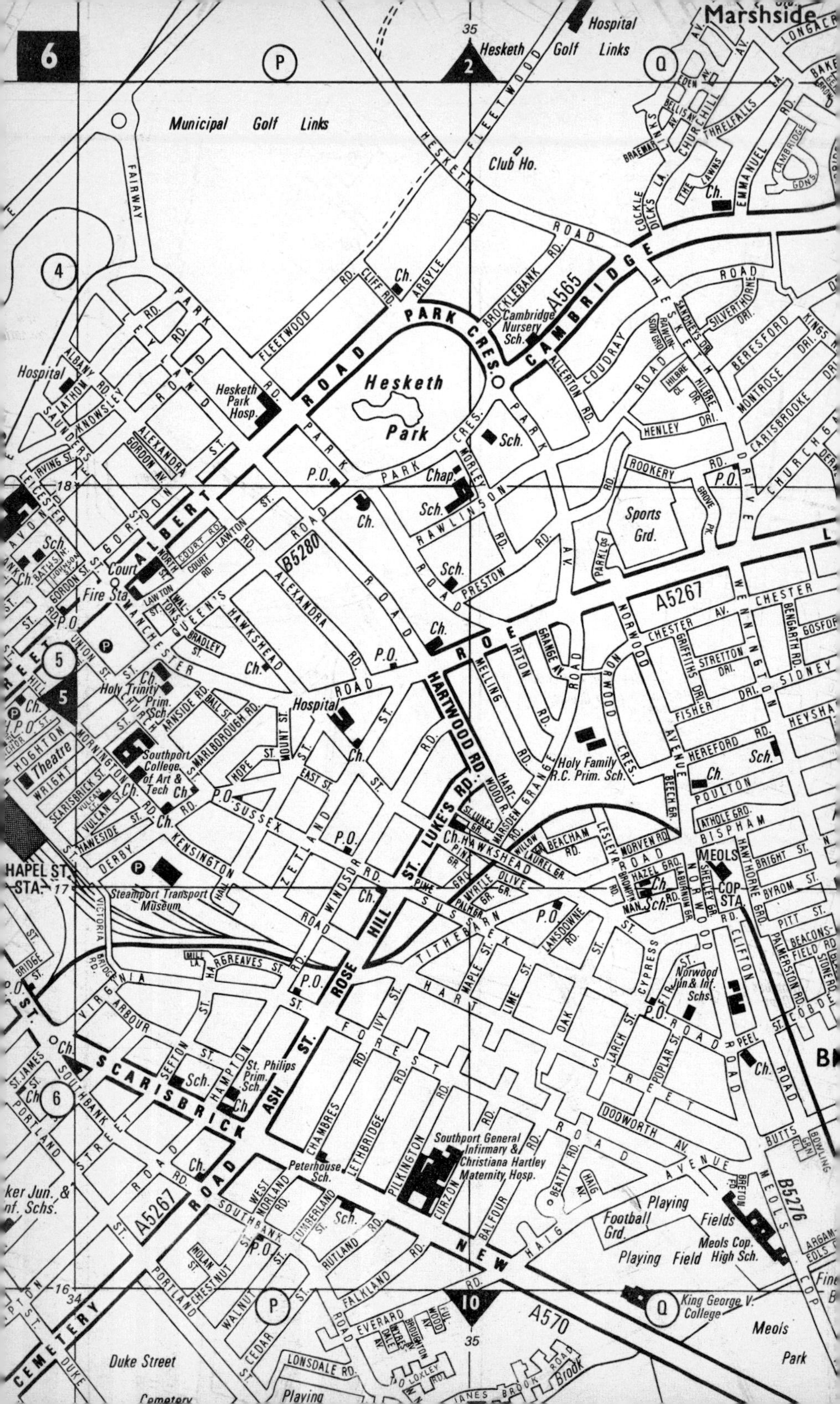
6
Marshside
Hesketh Golf Links
Municipal Golf Links
Hesketh Park
Southport General Infirmary & Christiana Hartley Maternity Hosp.
Steamport Transport Museum
Meols Cop High Sch.
King George V. College
Meols Park
Duke Street Cemetery

7
Sch. Playing Fields
LEE
CRES.
PRESTON
R
HIGHFIELD
BALMORAL
MERLEWOOD AV.
37
3
VERULAM RD.
BLUNDELL
Bankfield Farm
S
Waterway
Rye Hey
Ch.
Botanic Gardens
Sports Grd.
LANE
Nursery
SUNNY RD.
ST. CUTHBERT'S RD.
Churchtown Prim. Sch.
BANKFIELD
B5244
MANOR
CAMBRIDGE RD.
Botanic Gardens Museum
Bankfield Plantation
Fish Pond Covert
Church Bri.
BOTANIC RD.
LITTLE LA.
ST. CLAIR DRI.
P.O.
Churchtown
Ch.
CHURCHGATE
PEETS LA.
RD.
4
New Plantati
Meols Hall
Larkham Covert
MILL LA.
MILL LA. CR.
Gore Hey Covert
Old Nursery
Liby.
18
Wright's Wood
MOSS LANE
HIGH PARK RD.
WARREN RD.
FARM CL
Bridge Farm
FINEJANE'S WAY
PITTS HOUSE LA.
DOLLY'S
STRAIGHT UP
Pool House Farm
Wyke Hey Farm
TARLETON RD.
Ch.
WYKE LANE
DEVONSHIRE RD
Southport Old Links (Golf Course)
5
LAWSON ST.
All Saints Prim. Sch.
Simon & St. Judes
Ch.
The Pool
Pitts House Farm
SCOTT ST.
Ch.
TEDDER AV.
Pitts House Covert
RUSSELL RD.
VICTORY AV.
WAVELL AV.
Firework Factory
17
SALISBURY ST.
MONTGOMERY AV.
ROAD
Recreation Grd.
Brook Farm
Omnibus Dept.
Electricity Works
Gas Works
CROWLAND CL.
STREET
Wier
Brook Farm Bridge
CROWLAND
The Old Pool
6
Hodge's Farm
Sandy Brook
Twist's Covert
S
R
WYKE
COP
16
37
38
Sheepfold Farm

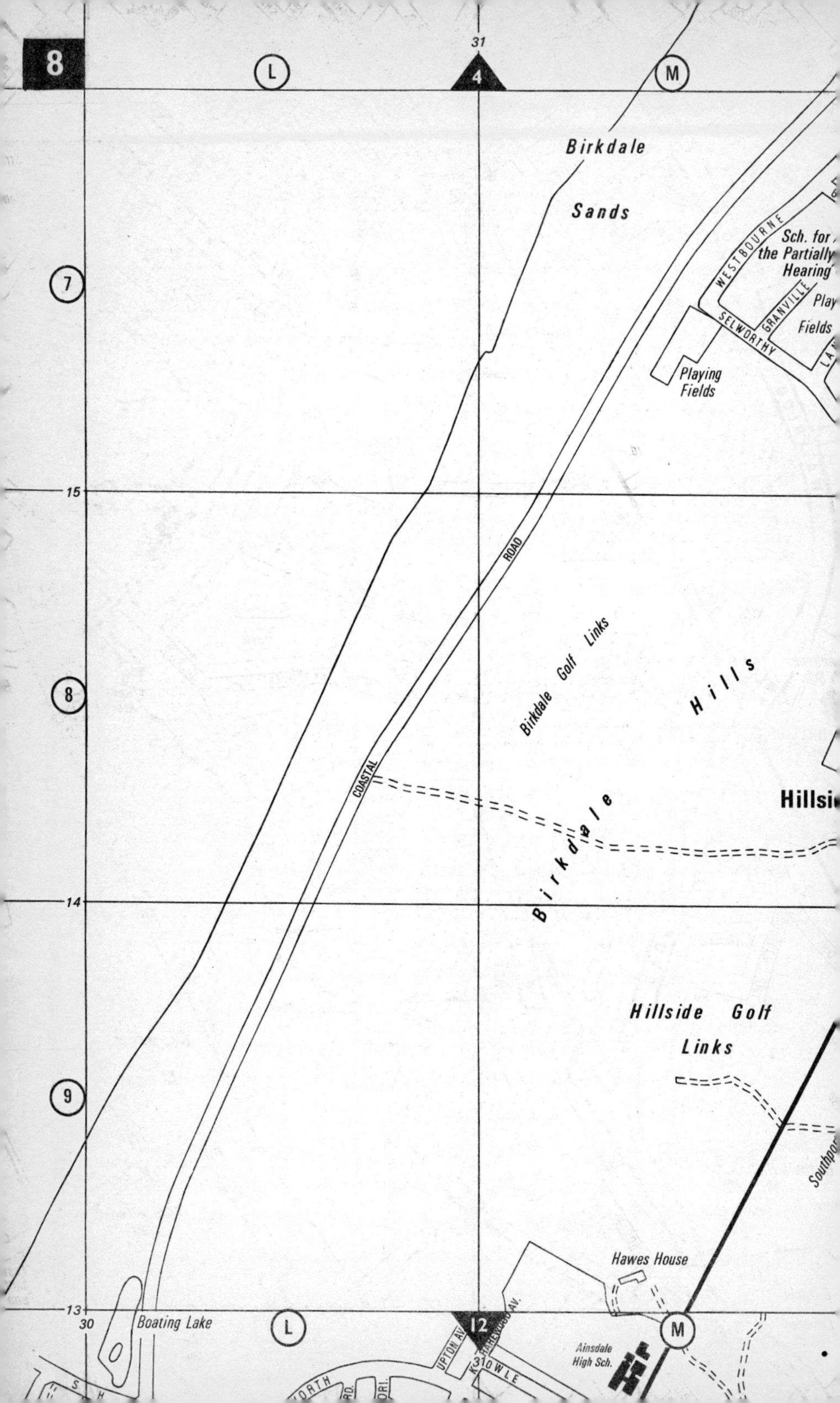

8

L   31   **4**   M

Birkdale

Sands

Sch. for
the Partially
Hearing

WESTBOURNE

SELWORTHY

GRANVILLE

LAW

Play
Fields

Playing
Fields

—7

—15

ROAD

Birkdale Golf Links

H i l l s

COASTAL

B i r k d a l e

Hillsi

—8

—14

Hillside Golf

Links

—9

Southpo

Hawes House

—13
30   *Boating Lake*   L   **12**   M

UPTON AV

KENILWORTH

310WLE

ORTH

RO.

ORI

*Ainsdale
High Sch.*

S. H

Birkdale
BIRKDALE STA.
HILLSIDE STA.
Bedford Park
Playing Field
Christ the King R.C. High Sch.
Cricket Grd.
Recreation Ground
Crantum Moss
Hollybrook Farm
Grave's Moss Farm
Gorsehill Farm
Boundary Farm
Crantum Farm West
Birkdale High Sch.
Under Hill Farm
Birkdale Cemetery
King's Covert
Brighthelmston Sch.
Birkdale Prim. Sch.
R.C. Prim. Sch.
Jun. & Inf. Schs.
Saxenholme Sch.
LIVERPOOL ROAD
WATERLOO ROAD
EASTBOURNE ROAD
CEMETERY ROAD
LULWORTH ROAD
A565
A5267
B5208
B5243
Fine Jane's Brook
NEW CUT LA.
CARR LA.
5
9
10
13

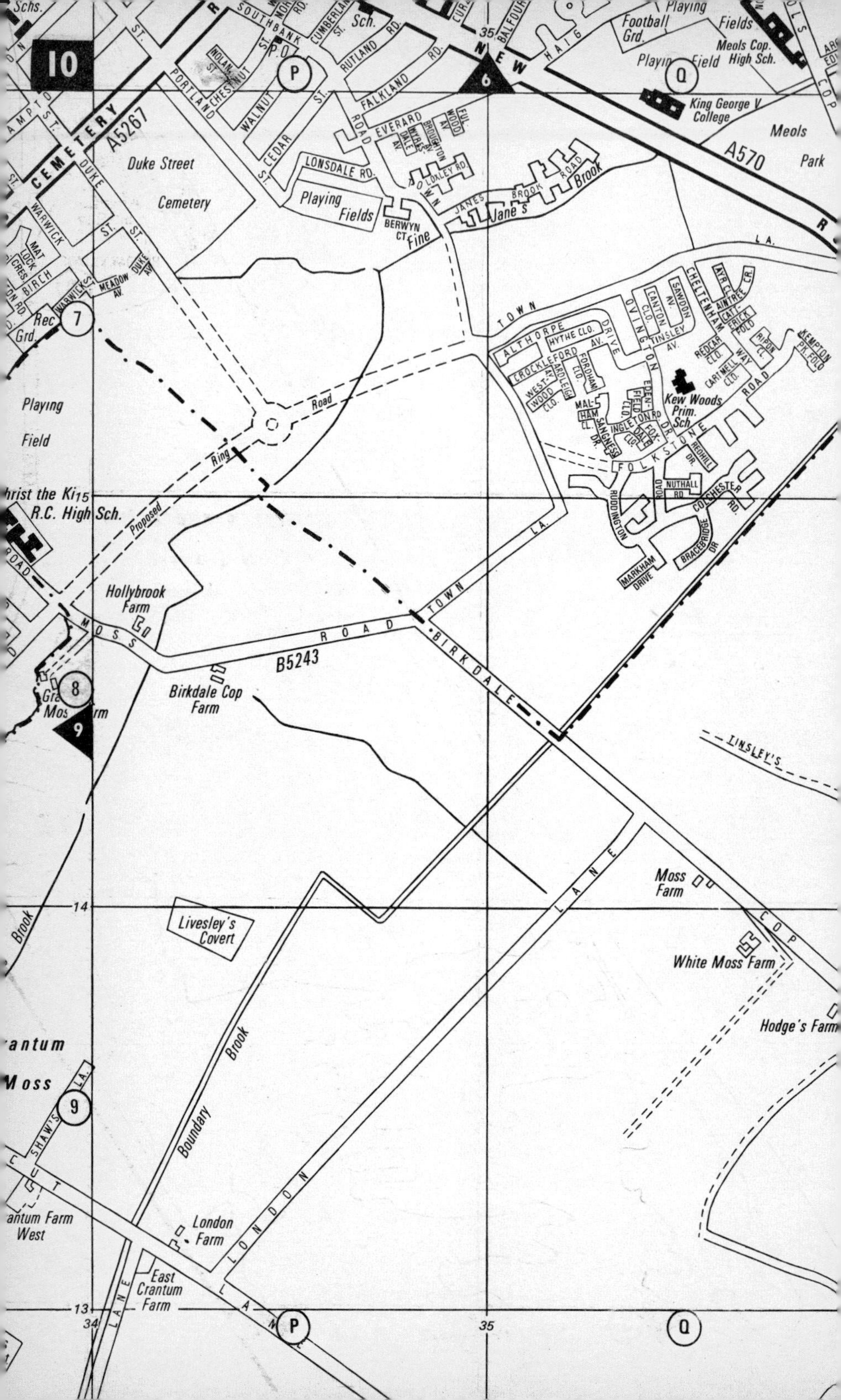

10
6
7
8
9
P
Q
35
15
14
13
34
Duke Street
Cemetery
A5267
A570
Playing Fields
Football Grd.
Playing Field
Meols Cop. High Sch.
King George V College
Meols
Park
Jane's Brook
Kew Woods Prim. Sch.
Playing
Field
Christ the Ki
R.C. High Sch.
Proposed
Ring
Road
Hollybrook Farm
B5243
Birkdale Cop Farm
Moss Farm
White Moss Farm
Hodge's Farm
Livesley's Covert
Boundary
Brook
London Farm
East Crantum Farm
Crantum Farm West
Crantum
Moss
TINSLEY'S

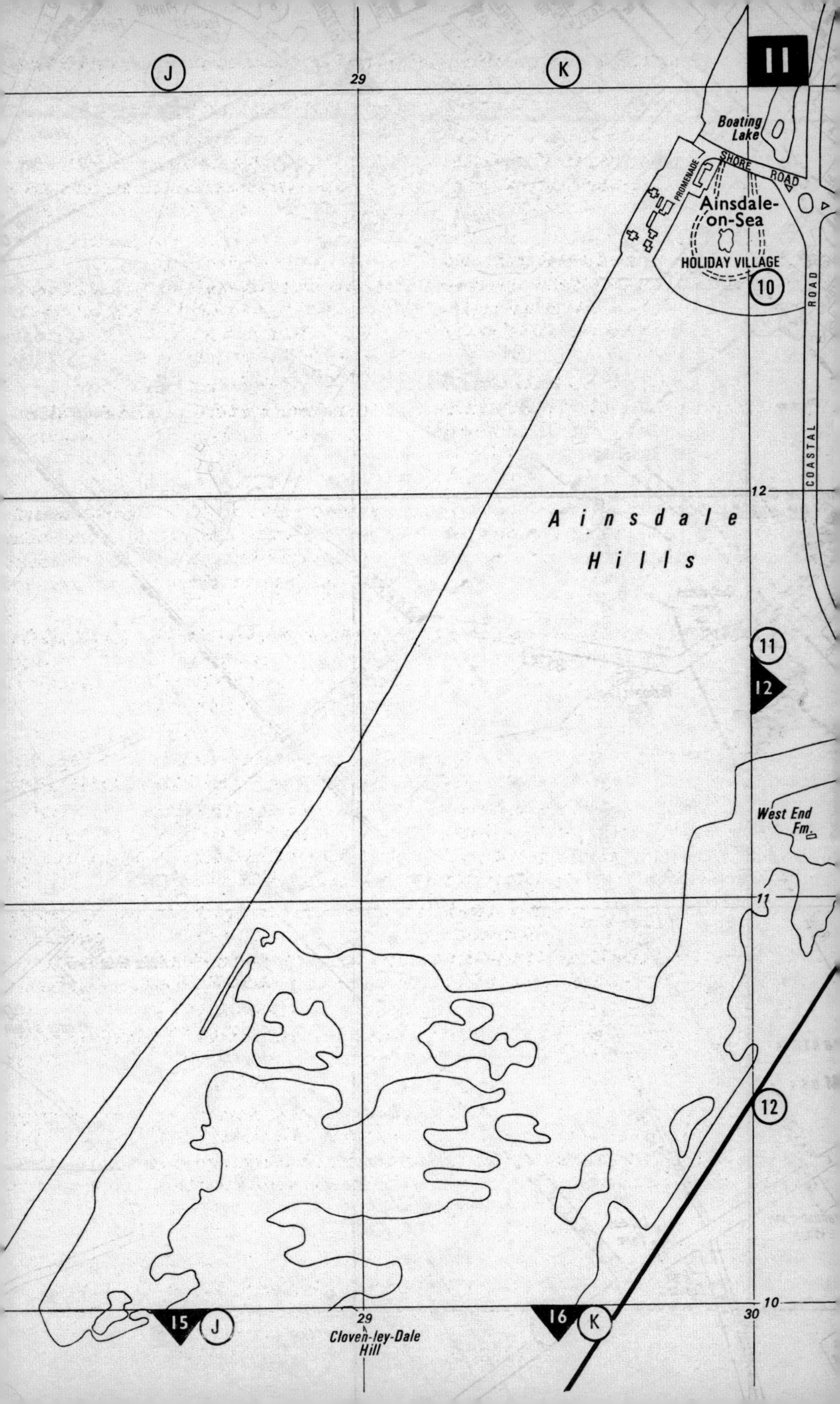

Boating
Lake

SHORE ROAD

PROMENADE

Ainsdale-
on-Sea

HOLIDAY VILLAGE

10

COASTAL ROAD

12

A i n s d a l e

H i l l s

11
12

West End
Fm.

11

12

15 J

29
Cloven-ley-Dale
Hill

16 K

30

10

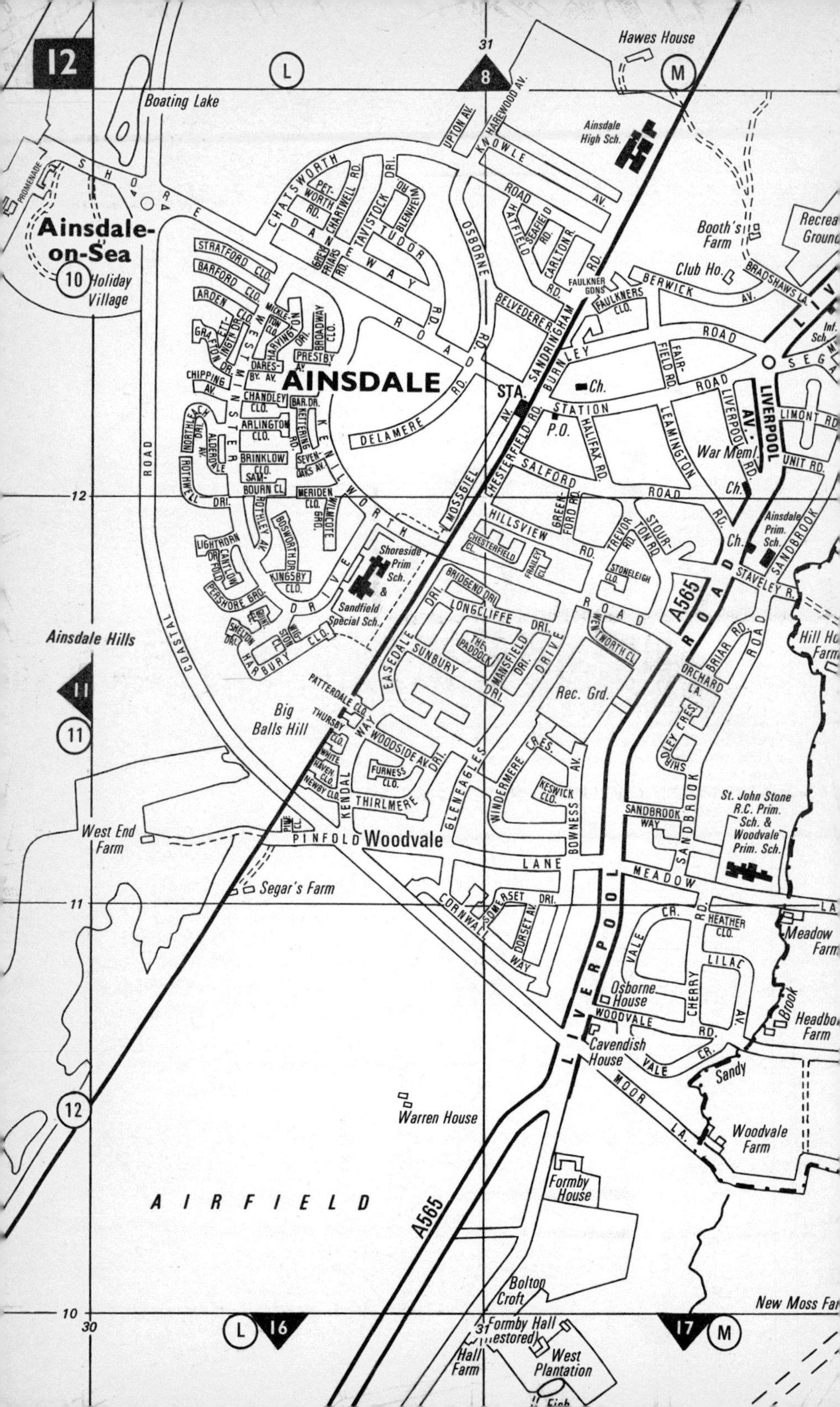
L
8
M
Hawes House
Boating Lake
Ainsdale High Sch.
PROMENADE
SHORE
Ainsdale-on-Sea
10
Holiday Village
CHATSWORTH
PETWORTH RD.
CHARTWELL RD.
TAVISTOCK DRI.
BLENHEIM RD.
UPTON AV.
HAREWOOD AV.
KNOWLE AV.
DANEWAY
TUDOR
OSBORNE RD.
HATFIELD
SEAFIELD RD.
CARLTON R.
Booth's Farm
Recrea Ground
STRATFORD CLO.
BARFORD CLO.
ARDEN CLO.
GREYFRIARS RD.
MICKLETON CLO.
HARVINGTON DRI.
BROADWAY CLO.
ROAD
BELVEDERE R.
FAULKNER GDNS
FAULKNERS CLO.
Club Ho.
BERWICK AV.
BRADSHAWS LA.
WESTMINSTER
ETTINGTON DR.
GRAFTON DR.
DARESBY AV.
PRESTBY AV.
CHIPPING AV.
AINSDALE
SANDRINGHAM RD.
BURNLEY ROAD
FAIRFIELD RD.
Ch.
Inf. Sch.
SEGAR
STA.
STATION ROAD
LIVERPOOL AV.
LIMONT RD.
CHANDLEY CLO.
BAR. DR.
ARLINGTON CLO.
KETTERING RD.
KENILWORTH
DELAMERE
CHESTERFIELD RD.
P.O.
HALIFAX RD.
LEAMINGTON
War Meml.
LIVERPOOL RD.
UNIT RD.
NORTHLEACH DRI.
ALDERDALE AV.
BRINKLOW CLO.
SEVENOAKS AV.
SAMBOURN CL.
MERIDEN CLO.
WILMCOTE GRO.
ROTHWELL DRI.
SALFORD ROAD
GREENFORD RD.
ROTHLEY AV.
BOSWORTH DR.
MOSSGIEL AV.
HILLSVIEW RD.
TREVOR RD.
STOURTON RD.
Ainsdale Prim. Sch.
SANDBROOK
12
LIGHTHORN DR.
CANTLOW FOLD
KINGSBY CLO.
Shoreside Prim Sch. & Sandfield Special Sch.
CHESTERFIELD CL.
FRAILEY CL.
STONELEIGH CLO.
A565
STAVELEY R.
PERSHORE GRO.
DRIVE
BRIDGEND DRI.
LONGCLIFFE DRI.
ROAD
Hill Ho Farm
Ainsdale Hills
SHELTON DRI.
WIGSTON CLO.
HARBURY CLO.
EASEDALE DRI.
SUNBURY DRI.
THE PADDOCK
MANSFIELD DRI.
DRIVE
WENTWORTH CL.
BRIAR RD.
ORCHARD LA.
COASTAL ROAD
11
PATTERDALE CLO.
Big Balls Hill
THURSBY CLO.
WAY
WOODSIDE AV.
Rec. Grd.
SHIRDLEY CRES.
WHITEHAVEN CLO.
NEWBY CLO.
FURNESS CLO.
DRI.
GLENEAGLES
WINDERMERE CRES.
KESWICK CLO.
BOWNESS AV.
KENDAL
THIRLMERE
SANDBROOK WAY
SANDBROOK
St. John Stone R.C. Prim. Sch. & Woodvale Prim. Sch.
West End Farm
PINFOLD CL.
PINFOLD
Woodvale
LANE
MEADOW
Segar's Farm
CORNWALL WAY
SOMERSET DRI.
DORSET AV.
VALE CR.
HEATHER CLO.
Meadow Farm
LILAC AV.
CHERRY RD.
LIVERPOOL
Osborne House
WOODVALE
Brook
Headbo Farm
Cavendish House
MOOR LA.
Sandy
Warren House
Woodvale Farm
Formby House
AIRFIELD
A565
Bolton Croft
New Moss Far
10
30
L
16
31
Formby Hall (restored)
Hall Farm
West Plantation
Fish
17
M

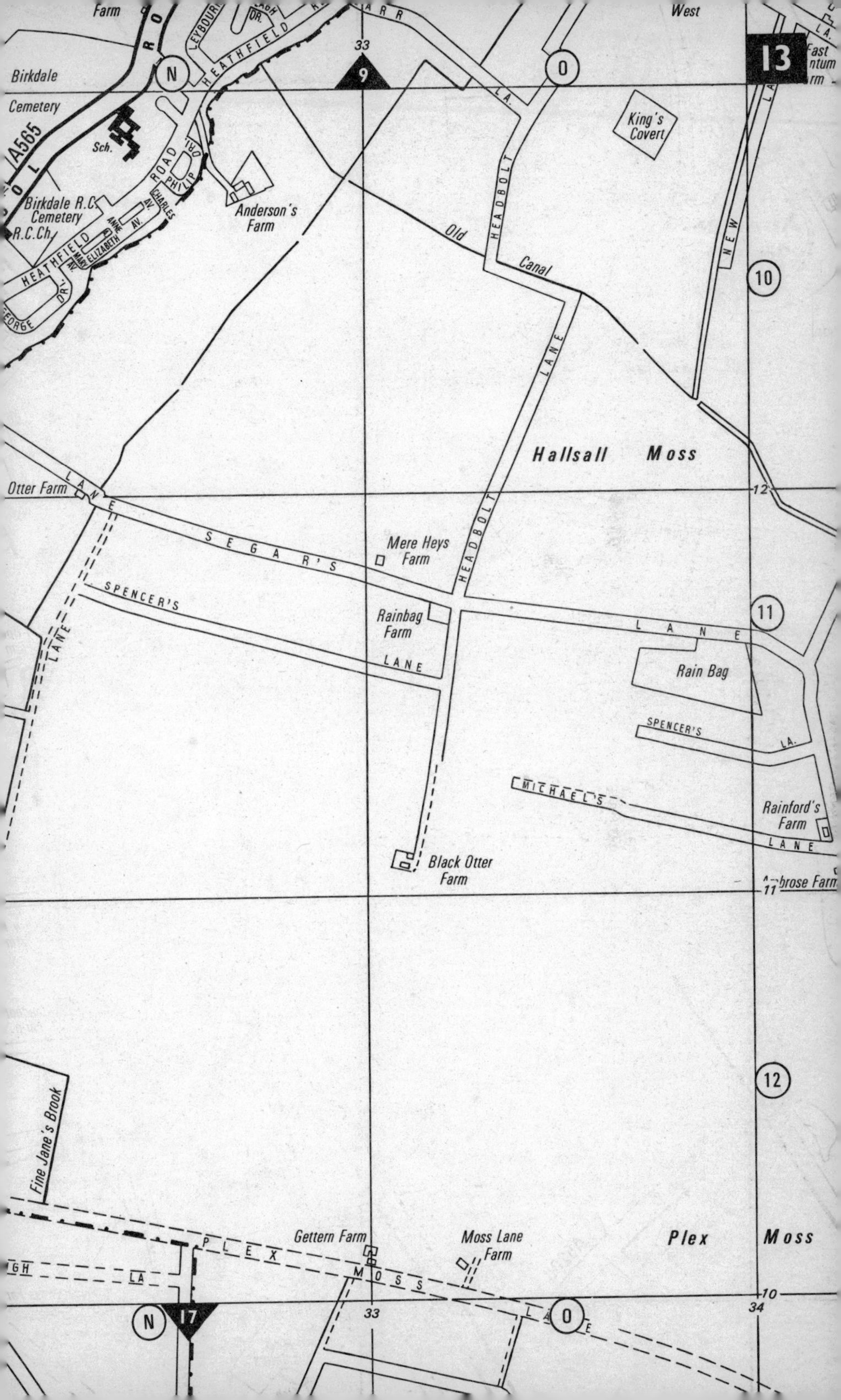

Farm

West

East
ntum
rm

Birkdale
Cemetery

N

33

9

0

10

King's
Covert

Sch.

HEATHFIELD

Anderson's
Farm

Birkdale R.C.
Cemetery
R.C.Ch.

Old

Canal

HEADBOLT

LANE

NEW

A565

HEATHFIELD DR

CHARLES

ELIZABETH AV.

GEORGE

Hallsall   Moss

12

Otter Farm

LANE

SEGAR'S

LANE

Mere Heys
Farm

HEADBOLT

LANE

11

SPENCER'S

Rainbag
Farm

LANE

LANE

Rain Bag

SPENCER'S

LA.

MICHAEL'S

Rainford's
Farm

Black Otter
Farm

LANE

Ambrose Farm

11

12

Fine Jane's Brook

PLEX

Gettern Farm

Moss Lane
Farm

Plex   Moss

GH

LA.

MOSS

LANE

10

34

N

17

33

0

F

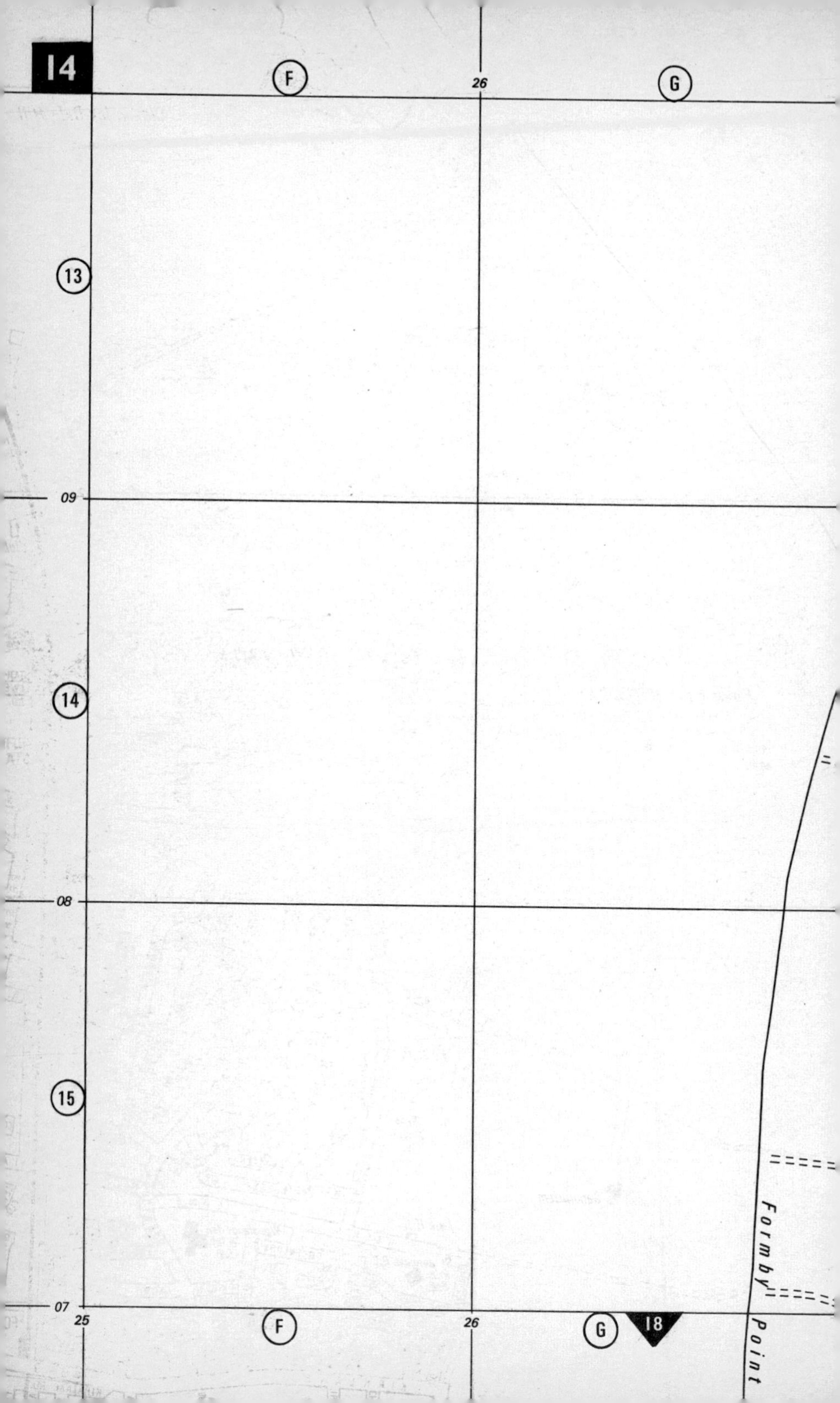

14

F

26

G

13

09

14

08

15

07

25

F

26

G

18

Formby" Point

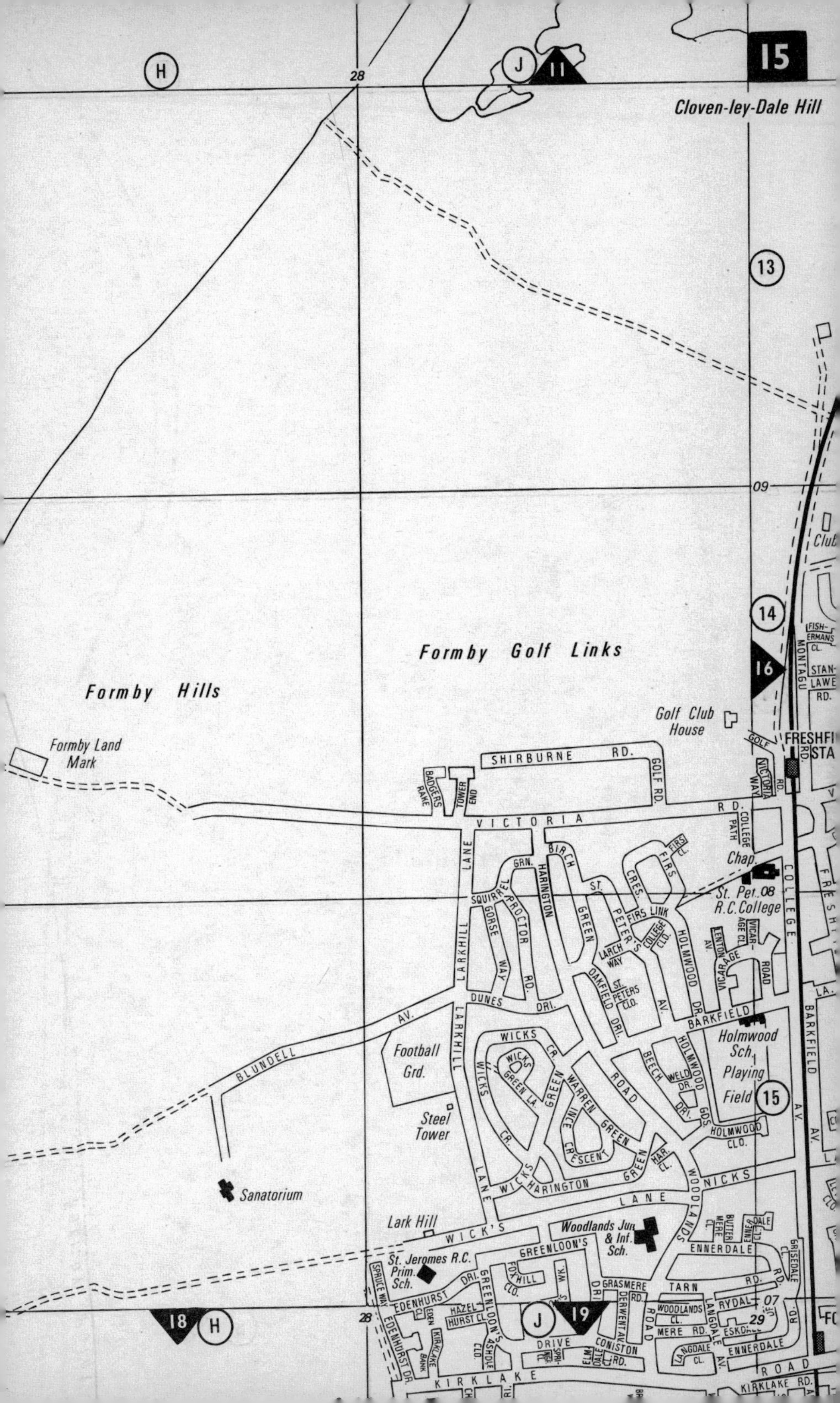

15
H
J
11
28
Cloven-ley-Dale Hill
13
09
14
16
Formby Golf Links
Formby Hills
Golf Club House
Formby Land Mark
SHIRBURNE RD.
GOLF RD.
BADGERS RAKE
TOWER END
VICTORIA RD.
VICTORIA WAY
COLLEGE PATH
Chap.
St. Pet. R.C. College
08
FRESHFI
STA
COLLEGE
MONTAGU RD.
FISHERMANS CL.
STANLAWE RD.
Club
LARKHILL LANE
SQUIRREL GRN.
HARINGTON
BIRCH GREEN
ST. PETER'S AV.
FIRS CRES.
FIRS CL.
FIRS LINK
COLLEGE CLO.
HOLMWOOD DR.
GORSE WAY
PROCTOR RD.
LARCH WAY
OAKFIELD DRI.
ST. PETERS CLO.
LENTON AV.
VICARAGE CL.
VICARAGE ROAD
DUNES DRI.
BLUNDELL AV.
Football Grd.
BARKFIELD
Holmwood Sch. Playing Field
BARKFIELD AV.
WICKS CR.
WICKS GREEN LA.
WARREN GREEN
BEECH ROAD
WELD DR.
HOLMWOOD GDS.
Steel Tower
INCE CRESCENT
HOLMWOOD CLO.
WICKS LANE
HARINGTON GREEN
HAR. CL.
WOODLANDS
Sanatorium
Lark Hill
WICK'S LANE
Woodlands Jun. & Inf. Sch.
MERE CL.
BUTTERMERE CL.
ENNERDALE
GRISEDALE CL.
St. Jeromes R.C. Prim. Sch.
GREENLOON'S DRI.
FOX HILL CLO.
GRASMERE RD.
TARN RD.
SPRUCE WAY
EDENHURST DRI.
EDENHURST CL.
EDEN
HAZEL HURST CL.
DERWENT AV.
ROAD
WOODLANDS CL.
LANGDALE AV.
RYDAL
07
29
18
19
DRIVE
CONISTON RD.
MERE RD.
ESKDALE
LANGDALE CL.
ENNERDALE
KIRKLAKE BANK
ASHDALE CLO.
ELMDALE
KIRKLAKE RD.

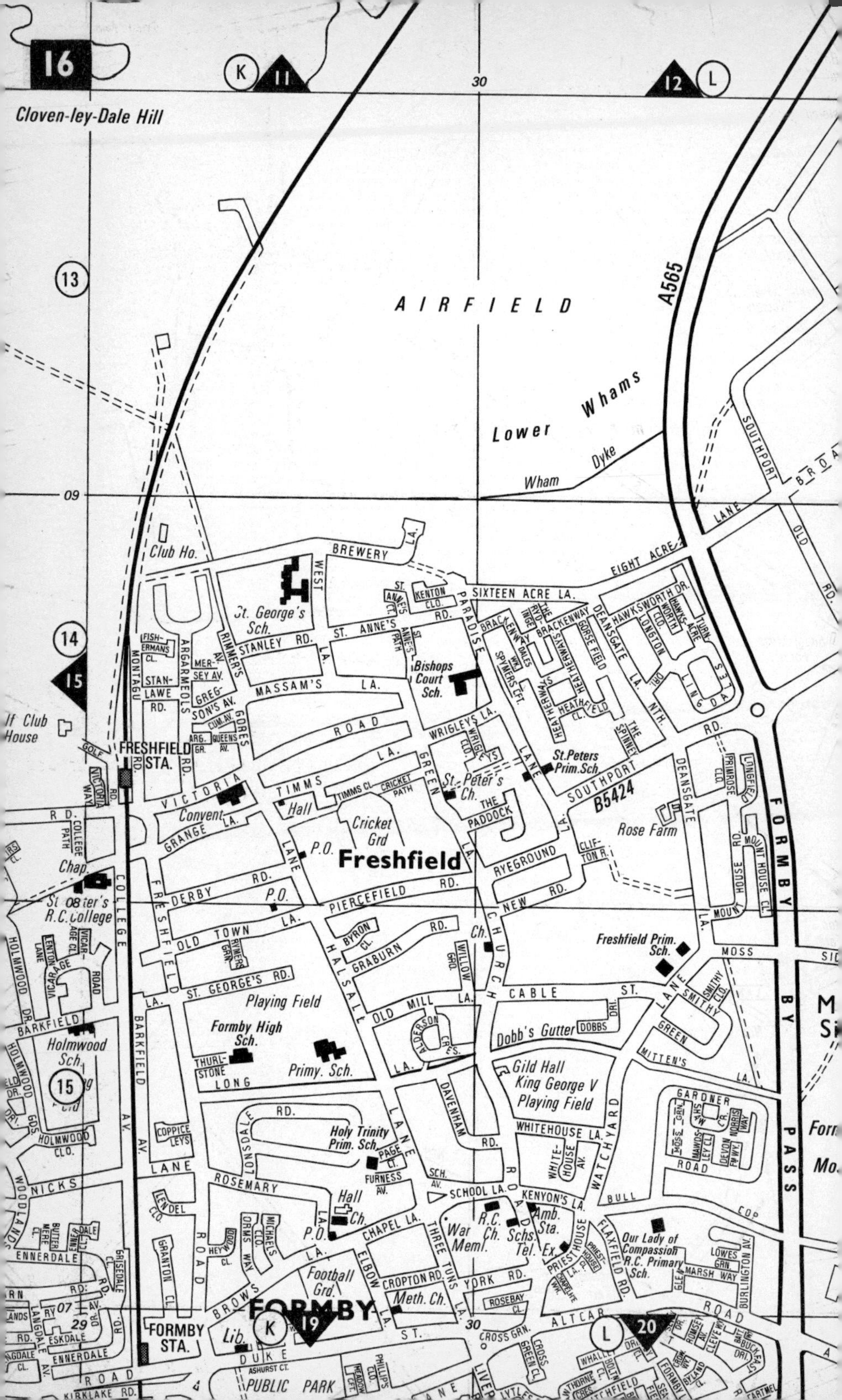
16
K
11
30
12
L
Cloven-ley-Dale Hill
13
AIRFIELD
A565
Lower Whams
Wham Dyke
SOUTHPORT
LANE
BROAD
OLD
RD.
09
Club Ho.
BREWERY LA.
WEST
EIGHT ACRE
SIXTEEN ACRE LA.
KENTON CLO.
ST. ANNE'S CT.
ST. ANNE'S RD.
ANNE'S PATH
PARADISE
BRACKENWAY
HAWKSWORTH DR.
HAWKS WORTH CLO.
HAWKS ACRE
TURN-ACRE
DEANSGATE LA. NTH.
LONGTON DRI.
LINGDALES
St. George's Sch.
14
15
FISH-ERMANS CL.
MONTAGU
ARGARMEOLS
RIMMER'S
STANLEY RD.
MERSEY AV.
GREGSON'S AV.
STAN-LAWE RD.
MASSAM'S LA.
Bishops Court Sch.
SPYMERS CFT.
DALES
HEATHERWAYS
GORSEFIELD
HEATHFIELD CL.
THE SPINNEY
If Club House
GOLF
FRESHFIELD RD.
FRESHFIELD STA.
CUM. AV.
QUEENS AV.
ARG. GR.
GORES
ROAD
WRIGLEYS LA.
WRIGLEYS CLO.
LANE
St. Peters Prim. Sch.
SOUTHPORT RD.
B5424
DEANSGATE
PRIMROSE CLO.
LONGFIELD
VICTORIA WAY
VICTORIA
TIMMS LA.
TIMMS CL.
CRICKET PATH
GREEN
St. Peter's Ch.
THE PADDOCK
Rose Farm
FORMBY
RD.
COLLEGE PATH
Convent
GRANGE LA.
Hall
Cricket Grd
LANE
P.O.
Freshfield
RYEGROUND
CLIFTON R.
MOUNT HOUSE RD.
MOUNT HOUSE CL.
Chap.
St. Peter's R.C. College
COLLEGE
FRESHFIELD
DERBY RD.
P.O.
PIERCEFIELD RD.
NEW RD.
MOUNT
BY
HOLMWOOD DR.
LENTON LANE
VICARAGE CL.
ROAD
OLD TOWN LA.
RYMERS GRN.
BYRON CL.
GRABURN RD.
HALSALE
Ch.
WILLOW GRO.
CHURCH
Freshfield Prim. Sch.
MOSS
SIDE
VICARAGE
ST. GEORGE'S RD.
Playing Field
OLD MILL LA.
CABLE ST.
LANE
SMITHY CLO.
SMITHY GREEN
M
BARKFIELD
Holmwood Sch.
LA.
Formby High Sch.
ALDERSON CRES.
Dobb's Gutter
DOBBS DRI.
MITTEN'S LA.
15
THURLSTONE
Primy. Sch.
LONG
LA.
Gild Hall
King George V Playing Field
GARDNER
MOSS GRN.
RD.
WAY
NORRIS
DAVENHAM RD.
WHITEHOUSE LA.
YARD
WATCH
WHITEHOUSE AV.
MAWDSLEY CL.
DEVON FM. WY.
ROAD
PASS
HOLMWOOD CLO.
COPPICE LEYS
LONSDALE
Holy Trinity Prim. Sch.
PAGE CT.
WOODLANDS
NICKS
LANE
ROSEMARY
LENDEL CLO.
FURNESS AV.
SCH. AV.
SCHOOL LA.
ROAD
KENYON'S LA.
BULL
COP
Hall
Ch.
LA.
CHAPEL LA.
War Meml.
R.C. Ch.
Schs.
Amb. Sta.
Tel. Ex.
HEYWOOD CL.
ORMS WAY
MICHAELS CLO.
BUTTERMERE CL.
ENNERDALE
GRISEDALE
RD.
GRANTON CL.
P.O.
Football Grd.
ELBOW LA.
THREE TUNS LA.
PRIEST HOUSE
PRIEST HOUSE LA. CL.
FLAXFIELD RD.
Our Lady of Compassion R.C. Primary Sch.
LOWES GRN.
BURLINGTON AV.
MARSH WAY
GLEN
CROPTON RD.
YORK RD.
Meth. Ch.
ROSEBAY CL.
07
29
LANGDALE
ESKDALE
ENNERDALE AV.
FORMBY STA.
ROAD
KIRKLAKE RD.
BROWS
FORMBY
K
19
Lib.
DUKE ST.
ASHURST CT.
PUBLIC PARK
PHILLIPS CLO.
MEADOW CFT.
30
ALTCAR ROAD
CROSS GRN.
GREEN CL.
CROSS
L
20
WHALLEY
ROMSEY AV.
CLEVEWD
BUCKFAST DRI.
FORMBY
HAWTHORNE CRES.
LITCHFIELD
LIVER

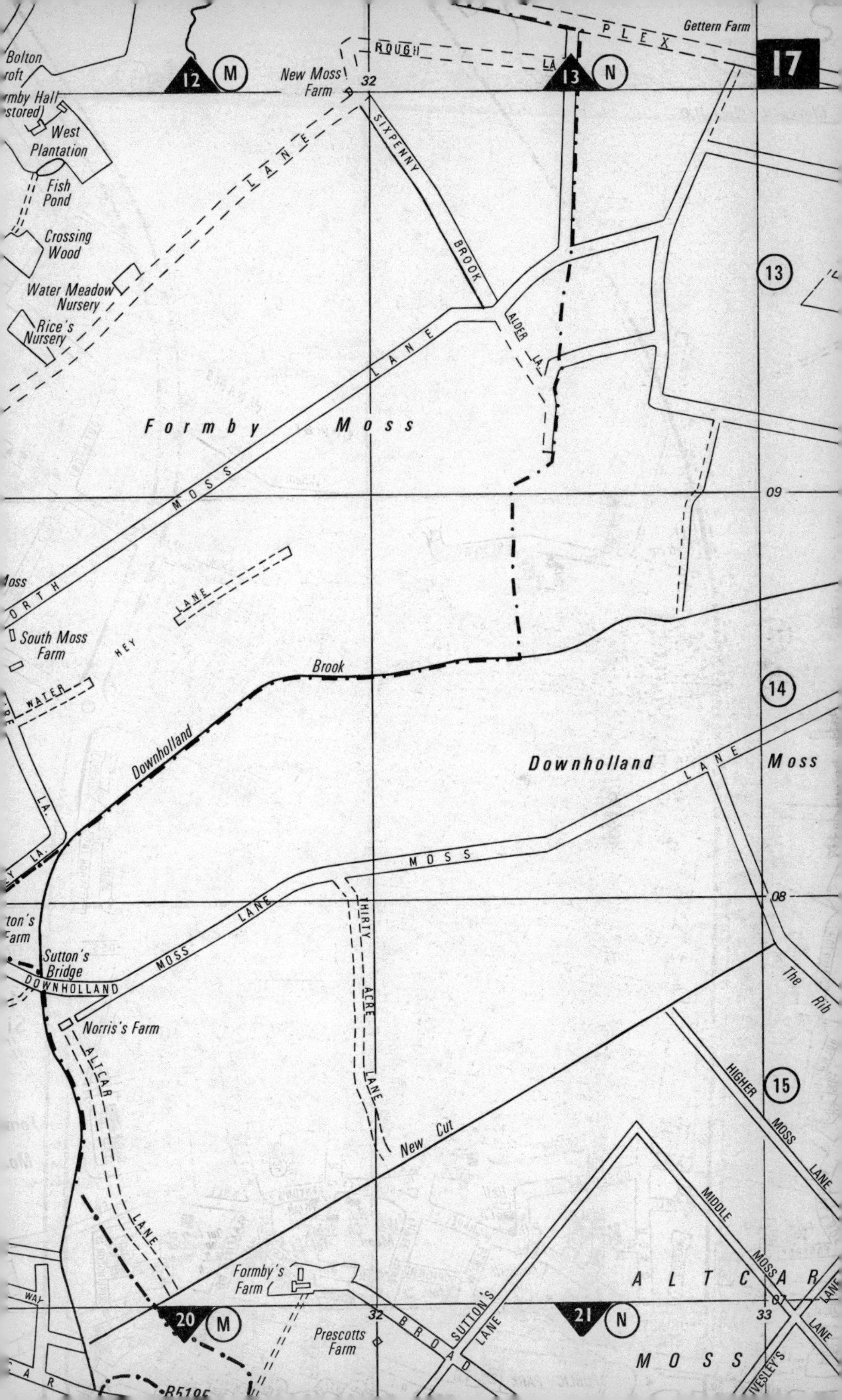

17
Gettern Farm
PLEX
ROUGH
LA
12
M
13
N
Bolton
roft
rmby Hall
stored)
New Moss
Farm
32
West
Plantation
Fish
Pond
Crossing
Wood
Water Meadow
Nursery
Rice's
Nursery
LANE
SIXPENNY
BROOK
ALDER
LA
LANE
Formby
Moss
MOSS
09
Moss
ORTH
LANE
HEY
South Moss
Farm
WATER
Brook
Downholland
LA.
LA.
Downholland
LANE
Moss
MOSS
MOSS
LANE
THIRTY
ACRE
LANE
08
ton's
Farm
Sutton's
Bridge
DOWNHOLLAND
Norris's Farm
The
Rib
ALTCAR
LANE
HIGHER
MOSS
LANE
New Cut
MIDDLE
MOSS
LANE
Formby's
Farm
ALTCAR
WAY
20
M
21
N
32
BROAD
SUTTON'S
LANE
Prescotts
Farm
33
07
MOSS
IVESLEY'S
LANE
B5195
13
14
15

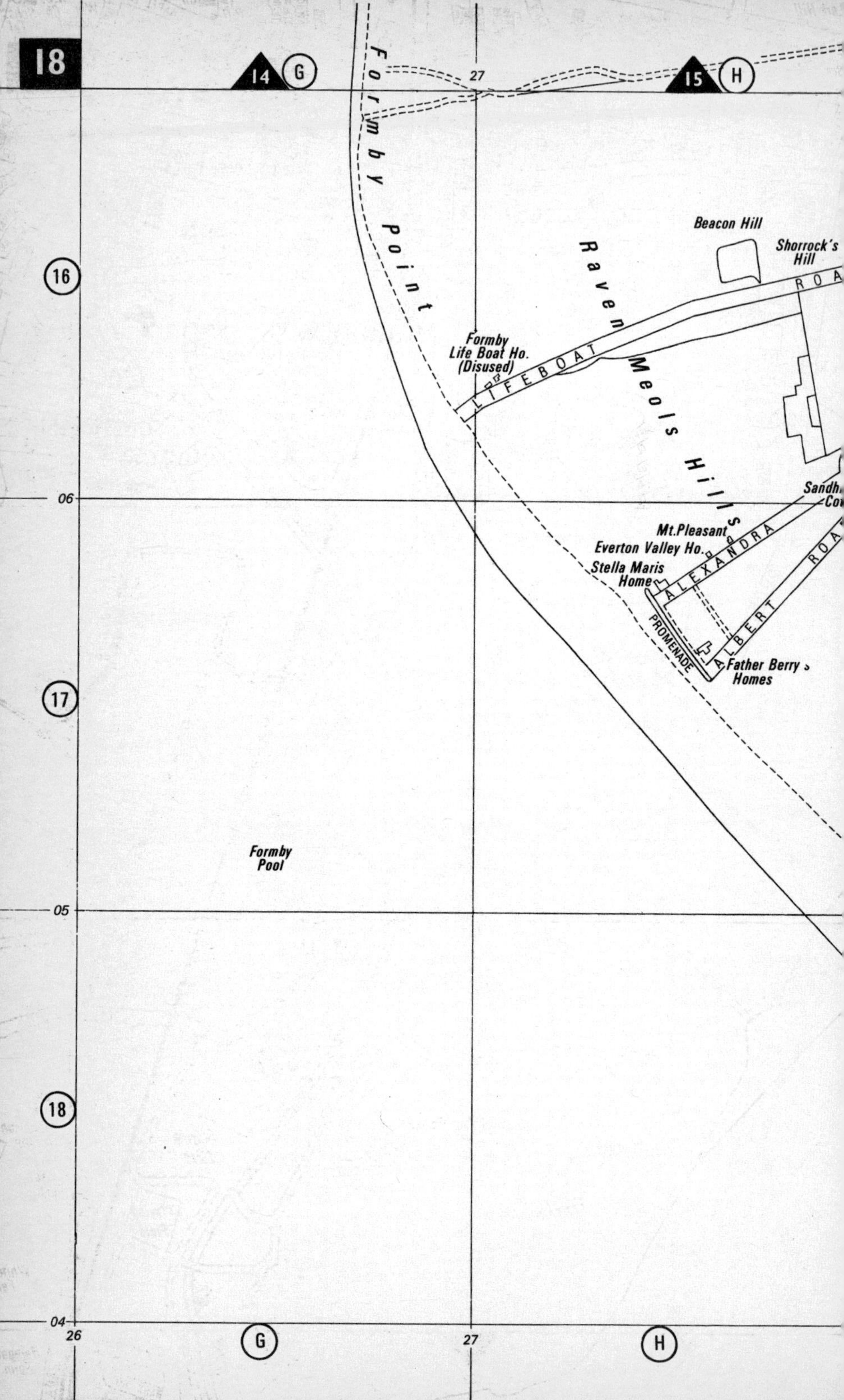

14 G
15 H
27
Formby Point
Beacon Hill
Shorrock's Hill
Raven Meols Hills
ROAD
Formby Life Boat Ho. (Disused)
LIFEBOAT
16
06
Mt.Pleasant
Everton Valley Ho.
Stella Maris Home
ALEXANDRA
ROAD
ALBERT
PROMENADE
Father Berry's Homes
17
Formby Pool
05
18
04
26
G
27
H

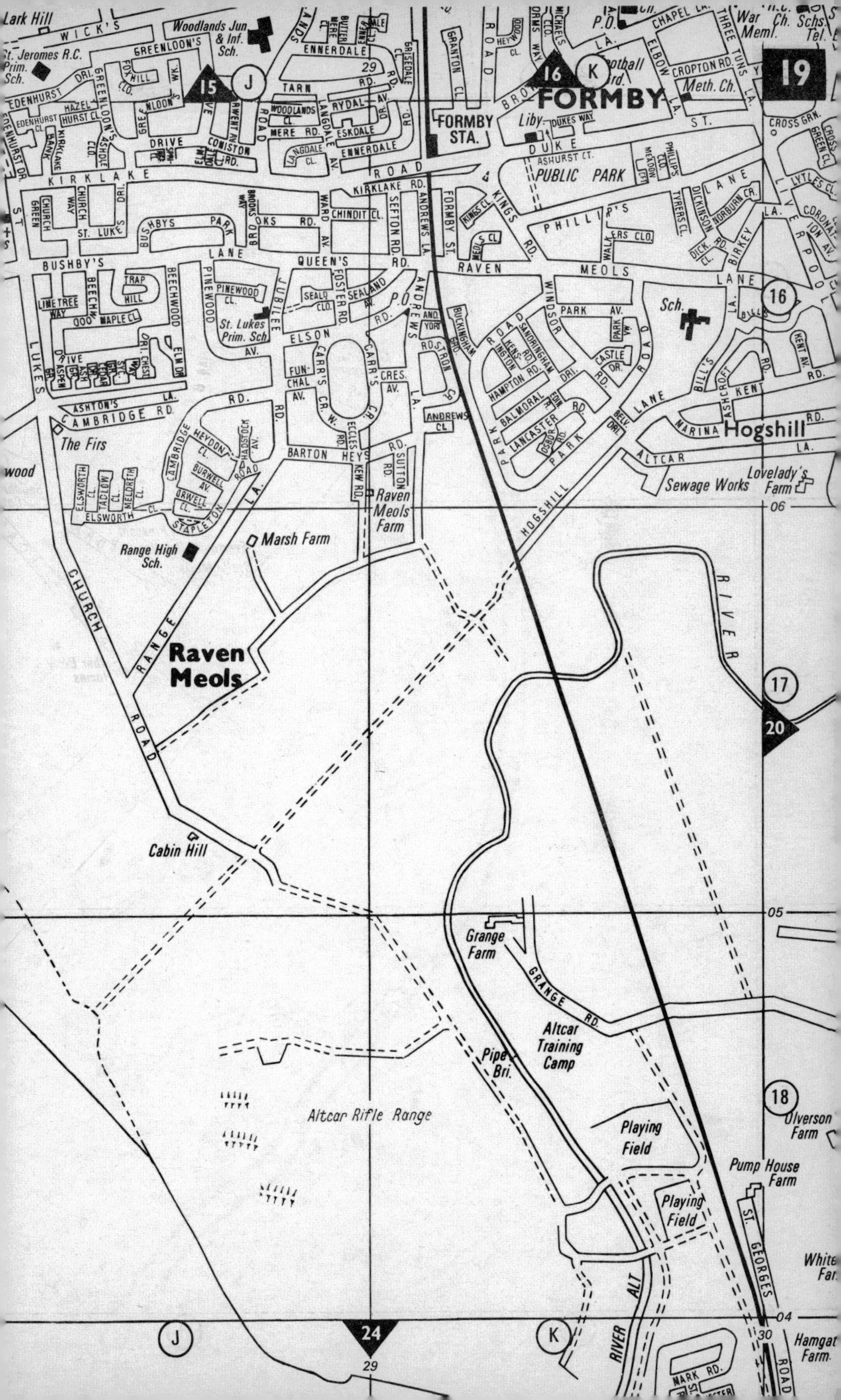

19
FORMBY
Formby Sta.
Raven Meols
Hogshill
Lark Hill
Woodlands Jun & Inf. Sch.
St. Jeromes R.C. Prim. Sch.
P.O.
Liby.
Meth. Ch.
War Meml.
Public Park
St. Lukes Prim. Sch.
Sch.
The Firs
Range High Sch.
Marsh Farm
Raven Meols Farm
Cabin Hill
Sewage Works
Lovelady's Farm
Grange Farm
Altcar Training Camp
Pipe Bri.
Altcar Rifle Range
Playing Field
Playing Field
Pump House Farm
Olverson Farm
Hamgate Farm
River Alt
Kirklake Road
Church Road
Range La.
Hogshill La.
Raven Meols Lane
Duke St.
Liverpool Rd.
Grange Rd.
Altcar La.
St. Georges Road
Phillip's Lane
Bushby's Lane
Queen's Rd.
Elson Rd.
Barton Heys Rd.
Cambridge Rd.
Park Road
Windsor Road
Freshfield Road
Three Tuns La.
Chapel La.
Elbow La.
Bill's La.
Kent Rd.
Marina Rd.
Formby St.
Kings Rd.
Sefton Rd.
Andrews La.
Foster Rd.
Jubilee Rd.
Pinewood Av.
Brooks Rd.
Ennerdale Rd.
Coniston Rd.
Greenloon's Drive
Wick's La.
Edenhurst Dri.
Kirklake Bank
St. Lukes Church Rd.
15
J
16
K
16
17
20
18
24
J
K
06
05
04
29
29
30

20
16
17
Our Lady of Compassion R.C. Prim. Sch.
Formby's Farm
Altcar Road
B5195
Rail Bridge
Sutton's Farm
St. Michael's
Redgate Prim. Sch.
Causeway
Formby
A565
Hogshill
Lovelady's Farm
Little Altcar
B5424
Road
Abraham's Bridge
New
Alt Bridge
River Alt
19
Arnold's Cop
Long Covert
Marsh Wood
Engine
Short
The Orchard
North End La.
North End Farm
Scaffold La.
Marsh Lane
North End
18
Olverson's Farm
Pump House Farm
Shire
Moss La.
Whitedge Farm
St. Georges Road
Hamgate Farm
25
Lady Green Farm
Orrell Hill Wood
Lady Green
06
05
04
30
31

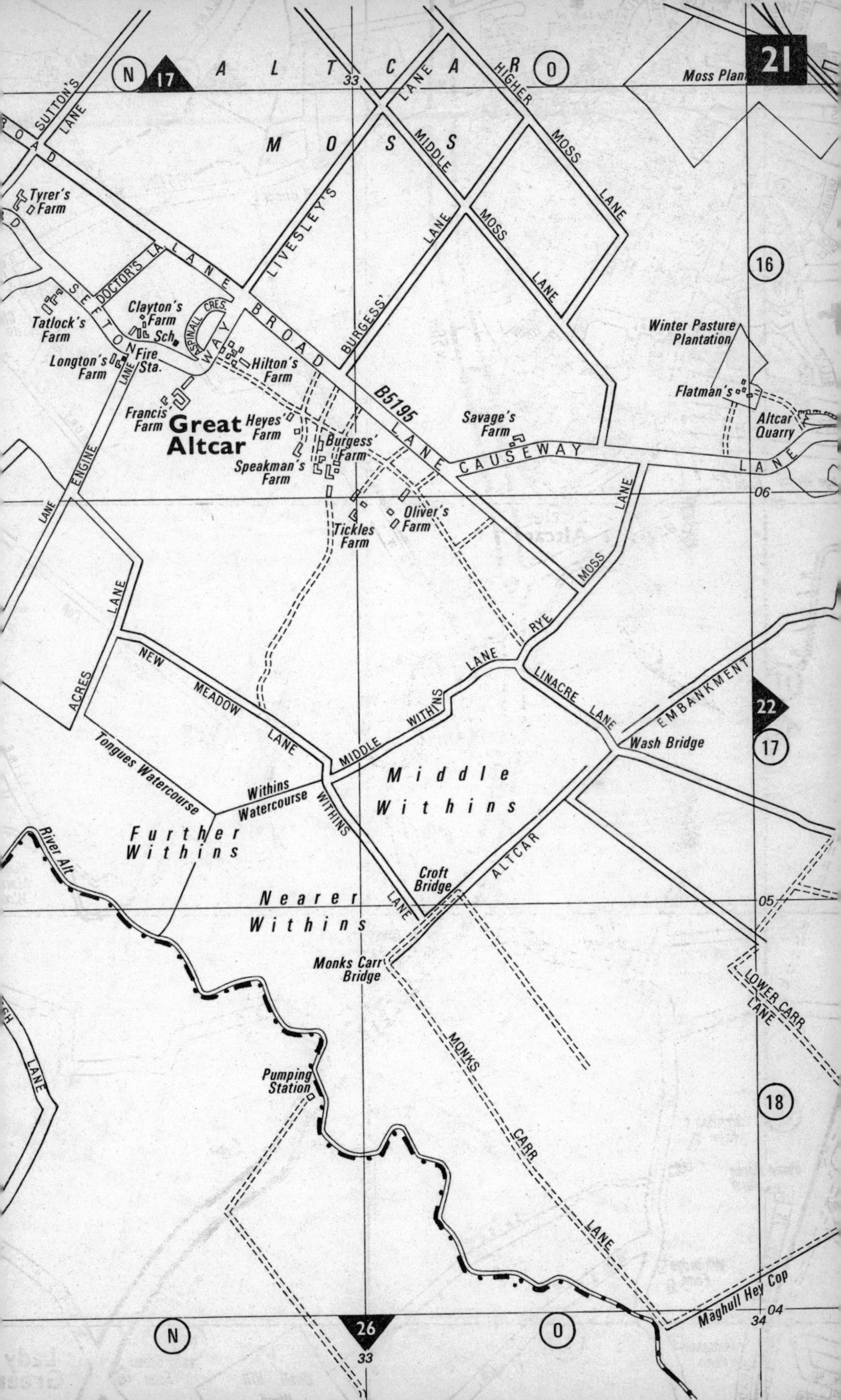

21
N
17
ALTCAR
O
MOSS
Moss Plan
SUTTON'S LANE
HIGHER MOSS LANE
MIDDLE MOSS LANE
LIVESLEY'S LANE
BURGESS' LANE
BROAD LANE
DOCTOR'S LA
SEFTON LANE
Tyrer's Farm
Tatlock's Farm
Clayton's Farm
Sch.
ASPINALL CRES.
WAY
Fire Sta.
Longton's Farm
Hilton's Farm
Francis' Farm
Great Altcar
Heyes' Farm
Burgess' Farm
Speakman's Farm
Tickles Farm
Oliver's Farm
B5195
Savage's Farm
CAUSEWAY LANE
Winter Pasture Plantation
Flatman's
Altcar Quarry
16
06
ENGINE LANE
ACRES LANE
NEW MEADOW LANE
MOSS LANE
RYE LANE
MIDDLE WITHINS LANE
LINACRE LANE
EMBANKMENT
22
17
Wash Bridge
Middle Withins
Tongues Watercourse
Withins Watercourse
WITHINS LANE
Further Withins
River Alt
ALTCAR
Croft Bridge
Nearer Withins
05
Monks Carr Bridge
LOWER CARR LANE
MONKS CARR LANE
Pumping Station
18
Maghull Hey Cop
04
34
N
26
33
O

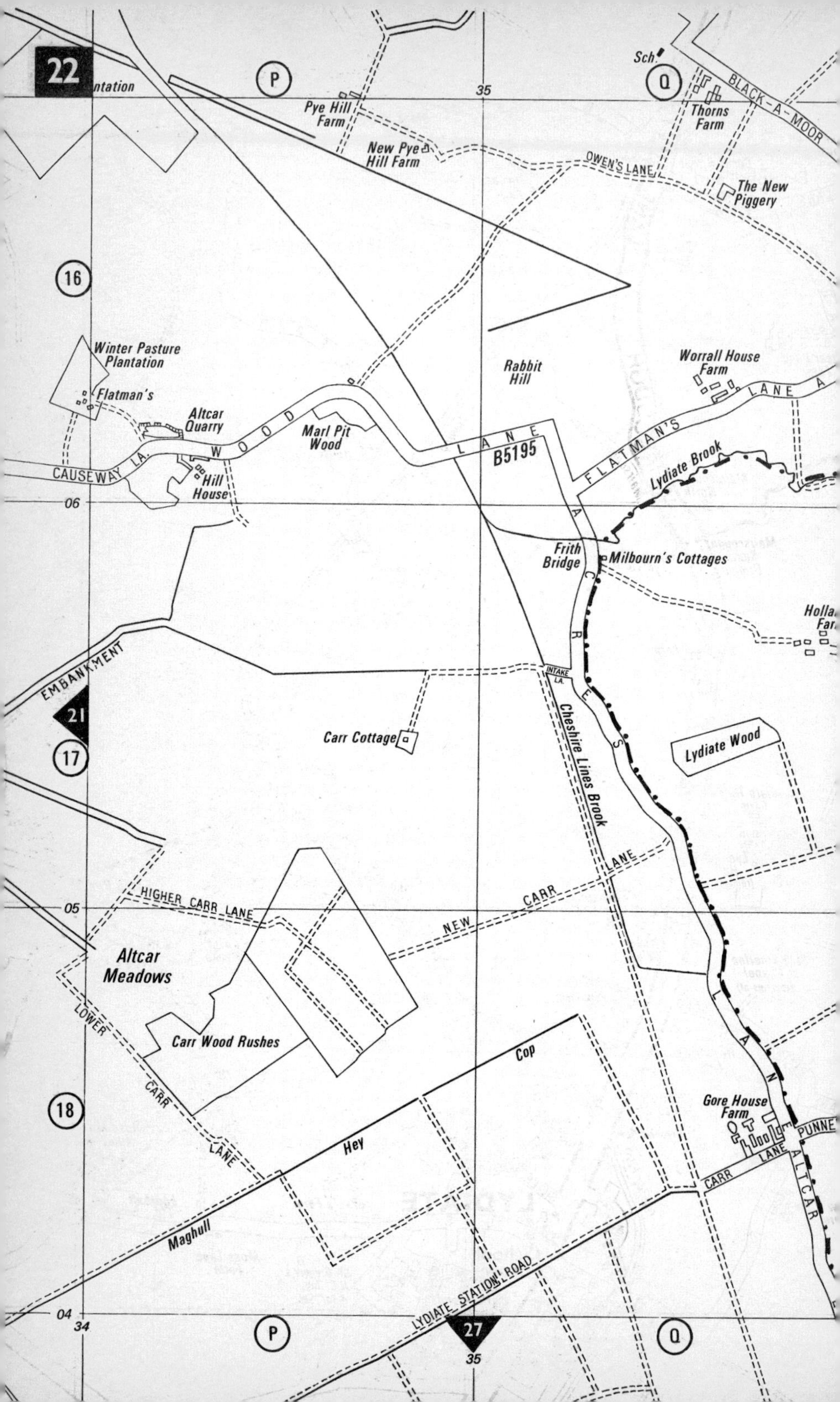

ntation
P
Q
35
Sch.
Pye Hill Farm
New Pye Hill Farm
Thorns Farm
BLACK-A-MOOR
OWEN'S LANE
The New Piggery
16
Winter Pasture Plantation
Flatman's
Rabbit Hill
Worrall House Farm
LANE
Altcar Quarry
Marl Pit Wood
WOOD LANE
B5195
FLATMAN'S
Lydiate Brook
CAUSEWAY LA.
Hill House
06
Frith Bridge
Milbourn's Cottages
ACRE
Holla Far
EMBANKMENT
INTAKE LA.
21
Carr Cottage
Cheshire Lines Brook
17
Lydiate Wood
LANE
HIGHER CARR LANE
05
NEW CARR
Altcar Meadows
LOWER CARR LANE
Carr Wood Rushes
Cop
18
Gore House Farm
PUNNE
Hey
CARR LANE
ALTCAR
Maghull
LYDIATE STATION ROAD
04
34
27
35

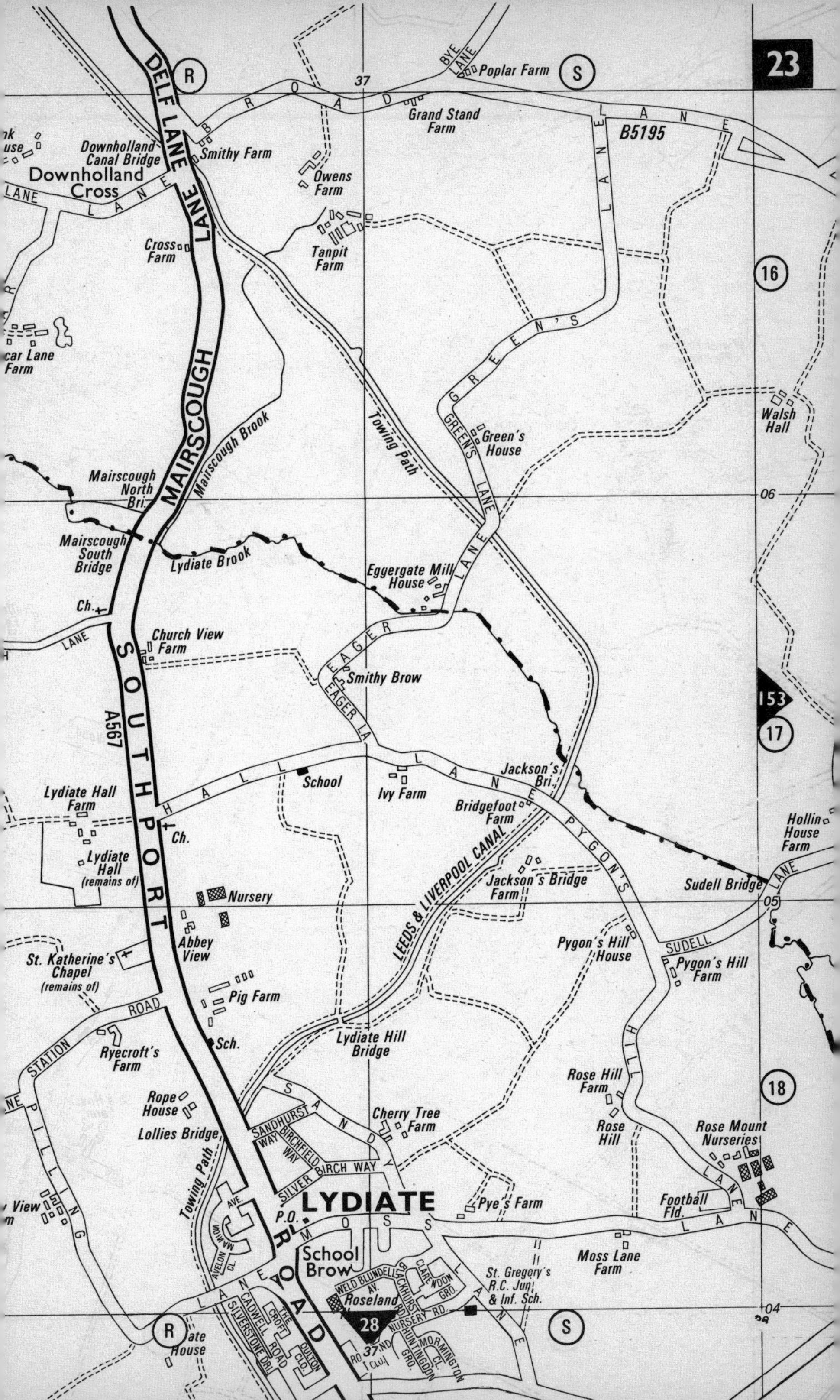

23
DELF LANE
BYE LANE
Poplar Farm
37
BROAD LANE
Grand Stand Farm
B5195
Smithy Farm
Downholland Canal Bridge
Downholland Cross
Owens Farm
Tanpit Farm
Cross Farm
MAIRSCOUGH LANE
Mairscough Brook
Towing Path
GREEN'S LANE
Green's House
Walsh Hall
16
Mairscough North Bri.
06
Mairscough South Bridge
Lydiate Brook
Eggergate Mill House
Ch.
Church View Farm
EAGER LANE
Smithy Brow
SOUTHPORT
A567
153
17
HALL LANE
School
Ivy Farm
Jackson's Bri.
Lydiate Hall Farm
Bridgefoot Farm
Ch.
LEEDS & LIVERPOOL CANAL
PYGON'S HILL
Hollin House Farm
Lydiate Hall (remains of)
Jackson's Bridge Farm
Sudell Bridge
Nursery
05
Abbey View
Pygon's Hill House
SUDELL LANE
Pygon's Hill Farm
St. Katherine's Chapel (remains of)
Pig Farm
STATION ROAD
Sch.
Lydiate Hill Bridge
Ryecroft's Farm
Rose Hill Farm
18
Rope House
Cherry Tree Farm
Rose Hill
Rose Mount Nurseries
Lollies Bridge
SANDY LANE
SANDHURST WAY
BIRCHFIELD WAY
SILVER BIRCH WAY
Towing Path
PILLING LANE
LYDIATE
Pye's Farm
Football Fld.
P.O.
MOSS LANE
AVE.
School Brow
Moss Lane Farm
AVELON CL.
WELD BLUNDELL AV.
BLACKHURST RD.
CLARENDON GRO.
St. Gregory's R.C. Jun. & Inf. Sch.
Roseland
04
R
S
ROAD
28
NURSERY RD.
CADWELL ROAD
SILVERSTONE DRI.
THE CROFT
OULTON CLO.
HUNTINGDON GRO.
MORNINGTON CL.
House

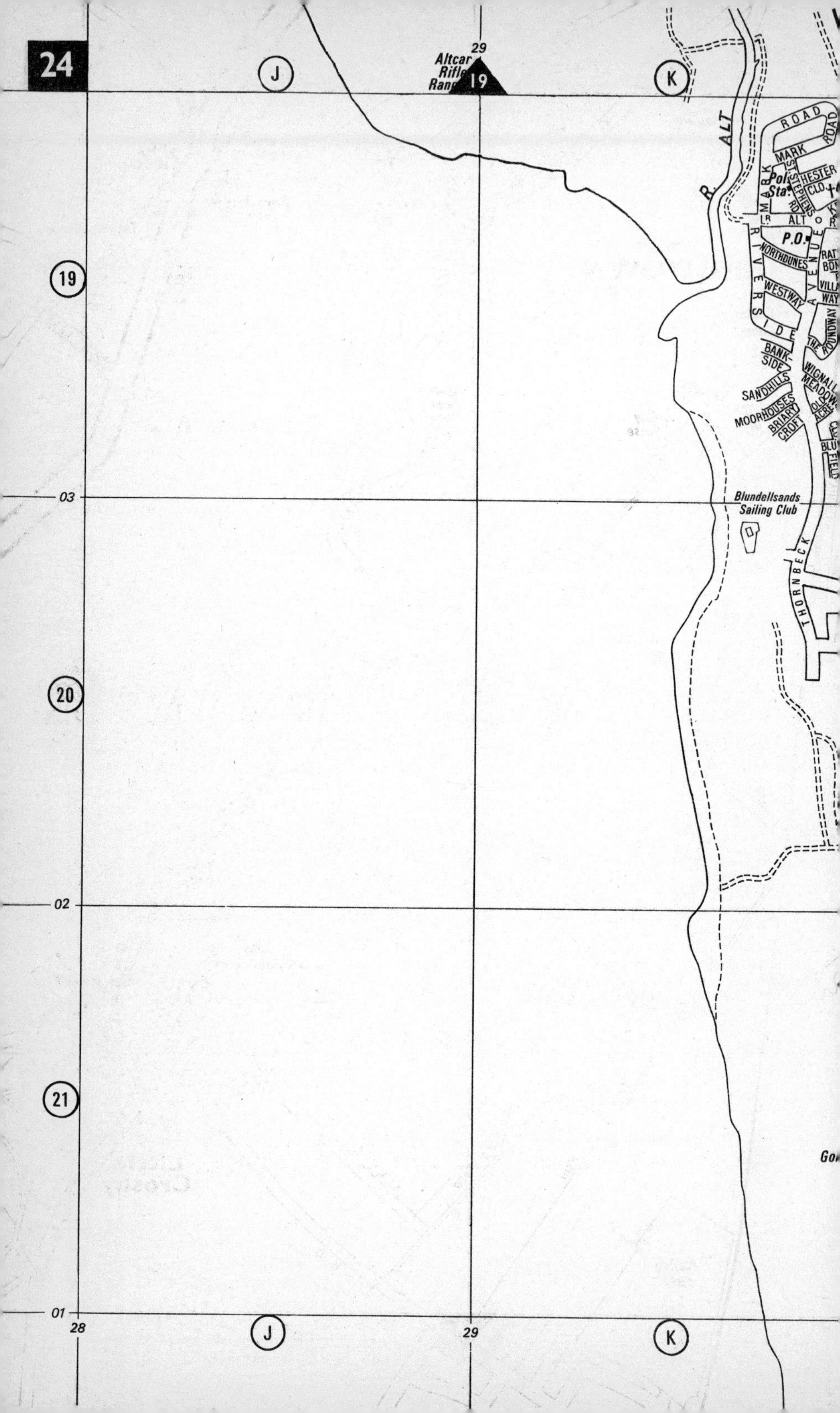

24

J
K

Altcar Rifle Range 29 19

19

R. ALT
ROAD
MARK
CHESTER
Pol. Sta.
P.O.
NORTHDUNES
WESTWAY
RIVERSIDE
WIGMALL MEADOW
BANK-SIDE
SANDHILLS
MOORHOUSES
BRIARY CROFT
BLUE FIELD

03

Blundellsands Sailing Club

THORNBECK

20

02

21

Gor

01

28

J

29

K

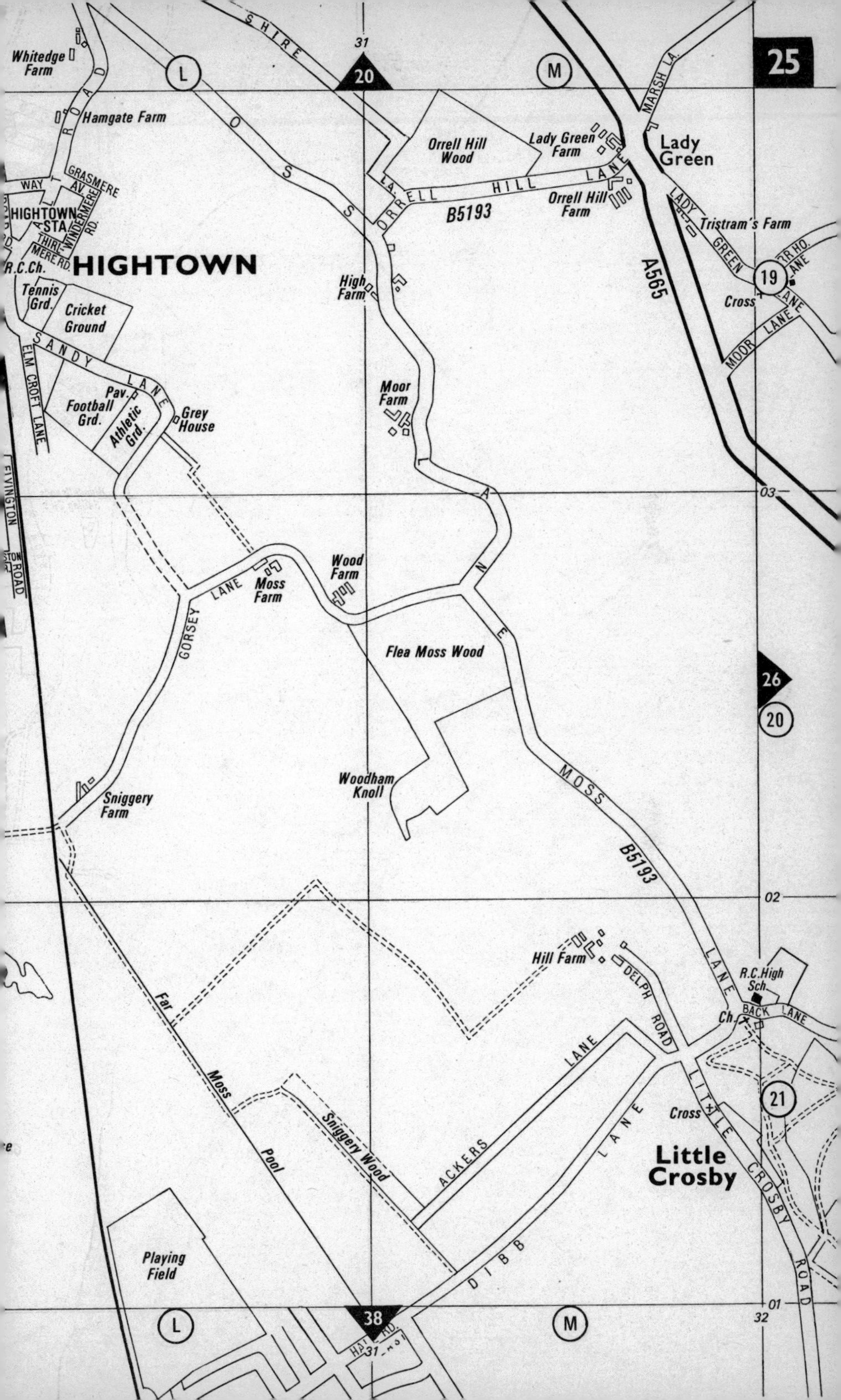
HIGHTOWN
Whitedge Farm
Hamgate Farm
ROAD
GRASMERE AV.
WAY
HIGHTOWN STA
WINDERMERE RD.
THIRLMERE RD.
R.C.Ch.
Tennis Grd.
Cricket Ground
SANDY LANE
ELM CROFT LANE
Pav.
Football Grd.
Athletic Grd.
Grey House
SHIRE
L
M
20
31
MOSS LANE
Orrell Hill Wood
Lady Green Farm
ORRELL HILL LANE
LA.
B5193
Orrell Hill Farm
MARSH LA.
Lady Green
LADY GREEN
Tristram's Farm
A565
19
Cross
MOOR LANE
High Farm
Moor Farm
03
Wood Farm
Moss Farm
GORSEY LANE
Flea Moss Wood
26
20
Woodham Knoll
Sniggery Farm
MOSS
B5193
02
Hill Farm
DELPH ROAD
LANE
R.C.High Sch.
BACK LANE
Ch.
Far Moss Pool
Sniggery Wood
ACKERS LANE
DIBB LANE
Cross
21
Little Crosby
LITTLE CROSBY ROAD
Playing Field
38
01
32
31

26
N
21
O
Lady Green
Carr Houses
Rigmaiden Farm
Tristram's Farm
CARR HOUSE LANE
HALL LANE
Kiln Farm
GREEN LA.
Ince Blundell
19
MOOR LA.
BACK O'TH TOWN LA.
VICTORIA RD.
Eccleston Farm
R.C.Prim.Sch.
Holt's Hey Wood
BLACKCARR LA.
CARR SIDE LA.
Carr Side Farm
PARK WALL ROAD
Home Farm
BARN LA.
CROSS
Ince Blundell Hall (Convalecent Home)
03
MOOR A565
Ince Blundell Park
Cricket Grd.
EAST LA.
25
20
Moss Wood
LANE
Sunnyfield Farm
PARK WALL ROAD
LONG LA.
Hunt's Brook
02
MOSS LA.
INCE
Holly Farm
Wrak's Farm
R.C.High Sch.
Ch.
Thornton Wood
BACK LANE
Little Crosby
Crosby Hall
21
LITTLE CROSBY RD.
B5193
INCE LA.
SOUTHPORT ROAD
INCE RD.
PARK DR.
WOODLAND VW.
SEFTON DR.
BRENDA CR.
The Cottage
Thornton
Meml. Chapel on site of Harkirke
VIRGIN'S LANE
HOLGATE PARK
HOLGATE
PARK VW.
RUTHWELLS
Burying Ground Plantation
01
32
N
39
33
O
BROOK RD.
CHELLOW DENE
QUARRY RD.
GREEN
HARTDALE RD.
Lib.
Holy Family R.C. High Sch.
WATER ST.
MOORLANDS
WESTBOURNE
NORTHWAY

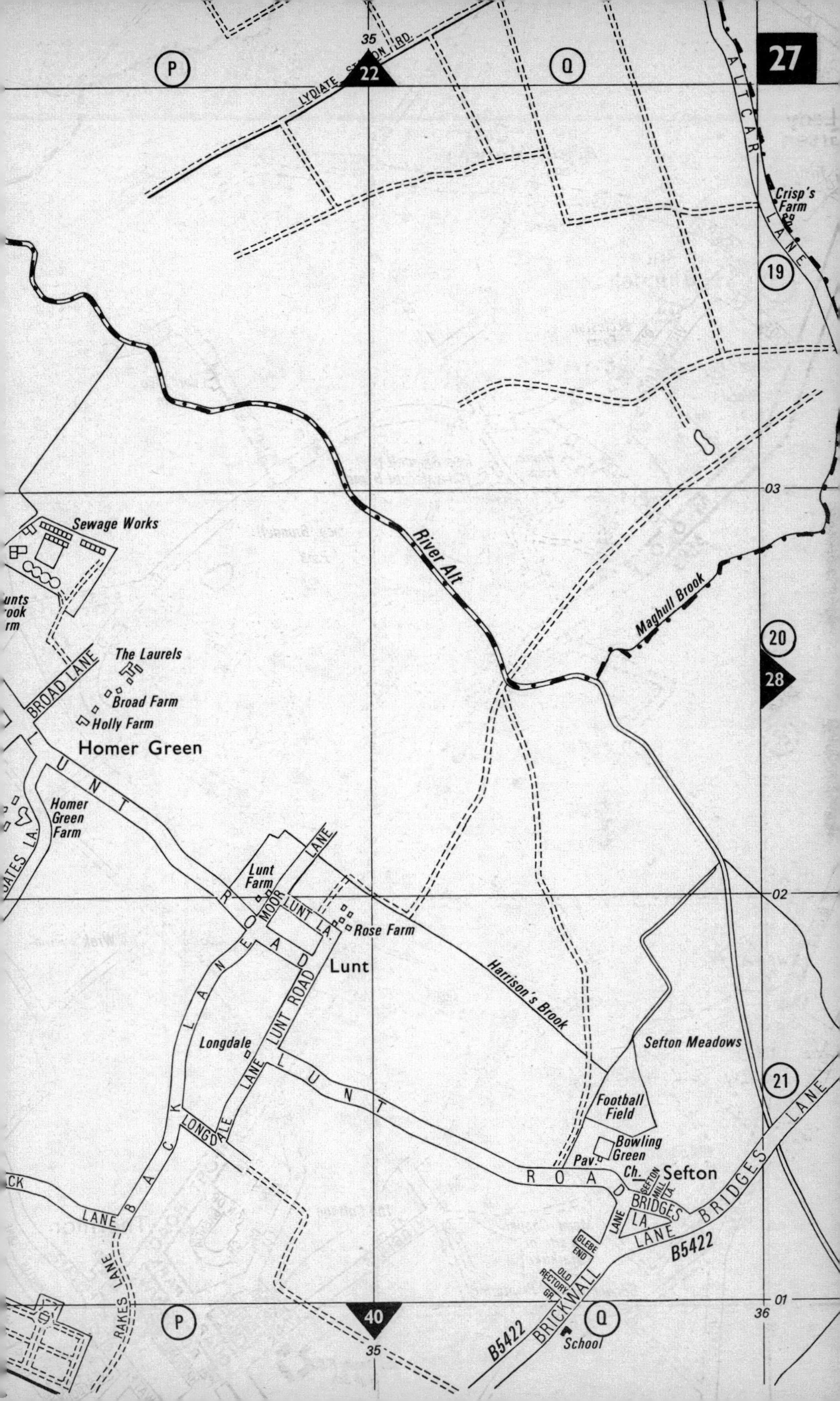
27
P
Q
35
22
LYDIATE STATION RD.
ALTCAR LANE
Crisp's Farm
19
03
River Alt
Sewage Works
Maghull Brook
20
28
The Laurels
Broad Farm
Holly Farm
BROAD LANE
Homer Green
LUNT ROAD
Homer Green Farm
GATES LA.
MOOR LANE
Lunt Farm
LUNT LA.
Rose Farm
02
Lunt
LUNT ROAD
Harrison's Brook
Sefton Meadows
Longdale
LONGDALE LANE
BACK LANE
Football Field
21
Bowling Green
Pav.
Ch.
Sefton
SEFTON MILL LA.
BRIDGES LA
BRIDGES LANE
GLEBE END
OLD RECTORY GR.
B5422
BRICKWALL LANE
RAKES LANE
01
36
40
35
School

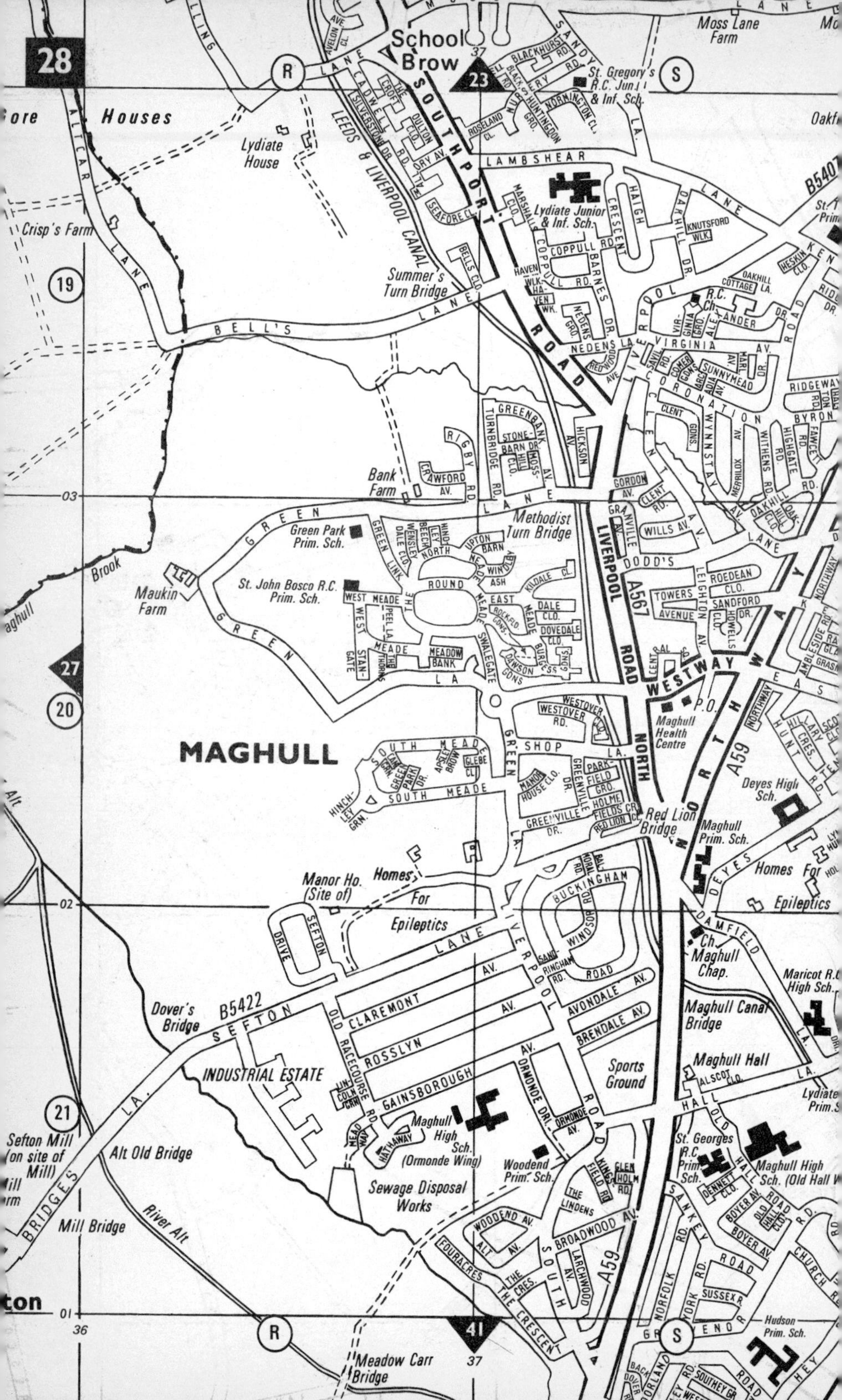
28
School Brow
23
Moss Lane Farm
St. Gregory's R.C. Jun. & Inf. Sch.
Houses
Lydiate House
LEEDS & LIVERPOOL CANAL
SOUTHPORT ROAD
LAMBSHEAR LANE
Lydiate Junior & Inf. Sch.
Crisp's Farm
ALTCAR LANE
19
Summer's Turn Bridge
BELL'S LANE
R.C. Ch.
VIRGINIA AV.
CORONATION ROAD
LIVERPOOL ROAD
Bank Farm
Green Park Prim. Sch.
St. John Bosco R.C. Prim. Sch.
Methodist
Turn Bridge
Brook
Maukin Farm
ROUND MEADE
GREEN LANE
27
20
MAGHULL
WESTWAY
NORTHWAY
A567
A59
Maghull Health Centre
P.O.
Deyes High Sch.
SOUTH MEADE
SHOP LA.
Red Lion Bridge
Maghull Prim. Sch.
Homes For Epileptics
Manor Ho. (Site of)
DAMFIELD LA.
Ch.
Maghull Chap.
Maricot R.C. High Sch.
Dover's Bridge
B5422
SEFTON LANE
INDUSTRIAL ESTATE
Maghull Canal Bridge
Maghull Hall
Sports Ground
Lydiate Prim.
21
Sefton Mill (on site of Mill)
Alt Old Bridge
Maghull High Sch. (Ormonde Wing)
Woodend Prim. Sch.
St. Georges R.C. Prim. Sch.
Maghull High Sch. (Old Hall Wing)
Sewage Disposal Works
Mill Bridge
River Alt
BRIDGES LA.
THE CRESCENT
Hudson Prim. Sch.
41
Meadow Carr Bridge
36
37
03
02
01

Aughton Chase
Riding Centre
Robbin's Bridge
Sudell Brook
T
U
39
153
Brookfields
Green
MOSS LANE
RD.
Highway Farm
Aspinall House
A59
HIGHWAY
Mill House Farm
BROOKFIELD LA.
Spring Farm
LANE
Elm House
BUTCHERS LANE
Cunscough
19
Millbank Farm
Brook
MILLBANK LANE
Maghull
Jun.
LATHOM DRIVE
PARK LANE
Bottle Corporation
Sanatorium
PARK BOURN
03
MOSS LANE
GILPIN AV.
RIBBLE AV.
WENNING AV.
LOWTHER AV.
CALDER
PENRITH CRES.
PATTERDALE CRES.
LANGDALE DR.
CARTMEL AV.
WINDERMERE DRIVE
DOUGLAS DRIVE
TRENT AV.
SUDELL AV.
MERSEY AV.
BRIDGE FARM DR.
Moss Side House
Moss Side Hospital
BEECHWAY
Moss Side Hosp.
20
30
DEYES LANE
Public Open Space
Public Open Space
LONGFOLD
MEADOW LA.
PENFOLD
HIGHFIELD
PARK
Moss Side
Junc 1.
Bradley's Farm
LAND END
Lyon's Farm
MAGHULL LANE
CROFTFIELD
BRIARS LA.
TWYFORD CLO.
DELLFIELD
HILLCREST
EASTWAY
WALTHO AV.
ALDYKES
LEATHWOOD
NEWLYN AVE
Guest Farm
02
ROAD
FOX HOUSE
ORCHARD HEY
Whinny Brook
The Old House
HOUSE LA.
POVERTY LANE
SPRING GDNS.
DAISY MT.
TAILOR'S LA.
KENNESSEE CL.
Sch.
Summer Hill Farm
HURST PARK
Summerhill Prim. Sch.
MAGHULL STA
P.O.
GRANGE
MELLING RD.
nessee
reen
WILLOW HEY
LANE
SUMMERHILL DR.
ASHLEIGH RD.
HEATHFIELD RD.
MOYNEUX RD.
M58
Moss Nook Farm
MOSS NOOK LA.
LANE
21
LEATHERBARROW'S LANE
WEAVER LANE
GIDDIGATE LANE
01
40
T
42
U
Pumping Sta.
39
BEDFORD AV.

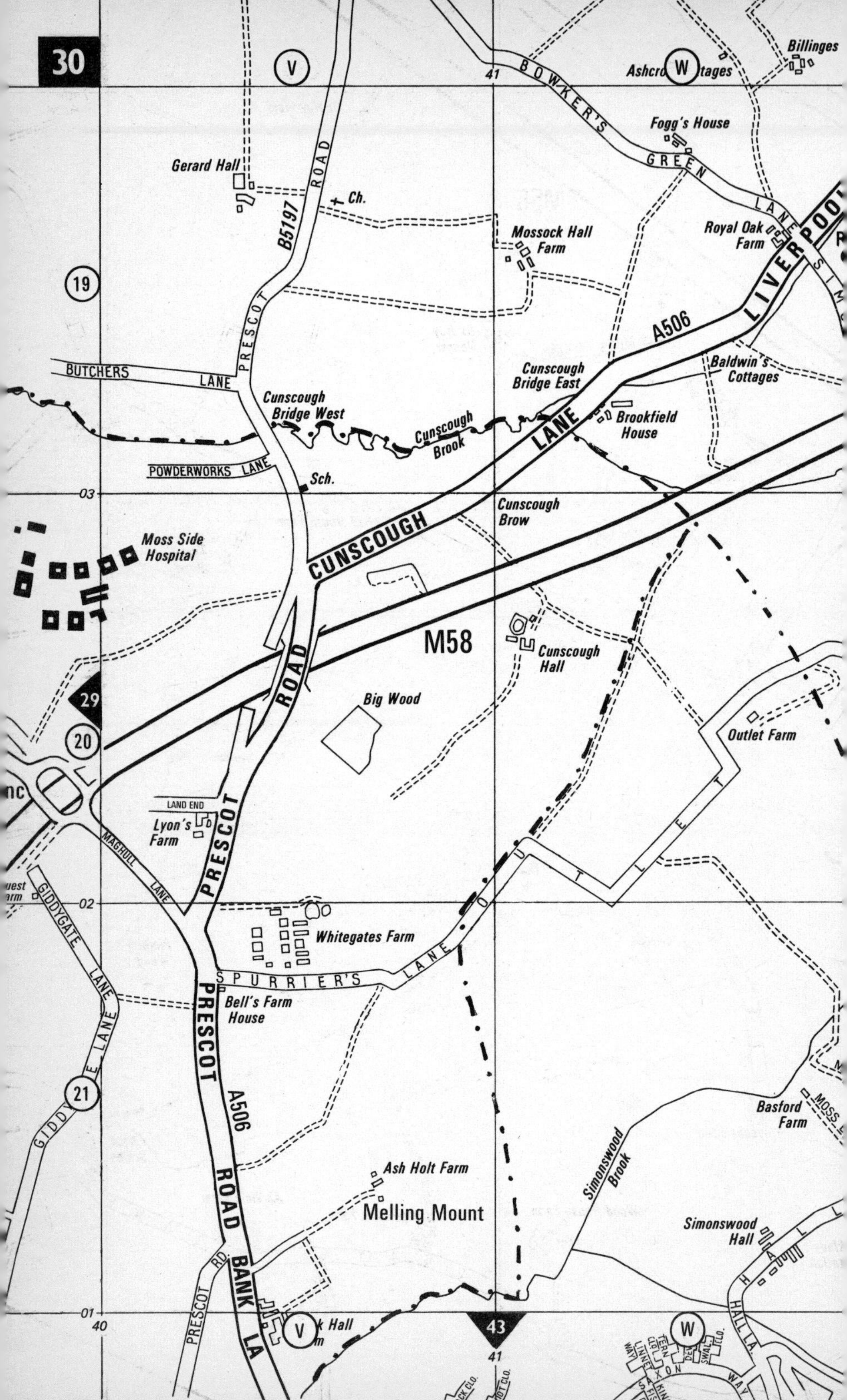
V
41
BOWKER'S GREEN LANE
W
Ashcroft Cottages
Billinges
Fogg's House
Gerard Hall
ROAD
Ch.
B5197
PRESCOT
Mossock Hall Farm
Royal Oak Farm
LIVERPOOL
19
A506
BUTCHERS LANE
Cunscough Bridge East
Baldwin's Cottages
Cunscough Bridge West
Cunscough Brook
LANE
Brookfield House
POWDERWORKS LANE
Sch.
03
Cunscough Brow
CUNSCOUGH
Moss Side Hospital
M58
Cunscough Hall
ROAD
Big Wood
29
20
Outlet Farm
LAND END
Lyon's Farm
PRESCOT
MAGHULL LANE
OUTLET LANE
GIDDYGATE LANE
02
Whitegates Farm
SPURRIER'S LANE
PRESCOT
Bell's Farm House
A506
21
Basford Farm
MOSS
Simonswood Brook
Ash Holt Farm
ROAD
Melling Mount
Simonswood Hall
PRESCOT RD.
BANK LA
HALL LA.
01
40
V
43
41
W
TERN CLO.
LINNET WAY
SAXON WAY
SWAL. CLO.

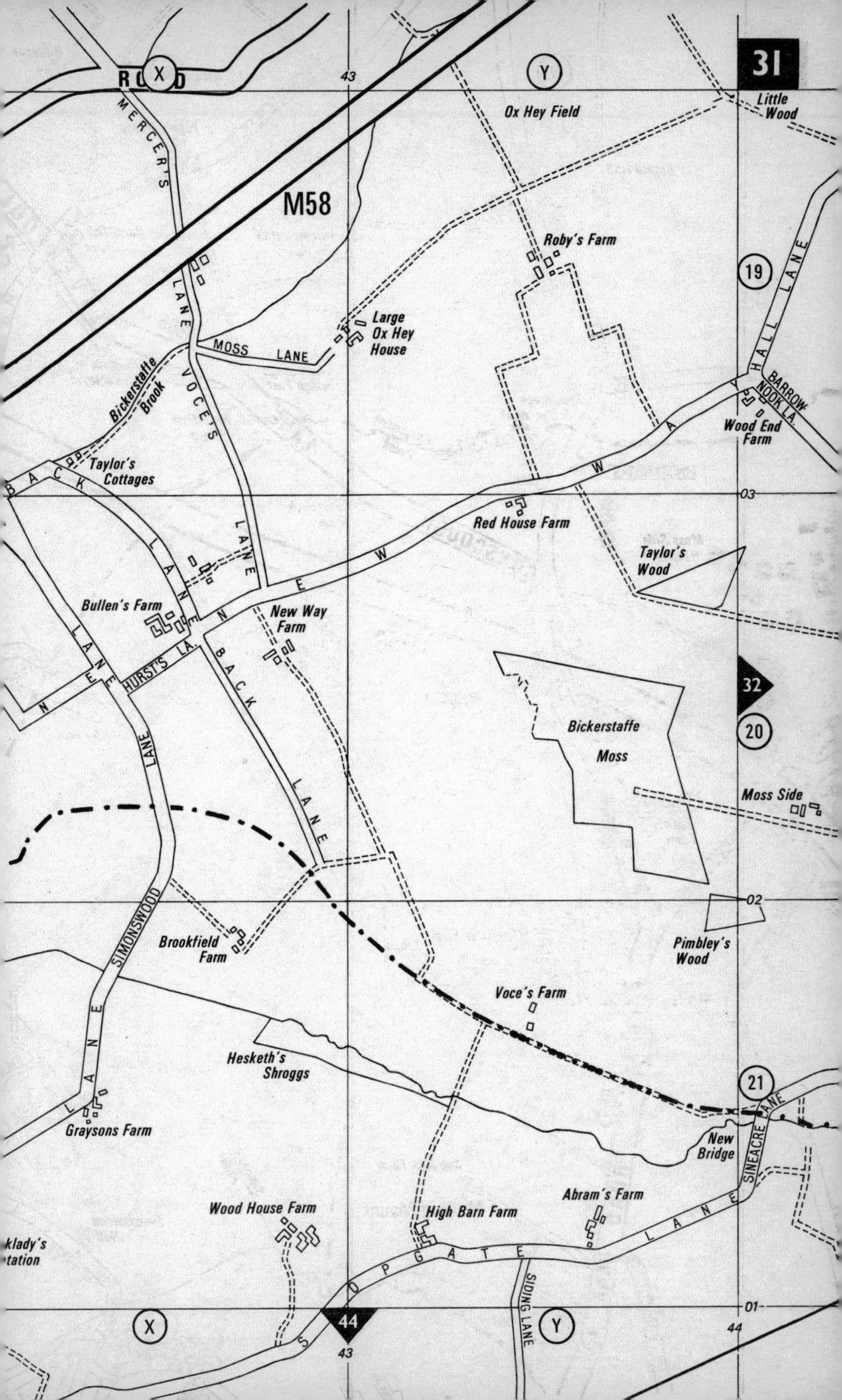
ROAD
MERCER'S
M58
Ox Hey Field
Little Wood
Roby's Farm
Large Ox Hey House
MOSS LANE
VOCE'S LANE
Bickerstaffe Brook
Taylor's Cottages
BACK LANE
HALL LANE
BARROW NOOK LA.
Wood End Farm
NEW WAY
Red House Farm
Taylor's Wood
Bullen's Farm
New Way Farm
HURST'S LA.
BACK LANE
LANE
Bickerstaffe Moss
Moss Side
SIMONSWOOD LANE
Brookfield Farm
Pimbley's Wood
Voce's Farm
Hesketh's Shroggs
Graysons Farm
New Bridge
SINEACRE LANE
Abram's Farm
Wood House Farm
High Barn Farm
SCOPGATE LANE
SIDING LANE
klady's
tation
X
Y
43
44
03
02
01
19
20
21
32
44

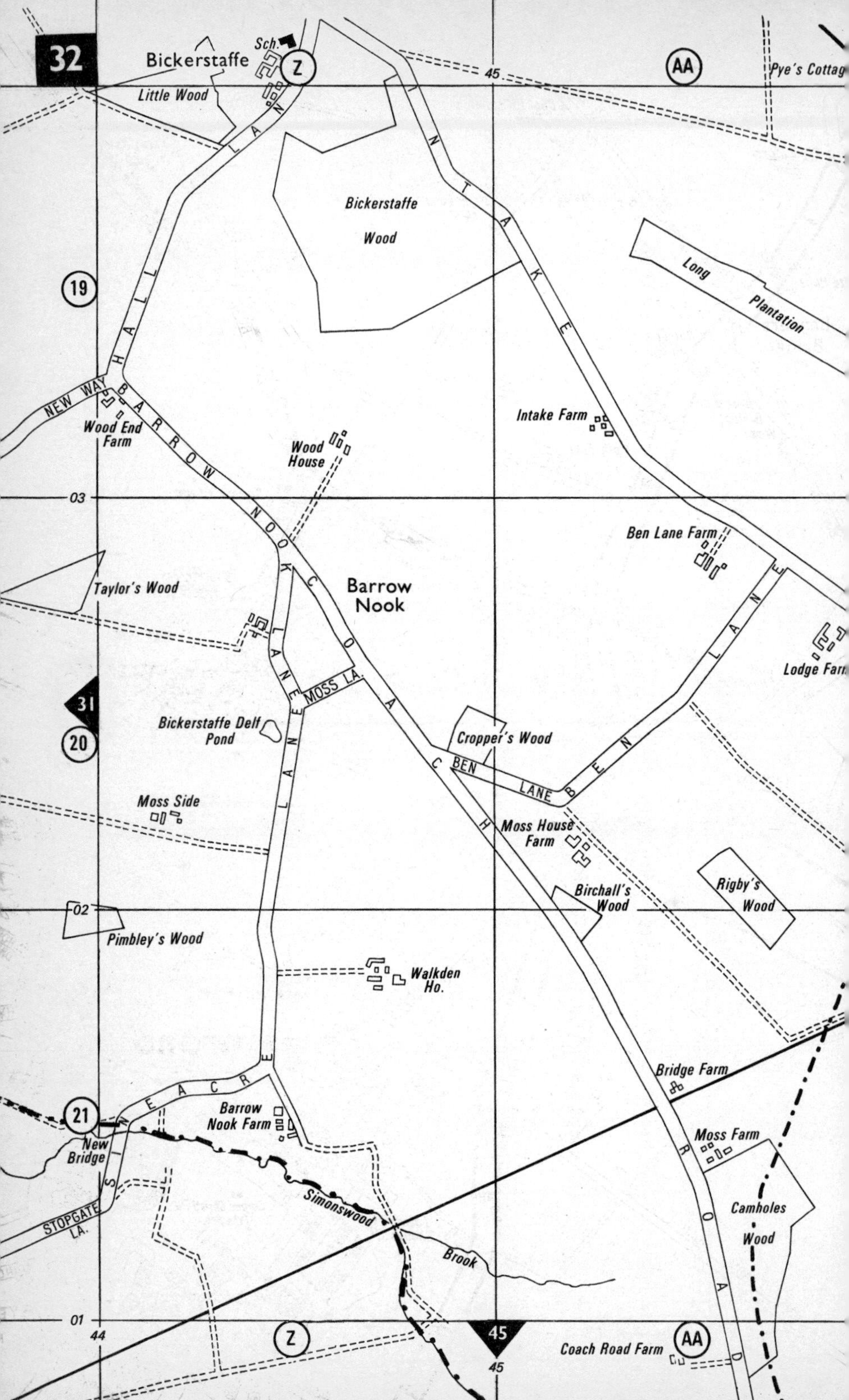
32
Bickerstaffe
Sch.
Little Wood
Z
AA
45
Pye's Cottag
HALL LANE
INTAKE
Bickerstaffe
Wood
Long
Plantation
19
NEW WAY
BARROW
Wood End
Farm
Wood
House
Intake Farm
03
Ben Lane Farm
NOOK LANE
COACH ROAD
Barrow
Nook
Taylor's Wood
Lodge Farm
MOSS LA.
31
Bickerstaffe Delf
Pond
20
Cropper's Wood
BEN
LANE
BEN LANE
Moss Side
Moss House
Farm
Birchall's
Wood
Rigby's
Wood
02
Pimbley's Wood
Walkden
Ho.
Bridge Farm
21
ACRE
Barrow
Nook Farm
New
Bridge
Moss Farm
SINE
STOPGATE
LA.
Simonswood
Camholes
Wood
Brook
01
44
Z
45
AA
45
Coach Road Farm

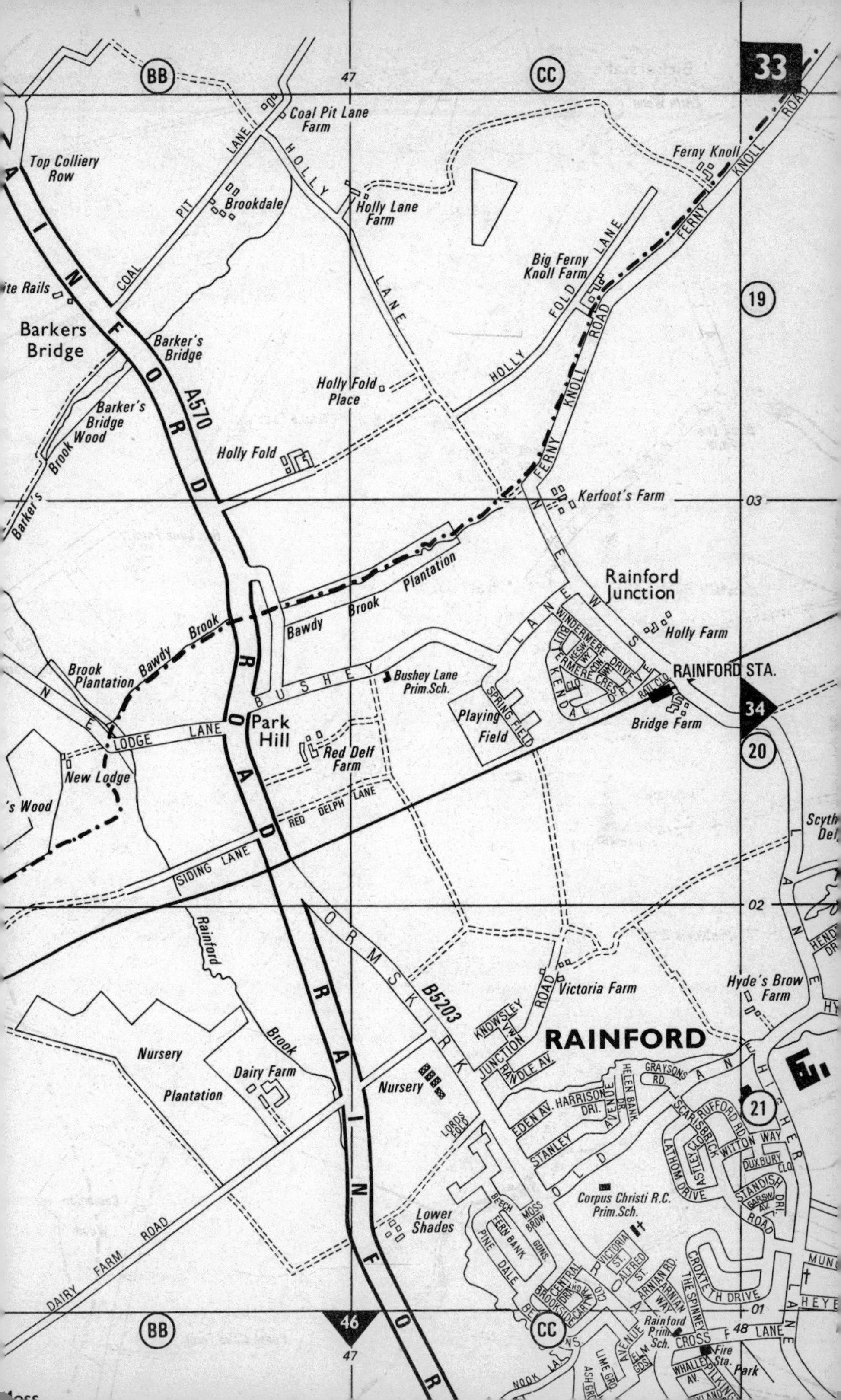

33
BB
CC
47
Coal Pit Lane Farm
COAL PIT LANE
Top Colliery Row
Brookdale
HOLLY LANE
Holly Lane Farm
Ferny Knoll
FERNY KNOLL ROAD
Big Ferny Knoll Farm
HOLLY FOLD LANE
19
ite Rails
Barkers Bridge
Barker's Bridge
A570
RAINFORD ROAD
Barker's Bridge Brook Wood
Holly Fold Place
Holly Fold
Barker's Brook
03
Kerfoot's Farm
NEWS LANE
Rainford Junction
Holly Farm
Bawdy Brook Plantation
Bawdy Brook
Brook Plantation
BUSHEY LANE
Bushey Lane Prim. Sch.
RAINFORD STA.
34
WINDERMERE DRIVE
BUTTERMERE CRES.
KESWICK WY.
CONISTON WY.
KENDAL DRIVE
KENDAL CLO.
RAIL CLO.
Bridge Farm
Playing Field
SPRING FIELD
LODGE LANE
Park Hill
Red Delf Farm
20
New Lodge
's Wood
RED DELPH LANE
SIDING LANE
Scyth Del
02
Rainford Brook
ORMSKIRK ROAD
B5203
KNOWSLEY ROAD
Victoria Farm
Hyde's Brow Farm
KNOWSLEY VW.
JUNCTION LANE
RANDLE AV.
RAINFORD
Nursery Plantation
Dairy Farm
Nursery
GRAYSONS RD.
HELEN BANK DR.
HARRISON DRI.
EDEN AV.
AVENUE
STANLEY AVENUE
OLD LANE
HIGHER LANE
21
SCARISBRICK CLO.
RUFFORD RD.
WITTON WAY
LATHOM DRIVE
ASTLEY CLO.
DUXBURY CLO.
STANDISH DRI.
GARSWOOD AV.
ROAD
LORDS FOLD
Corpus Christi R.C. Prim.Sch.
Lower Shades
BEECH
MOSS BROW
FERN BANK
PINE DALE
MOSS GDNS.
VICTORIA ST.
ALFRED ST.
ARNIAN RD.
ARNIAN WAY
THE SPINNEY
CROXTETH DRIVE
CENTRAL DRI.
BROOKSIDE
CARY
OLD
MUN
HEYE
DAIRY FARM ROAD
BB
46
47
CC
01
48
Rainford Prim. Sch.
CROSS LANE
Fire Sta.
Park
WHALLEY AV.
PILKINGTON
AVENUE
ELM GDS.
LIME GRO.
ASH GRO.
NOOK LA.
Moss

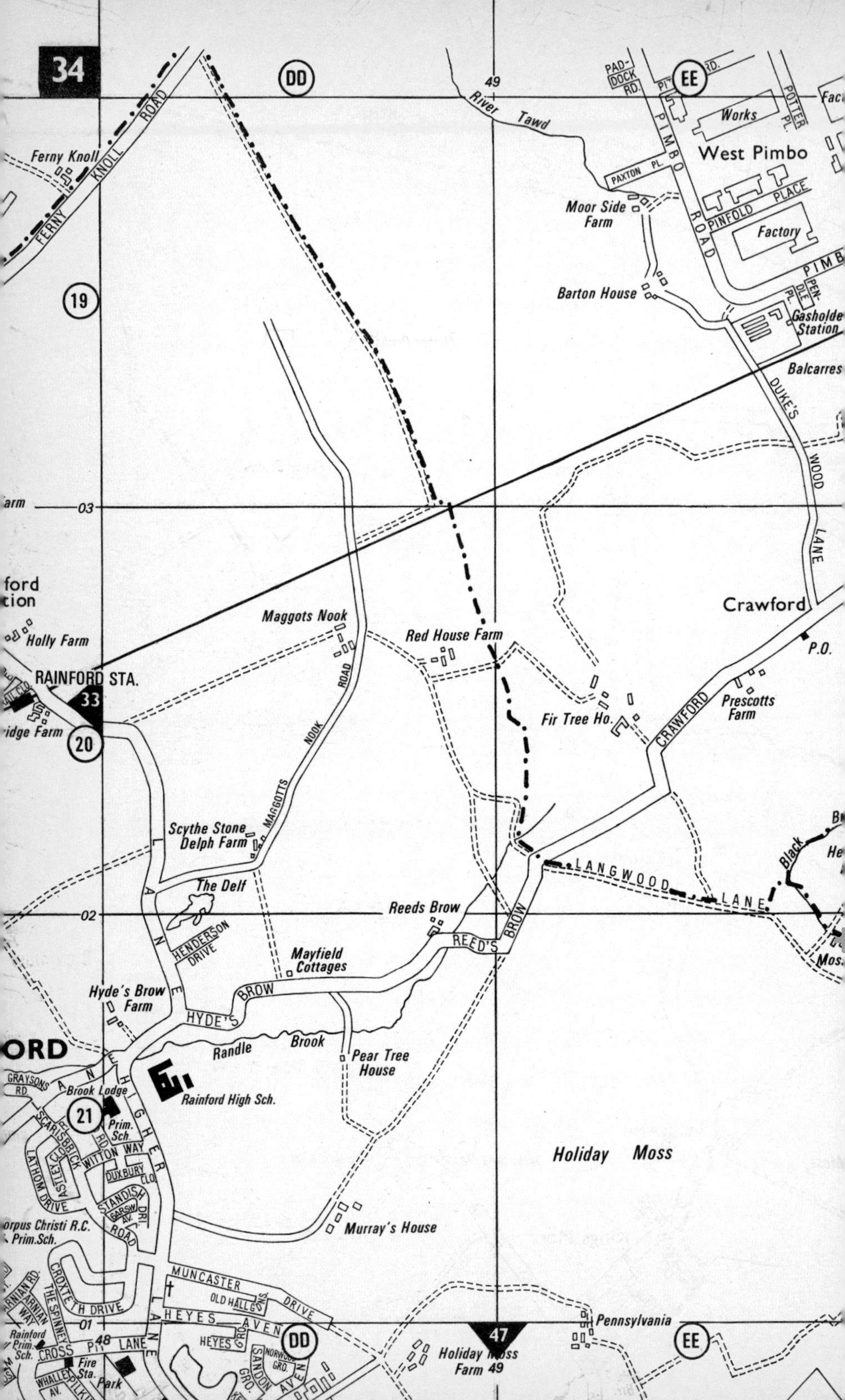
34
DD
EE
19
20
21
33
47
49
48
03
02
01
FERNY KNOLL ROAD
Ferny Knoll
River Tawd
PADDOCK RD.
West Pimbo
Works
POTTER PL.
PAXTON PL.
PIMBO ROAD
PINFOLD PLACE
Factory
Moor Side Farm
Barton House
PENDLE PL.
Gasholder Station
Balcarres
DUKE'S WOOD LANE
Crawford
P.O.
Prescotts Farm
CRAWFORD
Fir Tree Ho.
Red House Farm
Maggots Nook
MAGGOTS NOOK ROAD
Holly Farm
RAINFORD STA.
Scythe Stone Delph Farm
The Delf
HENDERSON DRIVE
LANE
Reeds Brow
REED'S BROW
LANGWOOD LANE
Black
Mayfield Cottages
Hyde's Brow Farm
HYDE'S BROW
Randle Brook
Pear Tree House
Rainford High Sch.
Brook Lodge
GRAYSONS RD.
HIGHER LANE
Prim. Sch.
SCARISBRICK RD
WITTON WAY
DUXBURY CLO
LATHOM DRIVE
ASTLEY CLO
STANDISH DRI
GARSW AV.
ROAD
Holiday Moss
Murray's House
Corpus Christi R.C. Prim.Sch.
CROXTETH DRIVE
THE SPINNEY
MUNCASTER DRIVE
OLD HALL GDNS.
HEYES AVENUE
HEYES GRO
NORWOOD GRO.
SANDON GRO.
AVENUE
Pennsylvania
Holiday Moss Farm
CROSS PIT LANE
Rainford Prim. Sch.
Fire Sta.
Park
WHALLEY AV.

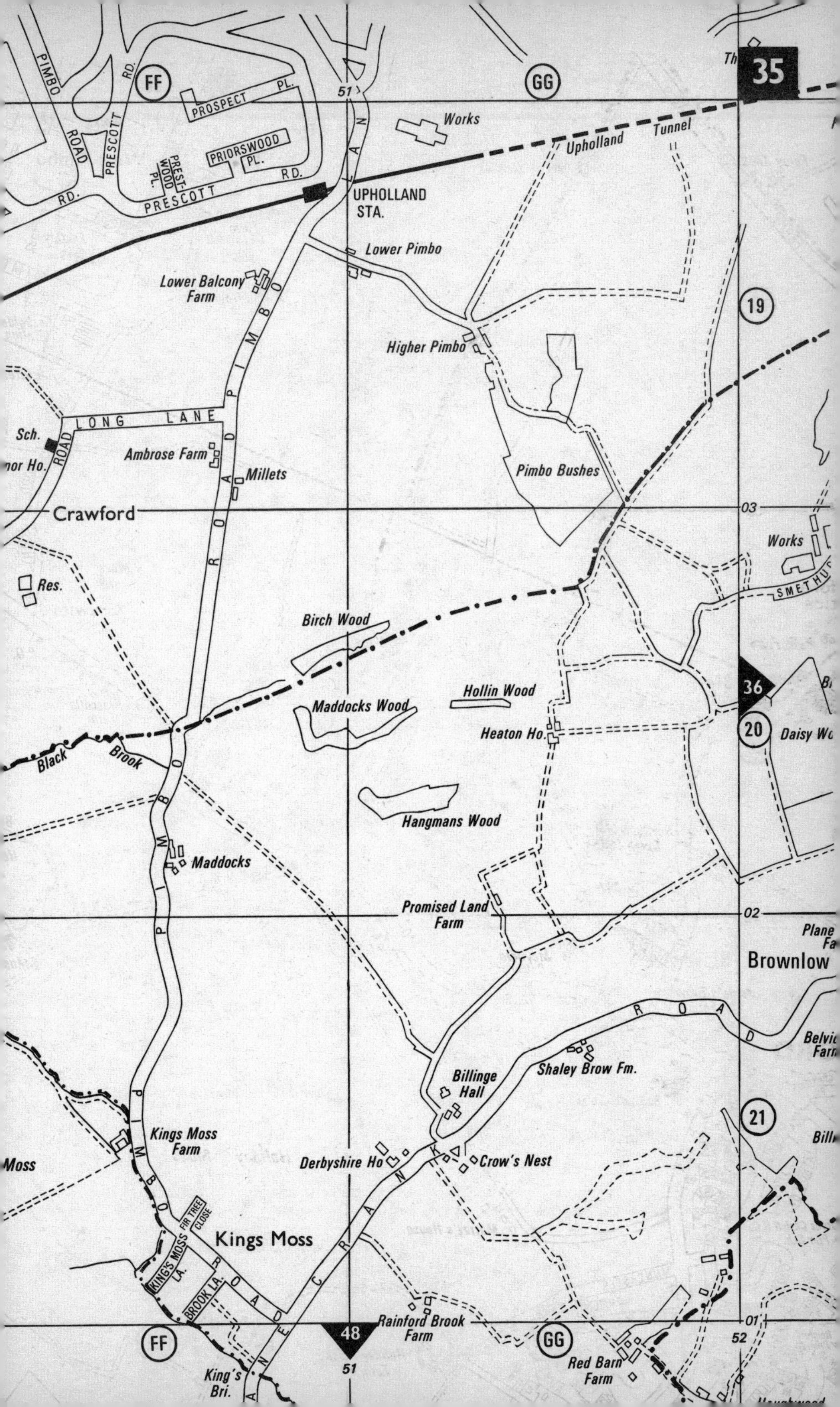
35
FF
GG
PIMBO ROAD
PRESCOTT RD.
PROSPECT PL.
PRIORSWOOD PL.
PREST-WOOD PL.
PRESCOTT RD.
RD.
51
Works
Upholland Tunnel
UPHOLLAND STA.
Lower Pimbo
Lower Balcony Farm
Higher Pimbo
19
LONG LANE
Sch.
nor Ho.
Ambrose Farm
Millets
Pimbo Bushes
Crawford
03
Works
Res.
Birch Wood
Hollin Wood
Maddocks Wood
36
Heaton Ho.
20
Daisy Wo
Black Brook
Hangmans Wood
Maddocks
Promised Land Farm
02
Plane Fa
Brownlow
ROAD
Belvic Farn
Billinge Hall
Shaley Brow Fm.
21
Kings Moss Farm
Bill
Moss
Derbyshire Ho
Crow's Nest
CRANK LANE
FIR TREE CLOSE
Kings Moss
KING'S MOSS LA.
BROOK LA.
ROAD
Rainford Brook Farm
48
01
52
King's Bri.
Red Barn Farm

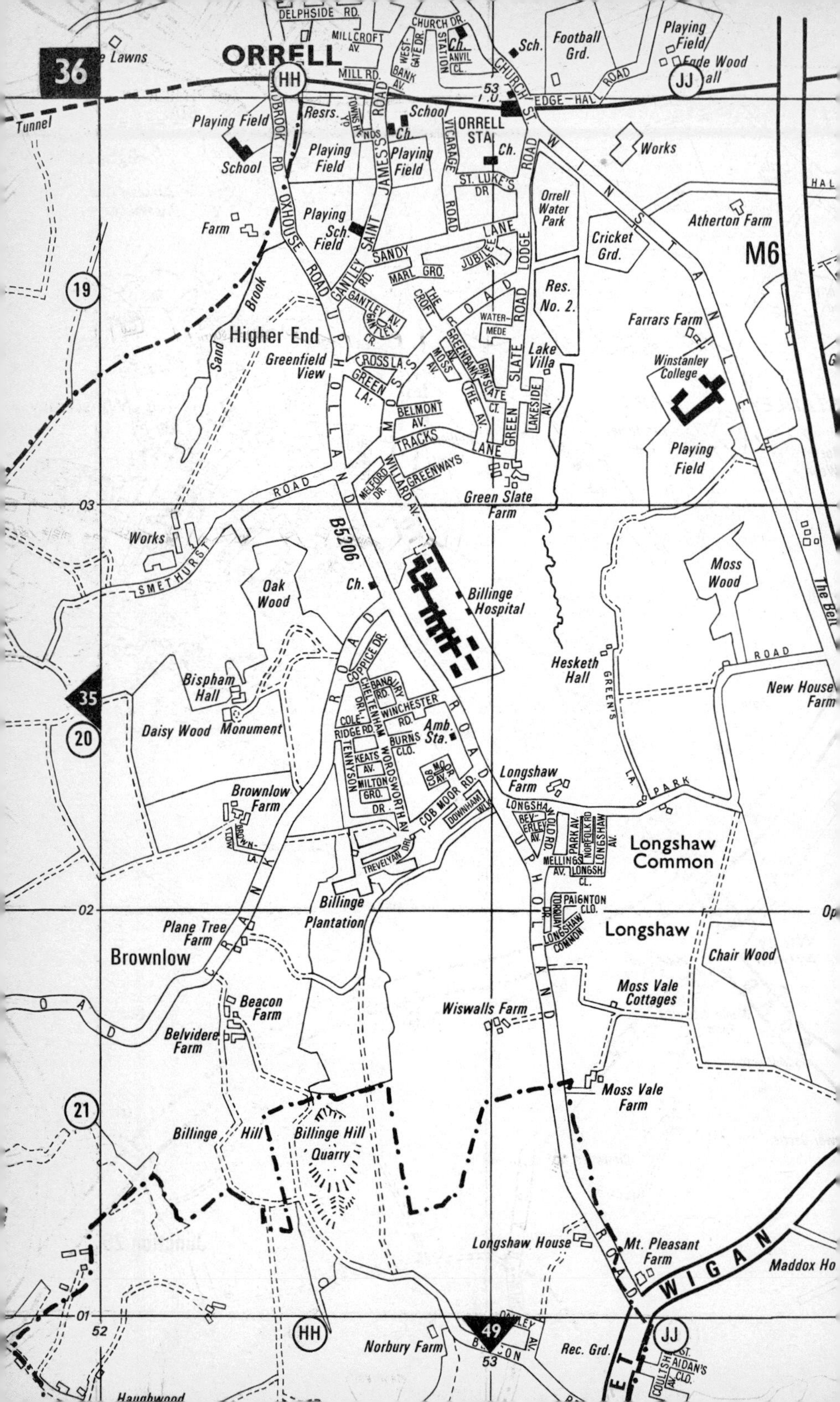
36
ORRELL
HH
JJ
DELPHSIDE RD.
CHURCH DR.
MILLCROFT AV.
WEST-GATE DR.
STATION
ANVIL CL.
Ch.
Sch.
Football Grd.
Playing Field
Lawns
MILL RD.
BANK AV.
53
CHURCH ST.
EDGE-HALL ROAD
Tunnel
Playing Field
Resrs.
School
Ch.
ORRELL STA.
Ch.
School
Playing Field
Playing Field
Works
VICARAGE ROAD
ST. LUKE'S DR.
SAINT JAMES'S ROAD
Orrell Water Park
Atherton Farm
M6
Farm
Playing Sch. Field
SANDY LANE
JUBILEE AV.
Cricket Grd.
MARL GRO.
GANTLEY RD.
GANTLEY AV.
GANTLEY CR.
THE CROFT
LODGE ROAD
Res. No. 2.
19
Higher End
Sand Brook
OXHOUSE ROAD
UPHOLLAND
WATERMEDE
GREENBANK AV.
MOSS AV.
SLATE ROAD
Farrars Farm
WINSTANLEY
Winstanley College
Lake Villa
Greenfield View
CROSS LA.
GREEN LA.
MOSS LA.
SLATE CT.
THE AV.
GREEN LANE
LAKESIDE AV.
BELMONT AV.
TRACKS LANE
Playing Field
ROAD
MELFORD DR.
WILLARD AV.
GREENWAYS
Green Slate Farm
03
B5206
Works
SMETHURST
Oak Wood
Ch.
Moss Wood
Billinge Hospital
The Bell
Hesketh Hall
GREEN'S LA.
ROAD
New House Farm
35
20
Bispham Hall
Daisy Wood
Monument
COPPICE DR.
BANBURY RD.
CHELTENHAM DR.
WINCHESTER RD.
COLERIDGE RD.
BURNS CLO.
Amb. Sta.
TENNYSON
KEATS AV.
WORDSWORTH AV.
MILTON GRO.
COB MOOR AV.
COB MOOR RD.
DOWNHAM WLK.
Longshaw Farm
PARK
Brownlow Farm
BROWNLOW LA.
TREVELYAN DR.
LONGSHAW
BEVERLEY AV.
WOLD RD.
PARK AV.
NORFOLK RD.
LONGSHAW AV.
MELLINGS AV.
LONGSH. CL.
Longshaw Common
Billinge Plantation
02
PAIGNTON CLO.
TORQUAY DR.
LONGSHAW COMMON
Longshaw
Plane Tree Farm
CRANK ROAD
Brownlow
Chair Wood
Beacon Farm
Moss Vale Cottages
Wiswalls Farm
Belvidere Farm
Moss Vale Farm
21
Billinge Hill
Billinge Hill Quarry
Longshaw House
Mt. Pleasant Farm
WIGAN ROAD
Maddox Ho
01
52
HH
49
OAKLEY AV.
BEACON
53
Norbury Farm
Rec. Grd.
JJ
COULTSHEAD AV.
ST. AIDAN'S CLO.
Haughwood

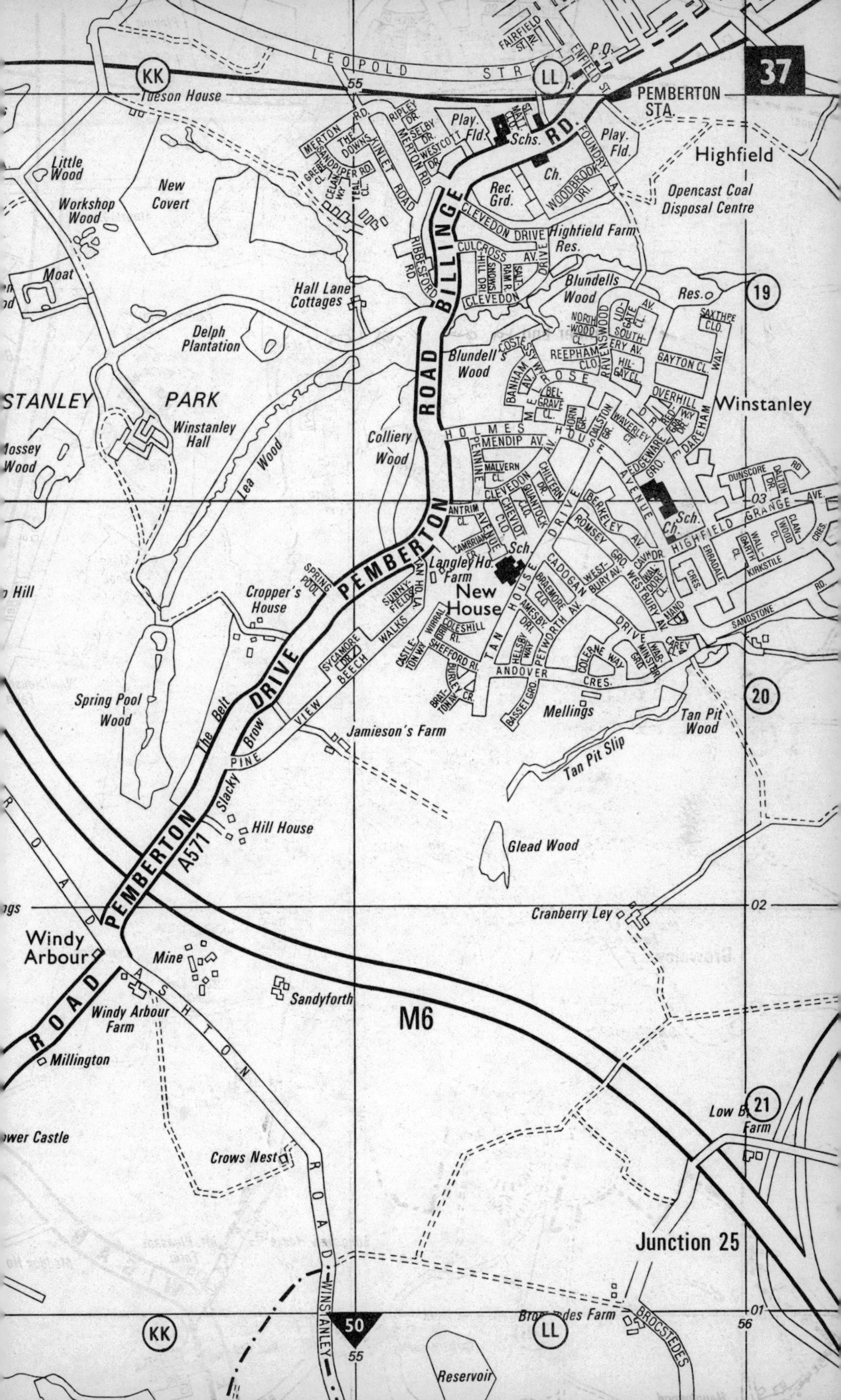

37
KK
LL
LEOPOLD STREET
FAIRFIELD ST.
AV.
ENFIELD ST.
P.O.
PEMBERTON STA.
Tueson House
55
MERTON RD.
THE DOWNS
RIPLEY DR.
SELBY DR.
WESTCOTT DR.
MERTON RD.
KINLET ROAD
SANDPIPER RD.
GREBE CL.
CELAN WY
TEAL CL.
Play. Fld.
Schs.
RD.
Play. Fld.
FOUNDRY LA.
Highfield
Opencast Coal Disposal Centre
Little Wood
New Covert
Workshop Wood
Rec. Grd.
Ch.
WOODBROOK DRI.
CLEVEDON DRIVE
Highfield Farm Res.
RIBBESFORD RD.
BILLINGE
CULCROSS AV.
HILL DRI.
SNOWDON
RAM R.
SALT.
DRIVE
CLEVEDON
Moat
Hall Lane Cottages
Blundells Wood
Res.
19
SAXTHPE CLO.
Delph Plantation
Blundell's Wood
ROAD
COSTESSY
NORTH-WOOD CL.
RAVENSWOOD
LUDGATE CL.
SOUTHERY AV.
REEPHAM CLO.
HILGAY CL.
GAYTON CL.
WAY
MELROSE
BANHAM AV.
BEL-GRAVE CL.
OVERHILL
DRIVE
DAREHAM
Winstanley
STANLEY PARK
Winstanley Hall
Mossey Wood
Lea Wood
Colliery Wood
HOLMES HOUSE
PENNINE
MENDIP AV.
MALVERN CL.
DALSTON GR.
WAVERLEY CL.
EDGEWARE GRO.
AVENUE
DUNSCORE RD
DALTON DR.
03
AVE.
HIGHFIELD GRANGE
CLEVEDON
CHILTERN DR.
QUANTOCK CLO.
CHEVIOT CLO.
DRIVE
BERKELEY AV.
ROMSEY GRO.
Sch.
Ch.
ANTRIM CL.
AVENUE
CAMBRIAN CR.
PEMBERTON
Sch.
CLANWOOD CL.
WALLGARTH CL.
ERRADALE CRES.
KIRKSTILE
CRES.
Langley Ho. Farm
SPRING POOL
TAN HO. LA.
SUNNYFIELDS
New House
CADOGAN
WESTBURY AV.
WESTBURY AV.
RD.
SANDSTONE
Hill
Cropper's House
BRAEMORE CLO.
AMESBY DRI.
PETWORTH AV.
DRIVE
HAND
WALKS
COLESHILL RI.
WIRRAL DR.
CASTLETON WY.
SHEFFORD RI.
TAN HOUSE
HELSBY WAY
COLERNE WAY
WARMINSTER GRO.
CAREY CL.
SYCAMORE DR.
BEECH
DRIVE
ANDOVER CRES.
BURLEY CR.
BRATTON CR.
Spring Pool Wood
The Belt
BASSET GRO.
Mellings
Tan Pit Wood
20
VIEW
Brow
Jamieson's Farm
PINE
Tan Pit Slip
ROAD
Slacky
Hill House
PEMBERTON
A571
Glead Wood
02
Cranberry Ley
Windy Arbour
Mine
ROAD
ASHTON
Sandyforth
Windy Arbour Farm
M6
Millington
Low B Farm
21
Crows Nest
ROAD
Junction 25
01
WINSTANLEY
50
55
56
Bromledes Farm
BROCSTEDES
Reservoir

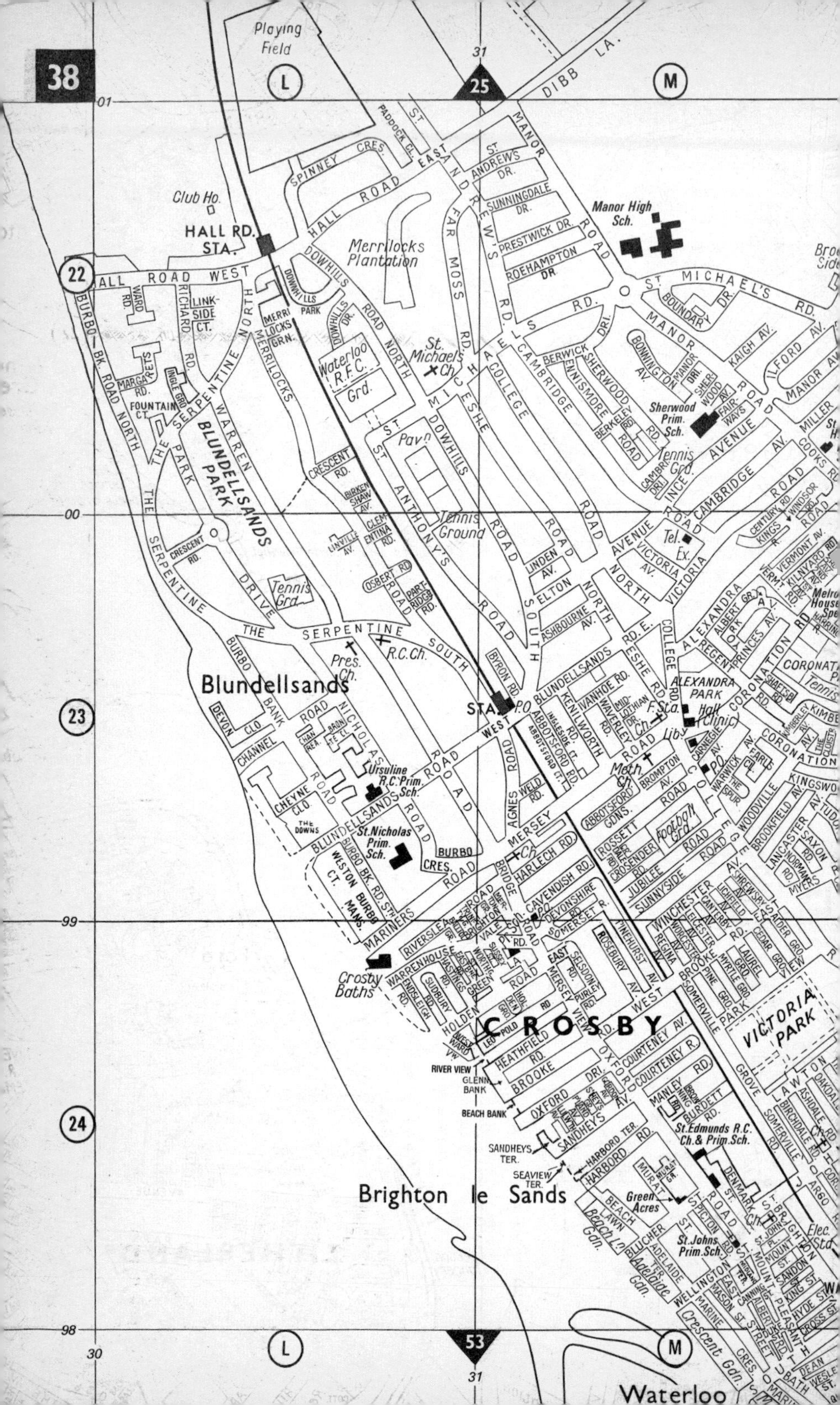
38
25
53
L
M
22
23
24
01
00
99
98
30
31
Playing Field
DIBB LA.
Club Ho.
HALL RD. STA.
HALL ROAD WEST
HALL ROAD EAST
SPINNEY CRES.
PADDOCK CL.
ST. ANDREWS DR.
SUNNINGDALE DR.
PRESTWICK DR.
ROEHAMPTON DR.
MANOR ROAD
Manor High Sch.
Merrilocks Plantation
DOWHILLS ROAD
DOWHILLS PARK
DOWHILLS DR.
FAR MOSS RD.
ST. ANDREW'S RD.
ST. MICHAEL'S RD.
BOUNDARY DR.
MANOR DRI.
BONNINGTON AV.
KAIGH AV.
ILFORD AV.
MANOR AV.
WARD RD.
RICHARD RD.
LINK-SIDE CT.
MERRI LOCKS GRN.
MERRILOCKS
BURBO BK. ROAD NORTH
MARGARETS RD.
INGLE GRO.
FOUNTAIN CT.
THE SERPENTINE NORTH
WARREN
BLUNDELLSANDS PARK
PARK
THE SERPENTINE
CRESCENT RD.
DRIVE
Tennis Grd.
THE SERPENTINE SOUTH
Waterloo R.F.C. Grd.
St. Michaels Ch.
MICHAELS
ESHE
COLLEGE
CAMBRIDGE
BERWICK
ENNISMORE
SHERWOOD
BERKELEY RD.
Sherwood Prim. Sch.
FAIRWAYS
Tennis Grd.
CAMBRIDGE AVENUE
INCE
CAMBRIDGE ROAD
CENTURY RD.
WINDSOR RD.
KINGS
VERMONT AV.
KILNYARD
Melrose House
CRESCENT RD.
BIRKENSHAW AV.
CLEMENTINA RD.
LINVILLE AV.
OSBERT RD.
PARTRIDGE RD.
Pavn
DOWHILLS ROAD
ST. ANTHONY'S ROAD
Tennis Ground
UNDEN AV.
ELTON
ASHBOURNE AV.
NORTH ROAD
SOUTH ROAD
AVENUE
VICTORIA AV.
VICTORIA ROAD
Tel. Ex.
ALEXANDRA
ALBERT GR.
YORK AV.
PRINCES AV.
CORONATION RD
REGENT
Pres. Ch.
R.C. Ch.
Blundellsands
BURBO BANK
DEVON CLO.
CHANNEL ROAD
NICHOLAS ROAD
Ursuline R.C. Prim. Sch.
CHEYNE CLO.
THE DOWNS
BLUNDELLSANDS ROAD
St. Nicholas Prim. Sch.
BURBO CRES.
BURBO BK. RD. STH.
WESTON CT.
BURBO MANS.
MARINERS ROAD
BYRON RD.
STA.
P.O.
BLUNDELLSANDS ROAD WEST
ABBOTSFORD RD.
KENILWORTH RD.
IVANHOE RD.
WAVERLEY RD.
MIDLOTHIAN DR.
ESHE RD.
COLLEGE RD.
ALEXANDRA PARK
F. Sta.
Hall (Clinic)
Liby.
CARNEGIE AV.
Ch.
Meth. Ch.
BROMPTON AV.
AGNES RD.
WELD RD.
MERSEY ROAD
ABBOTSFORD GDNS.
ROSSETT RD.
CROSENDER RD.
Football Grd.
JUBILEE ROAD
SUNNYSIDE ROAD
COLLEGE
WARWICK AV.
THE SPUR
WOODVILLE
BROOKFIELD AV.
LANCASTER AV.
SAXON RD.
KINGSWOOD
CORONATION
HARLECH RD.
CAVENDISH RD.
DEVONSHIRE RD.
SOMERSET R.
BRIDGE ROAD
RIVERSLEA ROAD
VALE RD.
WARRENHOUSE
Crosby Baths
ENDSLEIGH RD.
SUDBURY
HASTINGS
GREEN
HOLDEN
CROSBY
EAST RD.
MERSEY VIEW
SELSDON
PURLEY
ROSEBURY AV.
PINEHURST AV.
WEST
WINCHESTER AV.
REGINA AV.
LEICESTER
BROOKE RD.
MYRTLE GRO.
LAUREL GRO.
CEDAR GROVE
VIEW
PARK
SOMERVILLE
VICTORIA PARK
HEATHFIELD RD.
BROOKE
OXFORD DRI.
OXFORD
COURTENEY AV.
COURTENEY R.
RD.
RIVER VIEW
GLENN BANK
BEACH BANK
SANDHEYS AV.
SANDHEYS TER.
SEAVIEW TER.
HARBORD TER.
HARBORD RD.
MANLEY
BURDETT
St. Edmunds R.C. Ch. & Prim. Sch.
GROVE
LAWTON
BIRCHDALE RD.
ASHDALE
OAKDALE
Brighton le Sands
BEACH LAWN
Beach Lawn Gdn.
MURAT GR.
Green Acres
SPICTON
ST. ROAD
DENMARK ST.
St. Johns Prim. Sch.
BLUCHER ST.
ADELAIDE TER.
Adelaide Gdn.
WELLINGTON ST.
MARINE CRES.
Crescent Gdn.
MASON ST.
EAST ST.
MOUNT PLEASANT
SANDON ST.
KING ST.
HYDE ST.
CROSS ST.
DEAN ST.
BATH ST.
SOUTH RD.
ST. JOHNS RD.
BRIGHTON RD.
Elec. Std.
Waterloo

39
Mem! Chapel on site of Harkirke
Cross
Burying Ground
Plantation
The Cottage
VIRGINS LANE
Holy Family R.C. High Sch.
Crab Wood
Ronald House Special Sch.
Cricket Grd.
Ramblers Football Grd
A565
QUARRY RD.
GREEN LA.
LYDIATE
CEMETERY
Thornton
Thornton Prim. Sch.
St. William of York R.C. Inf. & Jun. Schs & Newfield Special Sch.
Birch Cotts.
Tan House Farm
Civil Service Sports Ground
MOOR LANE
THE BYPASS
Waterloo Pk Cricket Grd.
All Saints Ch.
Chesterfield High Sch.
Forefield Jun. Sch.
Recreation Ground
Forefield Inf. Sch.
Great Crosby
IND. ESTATE
Sacred Heart R.C. High Sch.
Sacred Heart R.C. High Sch. (Lower Sch.)
Rimrose Brook
Liverpool Canal
Ford
Ford Ho.
Our Lady Queen of Peace R.C. Prim. Sch.
Foot Br.
Hatton Hill Prim. Sch.
Litherland Tannery
LITHERLAND
Sefton Tannery
Recreation Ground
Chesterfield High Sch. (Annexe)
Chaffers Playing Fields
Waterloo Park
Hospital
Cent. Liby.
St. Faiths Ch.
Train. Centre
Tailors Arms
Clinic

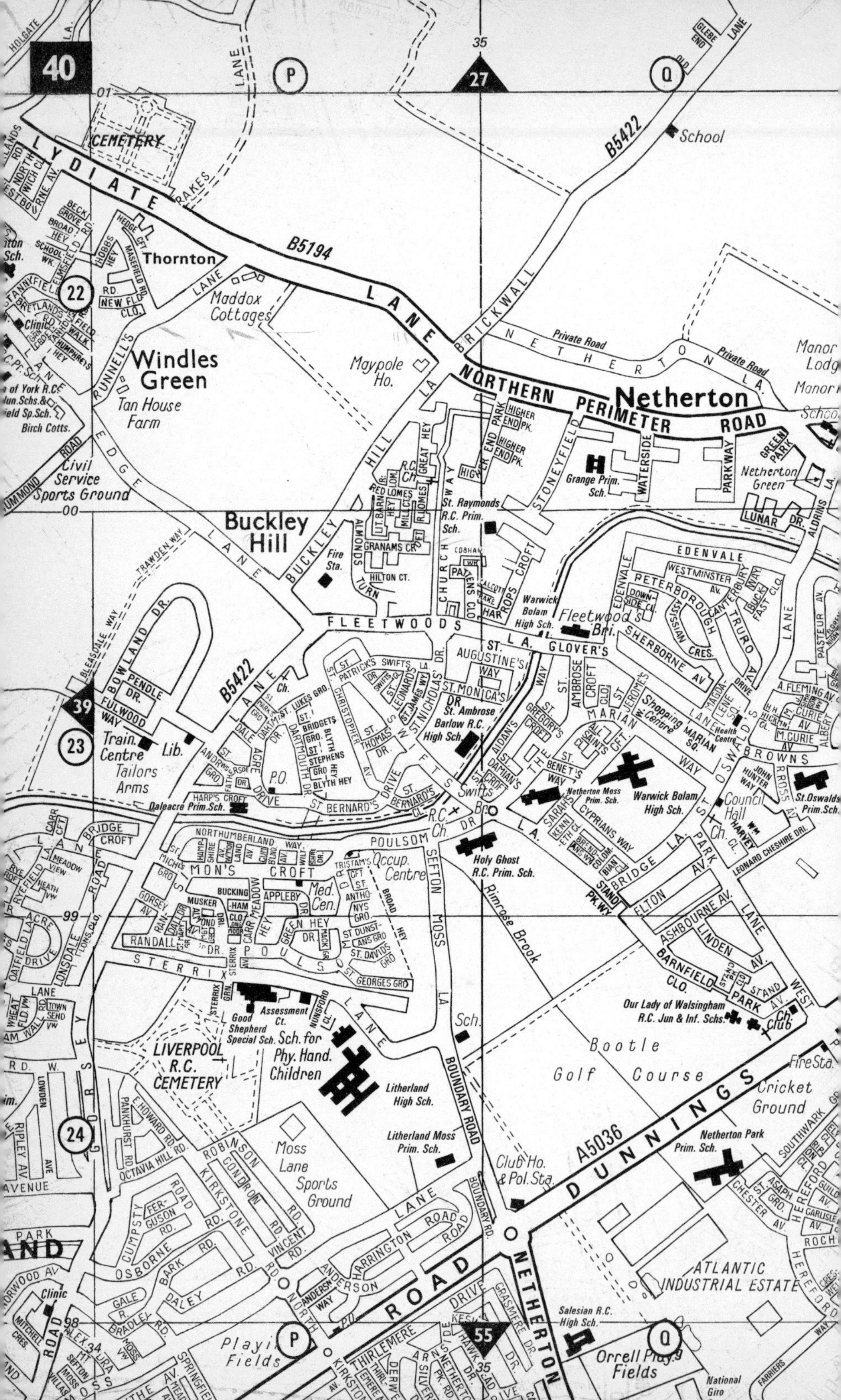

27
39
55
P
Q
35
01
00
99
98
34
22
23
24
CEMETERY
LYDIATE
LANE
B5194
Thornton
Maddox Cottages
Windles Green
Tan House Farm
RUNNELL'S LANE
Birch Cotts.
Civil Service Sports Ground
DRUMMOND ROAD
EDGE LANE
Buckley Hill
BUCKLEY HILL LA.
TRAWDEN WAY
BLEASDALE WAY
BOWLAND DR.
PENDLE DR.
FULWOOD WAY
B5422
Train. Centre
Lib.
Tailors Arms
Fire Sta.
Maypole Ho.
B5422
School
BRICKWALL
NETHERTON LA.
Private Road
NORTHERN PERIMETER ROAD
Netherton
Manor Lodge
HIGHER END PARK
HIGHER END PK.
GREAT HEY
ALMONDS TURN
GRANAMS CROFT
HILTON CT.
CHURCH WAY
St. Raymonds R.C. Prim. Sch.
PATTENS CLO.
HARROPS CROFT
STONEYFIELD
Grange Prim. Sch.
WATERSIDE
PARKWAY
GREEN PARK
Netherton Green
LUNAR DR.
ALDRINS LA.
FLEETWOODS LA.
Warwick Bolam High Sch.
Fleetwood's Bri.
GLOVER'S
EDENVALE
WESTMINSTER AV.
PETERBOROUGH
CANTERBURY WAY
TRURO AV.
SHERBORNE AV.
ASSISIAN CRES.
ST. AUGUSTINE'S WAY
ST. MONICA'S DR.
St. Ambrose Barlow R.C. High Sch.
SWIFTS LA.
ST. NICHOLAS' DR.
DALE ACRE DRIVE
P.O.
Daleacre Prim. Sch.
HARP'S CROFT
ST. BERNARD'S CL.
ST. THOMAS' DR.
ST. CHRISTOPHER AV.
DARTMOUTH DR.
BLYTH HEY
Swifts Bri.
R.C. Ch.
Holy Ghost R.C. Prim. Sch.
MARIAN WAY
Shopping Centre
MARIAN SQ.
Health Centre
Netherton Moss Prim. Sch.
Warwick Bolam High Sch.
CYPRIANS WAY
Council Hall
ST. OSWALDS LANE
BROWNS
St. Oswalds Prim. Sch.
LEONARD CHESHIRE DRI.
BRIDGE LA.
PARK LANE
ELTON AV.
ASHBOURNE AV.
LINDEN AV.
BARNFIELD CLO.
PARK AV.
WEST
Our Lady of Walsingham R.C. Jun & Inf. Schs.
Club
Ch.
BRIDGE CROFT
NORTHUMBERLAND WAY
POULSOM DR.
SIMON'S CROFT
Occup. Centre
Med. Cen.
APPLEBY DR.
GREEN HEY
BROAD HEY
STERRIX LANE
RANDALL DR.
GORSEY AV.
MUSKER
MEADOW
SEFTON MOSS LA.
Rimrose Brook
Assessment Ct.
Good Shepherd Special Sch.
Sch. for Phy. Hand. Children
LANE
Litherland High Sch.
Sch.
BOUNDARY ROAD
Bootle Golf Course
Fire Sta.
Cricket Ground
LIVERPOOL R.C. CEMETERY
Litherland Moss Prim. Sch.
Moss Lane Sports Ground
Club Ho. & Pol. Sta.
A5036
DUNNINGS
Netherton Park Prim. Sch.
ORRELL
LONSDALE
OATFIELD LA.
ACRE DRIVE
LOWDEN
RIPLEY AV.
AVENUE
ROBINSON
KIRKSTONE
CONDRON
VINCENT RD.
OCTAVIA HILL RD.
PANKHURST RD.
CUMPSTY ROAD
FERGUSON RD.
OSBORNE RD.
BARK RD.
DALEY RD.
GALE R.
BRADLEY RD.
MOSS VW.
Clinic
NORWOOD AV.
ROAD
NORTH RD.
ANDERSON WAY
HARRINGTON ROAD
LANE
ROAD
NETHERTON ROAD
BOUNDARY RD.
ATLANTIC INDUSTRIAL ESTATE
Salesian R.C. High Sch.
Orrell Play. Fields
Playing Fields
THIRLEMERE
KESWICK
GRASMERE DR.
National Giro
FARRIERS WAY
CHESTER AV.
HEREFORD
SOUTHWARK
ST. ASAPH GRO.
CARLISLE AV.
ROCH

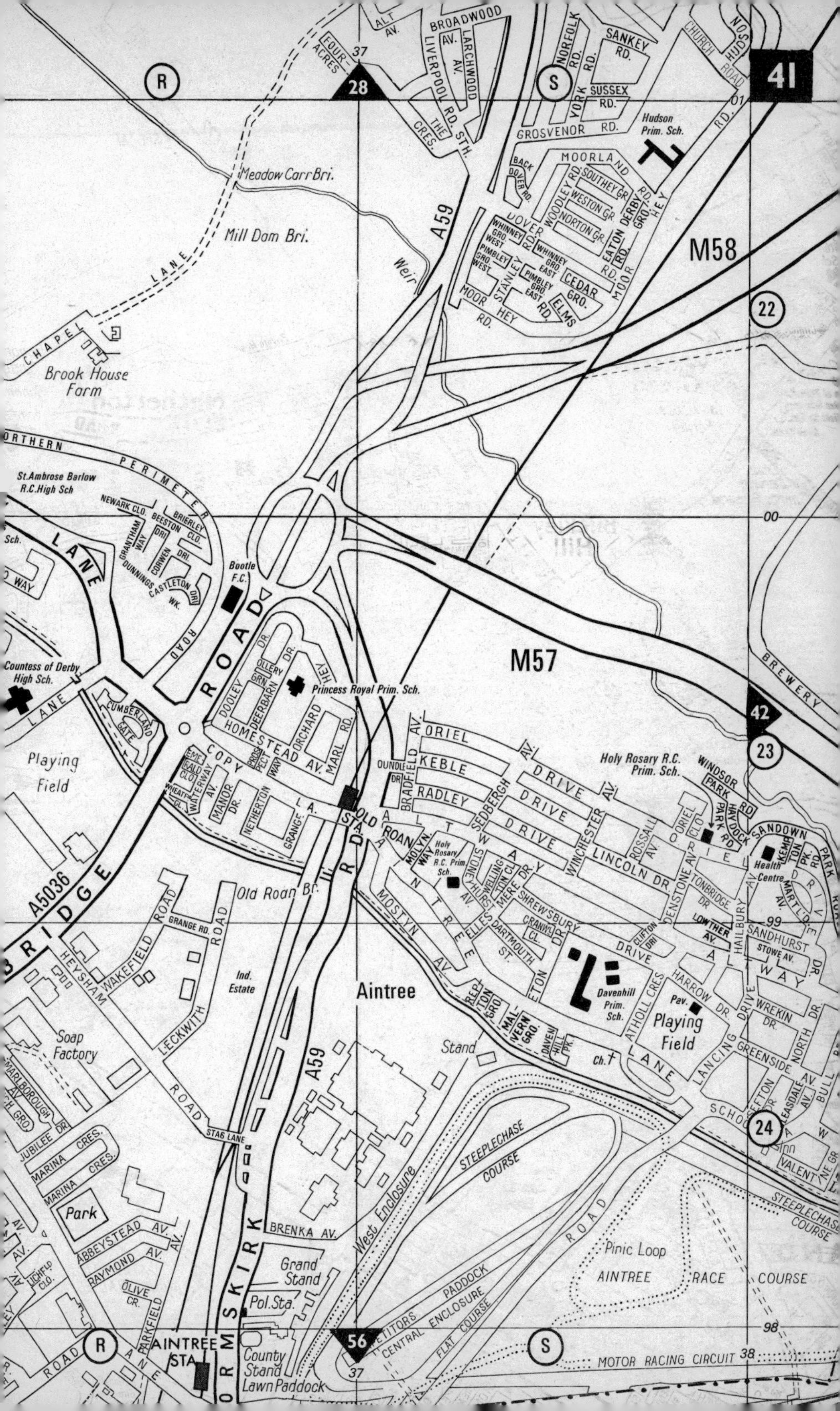

41
28
37
42
23
22
24
56
38
R
S
M58
M57
A59
A5036
Meadow Carr Bri.
Mill Dam Bri.
Weir
Brook House Farm
St.Ambrose Barlow R.C.High Sch.
Countess of Derby High Sch.
Bootle F.C.
Princess Royal Prim. Sch.
Hudson Prim. Sch.
Holy Rosary R.C. Prim. Sch.
Davenhill Prim. Sch.
Health Centre
Playing Field
Soap Factory
Ind. Estate
Aintree
Old Roan Br.
Park
Grand Stand
Pol.Sta.
County Stand
Lawn Paddock
AINTREE STA.
Pinic Loop
AINTREE RACE COURSE
STEEPLECHASE COURSE
MOTOR RACING CIRCUIT
West Enclosure
CENTRAL ENCLOSURE
FLAT COURSE
PADDOCK
Stand
Pav.
Ch.
NORTHERN PERIMETER ROAD
ORMSKIRK RD.
BRIDGE
GROSVENOR RD.
MOORLAND RD.
CHURCH ROAD
HUDSON RD.
SANKEY RD.
SUSSEX RD.
NORFOLK RD.
YORK RD.
BROADWOOD AV.
LARCHWOOD AV.
LIVERPOOL RD. STH.
ALT AV.
FOUR ACRES
THE CRES.
CHAPEL LANE
LANE
BREWERY
ORIEL DRIVE
KEBLE DRIVE
RADLEY DRIVE
LINCOLN DR.
SHREWSBURY DRIVE
WINCHESTER AV.
SEDBERGH AV.
ROSSALL AV.
OLD ROAN
ALTWAY
AINTREE LANE
MOSTYN AV.
HOMESTEAD AV.
COPY LA.
DOOLEY DR.
DEERBARN DR.
ORCHARD HEY
MARL RD.
WAKEFIELD ROAD
GRANGE RD.
LECKWITH ROAD
HEYSHAM ROAD
STAG LANE
BRENKA AV.
ABBEYSTEAD AV.
RAYMOND AV.
OLIVE CR.
PARKFIELD
MARINA CRES.
JUBILEE DR.
MARLBOROUGH AV.
SANDOWN PARK RD.
HAYDOCK PARK RD.
WINDSOR PARK RD.
TONBRIDGE DR.
LOWTHER AV.
HAILBURY AV.
SANDHURST DR.
STOWE AV.
HARROW DR.
LANCING DRIVE
GREENSIDE AV.
NORTH DR.
WREKIN DR.
VALENTINE GR.
SCHOOL

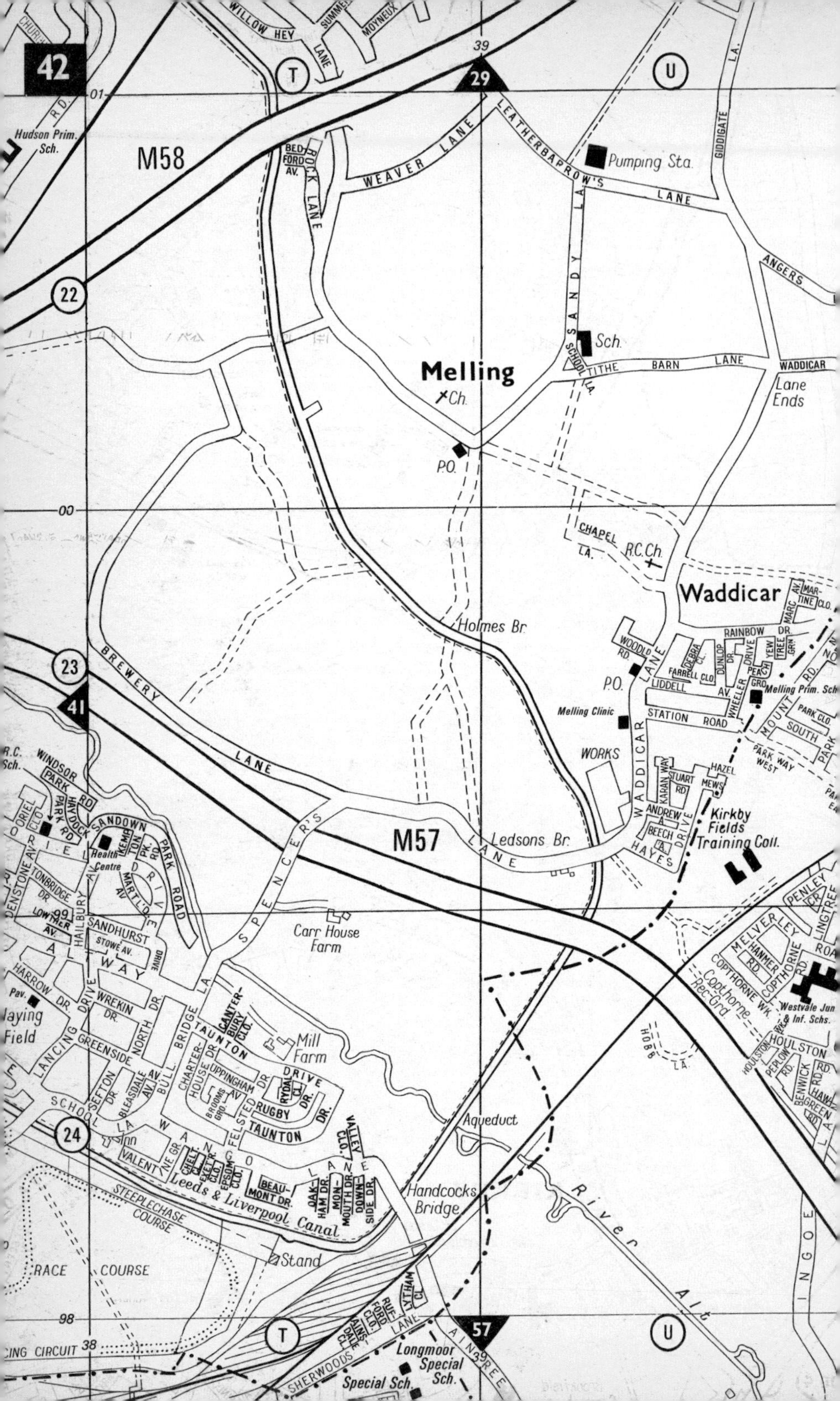
42
WILLOW HEY
SUMMER
MOYNEUX
LANE
39
T
29
U
01
RD.
Hudson Prim. Sch.
M58
BED FORD AV.
ROCK LANE
WEAVER LANE
LEATHERBARROW'S LANE
Pumping Sta.
GIDDIGATE LA.
SANDY LA.
ANGERS
22
Sch.
SCHOOL LA.
TITHE BARN LANE
WADDICAR
Lane Ends
Melling
Ch.
P.O.
00
CHAPEL LA.
R.C.Ch.
Waddicar
MARC AV.
MARTINE CLO.
Holmes Br.
WOODLD RD.
RAINBOW DR.
DEBRA CL.
DUNLOP DR.
DRIVE
YEW TREE
GRN.
FARRELL CLO.
PEACH GRO.
LIDDELL AV.
WHEELER
Melling Prim. Sch.
P.O.
Melling Clinic
STATION ROAD
MOUNT RD.
PARK CLO.
SOUTH PARK
23
41
BREWERY LANE
WORKS
WADDICAR LANE
KARAN WAY
STUART RD
HAZEL MEWS
PARK WAY WEST
R.C. Sch.
WINDSOR RD
PARK RD
HAYDOCK
ORIEL CLO.
SANDOWN PARK ROAD
KEMPTON PK. RD.
Health Centre
DRIVE
MARTLDE AV
ANDREW DRIVE
BEECH LA.
HAYES
Kirkby Fields Training Coll.
M57
Ledsons Br.
LANE
SPENCER'S LA.
TONBRIDGE DR
LOWTHER AV.
99
HAILBURY AV.
SANDHURST
STOWE AV.
WAY
DRIVE
Carr House Farm
PENLEY CR.
LINGTREE ROAD
MELVERLEY
HANMER RD.
COPTHORNE RD.
COPTHORNE WK.
Copthorne Rec.Grd.
Westvale Jun & Inf. Schs.
HARROW DR.
Pav.
Playing Field
WREKIN DR.
NORTH DR.
BULL BRIDGE LA.
CANTERBURY CLO.
TAUNTON DR.
Mill Farm
HOBB LA.
HOULSTON RD.
PEPLOW RD.
BENWICK RD.
HAWKS GREEN RD.
LANCING DRIVE
GREENSIDE AV.
SEFTON DR.
BLEASDALE AV.
CHARTERHOUSE DR.
UPPINGHAM AV.
BROOMS GRO.
RYDAL CL.
DRIVE
RUGBY DR.
FELSTED DR.
TAUNTON
VALLEY CLO.
Aqueduct
SCHOOL LA.
24
Inn
WANCO LANE
VALENTINE GR.
CHELT. CL.
EXETR. CLO.
EPSOM CLO.
BEAUMONT DR.
OAKHAM DR.
MONMOUTH DR.
DOWNSIDE DR.
Handcocks Bridge
Leeds & Liverpool Canal
STEEPLECHASE COURSE
River Alt
INGOE
RACE COURSE
Stand
98
T
LYTHAM CL.
RUFFORD CLO.
AINSDALE CL.
57
U
RACING CIRCUIT
38
LANE
SHERWOODS
AINTREE
Longmoor Special Sch.
Special Sch.

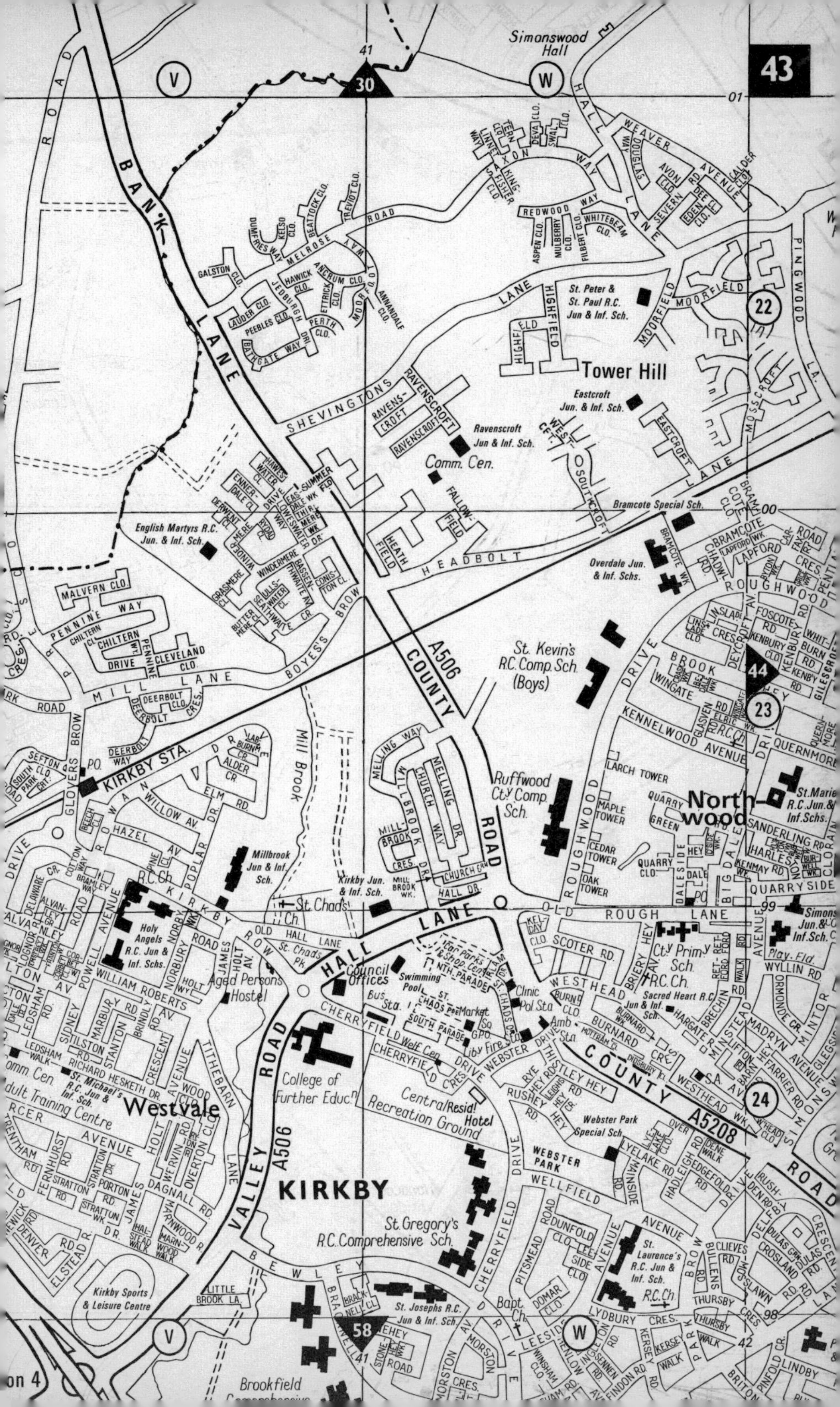
Simonswood Hall
30
BANK LANE
SHEVINGTONS LANE
HALL LANE
WEAVER AVENUE
SAXON WAY
REDWOOD WAY
MELROSE ROAD
St. Peter & St. Paul R.C. Jun & Inf. Sch.
MOORFIELD
Tower Hill
Eastcroft Jun. & Inf. Sch.
Ravenscroft Jun & Inf. Sch.
Comm. Cen.
MOSSCROFT LANE
Bramcote Special Sch.
HEADBOLT LANE
English Martyrs R.C. Jun. & Inf. Sch.
Overdale Jun. & Inf. Schs.
ROUGHWOOD DRIVE
St. Kevin's R.C. Comp. Sch. (Boys)
A506 COUNTY ROAD
PENNINE WAY
CHILTERN DRIVE
MILL LANE
BOYES'S BROW
KIRKBY STA.
Mill Brook
Ruffwood Cty Comp. Sch.
Northwood
St. Marie R.C. Jun. & Inf. Schs.
Millbrook Jun & Inf. Sch.
Holy Angels R.C. Jun & Inf. Schs.
Kirkby Jun. & Inf. Sch.
St. Chad's Ch.
OLD HALL LANE
OLD ROUGH LANE
Council Offices
Swimming Pool
Aged Persons Hostel
Cty Prim. Sch.
Sacred Heart R.C. Jun & Inf. Sch.
WESTHEAD AVENUE
A5208 COUNTY ROAD
College of Further Educn.
Central Recreation Ground
Resid! Hotel
Webster Park Special Sch.
Westvale
KIRKBY
VALLEY ROAD A506
St. Gregory's R.C. Comprehensive Sch.
St. Laurence's R.C. Jun & Inf. Sch.
Kirkby Sports & Leisure Centre
BEWLEY DRIVE
St. Josephs R.C. Jun & Inf. Sch.
58
44
22
23
24
Brookfield

44
Shacklady's Plantation
High Barn Farm
X
Y
31
43
01
SIDING LA.
STOPGATE LANE
Warren Farm
PINGWOOD LA.
MOORFIELD
22
MOSSCROFT
EASTCROFT
LANE
Woods Farm
Woodward's Plantation
Special Sch.
00
BRAMCOTE
DALE LANE
NORTH PERIMETER ROAD
DEPOT ROAD
KUDC Depot
WOODWARD ROAD
MARL ROAD
HAMMOND ROAD
BRADMAN ROAD
ASHCROFT ROAD
INDUSTRIAL ESTATE
MOSS
ROUGHWOOD DRIVE
SHACKLADY RD
PENTLAND RD
TRECASTLE RD
WARRENHOUSE RD
FALSTONE RD
FOSCOTE RD
KENBURY RD
WHITBURN RD
GILESCROFT AV
JARRETT RD
CHANGFORD RD
WATTS CLO.
DEYCROFT AV
BROOK
WINGATE
43
HEY DRIVE
QUERNMORE
ELWOOD AVENUE
23
North-wood
St. Marie's R.C. Jun.& Inf.Schs.
Warrenhouse Recreation Ground
Moss Lane Recreation Ground
SIMONSWOOD LANE
SANDERLING RD
DARMOND RD
CLORAIN RD
BIRBECK RD
HARLESDON
MOSS LANE
QUARRYSIDE DRIVE
99
Simonswood Jun.& Inf.Sch.
COLWALL
Play. Fld.
WYLLIN RD
Windy Arbour Recreation Ground
ARBOUR LANE
NEWSTET ROAD
BIRCHILL ROAD
STOCKPIT ROAD
DRAW WELL ROAD
KIRKBY BANK ROAD
WEBBER ROAD
KIRKBY
YARDLEY
CHARLEY WOOD ROAD
CORNFIELD ROAD
LEES ROAD
Charley
MINTOR
GLEGSIDE
SIMONSWOOD
WESTHEAD AVENUE
24
Football Ground
ROAD
A5208
Broad Lane Recreation Ground
CUSSON RD
DIXON RD
GORES ROAD
59
Y
X
42
98
Park Brow Jun. & Inf.Schs.
SOUTH
LINDBY ROAD
PO

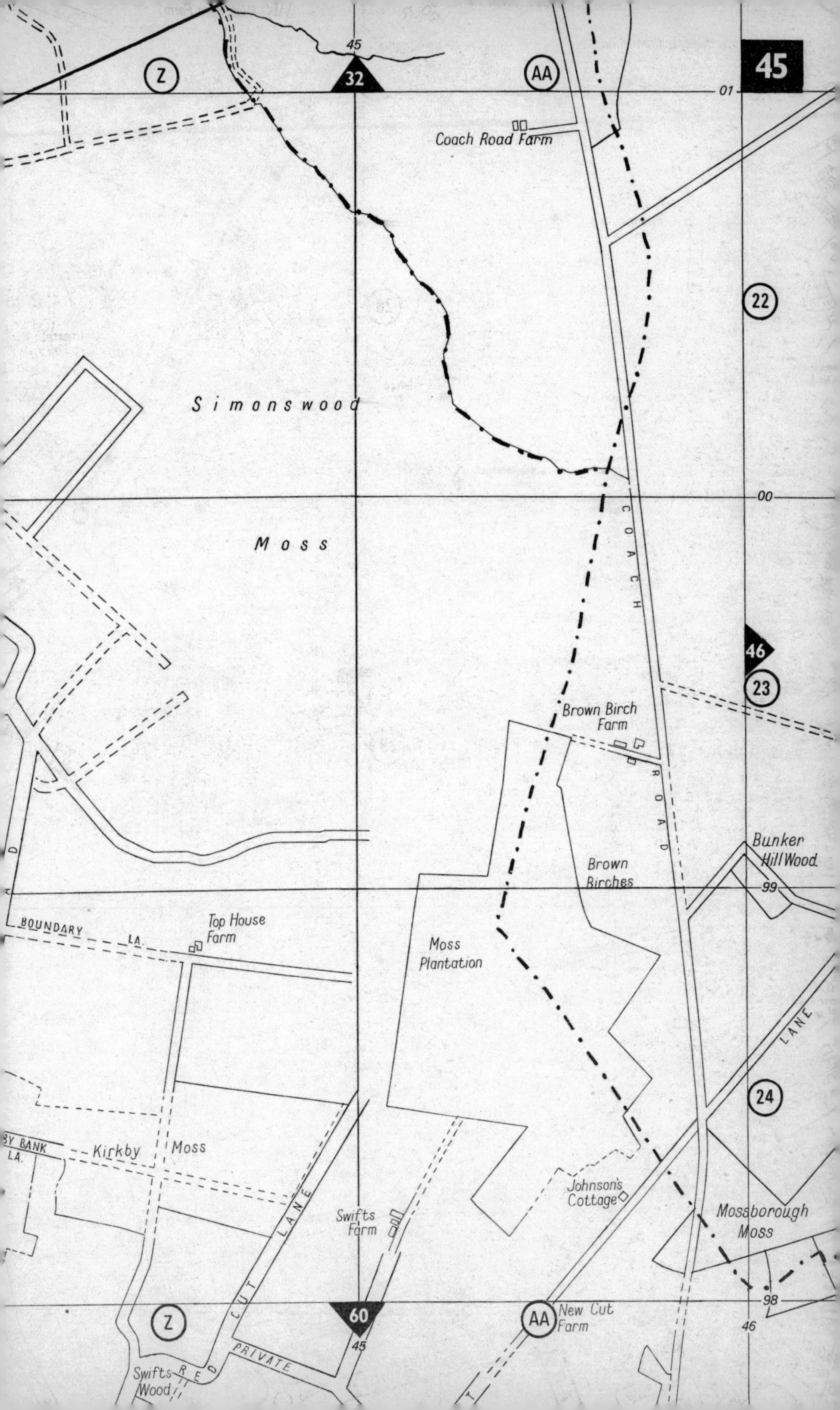

Z

32

AA

Coach Road Farm

22

Simonswood

Moss

COACH

00

46

23

Brown Birch
Farm

Bunker
Hill Wood

ROAD

99

BOUNDARY   LA.

Top House
Farm

Brown
Birches

LANE

Moss
Plantation

24

BY BANK

Kirkby   Moss

LA.

CUT

LANE

Swifts
Farm

Johnson's
Cottage

Mossborough
Moss

98

46

Z

60

RED

45

PRIVATE

AA

New Cut
Farm

Swifts
Wood

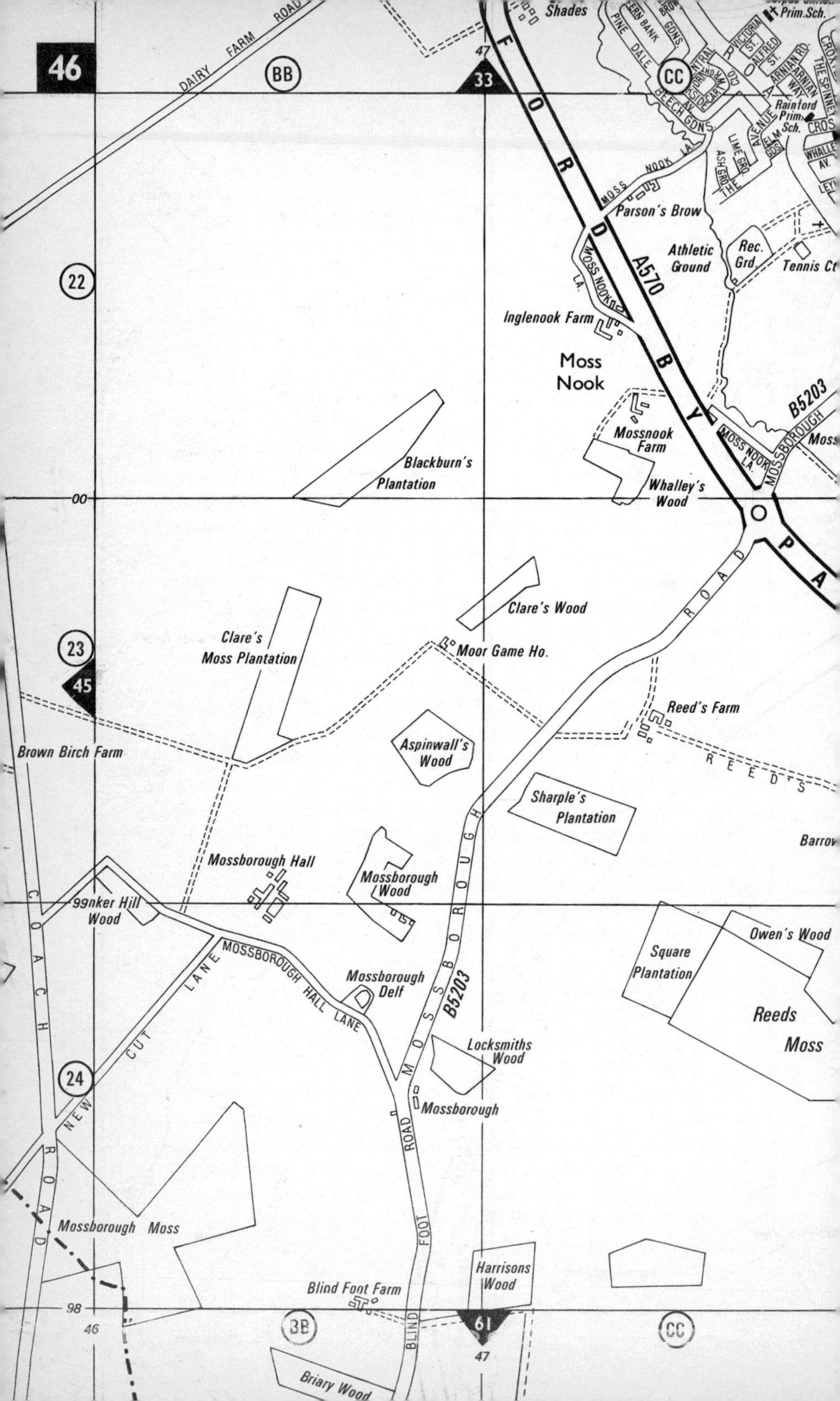

DAIRY FARM ROAD
BB
33
47
Shades
FORD BY PASS
A570
CC
Prim.Sch.
PINE DALE
FERN BANK
GDNS.
VICTORIA ST.
ALFRED ST.
ARNIAN RD.
ARNIAN WAY
BEECH GDNS.
AVENUE
Rainford Prim. Sch.
LIME GRO.
ASH GRO.
THE
ELM GDS
WHALLEY AV.
MOSS NOOK LA.
Parson's Brow
Athletic Ground
Rec. Grd.
Tennis Ct
22
Inglenook Farm
Moss Nook
B5203
Mossnook Farm
MOSSBOROUGH
Whalley's Wood
Blackburn's Plantation
00
ROAD
Clare's Wood
Clare's Moss Plantation
Moor Game Ho.
23
45
Reed's Farm
REEDS
Aspinwall's Wood
Brown Birch Farm
Sharple's Plantation
Barrow
Mossborough Hall
Mossborough Wood
Bunker Hill Wood
COACH ROAD
MOSSBOROUGH HALL LANE
NEW CUT LANE
Square Plantation
Owen's Wood
Mossborough Delf
MOSSBOROUGH ROAD
Reeds Moss
Locksmiths Wood
24
Mossborough
Mossborough Moss
BLIND FOOT ROAD
Harrisons Wood
Blind Foot Farm
98
46
BB
61
CC
47
Briary Wood

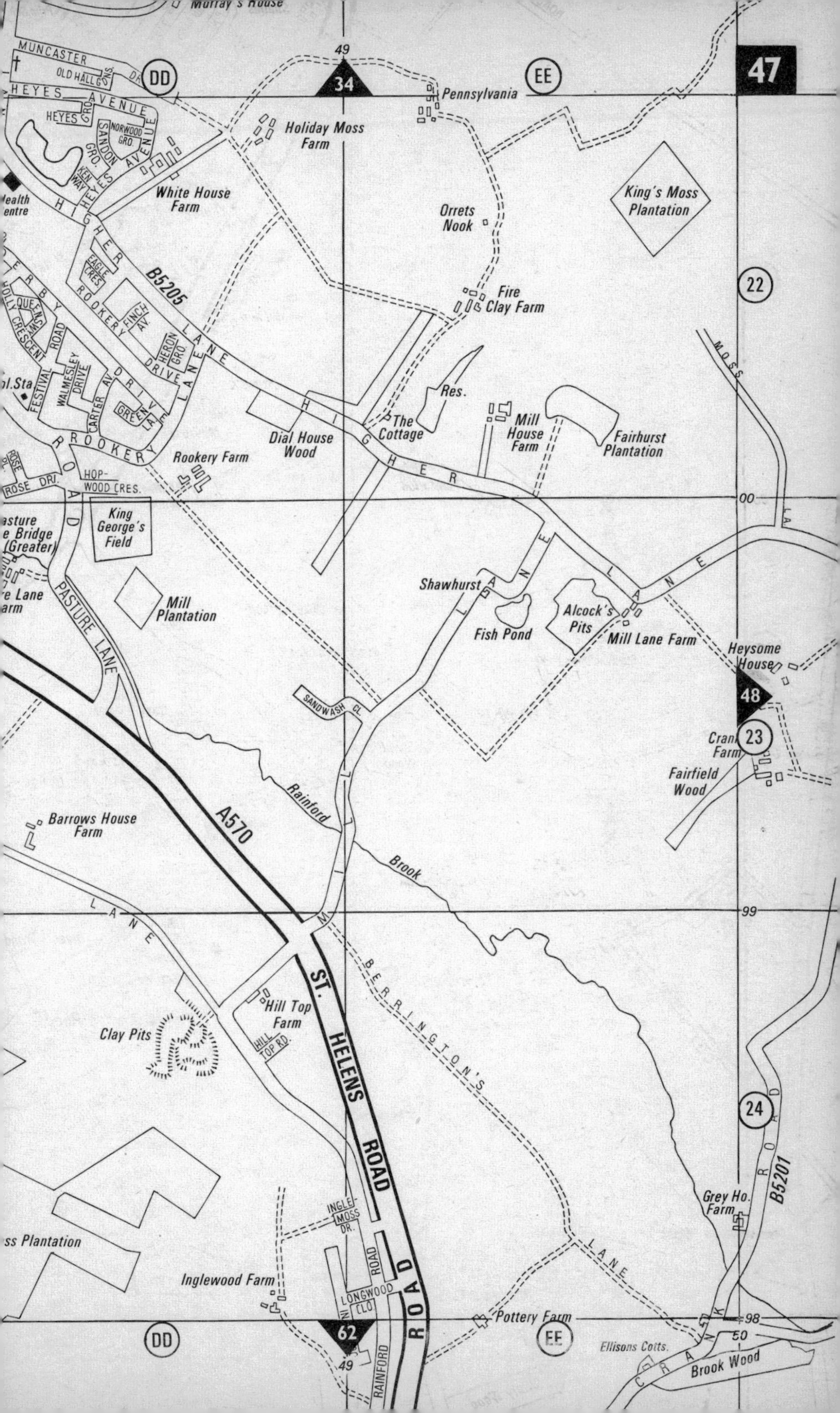
47
34
62
48
DD
EE
22
23
24
49
00
99
98
50
Murray's House
MUNCASTER DR.
OLD HALL GDNS.
HEYES AVENUE
HEYES GRO.
NORWOOD GRO.
SANDON GRO.
KEN WAY
HEYES AVENUE
Health Centre
HIGHER LANE
B5205
EAGLE CRES.
ROOKERY DRIVE
FINCH AV.
HERON GRO.
QUEENSWAY
HOLLY CRESCENT
FESTIVAL ROAD
WALMESLEY DRIVE
CARTER AV.
GREEN LA.
ROOKERY ROAD
ROSE DR.
ROSE DRI.
HOP-WOOD CRES.
Pol.Sta
Pennsylvania
Holiday Moss Farm
White House Farm
Orrets Nook
King's Moss Plantation
Fire Clay Farm
MOSS LA.
Res.
The Cottage
Mill House Farm
Fairhurst Plantation
Dial House Wood
Rookery Farm
King George's Field
Pasture Bridge (Greater)
Pasture Lane Farm
PASTURE LANE
Mill Plantation
Shawhurst
MILL LANE
Fish Pond
Alcock's Pits
Mill Lane Farm
Heysome House
Crank Farm
Fairfield Wood
SANDWASH CL.
Rainford Brook
A570
Barrows House Farm
LANE
BERRINGTON'S LANE
ST. HELENS ROAD
Hill Top Farm
HILL TOP RD.
Clay Pits
Moss Plantation
INGLE-MOSS DR.
ROAD
Inglewood Farm
LONGWOOD CLO.
RAINFORD ROAD
Pottery Farm
Ellisons Cotts.
Brook Wood
CRANK ROAD
B5201
Grey Ho. Farm

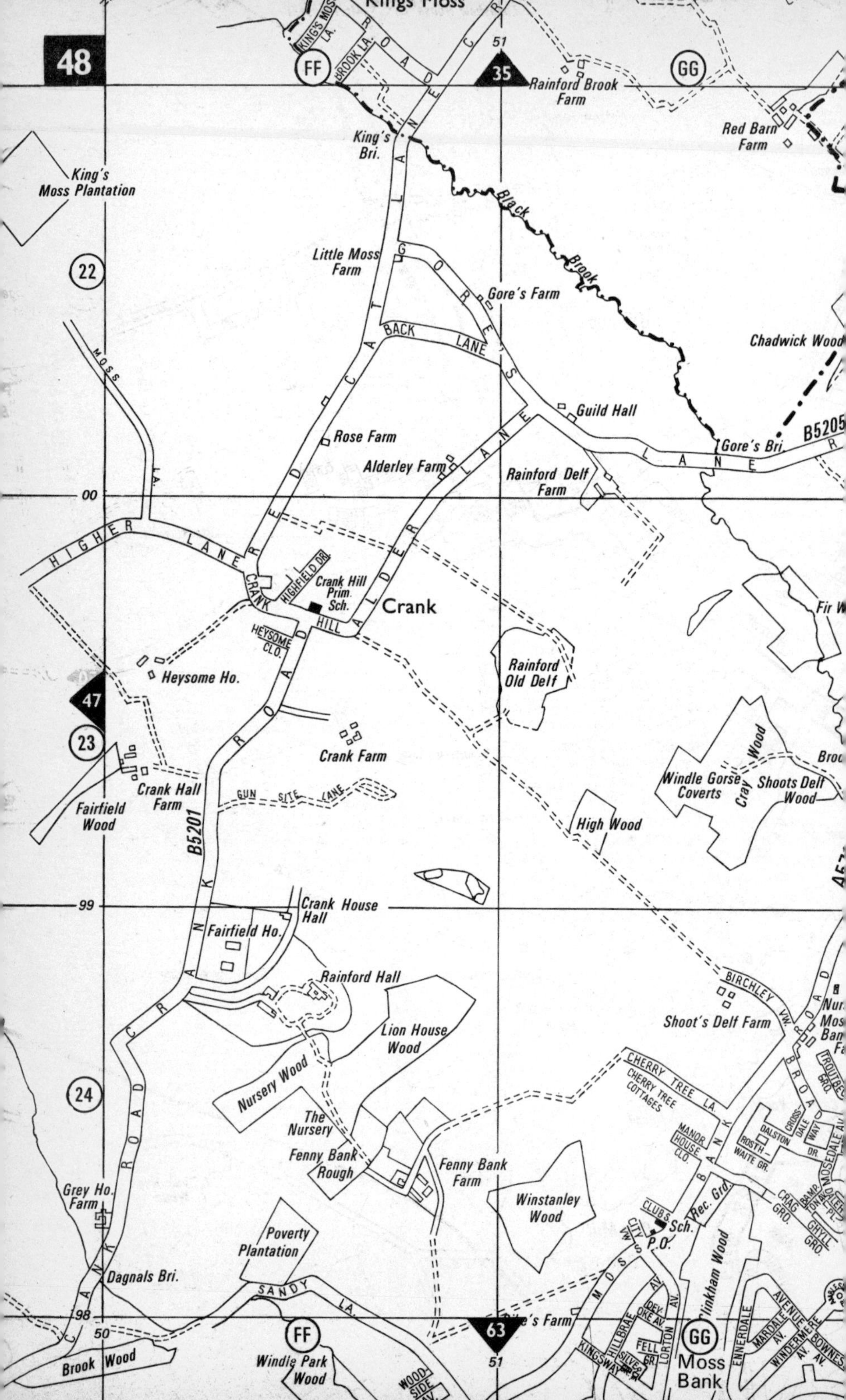

Kings Moss

48

FF

35 Rainford Brook Farm

GG

Red Barn Farm

King's Moss Plantation

King's Bri.

22

Little Moss Farm

Gore's Farm

Black Brook

Chadwick Wood

BACK LANE

Guild Hall

B5205

Rose Farm

Gore's Bri.

00

Alderley Farm

Rainford Delf Farm

HIGHER LANE

CRANK

Crank Hill Prim. Sch.

Crank

Fir

HEYSOME CLO.

Rainford Old Delf

47

Heysome Ho.

23

Crank Farm

Windle Gorse Coverts

Cray Wood

Shoots Dell Wood

Broo

GUN SITE LANE

B5201

Crank Hall Farm

Fairfield Wood

High Wood

AE

99

Crank House Hall

Fairfield Ho.

Rainford Hall

BIRCHLEY VW.

Shoot's Delf Farm

Nur Mos Ban

Lion House Wood

24

Nursery Wood

CHERRY TREE LA.

CHERRY TREE COTTAGES

ROSMERE AV.

DALSTON

NAVY

The Nursery

MANOR HOUSE CLO.

ROISTH

WAITE GR.

CRAG GRO.

CHYKL

Fenny Bank Rough

Fenny Bank Farm

CROSS

Grey Ho. Farm

Winstanley Wood

CLUB

Rec. Grd.

CITY

Sch.

P.O.

Poverty Plantation

Dagnals Bri.

SANDY LA.

MOSS

Rie's Farm

50

FF

98

Brook Wood

Windle Park Wood

63

51

GG

Moss Bank

WOOD SIDE AV.

KINGSWAY

HILLBRAE

DEV. AV.

FELL GR.

HILLBRAE AV.

CITY

AVENUE

ENNERDALE

MARSDALE AV.

WINDERMERE

BOWNES

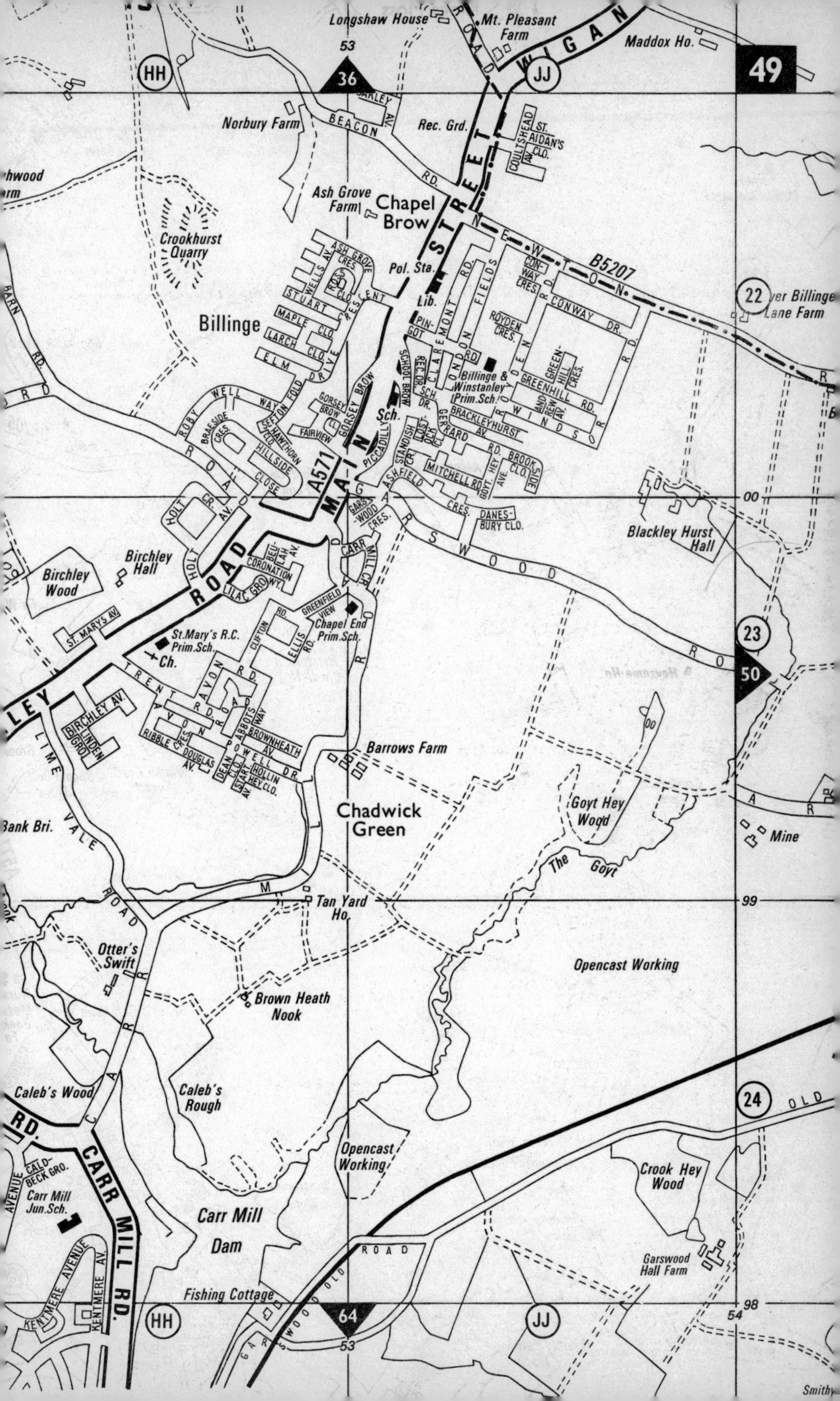
Longshaw House
Mt. Pleasant Farm
Maddox Ho.
WIGAN
ROAD
HH
JJ
36
53
BARLEY AV.
BEACON RD.
Norbury Farm
Rec. Grd.
COULTSHEAD AV.
ST. AIDAN'S CLO.
Ash Grove Farm
Chapel Brow
MAIN STREET
NEWTON
B5207
Crookhurst Quarry
ASH GROVE CRES.
ROSS CLO.
WELLS AV.
STUART CRESCENT
Pol. Sta.
Lib.
CON-WAY CRES.
CONWAY DR.
22
Lower Billinge Lane Farm
Billinge
MAPLE CLO.
LARCH CLO.
ELM DRIVE
PINGOT
CLAREMONT RD.
LONDON FIELDS
ROYDEN CRES.
ROYDEN RD.
GREENHILL CRES.
GREENHILL RD.
WINDSOR RD.
Billinge & Winstanley Prim.Sch.
ANDREW AV.
SCHOOL BROW
SCH. DR.
ROBY WELL WAY
SEFTON FOLD
BRAESIDE CRES.
HAWTHORN
HILLSIDE CLOSE
GORSEY BROW
FAIRVIEW
Sch.
PICCADILLY
STANDISH CR.
GERRARD AV.
BRACKLEYHURST AV.
BROOKSIDE CLO.
GOYT HEY AVE.
MITCHELL RD.
ASHFIELD CRES.
DANESBURY CLO.
A571
HOLT CR.
HOLT AV.
GARSWOOD CRES.
GARSWOOD ROAD
00
Blackley Hurst Hall
Birchley Hall
Birchley Wood
BEULAH AV.
CORONATION WY.
LILAC GRO.
CARR MILL CR.
GREENFIELD VIEW
Chapel End Prim.Sch.
CLIFTON RD.
ELLIS RD.
St.Mary's R.C. Prim.Sch.
Ch.
ST. MARYS AV.
TRENT RD.
AVON RD.
AVON ROAD
23
50
BIRCHLEY AV.
LINDEN GRO.
RIBBLE CRES.
DOUGLAS AV.
ABBOTS WAY
BROWNHEATH AV.
POWELL DR.
DEAN CLO.
STARTHEY AV.
HOLLIN HEY CLO.
Barrows Farm
LIME VALE ROAD
Bank Bri.
Chadwick Green
Goyt Hey Wood
The Goyt
Mine
MILL LANE
Tan Yard Ho.
99
Otter's Swift
Brown Heath Nook
Opencast Working
Caleb's Wood
Caleb's Rough
CARR MILL RD.
CALDBECK GRO.
AVENUE
Carr Mill Jun.Sch.
Carr Mill Dam
24
OLD
Crook Hey Wood
Garswood Hall Farm
KENTMERE AVENUE
KENTMERE AV.
Fishing Cottage
GARSWOOD OLD ROAD
64
98
54
Smithy

50
KK
37
55
LL
Brocstedes Farm
BROCSTEDES ROAD
Reservoir
WINSTANLEY ROAD
Barton Clough
Gladden Hey Brow
Booth's Brow Farm
Res.
22
Lower Billinge Lane Farm
Down Brook
LEYLAND GREEN LANE
Leyland Green Farm
Ch.
Rectory Prim.Sch
Football Grd.
Leyland Green
ROAD BILLINGE ROAD
Billinge Lane Farm
B5207
Weathercock Hill Farm
Downhall Green
00
Mine
Weathercock Hill
GARSWOOD ROAD
Club
Playing Field
Seneley Green Farm
Garswood
Torpen Wood
49
23
The Goyt
Chanity Farm
ARCH LANE
Mine
Arch Lane Farm
Gerard R.C. Prim.Sch
Garswood Prim. Sch.
Manor House Farm
GARSWOOD STA.
Tithe Barn Hillock
99
TITHE BARN
Tithe Barn Farm
Carter's Fold Farm
Reservoir
A58
24
OLD GARSWOOD ROAD
LIVERPOOL ROAD
Crook Hey Wood
Old Garswood Park
Pewfall
98
54
KK
65
55
LL
Depot
Smithy

51
52
66
Junction 25
Junction 24
ASHTON IN MAKERFIELD
North Ashton
Rose Hill
Bryn
Town Green
Home Farm
Garswood Park
Golf Course
Vista Plantation
Rookery Plantation
Haydock Boundary Plantation
New Hall Wood
Long Covert
Skitters
Down Brook
Millingford Brook
Oil Distribution Terminal
YEW TREE FARM TRADING ESTATE
OLD BOSTON TRADING ESTATE
INDUSTRIAL ESTATE
Hospital
Sports Centre
Jubilee Parks
King George's Fld.
Scrap Metal Works
Tanks
WIGAN ROAD
WARRINGTON ROAD
LIVERPOOL ROAD
BRYN ROAD
LODGE
LOW BANK ROAD
ALEXANDRA ROAD
GERARD ST.
BRYN ST.
M6
A49
B5207

52
00
59
PP
Baldwins
Coffin Lane
Brook
Opencast Working
Hospital
22
Lily Lane
Lily Fm.
RIDING LA.
ROAD
A58
INDUSTRIAL ESTATE
Stubshaw Cross
Stubshaw Cross Prim. Sch.
Rose
Potter's Farm
Town Green
23
51
Rec. Grd.
Jameson's Farm
B5207
Edge Green Farm
GREEN ROAD
King George's Fld.
Recreation Ground
BOLTON
New Barn
Edge Green
Sewage Pump Sta.
ASHTON ROAD
Works
Meth. Ch.
99
Millingford Brook
Ashton Heath
Ashton Heath Farm
HAYDOCK PARK STA. (Racedays Only)
24
Paddock
Car Park
Millingford Bridge
Park House Farm
Haydock Park Race Course
Haydock Lodge Hosp.
LODGE ROAD
98
58
00
67
59
PP

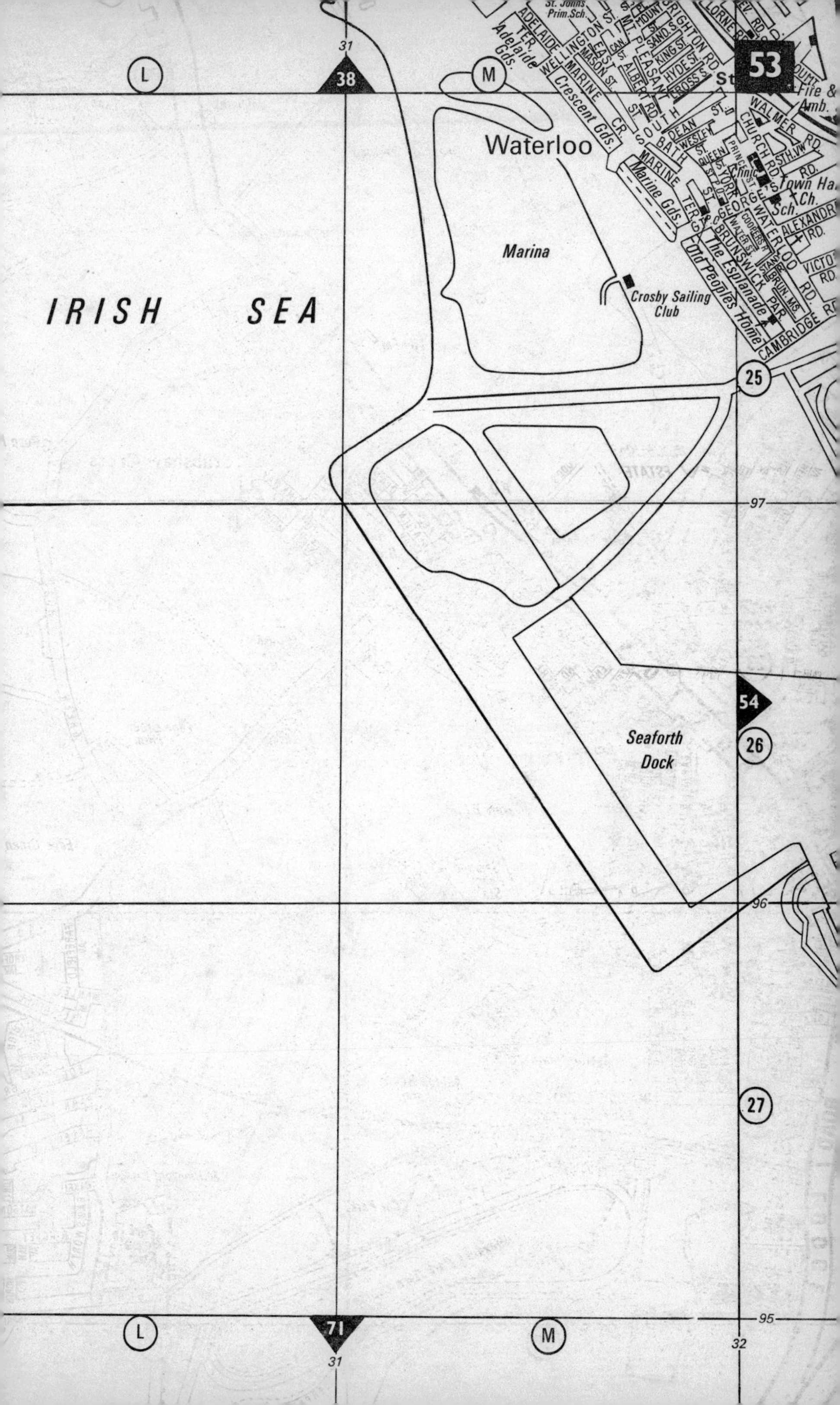

53
38
54
71
L
M
31
32
95
96
97
25
26
27
IRISH SEA
Waterloo
Marina
Crosby Sailing Club
Seaforth Dock
St. Johns Prim.Sch.
Adelaide Gds.
ADELAIDE TER.
WELLINGTON ST.
EAST ST.
MASON ST.
MARINE CR.
Crescent Gds.
ALBERT RD.
MT. PLEASANT
MOUNT ST.
KING ST.
HYDE ST.
CROSS S.
BRIGHTON RD.
LORNE RD.
SOUTH RD.
DEAN ST.
BATH ST.
WESLEY ST.
MARINE TER.
Marine Gds.
QUEEN ST.
YORK ST.
ST. GEORGE'S RD.
WATERLOO RD.
BRUNSWICK PAR.
The Esplanade
Old Peoples Home
CHURCH RD.
WALMER RD.
Clinic
Town Ha.
Ch.
Sch.
ALEXANDRA RD.
STH.VW RD.
CAMBRIDGE RD.
Fire & Amb.

54
LITHERLAND
Seaforth
Linacre
ROYAL SEAFORTH DOCK
GLADSTONE DOCK (Container Ships)
HORNBY DOCK
ALEXANDRA DOCK
BRANCH NO.2
BRANCH NO.1
BRANCH NO.3
GRAVING DOCK
Dock Entrance
Recreation Ground
BEACH RD INDUSTRIAL ESTATE
Crosby Sailing Club
The Esplanade
Old People's Home
Town Hall
Council Offices
CROSBY RD. SOUTH
A565
REGENT ROAD
A5036
DERBY ROAD
KNOWSLEY RD.
RIMROSE
MARSH LA.
LINACRE
HORNBY BOULEVARD
SEAFORTH RD.
PRINCESS WAY
CHURCH RD.
GROVE ST.
STRAND RD.
39
53
72
25
26
27
N
O
33
32
97
96
95

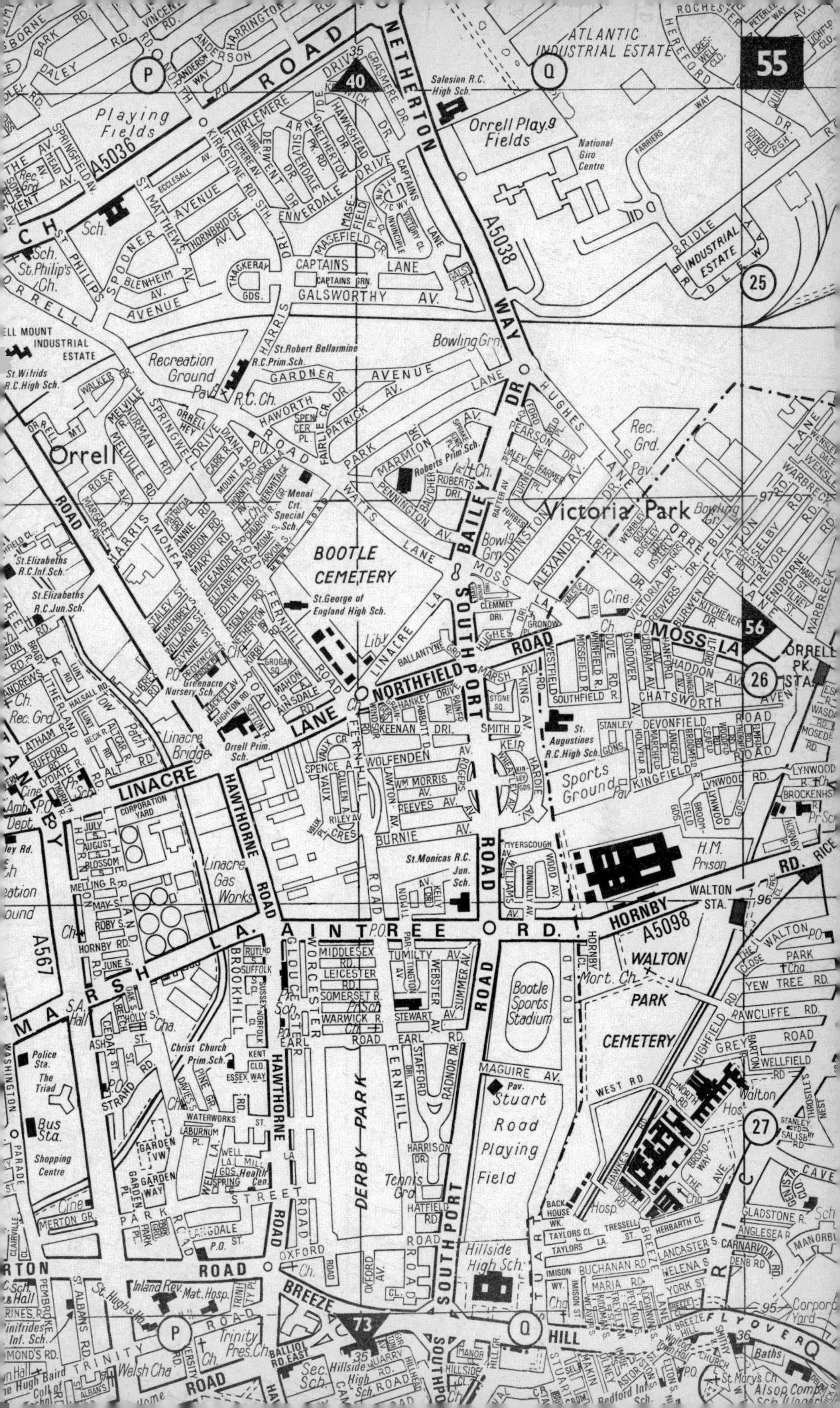

55
56
40
73
25
26
27
ATLANTIC INDUSTRIAL ESTATE
Salesian R.C. High Sch.
Orrell Play.g Fields
National Giro Centre
INDUSTRIAL ESTATE
BRIDLE WAY
NETHERTON WAY
A5038
A5036
ROAD
Playing Fields
Sch.
St.Philip's Ch.
ORRELL
MOUNT INDUSTRIAL ESTATE
St.Wifrids R.C.High Sch.
Recreation Ground
St.Robert Bellarmine R.C.Prim.Sch.
R.C.Ch.
CAPTAINS LANE
GALSWORTHY AV.
ENNERDALE
GARDNER AVENUE
Bowling Grn.
HUGHES LANE
Rec. Grd.
Victoria Park
Orrell
Roberts Prim.Sch.
BAILEY DR.
Menai Crt. Special Sch.
BOOTLE CEMETERY
St.George of England High Sch.
St.Elizabeths R.C.Inf.Sch.
St.Elizabeths R.C.Jun.Sch.
WATTS LANE
LINACRE LA.
NORTHFIELD ROAD
MOSS LA.
SOUTHPORT ROAD
Greenacre Nursery Sch.
Orrell Prim. Sch.
Linacre Bridge
LINACRE
CORPORATION YARD
Linacre Gas Works
HAWTHORNE ROAD
St. Augustines R.C.High Sch.
Sports Ground
H.M. Prison
St.Monicas R.C. Jun. Sch.
WALTON STA.
HORNBY RD.
A5098
RICE LANE
AINTREE RD.
A567
MARSH LA.
WALTON PARK CEMETERY
Bootle Sports Stadium
Stuart Road Playing Field
DERBY PARK
Tennis Grd
Christ Church Prim.Sch.
Police Sta.
The Triad
Bus Sta.
Shopping Centre
Walton Hosp.
Hillside High Sch.
Inland Rev.
Mat. Hosp.
Trinity Pres.Ch.
Welsh Cha
BREEZE HILL
FLYOVER
Hillside High Sch
Walton Town Hall
St Mary's Ch
Baths
Corpor. Yard

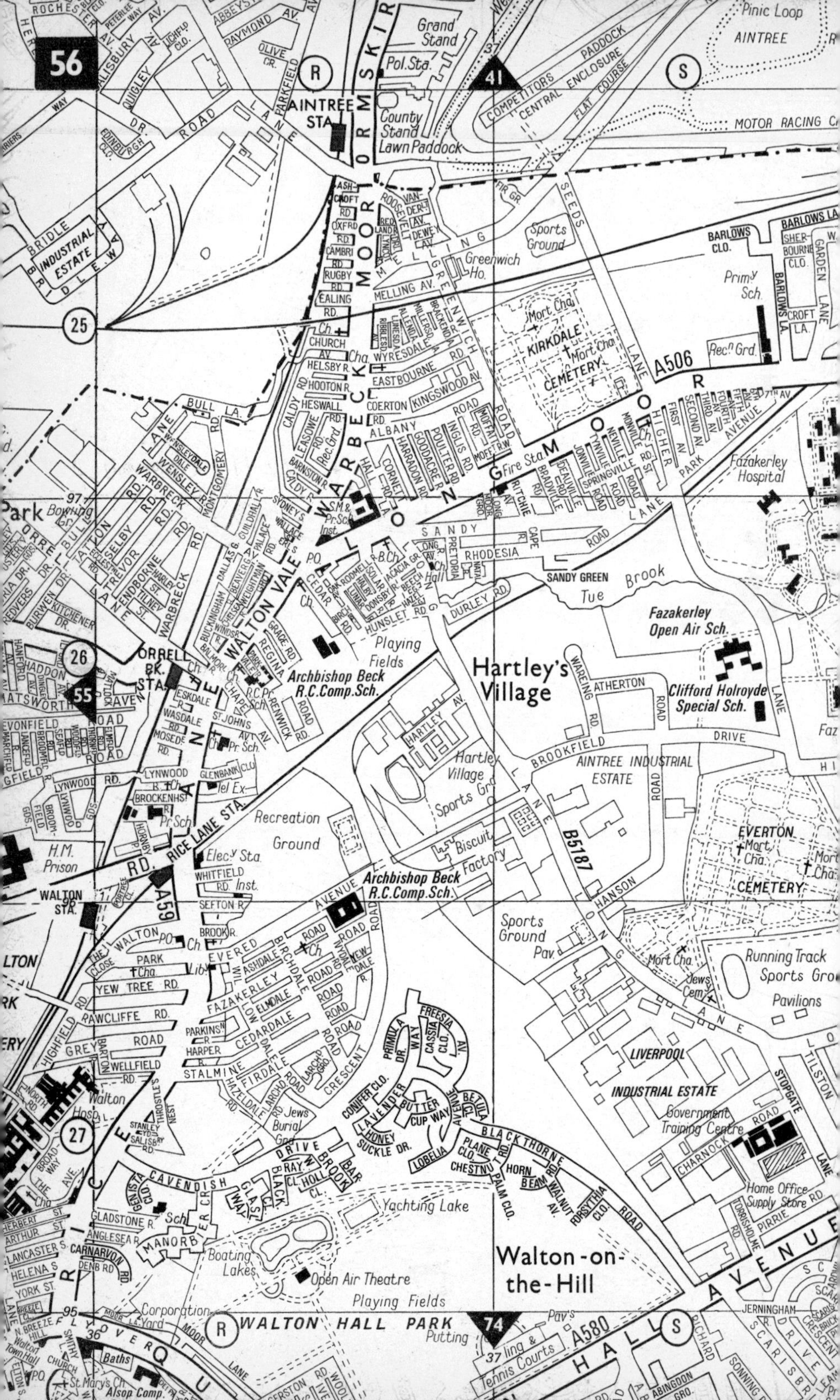
56
41
74
55
25
26
27
AINTREE STA.
Grand Stand
Pol. Sta.
County Stand
Lawn Paddock
COMPETITORS PADDOCK
CENTRAL ENCLOSURE
FLAT COURSE
MOTOR RACING
Pinic Loop
AINTREE
ORMSKIRK
INDUSTRIAL ESTATE
BRIDLE WAY
Sports Ground
Greenwich Ho.
MELLING AV.
KIRKDALE CEMETERY
A506
LONGMOOR
WARBECK MOOR
BARLOWS CLO.
Rec.n Grd.
Fazakerley Hospital
Fire Sta.
SANDY GREEN
Tue Brook
Fazakerley Open Air Sch.
Hartley's Village
Clifford Holroyde Special Sch.
Archbishop Beck R.C.Comp.Sch.
Playing Fields
WALTON VALE
ORRELL PK. STA.
RICE LANE STA.
AINTREE INDUSTRIAL ESTATE
BROOKFIELD DRIVE
Hartley Village Sports Grd
Recreation Ground
Biscuit Factory
B5187
EVERTON CEMETERY
H.M. Prison
WALTON STA.
A59
Sports Ground
Running Track
Sports Gro
Pavilions
LIVERPOOL INDUSTRIAL ESTATE
Government Training Centre
Home Office Supply Store
Walton Hosp.
Jews Burial Gnd.
BLACKTHORNE ROAD
Yachting Lake
Boating Lakes
Open Air Theatre
Playing Fields
Walton-on-the-Hill
WALTON HALL PARK
A580
HALL AVENUE
Corporation Yard
Baths
St. Mary's Ch.
Alsop Comp.

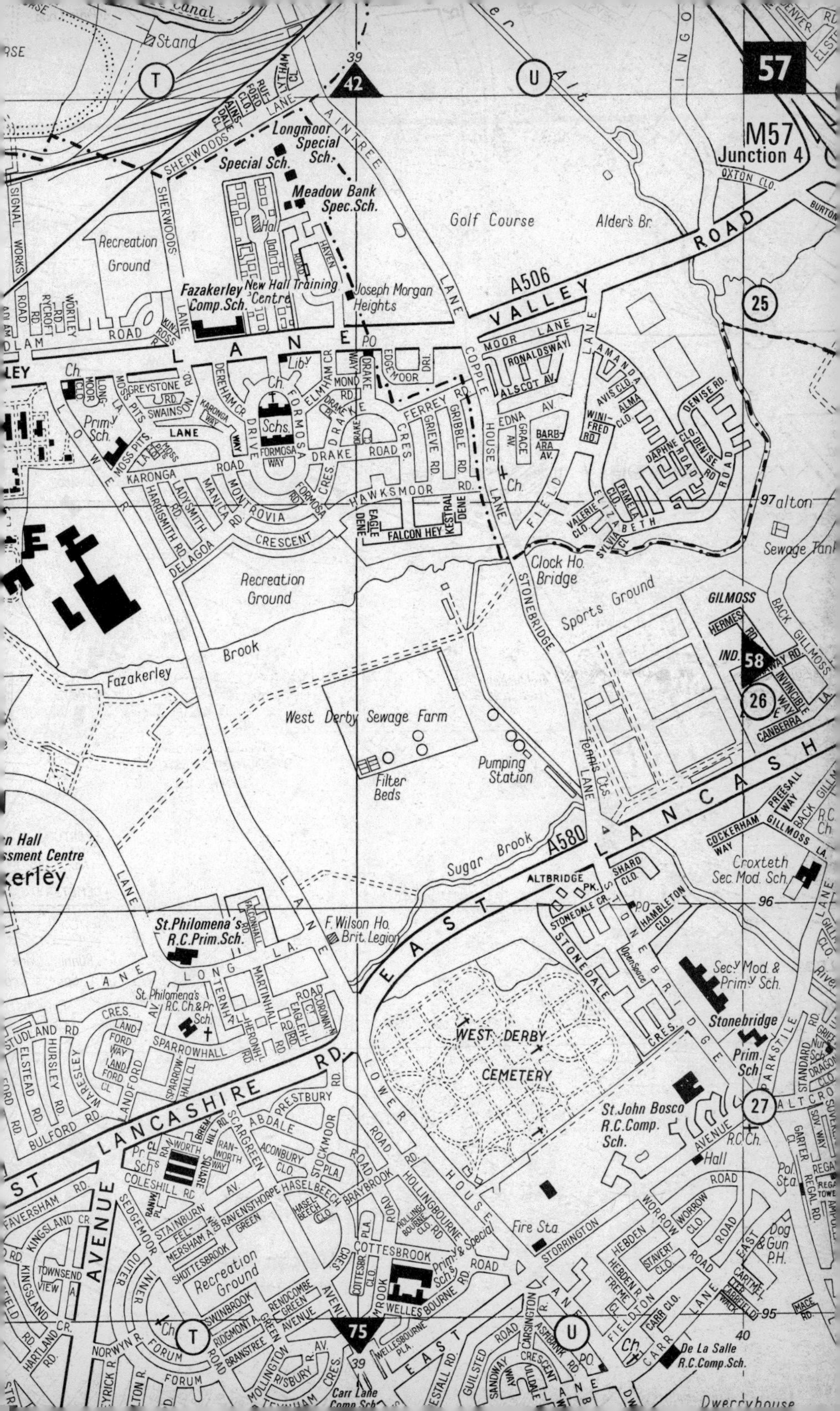
57
Canal
Stand
T
U
42
39
M57
Junction 4
OXTON CLO.
BURTON
LYTHAM CL.
RUFFORD CLO.
AINSDALE CL.
LANE
SHERWOODS
Longmoor Special Sch.
Special Sch.
Meadow Bank Spec.Sch.
AINTREE
Golf Course
Alder's Br.
ROAD
A506
VALLEY
25
SIGNAL WORKS ROAD
Recreation Ground
Hall
HAVEN
Fazakerley Comp.Sch.
New Hall Training Centre
Joseph Morgan Heights
LANE
WORTLEY RD.
RYCROFT RD.
ROAD
KINROSS
PO
Liby
EDGEMOOR DRI.
MOOR LANE
RONALDSWAY
ALSCOT AV.
COPPLE HOUSE LANE
AMANDA
DENISE RD.
AVIS CLO.
ALMA CLO.
Ch.
MOSS PITS LANE
GREYSTONE RD.
SWAINSON RD.
DEREHAM CR.
KARONGA WAY
ELMHAM CR.
MOND RD.
DRAKE
FERREY
GRIEVE RD.
GRIBBLE RD.
EDNA AV.
GRACE AV.
BARBARA AV.
WINIFRED RD.
Prim.y Sch.
Schs.
FORMOSA WAY
FORMOSA DRIVE
DRAKE ROAD
CRES.
DAPHNE CLO.
DENISE ROAD
KARONGA ROAD
HARRISMITH RD.
LADYSMITH RD.
MANICA RD.
MONTROVIA
HAWKSMOOR RD.
EAGLE DENE
FALCON HEY
KESTRAL DENE
FIELD LANE
VALERIE CLO.
ELIZABETH
PAMELA CLO.
SYLVIA CL.
97
Sewage Tank
DELAGOA
CRESCENT
Recreation Ground
Clock Ho. Bridge
STONEBRIDGE
Sports Ground
GILMOSS
HERMES RD.
IND.
58
BACK GILLMOSS
Brook
Fazakerley
West Derby Sewage Farm
Filter Beds
Pumping Station
Tennis Ct.s
26
INVINCIBLE WAY
CANBERRA
LANE
LOWER LANE
A580
EAST LANCASHIRE
PREESALL WAY
COCKERHAM WAY
GILLMOSS LA.
BACK GILLMOSS
R.C. Ch.
Croxteth Sec.Mod.Sch.
Sugar Brook
...n Hall
...ssment Centre
...kerley
ALTBRIDGE PK.
SHARD CLO.
PO
HAMBLETON CLO.
STONEDALE CR.
96
St.Philomena's R.C.Prim.Sch.
FALCONHALL RD.
F. Wilson Ho. Brit. Legion
Open Space
STONEDALE CRES.
Sec.y Mod. & Prim.y Sch.
LONG LANE
St.Philomena's R.C.Ch.& Pr.Sch.
MARTINHALL RD.
CORONATION RD.
Stonebridge Prim. Sch.
WEST DERBY CEMETERY
STUDLAND RD
HURSLEY RD.
ELSTEAD RD.
WARESLEY CRES.
LANDFORD AV.
SPARROWHALL
PARKSTILE
STANDARD RD.
27
ALTCROSS
St.John Bosco R.C.Comp. Sch.
AVENUE
R.C.Ch.
Hall
BULFORD RD.
EAST LANCASHIRE RD.
PRESTBURY
ABDALE
SCARGREEN
STOCKMOOR
ACONBURY CLO.
LOWER HOUSE LANE
ROAD
Pol. Sta.
GARTER CL.
REGAL RD.
FAVERSHAM RD.
COLESHILL RD
HASELBEECH
BRAYBROOK
HOLLINGBOURNE RD.
WORROW ROAD
KINGSLAND CR
AVENUE
SEDGEMOOR
RAVENSTHORPE GREEN
Fire Sta.
STORRINGTON
HEBDEN
STAVERT CLO.
EAST LANE
Dog & Gun P.H.
TOWNSEND VIEW
Recreation Ground
SHOTTESBROOK
COTTESBROOK
Prim.y & Special Sch.s
CARTMEL
INNER FORUM
OUTER FORUM
SWINBROOK
RENDCOMBE GREEN
WELLESBOURNE RD.
ROAD
FIELDTON
CARR CLO.
95
MACE RD.
KINGSLAND RD.
HARTLAND RD.
Ch.
T
RIDGMONT A.
BRANSTREE
AVENUE
75
WELLESBOURNE PLA.
EAST
GUILSTED ROAD
CARSINGTON
U
CARR LANE
De La Salle R.C.Comp.Sch.
40
NORWYN R.
MOLLINGTON
RISBURY R. AV.
CRES.
Carr Lane Comp.Sch.
ESTALL RD.
SANDWAY
CRESCENT
ASHBANK RD.
PO.
Dwerryhouse

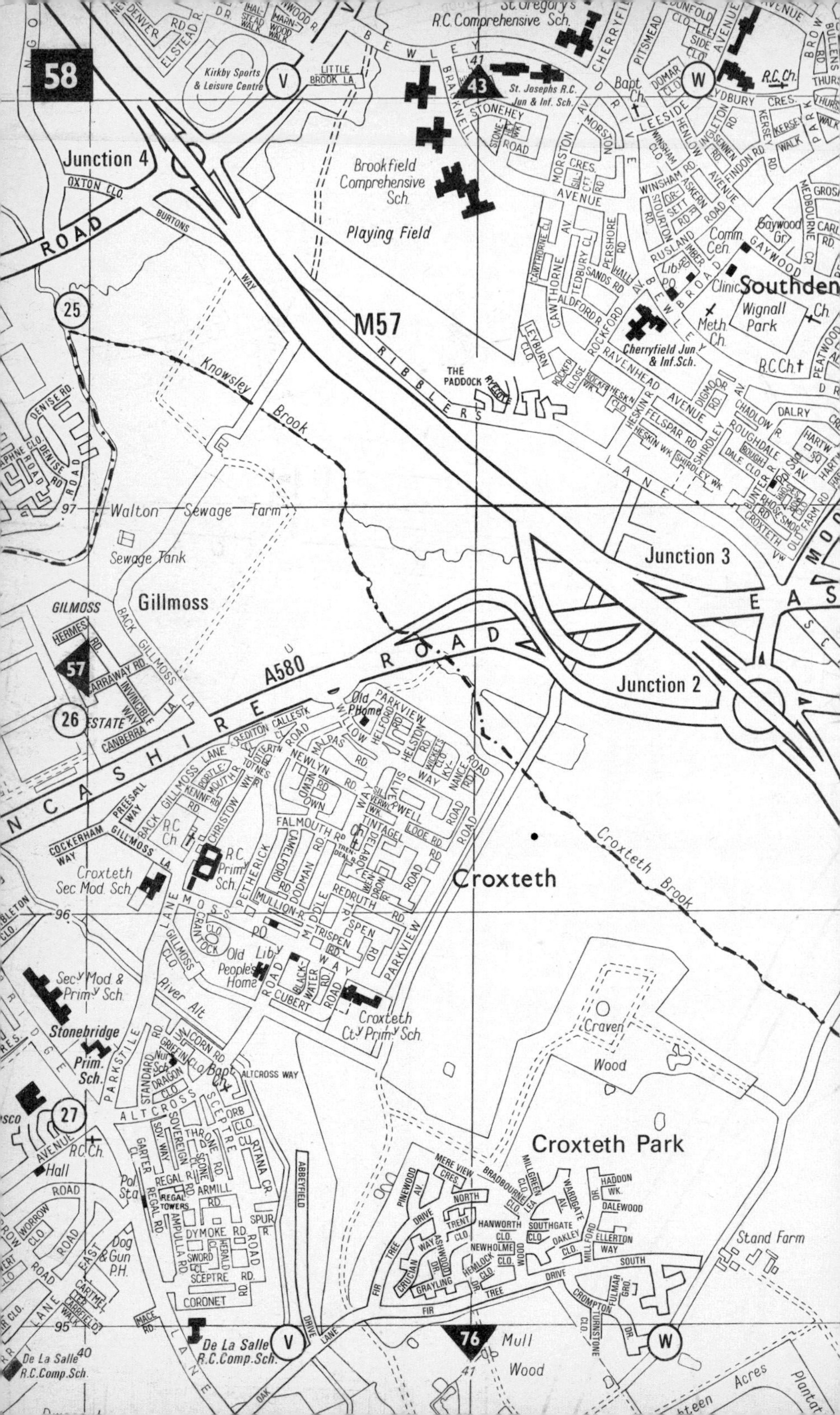

58
St. Gregory's R.C. Comprehensive Sch.
Kirkby Sports & Leisure Centre
V
W
43
St. Josephs R.C. Jun & Inf. Sch.
Junction 4
Brookfield Comprehensive Sch.
Playing Field
M57
Ribblers Lane
The Paddock
Southden
Wignall Park
Cherryfield Jun. & Inf. Sch.
Bewley Drive
Cherryfield Drive
Knowsley Brook
25
Walton Sewage Farm
Sewage Tank
Gillmoss
Junction 3
Junction 2
57
26
Gillmoss Estate
A580
Lancashire Road
East Lancashire Road
Croxteth
Croxteth Brook
Croxteth Sec. Mod. Sch.
R.C. Prim. Sch.
Old People's Home
Croxteth Ct. Prim. Sch.
Sec. Mod. & Prim. Sch.
Stonebridge Prim. Sch.
River Alt
27
Craven Wood
Croxteth Park
Stand Farm
Dog & Gun P.H.
Pol. Sta.
De La Salle R.C. Comp. Sch.
76
Mull Wood
97
96
95
40
41

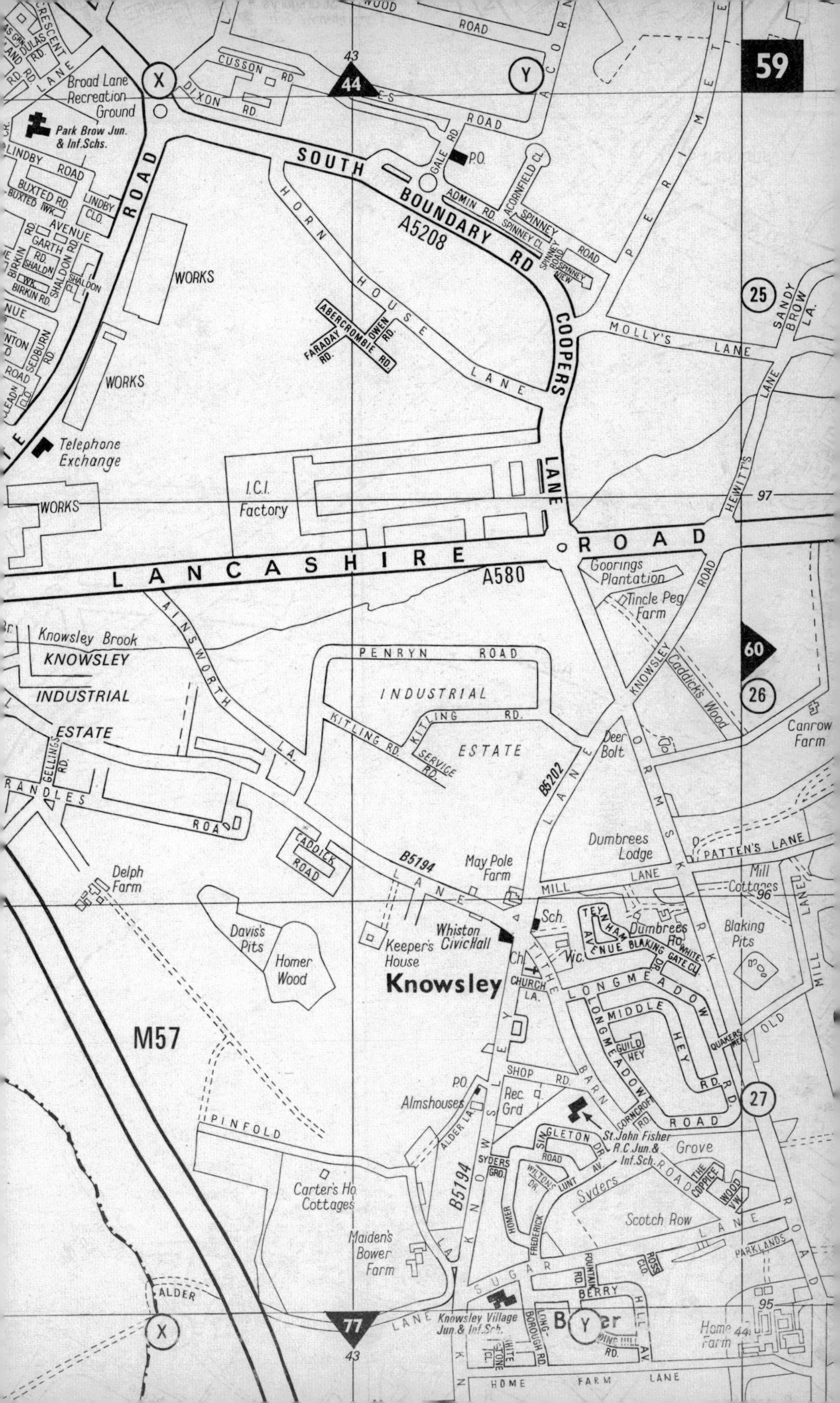

59
44
43
X
Y
Broad Lane Recreation Ground
Park Brow Jun. & Inf. Schs.
CRESCENT
DULAS RD.
LANE
CUSSON RD
DIXON RD.
ROAD
WOOD ROAD
ACORN
PERIMETER
LINDBY ROAD
BUXTED RD.
BUXTED WK.
LINDBY CLO.
AVENUE
GARTH RD.
SHALDON RD.
SHALDON CL.
BIRKIN RD.
SEDBURN RD.
SOUTH BOUNDARY RD
A5208
GALE RD.
P.O.
ADMIN RD.
ACORNFIELD CL.
SPINNEY ROAD
SPINNEY CL.
SPINNEY VIEW
HORN HOUSE LANE
ABERCROMBIE RD.
FARADAY RD.
OWEN RD.
WORKS
Telephone Exchange
COOPERS LANE
MOLLY'S LANE
SANDY BROW LA.
HEWITT'S LANE
25
I.C.I. Factory
97
LANCASHIRE ROAD
A580
Goorings Plantation
Tincle Peg Farm
KNOWSLEY ROAD
Caddick's Wood
60
26
Canrow Farm
Knowsley Brook
KNOWSLEY INDUSTRIAL ESTATE
AINSWORTH LA.
PENRYN ROAD
INDUSTRIAL ESTATE
KITLING RD.
KITLING SERVICE RD.
GELLINGS RD.
RANDLES ROAD
CADDICK ROAD
B5202
LANE
Deer Bolt
ORMSKIRK
Dumbrees Lodge
PATTEN'S LANE
Mill Cottages
96
Delph Farm
B5194
LANE
May Pole Farm
MILL LANE
Sch.
Whiston Civic Hall
Davis's Pits
Homer Wood
Keeper's House
Knowsley
Ch.
Vic.
CHURCH LA.
TITHE BARN
TEYNHAM AVENUE
Dumbrees Ho.
BLAKING DR.
WHITEGATE CL.
Blaking Pits
LONGMEADOW
MIDDLE HEY RD.
GUILD HEY
QUAKERS MEA.
OLD MILL LANE
M57
SHOP RD.
P.O.
Almshouses
Rec. Grd
CORNCROFT RD.
ROAD
27
PINFOLD
ALDER LA.
SINGLETON DR.
ROAD
St.John Fisher R.C. Jun. & Inf. Sch.
Grove ROAD
SYDERS GRO.
WILTONS DR.
LUNT AV.
Syders
THE COPPICE
WOOD VW.
Carter's Ho. Cottages
B5194
KNOWSLEY LANE
HOMER
FREDERICK
Scotch Row
LANE
Maiden's Bower Farm
SUGAR
FOUNTAIN RD.
ROSS CLO.
PARKLANDS
ROAD
BERRY HILL AV.
ALDER
LANE
77
Knowsley Village Jun.& Inf.Sch.
LONGBOROUGH RD.
WHITESTONE CL.
RD.
95
Home Farm
44
HOME FARM LANE

60
Swifts Farm
45
Z
AA
New Cut Farm
RED CUT LANE
PRIVATE ROAD
Swifts Wood
NEW CUT
Grab Tree Plantation
SANDY BROW LANE
25
Sandy Lane Farm
CUT LANE
LANE
HEWITT'S LANE
Moss Cottages
Lydiate Moss Plantation
97
LANCASHIRE ROAD
A580
ROAD
Moss Wood
59
Caddick's Wood
Moss Plantation
Canrow Farm
26
Scamper Plantation
PATTEN'S LANE
Mill Cottages
96
Mill Plantation
Patten's Bank
Blaking Pits
WHITE GATE CL
MILL LANE
Avenue Plantation
Pony Coppice
OLD
QUAKERS
HEY RD.
Pheasantry
Berry Hill Plantation
ROAD
27
Grove
THE COPPICE
WOOD VW
KNOWSLEY PARK
LANE
PARKLANDS
The
Kennels
Berry Hill
95
Z
78
AA
Home Farm
44
JACK'S BROW
45
Dock Plantation
DAMS
Nightcap
Jack's Brow Plantation

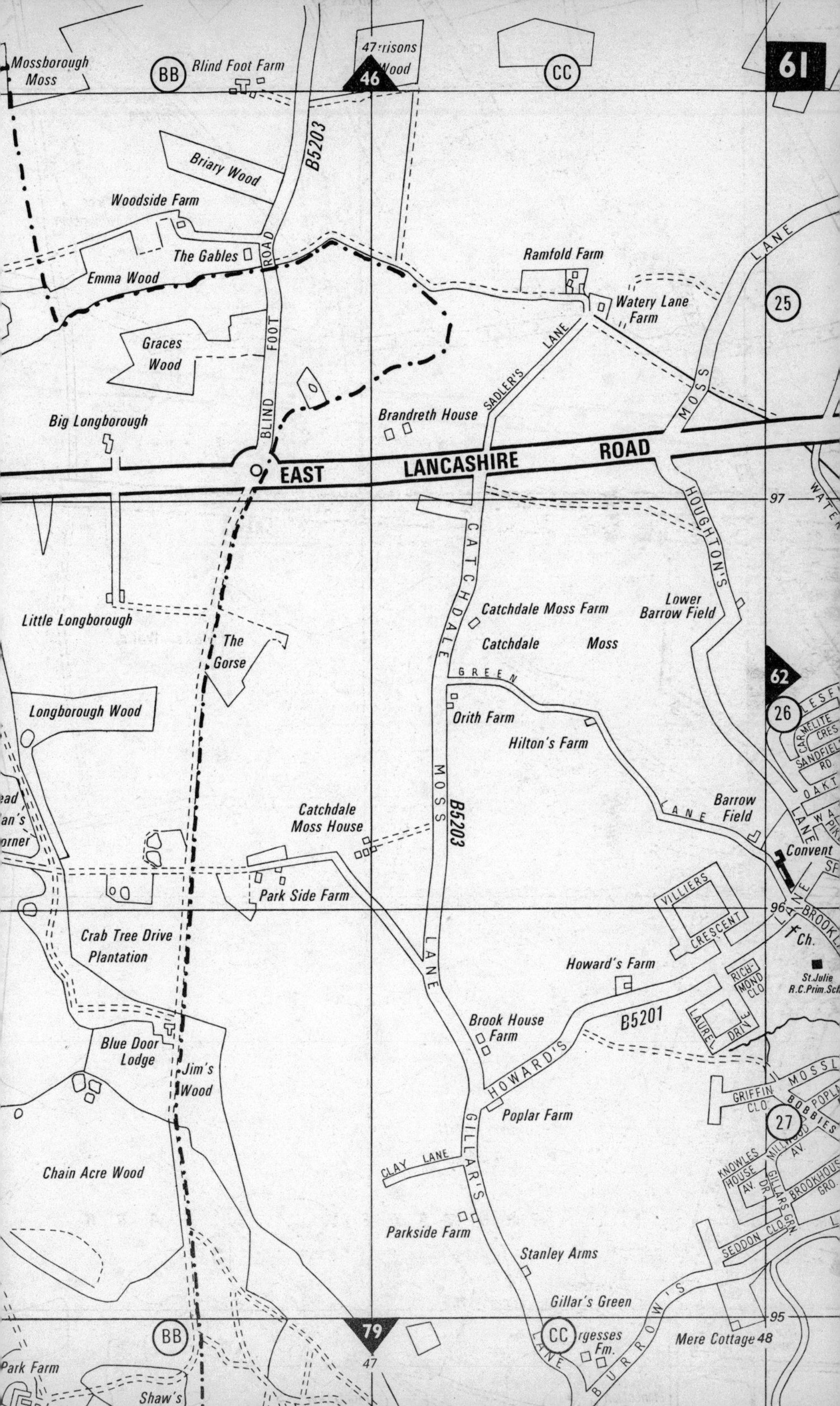
61
46
62
79
BB
CC
25
26
27
97
96
95
47
48
Mossborough Moss
Blind Foot Farm
Briary Wood
B5203
Woodside Farm
The Gables
Emma Wood
Graces Wood
Big Longborough
BLIND FOOT ROAD
Ramfold Farm
Watery Lane Farm
SADLER'S LANE
MOSS LANE
Brandreth House
EAST LANCASHIRE ROAD
HOUGHTON'S LANE
CATCHDALE MOSS LANE
Catchdale Moss Farm
Catchdale Moss
Lower Barrow Field
Little Longborough
The Gorse
GREEN LANE
Orith Farm
Hilton's Farm
Longborough Wood
CARMELITE CRES.
SANDFIELD RD.
Barrow Field
Convent
Catchdale Moss House
Park Side Farm
VILLIERS CRESCENT
BROOK
Ch.
Crab Tree Drive Plantation
Howard's Farm
St.Julie R.C.Prim.Sch.
RICH-MOND CLO.
LAUREL DRIVE
Brook House Farm
B5201
HOWARD'S LANE
Blue Door Lodge
Jim's Wood
Poplar Farm
GRIFFIN CLO.
BOBBIES
KNOWLES HOUSE AV.
MILLWOOD AV.
GILLARS GRN. DR.
BROOKHOUSE GRO.
GILLAR'S LANE
Chain Acre Wood
CLAY LANE
Parkside Farm
SEDDON CLO.
Stanley Arms
Gillar's Green
BURROW'S LANE
Mere Cottage
Park Farm
Shaw's

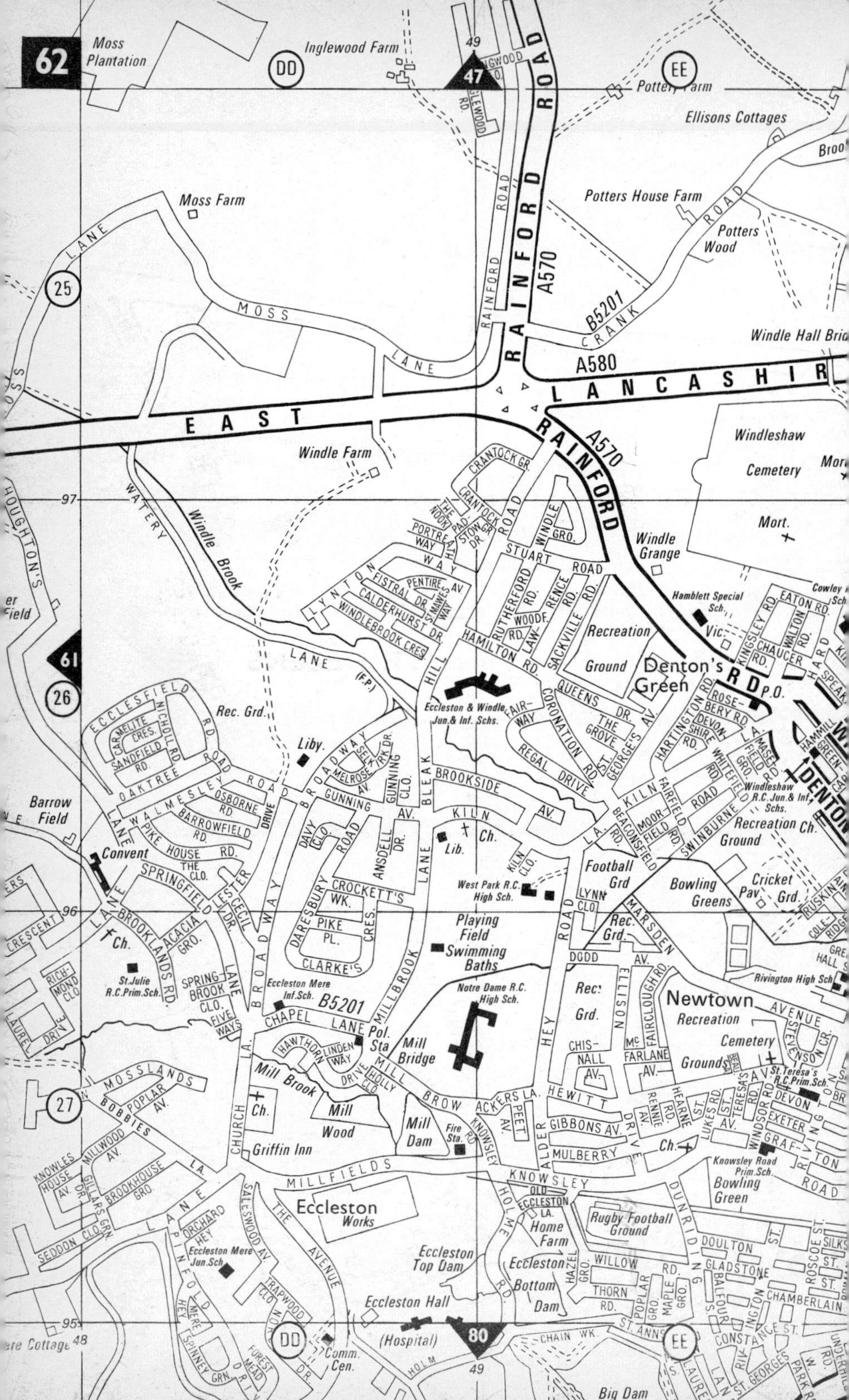
Moss Plantation
Inglewood Farm
DD
EE
47
Pottery Farm
Ellisons Cottages
RAINFORD ROAD
A570
Moss Farm
Potters House Farm
Potters Wood
MOSS LANE
B5201
CRANK ROAD
Windle Hall Bridge
25
A580
EAST LANCASHIRE ROAD
Windle Farm
Windleshaw Cemetery
Mort.
97
WATERY LANE
Windle Brook
CRANTOCK GR.
STUART ROAD
WINDLE GRO.
Windle Grange
LYNTON WAY
FISTRAL DR.
CALDERHURST DR.
WINDLEBROOK CRES.
PENTIRE AV.
RUTHERFORD RD.
LAWRENCE RD.
SACKVILLE RD.
Recreation Ground
Hamblett Special Sch.
Vic.
HAMILTON RD.
Denton's Green
DENTON'S RD
P.O.
61
26
ECCLESFIELD RD.
Rec. Grd.
Liby.
Eccleston & Windle Jun.& Inf. Schs.
FAIRWAY
QUEENS DR.
THE GROVE
CORONATION RD.
REGAL DRIVE
ST. GEORGE'S AV.
HARTINGTON RD.
ROSEBERY RD.
DEVONSHIRE RD.
WHITEFIELD RD.
Windleshaw R.C. Jun.& Inf. Schs.
OAKTREE ROAD
WALMESLEY ROAD
OSBORNE RD.
BARROWFIELD RD.
Barrow Field
BROADWAY
GUNNING AV.
BROOKSIDE AV.
BLEAK HILL
KILN LANE
Ch.
Lib.
BEACONSFIELD RD.
MOORFIELD RD.
SWINBURNE ROAD
Recreation Ground
Convent
PIKE HOUSE RD.
SPRINGFIELD LANE
DAVY CLO.
ANSDELL DR.
CROCKETT'S WK.
West Park R.C. High Sch.
Football Grd
LYNN CLO.
MARSDEN AV.
Bowling Greens
Cricket Grd.
Pav.
96
CRESCENT
BROOKLANDS RD.
ACACIA GRO.
DARESBURY RD.
PIKE PL.
CLARKE'S CRES.
Playing Field
Swimming Baths
HEY ROAD
Rec. Grd.
DODD AV.
Rivington High Sch.
St.Julie R.C.Prim.Sch.
SPRINGBROOK CLO.
Eccleston Mere Inf.Sch.
B5201
MILLBROOK LANE
Notre Dame R.C. High Sch.
ELLISON
FAIRCLOUGH RD.
Newtown
Recreation Grounds
AVENUE
Cemetery
FIVE WAYS
CHAPEL LANE
Pol. Sta
Mill Bridge
HAWTHORN DRIVE
LINDEN WAY
HOLLY CLO.
CHISNALL AV.
McFARLANE AV.
St. Teresa's R.C.Prim.Sch.
27
MOSSLANDS
BOBBIES LA.
POPLAR AV.
Mill Brook
Mill Wood
MILL BROW
ACKERS LA.
HEWITT
Ch.
Mill Dam
Fire Sta.
PEET AV.
GIBBONS AV.
ALDER DRIVE
RENNIE AV.
HEARNE RD.
ST. LUKES RD.
ST. TERESA'S AV.
WINDSOR RD.
DEVON
EXETER
GRAFTON
RIVINGTON ROAD
CHURCH LA.
Griffin Inn
MILLWOOD AV.
KNOWLES HOUSE AV.
GILLARS GRN.
BROOKHOUSE GRO.
MILLFIELDS
MULBERRY
KNOWSLEY RD.
Ch.
Knowsley Road Prim.Sch.
Bowling Green
KNOWSLEY
OLD ECCLESTON LA.
HOLME RD.
Eccleston Works
Home Farm
Rugby Football Ground
DUNRIDING
SEDDON CLO.
ORCHARD HEY
SALESWOOD AV.
THE AVENUE
Eccleston Top Dam
Eccleston Bottom Dam
HAZEL GRO.
WILLOW RD.
THORN RD.
POPLAR GRO.
MAPLE GRO.
DOULTON ST.
GLADSTONE ST.
BALFOUR
CHAMBERLAIN
ROSCOE ST.
SILKSTONE ST.
Eccleston Mere Jun.Sch.
PINFOLD LANE
TRAPWOOD CLO.
Eccleston Hall
(Hospital)
80
CHAIN WK.
ST. ANNS
CONSTANCE ST.
95
48
49
Comm. Cen.
MERE HEY
SPINNEY GRN.
FOREST MEAD
HOLM
ST. GEORGES
PARK RD.
LAUREL
Big Dam

ST. HELENS
Windle Park Wood
Rainford Brook
Windle Hall Farm
Windle Hall
Moss Bank
Clinkham
SANDY LA.
MOSS BANK RD.
KINGSWAY
QUEENSWAY
BASSENTHWAITE AV.
WINDERMERE
THIRLMERE AV.
ULLSWATER AV.
GRIZEDALE AV.
BOWNESS AVENUE
WASDALE AV.
WYTHBURN
KIRKSTONE CRES.
YEWDALE
KENTMERE
Lib. Health Centre
Carr Hill Inf.Sch.
ROAD
WASHWAY LANE
CITY RD.
WINDLE HALL DRIVE
WYRESDALE AV.
WHALLEY AV.
CARTMELL AV.
PRIORY GDNS.
Bowling Greens
Playing Fields
Football Grd.
WINDLE CITY
Football Ground
St.Alban's R.C.High Sch.
Gerard's Bridge Farm
Res.
Gerard's Bridge Works
GREEN LEACH LANE
GRASMERE AV.
LANGDALE GRO.
CONISTON GRO.
RYDAL GRO.
DERWENT RD.
NEWLANDS
St.Peter & St.Paul R.C.Prim.Sch.
SHIREBOURN AV.
Haresfinch
Haresfinch Park
WOODLANDS
HARESFINCH RD.
HARESFINCH VW.
A571
LINCOLN CR.
EWART RD.
ISLANDS BROW
Sand Lodge
Canal (Disused)
New Double Locks
Gerard's Bridge
Atlas Works
Pocket
Hurst Special Sch.
Windlehurst Prim.Sch.
GAMBLE AV.
MARTIN AV.
Rec. Grd.
WINDLEHURST AV.
RIVINGTON AV.
Victoria Park
Youth Centre
Rivington Prim. Sch.
Athletic Grd.
Tennis Ct.
PRINCESS AV.
Mat. Hosp.
BALKER DR.
COWLEY LA.
Athletic Grd. Sch's
BISHOP
WYNNE
RUTLAND
STANHOPE
ARGYLE
NORTH
OLDFIELD
CHAPEL
WELLINGTON TER.
COWLEY STREET
HILL ST.
STREET
WINDLE
COWLEY HILL LANE
WOLSELEY RD.
KESWICK
GREEN LA.
LINGHOLME RD.
HARRIS
Bowl. Grn.
Queens Rec.Grd.
Lib. Sch.
Baths
CAMBRIDGE RD.
KIRKLAND ST.
DUKE STREET
Lowe House R.C.Jun.& Inf.Sch.
CRAB ST.
COLLEGE
Central High Sch.
Pol. Sta.
Law Cts.
Mus.
BALDWIN ST.
CORPORATION
Town Hall
HARDSHAW
CLIFTON
CANSFIELD
Parish Prim. Sch.
Holy Cross R.C.Prim.Sch.
Hospital
Theatre Royal
Hipp.
Coll.
STANDISH ST.
HOSPITAL ST.
STRICKLAND
WOODVILLE ST.
RAILWAY ST.
Canal (Disused)
POCKET NOOK
SHAW ST.
STA.
HIGHER PARR ST.
JACKSON ST.
BICKERSTAFFE ST.
The Hardshaw Centre
CHURCH ST.
PARR ST.
A570
WARRINGTON NEW RD.
WARRINGTON OLD RD.
PEASLEY CROSS LA.
STREET
Tech College
BRIDGE S.
CHALON WAY
WESTFIELD
LIVERPOOL RD
T.A. Centre
Electricity Wks.
ECCLESTON
LAWRENSON ST.
PRESCOT RD.
BOROUGH RD.
Sacred Heart R.C.Prim.Sch.
BOLD ST.
St.Helens
SUTTON LODGE RD.
FF
GG
48
81
64
25
26
27
51
52
95
96
97

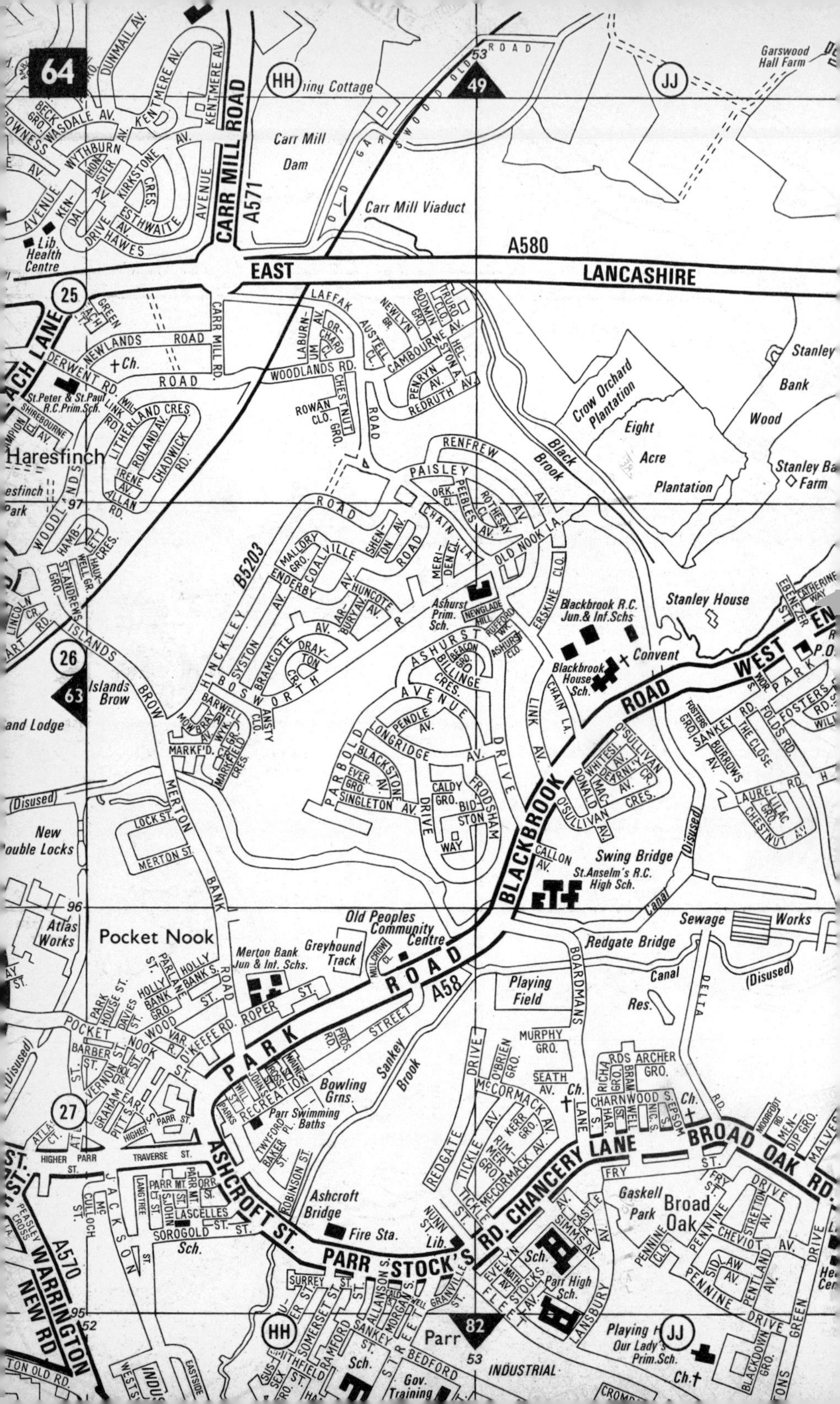

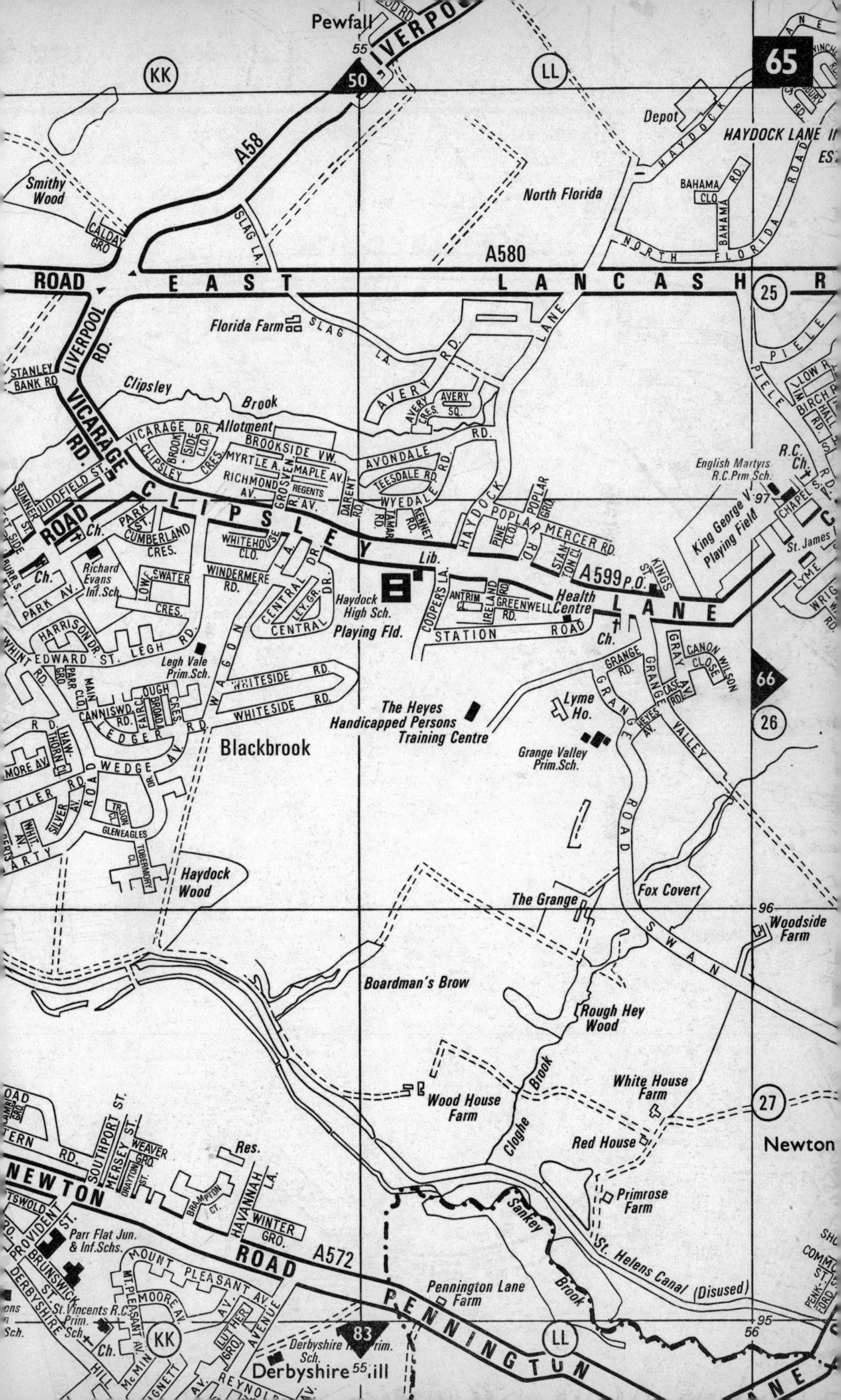
65
Pewfall
LIVERPOOL
50
KK
LL
Depot
HAYDOCK LANE
A58
Smithy Wood
CALDAY GRO
SLAG LA.
North Florida
BAHAMA CLO
BAHAMA RD.
NORTH FLORIDA ROAD
A580
ROAD EAST LANCASHIRE
25
Florida Farm
SLAG LA.
LIVERPOOL RD.
STANLEY BANK RD
Clipsley Brook
AVERY RD.
AVERY CRES.
AVERY SQ.
PIELE RD.
VICARAGE RD.
VICARAGE DR.
Allotment
BROOKSIDE VW.
BROOKSIDE CLO.
CLIPSLEY CRES.
MYRTLE A.
MAPLE AV.
AVONDALE RD.
TEESDALE RD.
RICHMOND AV.
GROSVENOR AV.
REGENTS AV.
DARENT RD.
WYEDALE RD.
TAMAR RD.
KENNET RD.
HAYDOCK LANE
POPLAR GRO.
POPLAR RD.
PINE CLO.
MERCER RD.
STANTON CL.
KINGS ST.
English Martyrs R.C.Prm.Sch.
R.C. Ch.
King George V Playing Field
CHAPEL ST.
St. James
LYME
SUMNER ST.
JUDDFIELD ST.
ROAD
CLIPSLEY LANE
A599
P.O.
Lib.
Ch.
PARK ST.
CUMBERLAND CRES.
WHITEHOUSE CLO.
CENTRAL DR.
LEY GR.
Richard Evans Inf.Sch.
LOWE
SWATER CRES.
WINDERMERE RD.
Haydock High Sch.
Playing Fld.
COOPERS LA.
ANTRIM CL.
IRELAND RD.
GREENWELL RD.
Health Centre
STATION ROAD
PARK AV.
HARRISON DR.
EDWARD ST.
LEGH RD.
Legh Vale Prim.Sch.
WAGON
WHITESIDE RD.
GRANGE RD.
GRANGE VALLEY
GRAY AV.
CANON WILSON CLOSE
CASE RD.
HEYES AV.
66
26
PARR GRO
MAIN
CANNISWD.
FAIRCL.
BROADA
LEDGER RD.
WEDGE AV.
WEDGE RD.
HAWTHORN CL.
MORE AV.
SILVER AV.
TROON CL.
GLENEAGLES
TOBERMORY CL.
The Heyes Handicapped Persons Training Centre
Blackbrook
Lyme Ho.
Grange Valley Prim.Sch.
GRANGE ROAD
Haydock Wood
The Grange
Fox Covert
SWAN
96
Woodside Farm
Boardman's Brow
Rough Hey Wood
White House Farm
27
Wood House Farm
Cloghe Brook
Red House
Newton
Res.
SOUTHPORT ST.
MERSEY ST.
WEAVER GRO
DRAYTON ST.
HAVANNAH LA.
BRAMPTON CT.
WINTER GRO.
NEWTON ROAD
A572
PROVIDENT ST.
Parr Flat Jun. & Inf.Schs.
BRUNSWICK ST.
DERBYSHIRE
MOUNT PLEASANT AV.
MT.PLEASANT AV.
MOORE AV.
Primrose Farm
Sankey Brook
St. Helens Canal (Disused)
Pennington Lane Farm
PENNINGTON LANE
St.Vincents R.C. Prim. Sch.
Ch.
83
Derbyshire Hill Prim. Sch.
Derbyshire Hill
LUTHER GRO.
AVENUE
95
56
55

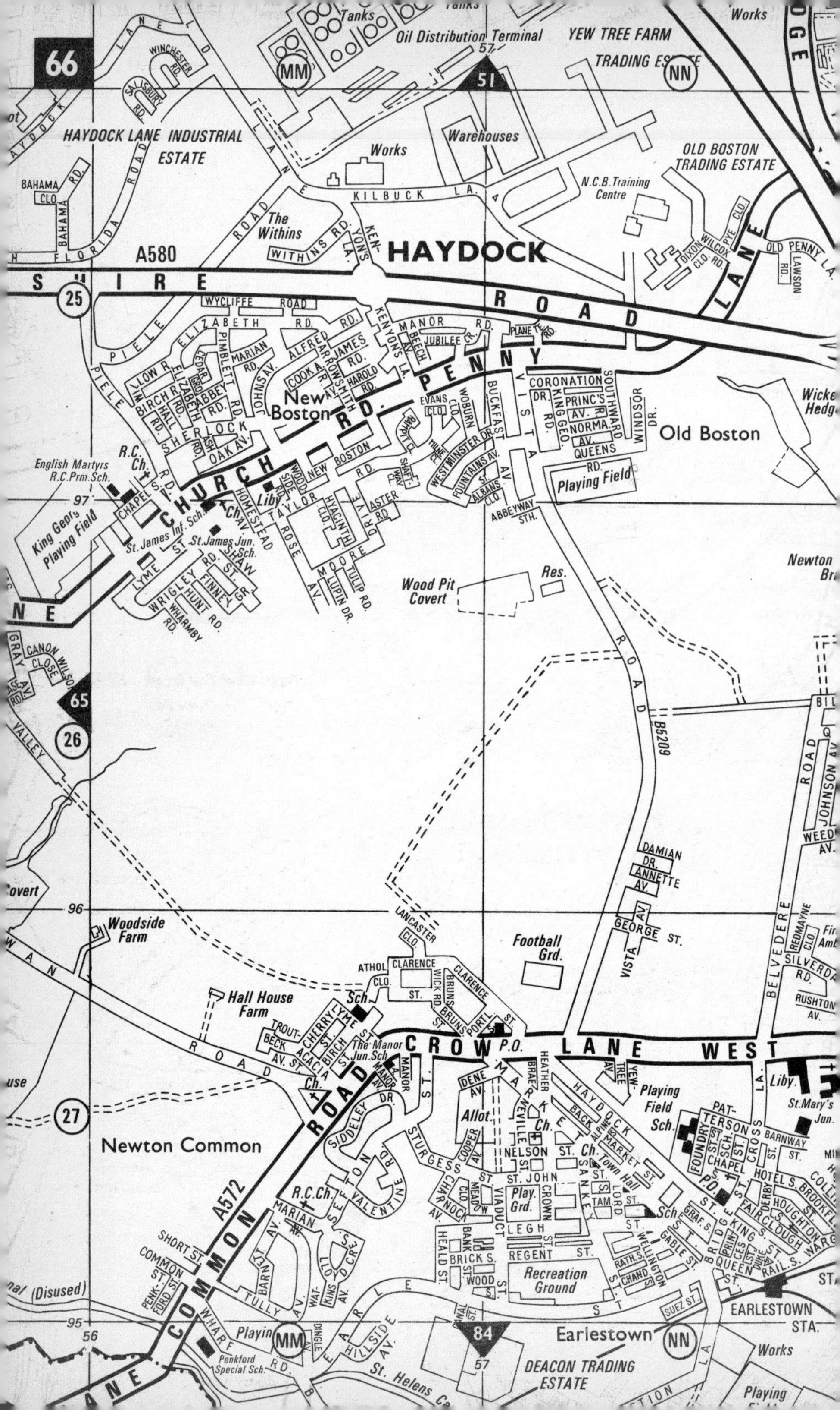

Tanks
Oil Distribution Terminal
YEW TREE FARM
TRADING ESTATE
Works
MM
NN
51
57
WINCHESTER RD.
SALISBURY RD.
HAYDOCK LANE INDUSTRIAL
ESTATE
Warehouses
Works
OLD BOSTON
TRADING ESTATE
N.C.B. Training
Centre
BAHAMA CLO.
BAHAMA RD.
FLORIDA ROAD
KILBUCK LA.
The Withins
WITHINS RD.
KENYON'S LA.
HAYDOCK
A580
SHIRE ROAD
25
WYCLIFFE ROAD
DIXON
WILCOX CLO. RD.
PYE CLO.
LANE
OLD PENNY LA.
LAWSON RD.
ELIZABETH RD.
ALFRED RD.
MANOR RD.
BEECH AV.
JUBILEE CR.
PLANET RD.
PIELE ROAD
PIMBLETT RD.
MARIAN RD.
JOHNS AV.
COOK A.
ARROWSMITH R.
JAMES RD.
HAROLD RD.
KENYONS LA.
PENNY
VISTA
CORONATION DR.
SOUTHWARD RD.
PRINC'S AV.
KING GEO. RD.
NORMA AV.
QUEENS RD.
WINDSOR DR.
New Boston
Old Boston
Wicke Hedge
BIRCH R.
HALL RD.
CEDAR GRO.
ELIZABETH RD.
ABBEY RD.
EVANS CLO.
WOBURN CLO.
BUCKFAST
WESTMINSTER DR.
FOUNTAINS AV.
ST. ALBANS CLO.
ABBEYWAY STH.
SHERLOCK AV.
OAK AV.
ASH RD.
CHURCH RD.
NEW BOSTON
TAYLOR RD.
WOODSIDE RD.
HYACINTH CLO.
DRIVE
ASTER RD.
SHAFTWAY CL.
Playing Field
R.C. Ch.
English Martyrs R.C. Prm. Sch.
97
CHAPEL ST.
King George Playing Field
St. James Inf. Sch.
St. James Jun. Sch.
Liby.
HOMESTEAD AV.
ROSE AV.
MOORE
TULIP RD.
LUPIN DR.
SHAW ST.
LYME ST.
WRIGLEY RD.
FINNEY GR.
HUNT RD.
WHARMBY RD.
Wood Pit Covert
Res.
Newton Br
ROAD
B5209
GRAY AV.
CANON WILSON CLOSE
VALLEY
65
26
DAMIAN DR.
ANNETTE AV.
GEORGE ST.
VISTA AV.
JOHNSON AV.
WEEDEN AV.
BELVEDERE ROAD
REDMAYNE CLO.
SILVERDALE RD.
RUSHTON AV.
Covert
96
Woodside Farm
LANCASTER CLO.
Football Grd.
ATHOL CLO.
CLARENCE ST.
CLARENCE
WICK RD.
BRUNS. ST.
PORTL. ST.
Hall House Farm
Sch.
CHERRY ST.
LYME ST.
BIRCH ST.
TROUTBECK AV.
ACACIA
The Manor Jun. Sch.
CROW LANE WEST
P.O.
HEATHER BRAE
MARKET
TREE AV.
YEW
Playing Field
Sch.
Liby.
St. Mary's Jun.
ROAD
27
Ch.
MANOR AV.
DENE AV.
Allot.
NEVILLE ST.
Ch.
HAYDOCK
BACK
ALPINE
PATTERSON ST.
FOUNDRY ST.
SCH. ST.
CHAPEL ST.
CROSS
BARNWAY ST.
Newton Common
SIDDELEY DR.
SEFTON RD.
VALENTINE RD.
STURGESS ST.
COOPER AV.
NELSON ST.
Ch.
Town Hall
ST. JOHN
SANKEY
P.O.
HOTEL S.
BROOKFIELD
A572
R.C.Ch.
CHARNOCK AV.
MEADOW CLO.
VIADUCT
Play. Grd.
CROWN
TAM
LORD ST.
Sch.
GRAF. S.
BRIDGE ST.
KING ST.
FAIRCLOUGH
HOUGHTON
DERBY
MARIAN AV.
BANK
HEALD ST.
LEGH ST.
REGENT ST.
WELLINGTON
GABLE ST.
QUEEN ST.
PRIN. ST.
DUKE ST.
RAIL. S.
SHORT ST.
COMMON ST.
PENKFORD ST.
BARN ST.
LLOYD CRES.
WAT-KINS AV.
BRICK S.
WOOD S.
Recreation Ground
RATH. S.
CHAND. S.
EARLESTOWN STA.
Canal (Disused)
COMMON
TULLY AV.
EARLE ST.
SUEZ ST.
95
56
WHARF RD.
Playing
DINGLE
HILLSIDE AV.
CANAL ST.
84
Earlestown
Works
Penkford Special Sch.
St. Helens Canal
57
DEACON TRADING ESTATE
LANE
Playing

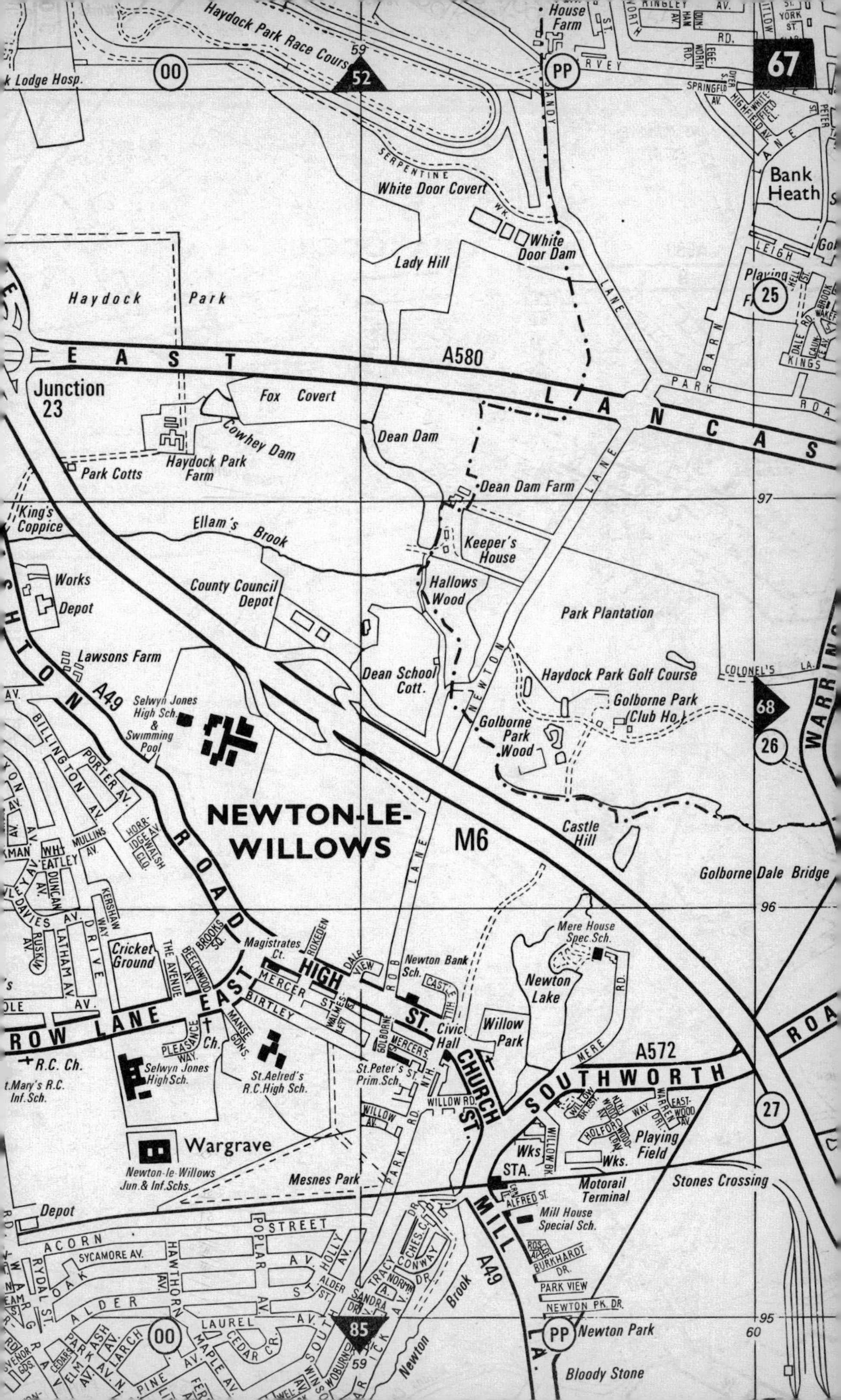
67
68
Haydock Park Race Course
Haydock Park
EAST LANCASHIRE ROAD
A580
Junction 23
Fox Covert
Cowhey Dam
Haydock Park Farm
Park Cotts
King's Coppice
Ellam's Brook
Works
Depot
Lawsons Farm
County Council Depot
Dean Dam
Dean Dam Farm
Keeper's House
Hallows Wood
Dean School Cott.
Park Plantation
Haydock Park Golf Course
Golborne Park (Club Ho.)
Golborne Park Wood
Castle Hill
Golborne Dale Bridge
White Door Covert
White Door Dam
Lady Hill
House Farm
Bank Heath
Playing Field
Colonel's La.
NEWTON-LE-WILLOWS
M6
A49
A572
Selwyn Jones High Sch. & Swimming Pool
Cricket Ground
Magistrates Ct.
High St.
Newton Bank Sch.
Civic Hall
Willow Park
Newton Lake
Mere House Spec. Sch.
Southworth Road
Church St.
Selwyn Jones High Sch.
St. Aelred's R.C. High Sch.
St. Peter's Prim. Sch.
R.C. Ch.
St. Mary's R.C. Inf. Sch.
Wargrave
Newton-le-Willows Jun. & Inf. Schs.
Mesnes Park
Depot
Wks.
Sta.
Motorail Terminal
Stones Crossing
Playing Field
Mill House Special Sch.
Mill La.
Newton Park
Bloody Stone
Newton Brook
Crow Lane East
Ashton Road
Newton Lane
Park Road
Acorn Street
Sycamore Av.
Alder St.
Park View
Newton Pk. Dr.
Burkhardt Dr.
Alfred St.
97
96
95
59
60
52
85
00
PP
25
26
27

68
GOLBORNE
Bank Heath
Golborne Bri.
Playing Field
Millingford Industrial Estate
Railway View
Works
Town Fm.
Lowton Heath Ho.
Rec.Grd.
Sports Ground
Manor House Farm
Stirrups Farm
Thompson's Farm
Holly Bank
A580
CASHIRE ROAD
Lowton Heath
Millingford Brook
Stone Pits
Mountain Farm
Lowton Heath
A572
Bamber Lodge
Byron's Farm
Golborne Junction
Golborne Dale Bridge
Holly House
Sandup Farm
Highfield Moss Farm
Sandfield Hall
Town of Lowton
Highfield Moss
Parkside Manchester Junction
Highfield Farm
Stones Crossing
M6
Moss Pits
WARRINGTON RD.
A573
NEWTON ROAD
PARKSIDE ROAD
STONE CROSS
LANE SLAG
HIGH ST.
BRIDGE ST.
67
86
25
26
27
QQ
RR
97
96
95
60
61

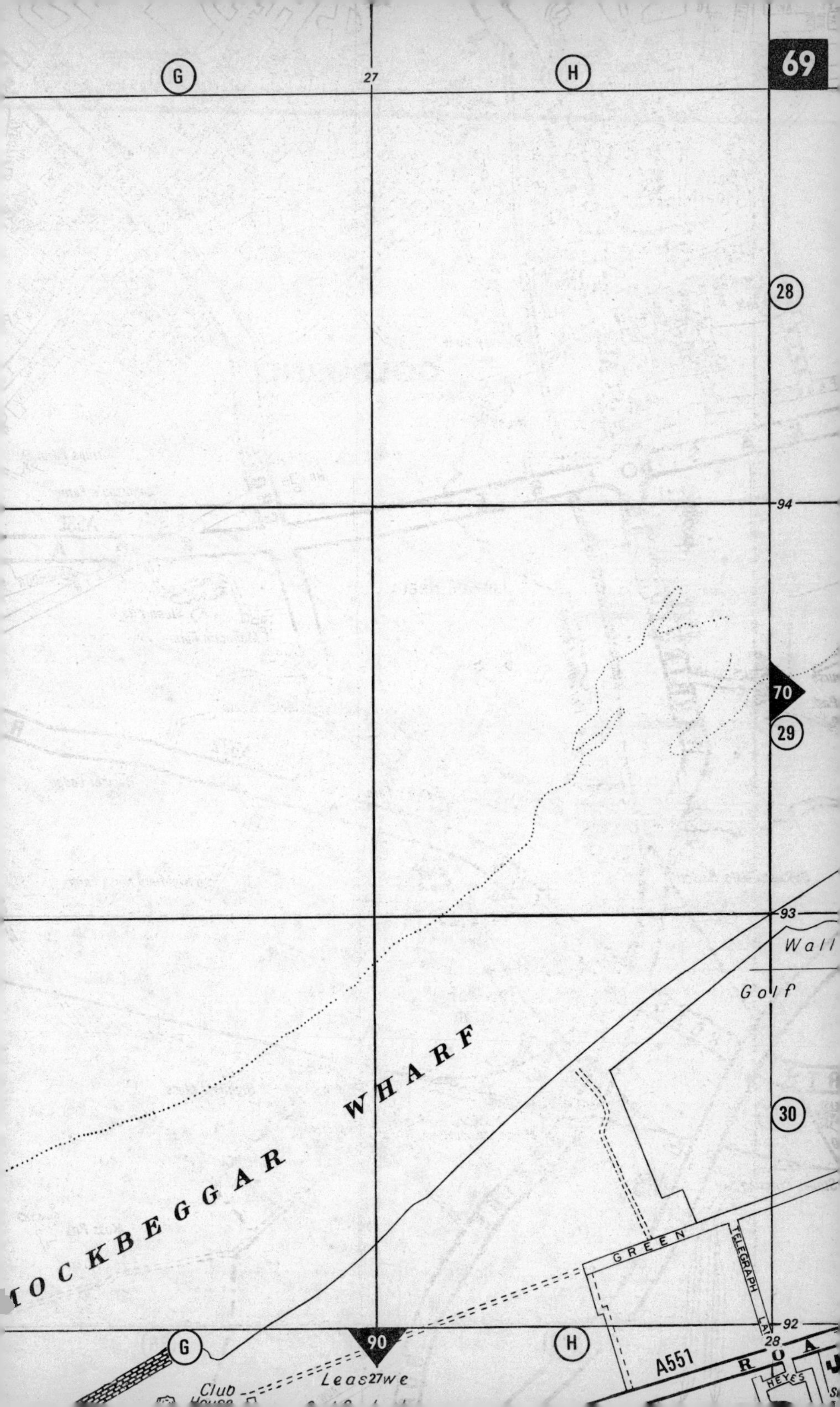

G 27 H

28

94

70
29

93

Wall

Golf

30

STOCKBEGGAR WHARF

GREEN

TELEGRAPH

92
28

G 90 H

A551

ROA

Club
House

Leas 27 we

J
29
K
28
94
29
69
93
30
92
28
91
KINGS PARADE
A554
Red Noses
COASTAL DRIVE
Wirral Line
HARRISON PARK
Warren Pk Municipal Golf Course
Miniature Golf Course
Wallasey Golf Links
Club House
Wallasey Grove Rd. Sta.
Bowling Green
BAYSWATER ROAD
SANDCLIFFE ROAD
WARREN DRIVE
HARRISON DR.
GLOUCESTER RD.
TAUNTON RD.
SANDY LANE
St. Mary's R.C. Coll.
STUDLEY RD.
WALLASEY
St Georges Prim. Sch.
Cricket Ground
Greenleas Prim. Sch.
Wallasey Village Sta.
LEASOWE ROAD
A551
WALLASEY VILLAGE
BROADWAY
St Hilary's Ch School
PROSPECT VALE
VYNER ROAD
BELVIDERE RECREATION GROUND
TELEGRAPH RD.
St. Mary's
NORTH

L
53
M
31
28
29
30
72
94
93
92
32
Rock
Perch Rock
Battery
Bathing
Pool
MARINE
LAKE
COASTAL DR.
Car Park
MARINE PROMENADE
Coastguard Lookout
Floating Stage
Coastguard Sta.
The Palace
Amuse Pk.
Victoria Gdns.
MARINE PARK
NEW BRIGHTON
PIER
TOWER GROUNDS
(Amusement Park)
NEW BRIGHTON
Tower
Winter
Gardens
New Brighton
Sta.
VICTORIA RD.
ROWSON ST.
TOWER PROMENADE
MAGAZINES
Reservoirs
(Covered)
St Peter
&
St Paul
R.C.
Sch.
ST GEORGES
PARK
OARLAND
VALE
VALE
PARK
Health Centre
New Brighton
Prim. Sch.
HOLLAND
ROAD
PROMENADE
MARINE
TERRACE
Weatherhead
High Sch.
for girls
Captain
Pit
Earlston
Library
EARLSTON
GARDENS
WALLASEY
CEMETERY
Mort.
Cha.
PENKETT
ROAD
PENKETT
GROVE
Westbourne Sch.
Wirral Metropolitan
Coll
Tennis Cts.
Bus
Depot
Pumping
Sta.
New Brighton
Footb. & Crick.
Gnd.
Recreation
Ground
Liscard Prim. Sch.
Masonic
Hall
Drill
Hall
Oldershaw
Sec. Sch.
Grosons Home
EGREMONT
KING'S PAR
LISCARD
LISCARD VILLAGE
Fire
Sta.
EGREMONT PROMENADE
KINGS ROAD

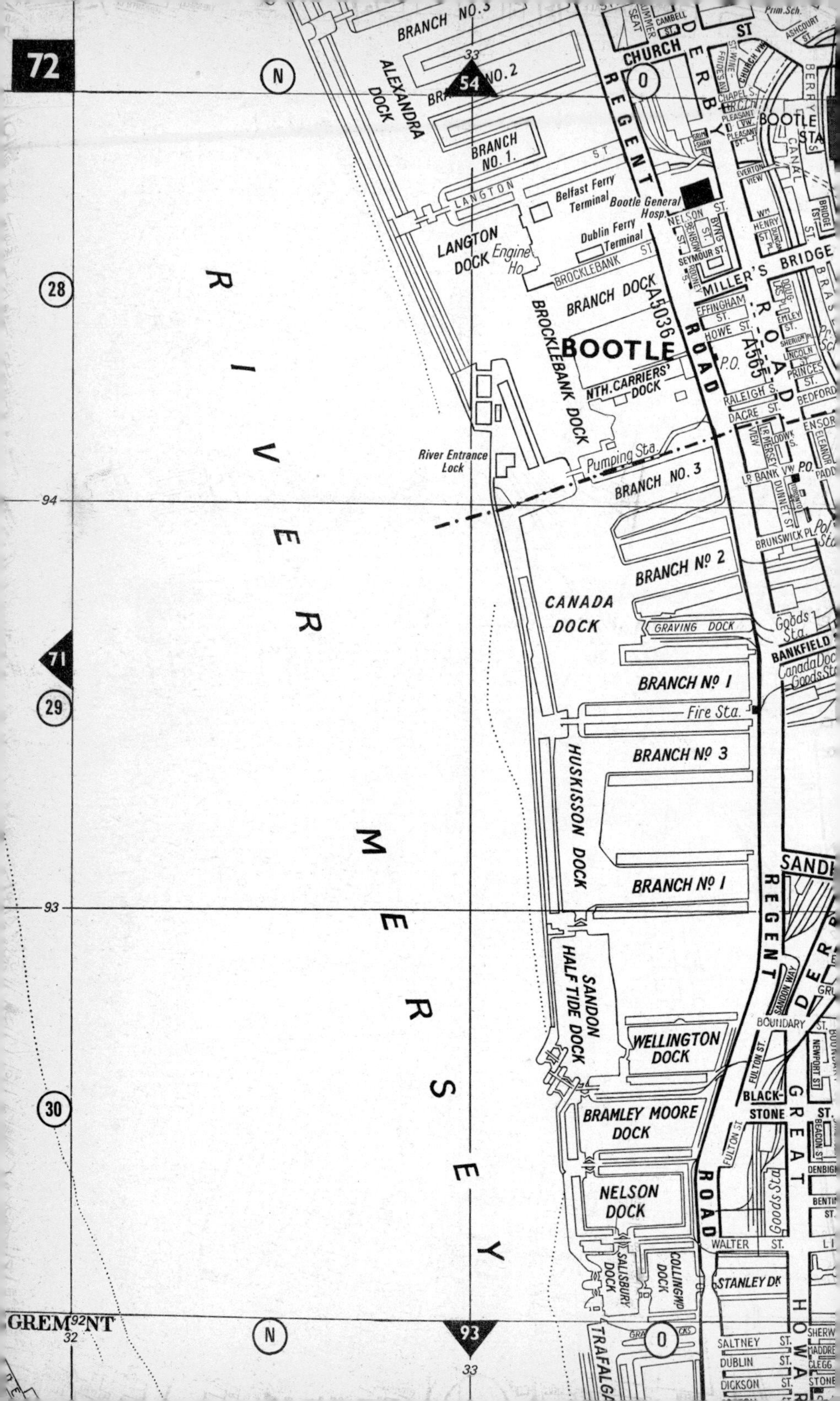

N

BRANCH NO. 3

BRANCH NO. 2

54

33

CHURCH ST

DERBY

Prim. Sch.

Ashcourt
SEAT

CAMPBELL

SUMMER

BERRY

Bootle Sta.

ALEXANDRA DOCK

BRANCH NO. 1

CHAPEL ST.

CHURCH ST.

PLEASANT ST.

PLEASANT VW.

EVERTON VIEW

BOOTLE

REGENT

LANGTON

Belfast Ferry Terminal

Dublin Ferry Terminal

Bootle General Hosp.

NELSON ST.

SEYMOUR ST.

HENRY

BYNG ST.

W.

BOOTLE

LANGTON DOCK

Engine Ho.

Brocklebank

BRANCH DOCK

A5036

BOOTLE

MILLER'S BRIDGE

ROAD A565

EFFINGHAM ST.

HOWE ST.

LINCOLN

PRINCES

BEDFORD

28

R I V E R

BROCKLEBANK DOCK

NTH. CARRIERS' DOCK

P.O.

RALEIGH ST.

DACRE ST.

ENSOR

River Entrance Lock

Pumping Sta.

LR BANK VW. P.O.

DUNNET ST.

94

BRANCH NO. 3

BRUNSWICK ST

PADD

BRANCH NO. 2

CANADA DOCK

GRAVING DOCK

Goods Sta.

BANKFIELD

71

Canada Doc Goods St

29

BRANCH NO. 1

Fire Sta.

M

BRANCH NO. 3

HUSKISSON DOCK

E

BRANCH NO. 1

SANDON

R

93

SANDON HALF TIDE DOCK

WELLINGTON DOCK

REGENT

DERBY

ARM NORTH

BOUNDARY

FULTON ST.

NEWPORT ST.

BLACK-STONE

GREAT

30

S

BRAMLEY MOORE DOCK

FULTON ST.

spoods spoods

NELSON DOCK

E

ROAD

WALTER ST.

STANLEY DK.

DENBIGH

BENTINC

SHERW

Y

SALISBURY DOCK

COLLINGWD DOCK

SALTNEY ST.

DUBLIN ST.

DICKSON ST.

HOWA

ADDRE

CLEGG

STONE

N

0

93

33

TRAFALGA

GRA

73
55
94
28
29
30
74
P
Q
MERTON ROAD
BREEZE HILL
FLYOVER
SOUTHPORT RD.
Hillside High Sch.
A5058
Inland Rev.
Trinity Pres.Ch.
TRINITY ROAD
Welsh Cha.
Town Hall
The Hugh Baird Coll. of Techn.
BALLIOL ROAD
BALLIOL RD. EAST
Tech.Coll.& Sch. of Art
Car Pk
Rec. Grd.
Cricket Ground
HAWTHORNE ROAD
Hillside High Sch
Sec. Sch.
CAMBRIDGE RD.
SIDNEY
GONVILLE
DOWNING
CLARE
Bedford Jun. Sch.
BREWSTER ST.
BEDFORD ROAD
BELLAMY
HAHNEMANN
MARGARET
PETER
CARISBROOKE
ROXBURGH
HALE RD.
Alsop Comp. Sch. (Lower)
Alsop Comp. Sch. (Upper)
Baths
St. Mary's Ch.
Bedford Inf. Sch.
COUNTY ROAD
WALTON LA.
WALTON
Everton F.C.
GWLADYS STREET
GOODISON RD.
Boating Lake
Bowling Green
Band Sq.
Stanley Park Comp.Sch.(Annexe)
ANFIELD
BACK ROCKFIELD RD.
ROCKFIELD RD.
WALTON BRECK RD.
A5089
KIRKDALE
Kirkdale
KIRKDALE STA.
BANK HALL STA.
BANKHALL STREET
MELROSE RD.
STANLEY ROAD
WESTMINSTER RD.
SELWYN ST.
Kirkdale Rec. Grd.
Prim. Sch.
WALTON ROAD
Lester Gdns.
Tech Coll.
EVERTON VALLEY
ST. DOMINGO ROAD
Notre Dame R.C. Comp. Sch.
Conv.
A565
COMMERCIAL ROAD
LAMBETH ROAD
Sec. Mod. Sch.
SMITH ST.
KIRKDALE ROAD
EVERTON ROAD
GREAT HOMER STREET
NETHERFIELD RD.
NORTHUMBERLAND
HEYWORTH STREET
Sir Thomas White Gdns.
Breckfield Comp. Sch. (Loraine Wing)
Breckfield Comp. Sch. (Downing Wing)
Everton Park Sports Centre
Everton
BOUNDARY STREET
St. Gerrard's R.C. Sch.
Gas Works
Liverpool Locks
St. Brigids R.C. Comp. Sch.
SILVESTER ST.
Rec. Grd.
BLENHEIM
LATIMER
GREAT MERSEY ST.
R.C. Sec. Sch.
LANE
MILE END
HAMILTON ROAD
A580
BRECK RD.
LLOYD HODSON PL.
ST. DOMINGO
SALISBURY
GRANTON
HERSCHELL
TOWSON
VENMORE
VIENNA
VENICE
SOUTH ST.
Rose Vale
ROSCOMMON
PORTLAND PL.
DORRINGTON ST.
Baths
35
92
93

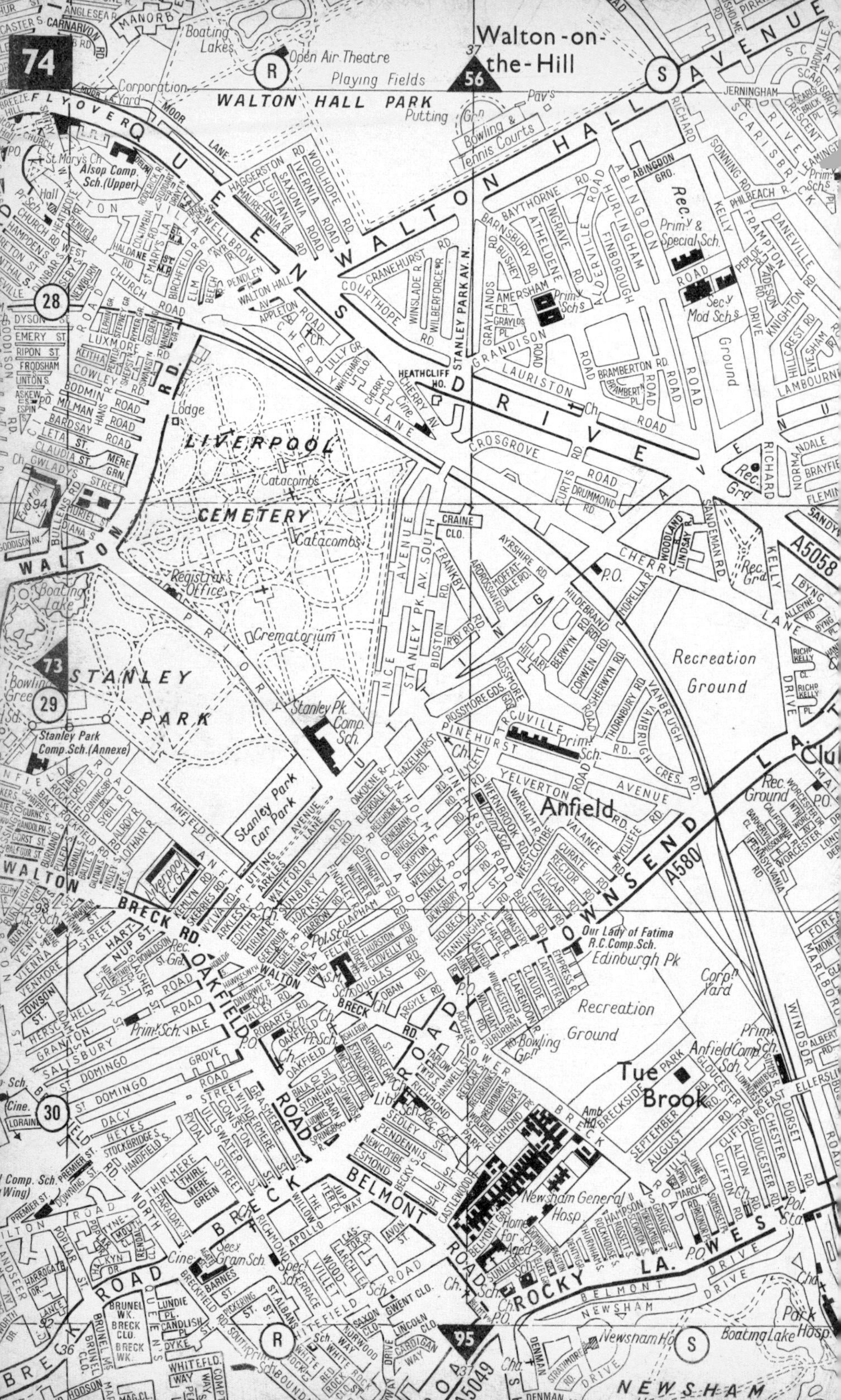

74
Walton-on-the-Hill
56
Boating Lakes
Open Air Theatre
Playing Fields
Corporation Yard
WALTON HALL PARK
Putting Grn
Bowling & Tennis Courts
FLYOVER
QUEENS DRIVE
WALTON HALL AVENUE
St Mary's Ch
Alsop Comp. Sch.(Upper)
28
LIVERPOOL CEMETERY
Catacombs
Registrar's Office
Crematorium
Lodge
STANLEY PARK
73
29
Stanley Park Comp.Sch.(Annexe)
Stanley Pk. Comp. Sch.
Stanley Park Car Park
Boating Lake
Everton F.C. Grd
Liverpool F.C. Grd
WALTON BRECK RD.
OAKFIELD ROAD
BRECK ROAD
BELMONT ROAD
TOWNSEND LA.
A580
A5058
A5049
Recreation Ground
Anfield
Our Lady of Fatima R.C.Comp.Sch.
Edinburgh Pk
Corpn Yard
Tue Brook
Anfield Comp. Sch.
Newsham General Hosp.
Home For Aged
ROCKY LA.
WEST DERBY RD
Newsham Hosp
Boating Lake
Park Hosp.
NEWSHAM
BELMONT DRIVE
Secy Gram.Sch.
Spec. Sch.
30
36
37
95
R
S

75
Norris Green
West Derby
Recreation Ground
Carr Lane Comp. Sch. (Upper)
Carr Lane Comp. Sch. (Lower)
De La Salle R.C. Comp. Sch.
Dwerryhouse Playing Field
Queen Mary Comp. Sch. (Lower)
Mencap Special Sch.
N.E. Liverpool Tech. Coll
Norris Green Park
Haig Mem! Homes
Almonds Green Farm
Margaret Beavan Sch.
St. Mary's Ch.
Village Hall
Sports Ground
Holly Lodge Play^g Flds.
Ernest Cookson Special Sch.
Holly Lodge Comp. Sch. (Upper)
Holly Lodge Comp. Sch. (Lower)
Athletic Ground
Bellefield Everton F.C. Sports Grd.
Walker Playing Fld.
Robt Davis Nurs^g Home
Nurses Ho.
Runnymede
St. Edward's Coll.
Sandfield Park Special Sch.
The Old Hall
West Derby Comp. Sch. (Bankfield Wing)
West Derby Comp. Sch. Gts (Quarry Wing)
Millbank Coll. of Commerce
Bankfield Ho.
R.C. Sec. Sch.
Jolly Miller
Grove Ho.
Playing Field
A5058
Townsend Avenue
Utting Avenue
Queens Drive
Muirhead Avenue
Muirhead Av. East
Eaton Road
Croxteth Lane
Mill Bank
West Derby Road
Lisburn Lane
Green Lane
Larkhill Gdns.
A.L.G.O. Sports Grd.
Derwent Ho.
57
76
96
28
29
30
93
94
92
39
40

76
58
97
75
28
29
30
V
W
Dog & Gun P.H.
De La Salle R.C.Comp.Sch.
Dwerryhouse Playing Field
Mull Wood
Eighteen Acres Plantation
Long Pond
Statue Pond
Croxteth Hall
CROXTETH PARK
Ewens
Cricket Ground
Pav.
Croxteth Country Park
E. Liverpool
West Derby
Grove Ho.
R.C. Ch.
Hall Brook
Deysbrook Ho.
Deysbrook Br.
Deys Brook
Sports Ground
Training Ground
Liby. (site for)
Melwood Liverpool F.C. Sports Grd.
Winterburn Heights
West Derby Golf Course
Club Ho.
Yewtree Playing Fields
Yewtree R.C.Cem.
R.C. Blind Sch.
Sefton R.U.F.C.
Leyfield Priory
Pond
Broughton Hall R.C. Comp. Sch.
Play Flds.
Cardinal Heenan R.C. Comp. Sch.
Carmel Convent
Liv.City Rugby League Club Grd.
Nurses Ho.
Alder Hey
Robt Davis Nurs Home
Nurses Ho.
The Old Hall
Special Sch.
Walker Playing Fld.
Sch.
R.C.Ch.
Bowl Gr.
Rec. Grd.
Pr. Sch.
Prim. Sch.
A53
CROXTETH HALL LANE
OAK LANE
CROXTETH DRIVE
DEYSBROOK LANE
PRINCESS DRIVE
MAB LANE
FINCH LANE
YEW TREE LANE
LEYFIELD ROAD
BLACKMOOR DRIVE
EATON ROAD
ALDER ROAD
KINGSHEATH AV
PRESCOT ROAD
WATERPARK DRIVE

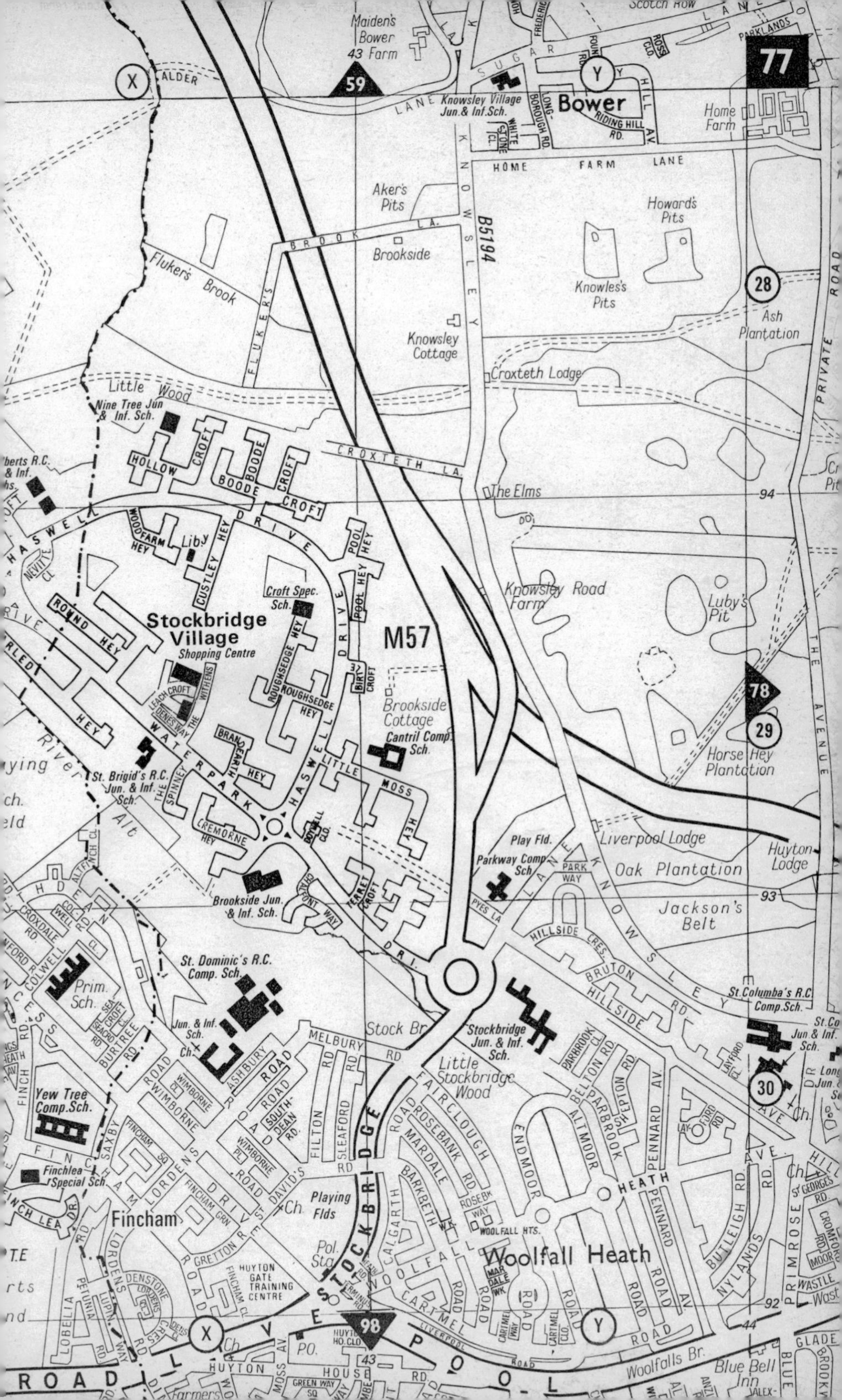

Maiden's Bower Farm
43
59
77
X
Y
ALDER
SUGAR
LANE
Scotch Row
PARKLANDS
ROSS CLO.
Knowsley Village Jun. & Inf. Sch.
Bower
LONG-BOROUGH RD.
WHITE STONE CL.
RIDING HILL RD.
HILL AV.
Home Farm
HOME FARM LANE
Aker's Pits
Howard's Pits
BROOK LA.
Brookside
B5194
KNOWSLEY
Fluker's Brook
FLUKER'S
Knowles's Pits
28
Ash Plantation
PRIVATE ROAD
Knowsley Cottage
Croxteth Lodge
Little Wood
Nine Tree Jun & Inf. Sch.
HOLLOW CROFT
BOODE CROFT
CROXTETH LA.
The Elms
94
HASWELL DRIVE
WOODFARM HEY
Liby
CUSTLEY HEY
POOL HEY
NEVITTE CL.
ROUND HEY
Stockbridge Village
Shopping Centre
Croft Spec. Sch.
M57
Knowsley Road Farm
Luby's Pit
THE AVENUE
ROUGHSEDGE HEY
BIRT CROFT
LEACH CROFT
DENES WAY
THE WITHENS
WATERPARK
Brookside Cottage
Cantril Comp. Sch.
78
29
Horse Hey Plantation
River
St. Brigid's R.C. Jun. & Inf. Sch.
BRAMBLE DEARTH HEY
THE SPINNEY
LITTLE MOSS HEY
Alt
CREMORNE HEY
DOTWELL CLO.
Play Fld.
Liverpool Lodge
Huyton Lodge
Parkway Comp. Sch.
PARK WAY
Oak Plantation
ALTFINCH CL.
Brookside Jun. & Inf. Sch.
CHALFONT WAY
FERRET CROFT
PYES LA.
93
Jackson's Belt
CROXDALE RD.
COLWELL RD.
HILLSIDE CRES.
St. Dominic's R.C. Comp. Sch.
BRUTON RD.
HILLSIDE RD.
St. Columba's R.C. Comp. Sch.
Prim. Sch.
SEACROFT
BURTREE RD.
Jun. & Inf. Sch.
Stock Br.
MELBURY RD.
Stockbridge Jun. & Inf. Sch.
PARBROOK CL.
BELTON RD.
SHEPTON RD.
LAYFORD CL.
Ch.
Yew Tree Comp. Sch.
ASHBURY ROAD
WIMBORNE
SOUTHDEAN RD.
FILTON RD.
SLEAFORD RD.
Little Stockbridge Wood
FAIRCLOUGH
ROSEBANK RD.
ENDMOOR
ALTMOOR
PARBROOK
PENNARD AV.
30
LAYFORD RD.
FINCHAM SQ.
LORDENS DRIVE
ST DAVID'S
STOCKBRIDGE
MARDALE
BARKRETH
HEATH
NYLANDS
BUTLEIGH RD.
PRIMROSE RD.
ST GEORGES RD.
Finchlea Special Sch.
FINCH LEA DR.
Fincham
FINCHAM GRN.
Playing Flds
CALGARTH
ROSEBK WAY
WOOLFALL HTS.
GRETTON RD.
Pol. Sta.
Woolfall Heath
MARDALE WK.
WASTLE
HUYTON GATE TRAINING CENTRE
FINCHAM CL.
WOOLFALL
CARTMEL
92
LOBELIA RD.
PETUNIA
LUPIN WAY
DENSTONE CRES.
98
ROAD
44
LIVERPOOL
HUYTON HO. CLO.
P.O.
43
HUYTON HOUSE RD.
MOSS AV.
GREEN WAY SQ.
Woolfalls Br.
Blue Bell Inn
GLADE

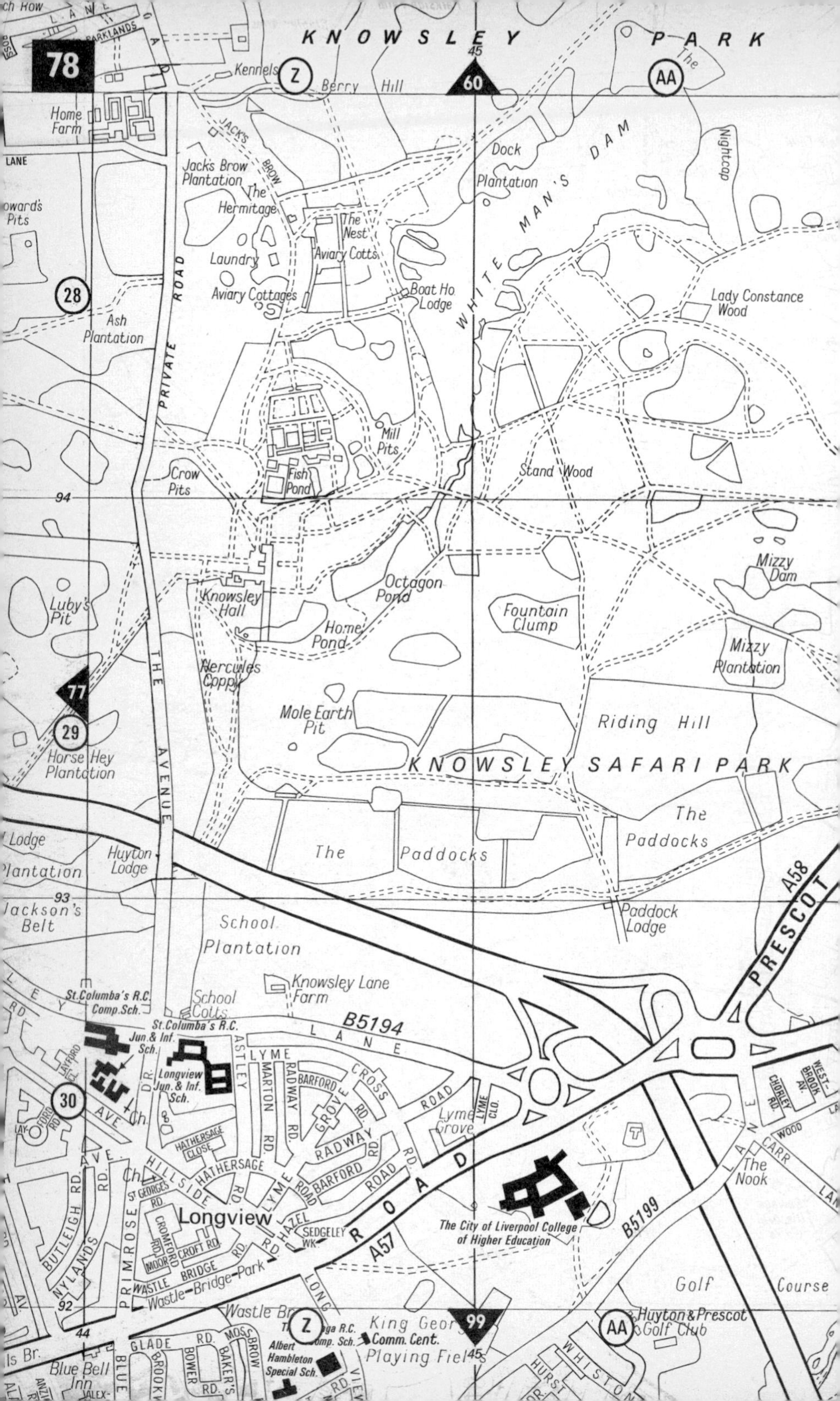
KNOWSLEY PARK
Kennels
Berry Hill
60
45
Home Farm
Jack's Brow Plantation
The Hermitage
The Nest
Aviary Cotts
Laundry
Aviary Cottages
Boat Ho. Lodge
Dock Plantation
WHITE MAN'S DAM
Nightcap
Lady Constance Wood
Ash Plantation
PRIVATE ROAD
Mill Pits
Crow Pits
Fish Pond
Stand Wood
94
Octagon Pond
Knowsley Hall
Home Pond
Luby's Pit
Fountain Clump
Mizzy Dam
Mizzy Plantation
Hercules Coppy
Mole Earth Pit
Riding Hill
77
29
Horse Hey Plantation
THE AVENUE
KNOWSLEY SAFARI PARK
The Paddocks
Huyton Lodge
Plantation
93
Jackson's Belt
School Plantation
Paddock Lodge
A58
PRESCOT
Knowsley Lane Farm
School Cotts
St.Columba's R.C. Comp.Sch.
St.Columba's R.C. Jun.& Inf. Sch.
B5194
LANE
Longview Jun.& Inf. Sch.
ASTLEY
LYME
MARTON RD.
RADWAY RD.
BARFORD
GROVE
CROSS RD.
ROAD
Lyme Grove
LYME CLO.
30
HATHERSAGE CLOSE
HATHERSAGE RD.
HILLSIDE
RADWAY
BARFORD RD.
ROAD
CHORLEY RD.
WESTBROOK AV.
CARR
WOOD
The Nook
ST GEORGES RD.
CROMFORD RD.
Longview
HAZEL RD
SEDGELEY WK.
ROAD
A57
The City of Liverpool College of Higher Education
B5199
BUTLEIGH RD.
NYLANDS
PRIMROSE
MOOR
CROFT RD.
WASTLE BRIDGE RD.
Wastle-Bridge-Park
Golf Course
92
Wastle Br.
LONG
Z
AA
99
Huyton & Prescot Golf Club
44
King George
Comm. Cent.
Playing Fields
45
GLADE RD.
MOSS
BROW
BAKER'S
BOWER RD.
BROOK
BLUE
Blue Bell Inn
Albert Hambleton Special Sch.
WHISTON
HURST DR.

Stanley Arms
's Green
Burgesses Fm.
Mere Cottage
BURROW'S LANE
B5201
Eccleston Mere
Park Farm
Shaw's Plantation
Knowsley Safari Park
Trap Wood
Mere View Farm
Burrows La. Farm
Singleton's Hill
Trapwood Cottage
Deer Paddocks
Trap Lodge
Roughley's Brow Farm
Sale's Wood
Gorse Plantation
Cricket Ground
Number 4 Reservoir
Number 3 Reservoir
Roughley's Brow House
Mizzy Plantation
Number 2 Reservoir
Eccleston Nursery
Knoll House
Yates Plantation
Number 1 Reservoir
War Mem.
Eccleston Lane Ends
Valencia
Knowsley Park Entrance
BY-PASS
ST. HELENS
PARK
Prescot Comp. Sch.(Park Wing)
Our Lady's R.C.Jun. & Inf.Sch.
Prescot Comp.Sch. (Latham Wing)
Playing Field
PRESCOT
Eccleston Park
Foot. Grd.
Evelyn Jun.& Inf.Sch.
Old Lane Ends Prim.Sch.
Lib.
Pol.Sta.
DERBY ST.
HIGH ST.
Prescot Trade Centre
Prescot Museum
Vic.
Cemetery
Prescot Jun. & Inf.Sch.
Prescot Coll. of Further Education
Ramhill High Sch.
Cable Works
SCOTCHBARN
Swimming Baths
WARRINGTON
A57
Prescot Sports & Leisure Cent.
St.Edmund Arrowsmith R.C.Comp.Sch.
Council Offices
Holt Lane Quarry
Sewage Disposal Works
Rye Hey
Prescot Hall
PRESCOT STA.
Sports Grd.
S.A. Citadel
Fire Sta.
Delph La Hospital
New Hall
Nurse's Home
High-hill
Prescot CE Jun. & Inf. Sch.
St.Lukes R.C Jun.& Inf. Schs
Whiston Hospital

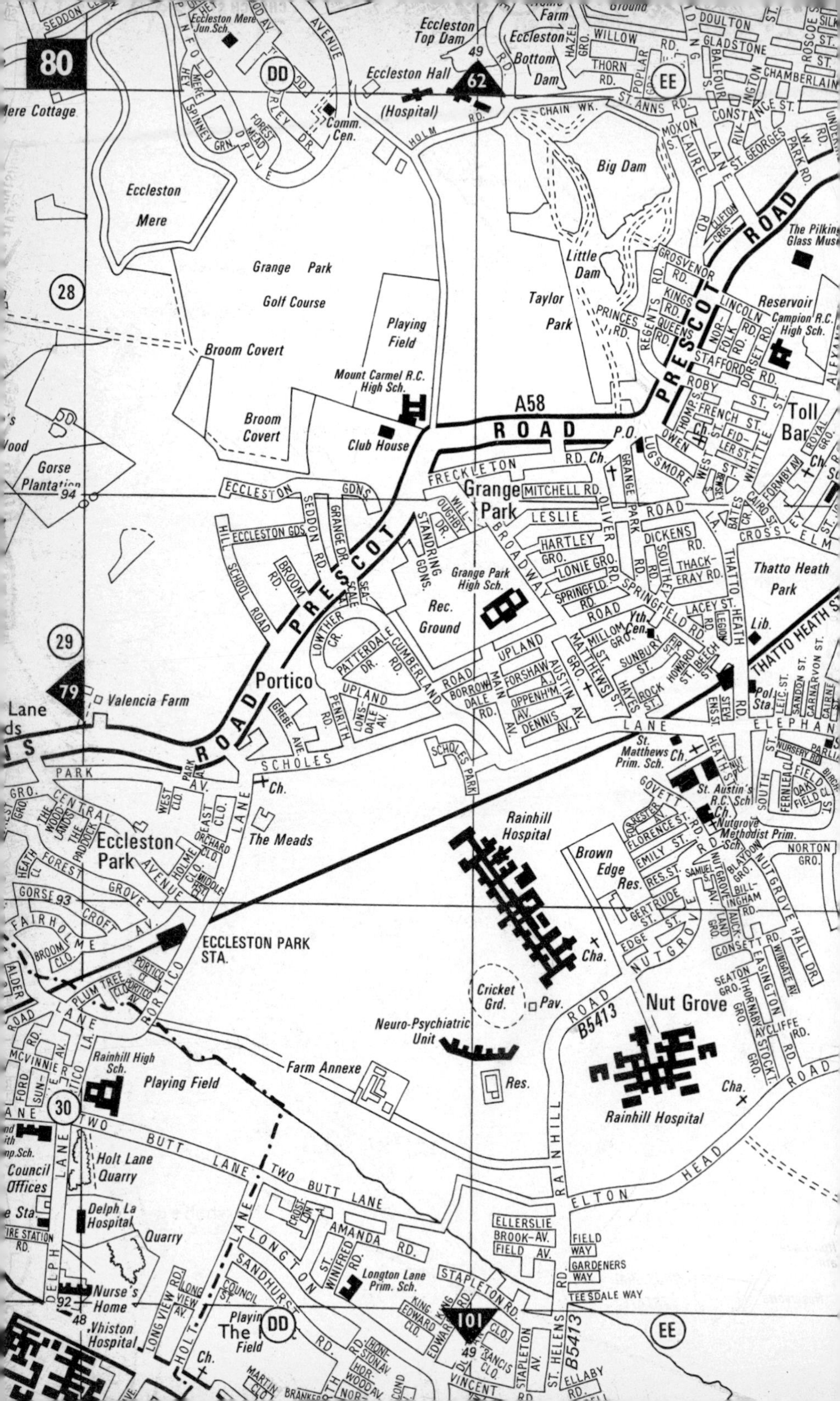
80
Eccleston Mere Jun. Sch.
DD
Eccleston Top Dam
Eccleston Bottom Dam
Eccleston Hall (Hospital)
62
49
EE
Doulton St.
Willow Rd.
Thorn Rd.
Gladstone
Balfour St.
Chamberlain
Roscoe St.
Constance St.
St. Anns Rd.
Chain Wk.
Holm Rd.
Comm. Cen.
Mere Cottage
Eccleston Mere
Big Dam
Moxon St.
Laurel
Lane
St. Georges
Park Rd.
Clifton Cres.
Prescot Road
The Pilkington Glass Museum
Little Dam
Grange Park Golf Course
Taylor Park
Grosvenor Rd.
Kings Rd.
Queens Rd.
Princes Rd.
Regents Rd.
Lincoln
Reservoir
Campion R.C. High Sch.
28
Playing Field
Broom Covert
Mount Carmel R.C. High Sch.
Norfolk Rd.
Dorset Rd.
Stafford Rd.
Roby St.
A58
Road
Club House
Toll Bar
P.O.
Freckleton Rd.
Ch.
Grange Park
Mitchell Rd.
Leslie
Lugsmore
Owen
French St.
Fidler St.
Whittle
Formby Av.
Royal
Gorse Plantation
94
Eccleston Gdns.
Seddon Rd.
Grange Dr.
Willoughby Dr.
Standring Gdns.
Broadway
Hartley Gro.
Lonie Gro.
Oliver Rd.
Dickens Rd.
Southey Rd.
Thackeray Rd.
Thatto Heath Rd.
Crossley
Elm
Thatto Heath Park
Eccleston Gds.
Hill School Road
Broom Rd.
Prescot
Grange Park High Sch.
Rec. Ground
Springfld. Rd.
Springfield Rd.
Lacey St.
Lib.
Thatto Heath St.
Lowther Cr.
Patterdale Dr.
Cumberland Rd.
Upland
Millom Gro.
Yth. Cen.
Sunbury St.
Fir St.
Howard St.
Beech St.
29
79
Valencia Farm
Portico
Upland Rd.
Borrowdale Rd.
Main Av.
Forshaw A.
Oppenh'm. Av.
Dennis Av.
Austin Av.
Matthews St.
Hayes St.
Rock St.
Stevens St.
Pol. Sta.
Leic. St.
Sandon St.
Carnarvon St.
Grebe Ave.
Penrith Rd.
Lonsdale Av.
Road
Scholes Park
Lane
Elephant
St. Matthews Prim. Sch.
Heath St.
Nutgrove
Nursery Rd.
Park
Scholes
Park Av.
Ch.
West Clo.
East Clo.
Lane
Govett Rd.
St. Austin's R.C. Sch.
Nutgrove Methodist Prim. Sch.
Fernlea Cl.
Oakfield Cl.
Central
The Woodlands
The Paddock
Eccleston Park
Avenue
Orchard Clo.
Holme Clo.
Middle Hey
The Meads
Rainhill Hospital
Forester Av.
Florence St.
Emily St.
Res. St.
Brown Edge Res.
Samuel St.
Blaydon Gro.
Billingham Rd.
Norton Gro.
Heath Cl.
Forest
Grove
Gorse
93
Croft
Av.
Fairholme
Gertrude St.
Edge
Nutgrove
Auckland Gro.
Consett Rd.
Wingate Av.
Hall Dr.
Broom Clo.
Eccleston Park Sta.
Cha.
Alder
Portico
Plum Tree Clo.
Portico Av.
Cricket Grd.
Pav.
Road
B5413
Nut Grove
Seaton Gro.
Easington
Thornaby Gro.
Aycliffe Rd.
Stockton Gro.
Neuro-Psychiatric Unit
McVinnie Rd.
Ford
Sunnyside Av.
Rainhill High Sch.
Playing Field
Farm Annexe
Res.
Cha.
Rainhill Hospital
30
Two Butt Lane
Holt Lane Quarry
Council Offices
Elton Head Road
Rainhill
Delph Lane
Delph La. Hospital
Quarry
Fire Station Rd.
Crostlow
Amanda Rd.
Ellerslie
Brook Av.
Field Av.
Field Way
Gardeners Way
Teesdale Way
St. Winifred Rd.
Longton Lane Prim. Sch.
Stapleton Rd.
Nurse's Home
92
48
Whiston Hospital
Longview Rd.
Long View Av.
Council St.
Sandhurst Rd.
Holt Lane
King Edward Clo.
101
Francis Clo.
Stapleton Av.
St. Helens Rd.
B5413
Ellaby Rd.
Ch.
Vincent
Martin Clo.
Branker
Honiston Av.
Horwood Av.

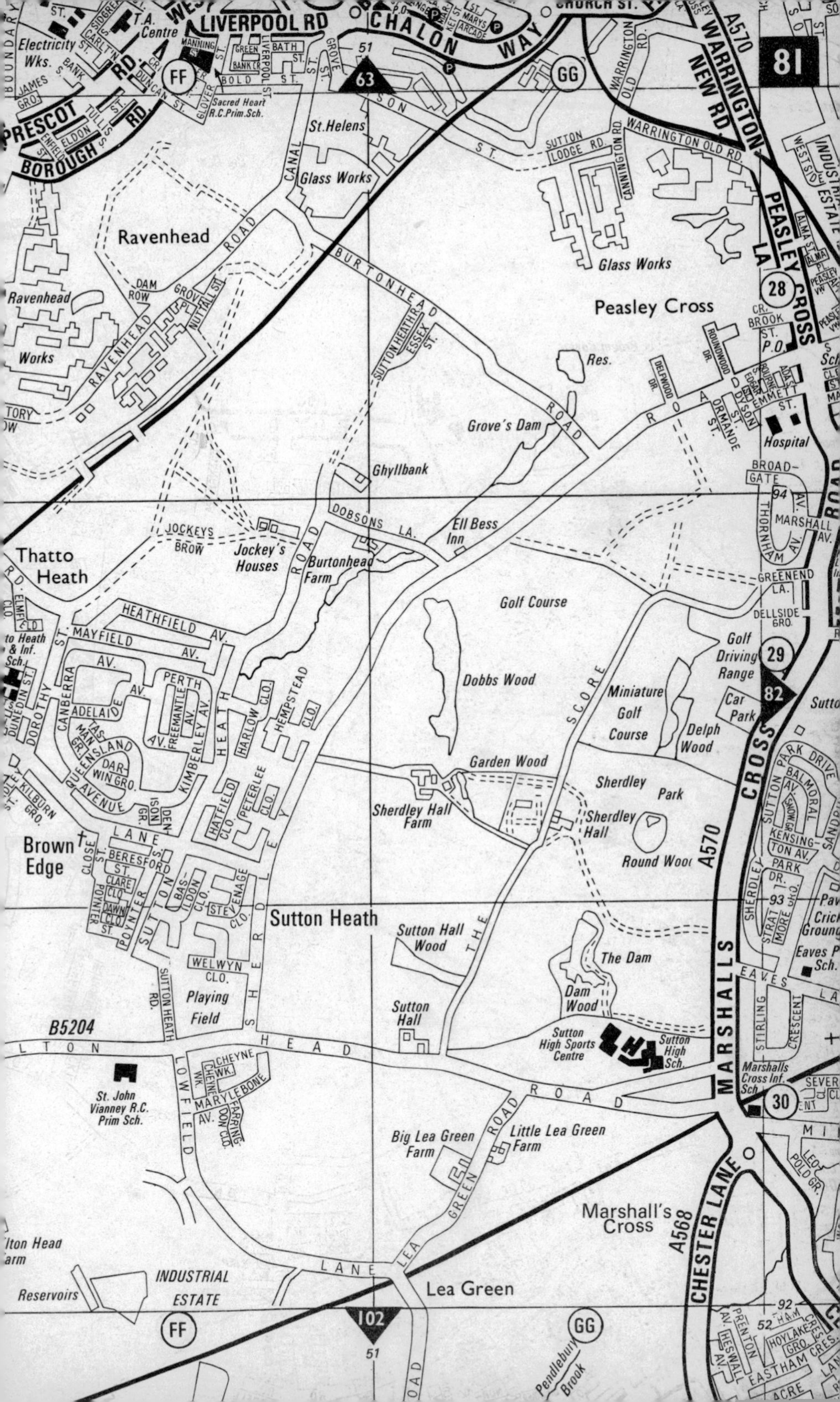
81
LIVERPOOL RD
CHALON WAY
CHURCH ST.
T.A. Centre
Electricity Wks.
PRESCOT RD.
BOROUGH RD.
FF
GG
63
51
Sacred Heart R.C.Prim.Sch.
St.Helens
Glass Works
CANAL
WARRINGTON NEW RD.
A570
WARRINGTON OLD RD.
SUTTON LODGE RD.
CANNINGTON RD.
Ravenhead
Ravenhead Works
BURTONHEAD ROAD
RAVENHEAD ROAD
Glass Works
Peasley Cross
PEASLEY CROSS LA
28
Res.
Grove's Dam
Ghyllbank
SUTTON HEATH RD.
ESSEX ST.
DELFWOOD DR.
ROUNDWOOD DR.
Hospital
BROADGATE
MARSHALL AV.
THORNHAM AV.
94
Thatto Heath
JOCKEYS BROW
Jockey's Houses
DOBSONS LA.
Ell Bess Inn
Burtonhead Farm
Golf Course
GREENEND LA.
DELLSIDE GRO.
Golf Driving Range
29
82
Car Park
HEATHFIELD AV.
MAYFIELD AV.
CANBERRA AV.
PERTH AV.
ADELAIDE AV.
FREEMANTLE AV.
KIMBERLEY AV.
QUEENSLAND AVENUE
DORORTHY ST.
DUNEDIN ST.
KILBURN GRO.
HARLOW CLO.
HEMPSTEAD CLO.
Dobbs Wood
Miniature Golf Course
Delph Wood
SCORE
Garden Wood
Sherdley Park
Sherdley Hall Farm
Sherdley Hall
Round Wood
HATFIELD CLO.
PETERLEE CLO.
Brown Edge
BERESFORD ST.
CLARE CLO.
POYNTER ST.
SUTTON HEATH RD.
BASILDON CLO.
STEVENAGE CLO.
WELWYN CLO.
Sutton Heath
SHERDLEY RD.
THE SCORE
Sutton Hall Wood
The Dam
Dam Wood
MARSHALLS CROSS RD.
SUTTON PARK DRIVE
BALMORAL AV.
KENSINGTON AV.
93
Eaves Sch.
EAVES LA.
STIRLING CRESCENT
Playing Field
B5204
Sutton Hall
Sutton High Sports Centre
Sutton High Sch.
HEAD ROAD
CHEYNE WK.
MARYLEBONE AV.
LOWFIELD
St. John Vianney R.C. Prim Sch.
Marshalls Cross Inf. Sch.
30
Big Lea Green Farm
Little Lea Green Farm
LEA GREEN ROAD
CHESTER LANE
A568
Marshall's Cross
LEOPOLD GR.
INDUSTRIAL ESTATE
Reservoirs
LANE
Lea Green
102
92
PRENTON
HESWALL AV.
HOYLAKE GRO.
EASTHAM CRES.
Pendlebury Brook

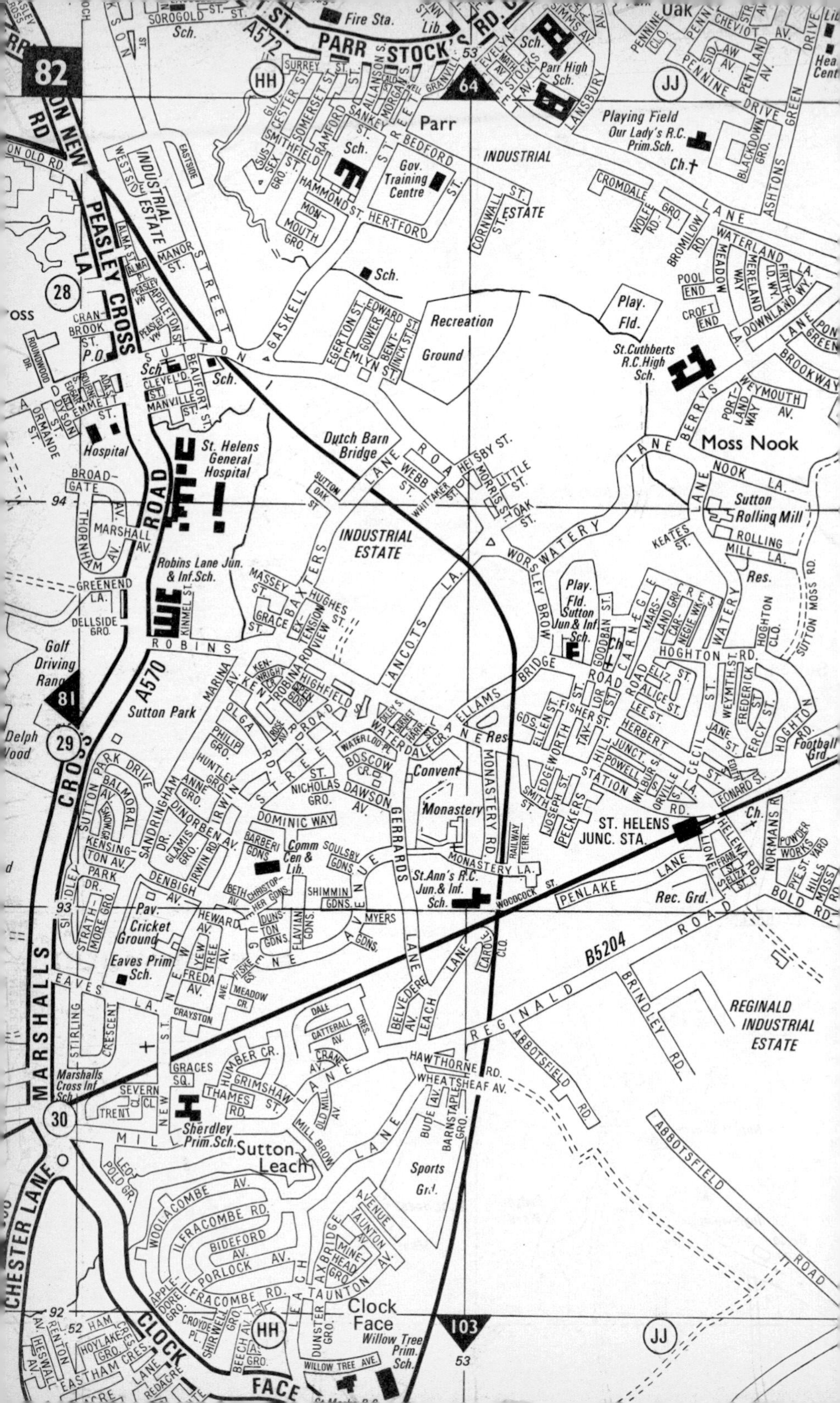

82
81
64
103
HH
JJ
28
29
30
94
93
92
53
Parr
INDUSTRIAL
ESTATE
PARR STOCK'S RD.
A572
Fire Sta.
Parr High Sch.
Playing Field
Our Lady's R.C. Prim.Sch.
Ch.
Gov. Training Centre
Recreation Ground
Play. Fld.
St.Cuthberts R.C.High Sch.
Moss Nook
Sutton Rolling Mill
Dutch Barn Bridge
INDUSTRIAL ESTATE
St. Helens General Hospital
Hospital
Robins Lane Jun. & Inf.Sch.
Golf Driving Rang
Sutton Park
A570
Delph Wood
PEASLEY CROSS
P.O.
Play. Fld. Sutton Jun & Inf. Sch.
Res.
Convent
Monastery
ST. HELENS JUNC. STA.
Football Grd.
Rec. Grd.
B5204
REGINALD ROAD
REGINALD INDUSTRIAL ESTATE
Comm Cen & Lib.
St.Ann's R.C. Jun.& Inf. Sch.
Pav.
Cricket Ground
Eaves Prim Sch.
Marshalls Cross Inf. Sch.
Sherdley Prim.Sch.
Sutton Leach
Sports Grd.
Clock Face
Willow Tree Prim. Sch.
MARSHALLS CROSS
CHESTER LANE
CLOCK FACE
ABBOTSFIELD ROAD
BRINDLEY RD.
ABBOTSFIELD RD.
HAWTHORNE RD.
WHEATSHEAF AV.
WOOLACOMBE AV.
ILFRACOMBE RD.
BIDEFORD AV.
PORLOCK AV.
TAUNTON
WATERY LANE
BERRYS LANE
WORSLEY BROW
LANCOTS LA.
GERRARDS LANE
MONASTERY RD.
PENLAKE LANE
BOLD RD.
HOGHTON RD.
STATION RD.
ROBINS LANE
SUTTON PARK DRIVE
EAVES LA.
MILL LANE

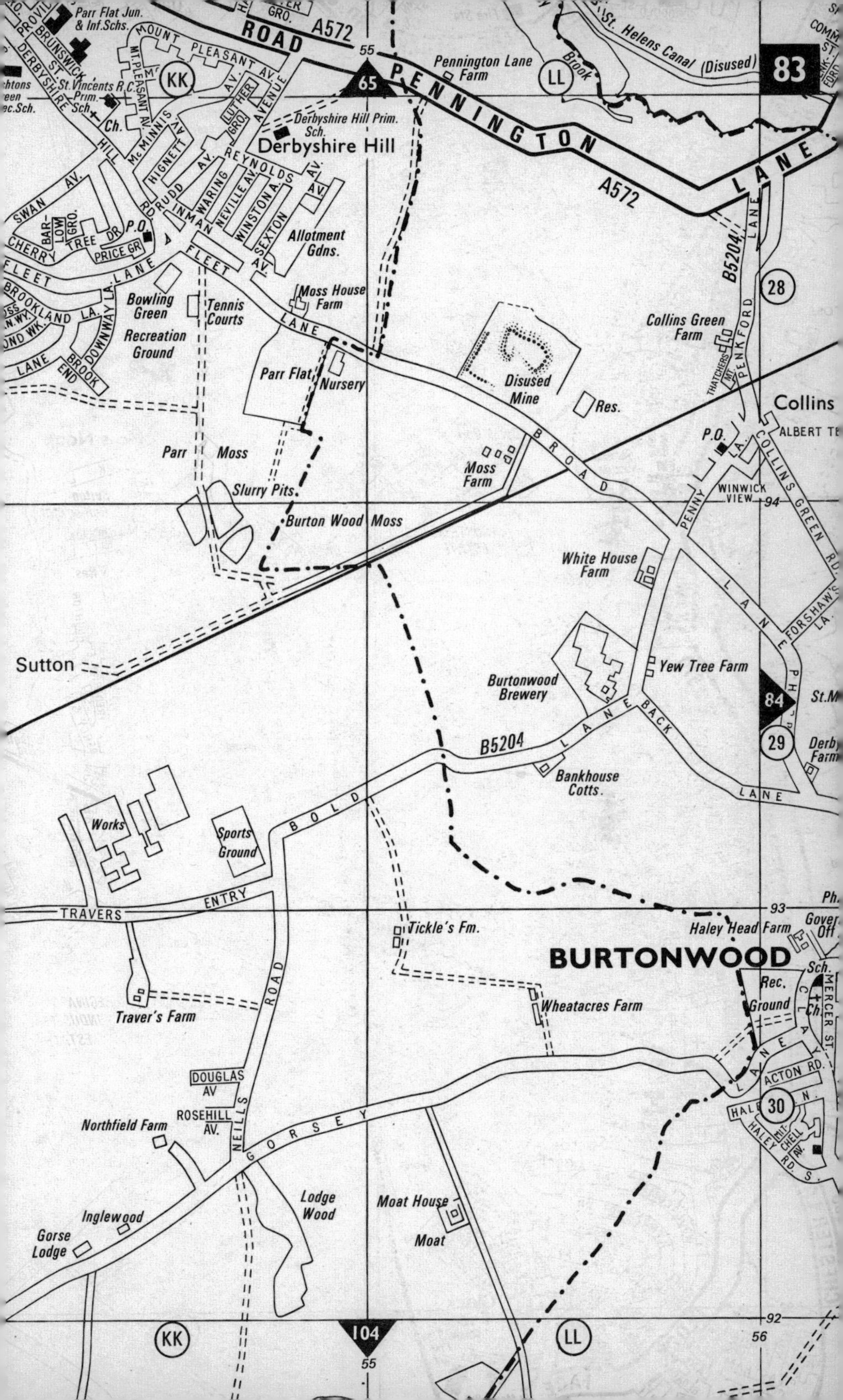

83
84
104
65
A572
ROAD
PENNINGTON
LANE
Pennington Lane Farm
St. Helens Canal (Disused)
Brook
Parr Flat Jun. & Inf. Schs.
BRUNSWICK ST.
DERBYSHIRE
MOUNT PLEASANT AV.
MT. PLEASANT AV.
St. Vincents R.C. Prim. Sch.
Ch.
KK
LL
LUTHER GRO.
AVENUE
Derbyshire Hill Prim. Sch.
Derbyshire Hill
HILL
McMINNIS
HIGNETT AV.
RUDD AV.
REYNOLDS
WARING
NEVILLE AV.
WINSTON AV.
SEXTON AV.
INMAN
SWAN AV.
BARLOW GRO.
CHERRY TREE DR.
P.O.
PRICE GR.
RD.
FLEET LANE
Allotment Gdns.
BROOKLAND LA.
DOWNWAY LA.
Bowling Green
Tennis Courts
Recreation Ground
Moss House Farm
LANE
BROOK
LANE END
Parr Flat
Nursery
Disused Mine
Res.
Parr Moss
Slurry Pits
Burton Wood Moss
Moss Farm
BROAD
LANE
B5204
LANE
PENKFORD
THATCHERS MT.
Collins Green Farm
28
Collins
ALBERT TE
P.O.
PENNY LA.
COLLINS GREEN RD.
WINWICK VIEW
94
White House Farm
FORSHAWS LA.
Sutton
Yew Tree Farm
Burtonwood Brewery
29
St.M
Derby Farm
B5204
BACK
LANE
Bankhouse Cotts.
BOLD
Works
Sports Ground
TRAVERS
ENTRY
93
Tickle's Fm.
Haley Head Farm
BURTONWOOD
Sch.
Rec. Ground
Ch.
MERCER ST.
CLAY
Traver's Farm
Wheatacres Farm
ROAD
DOUGLAS AV.
ROSEHILL AV.
NEILLS
Northfield Farm
GORSEY
ACTON RD.
30
HALEY RD.
MITCHELL AV.
Lodge Wood
Moat House
Moat
Inglewood
Gorse Lodge
92
KK
LL
55
56

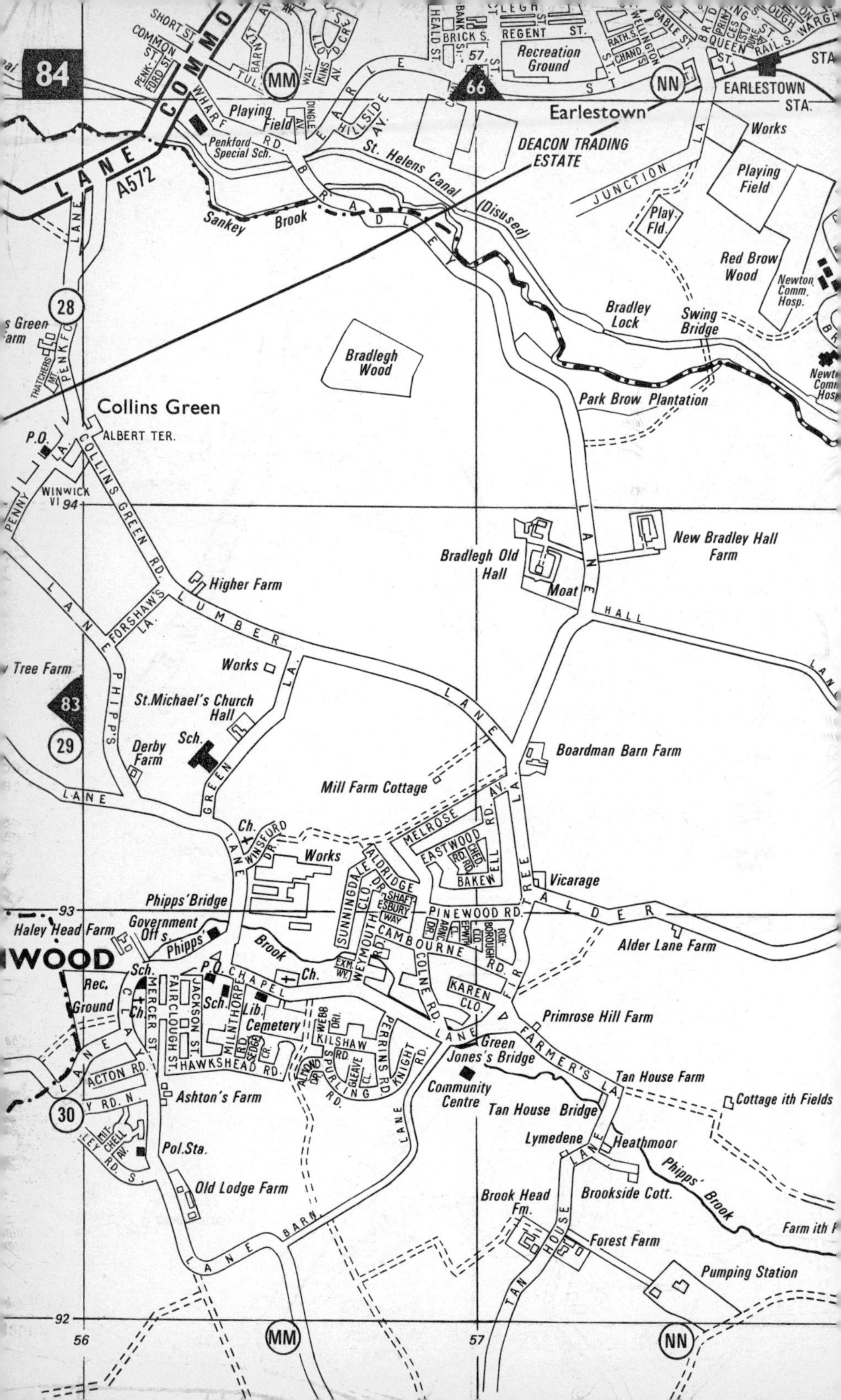

84
66
83
Short St.
Common St.
Penkford St.
Common Lane
Wharf Rd.
A572
Lane
Barnet Av.
Lloyd Cres.
Watkins Av.
MM
NN
Heald St.
Bank St.
Brick S.
Regent St.
Recreation Ground
Wellington
Gable St.
Queen St.
Rail. S.
Earlestown
Earlestown Sta.
Playing Field
Dingle Av.
Hillside Av.
Penkford Special Sch.
Deacon Trading Estate
St. Helens Canal (Disused)
Sankey Brook
Bradley Lane
Junction La.
Works
Playing Field
Play. Fld.
Red Brow Wood
Newton Comm. Hosp.
Bradley Lock
Swing Bridge
Park Brow Plantation
28
Thatchers Mt.
Penkford
Bradlegh Wood
Collins Green
Albert Ter.
P.O.
Penny Lane
Winwick Vi
94
Collins Green Rd.
New Bradley Hall Farm
Bradlegh Old Hall
Moat
Higher Farm
Forshaw's La.
Lumber Lane
Hall Lane
Tree Farm
Works
St.Michael's Church Hall
Sch.
29
Derby Farm
Phipps' Lane
Green Lane
Boardman Barn Farm
Mill Farm Cottage
Melrose Av.
Eastwood Rd.
Bakewell
Winsford Dr.
Ch.
Works
Aldridge Dr.
Sunningdale Clo.
Shaftesbury Way
Vicarage
Fir Tree La.
Alder Lane
Phipps' Bridge
93
Pinewood Rd.
Camborne
Roxborough Rd.
Haley Head Farm
Government Offs.
Phipps' Brook
Alder Lane Farm
WOOD
Rec. Ground
Sch.
Ch.
P.O.
Chapel Lane
Weymouth Rd.
Colne Rd.
Karen Clo.
Primrose Hill Farm
Clay Lane
Mercer St.
Fairclough St.
Jackson St.
Milnthorpe Rd.
Lib.
Cemetery
Webb Dri.
Kilshaw Rd.
Perrins Rd.
Knight Rd.
Green
Jones's Bridge
Farmer's La.
Hawkshead Rd.
Acton Rd.
Spurling Rd.
Gleave Cl.
Community Centre
Tan House Farm
Ashton's Farm
30
Mitchell Av.
Pol.Sta.
Tan House Bridge
Cottage ith Fields
Lymedene
Heathmoor
Old Lodge Farm
Brook Head Fm.
Brookside Cott.
Phipps' Brook
Farm ith
Barn Lane
Tan House Lane
Forest Farm
Pumping Station
92
56
57
MM
NN

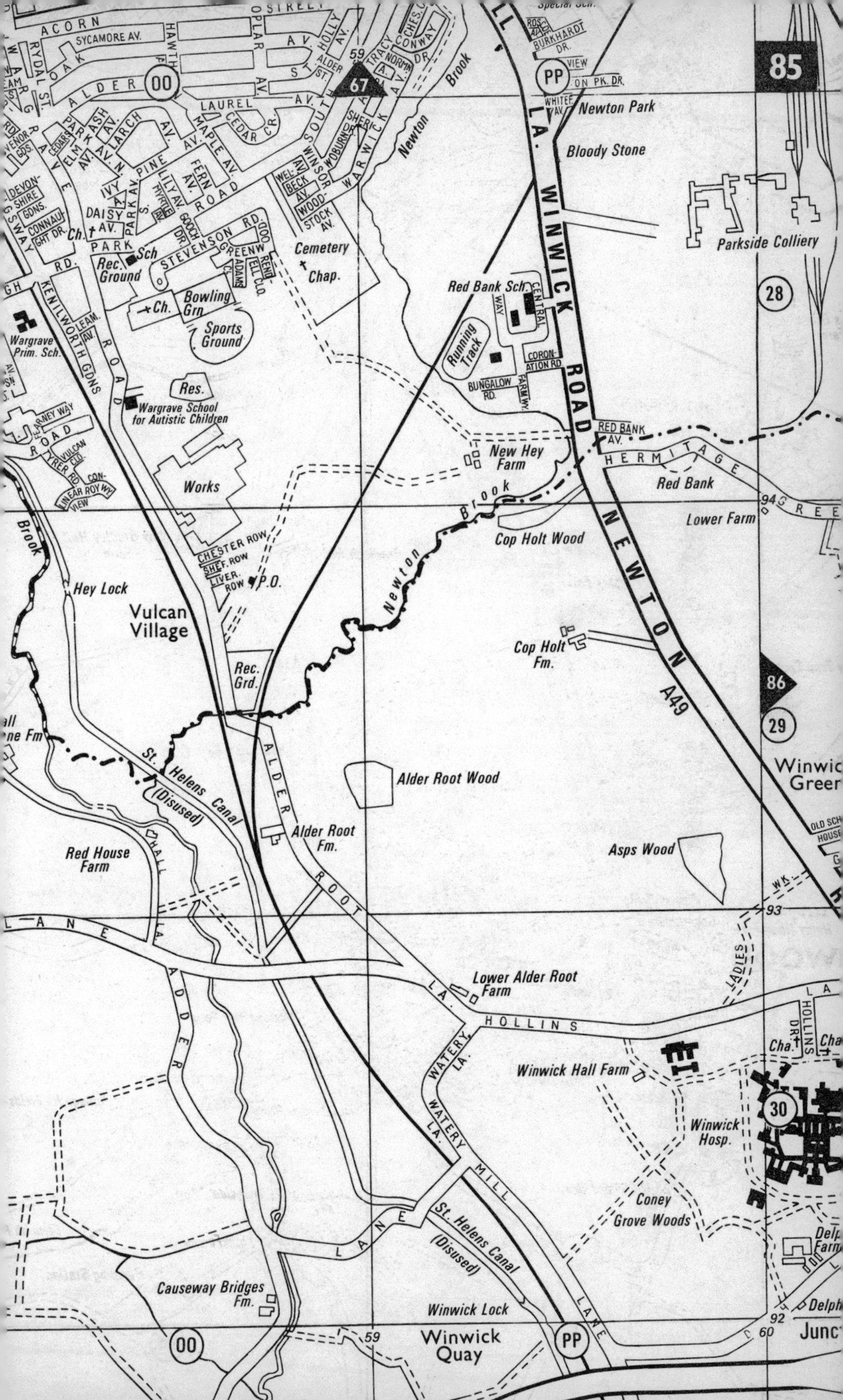
85
86
67
Newton Park
Bloody Stone
Parkside Colliery
Red Bank Sch.
Running Track
New Hey Farm
Red Bank
Lower Farm
Cop Holt Wood
Cop Holt Fm.
Newton Brook
WINWICK LA.
NEWTON ROAD
A49
Winwick Green
Wargrave Prim. Sch.
Wargrave School for Autistic Children
Works
Hey Lock
Vulcan Village
Rec. Grd.
Cemetery Chap.
Sports Ground
Bowling Grn
Rec. Ground
Res.
P.O.
Alder Root Wood
Alder Root Fm.
St. Helens Canal (Disused)
Red House Farm
Asps Wood
Lower Alder Root Farm
HOLLINS LA.
Winwick Hall Farm
Winwick Hosp.
Coney Grove Woods
Causeway Bridges Fm.
Winwick Lock
Winwick Quay
MILL LANE
WATERY LA.
ALDER ROOT LA.
HERMITAGE GREEN
ACORN
SYCAMORE AV.
ALDER AV.
LAUREL AV.
STEVENSON RD.
KENILWORTH GDNS
LEAM. AV.
CHESTER ROW
SHEF. ROW
LIVER. ROW
BUNGALOW RD.
CORONATION RD
RED BANK AV.
Delph Farm
Junc
00
PP
28
29
30
59
60
92
93
94

QQ
68
61
RR
Moss Pits
28
29
85
30
Parkside Colliery
BARROW LANE
ROAD
M6
Wood Head
Oven Back
WINWICK LANE
A579
St.Oswald's Well
Piper Hole
Rough Farm
Hermitage Farm
Bank
Lower Farm
94
GREEN LA.
GEROSA AV.
Rose Mount
Hermitage Green
Junction 22
LANE
HIGHFIELD
LINK ROAD
GOLBORNE ROAD
A573
Highfields
Winwick Green
A49
Winwick Cott.
OLD SCHOOL HOUSE LA.
GREEN LANE CL.
GREEN LA.
Res.
Ch.
WINWICK
The Lodge
LANE
SOUTHWORTH LANE
DELPH LA.
The Priory
93
HORNBY LA.
WATERWORKS
ILEX
OSWALDS AV.
OSWALDS CLO.
PILGRIM CL.
CH.WK.
Ch.
MYDDLETON LANE
ASH RD.
MAPLE AV.
ROAD
Arbury
Penrhyn
Delph Far
LADIES WK.
LANE
P.O.
Sch.
Playing Field
Leisure Centre
HOLLINS DR.
Cha.
RECTORY LA.
REC. CL.
FARINGDON RD.
FALCONDALE
LINKSIDE AV.
ARBURY
Gorsey Brow
WINWICK
Winwick Hosp.
Rec. Grd.
Spa W House
Bowling Green
Delph Farm
LANE
TOWNSFIELD RD.
Delph Hospital
Midhops Plantatio
Delph Cottage
DELPH
Arbury Pits
F.B.
M6
92
60
Junction 9
QQ
61
RR

31

91

▶
88

32

IRISH   SEA

90

Bowling Greens

West Kirby Gram
Sch.for
Girls

Baths

PROMENADE

Tennis
Cts.

M.Gdns.

HOYLE

SANDHEY

DENESHEY

SAXON   RD.

QU.
Co.

DOVEDALE
CLYDESDLE

AVONDALE

RD.

RD.

33

Y.M.C.A.

NEWTON

PARADE

PROM.

LAKE RD.

TRINITY

SCHOOL   RD.

SEA VW.

NEWT'N
RD.

STRAND

MARINE

GOVERNMT.

Holy Trinity
Prim. Sch.

Ch.

WAVERLEY   RD.

ST.

H.P.O.

ELM T. RD.

Lifeboat House

Cine

GROVE PL.

ALDERLEY

GROVE RD.

SHAW ST.

GRO. NORWOOD
RD.

HADFDA.

RD.

SEA VW.

GROVEL RD.

STAN. PL.

WALKER ST.

HOLD ST.

MELROSE

NORTH

RD.

RD.

Ch.

RD.

HOYLAKE

MARINE

CABLE

QUEENS

ST.

VILLA

RD.

MARKET

RD.

KING'S

WARREN   RD.

Ch.

CURZON ROAD

COURTENAY

ST. MARY'S R.

KING'S

RD.

RD.

Spa

SPI

89

PROCTOR

RD.

CARHAM RD.

CARS.

21

GAP

Town
Hall

CHARLES

GROSVENOR

H.P.O.

Ch.

HOYLAKE

88

C · 23 · D

31

91

87
32

Dove Point · Parkfields

PARADE ROAD

Newlyn · Rake · GUFFITTS CLO.
Lelt- · Win · GUFFITTS DRI.
Great Meols · Centurion · FAMIL CLO.
Prim.Sch. · DRI. · Barny · Clo.

BENNETS LANE · PARK

P A R A D E   R O A D

Meols · Sand · THE GOOSE GRN. · FOREST · Beachcroft · Meadow · LA. W.
Firshaw · Field Av. · Sand · ROMAN · GLO · FOR EST · Dovepoint · Rd. · FLOWER MEAD CLO.
Garden Hey · Wood · Landon · Wood RD. · SCHOOL · Park · ASHLEY RD.
Wynnstay · RD. · Shaws · DRI. · Mumfords · LA. W. · LYNDH · CRANBOURN · RD.
Tennis · Ashford · RD. · Green- · Celtic · WYM · RD.
Cts. · SANDHE · Redstone · EGBERT · CL. · KINGS · Park · CLEVELEY RD.
Gdns. · DENESHEY · ETHEL · RD. · BERT · RD. · SCH · CL. · Way · P.O.
Greens · HOYLE · SAXON RD. · Qn.Eliz. II · Egbert · AV. · Banks · FRANKBY RD. · LEIGHTON AV. · DERWENT RD.
Kirby Gram · Coronation · Bertram · AV. · Foxfield · GORSE · AV. · RD.
Sch. for · Park · Tel. Ex · Meols · DRI. · MEOLS STATION
Girls · Cottage · BERT · Bertram · DRI. N. · Queens · Fish Pond
AVONDALE · Hosp. · CARLION · RAM · AV. · RYECROFT · RD.
FERN · CHAPEL · SANDRINGHAM · Kingsmead · SAND · BIRCH RD. · BARN HEY CRES
33 · Y.M.C.A. · Sch. · AV. · SHERWOOD RD.
AV. · MANOR RD. · NEWTON RD. · A553
Ch. · Sch. · CARTER · HORNBY
Holy Trinity · WAVERLEY · RD.
Prim. Sch. · HADFDA · EW. GRO · CORMEREND
SHAW · HARRING · MANOR RD.
WALKER · MELROSE · STA.
MARKET · HADFDA · Football · FORMAL'S GREEN LA. · THE RIDGEWAY · FIELD WAY · ACRES
RD. · Grd. · Sports · BISPHAM DR.
89 · Grd.
22 · Industrial Esta · C · The · Birket · D
PROCTOR RD. · 106
CARHAM RD. · CARTERTON · 23
CARSIDE RD.
CARS
THORNE RD.
OYLAKE

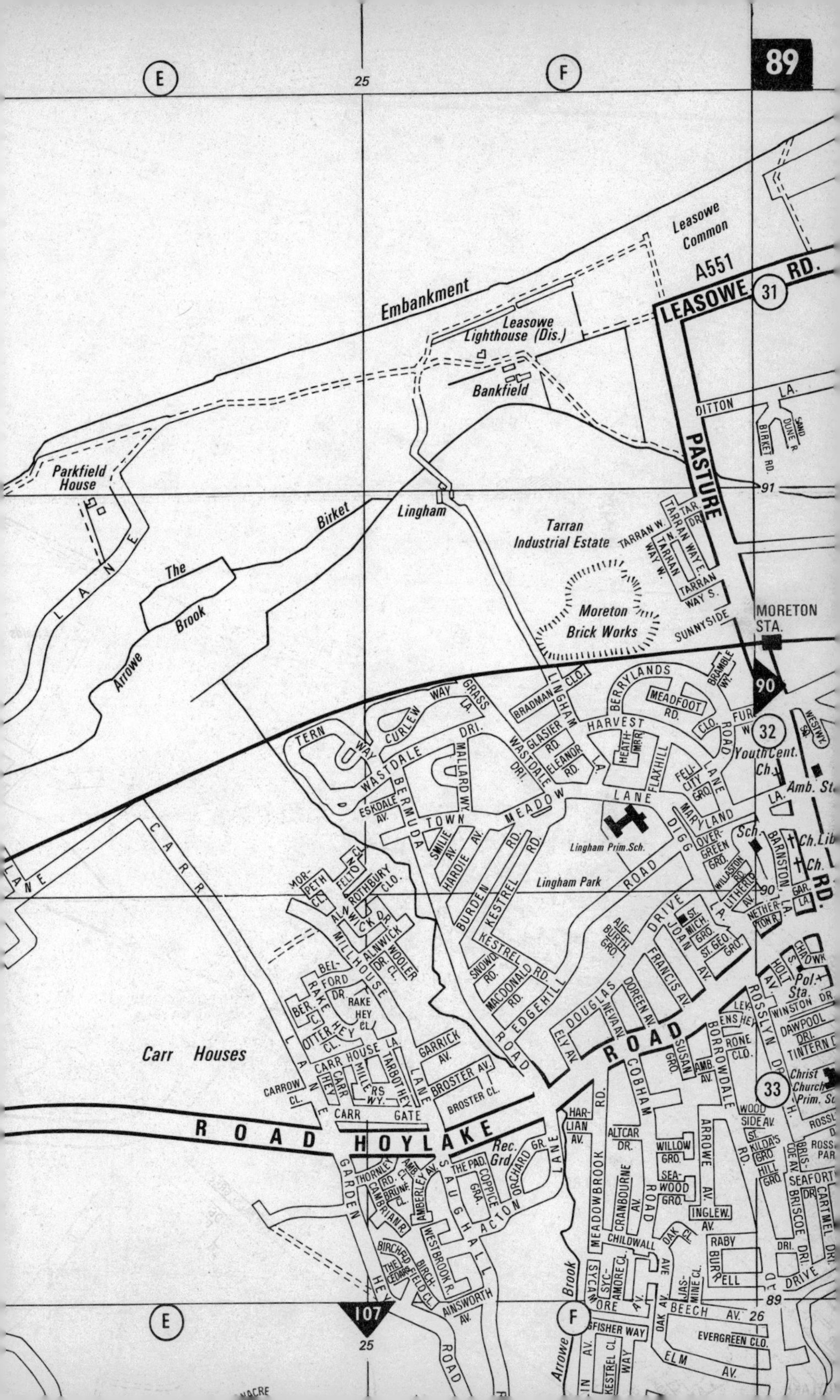
E
F
25
Leasowe Common
A551
LEASOWE RD.
31
Embankment
Leasowe Lighthouse (Dis.)
Bankfield
Parkfield House
DITTON LA.
BIRKET RD.
SAND DUNE R.
PASTURE
91
Lingham
Birket
LANE
The Brook
Arrowe
Tarran Industrial Estate
TARRAN W.
TARRAN WAY N.
TAR. DRI.
TARRAN WAY E.
TARRAN WAY W.
TARRAN WAY S.
Moreton Brick Works
SUNNYSIDE
MORETON STA.
90
BERRYLANDS
BRAMBLE WY.
MEADFOOT RD.
BRADMAN CLO.
LINGHAM
GRASS LA.
CURLEW WAY
TERN WAY
WASTDALE DRI.
MALLARD WY.
GLASIER RD.
HARVEST
ELEANOR RD.
HEATH-MRR.
FLAXHILL
CLO.
FELICITY GRO.
LANE
ROAD
32
Youth Cent.
Ch.
Amb. St.
MEADOW LANE
BERMUDA
ESKDALE AV.
TOWN
SMILIE AV.
HARDIE AV.
RD.
Lingham Prim. Sch.
MARYLAND
DIGG
OVERGREEN GRO.
Sch.
BARNSTON LA.
Ch. Lib
Ch.
RD.
CARR
LANE
MORPETH CL.
FELTON CL.
ROTHBURY CLO.
ALNWICK DR.
Lingham Park
BURDEN
KESTREL
WILLASTON RD.
LITHERLAND AV.
90
GAR.
NETHERTON R.
AIGBURTH GRO.
DRIVE
ST. MICH. GRO.
JOAN
ST. GEO. GRO.
FRANCIS AV.
MILLHOUSE
ALNWICK DR.
WOOLER CL.
KESTREL RD.
SNOWDON RD.
MACDONALD RD.
EDGEHILL
BELFORD DR.
RAKE
BER. CL.
RAKE HEY CL.
OTTER HEY CL.
DOUGLAS
NEVAN
DOREEN AV.
ROSSLYN DR.
HOLT AV.
Pol. Sta.
WINSTON DR.
DAWPOOL DRI.
TINTERN
Carr Houses
CARR HOUSE LA.
CARR HEY
MILLERS WY.
TARBOTHEY
GARRICK AV.
BROSTER AV.
BROSTER CL.
ROAD
ELY AV.
COBHAM
SUSAN GRO.
AMB. AV.
BORROWDALE
RONE CLO.
Christ Church Prim. Sch.
33
CARROW CL.
CARR GATE
ROAD HOYLAKE
Rec. Grd
ORCHARD GR.
HARLIAN AV.
RD.
ALTCAR DR.
WILLOW GRO.
SEAWOOD GRO.
ARROWE
WOODSIDE AV.
ST. KILDA'S GRO
HILL GRO.
BRISCOE AV.
SEAFORTH
GARDEN
THORNLEY RD.
AMB.
BRUNE CL.
CAMBRIAN R.
AMBERLEY AV.
SAUGHALL
THE PAD.
COPPICE GRA.
ACTON
LANE
MEADOWBROOK
CRANBOURNE AV.
ROAD
INGLEW. AV.
BRISCOE DR.
CARTMEL DRI.
CHILDWALL
OAK CL.
RABY DRI.
BURRELL
BIRCHFIELD
THE CEDARS
BIRCHFIELD CL.
WESTBROOK R.
HEY
Brook
SYCAMORE AV.
SYCAMORE CL.
AVE
JASMINE CL.
DRIVE
89
E
107
25
AINSWORTH AV.
ROAD
F
Arrowe
KINGFISHER WAY
KESTREL CL.
WAY
OAK AV.
BEECH AV.
26
EVERGREEN CLO.
ELM AV.

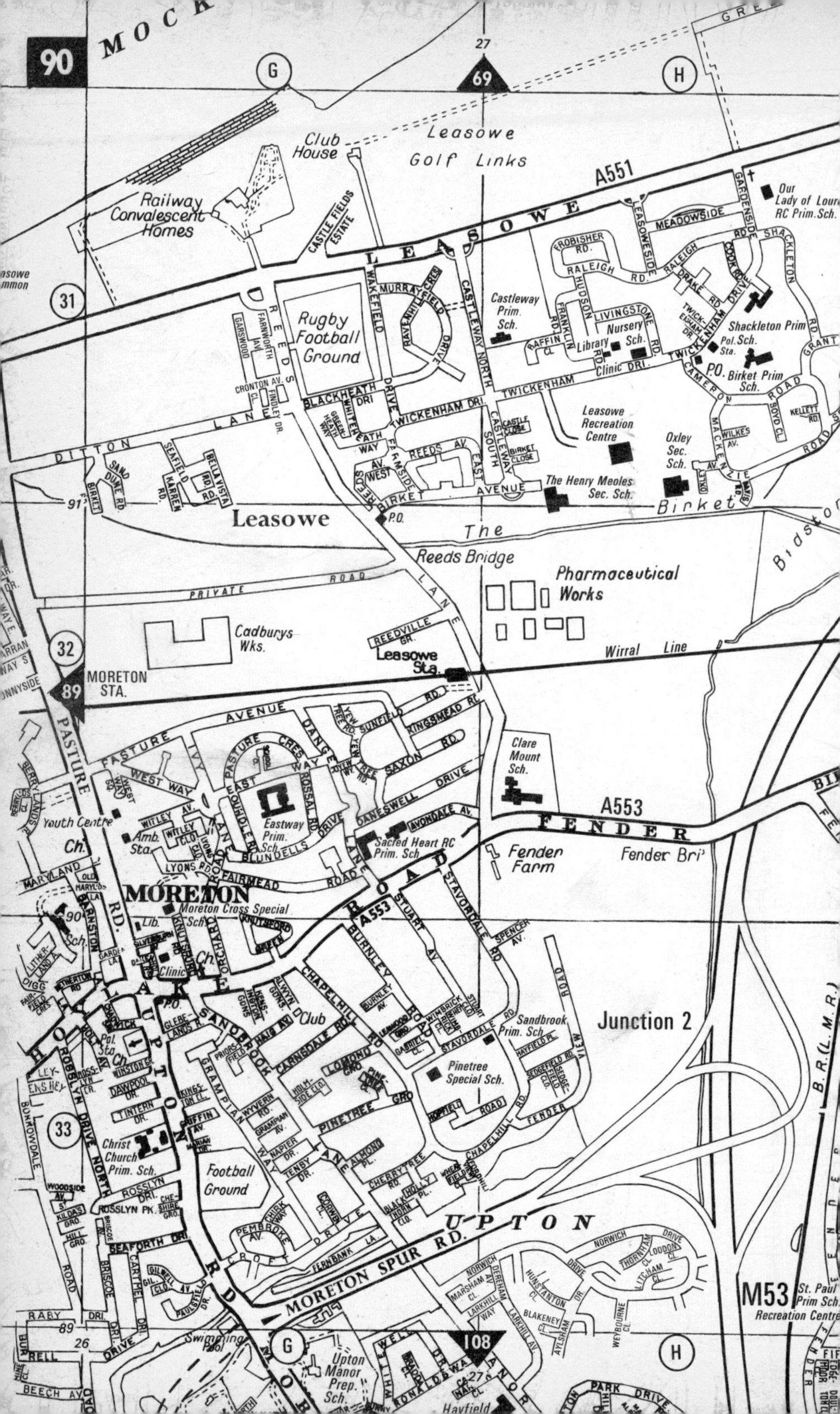

MOCK
69
27
G
H
Club House
Leasowe Golf Links
Railway Convalescent Homes
A551
LEASOWE
CASTLE FIELDS ESTATE
MEADOWSIDE
FROBISHER RD.
RALEIGH RD.
LEASOWESIDE
GARDENSIDE
SHACKLETON RD.
Our Lady of Lourdes RC Prim. Sch.
31
REEDS LANE
Rugby Football Ground
WAKEFIELD DRIVE
MURRAYFIELD DRIVE
RAVENHILL CRES.
CASTLEWAY NORTH
Castleway Prim. Sch.
HUDSON RD.
FRANKLIN RD.
RAFFIN CL.
LIVINGSTONE
Nursery Sch.
Library
Clinic DRI.
TWICKENHAM
Shackleton Prim. Sch.
Pol. Sta.
P.O.
Birket Prim. Sch.
CAMERON ROAD
GRANT RD.
GARSWOOD
FARNWORTH AV.
CRONTON AV.
FINDLEY DR.
BLACKHEATH DRI.
GREEN HEATH WAY
WHITEHEATH WAY
TWICKENHAM DRI.
CASTLEWAY SOUTH
CASTLE CLOSE
BIRKET CLOSE
Leasowe Recreation Centre
Oxley Sec. Sch.
MACKENZIE AV.
WILKES AV.
BOYD CL.
KELLETT RD.
DITTON LANE
SAND DUNE RD.
BIRKET
SEAFIELD RD.
KARREN RD.
BELLAVISTA RD.
REEDS AV.
FARMSIDE
WEST
EAST
BIRKET AVENUE
The Henry Meoles Sec. Sch.
Birket
Leasowe
P.O.
The
Reeds Bridge
Bidston
Pharmaceutical Works
PRIVATE ROAD
LANE
Cadburys Wks.
REEDVILLE GR.
Leasowe Sta.
Wirral Line
32
89
MORETON STA.
PASTURE RD.
AVENUE
PASTURE CRES.
KINGSMEAD RD.
SUNFIELD RD.
YEW TREE RD.
SAXON RD.
WEST WAY
EAST WAY
DANGER
ROSSAL RD.
Eastway Prim. Sch.
DANESWELL DRIVE
AVONDALE AV.
Clare Mount Sch.
A553
FENDER
Fender Farm
Fender Bri
BERRYLANDS RD.
Youth Centre
WITLEY AV.
WITLEY CL.
Amb. Sta.
LYONS RD.
BLUNDELLS
FAIRMEAD
ROAD
Sacred Heart RC Prim. Sch.
ROAD
STAVORDALE RD.
Ch.
MARYLAND
OLD MARYLDS
MORETON
Moreton Cross Special Sch.
BARNSTON LA.
90
Sch.
KNUTSFORD
GRIFFIN
Lib.
ORCHARD
Clinic
Ch.
STUART AV.
BURNLEY AV.
SPENCER AV.
LITHERLAND AV.
DIGG
FAIRFIELD CRES.
ETHERTON RD.
HOYLAKE
UPTON
P.O.
GLEBELANDS R.
SANDBROOK
HAIG AV.
Club
CHAPELHILL RD.
WIMBRICK CL.
STAVORDALE RD.
Sandbrook Prim. Sch.
HAYFIELD PL.
VIEW ROAD
Junction 2
Pol. Sta.
Ch.
ROBSLYN DRIVE NORTH
LEY
ENSHEY
ROSS
WINSTON GR.
DAWPOOL DR.
TINTERN DR.
KINGSTON CL.
GRAMPIAN WAY
PRIORSFIELD
CARNSDALE RD.
LOMOND GRO.
HOLMSIDE CLO.
PINEWOOD
Pinetree Special Sch.
SEDGEFIELD RD.
HOPFIELD ROAD
FENDER
CHAPELHILL RD.
B.R. (L.M.R.)
33
Christ Church Prim. Sch.
GRIFFIN
WYVERN RD.
GRAMPIAN AV.
NAPIER DR.
PINETREE GRO
ALMOND PL.
CHERRYTREE
HOLLY PL.
TENBY DR.
Football Ground
BOUNDSDALE
WOODSIDE AV.
ST. KILDAS GRO.
HILL GRO.
ROSSLYN
ROSSLYN PK.
CHESHIRE GRO.
PEMBROKE AV.
CHIRK WAY
CROFT DRIVE
FERNBANK LA.
UPTON
MORETON SPUR RD.
NORWICH
THORNHAM DRIVE
LODDON CL.
LITCHAM CL.
HUNSTANTON CL.
DEREHAM
MARSHAM AV.
LARKHILL WAY
BLAKENEY CL.
AYLSHAM DR.
WEYBOURNE CL.
M53
St. Paul Prim. Sch.
Recreation Centre
SEAFORTH DRI.
BRISCOE DRI.
CARTMEL DRI.
GILWELL AV.
PAULSFIELD DR.
RABY DRI.
89
26
BURRELL DRIVE
BEECH AV.
Swimming Pool
G
Upton Manor Prep. Sch.
108
27
RONALDS WAY
PARK DRIVE
H
Hayfield

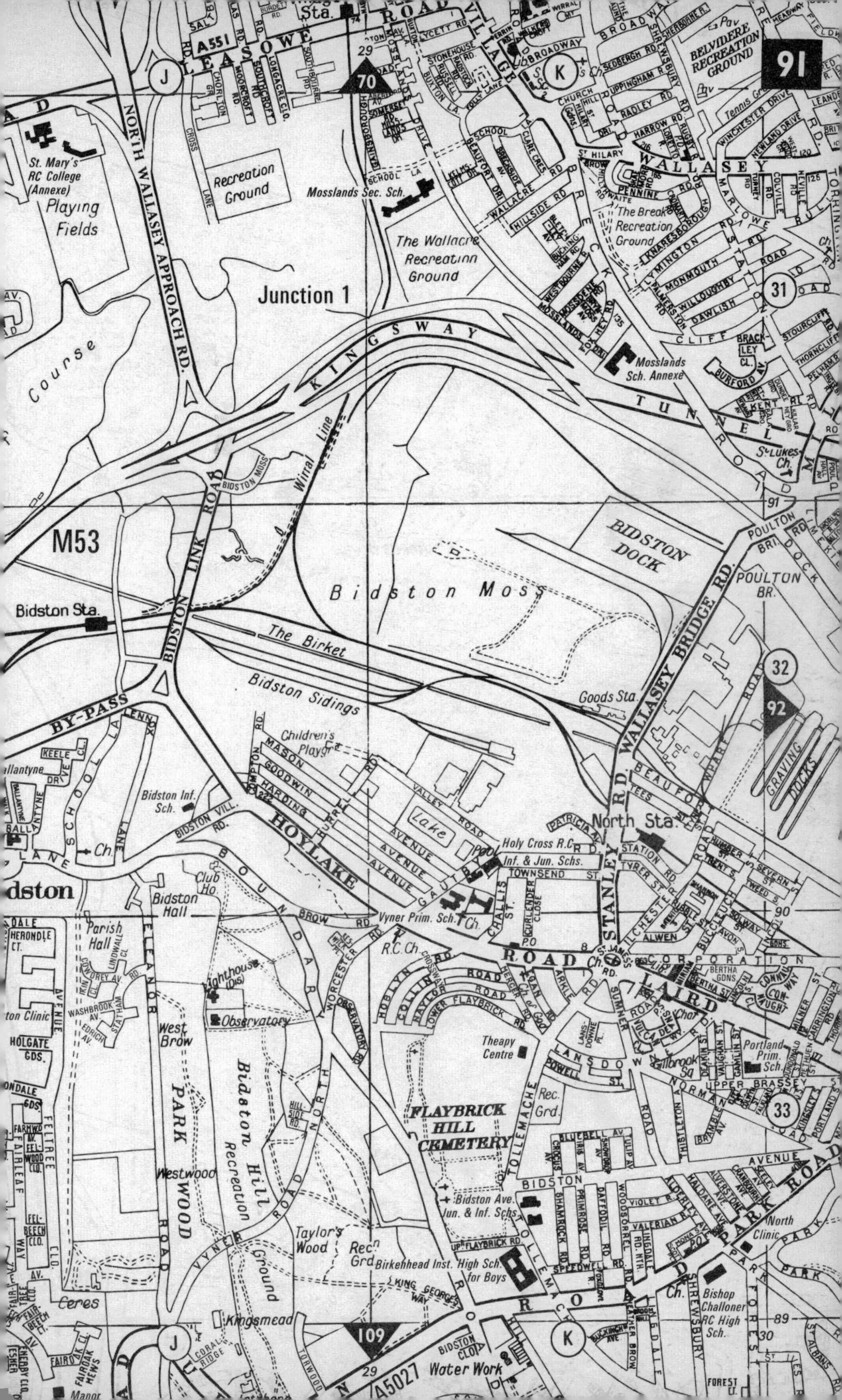
91
70
Leasowe Road
A551
Belvidere Recreation Ground
Wallasey
Broadway
St. Mary's RC College (Annexe)
Playing Fields
Recreation Ground
Mosslands Sec. Sch.
The Wallacre Recreation Ground
The Breck Recreation Ground
North Wallasey Approach Rd.
Junction 1
Kingsway
Course
Tunnel Road
Mosslands Sch. Annexe
St. Lukes Ch.
Wirral Line
Bidston Link Road
Bidston Moss
M53
Bidston Dock
Poulton Br.
Bidston Sta.
The Birket
Bidston Sidings
Goods Sta.
Wallasey Bridge Rd.
32
92
Graving Docks
By-Pass
Children's Playgr.
Lake
Valley Road
Bidston Inf. Sch.
Hoylake
North Sta.
Holy Cross R.C. Inf. & Jun. Schs.
Stanley Rd.
Bidston
Bidston Hall
Vyner Prim. Sch.
Parish Hall
Lighthouse (Dis)
Observatory
Laird
Corporation Road
Theapy Centre
Portland Prim. Sch.
33
West Brow
Park Wood
Bidston Hill Recreation Ground
Flaybrick Hill Cemetery
Rec. Grd.
Westwood
Bidston Ave. Jun. & Inf. Schs.
Taylor's Wood
Rec. Grd
Birkenhead Inst. High Sch. for Boys
King Georges Way
North Clinic
Bishop Challoner RC High Sch.
Park Road
Ceres
Kingsmead
109
A5027
Water Work
Manor

92
71
91
110
31
32
33
EGREMONT
LISCARD
LISCARD ROAD
GROSVENOR
PARK ST.
ST. ALBANS RD.
WOODSTOCK RD.
TORRINGTON
Victoria Central Hospital
Cricket Ground
Football Ground
CENTRAL PARK
A551
Wirral Metropolitan Coll.
St. John's Ch.
Park Prim. Sch.
Bowling Grn.
Recreation Ground
Health Clinic
Prim. Sch.
POULTON ROAD
Poulton
POULTON BR.
Somerville
Orrets Meadow Special Sch.
Playing Field
Kingsway Prim. Sch.
GORSEY LA.
GORSEDALE
DOCK APPROACH
Electr. Gener. Sta.
Gas Works
Wallasey Mills
OLD GORSEY LA.
Flour Mills
GRAVING DOCKS
WEST FLOAT
EAST FLOAT
Gill Brook Basin
Duke Street Bridge
Cavendish Wharf
Duke Street Wharf
Vittoria Wharf
VITTORIA DOCK
CORPORATION ROAD
CLEVELAND ST.
Refuse Destructor
Bus Depot
R.C. Prim. Sch.
OLD BIDSTON RD.
BRASSEY ST.
UPPER BRASSEY STR.
Park Sta.
DUKE ST.
PARK ROAD NORTH
A553
Birkenhead Park Rugby Union F.C.
Football Ground
North Clinic
Pond
BIRKENHEAD PARK
Refreshment Room
Boat Ho. Pond
Bowling Greens
Playing Field
Health Centre
Bishop Challoner RC High Sch.
CLAUGHTON
Tennis Ground

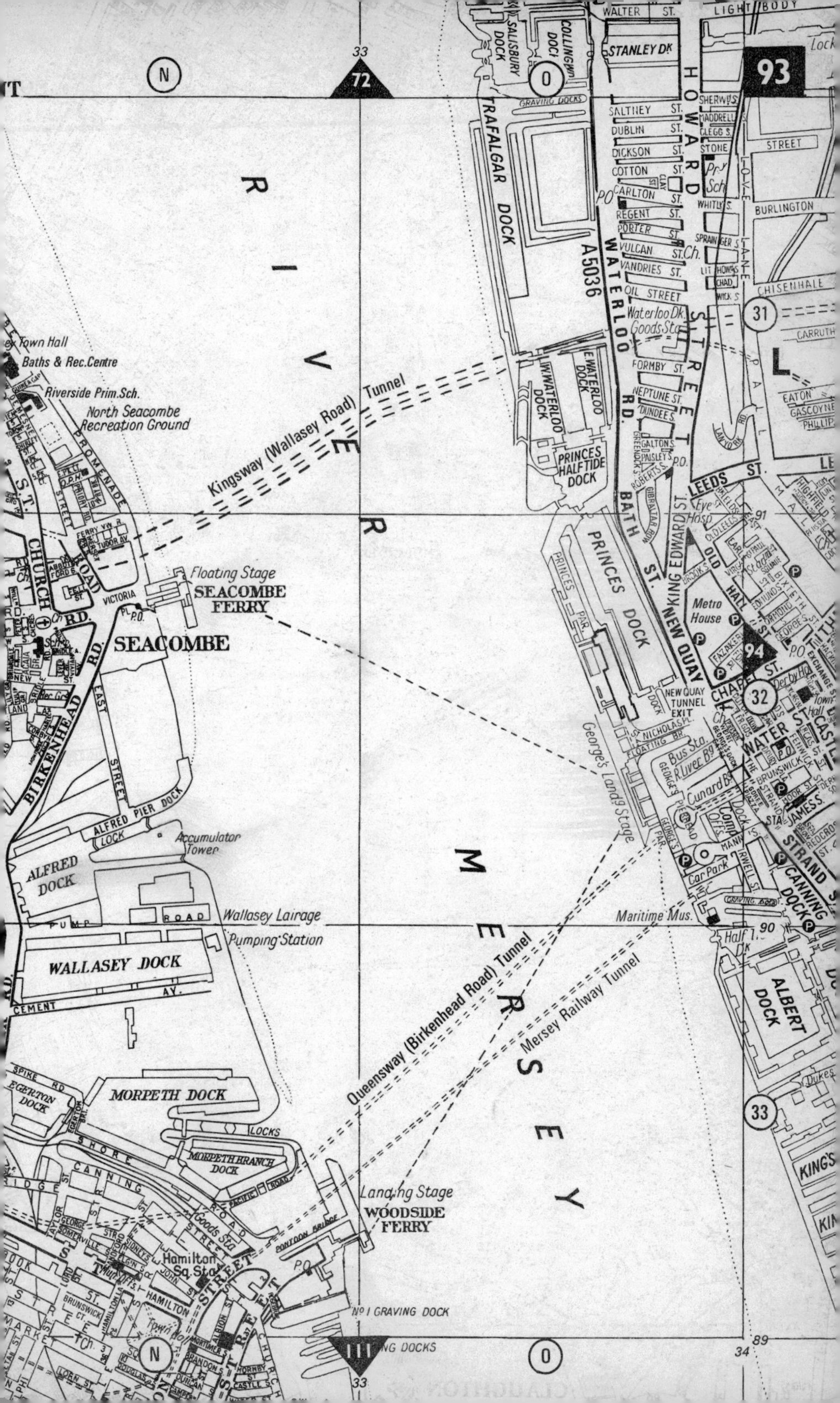

72
93
94
111
RIVER MERSEY
Kingsway (Wallasey Road) Tunnel
Queensway (Birkenhead Road) Tunnel
Mersey Railway Tunnel
SALISBURY DOCK
COLLINGWD. DOCK
STANLEY DK.
GRAVING DOCKS
TRAFALGAR DOCK
WALTER ST.
LIGHTBODY
SALTNEY ST.
DUBLIN ST.
DICKSON ST.
COTTON ST.
CARLTON ST.
REGENT ST.
PORTER ST.
VULCAN ST.
VANDRIES ST.
OIL STREET
HOWARD
STREET
BURLINGTON
CHISENHALE
A5036
WATERLOO RD.
Waterloo Dk. Goods Sta.
W. WATERLOO DOCK
E. WATERLOO DOCK
PRINCES HALFTIDE DOCK
FORMBY ST.
NEPTUNE ST.
DUNDEE S.
LEEDS ST.
BATH ST.
GIBRALTAR ROW
KING EDWARD ST.
Eye Hosp.
PRINCES DOCK
PRINCES PAR.
NEW QUAY
NEW QUAY TUNNEL EXIT
Metro House
OLD HALL ST.
CHAPEL ST.
WATER ST.
Derby Hse.
Town Hall
ST. NICHOLAS PL.
FLOATING BR.
Bus Sta.
R. Liver Bg.
Cunard Bg.
George's Landg. Stage
GEORGE'S PIERHEAD
Car Park
Maritime Mus.
STRAND ST.
JAMES S.
CANNING DOCK
Half T. Dk.
ALBERT DOCK
KING'S
Town Hall
Baths & Rec. Centre
Riverside Prim. Sch.
North Seacombe Recreation Ground
PROMENADE
CHURCH RD.
VICTORIA PL.
Floating Stage
SEACOMBE FERRY
SEACOMBE
BIRKENHEAD RD.
EAST STREET
ALFRED PIER DOCK
ALFRED LOCK
Accumulator Tower
ALFRED DOCK
PUMP ROAD
Wallasey Lairage
Pumping Station
WALLASEY DOCK
CEMENT AY.
SPIKE RD.
EGERTON DOCK
MORPETH DOCK
LOCKS
MORPETH BRANCH DOCK
SHORE RD.
CANNING ST.
Goods Sta.
Landing Stage
WOODSIDE FERRY
PONTOON BRIDGE
Hamilton Sq. Sta.
HAMILTON ST.
Town Hall
No. 1 GRAVING DOCK
GRAVING DOCKS
MARKET
33
34
89
90
91

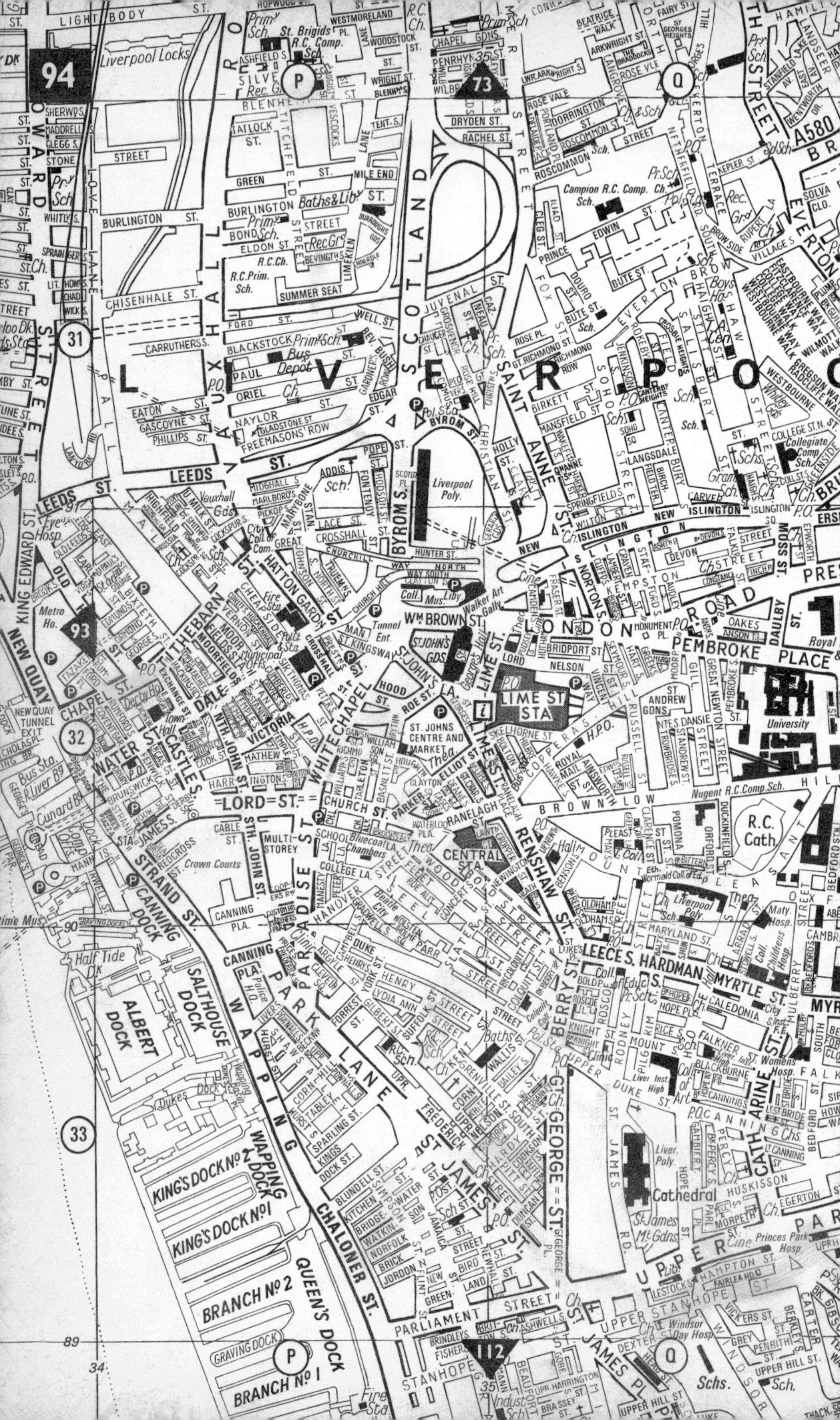

94
Liverpool Locks
LIGHTBODY ST.
HOPWOOD ST.
WESTMORELAND PL.
WOODSTOCK ST.
St. Brigids R.C. Comp. Sch.
ASHFIELD S.
P
WRIGHT ST.
CHAPEL GDNS.
PENRHYN ST.
35
73
BEATRICE WALK
FAIRY ST.
ARKWRIGHT ST.
ST. GEORGES HEIGHTS
THE BRADDOCKS
LANGROVE
ROSE VALE
LWR. ARKWRIGHT S.
Q
HAMILTON
STANFIELD
LANDSEER
WENTWORTH DR.
A580
SHERWOOD S.
MADDRELL S.
CLEGG S.
STONE
TATLOCK ST.
BLENHEIM
DRYDEN ST.
RACHEL ST.
ROSE VALE
DORRINGTON ST.
ROSCOMMON ST.
ROSCOMMON
STREET
SCOTLAND
STREET
GREEN
MILE END
BURLINGTON ST.
BURLINGTON
Baths & Liby
Campion R.C. Comp. Sch.
KEPLER ST.
SOLVA CLO.
BOND
ELDON ST.
Rec Grd
BEVINGTON S.
EDWIN
EVERTON
R.C. Ch.
R.C. Prim. Sch.
SUMMER SEAT
PRINCE
BUTE ST.
EVERTON BROW
VILLAGE S.
CHISENHALE ST.
JUVENAL ST.
FOX
DOURO
WESTBOURNE WALK
WILMOTT ST.
FORD ST.
WELL ST.
31
CARRUTHERS S.
BLACKSTOCK
Bus Depot
ROSE PL.
GT. RICHMOND ST.
RICHMOND ROW
SALISBURY
L V E R P O O
PAUL
ORIEL ST.
EDGAR
GREGSON
RADCLIFFE
WESTBOURNE
EATON ST.
GASCOYNE ST.
PHILLIPS ST.
NAYLOR
GLADSTONE ST.
FREEMASONS' ROW
BYROM ST.
CHRISTIAN
SAINT ANNE
BIRKETT ST.
MANSFIELD ST.
CANTERBURY HEIGHTS
COLLEGE ST. N.
Collegiate Comp. Sch.
LEEDS
LEEDS ST.
ADDIS. Sch.
Liverpool Poly.
HOLLY
LANGSDALE
SOHO SQ
Gram. Sch.
Vauxhall Gds.
MARYBONE
FONTENOY
SPRINGFIELD S.
ISLINGTON
CARVER
KING EDWARD ST.
Eye Hosp.
City Coll. of Com.
LACE ST.
CROSSHALL ST.
GREAT
HUNTER ST.
CHURCHILL WAY NORTH
WAY SOUTH
NEW
ISLINGTON
DEVON
STREET
MOSS ST.
EPWORTH
NEW QUAY
Metro Ho.
93
TITHEBARN
HATTON GARDEN
Fire Sta.
ST. JOHN'S GDS.
Walker Art Gally.
LONDON ROAD
MONUMENT PL.
OAKES
ANSON ST.
DAULBY ST.
Royal
MOORFIELDS
Municipal Offs.
Tunnel Ent.
Wm BROWN ST.
LIME ST.
LORD
NELSON
BRIDPORT ST.
PEMBROKE PLACE
CHAPEL ST.
DALE
HOOD ST.
ROE ST.
ST. JOHN'S LA.
LIME ST STA
ANDREW GDNS.
GREAT NEWTON STREET
University
NEW QUAY TUNNEL EXIT
Town Hall
WHITECHAPEL
ST. JOHNS CENTRE AND MARKET
SKELHORNE ST.
COPPERAS HILL
32
WATER ST.
CASTLE S.
VICTORIA
MATHEW
H.P.O.
ROYAL MAIL ST.
Bus Sta.
Liver Bg
BRUNSWICK
HARRINGTON S.
ELLIOT ST.
Nugent R.C. Comp. Sch.
HILL
Cunard Bg
LORD ST.
CHURCH ST.
PARKER
RANELAGH
BROWNLOW
POMONA
R.C. Cath
STRAND
JAMES S.
CABLE ST.
MULTI-STOREY
SCHOOL LA.
Bluecoat Chambers
CENTRAL STA.
RENSHAW
MOUNT PLEASANT
STRAND ST.
Crown Courts
COLLEGE LA.
HANOVER
WOOD ST.
Wormald Coll. of Ed.
Liverpool Poly.
CANNING DOCK
CANNING
PARADISE ST.
DUKE
BOLD ST.
Maty. Hosp.
Childrens Hosp.
MARYLAND ST.
90
GRAVING DOCKS
CANNING PLA.
Police H.Q.
HENRY
SLATER
LEECE S. HARDMAN S.
MYRTLE ST.
Half Tide Dk
SALTHOUSE DOCK
ALBERT DOCK
WAPPING
PARK LANE
LYDIA ANN
FORREST ST.
SUFFOLK ST.
BERRY ST.
RODNEY
HOPE PL.
CALEDONIA
MULBERRY
Baths
WALLIS ST.
KNIGHT ST.
RICE S.
FALKNER ST.
Womens Hosp.
Coll. of Art
BLACKBURNE
CATHARINE ST.
Dukes Dock
CORNHILL
UPR. FREDERICK
GRENVILLE ST. SOUTH
UPPER DUKE ST.
Liver Inst. High
CANNING ST.
33
WAPPING DOCK
KING'S DOCK No 2
TABLEY
SPARLING ST.
KINGS DOCK ST.
ST. JAMES ST.
ST. JAMES RD.
Liver. Poly.
Cathedral
HUSKISSON
EGERTON
KING'S DOCK No 1
BLUNDELL ST.
KITCHEN
BRIDGEWATER ST.
JAMAICA
St James Mt Gdns.
PRINCES PARK
Princes Park Hosp
QUEEN'S DOCK
BRANCH No 2
WATKINSON
NORFOLK
BRICK
JORDON
NEW BIRD ST.
GREEN LAND
UPPER
HAMPTON ST.
FAIRLEA HO.
PARLIAMENT
STREET
UPPER STANHOPE
Windsor Day Hosp
VICKERS ST.
BERKLEY S.
CARTER
89
GRAVING DOCK
P
BRINDLEYS
FISHER
112
DEXTER ST.
Q
GREY
PENRITH
UPPER HILL ST.
34
BRANCH No 1
STANHOPE
35
Indust.
BEAUFORT
UPR HARRINGTON
JAMES PL.
Schs.
Sch.
Fire Sta.
BRASSEY
UPPER HILL ST.

95
74
96
113
31
32
33
R
S
ROCKY LA.
BELMONT DRIVE
NEWSHAM DRIVE
Newsham Ho.
Boating Lake
Park Hosp.
Rec. Grd.
NEWSHAM PARK
Tennis Ground
GARDNER'S DRIVE
A5049
SHEIL PARK
SHEIL ROAD
DENMAN DRIVE
JUDGES DRIVE
BERWICK CLO.
KENLEY CLO.
WEST DERBY ROAD
BOUNDARY LANE
WHITEFIELD ROAD
Mill Road Mat. Hosp.
Greatside Spec. Sch.
St. Georges Indust. Sch.
Grafton Rooms
BUTLER CRES.
GUTHRIE WAY
PHYTHIA CLO.
MOLYNEUX ROAD
HAMPSTEAD RD.
HUNTLEY RD.
RADSTOCK RD.
SWISS RD.
GENEVA RD.
BALMORAL ROAD
PROSPECT VALE
FAIRFIELD CRES.
Cricket Ground
Band Std.
PRESCOT DR.
PRESCOT ROAD
KENSINGTON
A57
Jews Cem.
Ice Rink
HOLLY RD.
University Hall
KENSINGTON GARDENS
Covered Res.
Baths & Ldy.
EDINBURGH RD.
CONNAUGHT RD.
JUBILEE DRIVE
EDGE LANE
Prim. Sch.
Sec. Sch.
A5080
Bus Depot
Botanic Gardens
BOTANIC ROAD
WAVERTREE PARK
WAVERTREE BOULEVARD
LEIGH ROAD
PICTON ROAD
EDGE HILL STA.
Goods Sta.
Gas Works
SPEKELAND RD.
IRVINE ST.
Paddington Comp. Sch.
Traffic Pol. Headquarters
SMITHDOWN LANE
WAVERTREE ROAD
MYRTLE GARDENS
Edge Hill
FALKNER ST.
Nugent R.C. Comp. Sch.
TUNNEL ROAD
DURNING ROAD
EARLE ROAD
SMITHDOWN ROAD
A562
UPPER PARLIAMENT STREET
Princes Spec. Sch.
Windsor
School
LODGE LANE
KINGSLEY
TOXTETH PARK CEMETERY
WELLINGTON RD.
90
91
89
37
38

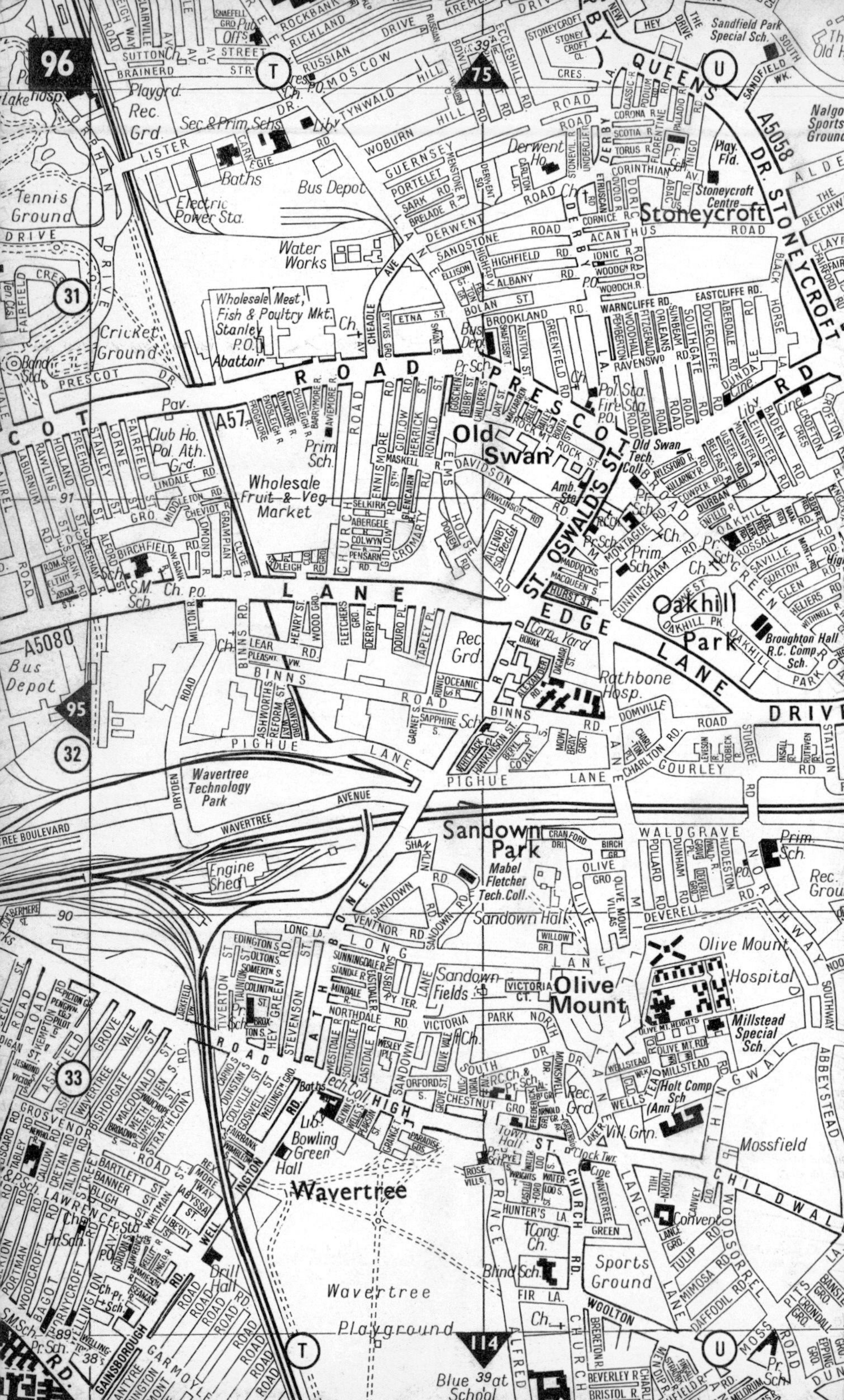

96
75
114
95
T
U
31
32
33
Stoneycroft
Old Swan
Oakhill Park
Sandown Park
Olive Mount
Wavertree
PRESCOT ROAD
EDGE LANE
A57
A5080
A5058
QUEENS DR. STONEYCROFT
Wholesale Meat, Fish & Poultry Mkt.
Wholesale Fruit & Veg. Market
Wavertree Technology Park
WAVERTREE BOULEVARD
Engine Shed
Electric Power Sta.
Water Works
Bus Depot
Cricket Ground
Tennis Ground
Rathbone Hosp.
Olive Mount Hospital
Mabel Fletcher Tech. Coll.
Sandown Hall
Sandown Fields
Broughton Hall R.C. Comp. Sch.
Millstead Special Sch.
Holt Comp. Sch.
Old Swan Tech. Coll.
Stoneycroft Centre
Sandfield Park Special Sch.
Nalgo Sports Ground
Bowling Green Hall
Wavertree Playground
Drill Hall
Blind Sch.
Sports Ground
Mossfield
Convent
Blue School

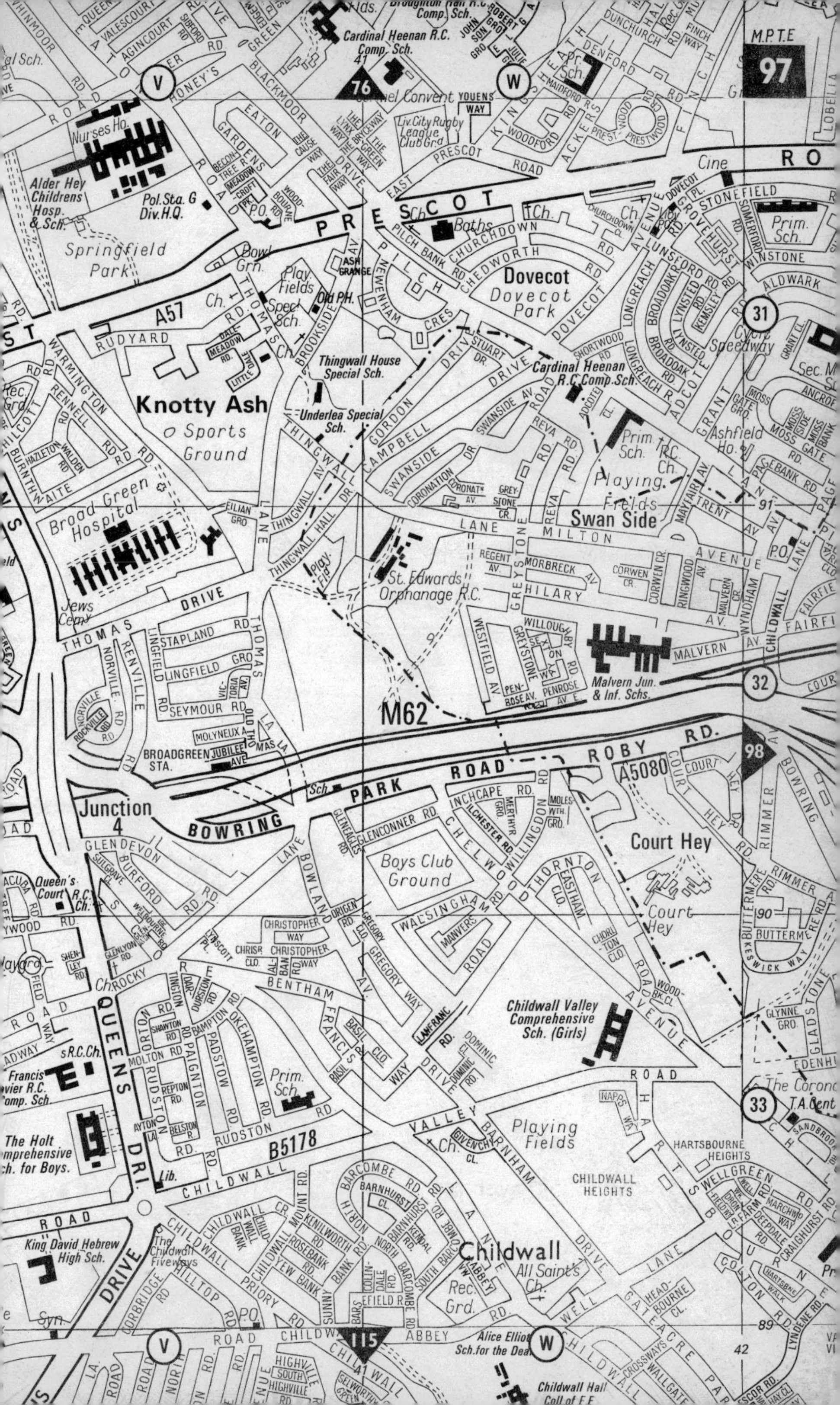

M.P.T.E
97
76
41
V
W
Cardinal Heenan R.C. Comp. Sch.
Alder Hey Childrens Hosp. & Sch.
Nurses Ho.
Pol. Sta. G Div. H.Q.
Springfield Park
PRESCOT ROAD
EAST PRESCOT ROAD
Liv. City Rugby League Club Grd.
Baths
Dovecot
Dovecot Park
Cine
Prim. Sch.
31
Cycle Speedway
A57
Knotty Ash
Sports Ground
Thingwall House Special Sch.
Underlea Special Sch.
Cardinal Heenan R.C. Comp. Sch.
Ashfield Ho.
Swan Side
Playing Fields
91
Broad Green Hospital
Jews Cemy.
St. Edwards Orphanage R.C.
Malvern Jun. & Inf. Schs.
32
M62
98
ROBY RD.
A5080
PARK ROAD
BOWRING
Junction 4
BROADGREEN STA.
Court Hey
Boys Club Ground
90
Queen's Court R.C. Ch.
Childwall Valley Comprehensive Sch. (Girls)
QUEENS DRI.
Francis Xavier R.C. Comp. Sch.
The Holt Comprehensive Sch. for Boys
Prim. Sch.
B5178
Playing Fields
33
The Coronet
T.A. Cent.
HARTSBOURNE HEIGHTS
CHILDWALL HEIGHTS
King David Hebrew High Sch.
The Childwall Fiveways
Childwall
All Saints Ch.
Rec. Grd.
89
115
Alice Elliot Sch. for the Deaf
42
Childwall Hall Coll of F.E.

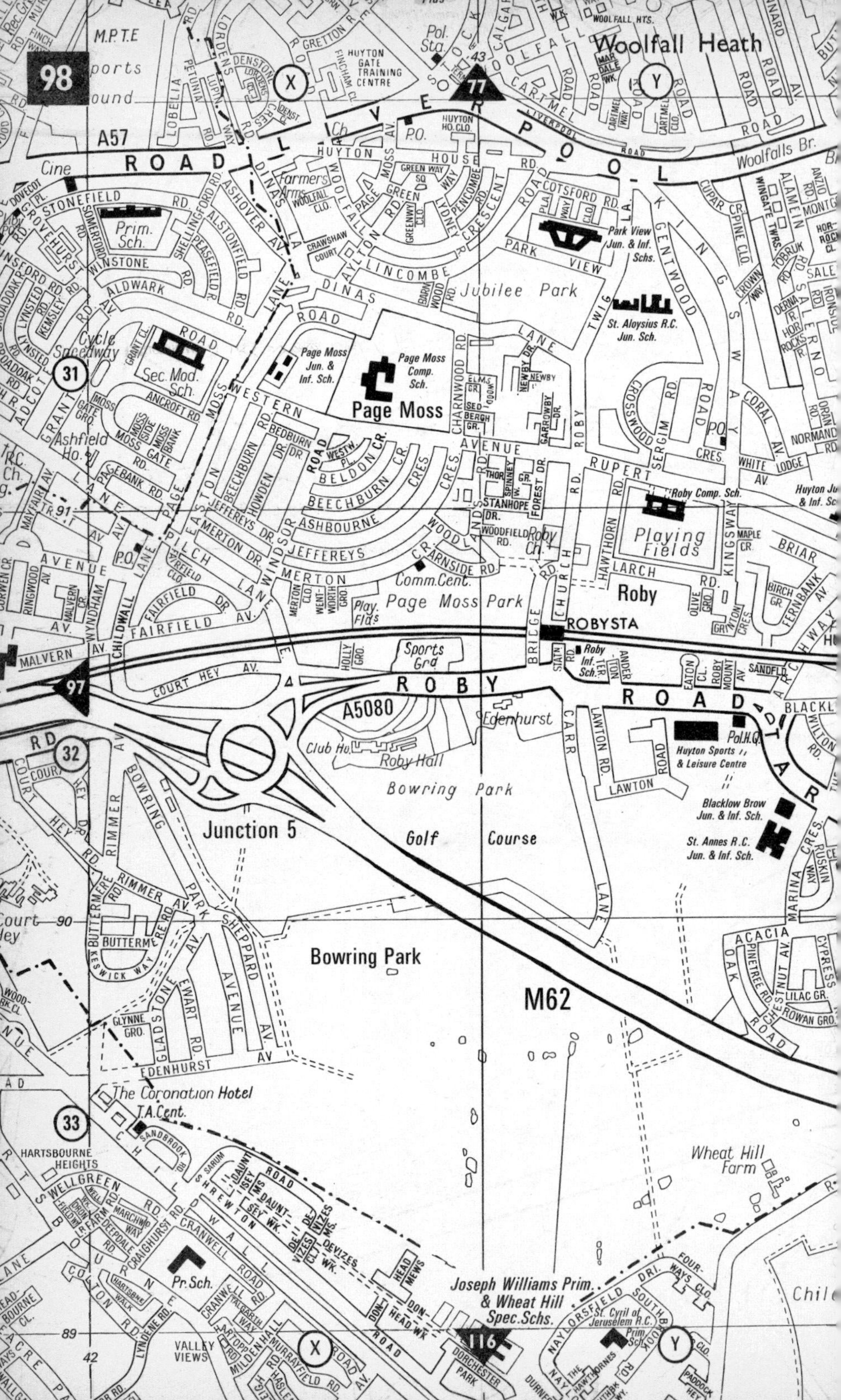
M.P.T.E
Sports Ground
Woolfall Heath
WOOLFALL HTS.
Huyton Gate Training Centre
Pol. Sta.
77
X
Y
A57
LIVERPOOL ROAD
Woolfalls Br.
Cine
Farmers Arms
P.O.
Prim. Sch.
Park View Jun. & Inf. Schs.
Jubilee Park
St. Aloysius R.C. Jun. Sch.
Cycle Speedway
Sec. Mod. Sch.
31
Page Moss Jun. & Inf. Sch.
Page Moss Comp. Sch.
Page Moss
Ashfield Ho.
R.C. Ch.
91
Roby Comp. Sch.
Playing Fields
Roby Ch.
Comm. Cent.
Page Moss Park
Roby
ROBY STA
Roby Inf. Sch.
Sports Grd
Play. Flds
Huyton Jun. & Inf. Sch.
97
ROBY ROAD
A5080
Edenhurst
Club Ho.
Roby Hall
Bowring Park
Golf Course
Pol. H.Q.
Huyton Sports & Leisure Centre
Blacklow Brow Jun. & Inf. Sch.
St. Annes R.C. Jun. & Inf. Sch.
32
Junction 5
Court Hey
90
Bowring Park
M62
The Coronation Hotel
T.A. Cent.
33
Hartsbourne Heights
Wheat Hill Farm
Pr. Sch.
Joseph Williams Prim. & Wheat Hill Spec. Schs.
St. Cyril of Jeruselem R.C. Prim. Sch.
116
89
42
Valley Views
Child

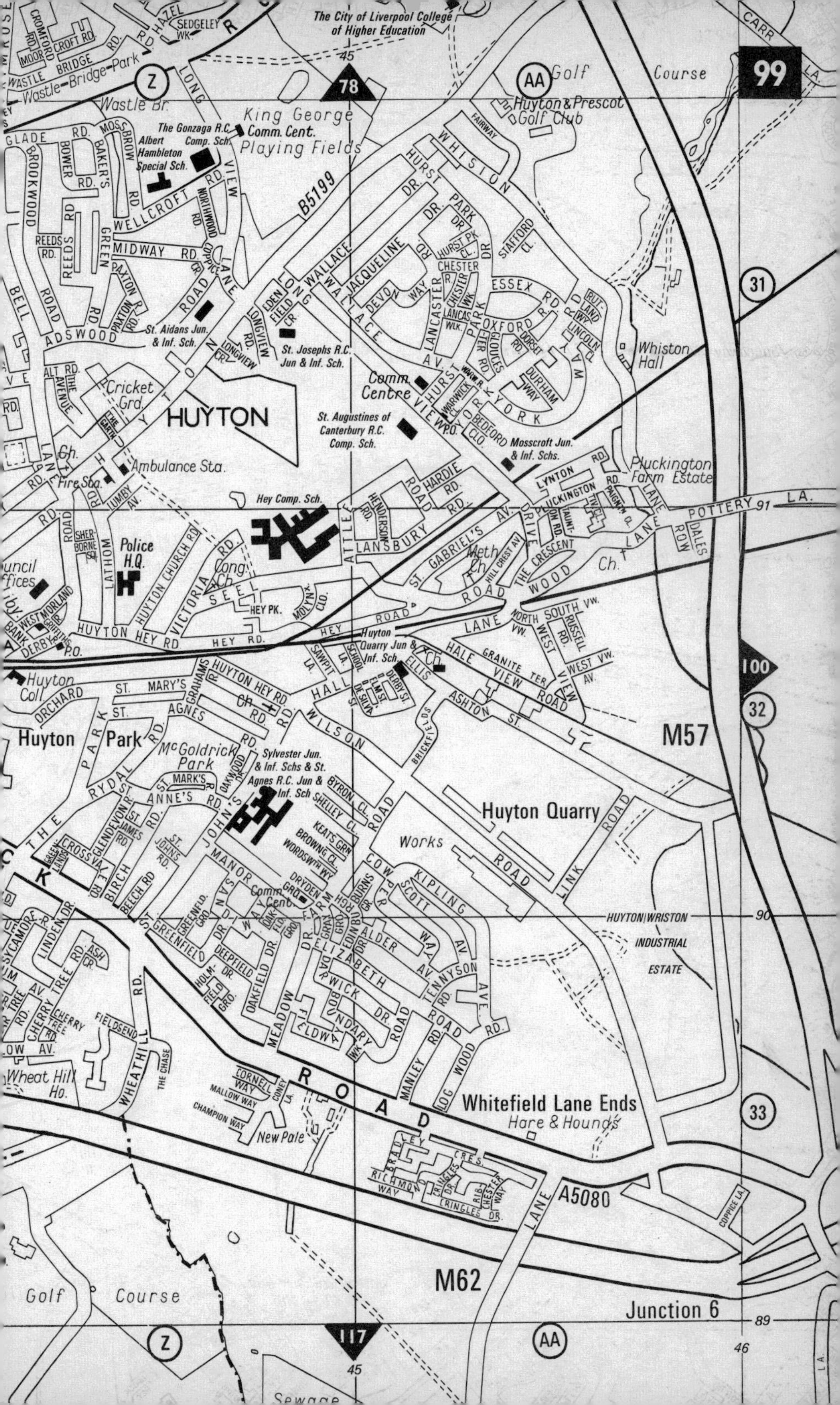

99
78
100
117
The City of Liverpool College of Higher Education
Golf Course
Huyton & Prescot Golf Club
King George Playing Fields
Comm. Cent.
The Gonzaga R.C. Comp. Sch.
Albert Hambleton Special Sch.
Wastle Bridge Park
Wastle Br.
Sedgeley Wk.
Hazel Rd.
Long
B5199
Whiston
Hurst Park Dr.
Fairway
Stafford Cl.
Wallace Dr.
Jacqueline
Devon Way
Lancaster Rd.
Chester
Essex Rd.
Oxford Rd.
Rutland Wy.
Lincoln Cl.
Durham Way
York
Bedford Clo.
Whiston Hall
St. Aidans Jun. & Inf. Sch.
St. Josephs R.C. Jun & Inf. Sch.
Comm. Centre
St. Augustines of Canterbury R.C. Comp. Sch.
Mosscroft Jun. & Inf. Schs.
Pluckington Farm Estate
Pottery La.
HUYTON
Cricket Grd.
Ambulance Sta.
Fire Sta.
Hey Comp. Sch.
Police H.Q.
Huyton Church Rd.
Victoria Rd.
Seel
Hey Pk.
Lansbury
Hardie Rd.
St. Gabriel's Av.
The Crescent
Wood Road
Lynton Rd.
Huyton Hey Rd.
Huyton Quarry Jun & Inf. Sch.
Hale View Road
Granite Ter.
Ashton St.
Wilson Rd.
Huyton Coll.
Huyton Park
McGoldrick Park
Sylvester Jun. & Inf. Schs & St. Agnes R.C. Jun & Inf. Sch
St. John's Rd.
Huyton Quarry
Works
M57
Link Road
HUYTON/WRISTON INDUSTRIAL ESTATE
Kipling Av.
Tennyson Rd.
Elizabeth Rd.
Boundary Dr.
Manley Rd.
Log Wood Rd.
Wheathill Rd.
Wheat Hill Ho.
The Chase
Cornell Way
Mallow Way
Champion Way
New Pale
ROAD
Whitefield Lane Ends
Hare & Hounds
Bradley Cres.
Richmond Way
Cringles Dr.
Ribchester Way
A5080
Coppice La.
M62
Junction 6
Golf Course
Sewage
31
32
33
Z
AA
45
46
89
90
91

100
Sewage Disposal Works
Prescot Hall
New Hall
High-hill
Sports Grd.
Citadel
79
47
Prescot CE Jun. & Inf. Sch.
Whiston
Whiston Cross
Platts Bridge
Health Cen.
Willis Jun.& Inf.Sch.
Halsnead Jun.& Inf.Sch.
St.Leo's R.C.Jun.& Inf.& Southmead Jun. & Inf. Schs.
St.Luke's R.C Jun.& Inf. Schs.
Play Area
Sandfield
M57
31
32
99
33
Rec. Ground
Princes House
Halsnead Park
Cherry Tree Farm
Fox Clump
Snape Gate Barn
Round Clump
Big Water
Carrs Farm
Windy Arbor
Junction 6
M62
Old Halsnead
Mine
Fox's Bank Cottages
CRONTON ROAD
A5080
118
BB
CC
90
89
46
47
91

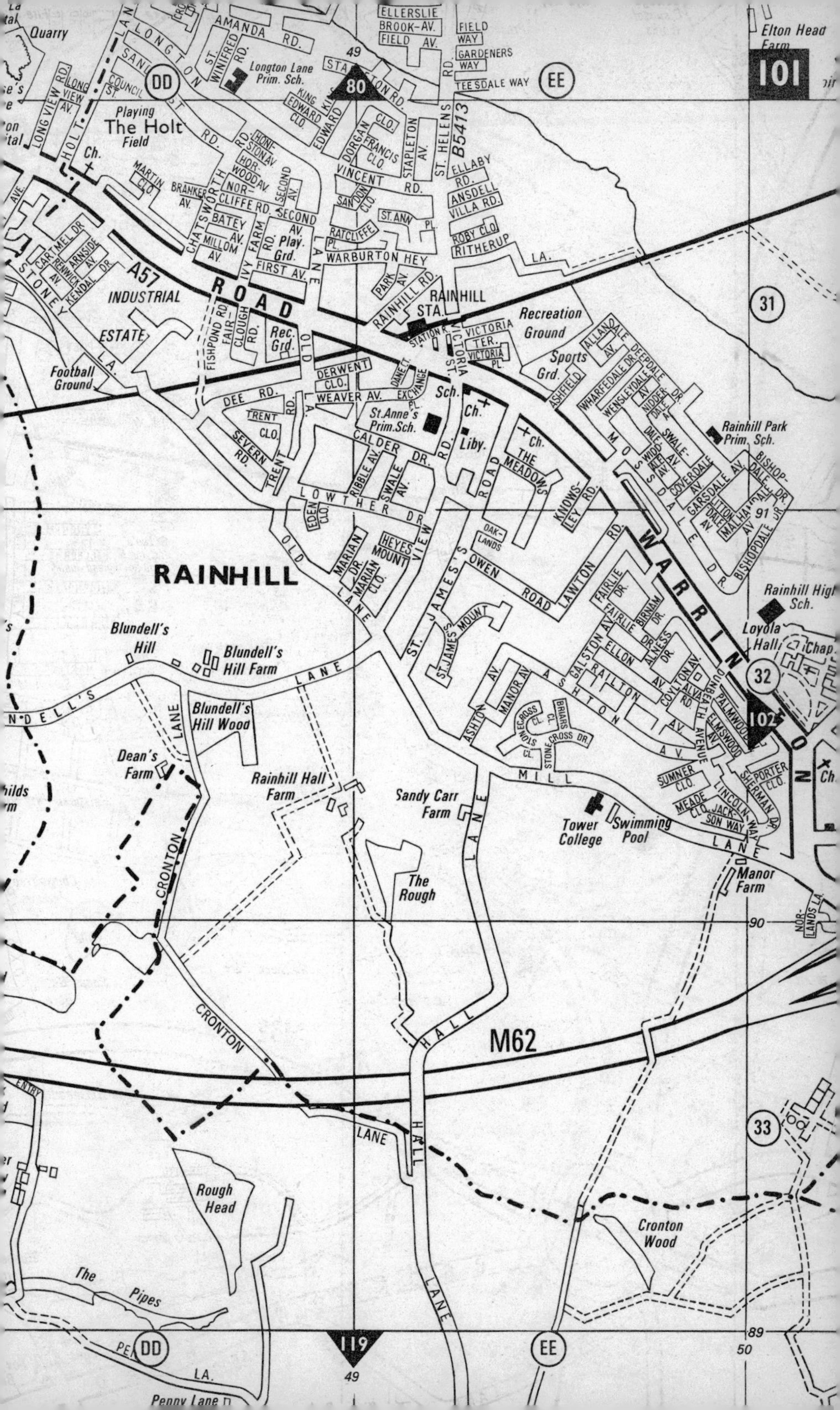

101
80
119
102
DD
EE
31
32
33
49
50
89
90
91
RAINHILL
A57
B5413
M62
WARRINGTON ROAD
RAINHILL STA.
Quarry
The Holt Playing Field
INDUSTRIAL ESTATE
Football Ground
Longton Lane Prim. Sch.
St. Anne's Prim. Sch.
Recreation Ground
Sports Grd.
Rainhill Park Prim. Sch.
Rainhill High Sch.
Loyola Hall
Elton Head Farm
Blundell's Hill
Blundell's Hill Farm
Blundell's Hill Wood
Dean's Farm
Rainhill Hall Farm
Sandy Carr Farm
Tower College
Swimming Pool
Manor Farm
The Rough
Rough Head
Cronton Wood
The Pipes
Penny Lane

Elton Head Farm
Reservoirs
INDUSTRIAL ESTATE
FF
81
Lea Green
GG
Marshall's Cross
CHESTER
Pendlebury Brook
Ansdell's Wood
LEA GREEN ROAD
31
Micklehead Green Farm
WALKERS LA.
Walkers Bridge
Rec.
FARNDON
BUDWORTH
ALFORD AV.
KELSALL AV.
PARK-SIDE AV.
LATHWAITE
St. The Grd.
Rainhill Park Prim. Sch.
BISHOPDALE DR.
COVERDALE AV.
GARSDALE AV.
91
Brookhouse Bridge
LANE
FOREST RD.
SCOTTS AV.
WORDSWORTH AV.
SHAKESPEARE RD.
BURNS RD.
DELAMERE AV.
EPPING AV.
BOWLAND AV.
Sutton Manor Prim. Sch.
TENNYSON
PRESTON ST.
MILTON ST.
SHELLEY ST.
DEAN WAY
ROAD
Home Farm
Rainhill High Sch.
A57
Loyola Hall
Chap
Chapel House Farm
CHAPEL
Wood's House Farm
Yew Tree Farm
Sutton Road Farm
BELL LANE
Sutton Manor
A568
101
32
MOORWAY
WHITMOOR CLO.
Rainhill Stoops
Ch.
St. Bartholomew's R.C. Prim. Sch.
M62
SCHOOL LANE
SUMNER CLO.
PORTER CLO.
MEADE CLO.
JACKSON WAY
LINCOLN WAY
HERMAN DR.
DUNBEATH AVENUE
COYLTON AV.
ALVA RD.
Manor Farm
CAXTON RD.
FAWLEY RD.
NORLANDS LA.
90
Junction 7
UNION
Union Bank Farm
JUBITS LANE
Sandhill Farm
ROAD
A57
Rainhill Pla. Farm
Old Brook Hall
WARR
Works
33
Wilmere House
NORLANDS LANE
A569
Rose Farm Cottages
Fairview House
89
50
FF
120
51
GG

103
82
53
HH
JJ
Clock Face
Willow Tree Prim. Sch.
St.Marks R.C. Prim.Sch.
CLOCK FACE ROAD
ILFRACOMBE
BIDEFORD AV.
PORLOCK AV.
TAUNTON AV.
AXBRIDGE
MINEHEAD GRO.
LEACH
TAUNTON
DUNSTER GRO.
WILLOW TREE AVE.
APPLEDORE GRO.
CROYDE PL.
SHIRWELL GRO.
BEECH AV.
ASH GRO.
CRES.
LANE
REDACRE
WHITE ACRE
PASTURE CLO.
GREENACRE CLO.
LEY CLO.
BLUE ACRE
HORNBY CRES.
DUNSOP AV.
WRAY AV.
BODDEN ST.
LINDALE AV.
FURNAGE AV.
PENDLEBURY ST.
POLLITT CR.
JERSEY ST.
AGNES ST.
LEVER ST.
BENTLEY
HAMMERSLEY ST.
LANE
Ch.
TUNSTALLS WAY
CRAWFORD CL.
BACK CRAWFORD ST.
CRAWFORD ST.
Football Grd
Cricket Grd.
P.O.
BALNIEL ST.
HALL
WILBS ST.
LINDSAY ST.
GORSEY LA.
FIELD CL.
FIELD RD.
PADDOCK GRO.
FARM CL.
FARM RD.
JAMES ST.
St.Aidan's Prim.Sch.
CRANSHAW AV.
FINCH AV.
CLO.
ABBOTS HALL
BUSHELS DR.
ECCLES GRO
OAKS CLO.
Clock Face Colliery
French Fields
31
91
Works
Currant Dam Plantation
Bushel's Farm
JOY LANE
BRIDGE RD.
Sidney Farm
M62
104
32
A570
Currant Dam Plantation
Coney Green Wood
FINGER HOUSE LANE
Union Bridge
The Cottage
Crow's Nest
ROAD
90
Tibb's Cross Cottage
CROSS LANE
Kebb's Farm
CLOCK FACE RD.
Union Bank Farm Cott.
Tibb's Cross Farm
TIBB'S
Bold Br.
Bold Bridge Cottages
Eccles Plantation
33
Holly Nursery
Nursery Farm
Holly Ho.
SCHOOL LA.
Sch.
Bold Heath Plantation
TWYFORD
Bridge Farm
ROAD
LIVER
A57
Model Farm
Bold Heath
P.O.
LA.
FERNDALE CLO.
Bold Heath Farm
89
54
121
53
ENTRY

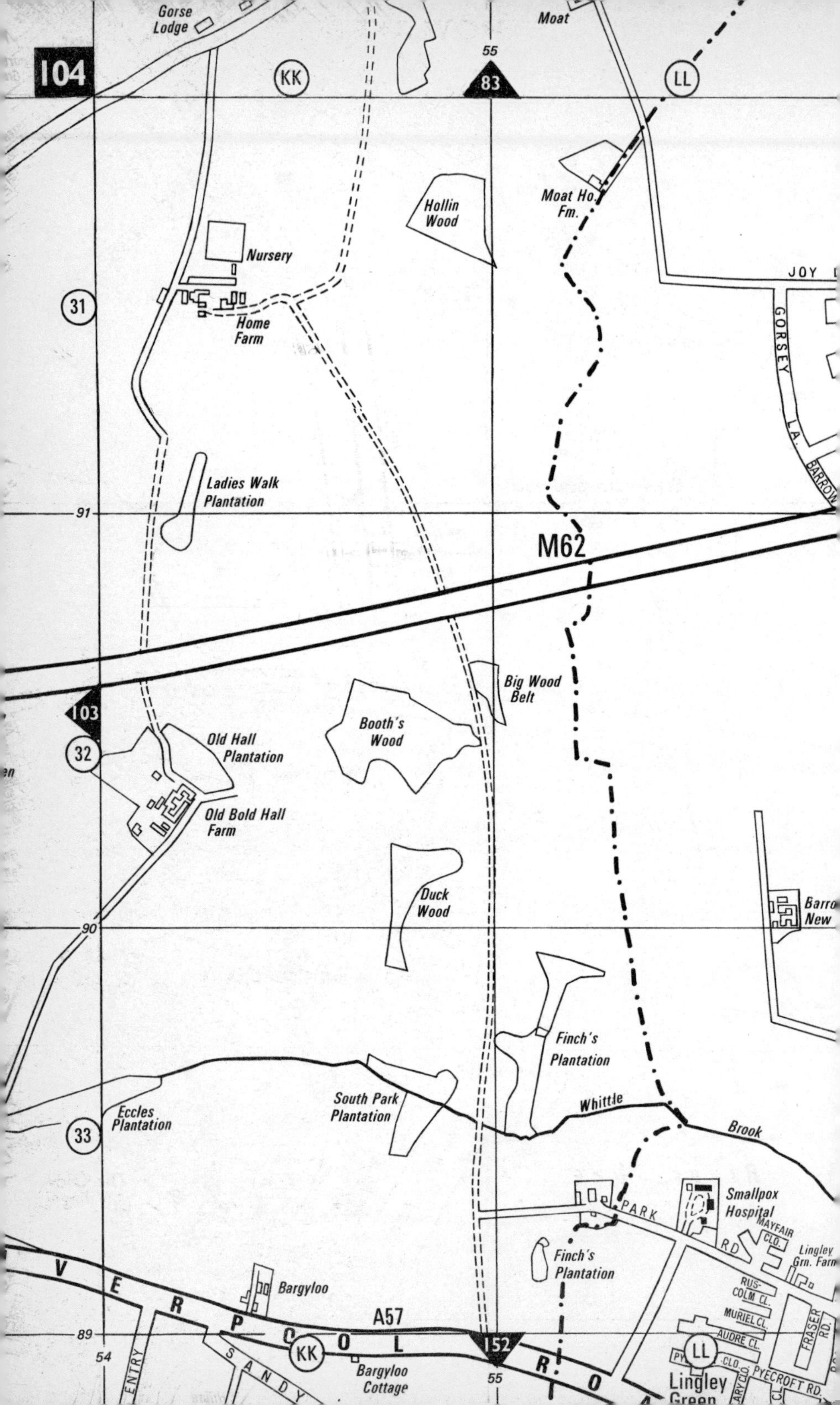

104

KK

55
83

LL

Moat

Gorse
Lodge

JOY

GORSEY LA.

Moat Ho.
Fm.

Hollin
Wood

Nursery

31

Home
Farm

BARROW

Ladies Walk
Plantation

91

M62

103

32

Big Wood
Belt

Old Hall
Plantation

Booth's
Wood

Old Bold Hall
Farm

Barro
New

90

Duck
Wood

Finch's
Plantation

Eccles
Plantation

South Park
Plantation

Whittle

Brook

33

Smallpox
Hospital

MAYFAIR

PARK

Lingley
Grn. Farm

RD.

RUS-
COLM CL.

Finch's
Plantation

MURIEL CL.

FRASER
RD.

V
E
R
P
O
O
L
R
O

AUDRE CL.

Bargyloo

A57

152

LL

PYECROFT RD.

89

54

KK

55

Bargyloo
Cottage

Lingley
Green

SANDY

ENTRY

HOYLAKE

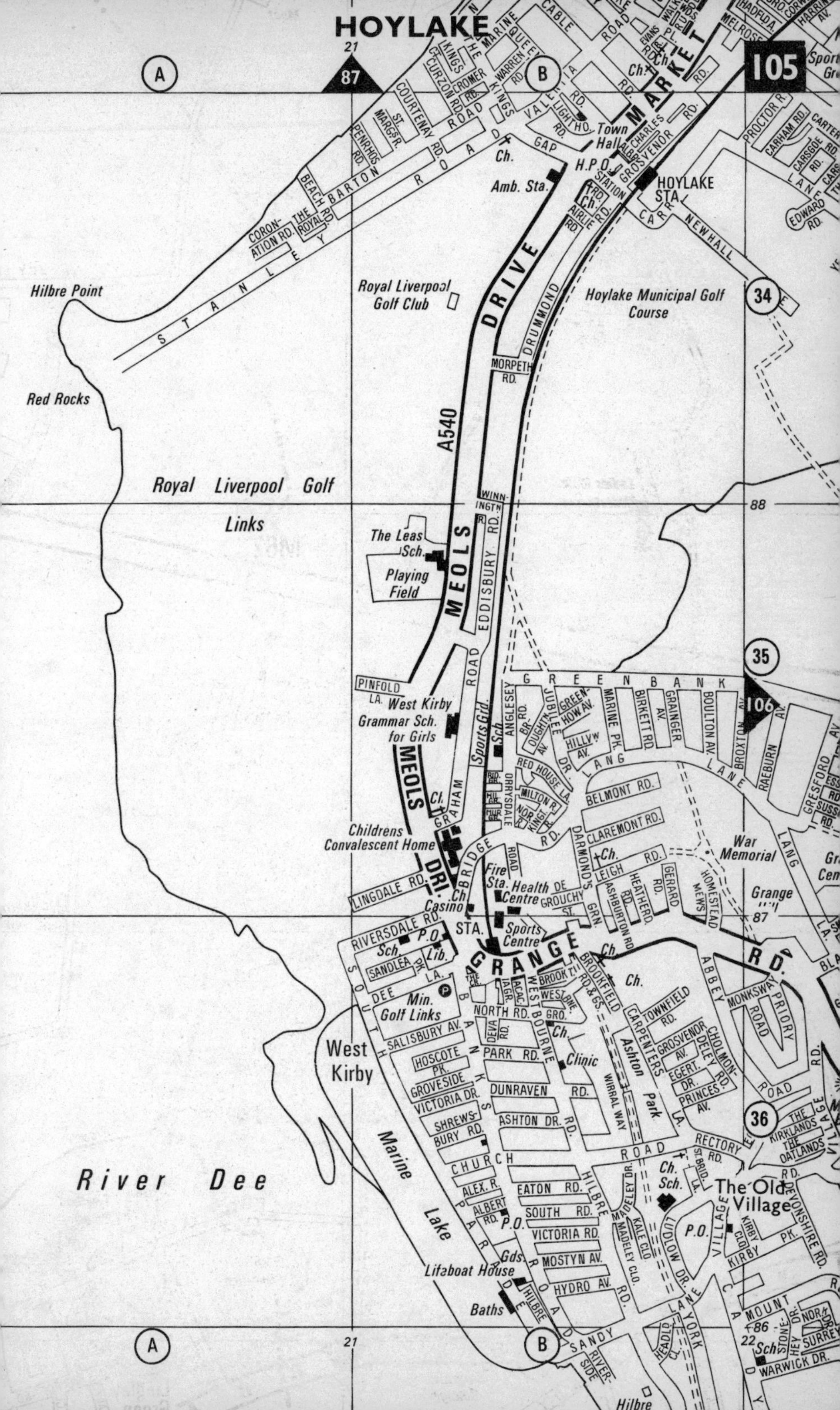

Hilbre Point

Red Rocks

STANLEY

BEACH RD

THE ROYAL RD

BARTON RD

PENRHOS RD

ST MARGS

COURTENAY ROAD

KINGS RD

CROMER

CURZON

WARREN

QUEEN

MARINE

CABLE

ROAD

KINGS RD

MARKET

Town Hall

H.P.O.

STATION RD

GROSVENOR

CHARLES

VALE RD

GAP

Amb. Sta.

HIGH HO

AIRLIE RD

Ch.

HOYLAKE STA.

CARR RD

NEWHALL

PROCTOR R.

CABHAM LANE

CASSOLE RD

CARR

EDWARD RD

105

34

DRIVE

DRUMMOND

Royal Liverpool
Golf Club

Hoylake Municipal Golf
Course

A540

MORPETH RD.

Royal   Liverpool   Golf

Links

WINN-INGTN RD.

EDDISBURY

MEOLS

ROAD

The Leas
Sch.

Playing
Field

88

PINFOLD LA.

West Kirby
Grammar Sch.
for Girls

Sports Grd.

Sch.

ANGLESEY RD

JUBILEE

GREEN HOW AV.

OSBORNE

RED HOUSE LA.

MILTON R.

NORTH R

MARINE PK.

BIRKETT RD.

GRANGER AV.

BOULTON AV.

GREENBANK

HILLV

LANE

BELMONT RD.

BROXTON

RAEBURN

106

35

CRESFORD

GRESFORD

SUSS

CAM

MEOLS DRI.

GRAHAM

BRIDGE

Ch.

Childrens
Convalescent Home

DUNSDALE

RD.

CLAREMONT RD.

Ch.

LEIGH RD

ASHBURTON

GERARD

HEATHER

CROUCHY

DARMOND'S GRN.

HOMESTEAD MEWS

War
Memorial

Grange
87

LANE

Gra
Cen

LINGDALE RD.

Casino

Ch.

STA.

Fire
Sta.

Health
Centre

DE

Sports
Centre

PRIORY

MONKSWAY

ROAD

ABBEY

GRANGE

RD.

RIVERSDALE RD.

Sch

SANDLEA

SOUTH

Lib.

P.O.

LA.

DEE

Min.
Golf Links

SALISBURY AV.

P

THE

BROOK RD

WEST BOURNE

NORTH RD.

GRO.

WESTOR

BROOKFIELD RD.

Ch.

TOWNFIELD
RD.

GROSVENOR
AV.

CARPENTERS

CHOLMON-DELEY RD

EGERT.

PRINCES
AV.

Park

ASHTON

36

KIRKLANDS

THE
OATLANDS

DEVONSHIRE RD.

LA.

West
Kirby

HOSCOTE
PK.

GROVESIDE

VICTORIA DR.

SHREWS-BURY RD.

PARK RD.

DUNRAVEN

Clinic

ASHTON DR.

RD.

WIRRAL WAY

RECTORY RD.

The Old
Village

VILLAGE

KIRBY PK.

MOUNT

River   Dee

Marine   Lake

CHURCH

ALEX. R.

ALBERT P.O.

Gds.

Lifeboat House

Baths

EATON RD.

SOUTH RD.

VICTORIA RD.

MOSTYN AV.

HYDRO AV.

HOYLAKE RD

Ch. Sch.

P.O.

HADLEY GLO.

KALE GLO.

MODLEY DR.

LUDLOW DR.

VILLAGE RD

SANDY

RIVER-SIDE

Hilbre

86

22

STONE

HEY

NOR

SURREY

WARWICK RD.

106
Football Grd.
Sports Grd.
C
88
23
D
Industrial Estate
HOYLAKE STA.
Cricket Ground
NEWHALL LANE
34
CARR LANE
SAUGHALL
ROAD
Grange
35
105
P.O.
GILROY
PATON CLO.
MASSIE
Black Horse Hill Jun. Sch.
Black Horse Hill Inf. Sch.
Hilbre Sec. Sch.
FARNDON DR.
FULTON AV.
NEWBOLD CR.
LARTON RD.
FARM CRES.
SPRINGFIELD
War Memorial
Grange Cemetery
Grange Hill
B5139
FRANKBY
QUEENSBURY
KINGSBURY
GRANGE MOUNT
Ch.
Newton
87
ENNISDALE
HILLSIDE RD.
COVERTSIDE
BEACON DRIVE
KINGSWALK
BURLINGHAM AV.
CROOME DR.
Grange
COLUMN
Mariner's Beacon
Swimming Baths
Sports Ground
SCHOOL LANE
GRAMMAR
Calday Grange Grammar Sch. for Boys
Recreation Ground
GRANGE CROSS LA.
36
The Old Village
P.O.
Liberty Park
Heather Lea
86
22
C
122
23
A540
D
B5139

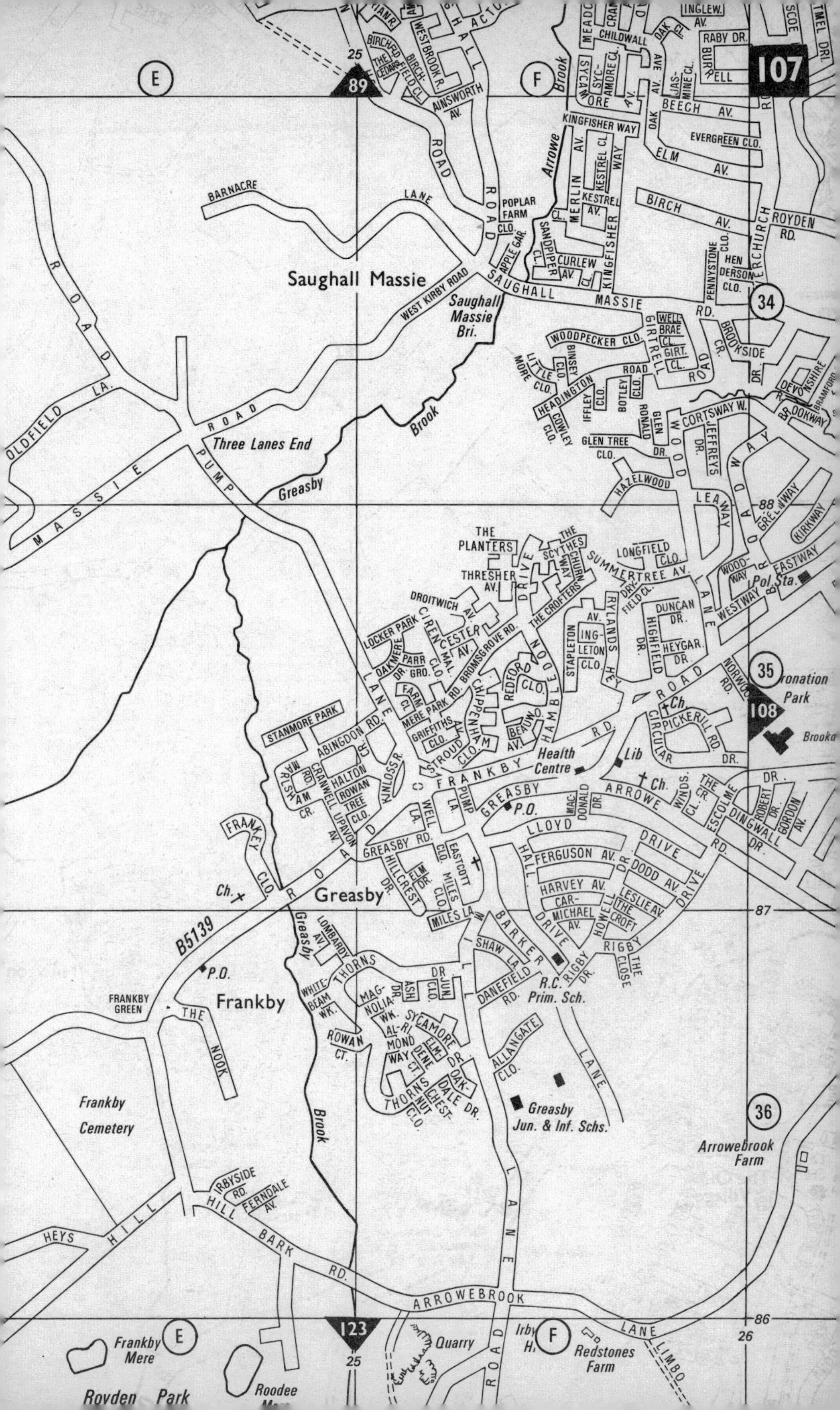

E
F
89
107
25
Saughall Massie
Saughall Massie Bri.
Three Lanes End
Greasby
Frankby
Frankby Cemetery
Frankby Mere
Royden Park
Quarry
Redstones Farm
Arrowebrook Farm
Health Centre
Lib
P.O.
Pol. Sta.
Ch.
R.C. Prim. Sch.
Greasby Jun. & Inf. Schs.
Coronation Park
B5139
34
35
36
88
87
86
26
108
123
ARROWE BROOK
GREASBY BROOK
BARNACRE LANE
SAUGHALL MASSIE RD.
WEST KIRBY ROAD
POPLAR FARM CLO.
APPLE GAR.
SANDPIPER CL.
CURLEW AV.
KINGFISHER WAY
KINGFISHER CL.
MERLIN AV.
KESTREL CL.
KESTREL AV.
BIRCH AV.
ELM AV.
EVERGREEN CLO.
BEECH AV.
SYCAMORE AV.
SYCAMORE CL.
CHILDWALL AV.
OAK AV.
JASMINE CL.
RABY DR.
BURRELL
INGLEW. AV.
ROYDEN RD.
UPTON PENNYSTONE CLO.
HENDERSON CLO.
OVERCHURCH RD.
AINSWORTH AV.
WESTBROOK R.
BIRCHFIELD CL.
THE CEDARS
ACTON
HALL ROAD
OLDFIELD LA.
MASSIE ROAD
PUMP
WOODPECKER CLO.
WELLBRAE CL.
GIRTRELL ROAD
GIRT. CL.
BROOKSIDE CR.
BROOKSIDE DR.
DEVONSHIRE
BROOKWAY
BRAMFORD
LITTLEMORE CLO.
BINSEY CLO.
HEADINGTON CLO.
COWLEY CLO.
IFFLEY CLO.
BOTLEY CLO.
RONALD RD.
GLEN DR.
GLEN TREE CLO.
CORTSWAY W.
WOODWAY ROAD
JEFFREYS DR.
HAZELWOOD
LEAWAY
GREENWAY
KIRKWAY
EASTWAY
WOODWAY
WESTWAY
THE PLANTERS
THE SCYTHES
CHURN WAY
THRESHER AV.
DRIVE
THE CROFTERS
LONGFIELD CLO.
SUMMERTREE AV.
DRYFIELD CL.
DUNCAN DR.
HIGHFIELD DR.
HEYGAR. DR.
RYLANDS HEY
STAPLETON AV.
INGLETON CLO.
DROITWICH AV.
CIRENCESTER AV.
MAL. CLO.
LOCKER PARK
OAKMERE DR.
PARR GRO.
BROMSGROVE RD.
REDFORD CLO.
HAMBLEDON
CHIPPENHAM AV.
BEAUWO. AV.
FARM CL.
MERE PARK RD.
GRIFFITHS CLO.
STROUD CLO.
STANMORE PARK
ABINGDON RD.
MARLSHAM RD. CR.
CRANWELL CR.
HALTON
ROWAN TREE CLO.
UPAVON AV.
KINLOSS R.
FRANKBY ROAD
PUMP LA.
WELL LA.
GREASBY RD.
HILLCREST DR.
ELM DR.
EASTCOTT CLO.
MILES CLO.
MILES LA.
CIRCULAR ROAD
PICKERILL RD.
ARROWE RD.
WINDS. CL.
THE CR.
ESCOLME DR.
DINGWALL DR.
ROBERT DR.
GORDON AV.
NORWOOD
MACDONALD DR.
LLOYD DRIVE
HALL
FERGUSON AV.
DODD AV.
LESLIE AV.
HARVEY AV.
CARMICHAEL AV.
HOWELL DR.
THE CROFT
BARKER DRIVE
RIGBY DR.
THE CLOSE
MILL LANE
SHAW LA.
DANEFIELD RD.
ALLANGATE CLO.
LANE
FRANKBY CLO.
LOMBARDY AV.
THORNS DR.
WHITEBEAM WK.
ASH DR.
JUN. CLO.
MAGNOLIA WK.
SYCAMORE DR.
ALMOND WAY
ELM DENE
CHESTNUT CT.
OAKDALE DR.
ROWAN CT.
THE NOOK
FRANKBY GREEN
IRBYSIDE RD.
FERNDALE AV.
HEYS HILL
HILL BARK RD.
ARROWEBROOK LANE
LIMBO
ROAD
Irby H.
Roodee Mere

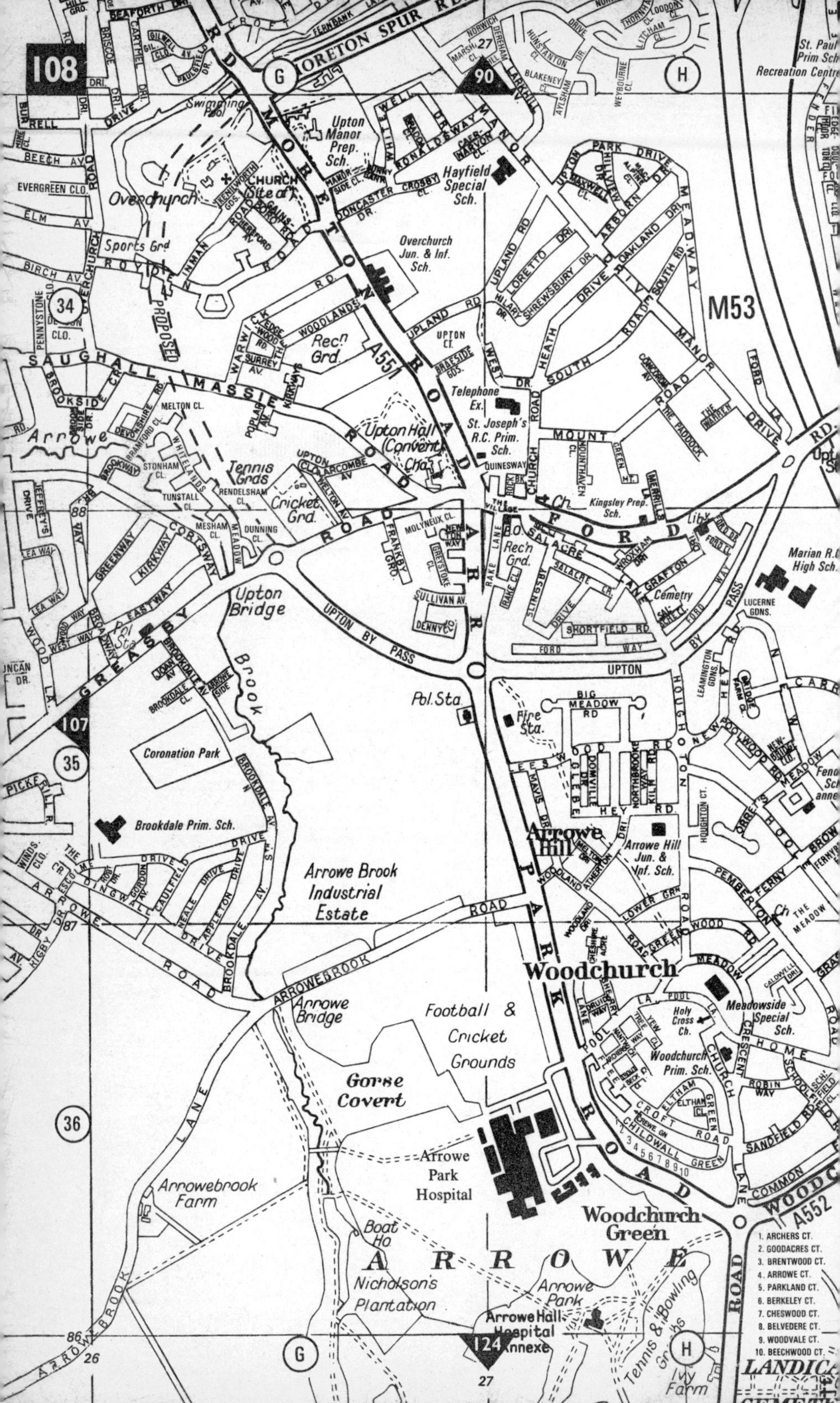

108
90
107
124
G
H
34
35
36
86
87
88
26
27
MORETON SPUR RD.
MORETON ROAD
A551
SEAFORTH DR.
CARTMEL
BRISCOE
GILWELL CLO.
PAULSFIELD DR.
FERNBANK
CROFT
NORWICH
DERHAM
MARSH CL.
HUNSTANTON CL.
BLAKENEY CL.
AYLSHAM
WEYBOURNE CL.
LITCHAM CL.
LODDON CL.
LARKHILL AV.
St. Paul's Prim Sch
Recreation Centre
BURRELL
BEECH AV.
EVERGREEN CLO.
ELM AV.
BIRCH AV.
OVERCHURCH ROAD
Swimming Pool
Upton Manor Prep. Sch.
CHURCH (Site of)
Overchurch
KENILWORTH GDS.
HEREFORD AV.
INMAN
Sports Grd
ROYDEN
PROPOSED
RONALDSWAY
CAERNARVON CL.
MANOR SIDE CL.
DONCASTER DR.
CROSBY CL.
Hayfield Special Sch.
Overchurch Jun. & Inf. Sch.
UPTON PARK DRIVE
MAXWELL CL.
HILLVIEW DR.
ARBORN DR.
OAKLAND DRI.
MEADWAY
UPLAND RD.
LORETTO DRI.
SHREWSBURY DR.
SOUTH RD.
HILARY DR.
HEATH DRIVE
M53
PENNYSTONE CLO.
SAUGHALL MASSIE ROAD
WOODLANDS RD.
EDGEWOOD RD.
SURREY AV.
WARWICK
Rec^n Grd.
UPTON CT.
BRAESIDE GDS.
WEST DR.
SOUTH DRIVE
MANOR DRIVE
FORD LA.
BROOKSIDE CR.
DEVONSHIRE RD.
MELTON CL.
POPLAR AV.
KIRKWAYS
Telephone Ex.
St. Joseph's R.C. Prim. Sch.
Upton Hall (Convent)
Cha.
CHURCH RD.
MOUNT RD.
MOUNTHAVEN CL.
GREEN MT.
THE PADDOCK
THE WARREN
Arrowe
BRAMFORD CL.
WHITELANDS
STONHAM CL.
Tennis Grds
UPTON CL.
ARCOMBE AV.
WELTON AV.
Cricket Grd.
QUINESWAY
THE VILLAGE
ROCK BK.
Kingsley Prep. Sch.
Ch.
MERRILLS
FORD DRIVE
Liby
Marian R.C. High Sch.
JEFFERYS DRIVE
LEA WAY
TUNSTALL CL.
RENDELSHAM CL.
MESHAM CL.
DUNNING CL.
MEADOW
CORTSWAY
KIRKWAY
GREENWAY
EASTWAY
WEST WAY
BROADWAY
Pol Sta
FRANKBY GRO.
MOLYNEUX CL.
NEW WAY
GREYSTOKE CL.
SULLIVAN AV.
DENNY CL.
ARROWE PARK ROAD
RAKE LANE
RAKE CL.
Rec^n Grd.
SALACRE LA.
SALACRE CR.
WROXHAM DRI.
GRAFTON DR.
Cemetery
STINGSBY DRIVE
SHORTFIELD RD.
FORD WAY
UPTON BY PASS
LUCERNE GDNS.
Upton Bridge
GREASBY ROAD
WOOD LA.
DUNCAN DR.
JOAN AV.
BROOKDALE AV.
ARROWE SIDE
Brook
Pol. Sta.
BIG MEADOW RD
Fire Sta.
HOUGHTON RD.
LEAMINGTON GDNS.
HEY RD.
NEW HEY RD.
OLDWOOD RD.
NEWBRIDGE CLO.
MEADOW
Coronation Park
LEESWOOD
MAVIS DR.
GLEBE
DOMVILLE
NORTHBROOKE WAY
KILN RD.
HEY RD.
HOUGHTON CT.
ORRETS MEADOW RD.
PICKERILL R.
Brookdale Prim. Sch.
Arrowe Hill
Arrowe Hill Jun. & Inf. Sch.
MELTON DR.
ATHERTON DRI.
WOODLAND
PEMBERTON
FERNY BROW
WINDSCLO.
THE CRESCENT
DINGWALL DR.
ROSE DR.
GORDON AV.
CAULFIELD DRIVE
NEALE DRIVE
APPLETON DRIVE
Arrowe Brook Industrial Estate
LOWER GREEN
GREENWOOD RD.
THE MEADOW
ARROWE PARK ROAD
RIGBY DR.
ARROWEBROOK ROAD
WOODLAND AV.
CHESHIRE ACRE
Woodchurch
MEADOW
CALDWELL DRI.
Arrowe Bridge
Football & Cricket Grounds
DRUIDS WAY
POOL LANE
Holy Cross Ch.
Meadowside Special Sch.
HOME
ROBIN WAY
SCHOOLFIELD RD.
YEW CL.
Woodchurch Prim. Sch.
CHURCH
ELTHAM GREEN
ELTHAM CL.
CROFT ROAD
CREWE GN
CHILDWALL GREEN
SANDFIELD RD.
Gorse Covert
Arrowe Park Hospital
COMMON
WOODCHURCH ROAD
A552
Arrowebrook Farm
LANE
Woodchurch Green
Boat Ho.
ARROWE
Nicholson's Plantation
Arrowe Park
Arrowe Hall Hospital Annexe
Tennis & Bowling Greens
Ivy Farm
LANDICAN CEMETERY
1 2 3 4 5 6 7 8 9 10
1. ARCHERS CT.
2. GODDACRES CT.
3. BRENTWOOD CT.
4. ARROWE CT.
5. PARKLAND CT.
6. BERKELEY CT.
7. CHESWOOD CT.
8. BELVEDERE CT.
9. WOODVALE CT.
10. BEECHWOOD CT.

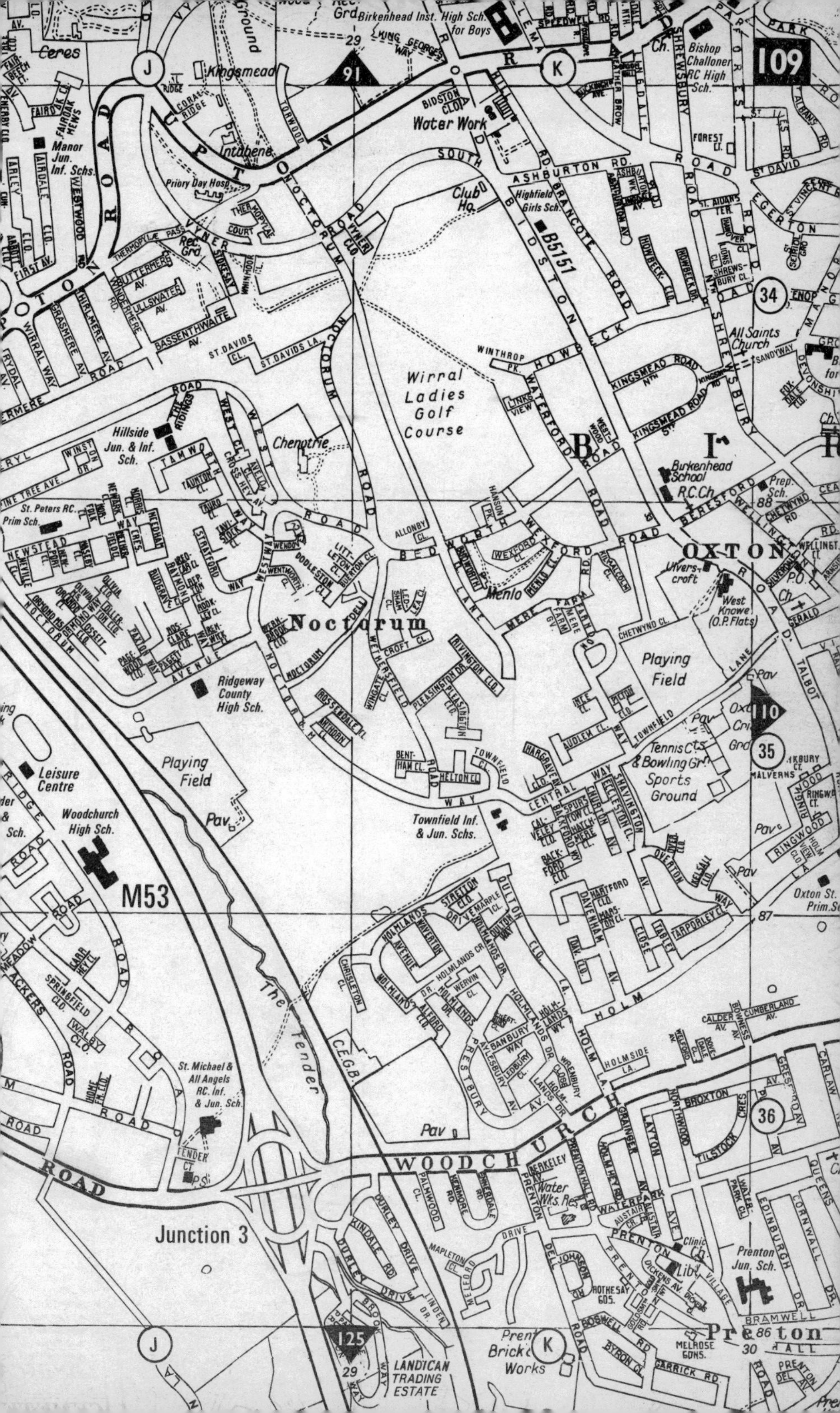

109
91
110
125
Birkenhead Inst. High Sch. for Boys
Bishop Challoner RC High Sch.
Ceres
Kingsmead
Manor Jun. Inf. Schs.
Intabene
Priory Day Hosp.
Water Work
Club Ho.
Highfield Girls Sch.
B5151
All Saints Church
Wirral Ladies Golf Course
Chenotrie
Hillside Jun. & Inf. Sch.
St. Peters RC. Prim Sch.
Birkenhead School
R.C.Ch.
OXTON
Uverscroft
West Knowe (O.P. Flats)
Menlo
Noctorum
Ridgeway County High Sch.
Playing Field
Leisure Centre
Woodchurch High Sch.
M53
Townfield Inf. & Jun. Schs.
Tennis Cts. & Bowling Gr.
Sports Ground
Oxton St. Prim.Sch.
St. Michael & All Angels RC. Inf. & Jun. Sch.
The Fender
C.E.G.B.
Junction 3
Water Wks. Res.
Prenton Jun. Sch.
Prenton
Prenton Brick Works
LANDICAN TRADING ESTATE
UPTON ROAD
NOCTORUM ROAD
BIDSTON ROAD
WOODCHURCH ROAD
SHREWSBURY ROAD
HOWBECK ROAD
WATERFORD ROAD
CENTRAL WAY
TOWNFIELD LANE
HOLM LA.
DURLEY DRIVE

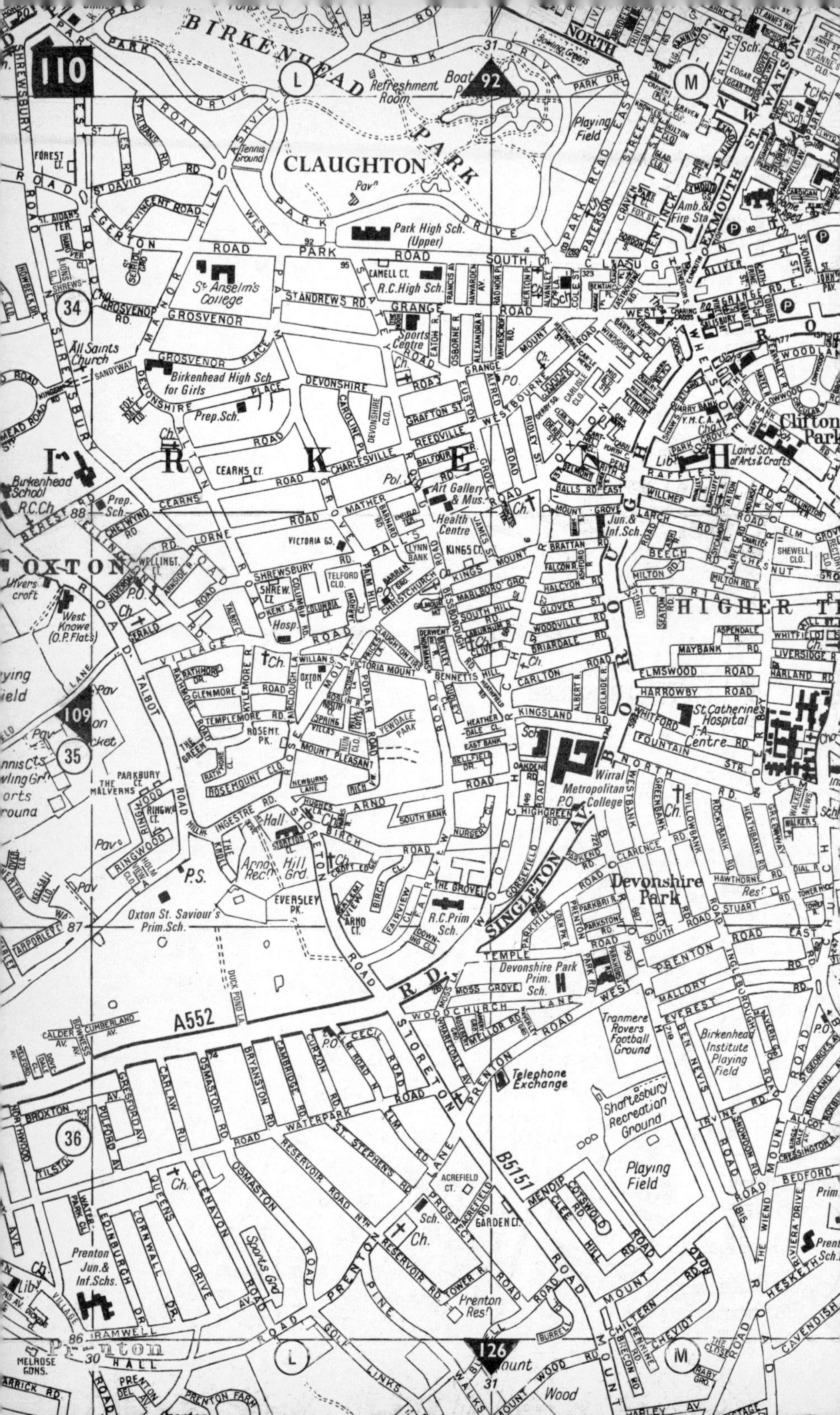

110
92
109
126
34
35
36
BIRKENHEAD PARK
CLAUGHTON
Park High Sch. (Upper)
St Anselm's College
R.C. High Sch.
Birkenhead High Sch for Girls
Birkenhead School
OXTON
Art Gallery & Mus.
Health Centre
Laird Sch. of Arts & Crafts
Clifton Park
HIGHER TRANMERE
St Catherine's Hospital
Wirral Metropolitan College
Devonshire Park
Tranmere Rovers Football Ground
Shaftesbury Recreation Ground
Birkenhead Institute Playing Field
Telephone Exchange
Prenton Jun. & Inf. Schs.
Prenton Res.
Oxton St. Saviour's Prim. Sch.
A552
B5151
Prenton

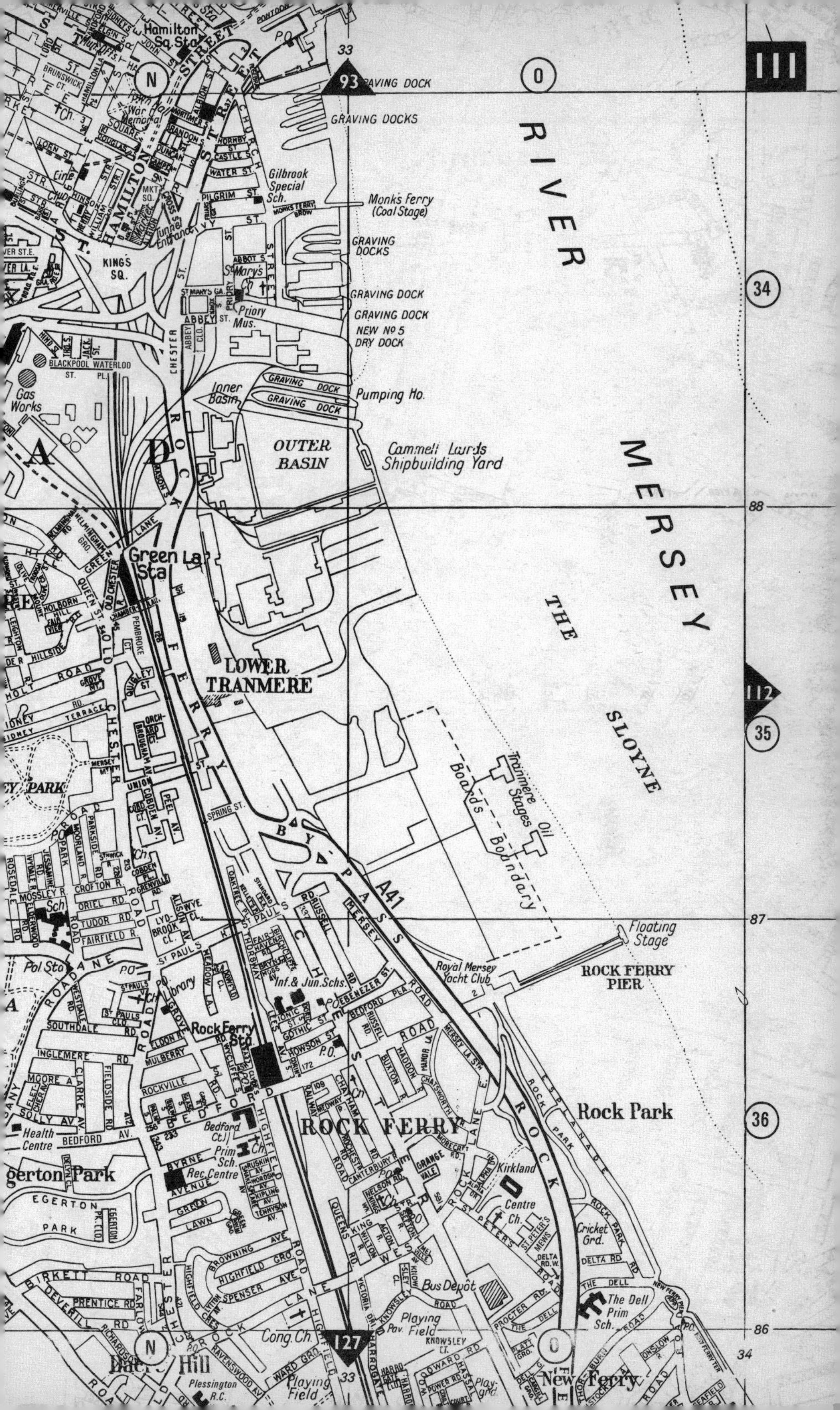

111
93
112
127
33
34
35
36
86
87
88
Hamilton Sq. Sta
Hamilton Square
War Memorial
Lorn St.
Cine
Hamilton St.
King's Sq.
Tunnel Entrance
Mkt. Sq.
Market
Church Street
Albion St.
Mortimer St.
Brandon St.
Duncan St.
Hornby St.
Castle St.
Water St.
Pilgrim St.
Monks Ferry Brow
Gilbrook Special Sch.
Monk's Ferry (Coal Stage)
Graving Dock
Graving Docks
Graving Dock
Graving Dock
New No 5 Dry Dock
Abbot St.
St. Mary's Ch.
Priory St.
St. Mary's Ga.
Abbey St.
Abbey Clo.
Priory Mus.
Chester St.
Blackpool
Waterloo Pl.
Gas Works
Inner Basin
Outer Basin
Pumping Ho.
Cammell Lairds Shipbuilding Yard
River Mersey
The Sloyne
Rock Ferry
Green Lane
Green La. Sta
Queen St.
Old Chester Rd.
Holborn Hill
Hillside
Holt Road
Grove Mt.
Sidney Terrace
Pembroke Ct.
Quigley St.
Lower Tranmere
Orchard
Brougham Av.
Mersey St.
Union St.
Cobden Av.
Peel Av.
Spring St.
By-Pass
A41
Tranmere Oil Stages
Boards Boundary
Floating Stage
Rock Ferry Pier
Royal Mersey Yacht Club
Rosedale Rd.
Mossley Rd.
Crofton R.
Oriel Rd.
Tudor Rd.
Fairfield R.
Grenville
Lydbrook Cl.
Alison Wye Cl.
St. Pauls Rd.
Oaktree Pl.
Fairhaven
Horsway
Russell Rd.
Mersey Road
Ebenezer St.
Bedford Pla.
Inf. & Jun. Schs.
Pol. Sta.
Lane
Westdale Rd.
St. Pauls Clo.
Southdale Rd.
Library
Rock Ferry Sta
Ionic St.
Gothic St.
Howson St.
P.O.
Inglemere Rd.
Moore Av.
Clarke Av.
Fieldside Rd.
Solly Av.
Eldon Rd.
Mulberry
Rockville
Wycliffe Rd.
Bedford Rd.
Health Centre
Bedford Av.
Bedford Ctl.
Prim. Sch.
Byrne Avenue
Rec. Centre
Egerton Park
Buxton R.
Haddon R.
Manor La.
Mersey La. Sth.
Chatsworth Av.
Morecroft Rd.
Grange
Canterbury
Rock Lane E.
Kirkland Centre
Ch.
Esplanade
Rock Park
Cricket Grd.
Delta Rd.
The Dell
The Dell Prim. Sch.
New Ferry Rd.
Highfield
Railway
Chatham
Queens Rd.
King
Wilton
Acton
Tennyson Av.
Kipling Av.
Ruskin Av.
Green Lawn
Browning Ave.
Highfield Gro.
Spenser Ave.
Birkett Road
Deverill Rd.
Prentice Rd.
Farlow
Richardson
Rock Lane
Bus Depot
Knowsley Rd.
Victoria Dr.
Playing Field
Pav.
Procter Rd.
St. Peter's Mews
St. Peter's Road
Cong. Ch.
Ravenswood Av.
Ward Gro.
Harrogate
Tranmere Hill
Plessington R.C.
Woodward Rd.
Power Rd.
Knowsley Ct.
Play. grd.
New Ferry
Onslow
Seafield

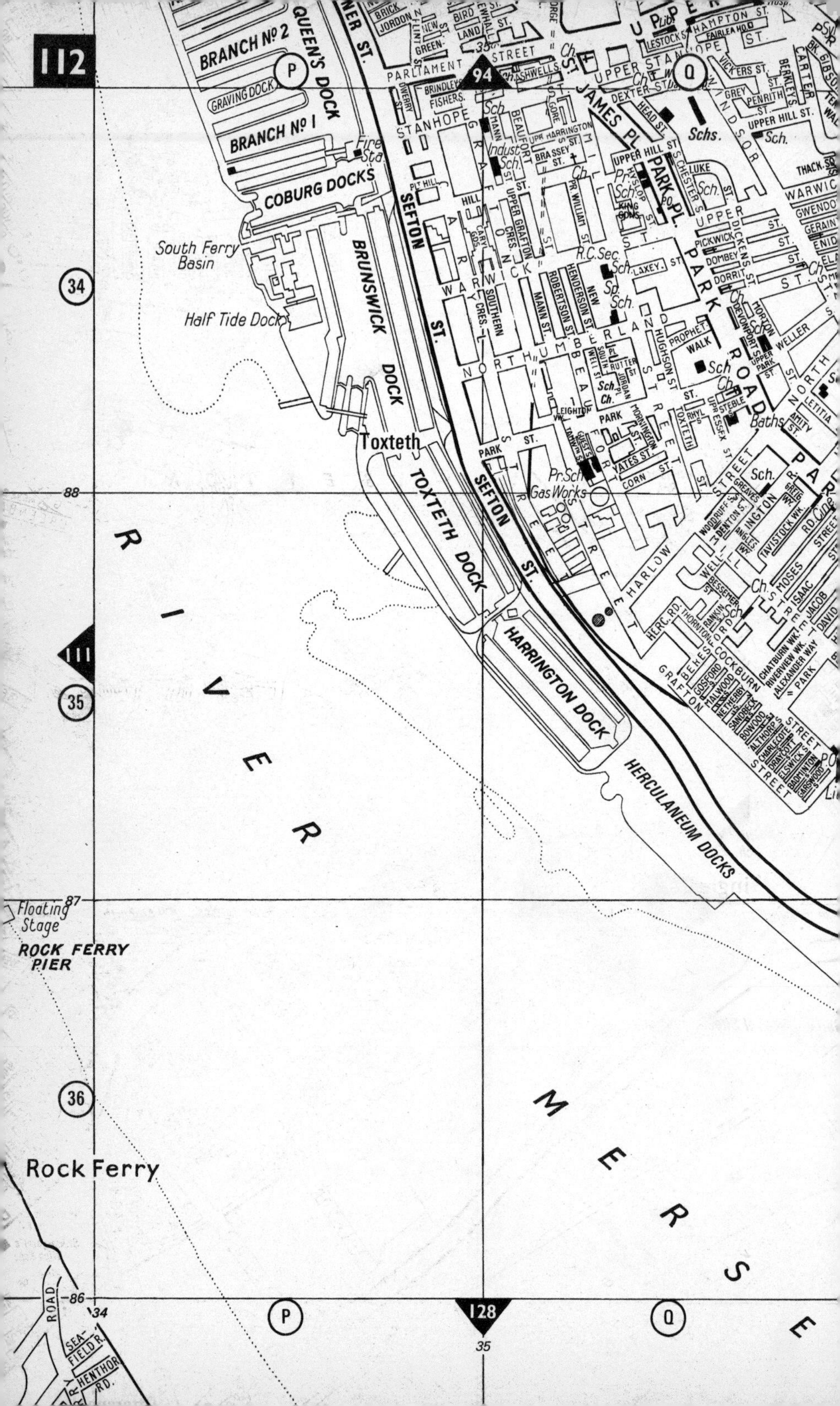
94
128
P
Q
34
35
36
88
87
86
QUEEN'S DOCK
BRANCH No 2
GRAVING DOCK
BRANCH No 1
COBURG DOCKS
South Ferry Basin
Half Tide Dock
BRUNSWICK DOCK
Toxteth
TOXTETH DOCK
HARRINGTON DOCK
HERCULANEUM DOCKS
SEFTON ST.
PARK ROAD
UPPER PARK ST.
NORTHUMBERLAND ST.
WARWICK ST.
GRAFTON ST.
PARK ST.
Gas Works
Baths
RIVER MERSEY
Floating Stage
ROCK FERRY PIER
Rock Ferry
SEAFIELD RD.
HENTHORN RD.

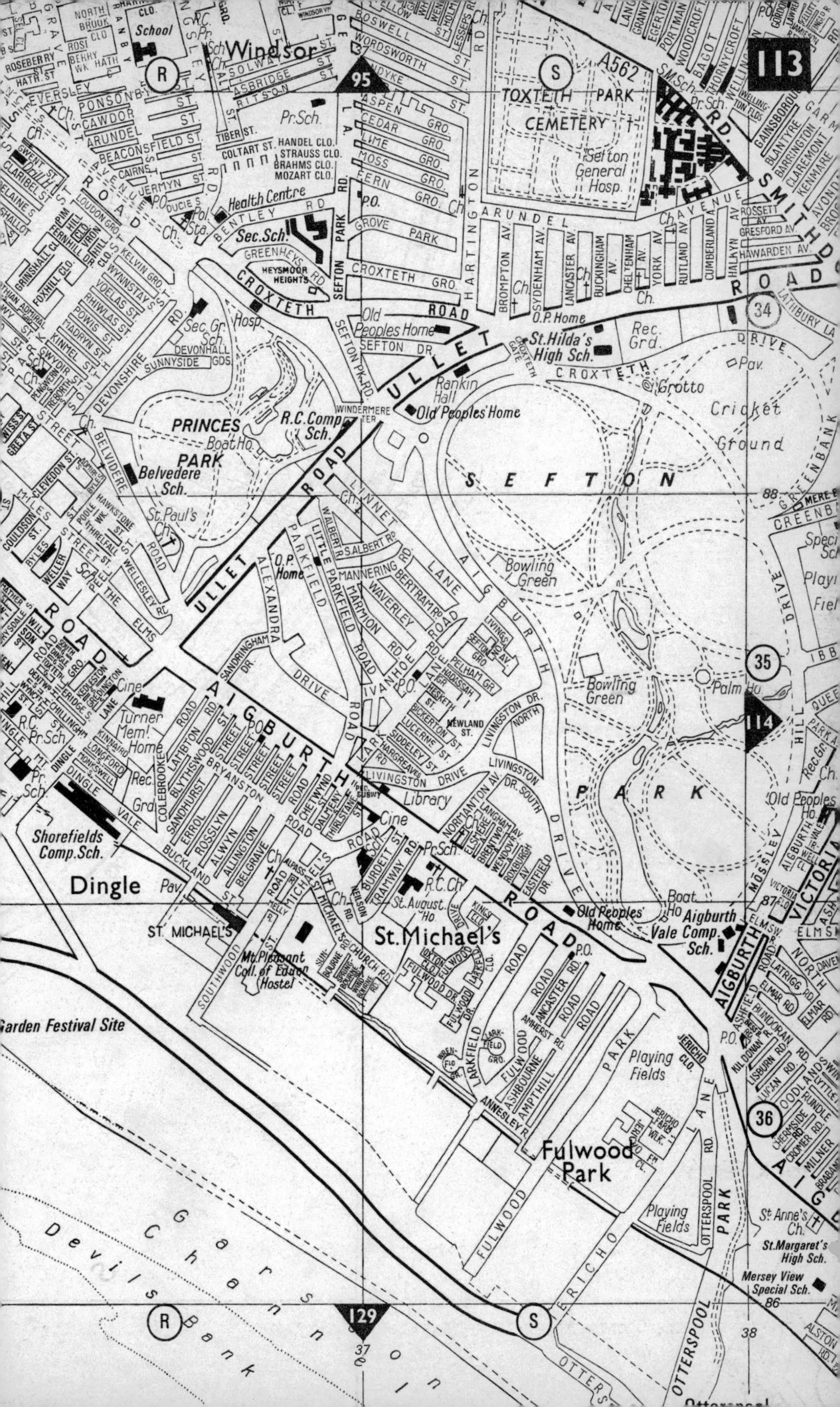

113
95
129
114
34
35
36
37
38
86
87
88
A562
Windsor
School
Health Centre
Sec.Sch.
Pr.Sch.
TOXTETH PARK CEMETERY
Sefton General Hosp.
SMITHDOWN RD.
CROXTETH ROAD
ARUNDEL AVENUE
HARTINGTON RD.
SEFTON PARK RD.
ULLET ROAD
PRINCES PARK
Boat Ho.
Belvedere Sch.
R.C.Comp Sch.
Old Peoples Home
St.Hilda's High Sch.
Rankin Hall
Grotto
Cricket Ground
SEFTON PARK
Bowling Green
Palm Ho.
Rec.Grd.
AIGBURTH ROAD
AIGBURTH DRIVE
LARK LANE
Library
Cine
Turner Meml. Home
Shorefields Comp.Sch.
Dingle
ST. MICHAEL'S
St.Michael's
Mt.Pleasant Coll.of Educn Hostel
St.August. Ho
R.C.Ch
Old Peoples' Home
Aigburth Vale Comp. Sch.
Boat Ho
Playing Fields
Fulwood Park
FULWOOD
JERICHO LANE
OTTERSPOOL RD.
OTTERSPOOL PARK
Garden Festival Site
Garston Channel
Devils Bank
St Anne's Ch.
St.Margaret's High Sch.
Mersey View Special Sch.
VICTORIA
MOSSLEY HILL
GREENBANK DRIVE

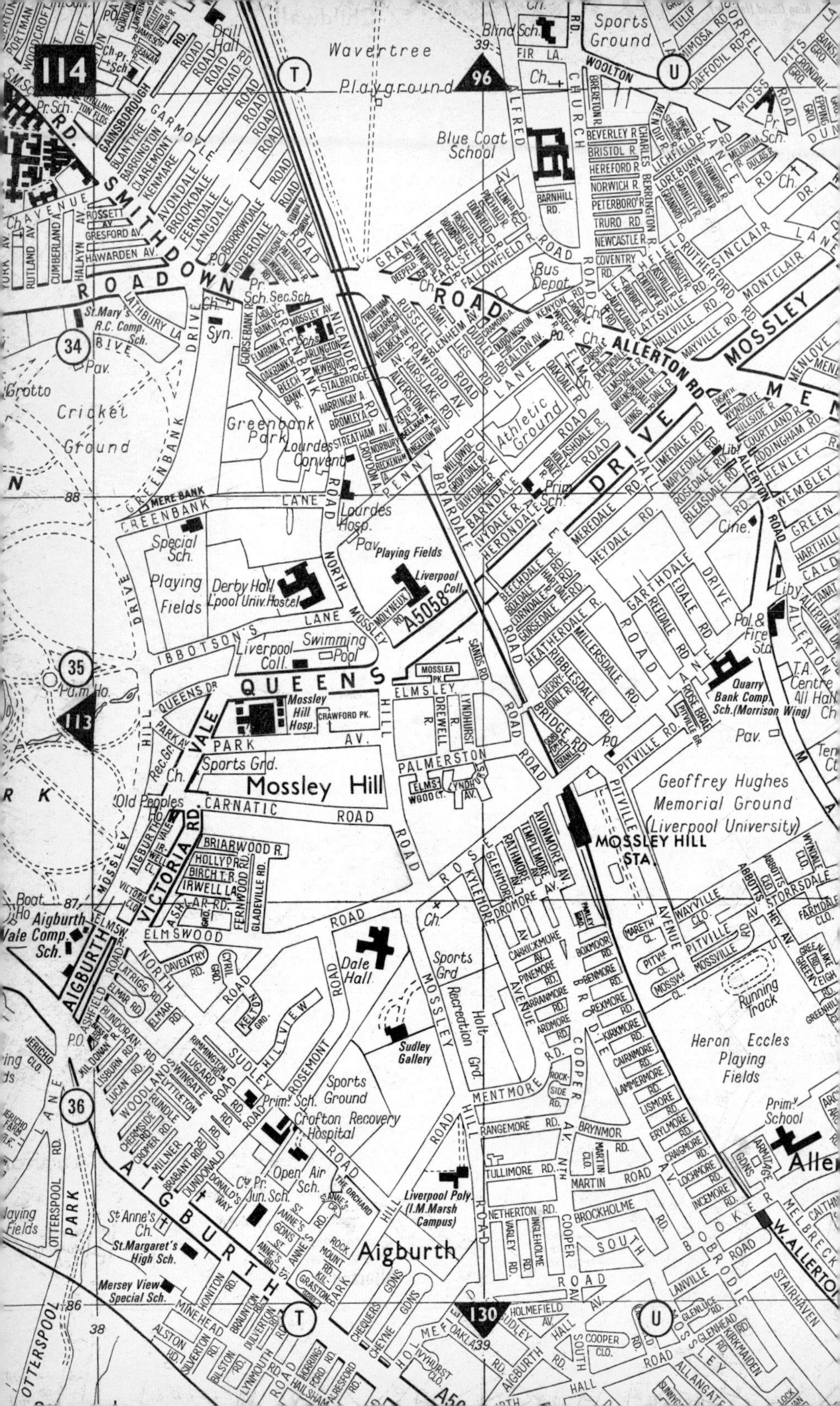

114
96
113
130
T
U
34
35
36
Wavertree
Playground
Blue Coat School
Sports Ground
Blind Sch.
Drill Hall
SMITHDOWN RD.
ROAD
DOWN
St.Mary's R.C. Comp. Sch.
Cricket Ground
Grotto
Greenbank Park
Lourdes Convent
Lourdes Hosp.
Special Sch.
Playing Fields
Derby Hall L'pool Univ. Hostel
Liverpool Coll.
Swimming Pool
A5058
QUEENS
Mossley Hill Hosp.
Mossley Hill
Sports Grd.
Old Peoples Ho.
Aigburth Vale Comp. Sch.
Dale Hall
Sudley Gallery
Recreation Grd.
Sports Ground
Crofton Recovery Hospital
Open Air Sch.
Liverpool Poly. (I.M.Marsh Campus)
Aigburth
St Anne's Ch.
St.Margaret's High Sch.
Mersey View Special Sch.
Athletic Ground
Bus Depot
ALLERTON RD
DRIVE
MOSSLEY
Quarry Bank Comp. Sch.(Morrison Wing)
Geoffrey Hughes Memorial Ground (Liverpool University)
MOSSLEY HILL STA.
Heron Eccles Playing Fields
Running Track
Prim.y School
Pal.& Fire Sta.
T.A. Centre
WOOLTON
VICTORIA RD.
AIGBURTH
PENNY LANE
ROSE LANE
MOSSLEY HILL ROAD
OTTERSPOOL PARK
W. ALLERTON

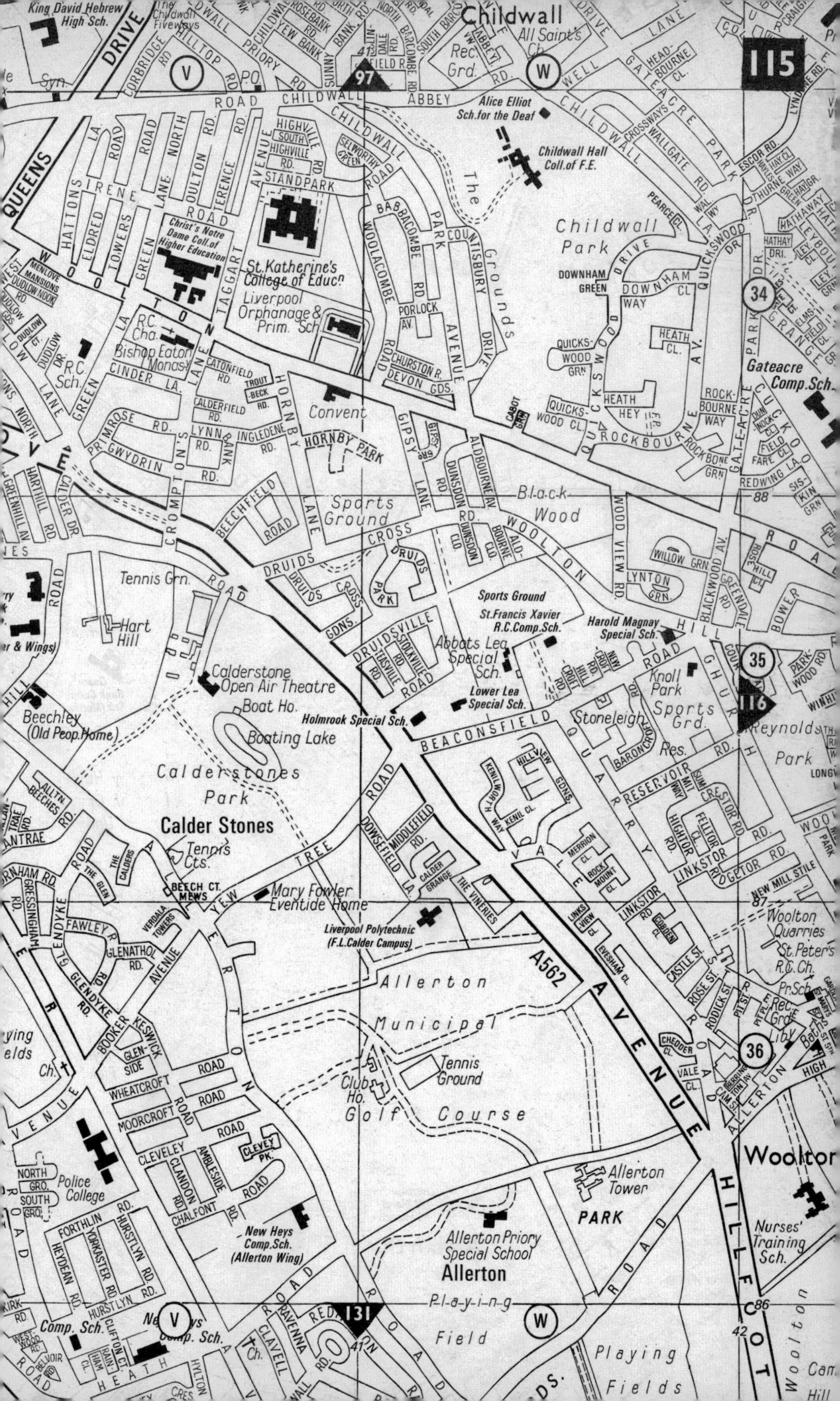
115
Childwall
All Saint's Ch.
King David Hebrew High Sch.
Syn.
The Childwall Fiveways
Rec. Grd.
Alice Elliot Sch. for the Deaf
Childwall Hall Coll. of F.E.
The Grounds
Childwall Park
Christ's Notre Dame Coll. of Higher Education
St. Katherine's College of Educn
Liverpool Orphanage & Prim. Sch.
R.C. Cha.
Bishop Eaton Monas.
R.C. Sch.
Convent
Hornby Park
Sports Ground
Black Wood
Gateacre Comp. Sch.
Tennis Grn.
Hart Hill
Beechley (Old Peop. Home)
Calderstone Open Air Theatre
Boat Ho.
Boating Lake
Calderstones Park
Calder Stones
Tennis Cts.
Sports Ground
St. Francis Xavier R.C. Comp. Sch.
Harold Magnay Special Sch.
Abbats Lea Special Sch.
Lower Lea Special Sch.
Holmrook Special Sch.
Knoll Park Sports Grd.
Stoneleigh
Res.
Reynolds Park
Mary Fowler Eventide Home
Liverpool Polytechnic (F.L. Calder Campus)
Allerton Municipal Golf Course
Club Ho.
Tennis Ground
A562
Woolton Quarries
St. Peter's R.C. Ch.
Pr. Sch.
Rec. Grd.
Liby.
Baths
Woolton
Nurses' Training Sch.
Allerton Tower Park
Allerton Priory Special School
Allerton
Playing Field
Playing Fields
Police College
New Heys Comp. Sch. (Allerton Wing)
New Heys Comp. Sch.
Comp. Sch.
Ch.
Playing Fields
Woolton Road
Queens Drive
Woolton Road
Childwall Abbey Road
Yew Tree Road
Menlove Avenue
Allerton Road
Quarry Street
Hillfoot Road
Booker Avenue
Mather Avenue
Beaconsfield Road
Hornby Lane
Druids Cross Road
Gipsy Lane
Taggart Avenue
Green Lane
Quickswood Drive
Gateacre Park Drive
Vale Road
Reservoir Road
Childwall Park Avenue
97
116
131
34
35
36
V
W
86
87
88
41
42

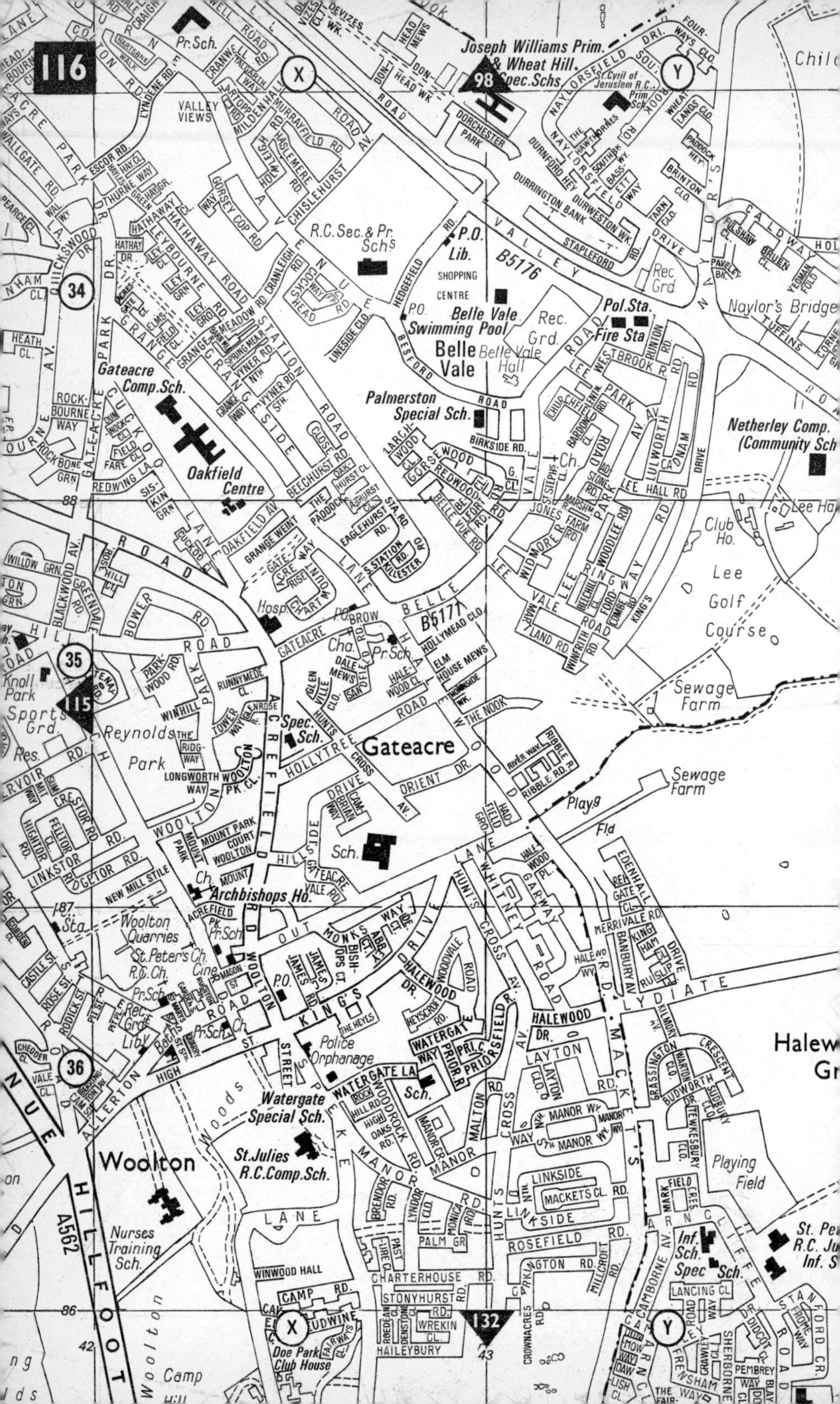

116
X
Y
98
115
132
34
35
36
Joseph Williams Prim. & Wheat Hill Spec. Schs
St. Cyril of Jerusalem R.C. Prim. Sch.
Valley Views
Pr. Sch.
R.C. Sec. & Pr. Schs
P.O. Lib.
Shopping Centre
B5176
Belle Vale Swimming Pool
Belle Vale
Belle Vale Hall
Rec. Grd.
Pol. Sta.
Fire Sta.
Naylor's Bridge
Palmerston Special Sch.
Netherley Comp. (Community Sch
Gateacre Comp. Sch.
Oakfield Centre
Lee Hall Rd
Club Ho.
Lee Golf Course
Sewage Farm
B5171
Hosp.
Gateacre
Spec. Sch.
Reynolds Park
Knoll Park Sports Grd.
Res.
Playg Fld
Sch.
Archbishops Ho.
Woolton Quarries
St. Peter's Ch.
R.C. Ch.
Cine
Police Orphanage
Watergate Special Sch.
St. Julies R.C. Comp. Sch.
Woolton
Nurses Training Sch.
A562
Hillfoot
Woolton Camp Hill
Winwood Hall
Doe Park Club House
Playing Field
Inf. Sch.
Spec. Sch.
St. Pe R.C. Ju Inf. S
Halew Gr
Station Road
Gateacre Park Dr.
Acrefield Rd.
Woolton Road
Kings Drive
Hillside Rd.
Mackets Lane
Lydiate Lane
Arncliffe Road
Naylorsfield Drive
Belle Vale Road
Lee Park Av.
Hunts Cross Av.
Manor Road
Charterhouse Rd.
Haileybury
Rosefield Rd.
Linkside
High St.
Allerton Rd.
Speke Road
Orient Dr.
Hollytree Road
Grange Lane
Cuckoo Lane
Woodlee Rd.
88
86
187
42
43

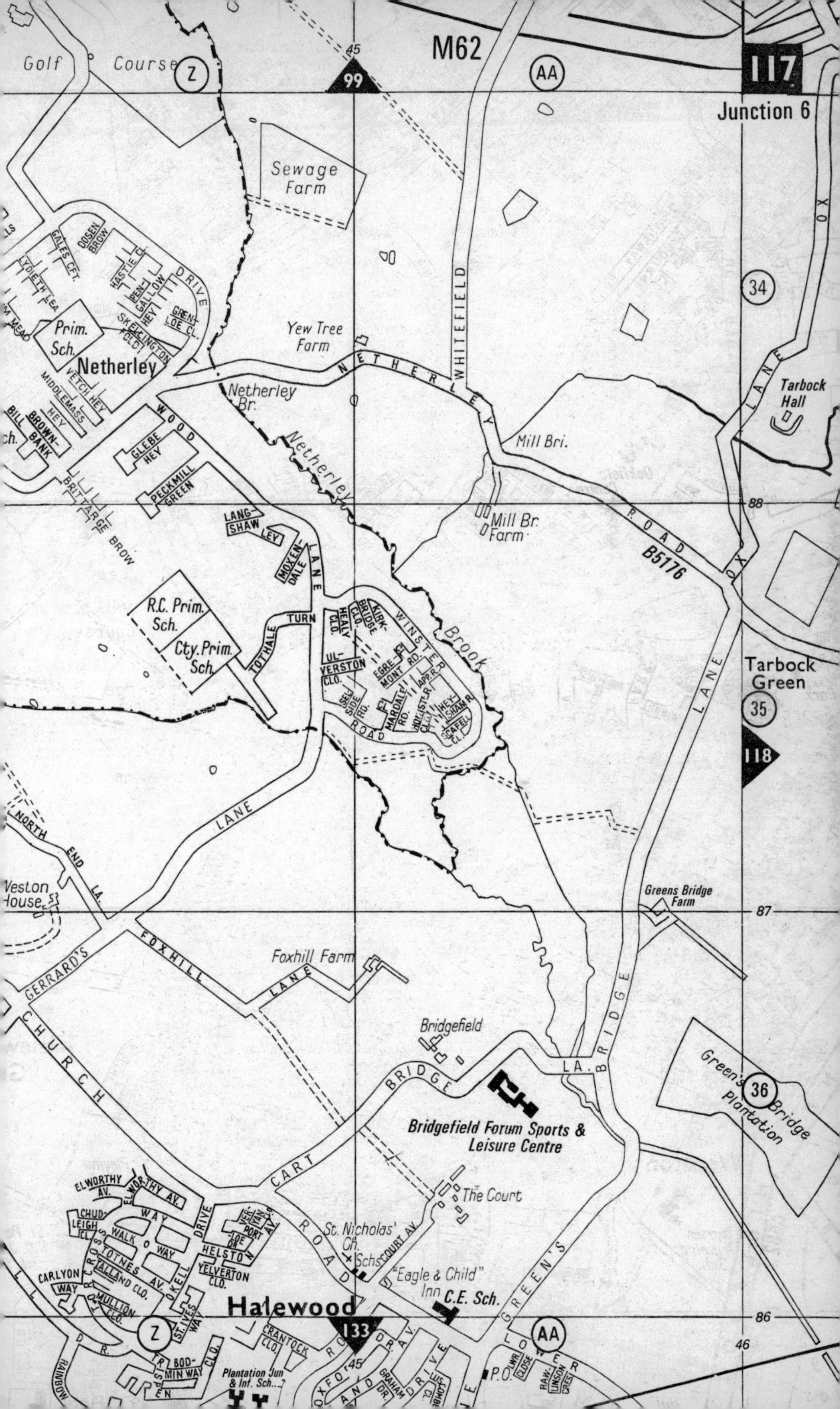

Golf Course
Z
45
99
M62
AA
117
Junction 6
Sewage Farm
Netherley
Prim. Sch.
DOSEN BROW
GALES CFT.
LYDIETH LEA
HASTIE CL.
PEN-GALLOW
HEY
GREN-LOE CL.
DRIVE
SKELLINGTON FOLD
VETCH HEY
MIDDLEMASS HEY
BILL
BROWN-BANK
WOOD
GLEBE HEY
PECKMILL GREEN
BRITTARGE BROW
LANG-SHAW
LEY
MOXEN-DALE
LANE
Yew Tree Farm
Netherley Br.
Netherley Brook
NETHERLEY ROAD
WHITEFIELD
Mill Bri.
Mill Br. Farm
B5176
34
OX LANE
Tarbock Hall
88
R.C. Prim. Sch.
Cty. Prim. Sch.
TOTHALE
TURN
HEALY CLO.
KIRK-BRIDGE CLO.
WINSTER
UL-VERSTON CLO.
EGRE-MONT RD.
SELL-SIDE RD.
MARDALE RD.
HEY-SHAM R.
SCAFELL CL.
ROAD
Tarbock Green
35
118
NORTH END LA.
Weston House
87
Greens Bridge Farm
GERRARD'S
FOXHILL LANE
Foxhill Farm
CHURCH
BRIDGE LANE
Bridgefield
LA.
CART BRIDGE ROAD
Bridgefield Forum Sports & Leisure Centre
Green's Bridge Plantation
36
The Court
St. Nicholas' Ch.
Schs.
COURT AV.
"Eagle & Child" Inn
C.E. Sch.
GREEN'S
ELWORTHY AV.
ELWORTHY AV.
WAY
CHUD-LEIGH CL.
WALK
TOTNES AV.
TALLAND CLO.
CARLYON WAY
MULLION CLO.
OKELL
DRIVE
HELSTON
YELVERTON CLO.
ST. IVES WAY
Halewood
133
86
AA
Z
CRANTOCK CLO.
BODMIN WAY
Plantation Jun & Inf. Sch.
RAINBOW
OXFORD
GRAHAM DR.
P.O.
46
RAW-LINSON CRES.
LOWE

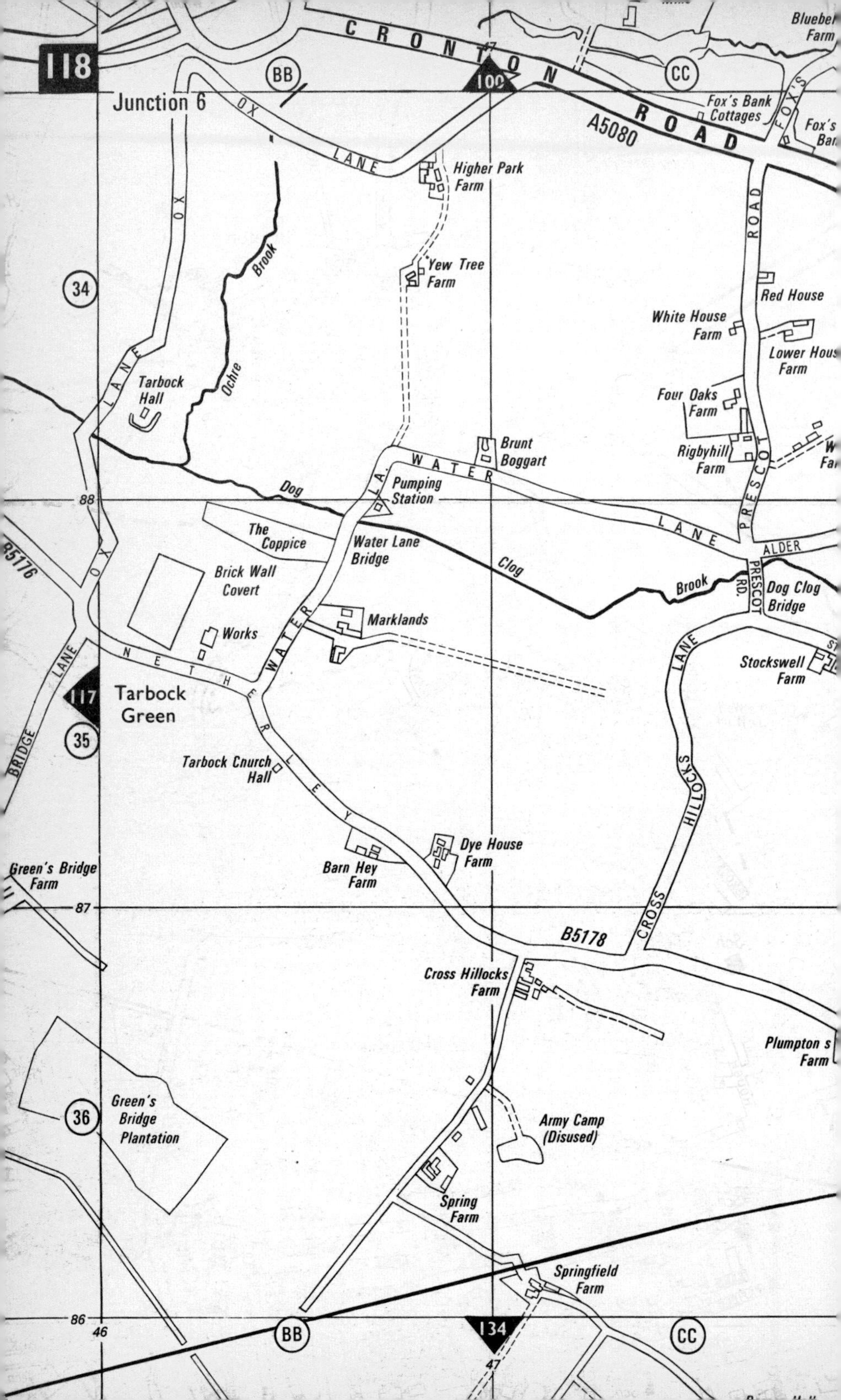

118
CRONTON ROAD
A5080
100
BB
CC
47
Junction 6
OX LANE
Bluebell Farm
Fox's Bank Cottages
FOX'S
Fox's Ban
Higher Park Farm
Yew Tree Farm
Ochre Brook
Red House
White House Farm
Lower House Farm
Four Oaks Farm
Rigbyhill Farm
PRESCOT ROAD
34
Tarbock Hall
Brunt Boggart
WATER LANE
LA.
Pumping Station
Dog Clog Brook
88
The Coppice
Water Lane Bridge
B5176
ALDER
PRESCOT RD.
Dog Clog Bridge
Brick Wall Covert
Marklands
Works
NETHERLEY
WATER
Stocks well Farm
BRIDGE LANE
117
Tarbock Green
35
Tarbock Cnurch Hall
CROSS HILLOCKS LANE
Dye House Farm
Barn Hey Farm
Green's Bridge Farm
87
B5178
Cross Hillocks Farm
Plumpton s Farm
36
Green's Bridge Plantation
Army Camp (Disused)
Spring Farm
Springfield Farm
86
46
134

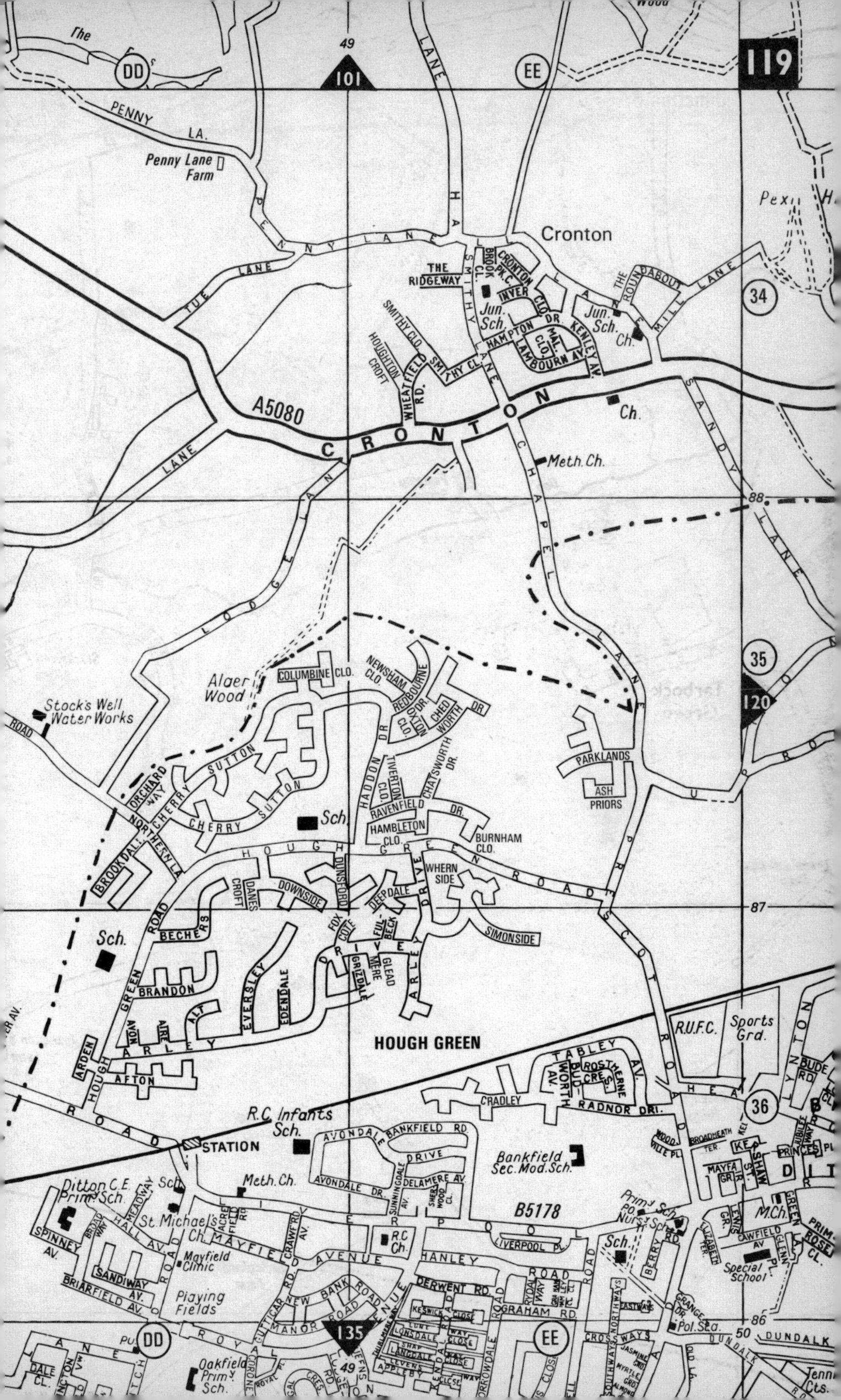

119
101
49
DD
EE
The
PENNY LA.
Penny Lane Farm
PENNY LANE
TUE LANE
HALL LANE
Cronton
THE RIDGEWAY
BROOK CL.
CRONTON PK. C.
INVER CLO.
Jun. Sch.
HAMPTON DR.
MAL. CLO.
LAMBOURN AV.
KENLEY AV.
THE ROUNDABOUT
MILL LANE
Jun. Sch.
Ch.
34
Pex
SMITHY CLO.
HOUGHTON CROFT
WHEATFIELD RD.
SMITHY CL.
SMITHY LANE
A5080
CRONTON
Ch.
SANDY LANE
LANE
Meth. Ch.
CHAPEL LANE
LODGE LANE
88
35
120
Alaer Wood
Stock's Well Water Works
ROAD
COLUMBINE CLO.
NEWSHAM CLO.
REDBOURNE DR.
NOXON CLO.
CHEDWORTH DR.
HADDON DR.
TIVERTON CLO.
CHATSWORTH DR.
RAVENFIELD DR.
HAMBLETON CLO.
BURNHAM CLO.
PARKLANDS
ASH PRIORS
ORCHARD WAY
SUTTON
CHERRY
CHERRY SUTTON
Sch.
NORTHERN LA.
BROOKDALE
HOUGH GREEN ROAD
DUNSFORD
DOWNSIDE
DANES CROFT
DEEPDALE
DRIVE
WHERN SIDE
SIMONSIDE
FOX COTE
FULBECK
87
Sch.
BECHERS
GREEN ROAD
BRANDON
EVERSLEY
EDENDALE
GRIZDALE
MERE
GLEAD
ARLEY DRIVE
AVON
AIRE
ALT
ARLEY
HOUGH GREEN
ARDEN
HOUGH
AFTON
ROAD
R.U.F.C.
Sports Grd.
TABLEY AV.
BUDWORTH AV.
ROSTHERNE CRES.
CRADLEY
RADNOR DRI.
LYNTON
BUDE RD.
36
R.C. Infants Sch.
STATION
AVONDALE
BANKFIELD RD.
DRIVE
SUNNINGDALE AV.
DELAMERE AV.
AVONDALE DR.
SHERWOOD CL.
Bankfield Sec. Mod. Sch.
WOODVILLE PL.
BROADHEATH TER.
KESHAW ST.
MAYFAIR GR.
PRINCES PL.
JUBILEE WAY
Ditton C.E. Prim. Sch.
MEADWAY
Sch.
Meth. Ch.
St. Michael's Ch.
LIVERPOOL
B5178
Prim. Sch.
PO.
Nurs. Sch.
LEWIS GR.
M.Ch.
GREEN LA.
PRIM. ROSE CL.
SPINNEY AV.
BROADWAY
HALL AV.
MAYFIELD AVENUE
R.C. Ch.
HANLEY
LIVERPOOL PL.
Sch.
BERRY RD.
ELIZABETH TER.
CAWFIELD AV.
GLENN PL.
Special School
SANDIWAY AV.
Mayfield Clinic
CRAWFORD AV.
ROAD
BRIARFIELD AV.
Playing Fields
GUTTICAR RD.
NEW BANK ROAD
DERWENT RD.
RYDAL WAY
NORTHWAYS
EASTWAYS
GRANGE DR.
MANOR ROAD
KESWICK CLOSE
GRAHAM RD.
Pol. Sta.
86
50
DUNDALK
PU.
DD
135
EE
ROYAL
LONSDALE
LANGDALE
APPLEBY
LEVENS WAY
CROSSWAYS
SOUTHWAYS
JASMINE GRO.
MYRTLE GRO.
ALMOND GRO.
DALE CL.
Oakfield Prim. Sch.
ROYAL PL.
Tennis Cts.

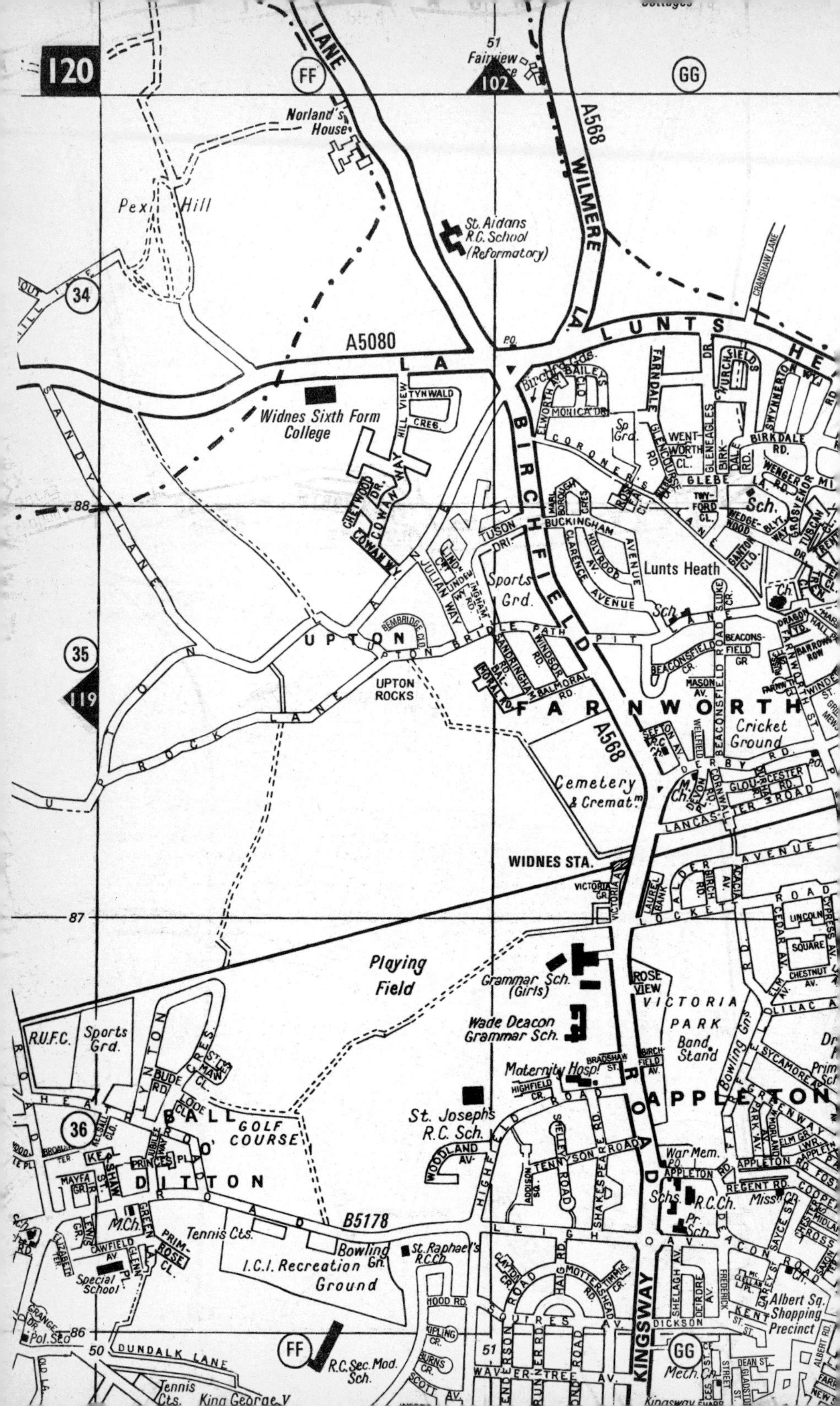

120
FF
GG
102
119
34
35
36
88
87
86
50
51
Fairview
Norland's House
Pex Hill
St. Aidans R.C. School (Reformatory)
A568
WILMERE LA.
LANE
A5080
LUNTS HEATH
Widnes Sixth Form College
TYNWALD CRES.
HILL VIEW
COWAN WAY
CHELWOOD DR.
SANDY LANE
BIRCHFIELD
P.O.
BAILEYS CL.
MONICA DR.
ELWORTH AV.
CORONERS LANE
FARNDALE
GLENCOURSE RD.
WENTWORTH CL.
GLENEAGLES
BIRKDALE RD.
CHURCHFIELDS
SWYNNERTON WAY
BIRKDALE RD.
WENGER RD.
GLEBE
TWYFORD CL.
Sch.
WEDGEWOOD
GROSVENOR
TUSCAN
Sp Grd.
MARLBOROUGH CRES.
BUCKINGHAM AVENUE
CLARENCE AV.
HOLYROOD AV.
AVENUE
Lunts Heath
Sch.
SLUKE LANE
TUSON DRI.
JULIAN WAY
INGHAM RD.
Sports Grd.
UPTON
BEMBRIDGE CLO.
UPTON ROCKS
BRIDLE PATH
PIT
SANDRINGHAM
WINDSOR RD.
BALMORAL RD.
BEACONSFIELD CR.
BEACONSFIELD ROAD
BEACONSFIELD GR
MASON AV.
DRAGON YD.
FARNWORTH ST.
BARROWS ROW
FARNWORTH
Cricket Ground
A568
SEFTON AV.
R.C. Ch.
WELLFIELD
DERBY RD.
P.O.
GLOUCESTER RD.
DURHAM
Cemetery & Cremat^m
M. Ch.
DEVON PL.
CORNWALL RD.
LANCASTER ROAD
ROCK LANE
WIDNES STA.
VICTORIA GR.
VICTORIA AV.
LAUREL BANK
ALDER AV.
BIRCH RD.
ACACIA
AVENUE
LOCKET ROAD
CEDAR AV.
LINCOLN SQUARE
CYPRESS AV.
CHESTNUT AV.
ELM AV.
LILAC
Playing Field
Grammar Sch. (Girls)
Wade Deacon Grammar Sch.
ROSE VIEW
VICTORIA PARK
Band Stand
Bowling Gns.
SYCAMORE
BIRCHFIELD AV.
BRADSHAW ST.
Maternity Hosp.
HIGHFIELD CR.
ROAD
APPLETON
GREENWAY
PARK AV.
MORLAND AV.
ELM GR.
R.U.F.C.
Sports Grd.
LYNTON
BUDE RD
CRES.
ST. MAWES CL.
LOOE CL.
HEATH ROAD
BALL O' DITTON
GOLF COURSE
St. Joseph's R.C. Sch.
WOODLAND AV.
HIGHFIELD
TENNYSON ROAD
SHELLEY RD.
SHAKESPEARE RD.
ADDISON SQ.
ROAD
War Mem.
P.O.
APPLETON RD.
APPLETON RD.
Schs.
R.C.Ch.
Pr. Sch.
REGENT RD.
Miss^n
BROADWAY TER.
KEASHAW ST.
JUBILEE WAY
PRINCES PL.
MAYFAIR GR.
M.Ch.
GREEN
PRIMROSE CL.
DITTON ROAD
B5178
Tennis Cts.
Bowling Gn.
St. Raphael's R.C.Ch.
I.C.I. Recreation Ground
LEIGH AV.
CLAYTON CR.
HAIG RD.
MOTTERSHEAD RD.
TIMMIS CR.
KINGSWAY
SHELAGH AV.
DEIRDRE AV.
FREDERICK
DEACON ROAD
SAYCE ST.
CARLEY ST.
KENT ST.
Albert Sq. Shopping Precinct
LEWIS
ELIZABETH TER.
LAWFIELD GLENN
Special School
GRANGE DR.
Pol. Sta.
HOOD RD.
KIPLING CR.
BURNS CR.
SCOTT AV.
SQUIRES AV.
DICKSON ST.
R.C. Sec. Mod. Sch.
DUNDALK LANE
Tennis Cts.
King George V
WAVERTREE AV.
ENDERSON
RUNNERRD
Mech. Ch.
DEAN ST.
GLADSTONE
ALBERT RD.

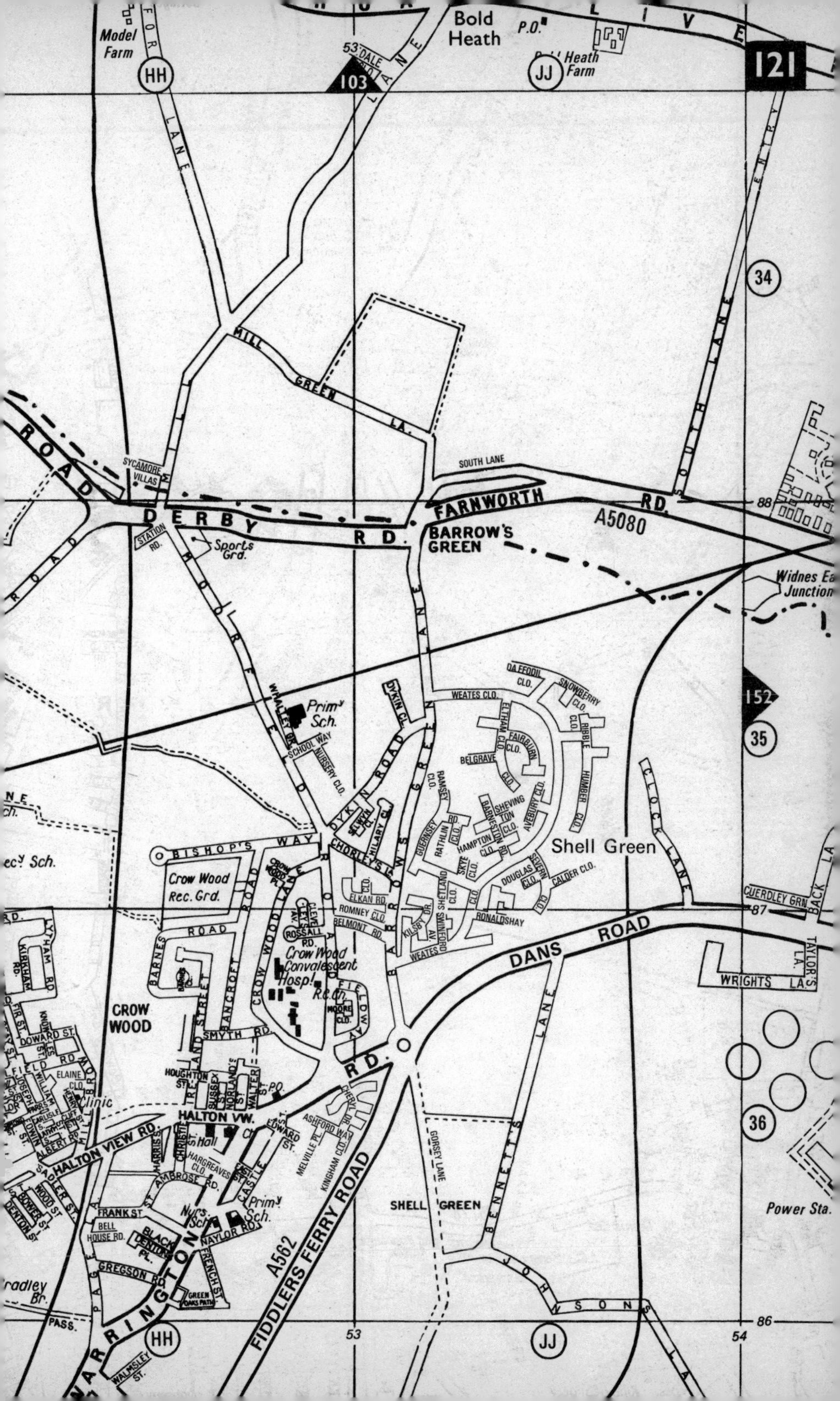

Bold Heath
P.O.
Model Farm
Bold Heath Farm
HH
JJ
103
121
DALE
LANE
MILL
GREEN
LA.
SOUTH LANE
SYCAMORE VILLAS
DERBY RD.
FARNWORTH RD.
A5080
BARROW'S GREEN
STATION RD.
Sports Grd.
ROAD
MOOR FIELD RD.
Widnes East Junction
34
35
36
152
88
87
86
53
54
DAFFODIL CLO.
SNOWBERRY CLO.
WEATES CLO.
ELTHAM CLO.
FAIRBURN CLO.
RIBBLE CLO.
BELGRAVE
HUMBER CLO.
RAMSEY CLO.
SHEVING TON
AVEBURY CLO.
BARNSTON RD.
RATHLIN RD.
HAMPTON CLO.
GUERNSEY
SKYE CLO.
DOUGLAS CLO.
CALDER CLO.
SHETLAND
RONALDSHAY
Shell Green
CLOCK LANE
CUERDLEY GRN.
BACK LA.
TAYLOR'S LA.
WRIGHTS LA.
DANS ROAD
Prim.y Sch.
WHALLEY GR.
SCHOOL WAY
NURSERY CLO.
DYKIN RD.
DYKIN CL.
SELWYN CL.
HILARY CL.
BARROW'S GREEN LANE
BISHOP'S WAY
CHORLEY'S LA.
Crow Wood Rec. Grd.
CROW WOOD PL.
CROW WOOD LANE
CLEVELEYS AV.
ROSSALL RD.
ELKAN RD.
ROMNEY CLO.
BELMONT RD.
KILSBY DR.
SWINEFORD AV.
WEATES
Crow Wood Convalescent Hosp.l
R.C.Ch.
FIELD WAY
MOORE CLO.
BARNES ROAD
STREET
BANCROFT
SMYTH RD.
RD.
CROW WOOD
HOUGHTON ST.
IRELAND
SUSSEX
NORLAND'S
WALTER ST.
P.O.
HALTON VW.
HALTON VIEW RD.
Clinic
Hall
Ch.
EDWARD ST.
CHERYL DR.
ASHFORD WAY
MELVILLE PL.
KINGHAM CLO.
HARGREAVES CLO.
AMBROSE RD.
CASTLE ST.
Prim.y Sch.
Nurs. Sch.
NAYLOR RD.
FRANK ST.
BELL HOUSE RD.
BLACK DENTON PL.
GREGSON RD.
FRENCH ST.
GREEN OAKS PATH
WARRINGTON
WALMSLEY ST.
PAGE LANE
FIDDLERS FERRY ROAD
A562
GORSEY LANE
BENNETTS LANE
SHELL GREEN
JOHNSON LA.
Power Sta.
Sec.y Sch.
LYTHAM RD.
KIRKHAM
DOWARD ST.
ELAINE CLO.
WILLIAM ST.
CARLISLE
ALBERT RD.
SADLER ST.
DENTON ST.
BOWER ST.
WOOD ST.
Bradley Br.
PASS.

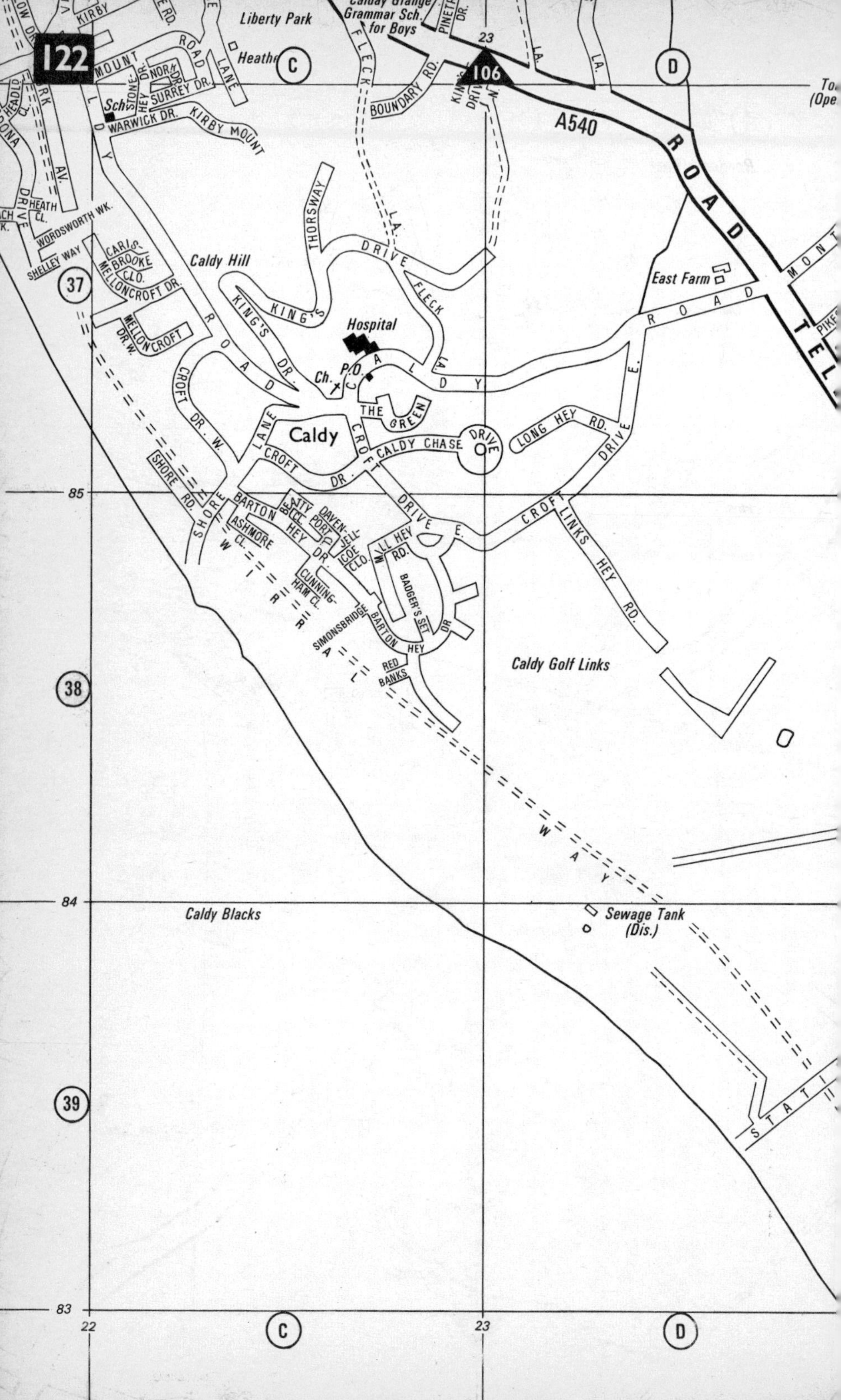

122
106
Liberty Park
Calday Grange Grammar Sch. for Boys
Heath
Caldy Hill
Hospital
Ch.
P.O.
Caldy
East Farm
Caldy Golf Links
Caldy Blacks
Sewage Tank (Dis.)
A540
KIRBY MOUNT
WARWICK DR.
SURREY DR.
MOUNT ROAD
BOUNDARY RD.
PINETREE DR.
THORSWAY
FLECK LA.
KING'S DRIVE
KING'S DR.
CALDY ROAD
CALDY CHASE DRIVE
THE GREEN
CROFT DR.
CROFT DR. W.
CROFT DRIVE E.
LONG HEY RD.
LINKS HEY RD.
MELLONCROFT DR.
MELLONCROFT DR. W.
CARISBROOKE CLO.
WORDSWORTH WK.
SHELLEY WAY
HEATH CL.
SHORE RD.
BARTON HEY DR.
ASHMORE CL.
BEATTY CL.
DAVENPORT
JELLICOE CLO.
MILL HEY RD.
BADGER'S SET DR.
CUNNINGHAM CL.
SIMONSBRIDGE
RED BANKS
WIRRAL WAY
C
D
22
23
37
38
39
83
84
85

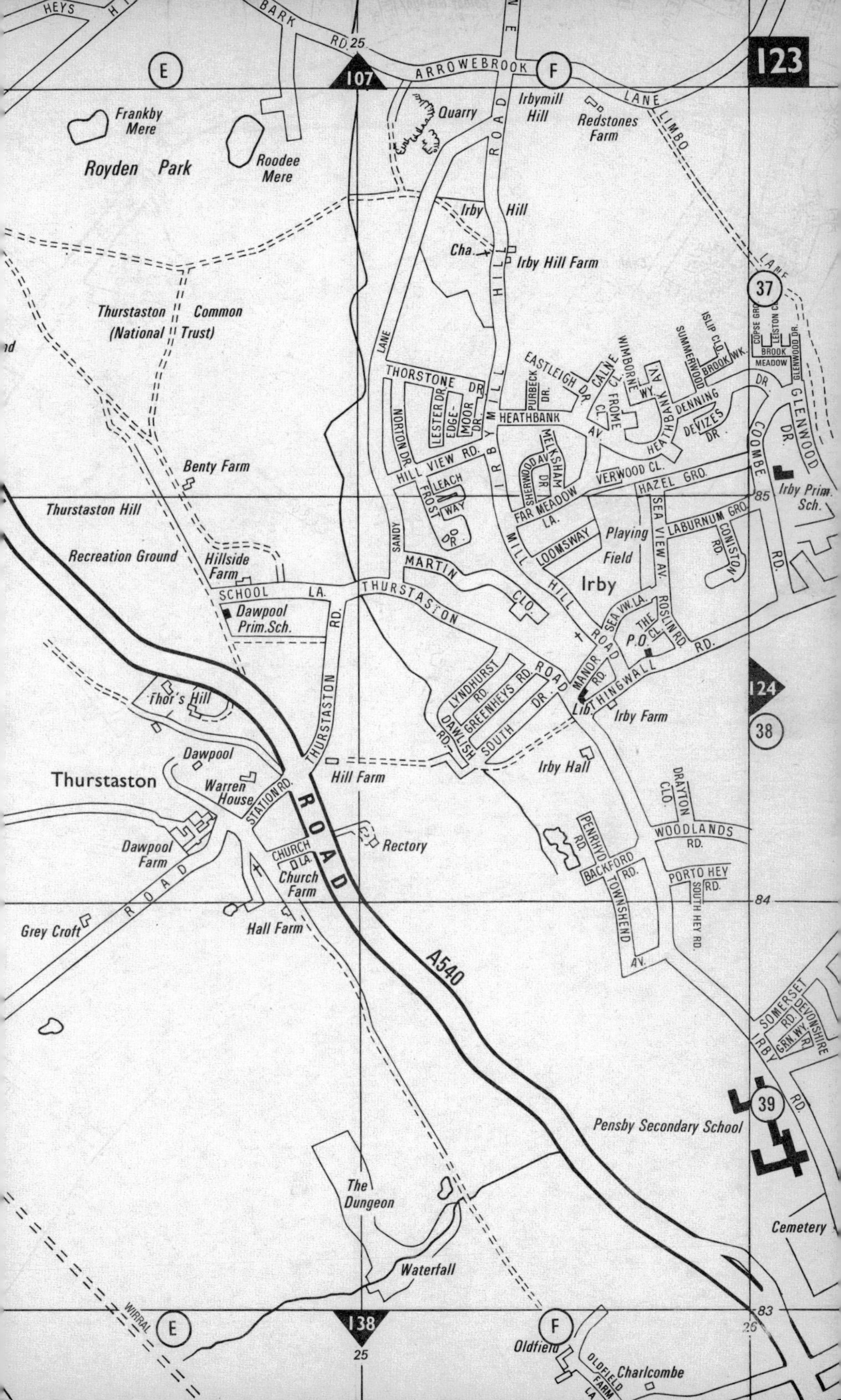
123
107
124
138
E
F
37
38
39
25
85
84
83
26
HEYS
BARK RD.
ARROWEBROOK LANE
LIMBO LANE
Frankby Mere
Roodee Mere
Royden Park
Quarry
Irbymill Hill
Redstones Farm
Irby Hill
Cha.
Irby Hill Farm
IRBY HILL ROAD
Thurstaston Common (National Trust)
SANDY LANE
THORSTONE DR.
NORTON DR.
LESTER DR.
EDGE-MOOR DR.
PURBECK DR.
EASTLEIGH DR.
CALNE CL.
FROME CL.
WIMBORNE WY.
HEATHBANK AV.
HEATHBANK
SUMMERWOOD
ISLIP CL.
BROOK WK.
COPSE GRO.
LEISTON CL.
BROOK MEADOW
GLENWOOD DR.
DENNING DR.
DEVIZES DR.
COOMBE RD.
HILL VIEW RD.
LEACH WAY
FROST DR.
MELKSHAM DR.
SHERWOOD AV.
FAR MEADOW LA.
VERWOOD CL.
HAZEL GRO.
Irby Prim. Sch.
LOOMSWAY
Playing Field
SEA VIEW AV.
LABURNUM GRO.
CONISTON RD.
Benty Farm
Thurstaston Hill
Recreation Ground
Hillside Farm
SCHOOL LA.
Dawpool Prim.Sch.
THURSTASTON RD.
MARTIN CLO.
MILL HILL ROAD
Irby
SEA VW. LA.
THE CL.
ROSLIN RD.
P.O.
THINGWALL RD.
MANOR RD.
Lib.
Irby Farm
THURSTASTON ROAD
LYNDHURST RD.
GREENHEYS RD.
DAWLISH RD.
SOUTH DR.
Thor's Hill
Dawpool
Thurstaston
Warren House
STATION RD.
Hill Farm
Irby Hall
OLD CLO.
DRAYTON
WOODLANDS RD.
PENRHYD RD.
BACKFORD RD.
TOWNSHEND AV.
PORTO HEY RD.
SOUTH HEY RD.
ROAD
Rectory
CHURCH LA.
Church Farm
Dawpool Farm
ROAD
Grey Croft
Hall Farm
A540
SOMERSET RD.
DEVONSHIRE RD.
GRN. WY.
IRBY RD.
Pensby Secondary School
The Dungeon
Cemetery
Waterfall
WIRRAL
Oldfield
OLDFIELD FARM LA.
Charlcombe

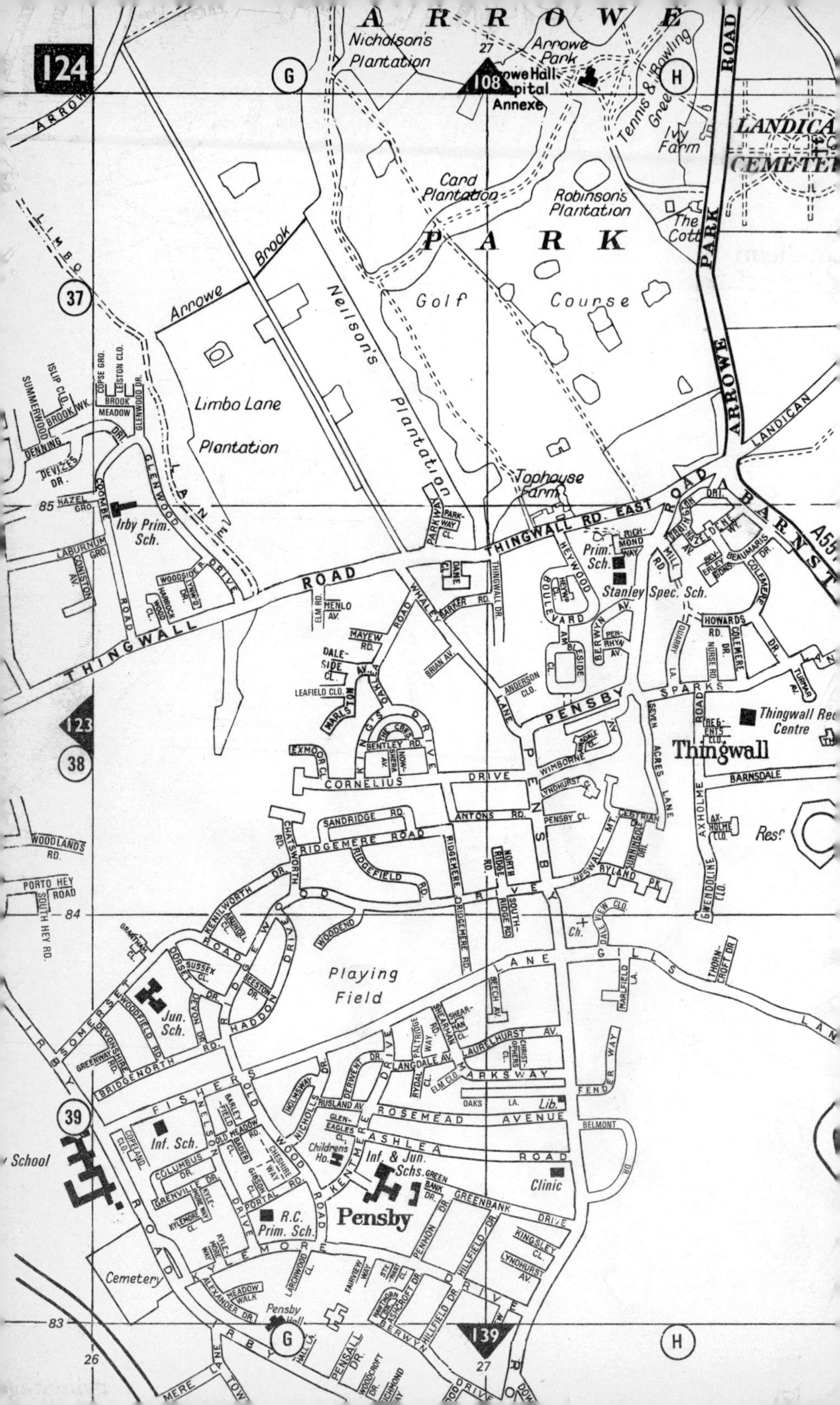
ARROWE
Nicholson's Plantation
Arrowe Park
Arrowe Hall Hospital Annexe
Tennis & Bowling Green
Ivy Farm
LANDICAN CEMETERY
ARROWE PARK ROAD
Card Plantation
Robinson's Plantation
The Cott
PARK
Golf Course
Arrowe Brook
Neilson's Plantation
Limbo Lane Plantation
Tophouse Farm
LIMBO LANE
LANDICAN
BARNSTON ROAD
A551
THINGWALL RD. EAST
THINGWALL ROAD
Irby Prim. Sch.
Prim. Sch.
Stanley Spec. Sch.
Thingwall Rec. Centre
Thingwall
Resr
PENSBY ROAD
PENSBY DRIVE
SPARKS LANE
SEVEN ACRES LANE
CORNELIUS DRIVE
KING'S DRIVE
RIDGEMERE ROAD
RIDGEWOOD DRIVE
HESWALL MT.
GILLS LANE
AXHOLME ROAD
BARNSDALE
Playing Field
Jun. Sch.
Inf. Sch.
Inf. & Jun. Schs.
Childrens Ho.
R.C. Prim. Sch.
Clinic
Lib.
Ch.
Pensby
Pensby Hall
Cemetery
School
ROSEMEAD AVENUE
ASHLEA ROAD
GREENBANK DRIVE
MARKSWAY
FENDER WAY
FISHERS LANE
KYLEMORE DRIVE
HILLFIELD DRIVE
IRBY ROAD
SOMERSET ROAD
BRIDGENORTH RD.
GLENWOOD DRIVE
COOMBE ROAD
WOODLANDS RD.
PORTO HEY ROAD
SOUTH HEY RD.
124
123
108
139
37
38
39
G
H
26
27
83
84
85

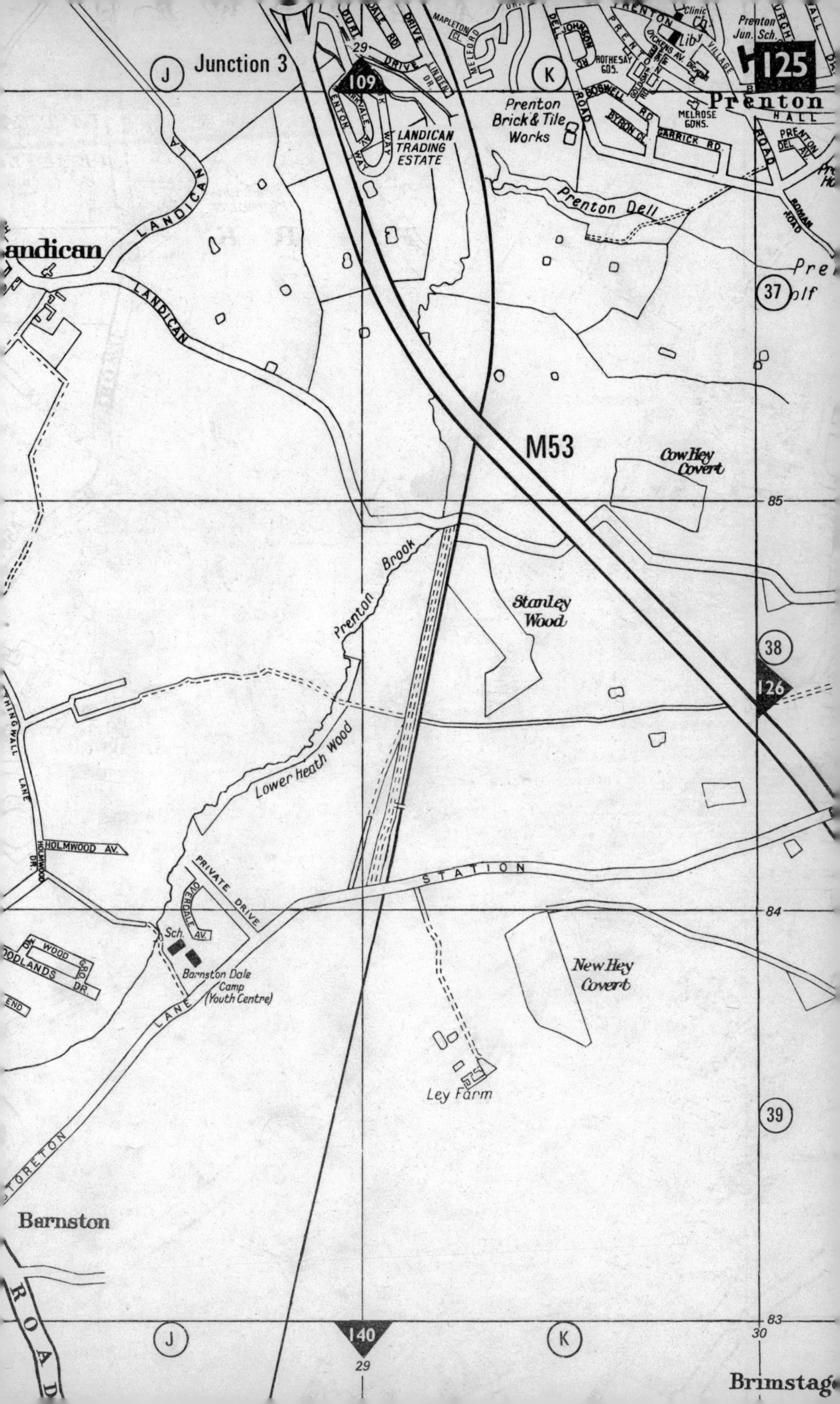

Junction 3
J
K
109
125
Prenton
Prenton Jun. Sch.
Clinic
Ch.
Lib.
Prenton Brick & Tile Works
LANDICAN TRADING ESTATE
Prenton Dell
Landican
LANDICAN LA.
LANDICAN
M53
Cow Hey Covert
Stanley Wood
Prenton Brook
Lower Heath Wood
37
38
39
126
85
84
83
STATION
PRIVATE DRIVE
OVERDALE AV.
HOLMWOOD AV.
HOLMWOOD DR.
THINGWALL LANE
Sch.
Barnston Dale Camp (Youth Centre)
New Hey Covert
Ley Farm
LANE
STORETON
Barnston
ROAD
140
29
30
Brimstage
MAPLETON CL.
MELFORD
JOHNSON RD.
ROTHESAY GDS.
BOSWELL RD.
BYRON CL.
CARRICK RD.
MELROSE GDNS.
DICKENS AV.
PRENTON DEL AV.
ROMAN ROAD
HALL

126
Prenton
Prenton Jun.& Inf.Sc
Ch.
Lib.
Prenton Hall
Prenton Hall Road
Prenton Farm Road
Roman Road
Melrose Gdns.
Prenton Del Av.
Golf Links Road
Golf Ho.
Pine Walks
Reservoir Rd.
Tower Rd.
Prenton Res.
110
Burrell Cl.
Mount Road
Mount Wood Rd.
Mount Wood
Chiltern
Pennine
Brecon Rd.
Cheviot
The Close
Raby Gro.
Cavendish
Hesketh
Sch.for
Harley Av.
Heswall Av.
Brimstage Av.
Gayton Av.
Thornton Av.
Thornton Rd.
Thornton Gro.
Claremont Way
Regents Way
The Ridge Way
Fieldway
Broadway
Kings Lane
Princes
Withert Av.
Bickerton Av.
Stanley Avenue
B5151
Prenton Golf Course
37
Causeway
Marsh Hey Covert
Marsh Lane
Kirkway
Kings Way
Mount Av.
Mount Dr.
Higher Bebington Hall
Kings Cl.
Linkside
Vic.
Ch.
Mill Road
Bentfield Gdns.
Rotherwood Cl.
Heather Bank
Millwood
Mill View Dr.
Well La.
Elm Ho.
Orchard Way
Acorn Cl.
Mount Villas
Millbut Cl.
King's Brow
Higher Bebington Jun.Sch.
Sandfield Cl.
Victoria Rd.
Teehey Cl.
Teehey Gdns.
Hey Covert
85
Lever Causeway
Storeton Grange
Storeton La.
Lit. Storeton La.
Landican Lane
Little Storeton
Storeton Hill
125
Ch.
Storeton Hall
Village Road
Hillfield Cl.
School La.
Mill Brow
HIGHER BEBINGTON
Mill Ter.
Calder Rd.
Conway Cl.
Kennet
Shallmarsh Cl.
Glenmarsh Cl.
Elmore Rd.
Derwent
Milstan
38
Road
Rest Hill Road
Storeton
Red Hill Road
Keepers La.
Storeton Lodge
Hillside Farm
Wishing Gate
Bracken La.
Brackenwood
Fern
84
Brimstage La.
Rake Hey Covert
M53
Brimstage Plantn.
Mount Road
B5151
Municipal Golf Course
Kennet
39
Umberstone Covert
83
30
31
L
M
141
Junction 4
Brimstage
Brimstage Road
A5137

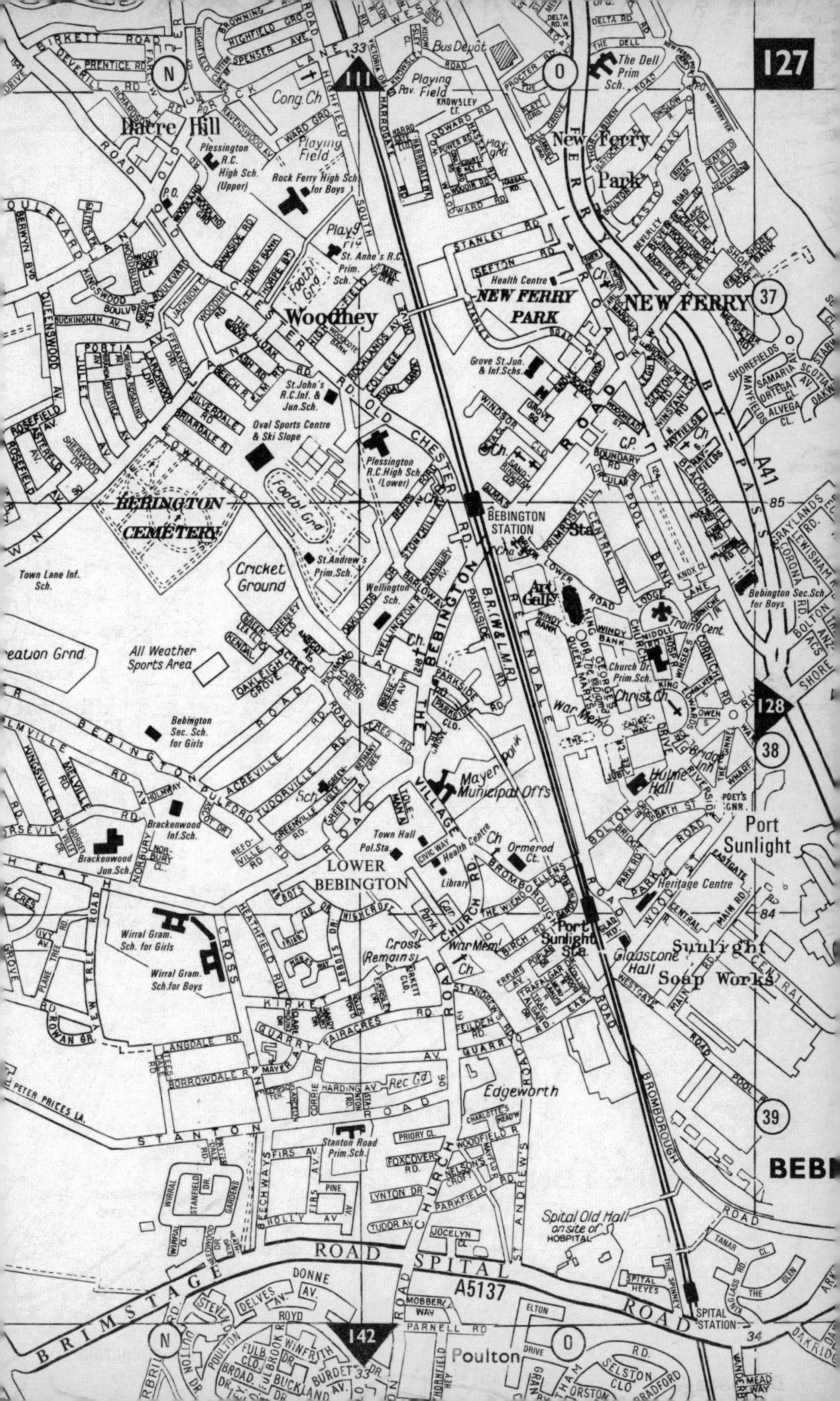
127
111
128
142
37
38
39
A41
A5137
Bus Depôt
Playing Field
Knowsley Ct.
Cong. Ch.
Tranmere
Rock Ferry High Sch. for Boys
Plessington R.C. High Sch. (Upper)
New Ferry Park
The Dell Prim. Sch.
NEW FERRY
NEW FERRY PARK
Health Centre
Woodhey
St. Anne's R.C. Prim. Sch.
Grove St. Jun. & Inf. Schs.
St. John's R.C. Inf. & Jun. Sch.
Oval Sports Centre & Ski Slope
Plessington R.C. High Sch. (Lower)
BEBINGTON CEMETERY
Town Lane Inf. Sch.
BEBINGTON STATION
Cricket Ground
St. Andrew's Prim. Sch.
Wellington Sch.
Art Gall.
Bebington Sec. Sch. for Boys
Church Dr. Prim. Sch.
Christ Ch.
War Mem.
Bridge Inn
Hulme Hall
Mayer Park
Municipal Offs
All Weather Sports Area
Bebington Sec. Sch. for Girls
Brackenwood Inf. Sch.
Brackenwood Jun. Sch.
Town Hall
Pol. Sta.
Health Centre
Library
Ormerod Ct.
LOWER BEBINGTON
Port Sunlight
Port Sunlight Sta.
Heritage Centre
Gladstone Hall
Sunlight Soap Works
Wirral Gram. Sch. for Girls
Wirral Gram. Sch. for Boys
Cross (Remains)
Rec. Gd.
Edgeworth
Stanton Road Prim. Sch.
Spital Old Hall on site of HOSPITAL
SPITAL STATION
Poulton
BEB
BRIMSTAGE ROAD
SPITAL ROAD
BEBINGTON ROAD
OLD CHESTER RD.
NEW FERRY BY-PASS
BROMBOROUGH ROAD
CHURCH ROAD
STANTON ROAD
TOWNFIELD LANE
NEW CHESTER ROAD
BOLTON RD.
POOL BANK
HIGHFIELD SOUTH
ROCK LANE WEST
BIRKETT ROAD

P
Q
35
112
RIVER
New Ferry
NEW FERRY BY-PASS
37
38
127
39
Bromborough Pool
Bromborough Dock
Warehouse
DOCK RD. NORTH
Works
Factory
Depot
Res.
Pav.
Cricket Grd.
Chap.
Bromborough Pool Prim.Sch.
Bromborough Pool Bridge
Sports Ground
YORK ST
MANOR PLACE
SOUTH VIEW
THE GREEN
POOL LANE
A41
NEW CHESTER ROAD
Port Sunlight
Heritage Centre
Sunlight Soap Works
CENTRAL ROAD
Amb. & Fire Sta.
DOCK ROAD
THERMAL ROAD
PORT CAUSEWAY
Factorys
Bromborough Pool
BEBINGTON
P.O.
TERMINUS ROAD
MAGAZINE ROAD
Allot Gds.
STADIUM ROAD
Storage Depot
COMMERCIAL RD.
Wks.
SPITAL RD.
SPITAL STATION
MEADWAY
Patrick's Well
HEATHER DENE
FAIRWAY STH
143
DINSDALE ROAD
WELTON RD.

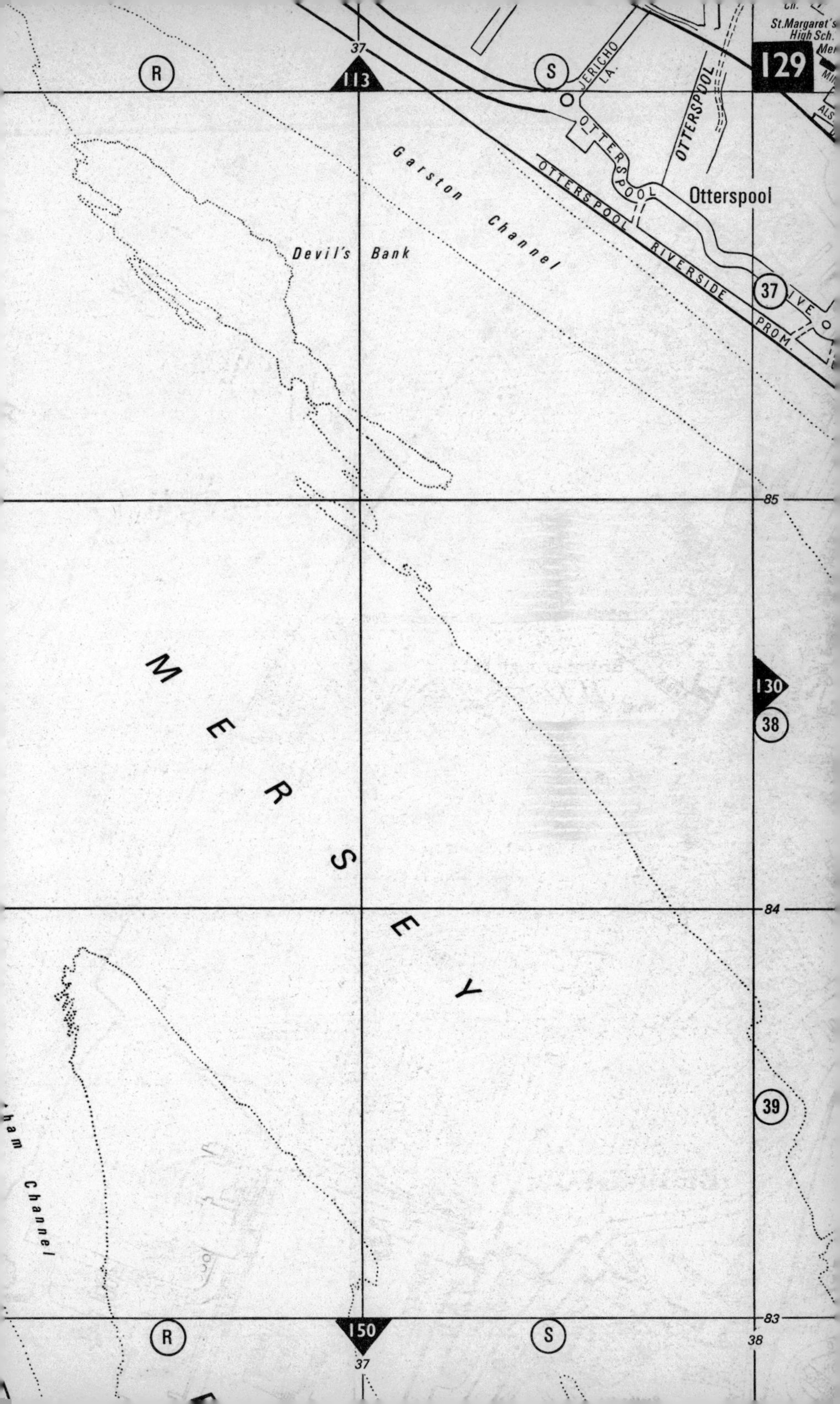

(R) ▼113
(S)
St.Margaret's
High Sch. Mer
■ 129

JERICHO LA.

OTTERSPOOL

Otterspool

Garston Channel

OTTERSPOOL RIVERSIDE PROM

37

37

Devil's Bank

85

M E R S E Y

▼130
38

84

39

...ham Channel

83

(R) ▼150
37
(S)
38

130
114
129
Aigburth
Otterspool
AIGBURTH STA.
Riversdale College of Technology
Liverpool Cricket Ground
Athletic Ground
College Hostel
Alfred Holt Rec. Grd.
Spec. Sch.
Beechwood Ho.
Grassendale
CRESSINGTON STA.
R.C. Secy. Gram. Sch.
Primy. Sch.
R.C.Ch.
Board of Trade Offices
Dock Master's Office
NORTH DOCK
OLD DOCK
STALBRIDGE DOCK
GRAVING DOCK
Garston Channel
RIVER MERSEY
OTTERSPOOL DRIVE
RIVERSIDE PROMENADE
GRASSENDALE PROM.
CRESSINGTON PROM.
AIGBURTH ROAD
A561
MERSEY ROAD
ALMA ROAD
RIVERSDALE ROAD
BEECHWOOD ROAD
KNOWSLEY ROAD
SALISBURY ROAD
EATON ROAD
DOCK ROAD
ST. MARY'S ROAD
W. ALLERTON
85
84
83
38
39
T
U
37
38
39

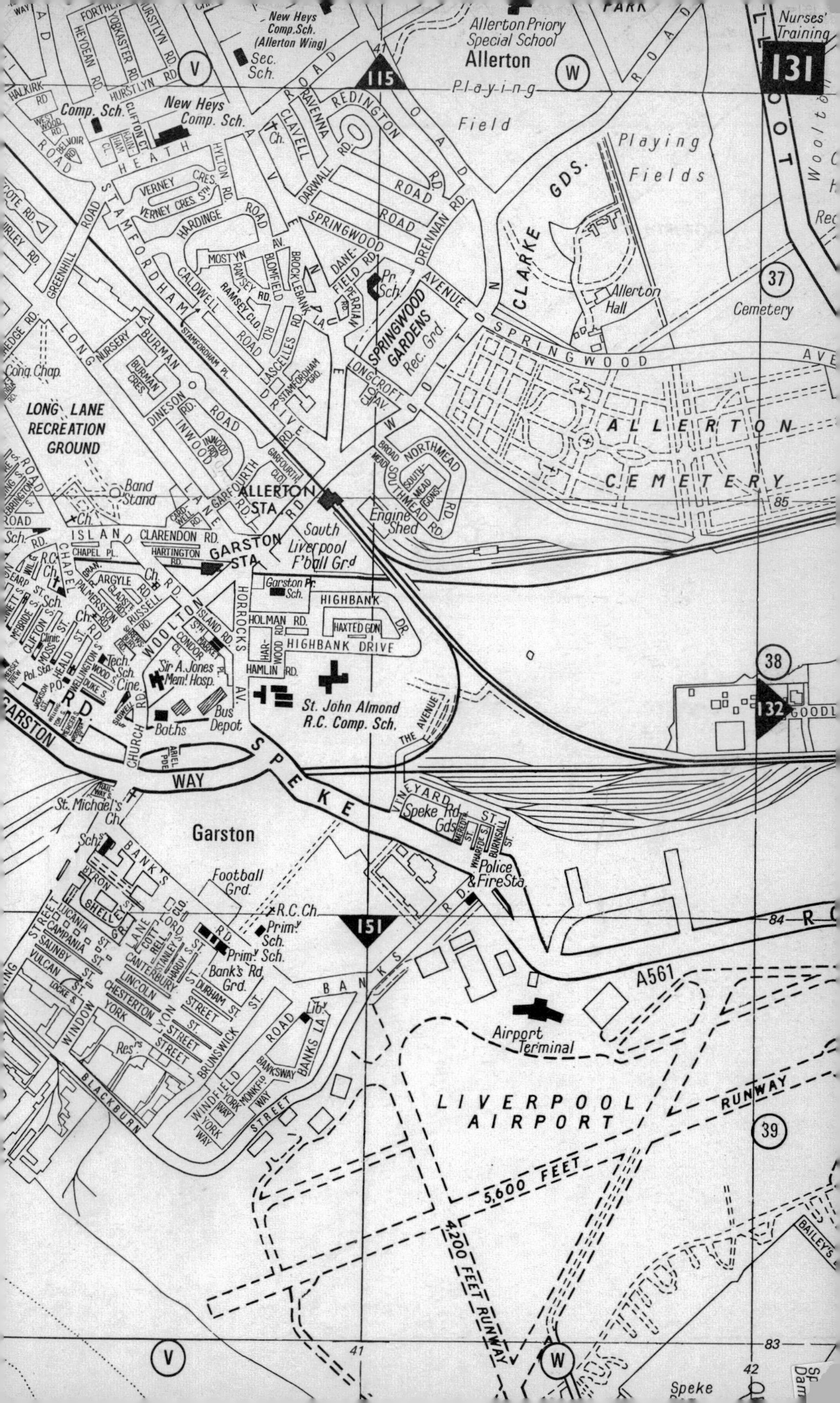

New Heys Comp.Sch. (Allerton Wing)
Sec. Sch.
Allerton Priory Special School
Allerton
PARK
Nurses' Training
131
115
V
W
FORTHLIN
HEYDEAN RD.
YORKASTER RD.
HURSTLYN RD.
HURSTLYN RD.
HALKIRK RD.
Comp. Sch.
New Heys Comp. Sch.
WESTWOOD RD.
CLIFTON CT.
HAINHAM CL.
BELVOIR RD.
ROAD
HEATH
HYLTON RD.
CLAVELL RD.
RAVENNA
REDINGTON RD.
ROAD
Ch.
Playing Field
Playing Fields
CLARKE GDS.
VERNEY CRES.
VERNEY CRES. Sth.
HARDINGE ROAD
STAMFORDHAM
GREENHILL ROAD
DARWALL RD.
ROAD
ROAD
SPRINGWOOD
DRENNAN RD.
AVENUE
MOSTYN AV.
RAMSEY RD.
RAMSEY CLO.
BLOMFIELD RD.
BROCKLEBANK LA.
DANEFIELD RD.
Pr. Sch.
PERRIAN RD.
SPRINGWOOD GARDENS
Rec. Grd.
Allerton Hall
37
Cemetery
CALDWELL ROAD
STAMFORDHAM PL.
LASCELLES RD.
STAMFORDHAM GRO.
LONGCROFT AV.
SPRINGWOOD AVE
WOOLTON
LONG LANE
NURSERY LA.
BURMAN RD.
BURMAN CRES.
Cong. Chap.
LONG LANE RECREATION GROUND
DINESON RD.
ROAD
INWOOD RD.
DRIVE
BROAD MEAD
NORTHMEAD
SOUTHMEAD RD.
SOUTHMEAD GDNS.
ALLERTON CEMETERY
GARFOURTH RD.
GARFOURTH CLO.
Band Stand
ALLERTON STA.
85
Engine Shed
ISLAND RD.
CLARENDON RD.
CHAPEL PL.
HARTINGTON RD.
GARSTON STA
South Liverpool F'ball Grd
Garston Pr. Sch.
HIGHBANK DR.
HOLMAN RD.
HAXTED GDN
HIGHBANK DRIVE
HARWOOD RD.
HAMLIN RD.
HORROCKS AV.
ARGYLE
GLADSTONE
PALMERSTON
RUSSELL RD.
WOOLTON
ISLAND RD.
CONDOR CL.
MARKET PL.
Tech. Sch.
Cine.
Sir A. Jones Mem. Hosp.
Bus Depot
Baths
St. John Almond R.C. Comp. Sch.
THE AVENUE
38
132
GOODL
Pol. Sta.
P.O.
Clinic
HEALD ST.
MOSS
CLIFTON S.
WELLINGTON S.
DUKE S.
R.D.
GARSTON
CHURCH RD.
ARIEL PDE.
WAY
SPEKE
St. Michael's Ch.
Garston
VINEYARD ST.
Speke Rd. Gds
MEREDITH ST.
WHARFEDALE ST.
BURNSALL ST.
Police & Fire Sta.
Sch.
BANKS
BYRON
SHELLEY GR.
Football Grd.
R.C. Ch.
Primy. Sch.
Primy. Sch.
151
84
LUCANIA
CAMPANIA ST.
SALINBY ST.
VULCAN ST.
STREET
LANE
COTTRELL
STANLEY
HARDY S.
DURHAM ST.
Bank's Rd. Grd.
CANTERBURY ST.
LINCOLN
CHESTERTON
YORK
LYON STREET
WINDOW
Resrs
STREET
BRUNSWICK ST.
ROAD
Liby.
BANKS LA.
BANKSWAY
A561
Airport Terminal
LIVERPOOL AIRPORT
RUNWAY
BLACKBURN
WINDFIELD
YORK WAY
MONKFIELD WAY
STREET
5,600 FEET
4,200 FEET RUNWAY
39
BAILEY'S
41
83
42
Speke

Nurses Training Sch.
WINWOOD HALL
JEUDWINE
Doe Park Club House
FAIRWAYS CL.
CHARTERHOUSE RD.
STONYHURST RD.
WREKIN CL.
HAILEYBURY
ROEDEAN CL.
DENSTONE CL.
PALM GR.
ROSEFIELD RD.
CARKINGTON RD.
MILLCROFT RD.
CROWNACRES
116
43
Inf. Sch.
Spec. Sch.
St. Peters R.C. Jun. & Inf. Sch.
CAMBORNE AV.
LANCING CL.
CAMBERLEY
ARNCLIFFE RD.
STANFORD CR.
FROME WAY
DIDCOT CL.
FRENSHAM
SHERBORNE AV.
PEMBREY WAY
THE FAIRWAYS
Arncliffe Special Sch.
Woolton Camp Hill Recreation Ground
Camp Hill
Woolton Road
Golf Course
Hunt's Cross
GREENACRE RD.
BANCROFT CL.
PINFOLD RD.
ROSKELL RD.
STUART AV.
YEW TREE RD.
R.C. Sec. Sch.
Play'g. Field
ANDOVER WAY
BALSHAM CL.
ABBERLEY
37
Cemetery
CAMPHILL RD.
HILLFOOT GRN.
Hillfoot Hey
Hillfoot Hey Comp Sch. (Boys)
SCHOOL
WAYLANDS DR.
SALCOMBE DR.
KINGSMEAD DR.
HUNTS CROSS STA.
St. Hilda's Ch.
TUDOR RD.
HIGHER AV.
SPEKE LANE
BOUNDARY DR.
BLACKBURNE DR.
PORTWAY
St. Andrews R.C. Jun. & Inf. Sch.
GRANGE AV.
HILLFOOT ROAD
HILLFOOT RD.
ALLERTON CEMETERY
ASHTON DR.
Lib'y (SITE FOR)
ARMSCOT
BOURTON CL.
LAXTON RD.
KINGSTHORNE RD.
Pr. Sch.
85
FARINGDON CL.
LEAFIELD
STONE RD.
BRAYDON CLO.
WOODEND
BARFORD ROAD
FLEMING RD.
Sports Ground
BOUNDARY
POULTON CL.
NORTH AVE.
38
131
GOODLASS RD.
EDWARD'S LANE
SPEKE
Pr. Sch.
SPEKE HALL RD.
INDUSTRIAL ESTATE
Bus Garage
SHAW
EVANS RD.
AVENUE
DELF LANE
ROAD
GASKILL RD.
84
SPEKE ROAD
136
A561
BARNHAM CLO.
PETWORTH CLO.
CHURCH RD.
RYCOT ROAD
BRAY ROAD
TONBRIDGE CLO.
BEX CL.
SAN CLO.
DYMCHURCH
LENHAM WAY
APPLEDORE CLO.
GERNETH CL.
SPEKE TOWN P.O.
WOODEND LA.
CLOUGH ROAD
TARBOCK ROAD
ILKLEY WK.
SHIPLEY WK.
WELLBROOK CL.
R.C. Pr. Sch.
RUNWAY
39
Playing Fields
HALL
SPEKE CHURCH RD.
GREYHOUND FARM RD.
BLACKROD AV.
RAMSBROOK CL.
STAPLETON
HAREFIELD GRN.
SPINDUS ROAD
BAILEY'S LA.
North Lodge
SPEKE INDUSTRIAL ESTATE
STOCKTON WOOD RD.
Lib'y
Pr. Sch.
Fire Sta.
SUTTON WOOD RD.
TEWIT HALL RD.
GOLDFINCH FARM RD.
LOVELL WY.
Speke Comp. Sch. (Lower)
WELTON CLO.
CENTRAL AV.
MARTON CLO.
Dunlop Sports Ground
Speke
FENTON CLO.
Speke Comp. Sch. (Upper)
83
42
WESTERN AV.
LINNER
DUNLOP RD.
DAM
SAINTS ROAD
HAREFIELD
CONLEACH
X
Y

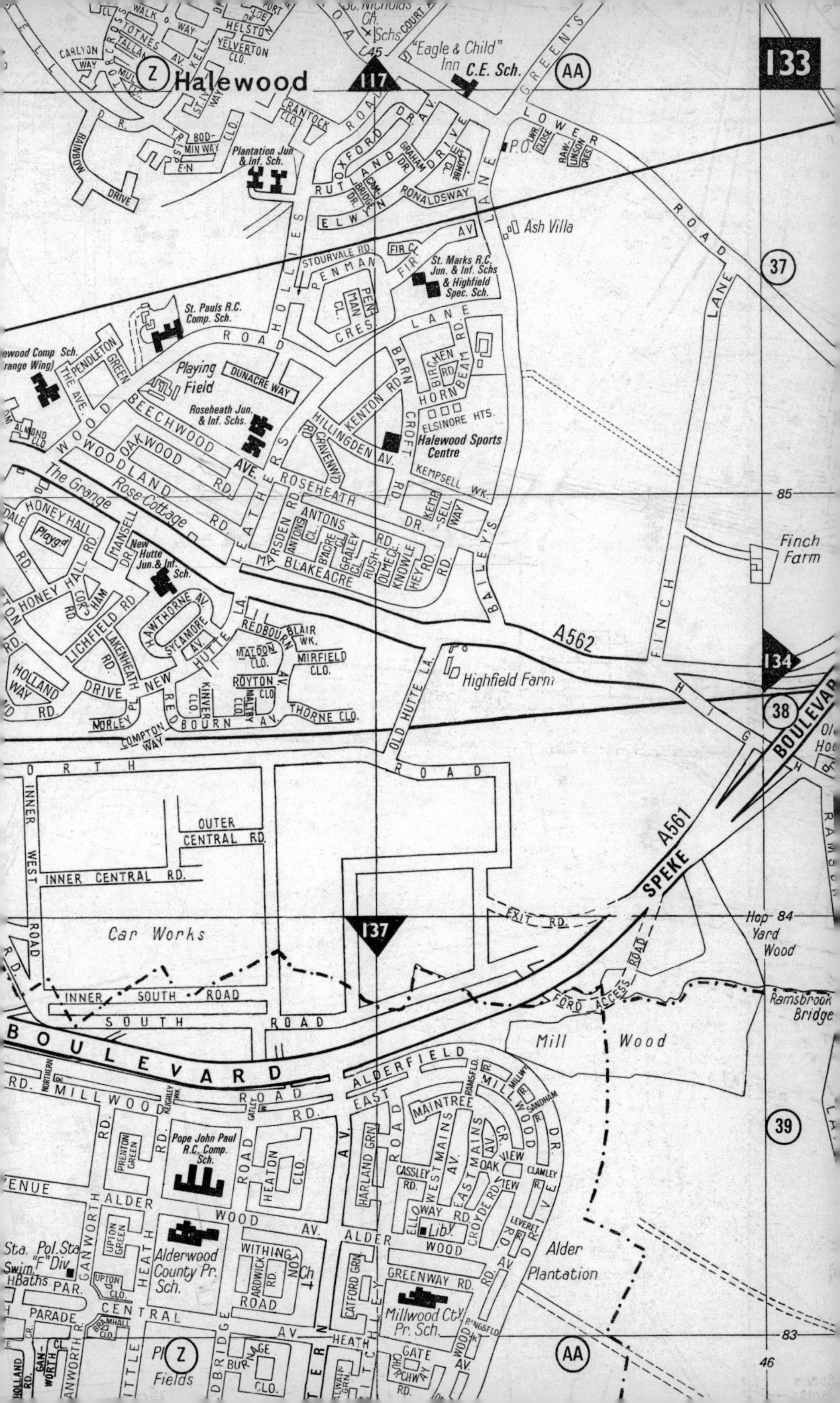
133
Halewood
Plantation Jun & Inf. Sch.
"Eagle & Child" Inn
C.E. Sch.
Ash Villa
St. Marks R.C. Jun. & Inf. Schs & Highfield Spec. Sch.
St. Pauls R.C. Comp. Sch.
Playing Field
Roseheath Jun. & Inf. Schs.
Halewood Sports Centre
New Hutte Jun. & Inf. Sch.
Finch Farm
Highfield Farm
A562
134
Car Works
137
A561
SPEKE
BOULEVARD
Hop Yard Wood
Ramsbrook Bridge
Mill Wood
Pope John Paul R.C. Comp. Sch.
Alderwood County Pr. Sch.
Millwood Cty Pr. Sch.
Alder Plantation
117
37
38
39
85
84
83
46

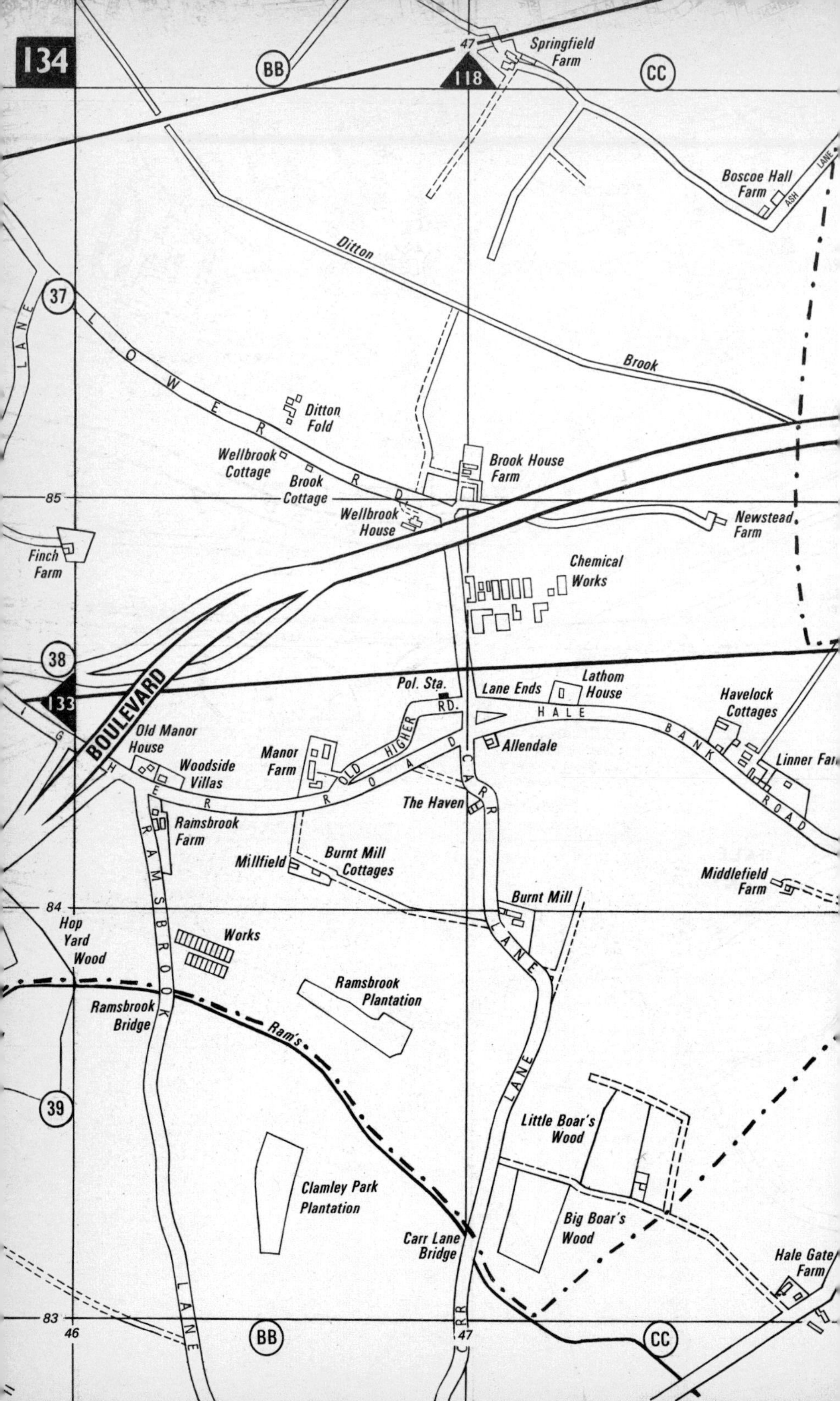
134
BB
47
118
Springfield Farm
CC
Boscoe Hall Farm
ASH LANE
Ditton
Brook
37
LANE
LOWER RD.
Ditton Fold
Wellbrook Cottage
Brook Cottage
Brook House Farm
85
Wellbrook House
Newstead Farm
Finch Farm
Chemical Works
38
133
BOULEVARD
Pol. Sta.
Lane Ends
Lathom House
Havelock Cottages
HALE BANK ROAD
OLD HIGHER RD.
HIGHER ROAD
Old Manor House
Woodside Villas
Manor Farm
Allendale
Linner Fa
CARR
The Haven
Ramsbrook Farm
Millfield
Burnt Mill Cottages
Middlefield Farm
84
Burnt Mill
Hop Yard Wood
Works
RAMSBROOK LANE
Ramsbrook Plantation
Ramsbrook Bridge
Ram's
39
LANE
Little Boar's Wood
Clamley Park Plantation
Big Boar's Wood
Carr Lane Bridge
Hale Gate Farm
83
46
BB
CARR
47
CC

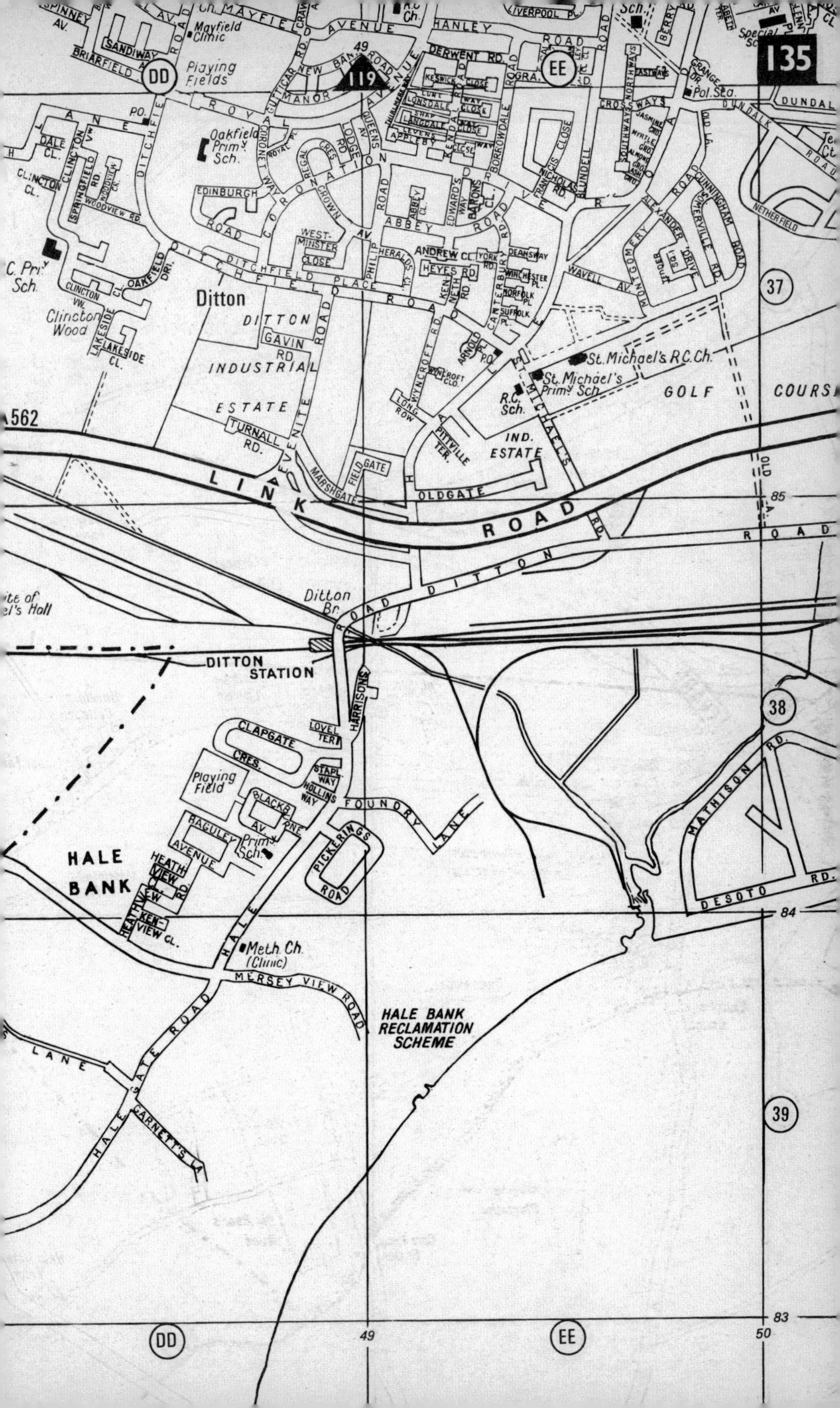
Mayfield Clinic
Playing Fields
DD
EE
119
49
MAYFIELD AVENUE
HANLEY ROAD
DERWENT RD.
LIVERPOOL PL.
SANDIWAY
BRIARFIELD
SPINNEY AV.
NEW BANK ROAD
CUTTICAR RD.
MANOR
ROYAL
QUEENS AV.
KESWICK CLOSE
LONSDALE CLOSE
LANGDALE
LEVENS
APPLEBY
BORROWDALE ROAD
CROSSWAYS
EASTWAYS
NORTHWAYS
SOUTHWAYS
Pol. Sta.
DUNDALK ROAD
NETHERFIELD
PO.
Oakfield Primy. Sch.
CORONET WAY
CORONATION
REGAL CRES
CROWN
LODGE RD
EDINBURGH
ROAD
DITCHFIELD
DITCHFIELD PLACE
DITCHFIELD ROAD
OAKFIELD DRI.
WEST-MINSTER CLOSE
PHILIP ROAD
HERALDS CL.
ABBEY
ANDREW CL.
HEYES RD.
KENNETH RD.
YORK RD.
DEANSWAY
WINCHESTER PL.
NORFOLK PL.
SUFFOLK PL.
CANTERBURY RD.
EDWARD'S WAY
BARONS CL.
FRANCIS CLOSE
NICHOLAS RD.
BLUNDELL
ALEXANDER DRIVE
MONTGOMERY
WAVELL AV.
CUNNINGHAM ROAD
SOMERVILLE RD.
37
DALE CL.
CLINCTON VW.
CLINCTON CL.
SPRINGFIELD RD.
WOODVIEW RD.
C. Primy. Sch.
CLINCTON VW.
Clincton Wood
LAKESIDE CL.
Ditton
DITTON INDUSTRIAL ESTATE
GAVIN RD
EVENITE ROAD
TURNALL RD.
WYNCROFT RD.
WYNCROFT CLO.
LONG ROW
ARNOLD PL.
P.O.
ST. MICHAEL'S RD.
St. Michael's R.C. Ch.
St. Michael's Primy. Sch.
R.C. Sch.
GOLF COURSE
IND. ESTATE
PITTVILLE TER.
FIELD GATE
MARSHGATE
OLDGATE
A562
LINK ROAD
OLD A.
85
ROAD
DITTON ROAD
Ditton Br.
DITTON STATION
HARRISONS
LOVEL TERR.
CLAPGATE CRES.
STAPL. WAY
HOLLINS WAY
Playing Field
BLACKSTONE AV.
FOUNDRY LANE
BAGULEY AVENUE
Primy. Sch.
PICKERINGS ROAD
HALE BANK
HEATH VIEW RD.
HEATHVIEW CL.
KENVIEW CL.
HALE
Meth. Ch. (Clinic)
MERSEY VIEW ROAD
HALE GATE ROAD
LANE
HALE
GARNETT'S LA.
HALE BANK RECLAMATION SCHEME
38
MATHISON RD.
DESOTO RD.
84
39
83
49
50
DD
EE

136
ROAD
SPEKE
SPEKE
ESTATE
EVANS RD.
AVENUE
ROAD
GASKILL RD.
43
X
Y
DELF LANE
BARNHAM CLO.
PETWORTH CLO.
CHURCH RD.
RYCOT
LA.
ROAD
CLOUGH
BRAY
ROAD
TARBOCK
TONBRIDGE CLO.
LENHAM WAY
BEX CL.
SAN. CLO.
DYMCHURCH
APPLEDORE
CLO.
WAY
RD.
GERNETH CL.
WOODEND
SPEKE TOWN
P.O.
THE CRES.
FARM RD.
HALL RD.
RAMSBROOK CL.
RAMSBROOK RD.
FARM RD.
AV.
ROAD
ROAD
WELLBROOK CL.
WELLBROOK GRN.
R.C. Pr. Sch.
ROAD
HAREFIELD GRN.
SHIPLEY WK.
ILKLEY WK.
151
RUNWAY
39
Playing Fields
HALL
SCHOOL
GERNETH L.
CHURCH RD.
GREYHOUND
BLACKROD AV.
BLACKLOCK
STOCKTON WOOD R.
Liby.
STAPLETON
SPEKE HALL
YEADON WK.
Fire Sta.
Pr. Sch.
GOLDFINCH
LOVELL WY.
Speke Comp. Sch. (Lower)
WELTON GRO.
WELTON CLO.
SPINDUS ROAD
BAILEY'S LA.
SPEKE
SUTTON WOOD RD.
SAINTS
TEWIT HALL RD.
TEWIT HALL CL.
CENTRAL
AV.
North Lodge
INDUSTRIAL
AVENUE
Dunlop Sports Ground
Speke
132
FENTON CLO.
FENTON GRN.
WESTERN
LINNER
LOVELL
Speke Comp. Sch. (Upper)
HAREFIELD
MARTON CLO.
MARTON GRN.
CONLEACH RD.
83
ESTATE
ROAD
DUNLOP RD.
DAM
BUCKLEY WK.
BRAMLEY WK.
HALE
HALE
OGLET LA.
Speke Farms
Stockton Wood
Farm
Hall
Airport Fire Sta.
40
LIVERPOOL
AIRPORT
NEW 7,500 FEET RUNWAY
82
41
RIVER
81
42
43
X
Y

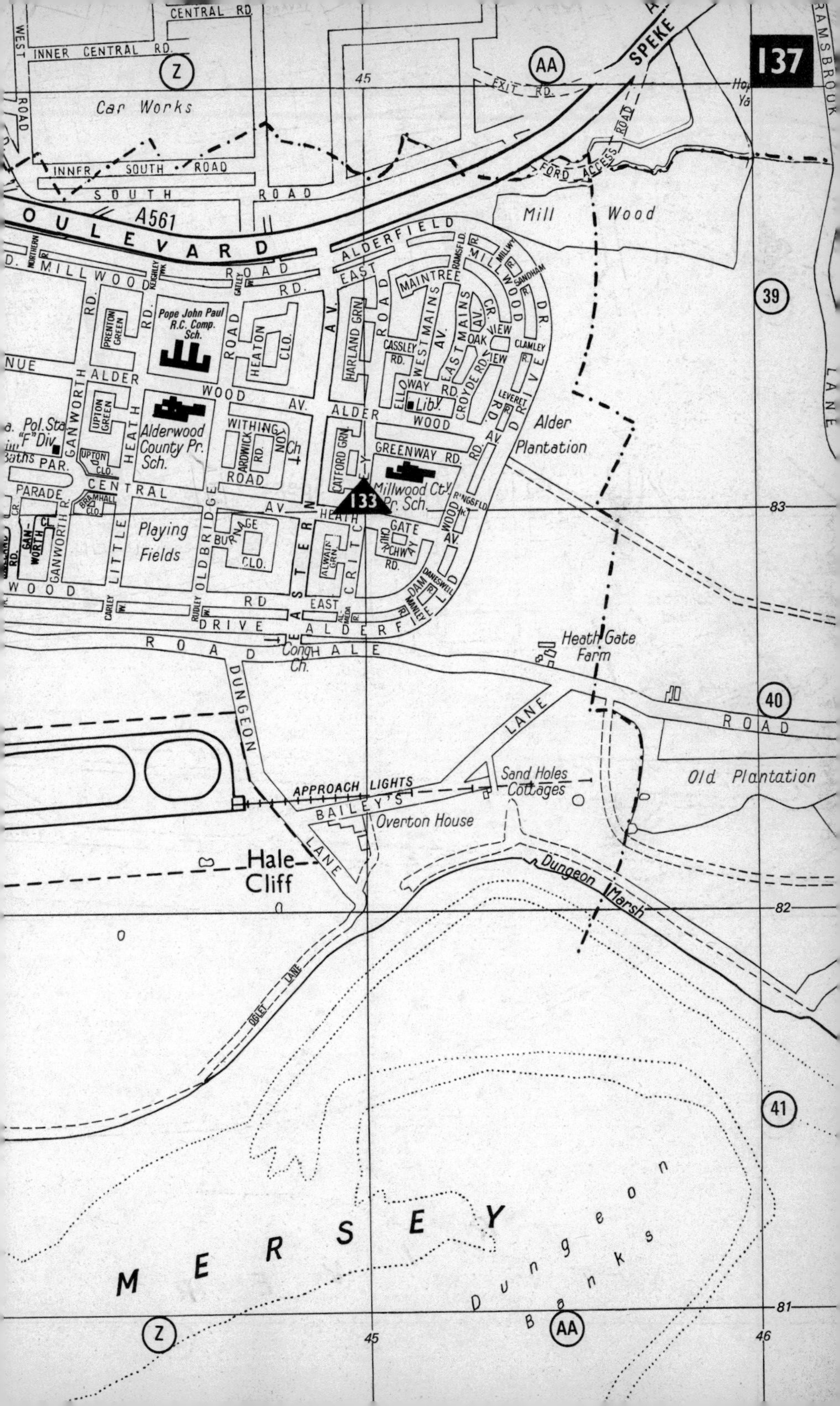
CENTRAL RD.
WEST
INNER CENTRAL RD.
ROAD
Z
AA
Car Works
45
EXIT RD.
SPEKE
INNER SOUTH ROAD
SOUTH ROAD
FORD ACCESS ROAD
A561
OULEVARD
Mill Wood
MILLWOOD ROAD
RD.
ALDERFIELD
EAST
MAINTREE
MILLWOOD DR.
SANDHAM
RAMSFLD.
MILLWY
WEST MAINS AV.
EAST MAINS
Pope John Paul R.C. Comp. Sch.
HEATON CLO.
HARLAND GRN.
CASSLEY RD.
PRENTON GREEN
OAK VIEW
CLAMLEY
CROYDE RD.
ALDER WOOD AV.
ALDERWOOD
NUE
GANWORTH RD.
UPTON GREEN
HEATH RD.
Alderwood County Pr. Sch.
WITHING
ARDWICK RD.
ROAD
Ch
ELLOWAY RD.
Lib'y.
LEVERET
DRIVE
Alder Plantation
Pol. Sta.
"F" Div.
Baths
UPTON CLO.
PAR.
PARADE
CENTRAL
CATFORD GRN.
GREENWAY RD.
Millwood Ct'y. Pr. Sch.
133
RINGSFLD.
HEATH AV.
83
BRAMHALL CLO.
GANWORTH CL.
Playing Fields
LITTLE
OLDBRIDGE
BURNAGE CLO.
EASTERN
CRITCHLEY
GATE
CHURCHWAY RD.
WOOD AV.
ALWAIN GRN.
DAMS
DANESWELL
MANLEY
WOOD
CARLEY
RUDLEY
RD
DRIVE
EAST ALDERFIELD
ROAD
Cong. Ch.
HALE
Heath Gate Farm
DUNGEON
LANE
40
ROAD
39
Sand Holes Cottages
Old Plantation
APPROACH LIGHTS
BAILEY'S
Overton House
LANE
Hale Cliff
Dungeon Marsh
82
OGLET LANE
41
M E R S E Y
Dungeon Banks
81
46

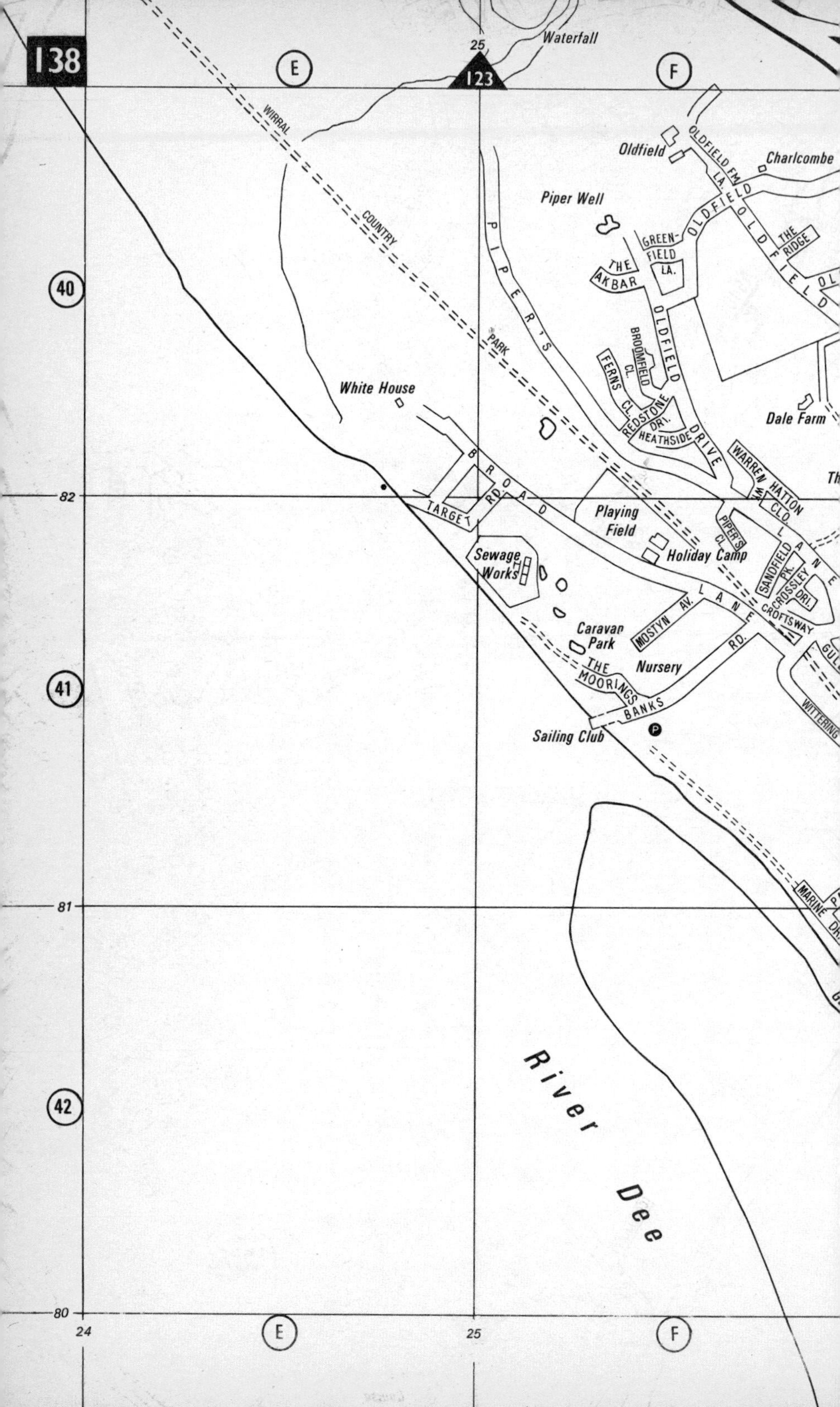

Waterfall
25
123
E
F
WIRRAL
COUNTRY
PARK
Oldfield
OLDFIELD FM. LA.
Charlcombe
Piper Well
PIPER'S
OLDFIELD
THE RIDGE
GREENFIELD LA.
THE AKBAR
OLDFIELD
BROOMFIELD CL.
FERNS CL.
REDSTONE DRI.
HEATHSIDE
DRIVE
Dale Farm
White House
BROAD
TARGET RD.
Playing Field
WARREN HATTON CLO.
PIPER'S CL.
Holiday Camp
SANDFIELD PK.
CROSSLEY DRI.
LANE
Sewage Works
MOSTYN AV.
CROFTSWAY
Caravan Park
THE MOORINGS
Nursery
RD.
BANKS
Sailing Club
WITTERING
MARINE
DR.
River Dee
40
41
42
82
81
80
24
25

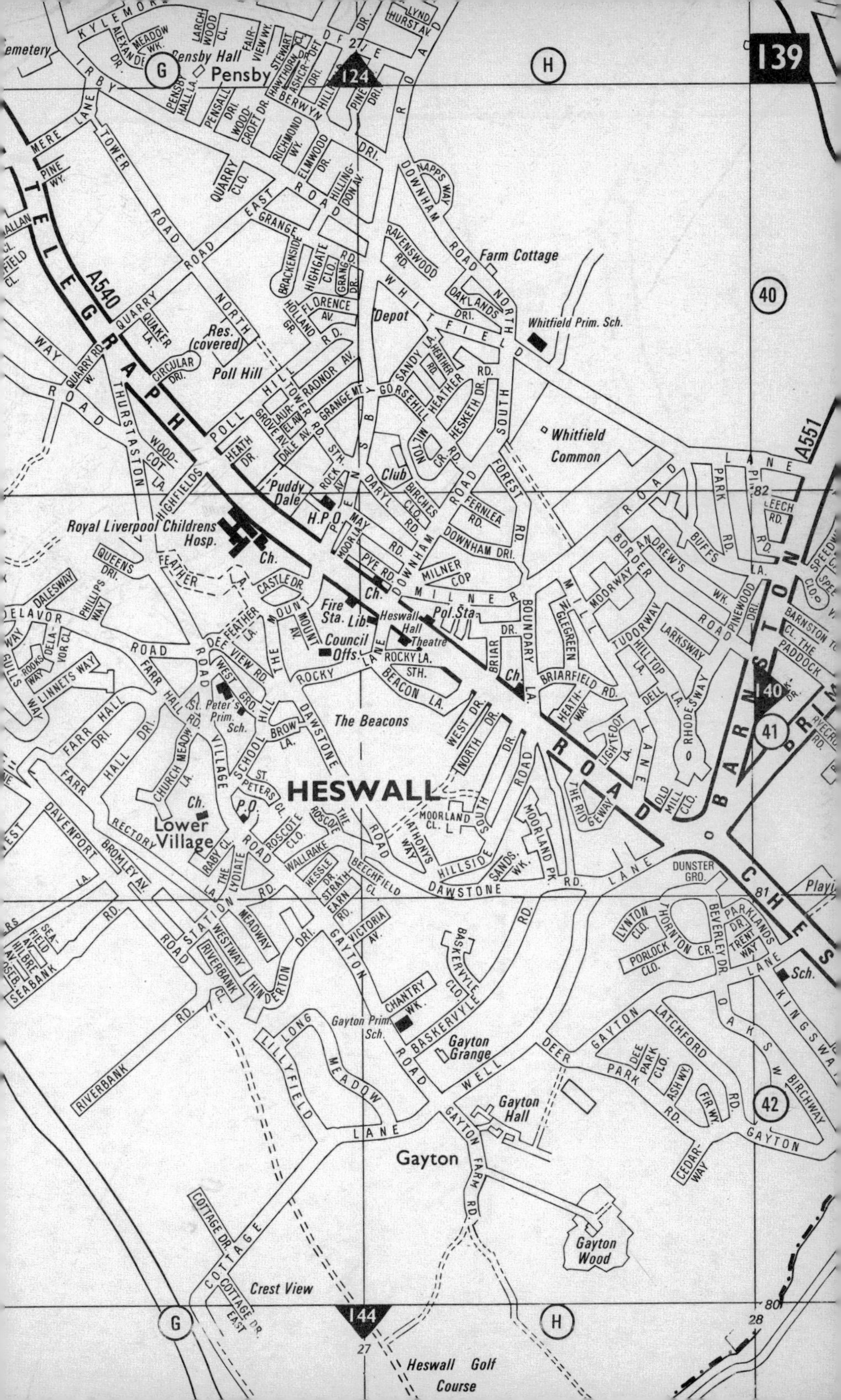
139
Cemetery
Pensby Hall
Pensby
G
H
124
27
KYLEMORE
ALEXANDER DR.
MEADOW WK.
LARCHWOOD CL.
FAIRVIEW WY.
STEWART CL.
HAWTHORN
ASHCROFT DRI.
LYNDHURST AV.
PENSBY HALL LA.
PENSALL DRI.
WOODCROFT DR.
BERWYN
HILLSIDE
PINE DRI.
IRBY
MERE LANE
PINE WY.
TOWER ROAD
QUARRY CLO.
RICHMOND WY.
ELMWOOD DR.
HILLINGDON AV.
DRI.
NAPPS WAY
DOWNHAM ROAD NORTH
GRANGE ROAD EAST
TELEGRAPH ROAD
A540
QUARRY ROAD
QUAKER LA.
BRACKENSIDE
HIGHGATE CLO.
GRANGE RD.
RAVENSWOOD RD.
WHITFIELD RD.
Farm Cottage
OAKLANDS DRI.
40
Whitfield Prim. Sch.
HOLLAND GR.
FLORENCE AV.
Depot
Res. (covered)
Poll Hill
CIRCULAR DRI.
QUARRY RD. W.
WAY
ROAD
THURSTASTON
RADNOR AV.
POLL HILL
TOWER RD.
GRANGE MT.
GORSEHILL
SANDY LA.
HEATHER RD.
HESKETH DR.
MILTON GR.
SOUTH
Whitfield Common
A551
LANE
PARK
82
LEECH RD.
WOODCOT LA.
HIGHFIELDS
HEATH DR.
LAUREL AV.
GROVE AV.
DALE AV.
STH.
Puddy Dale
ROCK AV.
Club
DARYL RD.
BIRCHES CLO.
FOREST RD.
FERNLEA RD.
DOWNHAM DRI.
H.P.O.
Royal Liverpool Childrens Hosp.
Ch.
MAY
MOORLA
PYE RD.
DOWNHAM
MILNER COP
MILNER
BORDER ROAD
ANDREW'S WK.
BUFFS RD.
BARNSTON
SPEEDWELL CLO.
QUEENS DRI.
FEATHER LA.
CASTLE DR
Fire Sta.
Lib.
Heswall Hall
Theatre
Pol. Sta.
BOUNDARY LA.
BRIAR DR.
MILL
WHEELGREEN
MOORWAY
TUDORWAY
HILLTOP LA.
LARKSWAY
PINEWOOD DRI.
BARNSTON CL.
THE PADDOCK
DALESWAY
DELAVOR
PHILLIPS WAY
THE MOUNT
MOUNT AV.
Council Offs.
ROCKY LA.
ROCKY LA. STH.
BEACON LA.
BRIARFIELD RD.
HEATHWAY
DELL
RHODESWAY
140
41
ROOKS WAY
DELAVOR CL.
GULLS WAY
LINNETS WAY
DEE VIEW RD.
WEST GRO.
St. Peter's Prim. Sch.
FARR HALL RD.
FARR HALL DRI.
HALL DRI.
SCHOOL HILL
BROW LA.
DAWSTONE
The Beacons
WEST DR.
NORTH DR.
LIGHTFOOT LA.
LANE
CHURCH MEADOW LA.
VILLAGE
ST. PETERS CL.
HESWALL
THE RIDGEWAY
OLD MILL CLO.
CHESTER
BRIMSTAGE
RYECROFT
FARR
DAVENPORT
RECTORY
BROMLEY AV.
Ch.
Lower Village
P.O.
ROSCOTE CLO.
THE ROSCOTE
ROAD
ANTHONY'S WAY
MOORLAND CL.
SOUTH
MOORLAND PK.
SANDS WK.
HILLSIDE
RABY CL.
THE LYDIATE
WALLRAKE
HESSLE DR.
BEECHFIELD CL.
STRATH
EARN RD.
DAWSTONE RD.
DUNSTER GRO.
81
Playi
LA.
STATION ROAD
MEADWAY
WESTWAY
RIVERBANK CL.
VICTORIA AV.
GAYTON
BASKERVYLE CLO.
LYNTON CLO.
THORNTON CR.
BEVERLEY DR.
PARKLANDS DR.
TRENT WAY
PORLOCK CLO.
LANE
Sch.
SEAFIELD AV.
HILBRE AV.
SEABANK
HINDERTON DRI.
CHANTRY WK.
Gayton Prim. Sch.
BASKERVYLE
Gayton Grange
DEER PARK
DEE PARK CLO.
ASH WY.
FIR WY.
LATCHFORD RD.
OAKS WAY
KINGSWAY
BIRCHWAY
42
RIVERBANK RD.
LONG MEADOW
LILLYFIELD
ROAD
WELL
Gayton Hall
CEDARWAY
GAYTON
Gayton
LANE
GAYTON FARM RD.
COTTAGE DR.
COTTAGE
Gayton Wood
Crest View
COTTAGE DR. EAST
144
27
80
28
Heswall Golf Course

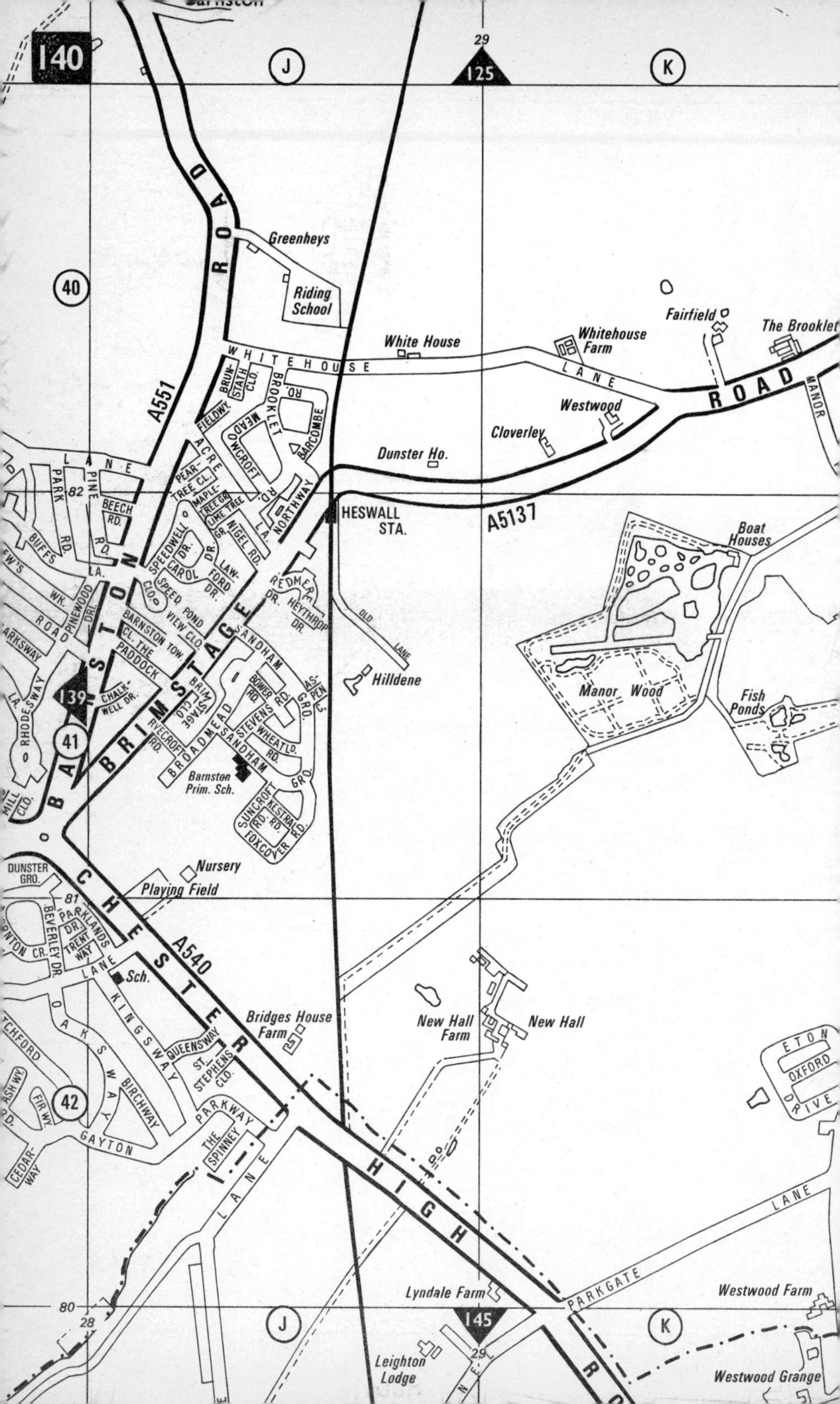
Barnston
140
J
29
125
K
ROAD
Greenheys
Riding School
40
A551
WHITEHOUSE LANE
White House
Whitehouse Farm
Fairfield
The Brooklet
ROAD
MANOR
Westwood
Cloverley
Dunster Ho.
BRUNSTATH CLO.
BROOKLET RD.
MEADOWCROFT
BARCOMBE
FIELDWY.
ACRE
PEAR-TREE CL.
MAPLE-TREE GR.
LIME TREE GR.
NIGEL RD.
LA.
NORTHWAY
HESWALL STA.
A5137
Boat Houses
LANE
PARK RD.
82
PINE RD.
BEECH RD.
BUFFS LA.
WK.
ROAD
PINEWOOD DR.
SPEEDWELL DR.
CAROL DR.
LAWFORD DR.
SPEED CLO.
POND VIEW CLO.
REDMERE DR.
HEYTHROP DR.
OLD LANE
Hilldene
BARNSTON
BRIMSTAGE
BARNSTON TOW.
CL. THE PADDOCK
SANDHAM
BRIMSTAGE CLO.
BOWER RD.
STEVENS RD.
ASPEN C.
GRO.
WHEATLD. RD.
Manor Wood
Fish Ponds
139
CHALKWELL DR.
RHODESWAY LA.
41
RYECROFT RD.
BROADMEAD
SANDHAM
Barnston Prim. Sch.
SUNCROFT RD.
KESTRAL RD.
FOXCOVER RD.
GRO.
MILL CLO.
DUNSTER GRO.
Nursery
Playing Field
CHESTER
A540
81
PARKLANDS DR.
BEVERLEY DR.
TRENT WAY
CR.
LANE
Sch.
OAKSWAY
KINGSWAY
QUEENSWAY
ST. STEPHENS CLO.
BIRCHWAY
Bridges House Farm
New Hall Farm
New Hall
ETON
OXFORD
DRIVE
42
FIR WY.
ASH WY.
GAYTON
CEDARWAY
PARKWAY
THE SPINNEY
LANE
HIGH
LANE
PARKGATE
Lyndale Farm
Westwood Farm
80
28
J
145
29
K
Leighton Lodge
Westwood Grange

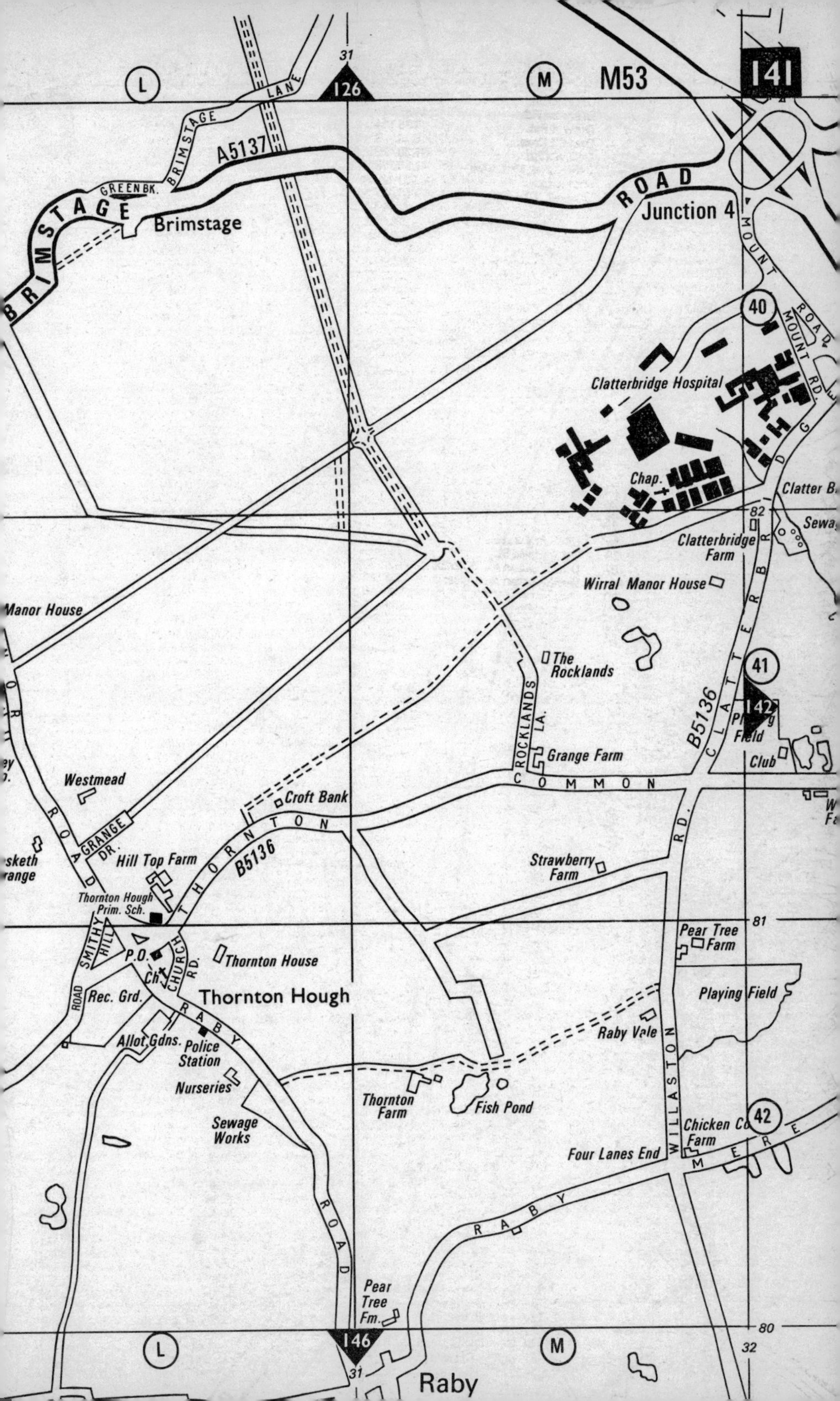

31
126
M53
141
L
M
BRIMSTAGE LANE
BRIMSTAGE
A5137
GREEN BK.
BRIMSTAGE
Brimstage
ROAD
Junction 4
MOUNT
ROAD
MOUNT RD.
40
Clatterbridge Hospital
Chap.
Clatter B
82
Sewa
Clatterbridge Farm
Wirral Manor House
Manor House
The Rocklands
ROCKLANDS LA.
41
142
Playing Field
Club
B5136
CLATTERBRIDGE
Grange Farm
COMMON
Westmead
Croft Bank
THORNTON
GRANGE DR.
ROAD
Hill Top Farm
B5136
sketh
range
Strawberry Farm
RD.
Thornton Hough Prim. Sch.
81
Pear Tree Farm
SMITHY HILL
P.O.
Ch.
CHURCH RD.
Thornton House
Thornton Hough
ROAD
Rec. Grd.
Playing Field
RABY
Raby Vale
Allot.Gdns.
Police Station
Nurseries
Thornton Farm
Fish Pond
Sewage Works
42
Chicken Co
Farm
WILLASTON
Four Lanes End
MERE
RABY
ROAD
Pear Tree Fm.
80
146
31
32
Raby

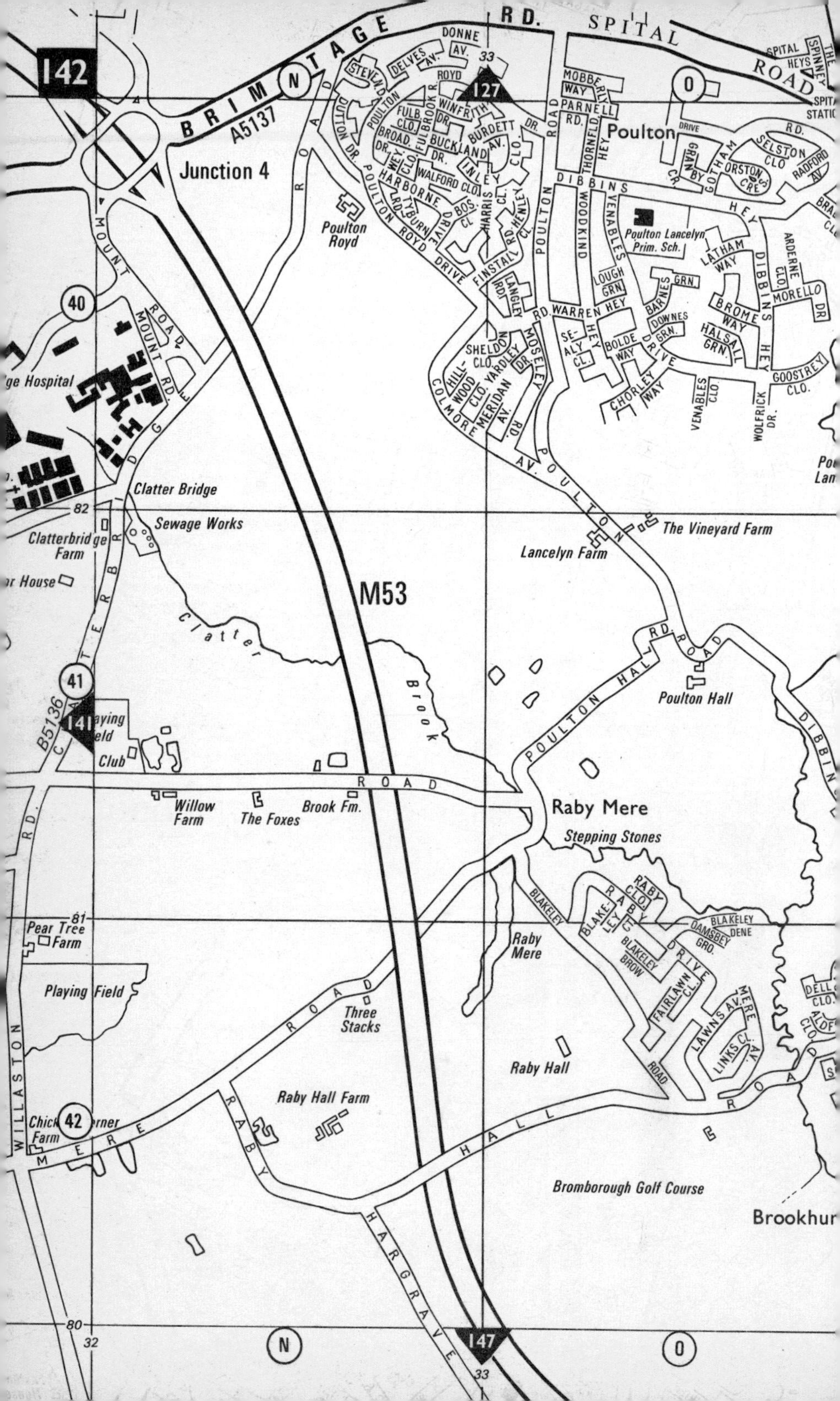

142
BRIMSTAGE RD.
SPITAL ROAD
A5137
Junction 4
127
33
Poulton
Poulton Royd
Poulton Lancelyn Prim. Sch.
Mount Road
40
Hospital
Clatter Bridge
Sewage Works
Clatterbridge Farm
82
M53
Clatter Brook
The Vineyard Farm
Lancelyn Farm
41
141
B5136
Clatterbridge Road
Club
Poulton Hall Road
Poulton Hall
Dibbins Hey
Raby Mere
Stepping Stones
Willow Farm
The Foxes
Brook Fm.
81
Pear Tree Farm
Playing Field
Three Stacks
Raby Hall
Raby Hall Farm
Raby Mere Road
Raby Hall Road
Bromborough Golf Course
Brookhur
42
Willaston Rd.
Hargrave
80
32
N
O
147

SPITAL ROAD
MILL RD.
HEATHER DENE
FAIRWAY S'TH
Allot Gds.
128
35
Storage Depot
COMMERCIAL RD.
Wks.
Power Sta.
ARKWOOD
GLEN
OAKRIDGE
OAKRIDGE CL.
PINE RIDGE CLO.
BIRCH CLO.
St. Patrick's Well
Brotherton Park
Sports Ground
SUMMERFIELD
Woodslee Prim. Sch.
CROFT AV.
CROFT AV. EAST
CALDBECK
THURSBY ROAD
WELTON RD.
DINSDALE ROAD
WELTON ROAD
Works
NORTH CLO.
UPLANDS RD.
CENTRAL AV.
Playing Field
RD.
STANHOPE DRIVE
CHUCHWOOD CLO.
Lib.
A41
NEW
CROFT
CROFT LA.
STANHOPE DR.
RAKE
HORNBY A.
HORNBY AV.
HORNBY RD.
BROSELEY
PALATINE
BELMONT AV.
ECCLESTON
FARLEY A.
HADLEY AV.
Ch.
Sch.
ATHELSTAN CLO.
MARK RAKE
P.O.
HIGH S.
QUEENS AV.
Rec. Grd.
LUDLOW GR.
Chap.
Civic Hall
ALLPORT LA.
BROMBOROUGH VILLAGE RD.
Pol. Sta.
HOWARD AV.
ROAD
THE VALLEY
PARK VIEW
BRADMOOR RD.
DALE AV.
FORWOOD RD.
Allot. Gdns.
GRATRIX AV.
HEYS R.
JUNE AV.
HARROW GR.
CAMBRIDGE RD.
CHESTNUT G.
BEECHWOOD
THE OAKS
ASHFIELD
MAINWARING R.
MAPLE GRO.
THE AVENUE
OAKFIELD RD.
OTELEY RD.
OTELEY AV.
LANE
HAWTHORN LA.
Playing Field
Mendell Prim. Sch.
ASHFLD. CR.
ACRE LA.
ACRE
MOSSLEY AV.
MEADOW RD.
NEVILLE RD.
Christ the King R.C. Prim. Sch.
Ch.
CUNNINGHAM DR.
Bromborough Sec. Sch.
Playing Field
GREENFIELDS AV.
DAWPOOL DR.
AMBLESIDE C.
GLYN C.
GORDON A.
ALLPORT RD.
THE ALLPORTS
BRANCOTE GDNS.
BRANCOTE DRIVE
ROAD
GRENVILLE CR.
CALDICOTT AV.
WOODYEAR RD.
BRIDLE
BROMBOROUGH STA.
MARTEN AV.
MARLINE AV.
WESTMINSTER
BRIDLE CLO.
Allot. Gdns.
Plymyard House
Playing Fields
Tennis Courts
MORLAND
Raeburn Prim. Sch.
MANOR RD.
MORLAND AV.
PRINCES AV.
KILBURN AV.
BRUCE CRES
ALISTAIR
ANGUS RD.
Brookhurst Prim. Sch.
MALCOLM CR.
DRIVE
BROOKHURST
FAIRHAVEN DR.
ROAD
Playing Field
THE CHASE
PLYMYARD
DEARNFORD AV.
SPRING AV.
BRONINGTON AV.
RAEBURN
Playing Field
Pav.
Eastham
BETTISFIELD
BRINLEY CLO.
WINGATE RD.
CROSSDALE RD.
DALE RD.
PLYMYARD CLO.
LANGFIELD GRO.
WOODLEA CLO.
HILLARY
Allot. Gdns.
Heygarth Jun. Sch.
ELGAR AV.
GORSEFIELD CLO.
GORSEFIELD AV.
OAKDENE CLO.
BROOKHURST CL.
KEITH DR.
BANFF
BOWNESS AV.
BROOKHURST RD.
WOODLEA DR.
EDGEWOOD
WHITE LODGE CL.
HEYGARTH
ATHOL CLO.
ATHOL DR.
CHESTERFIELD RD.
HARROGATE RD.
REDCAR DR.
CONISTON AV.
KESWICK
148
GRAMPIAN
SELKIRK AV.
RENFREW AV.
PAISLEY
GLENBURN
EDALE CLO.
WENSLEY AV.
ESKDALE AV.
DALE AV.
SWALE CL.
MALLOWDALE CL.
DARL. DR.
AVON DALE
Glenburn Inf. Sch.
ADASTON AV.
RAKE
P.O.
Lib.
STANLEY
CHURCH LA.
Eastham House
RIBBLES. CL.
WHARFEDALE DR.
MILLERSDALE CL.
CARLETT BOULEV.
HANDFORD AV.
ROAD
Rugby Football Ground
St. Mary's Prim. Sch.
EASTHAM VILLAGE RD.
DAVI
JOHN
42
War M
80
36
PARK RD.
Playing Field
Cemetery
Carlett Park
81
CHESTER ROAD
BROMBOROUGH
Leverhulme S
Playing Fields
Pav.
Sports Ground
41
150
Warren Farm
Cricket Ground
GREEN LANE
Playing Field
Eastham Country Park
Long Plantation
TEBAY ROAD
WRYNOSE ROAD
Factory
HARDKNOTT ROAD
GRISEDALE RD.
Oil Storage Depot
82
OLD HALL ROAD
Depot
Factory
Oak Wood
Playing Field
POWER ROAD
PLANTATION R.
Works
Works
40
Q
P

144

G   Crest View

27   **139**

H

Gayton Wood

COTTAGE DR.

COTTAGE DR. EAST

Heswall Golf Course

THE WIRRAL

COUNTRY

Backwood Fa

Backwood Hall

T.

The Lodge

PARK

43

Parkgate Baths (Dis.)

79

NORTH PDE

BOATHOUSE

THE

ACRE DR.

BARN
TOFT.

BROOK HEY

BEVYL

TITHE BARN

LOOMS

MEALORS WEINT

Sch.

P

ACRE R

SCHOO

44

Gayton

Sands

78

45

77

26   G   27   H

145
140
146
29
79
78
77
30
43
44
45
J
K
H
PARKGATE
ROAD
A540
CHE
Lyndale
Westwood Farm
Westwood Grange
Yew Tree Farm
Yew Tree House
Leighton Lodge
THE RUNNEL
BOATHOUSE LANE
B5135
Leighton Hall Farm
LEIGHTON RD.
Leighton Ho.
Windyridge
Ashfield Hall
Ashfield Farm
LIVERPOOL ROAD
Brook House
Five Ways
Oakland Farm
Leawood
Works
Cedar Ct.
WOOD LANE
Woodcote
LEIGHTON
B5136
Clayhill Industrial Estate
Windy Knowe
PADDOCK DR.
The Paddock
Ardmore
PINEHEY
FAIRHOLME AV.
RINGWAY
THE BIRCHES
THE WITTERING
MOORFIELD DR.
OAKLANDS RD.
Sch.
School
Playing Fields
Sports Complex
Parkgate
SPRINGCROFT
ROPEWALK
Field School
Sports Ground
THE SPINNEY
EARLE DRIVE
THE ROAD
PRIORY
ABBOTS WY.
EARLE CR.
MAYFIELD GDS.
LIVERPOOL
DRAKE RD.
SIDNEY RD.
HAWKINS RD.
RALEIGH RD.
GREN. RD.
PARK
Hin
Chap.
Cemetery
STATION RD.
Cricket Grd.
PARKGATE
WOODLANDS RD.
ALBERT DR.
The Woodlands
Club
THE LEIGHTONS
FROBISHER RD.
JONSON RD.
SHAKESPEARE RD.
MARL RD.
Playground
SYTCH CFT.
RABY
BREEZEHILL
BREE CL.
Oak Farm
NESTON
The Knoll
Autistic Centre
MANORIAL
Sports Ground
BUGGEN LA.
MILL ST.
Sch.
P.O.
STA.
PARK ST.
CHURCHILL WAY
Ch.
RABY RD.
Town Hall
BLACKEYS LA.
HIGHFIELD RD.
BREEZE-HILL PK.
GUNN GRO.
ROAD
Pol. Sta.
MOORSIDE AV.
Ch.
LA.
HERON CT.
ROAD
Lib.
ROAD
THE CROSS
BROOK
ST.
GLADSTONE RD.
OLIVE DR.
STANTON CT.
HINDERTON
THE QUILLET
Hinderton Lodge
MOORSIDE
OLD QUAY LANE
Manor Ho.
MANOR CLO.
Moorside
BEECHWAYS DR.
CHURCH LA.
HIGH ST.
CHESTER RD.
Ch.
BRIDGE ST.
Stanney Fields
BUSHELL RD.
STATION RD.
ELDON TER.
BURTON
Sch.
ROMNEY WY.
RAEBURN AV.
LANDSEER AV.
MORLAND AV.
MELLOCK
BENDEE
Clinic
Sch.
WATERFORD
DUNRAVEN RD.
RAYMOND
ROAD
BENDEE
FLINT MEADOW
Play Fld.
COTTAGE CLO.
ROMAN CT.
WINDERMERE CL.
DERWENT
FLAG LA.
NEW-TOWN
FLINT DR.
FLINT CL.
ALLANS CLO.
MEADOW
GRASMERE RD.
Works
RYDAL CL.
Sch.
TALBOT AV.
LANE
MELLOCK CLO.
THE GRN.
STONE-BANK RD.
MEADOW CLO.
WEST VALE
Little Neston

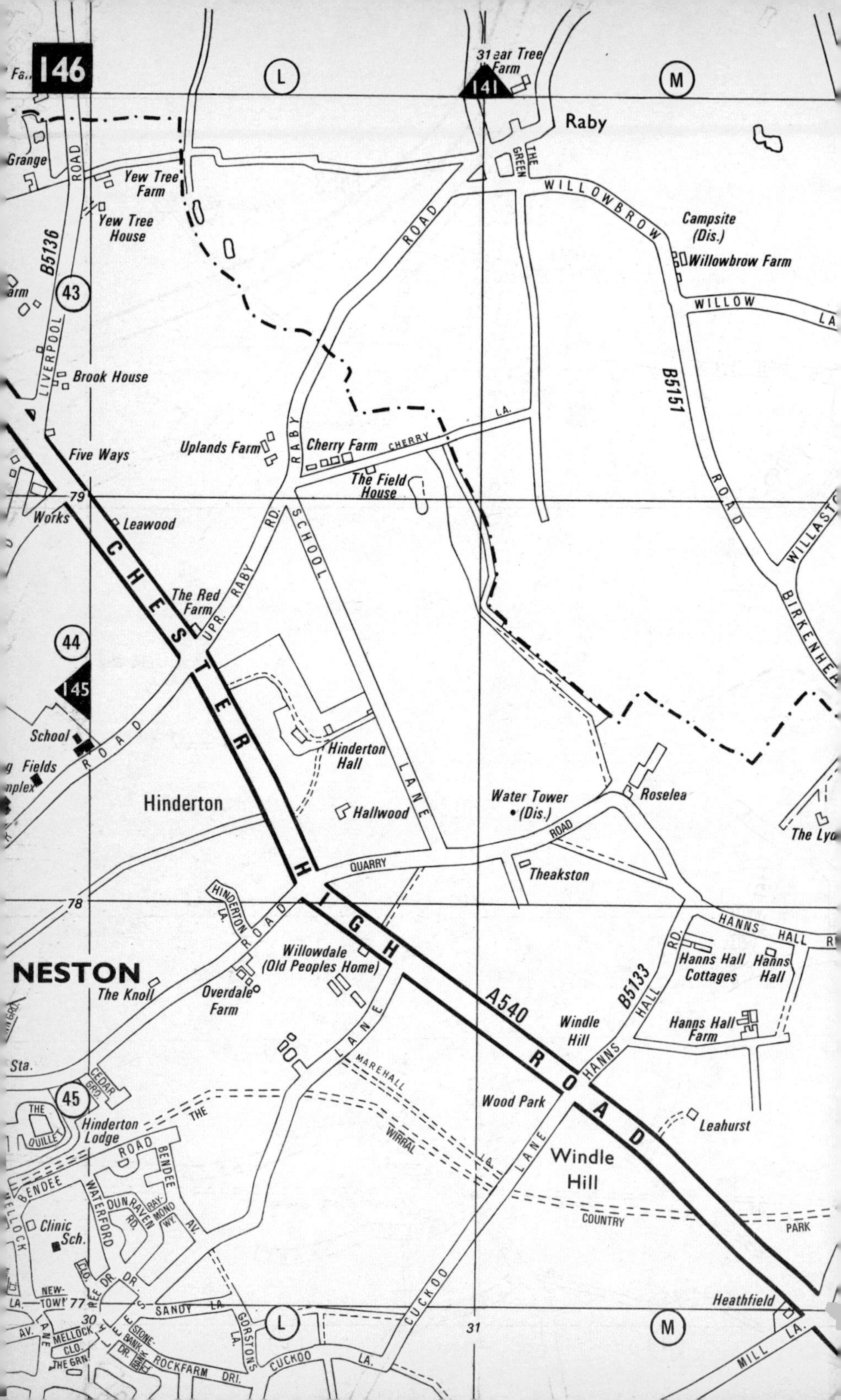
146
L
M
141
Pear Tree Farm
Raby
THE GREEN
WILLOWBROW
Campsite (Dis.)
Willowbrow Farm
WILLOW LA.
Grange
ROAD
Yew Tree Farm
Yew Tree House
B5136
43
LIVERPOOL
ROAD
Brook House
RAB
ROAD
Uplands Farm
Cherry Farm
CHERRY LA.
The Field House
B5151
ROAD
Five Ways
79
Works
Leawood
UPR. RABY RD.
SCHOOL
The Red Farm
CHESTER HIGH ROAD
WILLASTON
BIRKENHEAD
44
145
School
Fields
ROAD
Hinderton Hall
LANE
Water Tower (Dis.)
Roselea
Hinderton
Hallwood
ROAD
The Lyo
QUARRY
Theakston
78
HINDERTON LA.
ROAD
HANNS HALL RD.
Willowdale (Old Peoples Home)
Hanns Hall Cottages
Hanns Hall
NESTON
The Knoll
Overdale Farm
A540
B5133
Windle Hill
Hanns Hall Farm
LANE
HANNS
Sta.
CEDAR GRO.
MAREHALL
45
THE QUILLET
Wood Park
Hinderton Lodge
THE
WIRRAL
Leahurst
ROAD
BENDEE
LA.
LANE
Windle Hill
BENDEE
WATERFORD
DUNRAVEN RD.
RAYMOND WY.
AV.
COUNTRY
PARK
Clinic
Sch.
MELLOCK
CUCKOO
NEW-TOWN
LA.
77
SANDY LA.
GORSTONS LA.
Heathfield
30
L
31
M
AV.
MELLOCK CLO.
THE GRN.
STONEBANK DR.
ROCKFARM DRI.
CUCKOO LA.
MILL LA.

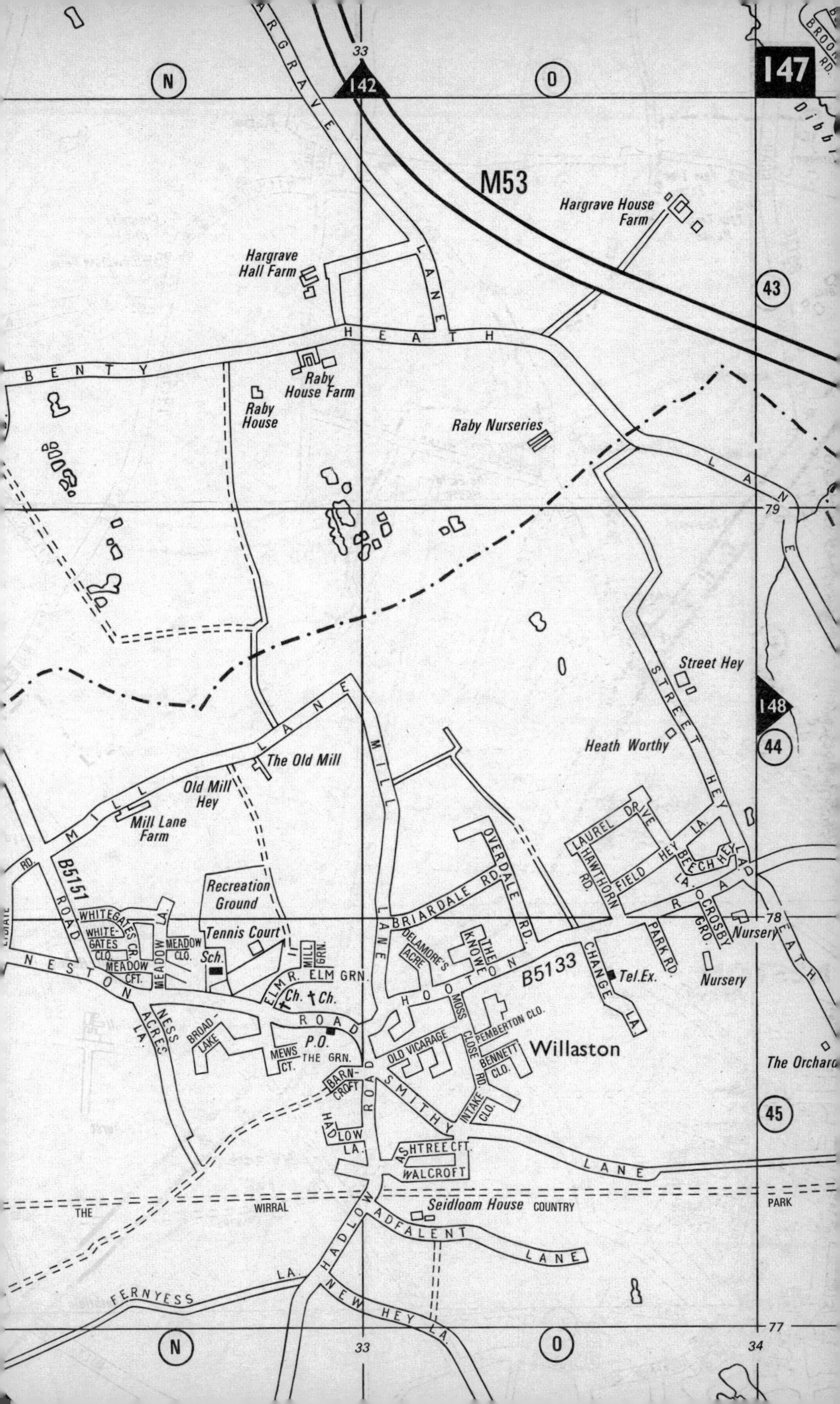

147
142
148
N
O
33
34
43
44
45
79
78
77
M53
HARGRAVE LANE
Hargrave House Farm
Hargrave Hall Farm
BENTY HEATH
Raby House Farm
Raby House
Raby Nurseries
LANE
Street Hey
STREET HEY
Heath Worthy
MILL LANE
The Old Mill
Old Mill Hey
Mill Lane Farm
B5151
ROAD
Recreation Ground
Tennis Court
WHITEGATES CR.
WHITEGATES CLO.
MEADOW CFT.
MEADOW LA.
MEADOW CLO.
Sch.
NESTON
ELM R.
ELM GRN.
MILL GRN.
Ch.
ROAD
P.O.
NESS ACRES
LA.
BROADLAKE
MEWS CT.
THE GRN.
BARNCROFT
HADLOW LA.
ROAD
SMITHY
ASHTREE CFT.
WALCROFT
LANE
OLD VICARAGE
MOSS CLOSE
PEMBERTON CLO.
BENNETT CLO.
INTAKE CLO.
RD.
Willaston
HOOTON
B5133
CHANGE LA.
Tel.Ex.
PARK RD.
CROSBY GRO.
Nursery
Nursery
BRIARDALE RD.
OVERDALE RD.
DELAMORE'S ACRE
THE KNOWE
LAUREL DRIVE
HAWTHORN RD.
FIELD HEY LA.
BEECH HEY LA.
HEY LA.
ROAD
HEATH
The Orchard
THE WIRRAL COUNTRY PARK
Seidloom House
HADLOW
ADFALENT LANE
FERNYESS LA.
NEW HEY LA.
BROOK RD.
Dibb

148
143
147
P
Q
43
44
45
79
78
77
34
35
Dibbinsdale Brook
Eastham Sec. Sch.
Mill Park Inf. & Jun. Schs.
Chap.
Ch.
Lib.
P.O.
Glenburn Inf. Sch.
Junction
M53
Clay Pit
Brick Works
Works
Street Hey
Hawthornden Ho.
HOOTON STA.
Oil Depot
HOOTON ROAD
Hooton Bridge
Woodland View
Hall
WATERWORKS LA.
DALE HEY
OAK RD.
SCHOOL
Hooton Farm
The Oaklands
Heathcote
OAKFIELD RD.
Heath Lodge
Heath Farm
Mayfield Lodge
Farre House
Nursery
The Orchard
Roseville Cottage
THE WIRRAL COUNTRY PARK
Heath Hey
The Grange
HEATH LANE
The Mill Nurs
SUTHERLAND DRIVE
EASTHAM MILL
KINGS AV.
PARK DRIVE
RAKE
BOWNESS AV.
BROOKHURST RD.
KESWICK AV.
DUNCANSBY DR.
GORSEFIELD AV.
CHESTERFIELD RD.
HARROGATE RD.
REDCAR DR.
GRAMPIAN WAY
ATHOL DR.
RENFREW AV.
PAISLEY AV.
GLENBURN AV.
ADASTON AV.
LYNDALE AV.
BERWICK AV.
ROTHSAY DR.
ARGYLL AV.
AIRDRE CLO.
DELAMERE AV.
ENNERDALE AV.
CAVELEY AV.
CROSTHWAITE AV.
CRAIGLEIGH GRO.
THORNLEIGH AV.
TARVIN RD.
HELSBY AV.
WILLINGTON AV.
CLIFTON AV.
MARSTON CL.
HATTON AV.
LOWFIELDS AV.
NORLEY AV.
KELSALL AV.
CROSBY GRO.
BEECH HEY LA.

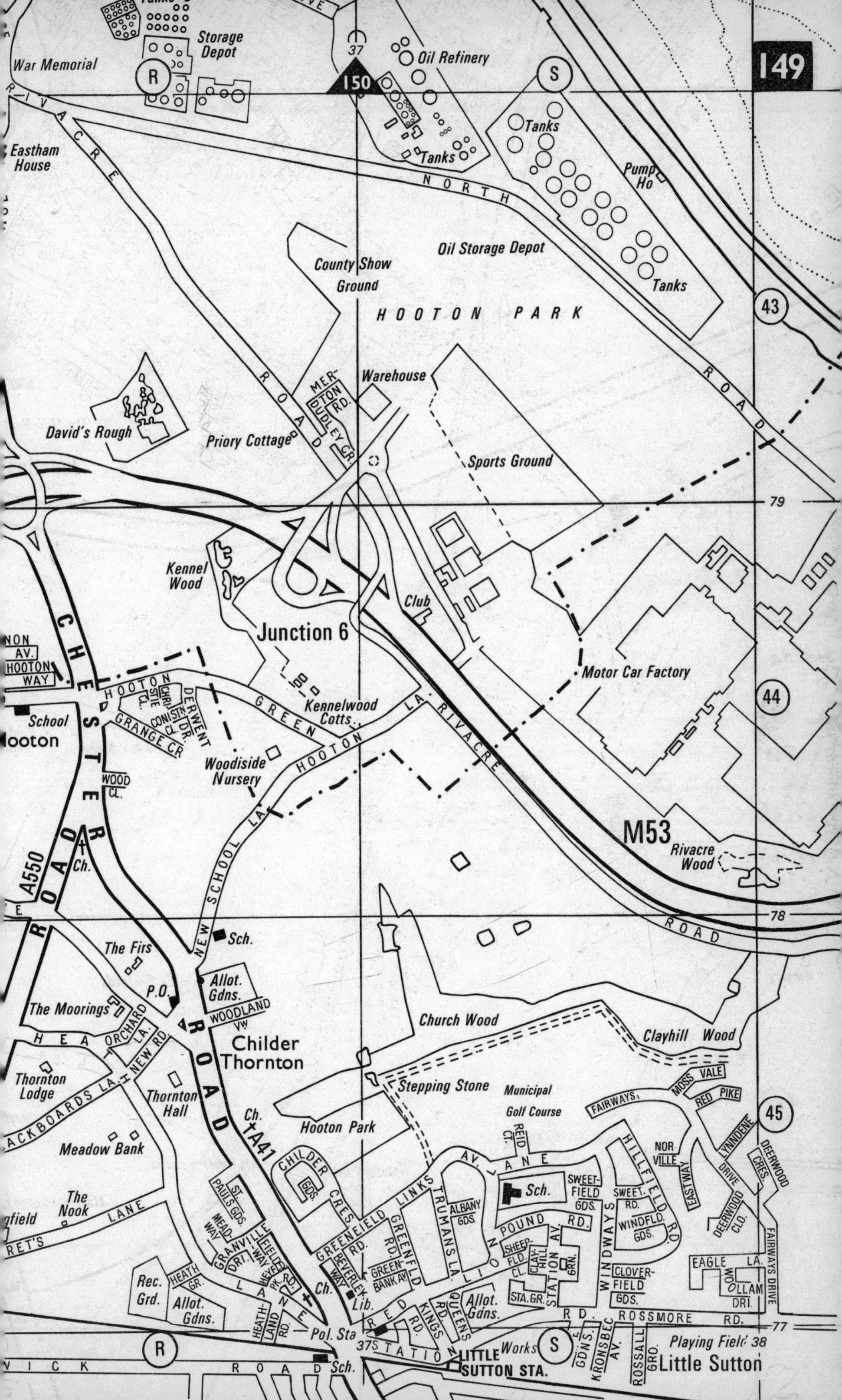
149
150
War Memorial
Storage Depot
Oil Refinery
Tanks
Eastham House
RIVACRE ROAD
NORTH ROAD
Pump Ho
Oil Storage Depot
County Show Ground
HOOTON PARK
43
Warehouse
MERTON RD.
DUDLEY CR.
David's Rough
Priory Cottage
Sports Ground
79
Kennel Wood
Junction 6
Club
CHESTER ROAD
HOOTON WAY
HOOTON GREEN
CHRISTIE CL.
CONISTON CL.
DERWENT DR.
GRANGE CR.
Kennelwood Cotts.
Motor Car Factory
44
School
Hooton
HOOTON LA.
RIVACRE ROAD
Woodiside Nursery
WOOD CL.
NEW SCHOOL LA.
M53
Rivacre Wood
A550
Ch.
78
Sch.
The Firs
Allot. Gdns.
P.O.
The Moorings
WOODLAND VW
ORCHARD LA.
Church Wood
Clayhill Wood
HEATH LA.
NEW RD.
Childer Thornton
Thornton Lodge
Thornton Hall
Stepping Stone
Municipal Golf Course
MOSS VALE
RED PIKE
FAIRWAYS
45
BLACKBOARDS LA.
Hooton Park
REID CT.
Meadow Bank
A41
CHILDER CRES.
LINKS AV.
LANE
NORVILLE
EASTWAY
LYNNDENE DRIVE
DEERWOOD CRES.
The Nook
ST. PAULS GDS.
MEADWAY
TRUMANS LA.
ALBANY GDS.
Sch.
SWEETFIELD GDS.
SWEET. RD.
HILLFIELD RD.
DEERWOOD CLO.
LANE
GRANVILLE DRI.
FIELDWAY
HEYFIELD PK. RD.
GREENFIELD RD.
GREENFLD RD.
GREENBANK AV.
BEVERLEY WAY
POUND RD.
SHEEPFLD. CL.
CLAYHILL GRN.
STATION AV.
WINDWAYS
WINDFLD. GDS.
CLOVERFIELD GDS.
EAGLE LA.
WOOLLAM DRI.
FAIRWAYS DRIVE
Rec. Grd.
HEATH GR.
Allot. Gdns.
HEATHLAND RD.
Ch.
Lib.
RED KINGS RD.
QUEENS RD.
Allot. Gdns.
STA. GR.
RD.
ROSSMORE RD.
77
Pol. Sta
37
STATION
LITTLE SUTTON STA.
Works
GDNS.
KRONSBEC AV.
ROSSALL GRO.
Playing Field
38
Little Sutton
ROAD
Sch.

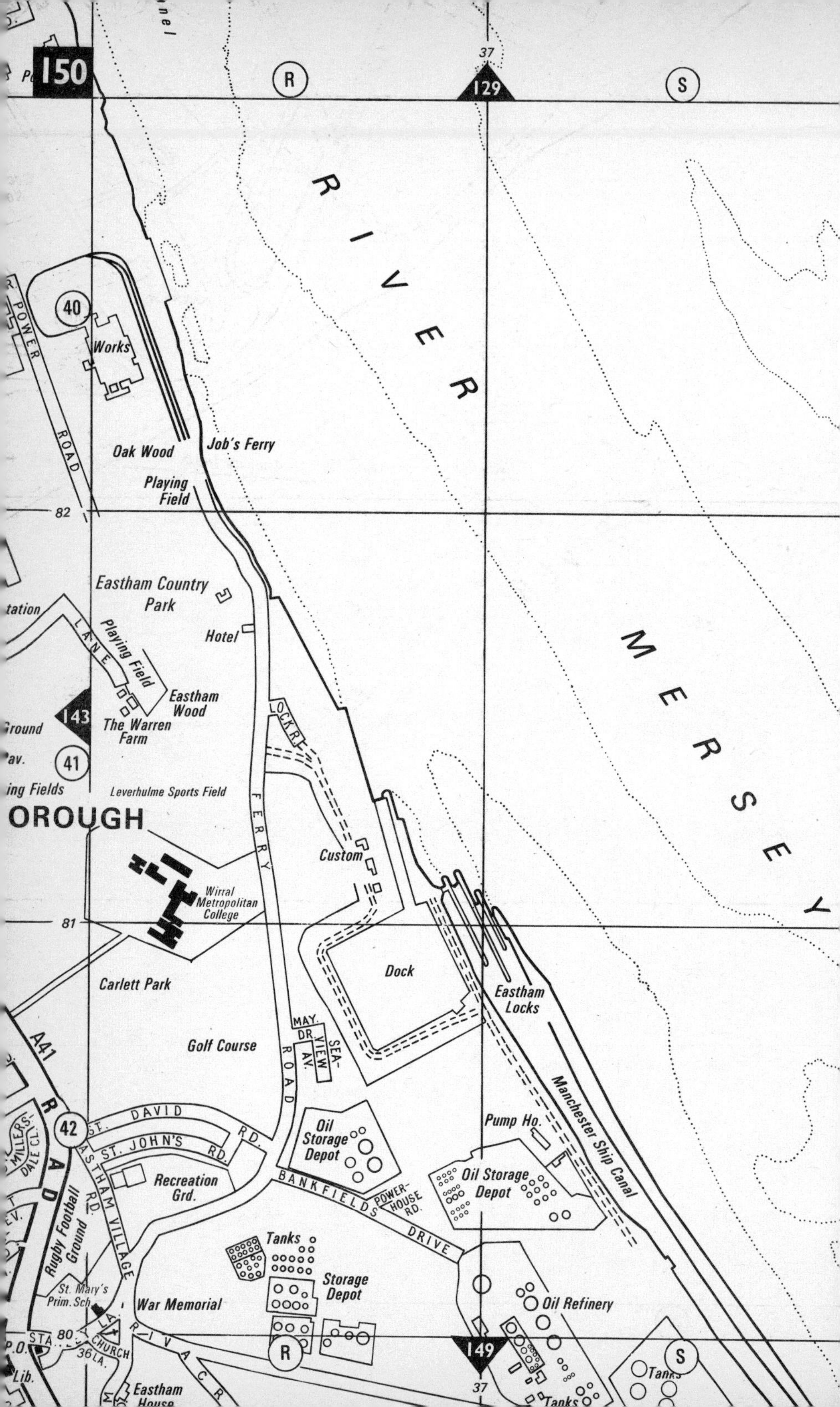

150
129
37
R
S
RIVER
MERSEY
POWER ROAD
40
Works
Oak Wood
Job's Ferry
Playing Field
82
Eastham Country Park
Hotel
LANE
Playing Field
Eastham Wood
143
The Warren Farm
41
Leverhulme Sports Field
OROUGH
LOCK RD.
FERRY
Custom
Wirral Metropolitan College
81
Dock
Eastham Locks
Carlett Park
Golf Course
A41
MAY. DR.
SEA-VIEW AV.
ROAD
ST. DAVID RD.
42
ST. JOHN'S RD.
Oil Storage Depot
Pump Ho.
Manchester Ship Canal
Oil Storage Depot
Recreation Grd.
BANKFIELDS DRIVE
POWER-HOUSE RD.
EASTHAM VILLAGE RD.
Rugby Football Ground
Tanks
Storage Depot
Oil Refinery
St. Mary's Prim. Sch.
War Memorial
80
CHURCH LA.
36
RIVACRE
149
Eastham House
Lib.
Tanks

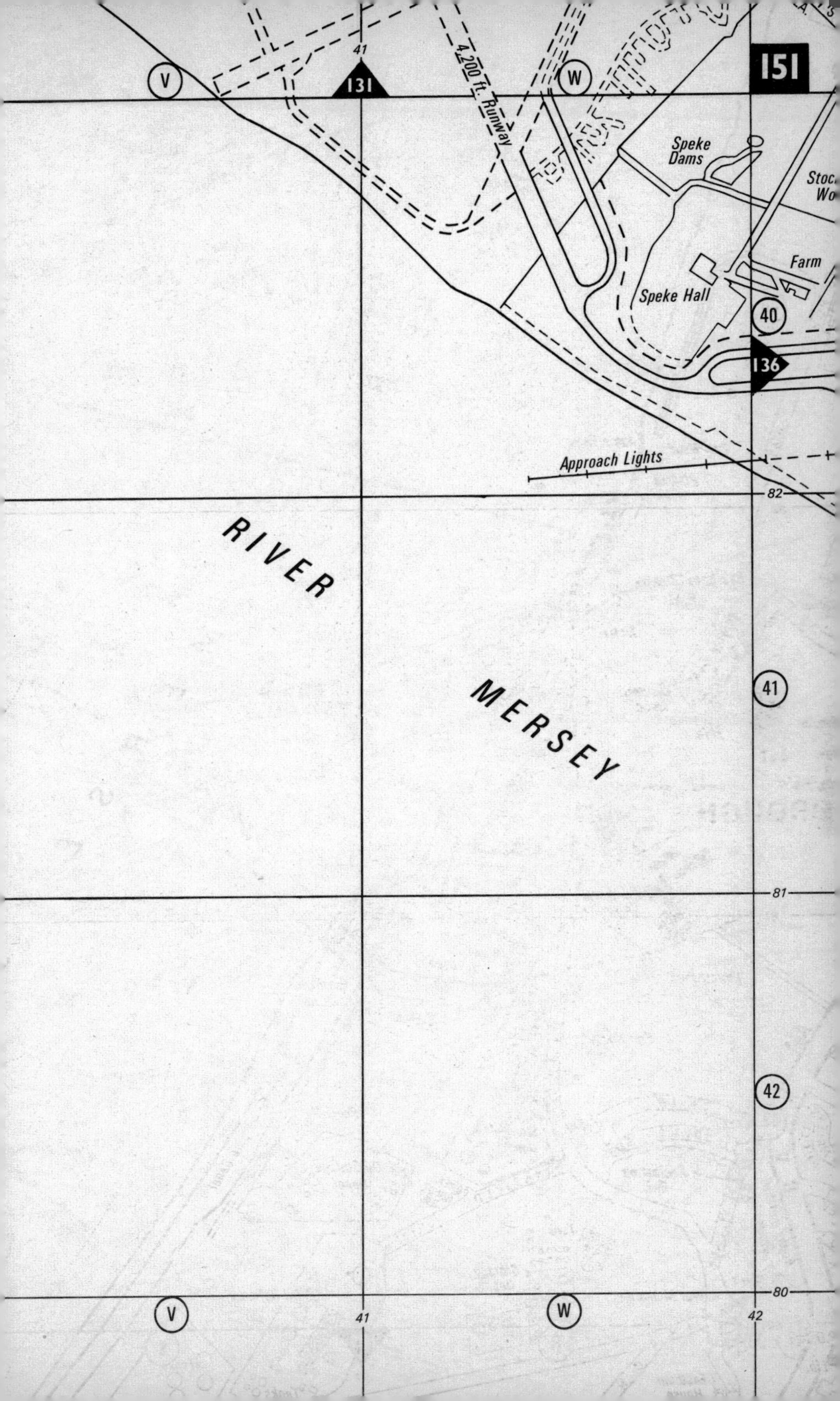

V

△ 131

4,200 Ft. Runway

W

Speke Dams

Stoc Wo

Farm

Speke Hall

40

▶ 136

Approach Lights

82

RIVER

MERSEY

41

81

42

V

41

W

42

80

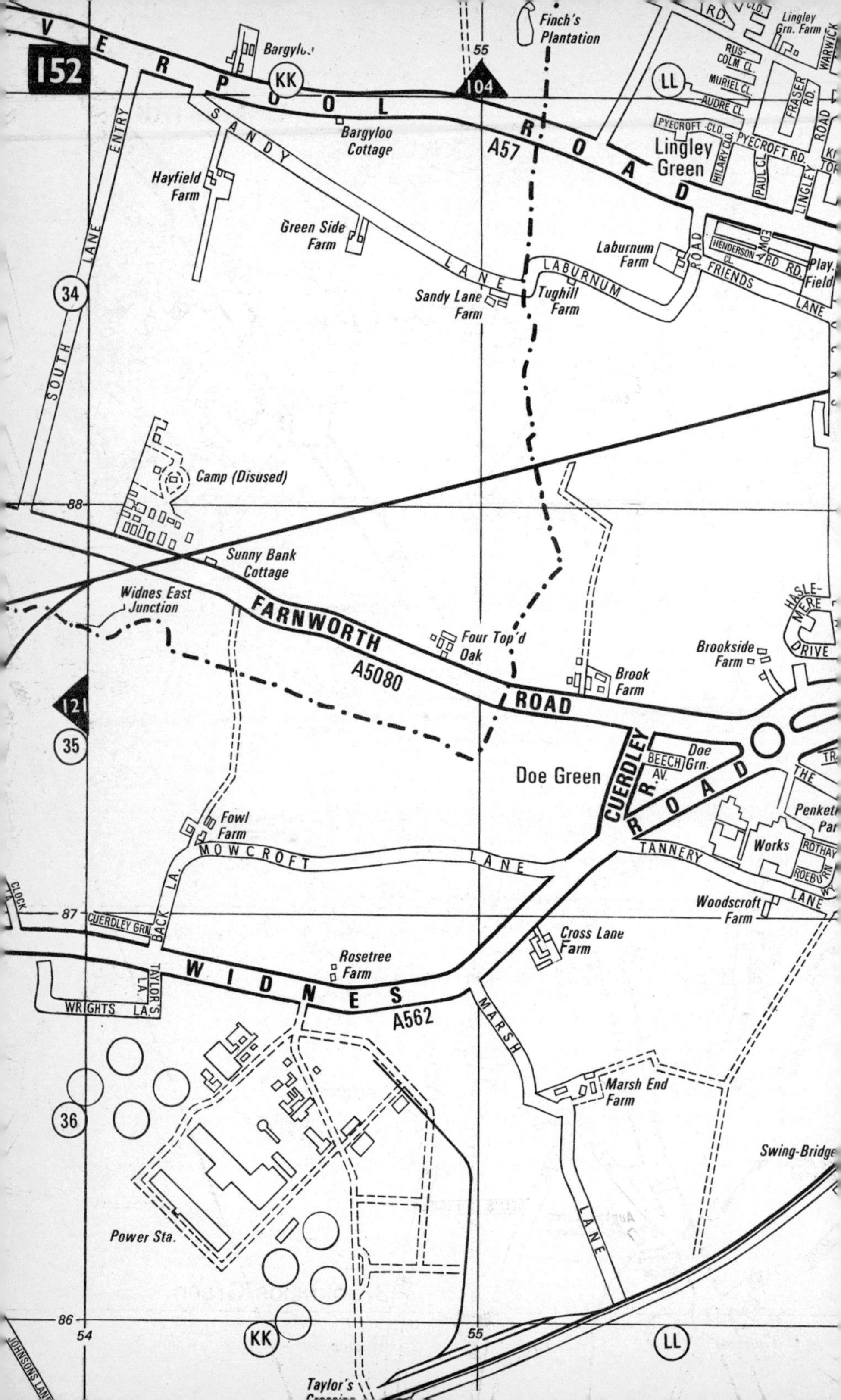

152
LIVERPOOL ROAD
A57
KK
104
Bargyloo
Bargyloo Cottage
Finch's Plantation
55
LL
Lingley Grn. Farm
WARWICK
RUSCOLM CL.
MURIEL CL.
AUDRE CL.
FRASER RD.
PYECROFT CLO.
PYECROFT RD.
HILARY CLO.
PAUL CL.
LINGLEY ROAD
Lingley Green
SOUTH LANE
ENTRY
SANDY LANE
Hayfield Farm
Green Side Farm
Laburnum Farm
LABURNUM ROAD
HENDERSON RD.
FRIENDS LANE
Play. Field
Sandy Lane Farm
Tughill Farm
34
Camp (Disused)
88
Sunny Bank Cottage
Widnes East Junction
FARNWORTH ROAD
A5080
Four Top'd Oak
Brook Farm
Brookside Farm
HASLEMERE DRIVE
121
35
CUERDLEY ROAD
BEECH AV.
Doe Grn.
Doe Green
Works
ROTHAY
ROEBURN
TANNERY LANE
Woodscroft Farm
Fowl Farm
MOWCROFT LANE
BACK LA.
CLOCK
87
CUERDLEY GRN
WIDNES
A562
Rosetree Farm
Cross Lane Farm
TAYLOR'S LA.
WRIGHTS LA.
MARSH LANE
Marsh End Farm
Swing-Bridge
36
Power Sta.
86
54
KK
55
LL
JOHNSONS LANE
Taylor's

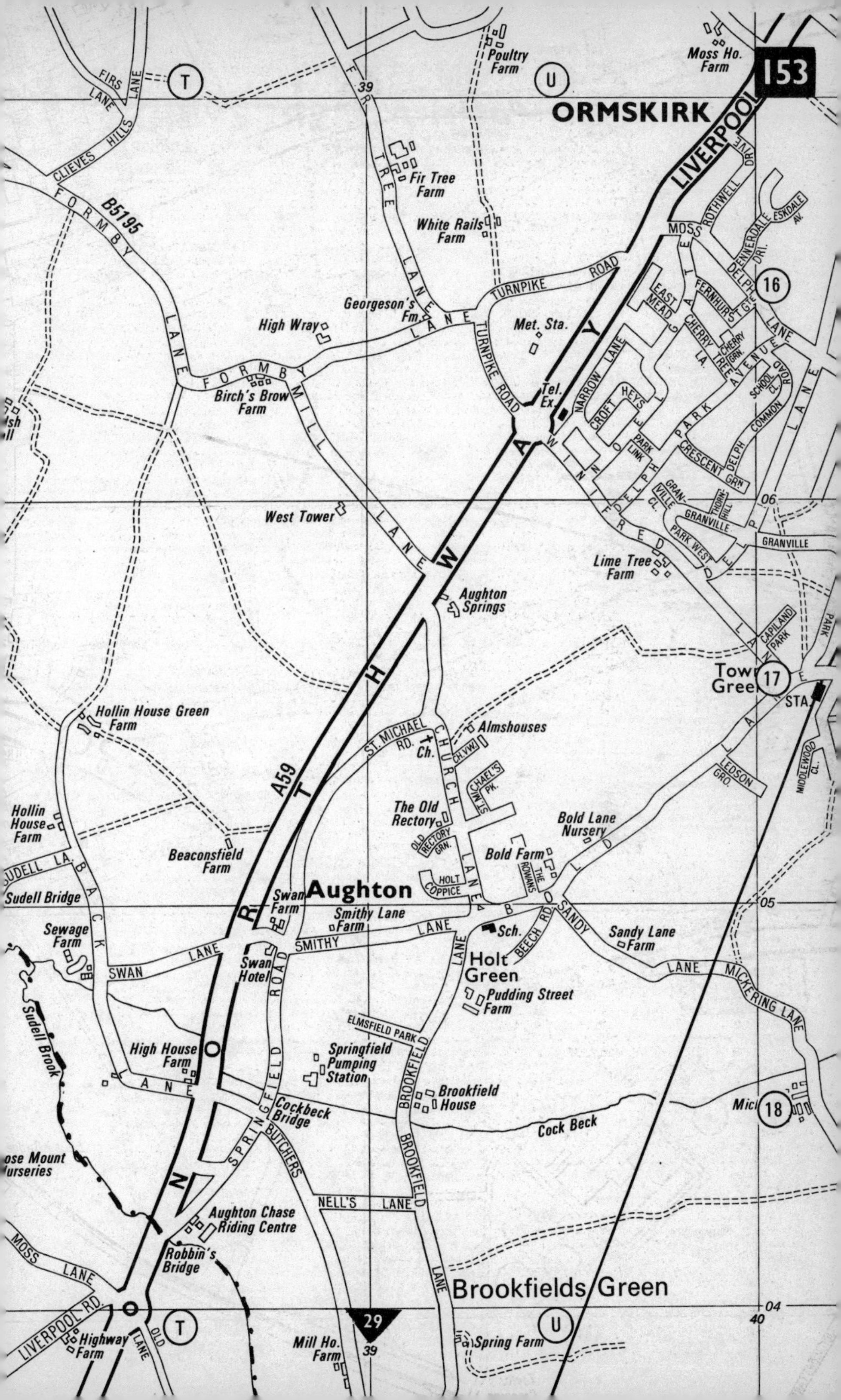

153
ORMSKIRK
Poultry Farm
Moss Ho. Farm
Fir Tree Farm
White Rails Farm
Georgeson's Fm.
High Wray
Met. Sta.
Tel. Ex.
Birch's Brow Farm
West Tower
Lime Tree Farm
Aughton Springs
Hollin House Green Farm
Almshouses
Ch.
The Old Rectory
Bold Lane Nursery
Bold Farm
Hollin House Farm
Beaconsfield Farm
Sudell Bridge
Swan Farm
Aughton
Smithy Lane Farm
Sch.
Sandy Lane Farm
Sewage Farm
Swan Hotel
Holt Green
Pudding Street Farm
Sudell Brook
High House Farm
Springfield Pumping Station
Brookfield House
Cock Beck
Cockbeck Bridge
Aughton Chase Riding Centre
Robbin's Bridge
Brookfields Green
Highway Farm
Mill Ho. Farm
Spring Farm
Town Green
STA.
LIVERPOOL ROAD
FIRS LANE
CLIEVES HILLS LANE
B5195
FORMBY LANE
FIR TREE LANE
TURNPIKE ROAD
MILL LANE
A59
NORTHWAY
WINIFRED LANE
MOSS GATE
PARK AVENUE
DELPH LANE
NARROW LANE
CROFT HEYS
EAST MEAD
CHERRY TREE LA.
FERNHURST GRO.
ROTHWELL DRIVE
ESKDALE AV.
PENNERDALE DRI.
SCHOOL CL.
COMMON ROAD
CRESCENT
GRANVILLE
PARK WEST
CAPILAND PARK
LEDSON GRO.
MIDDLEWOOD CL.
ST. MICHAEL RD.
CHURCH LANE
ST. MICHAEL'S PK.
OLD RECTORY GRN.
HOLT COPPICE
BOLD LANE
SANDY LANE
MICKERING LANE
BEECH RD.
SMITHY LANE
SWAN LANE
SUDELL LA.
BACK LANE
SPRINGFIELD ROAD
ELMSFIELD PARK
BROOKFIELD LANE
BUTCHERS LANE
NELL'S LANE
MOSS LANE
LIVERPOOL RD.
OLD LANE
39
06
05
04
40
16
17
18
29
T
U

INDEX TO
GEOGRAPHIA MERSEYSIDE
ATLAS

NOTE

A street name, followed by the name of another street in italics, does not appear on the map but will be found adjoining or near the latter.

GENERAL ABBREVIATIONS

Alley — All.
Approach — App.
Arcade — Arc.
Avenue — Av.

Back — Bk.
Bank — Bnk.
Boulevard — Boul.
Bridge — Br.
Buildings — Bldgs.

Churchyard — Chyd.
Circus — Cir.
Circle — Circ.
Close — Clo.
Corner — Cor.

Cottages — Cotts.
Court — Ct.
Crescent — Cres.
Croft — Cft.
Drive — Dr.
Dwellings — Dws.

East — E.
Esplanade — Esp.
Estate — Est.

Field — Fld.
Gardens — Gdns.
Grange — Gra.
Great — Gt.
Green — Grn.

Grove — Gro.

Heath — Hth.
Higher — Hr.
House — Ho.

King — Kg.

Lane — La.
Little — Lit.
Lodge — Lo.
Lower — Lwr.

Mansion — Mans.
Market — Mkt.
Mews — Ms.

Mount — Mt.

North — N.

Parade — Par.
Park — Pk.
Passage — Pass.
Place — Pl.
Promenade — Prom.
Prince
Princess   Pr.

Queen — Qn.

Road — Rd.

South — S.
Square — Sq.
Street — St.

Terrace — Ter.

Upper — Upr.

Valley — Vall.
View — Vw.
Villas — Vill.

Walk — Wk.
West — W.
Wharf — Wf.

Yard — Yd.

ABBREVIATIONS USED FOR DISTRICT NAMES

Aig. — Aigburth
Ain. — Aintree
Ains. — Ainsdale
All. — Allerton
Altcar
Anf. — Anfield
App. — Appleton
Asht. — Ashton-in-Makerfield
Augh. — Aughton

Beb. — Bebington
B. Green. — Broad Green
Bick. — Bickerstaffe
Bids. — Bidston
Bill. — Billinge
Bir. — Birkdale
Birk. — Birkenhead
Black. — Blackbrook
Boot. — Bootle
Brim. — Brimstage
Brom. — Bromborough
Burt. — Burtonwood

C. Cross — Cuerdley Cross
C. Face — Clock Face
C. Thornton — Childer Thornton
C. Wood — Crow Wood
Caldy
Carr Ho. — Carr Houses
Child. — Childwall
Claugh. — Claughton
Cron. — Cronton
Cros. — Crossens
Crosby
Crox. — Croxteth

Dingle
Ditton
Downhill G. — Downhill Green

Earls. — Earlstown
Easth. — Eastham
Eccl. — Eccleston
Edge H. — Edge Hill
Egre. — Egremont
Elles. — Ellesmere Port

Farn. — Farnworth
Faza. — Fazakerley
Ford
Formby
Frank. — Frank

Gars. — Garston
Gate. — Gateacre
Gol. — Golbourne
Gras. — Grassendale
Greas. — Greasby
Gr. Wood — Grow Wood
Gt. Crosby — Great Crosby

Gt. M. — Great Meols

H. Beb. — Higher Bebington
H. Cliff — Hale Cliff
H. Cross — Hunt's Cross
H. Green — Hough Green
H.V. — Hartleys Village
Hale Bk. — Hale Bank
Hale. — Halewood
Halt. — Halton
Ham. — Hamilton
Hay. — Haydock
Hes. — Heswall
High. — Hightown
Higher T. — Higher Tranmere
Hom. Grn. — Homer Green
Hoy. — Hoylake
Huy. — Huyton

Ince — Ince Blundell
Irby

Kirk. — Kirkdale
Kirkby
Know. — Knowsley

L. Alt. — Little Altcar
L. Beb. — Lower Bebington
L. Tran. — Lower Tranmere
Leas. — Leasowe
Ley. Green — Leyland Green
Liscard
Lith. — Litherland
Liver. — Liverpool
Lt. Cros. — Little Crosby
Lyd. — Lydiate

M. Nook — Moss Nook
Mag. — Maghull
Man. Rd. — Manning Road
Marsh. — Marshside
Mell. — Melling
More. — Moreton
Moss B. — Moss Bank
Moss H. — Mossley Hill
M. Nook — Moss Nook
Moss S. — Moss Side

N. Green — Norris Green
Nest. — Neston
Neth. — Netherton
New B. — New Brighton
New F. — New Ferry
Newt. — Newton-Le-Willows
Newton
Noct. — Noctorum

Oak Pk. — Oakhill Park
Old Swan
Olive. — Olive Mount

Orm. — Ormskirk
Orrell
Ox. — Oxton

P. Cross — Peasley Cross
Pen. — Pensby
Pren. — Prenton
Pres. — Prescot

R. Hill — Rainhill
R. Oak — Royal Oak
Raby
Rain. — Rainford
Roby
Rock. — Rock Ferry

S. Dene — Southdene
S. Port — Southport
St. H. — Saint Helens
St. Mich. — Saint Michaels
Sea. — Seaforth
Sefton
Som. — Somerville
Speke
Stone. — Stoneley
Stoney. — Stoneycroft
Sutt. — Sutton

Thatto Heath
Thing. — Thingwall
Thor. — Thornton
Thorn. — Thornton Hough
Thur. — Thurstaston

Upt. — Upton

Vic. Pk. — Victoria Park

W. Derby — West Derby
W. Green — Windles Green
W. Kirby — West Kirby
W. Lan. — West Lancashire
W. Park — West Park
Wadd. — Waddicar
Wall. — Wallesey
Walt. — Walton-on-the-Hill
War. — Wargrave
Warr. — Warrington
Wav. — Wavertree
Whist. — Whiston
Widnes
Wigan
Will. — Willaston
Wind. — Windsor
Win. — Winwick
Wirr. — Wirral
Wood. — Woodchurch
Woodhey
Wool. — Woolton
Wool H. — Woolfall Heath

Abacus Rd.	U31 96	Ada St.	HH28 82	Albert Rd., Crosby	M24 38
Abberley Rd.	Y37 132	Adair Pl.	T29 75	Albert Rd., Formby	H17 18
Abbey Clo., Birk.	N34 111	Adair Rd.	T29 75	Albert Rd., Hoy.	B34 105
Abbey Clo., Halton	EE37 135	Adam St.	S32 95	Albert Rd., Liver.	S30 74
Abbey Clo., Sefton	L16 20	Adam St., Anf.	Q30 73	Albert Rd., S.Port	P 5 6
Abbey Ct.	X36 116	Adams Clo.	OO28 85	Albert Rd., W.Kirby	B36 105
Abbey Gdns.	O 7 9	Adams Gro.	Q28 73	Albert Rd., Wirr.	M35 110
Abbey Rd., Halton	EE37 135	Adamson St.	NN23 51	Albert Schweizer Av.	Q23 40
Abbey Rd., Hay.	MM25 66	Adaston Av.	Q43 148	Albert St., Liver.	R32 95
Abbey Rd., Liver.	S30 74	Adcote Clo.	W31 97	Albert St., St.H.	GG26 63
Abbey Rd., St.H.	FF26 63	Adcote Rd.	W31 97	Albert St., Wigan	NN23 51
Abbey Rd., Wirr.	B36 105	Adder La.	OO30 85	Albert St., Wirr.	L29 71
Abbey St.	N34 111	Adderly St.	R32 95	*Egerton St.*	
Abbey Vw.	W33 97	Addingham Rd.	U34 114	Albert Ter.	MM28 84
Abbey Way S.	NN25 66	Addington St.	M31 92	Albion Pl.	L29 71
Abbeyfield Dr.	V27 58	Addison Sq.	GG36 120	Albion St., Birk.	N33 93
Abbeystead Av.	R24 41	Addison St., Sea.	O26 54	Albion St., Ham.	N34 111
Abbeystead Rd.	U33 96	*Byron St.*		Albion St., Liver.	Q30 73
Abbeyway N.	NN25 66	Addison St.	P31 94	Albion St., Newton	MM27 66
Buckfast Av.		Adelaide Av.	FF29 81	*Athol St.*	
Abbinger Clo.	FF27 63	Adelaide Pl.	Q31 94	Albion St., St.H.	FF27 63
Abbot St.	N34 111	Adelaide Rd., Liver.	R32 95	Albion St., Wall.	K29 70
Abbots Clo.	L16 20	Adelaide Rd., Sefton	N25 54	Albourne Rd.	X25 59
Abbots Dr.	N38 127	Adelaide Rd., Wirr.	M35 110	Albright Gro.	U33 96
Abbots Hall Av.	HH31 103	Adelaide St., Liver	Q30 73	Albury Rd.	W25 58
Abbots Way, Elles.	K44 145	Adelaide St., Wirr.	L32 92	Alcester Rd.	V30 76
Abbots Way, Sefton	L16 20	Adelaide Ter.	M24 38	Aldbourne Av.	W34 115
Abbots Way, St.H.	HH23 49	Adelphi St.	N34 111	Aldbourne Clo.	W35 115
Abbotsfield Rd.	JJ30 82	Adfalent La.	O45 147	Alder Av., Halton	GG35 120
Abbotsford Ct.	M23 38	Adkins St.	R30 74	Alder Av., Know.	AA33 99
Abbotsford Gdns.	M23 38	Adlam Cres.	T25 57	Alder Av., St.H.	HH22 49
Abbotsford Rd., Liver.	T28 75	Adlam Rd.	T25 57	*Maple Clo.*	
Abbotsford Rd., Sefton	M23 38	Admin Rd.	Y25 59	Alder Av., Wigan	MM22 51
Abbotsford St.	N32 93	Admiral Gro.	R34 113	Alder Clo.	CC30 79
Abbott Clo.	J34 109	Admiral St.	R34 113	Alder Cres.	V23 43
Abbott Dr.	Q26 55	Adshead Rd.	T29 75	Alder Gro.	M24 38
Abbotts Clo.	U35 114	Adstone Rd.	Y34 116	Alder Hey Rd.	EE27 62
Abbotts Way	C35 106	Adswood Rd.	Z31 99	Alder La., Burt.	NN29 84
Abbottshey Av.	U35 114	Africander Rd.	GG25 63	Alder La., Know.	Y27 59
Abdale Rd.	T27 57	Afton	DD36 119	Alder La., Sefton	N13 17
Abercrombie Rd.	X25 59	Agar Rd.	T29 75	Alder La., St.H.	FF23 48
Abercromby Sq.	Q32 94	Agate St.	R30 74	Alder Rd., H.Beb.	M39 126
Aberdale Rd.	U31 96	Agincourt Rd.	V30 76	Alder Rd., Know.	CC30 79
Aberdeen St., Wirr.	M33 92	Agnes Gro.	M30 71	Alder Rd., Stoney.	U31 96
Aberford Av.	K31 91	Agnes Rd., Birk.	M35 110	Alder Rd., W.Derby	V30 76
Abergele Rd.	T32 96	Agnes Rd., Sefton	M23 38	Alder Root La.	OO29 85
Abingdon Rd., Liver.	S28 74	Agnes St., Liver.	R32 95	Alder St.	OO27 67
Abingdon Rd., Wirr.	E35 107	Agnes St., St.H.	HH31 103	Alder Wood Av., Liver.	Z39 133
Abinger Rd.	LL23 50	Aigburth Dr.	S35 113	Alderdale Av.	L10 12
Abstone Rd.	Y34 116	Aigburth Gro.	F33 89	Alderfield Dr., Liver.	Z39 133
Abyssinia St.	T33 96	Aigburth Hall Av.	U37 130	Alderley Av., Wigan	RR25 68
Acacia Av., Halton	GG35 120	Aigburth Hall Rd.	U37 130	Alderley Av., Wirr.	K33 91
Acacia Av., Know.	Y32 98	Aigburth Rd.	R35 113	Alderley Clo.	JJ22 49
Acacia Clo.	F36 107	Aigburth St.	R33 95	*Ashfield Cres.*	
Thorns Dr.		Aigburth Vale	T35 114	Alderley Rd., Birk.	L31 92
Acacia Gro., Liver.	R26 56	Ainsdale Clo., Brom.	P42 143	Alderley Rd., Hoy.	B33 87
Acacia Gro., St.H.	DD27 62	*Brookhurst Rd.*		Alderson Cres.	K15 16
Acacia Gro., W.Kirby	B36 105	Ainsdale Clo., Liver.	T25 57	Alderson Rd.	S33 95
Acacia Gro., Wall.	N32 93	Ainsdale Clo., Thing.	H38 124	Alderton Dr.	NN23 51
Acacia St.	MM27 66	Ainsdale Rd.	P26 55	Alderville Rd.	S28 74
Acanthus Rd.	U31 96	Ainsworth Av.	F34 107	Aldford Clo.	O42 142
Access Rd.	V29 76	Ainsworth La.	X26 59	Aldford Rd.	W25 58
Acheson Rd.	T30 75	Ainsworth Rd.	EE26 62	Aldridge Dr.	MM29 84
Ackers Hall Av.	W30 76	Ainsworth St.	Q32 94	Aldrins La.	Q23 40
Ackers La., Sefton	M21 25	Aintree Cres.	Q 7 10	Aldwark Rd.	X31 98
Ackers La., St.H.	EE27 62	Aintree La., Liver.	U25 57	Aldwych Rd.	V30 76
Ackers Rd.	J36 109	Aintree La., Sefton	S23 41	Aldykes	T21 29
Ackers St.	BB30 79	Aintree Rd.	Q27 55	Alexander Dr., Halton	EE37 135
Acland Rd.	L31 92	Airdale Clo.	J34 109	Alexander Dr., Sefton	S19 28
Aconbury Pl.	T27 57	Airdale Rd.	T34 114	Alexander Dr., Wirr.	G39 124
Acorn Clo.	M38 126	Airdre Clo.	P43 148	Alexander Fleming Av.	Q23 40
Acorn St.	OO27 67	Aire	R20 28	Alexander Grn.	Z31 99
Acornfield Clo.	Y25 59	Airegate	R30 74	Alexander Way	Q35 112
Acornfield Rd.	Y24 44	Airlie Gro.	S30 74	Alexander Wk.	Q29 73
Acre Field Rd., Halton	DD36 119	Airlie Rd.	B34 105	*Florence St.*	
Acre La., Brom.	P41 143	Akbar, The	F40 138	Alexandra Dr.,	EE28 80
Acre La., Wirr.	J40 140	Akenside St.	O26 54	*Thatto Heath*	
Acrefield Ct.	L36 110	Alamein Rd.	Y31 98	Alexandra Dr., Birk.	N36 111
Acrefield Pk.	X35 116	Alastair Cres.	K36 109	Alexandra Dr., Liver.	R35 113
Acrefield Rd., Liver.	X35 116	Alban Rd.	V33 97	Alexandra Dr., Sefton	O26 55
Acrefield Rd., Wirr.	L36 110	Albany Av.	CC29 79	Alexandra Mt.	O25 54
Acres La.	Q17 22	Albany Gdns.	S45 149	Alexandra Rd.	U32 96
Acres La., W.Lan.	N17 21	Albany Rd., Edge H.	R32 95	Alexandra Rd., Birk.	L34 110
Acres Rd., Hoy.	D33 88	Albany Rd., H.V.	R25 56	Alexandra Rd., Crosby	M23 38
Acres Rd., L.Beb.	O38 127	Albany Rd., Know.	CC30 79	Alexandra Rd., Formby	H17 18
Acresgate Ct.	X34 116	Albany Rd., Sefton	O 4 5	Alexandra Rd., Liver.	S33 95
Acreville Rd.	N38 127	Albany Rd., Stone.	U31 96	Alexandra Rd., Marsh.	P 4 6
Acton La.	F33 89	Albany Rd., Wirr.	N36 111	Alexandra Rd., New.B.	L29 71
Acton Rake	Q22 40	Albemarle Rd.	M31 92	Alexandra Rd., Sea.	N25 54
Higher End Pk.		Albert Dr., Elles.	J45 145	Alexandra Rd., W.Kirby	B36 105
Acton Rd., Know.	V24 43	Albert Dr., Liver.	O26 55	Alexandra Rd., Wigan	NN23 51
Acton Rd., Warr.	MM30 84	Albert Edward Rd.	R32 95	Alexandra St., Liver.	U32 96
Acton Rd., Wirr.	O36 111	Albert Gro.	M23 38	Alexandra St., St.H.	EE29 80
Acton Way	S33 95	Albert Pl.	O 5 5	*St. John St.*	
Acuba Rd.	V32 97	Albert Rd., App.	GG36 120		

Alexandra Ter. FF28 81
Borough Rd.
Alexandria Rd., Liver. V37 131
Alfonso Rd. P29 73
Alford Av. GG31 102
Alford Clo. K36 109
Alford St. T32 96
Alfred Rd., Birk. L34 110
Alfred Rd., Liver. U34 114
Alfred Rd., St.H. MM25 66
Alfred Rd., Wall. N32 93
Alfred St., Newt. PP27 67
Alfred St., Rain. CC21 33
Alfred St., St.H. GG27 63
Alfriston Rd. U30 76
Alice St. JJ29 82
Alicia Wk., Know. U25 57
Amanda Rd.
Alison Av. N35 111
Alison Pl. T29 75
Alison Rd. T29 75
Alistair Dr. P42 143
All Saints Clo. Q23 40
All Saints Rd. Y39 132
Allan Rd. HH25 64
Allan St. HH29 82
Highfield St.
Allandale Av. EE31 101
Allangate Clo. F36 107
Allangate Rd. U37 130
Allans Clo. K45 145
Allans Meadow K45 145
Allanson St. HH28 82
Hammond St.
Allanson St. HH28 82
Allcot Av. M36 110
Allen St. HH29 82
Highfield St.
Allen St. HH29 82
Robins La.
Allenby Av. N24 39
Allenby Sq. U32 96
Allendale Av. R25 56
Allengate N22 39
Allerford Rd. V29 76
Allerton Beeches V35 115
Allerton Dr. U35 114
Allerton Grn. U35 114
Allerton Gro. M35 110
Allerton Rd., Birk. M35 110
Allerton Rd., Moss.H. U34 114
Allerton Rd., Sefton Q 4 6
Allerton Rd., Wirral K30 70
Allerton Rd., Wool. X36 116
Allesley Rd. W30 76
Alleyne Rd. S29 74
Allington St. R35 113
Allonby Clo. K35 109
Allport La. P40 143
Allport Rd. O42 142
Allports, The P41 143
Allscott Way OO23 52
Alma Clo. U25 57
Alma Clo. X23 44
Alma Pl. HH28 82
Alma St.
Alma Pl. HH28 82
Alma Rd., Liver T37 130
Alma Rd., Sefton O 7 9
Alma St. HH28 82
Alma St. NN27 66
Queen St.
Alma St., Hay. NN27 66
Suez St.
Alma St., Wirr. O37 127
Almacs Clo. L23 38
Burbo Bank Rd.
Almeda Rd. Z40 137
Almond Av. P23 40
Almond Clo. Z37 133
Almond Dr. MM30 84
Almond Gro. EE37 135
Almond Pl., Liver. R33 95
Almond Pl., Wirr. G33 90
Almond Ter. R33 95
Almond Way F36 107
Almonds Grn. U29 75
Almonds Gro. U29 75
Almonds Pk. U29 75
Almonds Turn P23 40
Alness Dr. EE32 101
Alnwick Dr. E33 89
Alpass Rd. R35 113
Alpha Dr. O36 111
Alpha St. O26 54
Alpine St. NN27 66
Alresford Rd. T37 130
Alroy Rd. R29 74
Alscot Clo. S21 28
Alscott Av. U25 57
Alston Clo. L40 143
Eccleston Av.
Alston Rd. T37 130
Alstonfield Rd. X31 98
Alt DD36 119
Alt Av. S21 28
Alt Rd., Boot. P26 55
Alt Rd., Formby L16 20
Alt Rd., High. L19 25
Alt Rd., Know. Z31 99
Alt St. R33 95
Altbridge Pk. U26 57
Altcar Av. S33 95
Altcar Dr. F33 89
Altcar Embankment O17 21
Altcar La. Q16 22
Altcar La., Formby K16 19
Altcar La., Sefton Q18 22
Altcar La., W.Lan. M15 17
Altcar Rd., Formby L16 20
Altcar Rd., Vic.Pk. P26 55
Altcross Rd. V27 58
Altcross Way V27 58
Altfield Rd. W29 76
Altfinch Clo. X29 77
Altham Rd. Q 7 10
Ruddington Rd.
Altham Rd. T29 75
Althorp St. Q35 112
Althorpe Dr. Q 7 10
Altmoor Rd. Y30 77
Alton Av. O24 39
Alton Clo. NN23 51
Alton Rd., Liver. S30 74
Alton Rd., Wirr. L34 110
Altway S23 41
Alun Dale Rd. W30 76
Alva Rd. EE32 101
Alvanley Grn. V24 43
Alvanley Pl. M34 110
Alvanley Rd. V24 43
Alvanley Rd. V30 76
Alvega Clo. P37 128
Alverstone Av. K33 91
Alverstone Rd., Liver. T34 114
Alverstone Rd., Wirr. M31 92
Alvina La. Q29 73
Alwain Grn. Z40 137
Alwen St. K33 91
Alwyn Dr. O24 39
Alwyn Gdns. G33 90
Alwyn St. R35 113
Amanda Rd., Liver. U25 57
Amanda Rd., St.H. DD30 80
Amanda Way U23 42
Wheeler Dr.
Amaury Clo. O22 39
Amaury Rd.
Amaury Rd. O22 39
Ambergate Rd. U37 130
Amberley Av. F33 89
Amberley Clo. F33 89
Amberly St. R33 95
Ambleside Clo. Q41 143
Ambleside Clo., Thing. H38 124
Ambleside Pl. GG24 48
Ambleside Rd., Liver. V36 115
Ambleside Rd., Sefton S20 28
Ambrose Rd. HH36 121
Amersham Clo. NN24 51
Newlyn Dr.
Amersham Rd. S28 74
Amery Gro. L36 110
Amesby Dr. LL20 37
Amherst Rd. S36 113
Amity St. Q34 112
Amos Av. P25 55
Ampthill Rd. S36 113
Ampulla Rd. V27 58
Amy Wk., Know. U25 57
Amanda Rd.
Ancaster Rd. S36 113
Anchor St. O 5 5
Ancient Meadows R25 56
Albany Rd.
Ancroft Rd. X31 98
Ancrum Clo. V22 43
Anderson Av. O27 54
Anderson Clo. EE32 101
Lincoln Way
Anderson Clo., Thing. H38 124
Anderson Rd. P24 40
Anderson St. Q30 73
Anderson Way P24 40
Anderton Sq. T33 96
Anderton Ter. Y32 98
Andover Cres. LL20 37
Andover Way Y37 132
Andrew Av., Sefton U23 42
Andrew Av., St.H. JJ22 49
Andrew Clo. EE37 135
Andrew St. Q28 73
Andrew St., Wall. M32 92
Andrews Clo. K16 19
Andrews La. K16 19
Andrews Wk. H41 139
Andrews Yort K16 19
Anfield Ct. R29 74
Anfield Rd. Q29 73
Angela St. R33 95
Angers La. U22 42
Angles Way Q35 112
Anglesea Rd. R27 56
Anglesey Rd., Birk. L31 92
Anglesey Rd., Hoy. B35 105
Angus Rd., Liver. T29 75
Angus Rd., Wirr. P42 143
Ankers Hall Clo. W30 76
Annan Gro. PP22 52
Lily St.
Annandale Clo. W22 43
Anne Av. N10 13
Anne Gro. HH29 82
Anne St. HH31 103
Balniel St.
Annerley St. S33 95
Annesley Rd., Liver. S36 113
Annesley Rd., Wirr. M31 92
Annette Av. NN26 66
Annie Rd. P26 55
Anscot Av. N38 127
Ansdell Dr. DD26 62
Ansdell Gro. R 3 3
Ansdell Rd. HH36 121
Ansdell Villa Rd. EE31 101
Anson St. Q32 94
Anson Ter. Q32 94
Anstey Rd. U31 96
Ansty Clo. HH26 64
Anthonys Way H41 139
Anthorn Clo. J35 109
Antonio St. P28 73
Antons Clo. Z38 133
Antons Rd., Know. Z38 133
Antons Rd., Wirr. G38 124
Antrim Clo., St.H. LL26 65
Antrim Clo., Wigan LL20 37
Antrim St. T29 75
Anzacs, The P38 128
Anzio Rd. Y31 98
Apollo Way, Ain. R23 41
Apollo Way, Liver. R30 74
Appin Rd. N34 111
Apple Ct. R31 95
Coleridge St.
Apple Gdn. F34 107
Appleby Clo., Widnes EE37 135
Appleby Dr. P23 40
Appleby Rd., Liver. AA35 117
Appledore Clo. X39 132
Appledore Ct. X39 132
Appledore Clo.
Appledore Gro. HH30 82
Appleton Dr. G36 108
Appleton Rd., Halton GG36 120
Appleton Rd., Liver. R28 74
Appleton Rd., Sefton O24 39
Appleton St. HH28 82
Approach Rd. L32 92
April Gro. S30 74
Apsley Av., L.Beb. O37 127
Apsley Av., Wall. L30 71
Apsley Brow R20 28
Apsley Rd. V30 76
Aragon Clo. T19 29
Arborn Dr. H34 108
Arbour La. X24 44
Arbour St. P 6 6
Arbury Av. HH26 64
Arbury La. RR30 86
Arcadia Av, S19 28
Arch La. KK23 50
Archer Clo. Q29 73
Archer St.
Archer Gro. JJ27 64

Archer St. Q29 73
Archerfield Rd. U36 114
Archers Ct. H36 108
Archers Way H36 108
Archway Rd. Y32 98
Arctic Rd. O27 54
Arden DD36 119
Arden Clo., Sefton L10 12
Ardennes Rd. Z31 99
Arderne Clo. O40 142
Ardleigh Av. Q 7 10
Ardleigh Clo. T32 96
Ardleigh Gro. T32 96
Ardleigh Pl. T32 96
Ardleigh Rd. T32 96
Ardmore Rd. U36 119
Ardrossan Rd. S29 74
Ardville Rd. S27 56
Ardwich St. GG27 63
Atlas St.
Ardwick Rd. Z39 133
Argameols Clo. Q 6 6
Argarmeols Gro. K14 16
Argarmeols Rd. K14 16
Argo Rd. M24 38
Argos Pl. P28 73
Argyle Rd., Anf. R30 74
Argyle Rd., Gars. V38 131
Argyle Rd., Sefton P 4 6
Argyle St. S. M34 110
Argyle St., Liver. P33 94
Argyle St., St.H. FF26 63
Argyle St., Wirr. N34 111
Argyll Av. P43 148
Argyll Clo. LL23 50
Ariel Par. V38 131
Arkle Rd. K33 91
Arkles La. R29 74
Arkles Rd. R30 74
Arkwood Clo. P39 128
Arkwright St. Q30 73
Arlescourt Rd. V30 76
Arley Clo. J34 109
Arley Dr. DD36 119
Arlington Av. T34 114
Arlington Clo. L10 12
Arlington Rd. K30 70
Armill Rd. V27 58
Armitage Gdns. U36 114
Armley Rd. R29 74
Armour Gro. U32 96
Rathbone Rd.
Armoury Bank NN23 51
Armscot Clo. X37 132
Armstrong St. O26 54
Arncliffe Rd. Y37 132
Arnhem Rd. Y31 98
Arnian Rd. CC21 33
Arnian Way CC21 33
Arno Ct. L35 110
Arno Rd. N35 110
Arnold Av. EE26 62
Ruskin Dr.
Arnold Clo. R34 113
Arnold Gro. U33 96
Arnold Pl. EE37 135
Arnold St. L30 71
Queens St.
Arnold St. L30 71
Arnolds Cop M17 20
Arnot St. Q28 73
Arnot Way M38 126
Arnside P25 55
Arnside Av. DD31 101
Arnside Av. KK26 65
Leigh Rd.
Arnside Rd., Birk. L35 110
Arnside Rd., Know. X32 98
Arnside Rd., Liver. S32 95
Arnside Rd., Sefton P 5 6
Arnside Rd., Wall. L30 71
Arrad St. Q33 94
Arran Clo. JJ26 64
Old Nook La.
Arranmore Rd. U36 114
Arrow Park Rd. G35 108
Arrowbrook La. F36 107
Arrowe Av. F33 89
Arrowe Brook Rd. G36 108
Arrowe Ct. H36 108
Arrowe Park Rd. H37 124
Arrowe Rd. F35 107
Arrowe Side G35 108
Arrowsmith Av. MM25 66
Arthur St., Boot. Q27 55
Arthur St., Wirr. M33 92
Arundel Av., Liver. S34 113
Arundel Av., Wirr. K30 70
Arundel Clo. G39 124
Arundel Clo. MM30 84
Colne Rd.
Arundel Rd. N 9 9
Arundel St., Boot. Q28 73
Arundel St., Wind. R34 113
Arvon St. P26 55
Asbridge St. R33 95
Asbury Rd. J30 70
Ascot Av. O25 54
Ascot Clo. N 6 5
Ascot Dr. N38 127
Ascot Park N23 39
Ash Av. OO28 85
Ash Dr. F36 107
Ash Grange V31 97
Ash Gro., Edge H. S33 95
Ash Gro., Formby J16 19
Ash Gro., Halton EE37 135
Ash Gro., Huy. Z33 99
Ash Gro., Know. CC30 79
Ash Gro., Lith. O26 54
Ash Gro., Rain. CC22 46
Ash Gro., St.H. HH31 103
Ash Gro., Wall. L29 71
Ash Gro., Whist. CC31 100
Ash Gro., Wigan QQ25 68
Ash Grove Cres. HH22 49
Ash La. CC37 134
Ash La. DD37 135
Ash Priors EE35 119
Ash Rd., Birk. M35 110
Ash Rd., L.Beb. N37 127
Ash Rd., Sefton O25 54
Ash Rd., St.H. MM25 66
Sherlock Av.
Ash Rd., Warr. QQ30 86
Ash St., Boot. P27 55
Ash St., Marsh. P 6 6
Ash St., Wigan NN22 51
Ash Way H42 139
Ashbank Rd. U28 75
Ashbourne Av., Boot. Q24 40
Ashbourne Av., Crosby M23 38
Ashbourne Cres. X31 98
Ashbourne Rd. S36 113
Ashburton Av. K34 109
Ashburton Rd., Birk. K34 109
Ashburton Rd., Wall. L31 92
Ashburton Rd., Wirr. B35 105
Ashburton Wk. K34 109
Ashbury Rd. X30 77
Ashcombe Rd. V31 97
Ashcourt St. O27 54
Ashcroft Dr. G39 124
Ashcroft Rd., Ain. R25 56
Ashcroft Rd., Formby K16 19
Ashcroft Rd., Know. Y23 44
Ashcroft St. HH27 64
Ashcroft St., Boot. O27 54
Ashdale Clo. J16 19
Ashdale Rd., H.V. R27 56
Ashdale Rd., Moss H. U34 114
Ashdale Rd., Sefton M24 38
Ashdown Dr. F36 107
Thorns Dr.
Ashfield Cres., Brom. P41 143
Ashfield Cres., St.H. JJ22 49
Ashfield Rd., Liver. T36 114
Ashfield Rd., Wirr. P41 143
Ashfield St. P30 73
Ashfield, Liver. S33 95
Ashfield, St.H. EE31 101
Ashford Rd., Birk. M35 110
Ashford Rd., Hoy. C33 88
Ashford Way HH36 121
Ashland Av. NN23 51
Ashlar Gro. T35 114
Ashlar Rd., Liver. T35 114
Ashlar Rd., Sefton N24 39
Ashlea Rd. G39 124
Ashleigh Barn Rd. R30 74
Ashleigh Rd. T21 29
Ashley Av. D32 88
Ashley Clo. EE32 101
Ashton Av.
Ashley St., Wirr. N36 111
Ashmore Clo. C38 122
Ashmuir Hey, Know. W24 43
Thistley Hey Rd.
Ashover Av. X31 98
Ashton Av. EE32 101
Ashton Clo. M43 148
Ashton Dr., Liver. X37 132
Ashton Dr., Wirr. B36 105
Ashton Heath OO24 52
Ashton Pl. Q32 94
Ashton Rd., Asht. PP23 52
Ashton Rd., Newt. OO26 67
Ashton Rd., Sefton N 8 9
Ashton Rd., Wigan KK21 37
Ashton St., St.H. GG27 63
Higher Parr St.
Ashton St., Stoney. U31 96
Ashtons Green Dr. JJ28 82
Ashtons La. J16 19
Ashtree Clo. L45 146
Ashtree Croft O45 147
Ashtree Dr. L45 146
Ashurst Clo., Liver. X34 116
Ashurst Clo., St.H. JJ26 64
Ashurst Ct. K16 19
Ashurst Dr. HH26 64
Ashville Rd., Claugh. L34 110
Ashville Rd., Wall. M32 92
Ashwell St. Q33 94
Ashwood Av., Asht. NN24 51
Ashwood Av., Gol. RR25 68
Ashwood Dr. V27 58
Ashworth St. T32 96
Askern Rd. W25 58
Askew Clo. F 5 92
Tobin St.
Askew St. Q28 73
Asland Gdns. S 3 3
Aspen Clo. J41 140
Aspen Clo., Kirkby W22 43
Aspen Gro., Liver. S34 113
Aspen Gro., Sefton J16 19
Aspendale Rd. M35 110
Aspes Rd. W29 76
Aspinal Pl. EE29 80
Springfield Rd.
Aspinall Cres. N16 21
Aspinall St., Know. BB30 79
Aspinall St., Wirr. M33 92
Asquith Av. L33 92
Asser Rd. T29 75
Assisslan Cres. Q23 40
Aster Rd. MM26 66
Asterfield Av. N37 127
Astley Clo. CC21 33
Astley Rd. Z30 78
Astonwood Rd. M35 110
Astor St. Q28 73
Atheldene Rd. S28 74
Athelstan Clo. P40 143
Atherton Clo. Q30 73
Atherton Dr. H35 108
Atherton Rd. S26 56
Atherton St. BB30 79
Eccleston St.
Atherton St. FF26 63
Atherton St., Claugh. M34 110
Atherton St., Know. BB30 79
High St.
Atherton St., Wall. L29 71
Athol Clo. MM27 66
Athol Dr. Q43 148
Athol St., Liver. P30 73
Athol St., St.H. MM27 66
Athol St., Wirr. N33 93
Athole Gro. Q 5 6
Atholl Clo. Q42 143
Atholl Cres. S24 41
Atlantic Rd. O27 54
Arlantic Way Q25 55
Atlas Ct. GG27 63
Atlas Rd. O27 54
Atlas St., St.H. GG27 63
Attlee Rd. Z32 99
Attwood St. Q29 73
Atwell St. R31 95
Aubrey St. Q31 94
Everton Rd.
Auburn Rd. L29 71
Auburn Rd. T30 75
Aubynes, The K30 70
Auckland Gro. EE30 80
Auckland Rd. U34 114
Audlem Clo. K35 109
Audley St. Q32 94
Audre Clo. LL34 152
Audrey Wk., Know. U25 57
Amanda Rd.
Aughton Clo. JJ22 49
Ashfield Cres.

Aughton Rd., Lith.	P26 55
Aughton Rd., S.Port	N 6 5
August Rd.	S30 74
August St., Lith.	P26 55
Augusta Clo.	U32 96
Rathbone Rd.	
Augustines Way	P23 40
Austair Cres.	K36 109
Austell Clo.	HH25 64
Austin Av., St.H.	EE29 80
Austin Av., Wigan	MM23 51
Autumn Gro.	N37 127
Bebington Rd.	
Avalon Rd.	V30 76
Avebury Clo.	JJ35 121
Avelon Clo.	J34 109
Avelon Clo.	R18 23
Avelon Clo.	V29 76
Avenue, The	Q27 55
Avenue, The	DD27 62
Avenue, The, Hale.	Z37 133
Avenue, The, Huy.	Z31 99
Avenue, The, Know.	Z29 78
Avenue, The, Liver.	W38 131
Avenue, The, New B.	L29 71
Avenue, The, Newt.	OO27 67
Avenue, The, Rain.	CC22 46
Avenue, The, Wigan	HH19 36
Avenue, The, Wirr.	P41 143
Averham Clo.	NN24 51
Newlyn Dr.	
Avery Cres.	LL25 65
Avery Rd.	LL25 65
Avery Sq.	LL25 65
Aviemore Rd.	T31 96
Avis Clo.	U25 57
Avon	DD36 119
Avon Clo., Know.	W22 43
Avon Clo., Liver.	Q29 73
Avon Ct.	N22 39
Avon Rd., St.H.	HH23 49
Avon Rd., Wigan	PP22 52
Avon St., Anf.	R30 74
Avon St., Edge H.	S33 95
Avon St., Wirr.	K33 91
Avondale Av., Brom.	Q42 143
Avondale Av., More.	G32 90
Avondale Av., Sefton	S21 28
Avondale Dr.	DD36 119
Avondale Rd., Liver.	T34 114
Avondale Rd., Sefton	O 5 5
Avondale Rd., St.H.	LL25 65
Avondale Rd., Wirr.	B33 87
Avonmore Av.	U35 114
Axbridge Av.	HH30 82
Axholme Av.	H38 124
Axholme Clo.	H38 124
Aycliffe Rd.	EE30 80
Aylesbury Av.	K36 109
Aylesbury Rd.	M29 71
Aylesford Rd.	U31 96
Aylsham Dr.	H33 90
Aylton Rd.	X31 98
Aylward Pl.	O27 54
Glover Pl.	
Ayr Clo.	Q 7 10
Ayr Rd.	R28 74
Ayrshire Rd.	S29 74
Aysgarth Av.	V30 76
Aysgarth Rd.	K30 70
Ayton La.	V33 97
Babbacombe Rd.	W34 115
Back Bath St.	O 5 5
Back Bedford St.	Q33 94
Back Berry St.	Q33 94
Back Bittern St.	Q32 94
Back Canning St.	Q33 94
Back Coloquitt St.	Q33 94
Back Crawford St.	JJ31 103
Back Devon St.	Q32 94
Back Dover Rd.	S22 41
Back Gibson St.	Q33 94
Back Gillmoss La.	V26 58
Back Grange Rd.	N34 111
Grange Rd. E.	
Back Guildford St.	Q31 94
Back Hope St.	Q33 94
Back House Wk.	Q27 55
Back King St.	M31 92
Back Knight St.	Q33 94
Back La., Anf.	T29 75
Back La., Augh.	T16 153

Back La., Burt.	LL29 83
Back La., Gars.	T38 130
Back La., High.	M21 25
Back La., Mag.	P21 27
Back La., R.Oak.	X19 31
Back La., Rain.	FF22 48
Back La., Warr.	KK36 152
Back Langham St.	Q29 73
Back Leeds St.	O32 93
Back Lime St.	P32 94
Back Lower House La.	U27 57
Back Market St.	NN27 66
Back Marshall St.	M33 92
Back Mulberry St.	Q33 94
Back o'th Town La.	N19 26
Back Percy St.	Q33 94
Back Price St.	M33 92
Back Rathbone St.	NN27 66
Sankey St.	
Back Renshaw St.	Q32 94
Back Rockfield St.	Q29 73
Back Rockfield Rd.	R29 74
Back Roe St.	P32 94
Back Roscommon St.	Q31 94
Back Sandon St.	Q33 94
Back Sea Vw.	B33 87
Grove Pl.	
Back South St.	N24 39
Hougoumont Av.	
Back St.	W38 131
Back St. Anne St.	M33 92
Back Stanley Rd.	P27 55
Back Stanley St.	P32 94
Back Towerland St.	R32 95
Back Water St.	M31 92
Back Winstanley Rd.	N24 39
Back York St.	Q30 73
Backford Clo.	K35 109
Backford Rd.	F38 123
Backford Way	K35 109
Backhouse Wk.	Q27 55
Baden Rd.	U31 96
Bader Clo.	G39 124
Badgers Rake	J14 15
Badgers Set	C38 122
Badminton St.	Q35 112
Baffin Clo.	H31 90
Bagnall St.	R29 74
Bagot St.	S33 95
Baguley Av.	DD38 135
Bahama Clo.	LL25 65
Bahama Rd.	LL25 65
Bailey Dr.	Q26 55
Baileys Clo.	GG34 120
Baileys La., Gars.	X39 132
Baileys La., Know.	AA38 133
Baileys La., Speke	Z40 137
Bainton Clo.	X25 59
Bainton Rd.	X25 59
Baird Av.	O27 54
Baker St.	HH27 64
Baker St., Liver.	R31 95
Hutchinson St.	
Baker Way	R31 95
Bakers Green Rd.	Z31 99
Bakers Green Rd.	Z31 91
Bakers La.	Q 3 2
Bakewell Rd.	MM29 84
Bala Gro.	K31 91
Bala St.	R30 74
Balcarres Av.	T34 114
Baldwin St.	GG27 63
Balfe St.	O26 54
Balfour Av.	O26 54
Balfour Rd. S.	Q 6 6
Balfour Rd., Birk.	L34 110
Balfour Rd., Lith.	O26 54
Balfour Rd., Wall.	L32 92
Balfour St., Liver.	Q29 73
Balfour St., St.H.	EE27 62
Balker Dr.	FF26 63
Ball Av.	L29 71
Ball St.	P 5 6
Ballant Gro.	T29 75
Ballant Pl.	T30 75
Ballantrae Rd.	V35 115
Ballantyne Dr.	J32 91
Ballantyne Gro.	Q26 55
Ballantyne Rd.	T30 75
Ballantyne Wk.	J32 91
Ballard Rd.	D35 106
Balliol Gro.	L24 38
Balliol Rd.	P28 73
Balliol Rd. E.	P28 73
Balliol Way	MM23 51

Ballpath Way	FF36 120
Princes Pl.	
Balls Rd.	L35 110
Balls Rd. E.	M34 110
Balm St.	R32 95
Balmer St.	EE29 80
Balmoral Av., Sefton	N23 39
Balmoral Av., St.H.	HH29 82
Balmoral Dr.	K16 19
Balmoral Dr.	R 3 3
Balmoral Rd., App.	GG35 120
Balmoral Rd., Edge H.	S31 95
Balmoral Rd., H.V.	R26 56
Balmoral Rd., Sefton	S20 28
Balmoral Rd., Wigan	NN23 51
Balmoral Rd., Wirr.	L29 71
Balniel St.	HH31 103
Balsham Clo.	Y37 132
Balte St.	Q33 94
Baltic Rd.	O27 54
Baltic St.	R29 74
Bamburgh Pl.	NN22 51
Bampton Av.	GG24 48
Bampton Rd.	V33 97
Banastre Rd.	O 6 5
Banastre St.	P31 94
Banbury Av.	Y36 116
Banbury Rd.	HH20 36
Banbury Way	K36 109
Bancroft Clo.	Y37 132
Bancroft Rd.	HH36 121
Banff Av.	P42 143
Bangor Rd.	J30 70
Bangor St.	P30 73
Banham Av.	LL19 37
Bank Dene	O37 127
Bank La.	V22 43
Bank Pace	S 2 3
Bank Rd.	O27 54
Bank Sq.	O 5 5
Bank St., Hay.	MM27 66
Bank St., St.H.	FF27 63
Bank St., Wirr.	N34 111
Bankburn Rd.	T30 75
Bankfield La.	R 4 7
Bankfield Rd., Halton	EE36 119
Bankfield Rd., Liver.	T30 75
Bankfield St.	O29 72
Bankfields Dr.	R42 150
Bankhall La.	P29 73
Bankhall St.	P29 73
Bankhouse Cotts.	LL29 83
Bankland Rd.	T30 75
Banks Av.	C33 88
Banks La.	V39 131
Banks Rd., Hes.	F41 138
Banks Rd., Liver.	V39 131
Banks Rd., Sefton	S 2 3
Banks Rd., W.Kirby	B36 105
Banks Way	V39 131
Bankside	K19 24
Bankside Rd.	N37 127
Bankville Rd.	M35 110
Banner Hey	BB32 100
Banner St., St.H.	FF27 63
Banner St., Wav.	T33 96
Bannerman St.	S33 95
Banning Clo.	M33 92
Banstead Gro.	U33 96
Banting Clo.	Q23 40
Barbara Av.	U25 57
Barbara St.	JJ31 103
Crawford St.	
Barber St.	HH27 64
Barberi Gdns.	HH29 82
Barbour Dr.	Q26 55
Barbrook Way	R27 56
Barclay St.	Q35 112
Mill St.	
Barcombe Rd.	J40 140
Bardon Clo.	Y34 116
Bardsay Rd.	R28 74
Barford Clo.	L10 12
Barford Rd., Birk.	H34 108
Barford Rd., Know.	Z30 78
Barford Rd., Liver.	X38 132
Bark Hill Rd.	T36 114
Bark Rd.	P24 40
Barkbeth Rd.	Y30 77
Barkbeth Wk.	Y30 77
Barkeley Dr.	N26 54
Barker La.	F36 107
Barker Rd.	G38 124
Barkerville Clo.	S29 74
Barkfield Av.	K15 16

Barkfield La. J15 15
Barley Field G39 124
Barlow Av. O38 127
Barlow Gro. KK28 83
Barlow La. Q29 73
Barlow St. Q29 73
Barlows Clo. S25 56
Barlows La. S25 56
Barmouth Rd. J30 70
Barmouth St. P30 73
Barn Croft Rd. AA37 133
Barn Hey Cres. D33 88
Barn Hey Grn. U30 75
Barn Hey Rd. X24 44
Barn La., Gol. PP25 67
Barn La., Warr. MM30 84
Barn Meadow Rd. X34 116
Barnacre Dr. H44 144
Barnacre La. E34 107
Barnard Rd. L34 110
Barncroft N45 147
Barncroft Pl. N22 39
Barndale Rd. U34 114
Barnes Dr. S19 28
Barnes Grn. O40 142
Barnes Rd. HH36 121
Barnes St. R30 74
Barneston Rd. JJ35 121
Barnet Clo. S33 95
Barnett Av. MM27 66
Barnfield Clo., Sefton Q24 40
Barnfield Clo., Wirr. D32 88
Barnfield Dr. U30 75
Barnham Dr. W33 97
Barnhill Rd. U34 114
Barnhouse Clo. X39 132
Barnhurst Clo. W33 97
Barnhurst Rd. W33 97
Barnsbury Rd. S28 74
Barnsdale Av. H38 124
Barnstaple Gro. HH30 82
Barnston La. G32 90
Barnston Rd., Liver. R25 56
Barnston Rd., Thing. H38 124
Barnston Rd., Wirr. H41 139
Barnston Tower Clo. J41 140
Barnton Clo. RR25 68
Barnton Clo. RR25 68
Barnway St. NN27 66
Barnwell Av. L31 92
Barnwood Rd. X31 98
Baroncroft Rd. W35 115
Barons Clo. EE37 135
Barons Hey W29 76
Barr St. P29 73
Barren Gro. L35 110
Barrett Rd. O 8 9
Barrington Dr. L10 12
Barrington Gro. NN23 51
Barrington Rd., Liver. T34 114
Barrington Rd., Wirr. M31 92
Barrow Clo. V28 76
Barrow Hall La. LL31 104
Barrow La. RR28 86
Barrow Nook La. Z19 32
Barrow St. OO22 52
Barrow St., St.H. GG27 63
Barrowdale Rd. QQ25 68
Barrowfield Rd. DD26 62
Barrows Green La. JJ36 121
Barrows Row GG35 120
Barrymore Rd. T31 96
Barrymore Way O42 142
Barsfield Rd. V33 97
Bartlett St. T33 96
Barton Clo., Sefton O24 39
Barton Clo., St.H. FF27 63
Barton Clough JJ22 49
Gerrard Rd.
Barton Clough JJ22 49
Mitchell Rd.
Barton Hey Dr. C38 122
Barton Heys Rd. J16 19
Barton Pl. R27 56
Barton Rd. B34 105
Barton St., Wigan QQ25 68
Barton St., Wirr. M34 110
Barwell Av. HH26 64
Basil Clo. W33 97
Basil Rd. V33 97
Basildon Clo. FF29 81
Basing St. V37 131
Baskervyle Clo. H42 139
Baskervyle Rd. H42 139
Basnett St. P32 94
Bass St. R33 95
Bassenthwaite Av., Wirr. J34 109
Bassenthwaite Av., Know. V23 43
Bassenthwaite Av., St.H. GG25 63
Bassett Gro. LL20 37
Bassett Way Y34 116
Bates Cres. E28 80
Batey Av. DD31 101
Bath St. N. O 5 5
Bath St., Crosby M25 53
Bath St., Liver. O32 93
Bath St., Sefton O 5 5
Bath St., St.H. FF27 63
Bath St., Wirr. O38 127
Bathgate Way V22 43
Bathhurst Rd. U37 130
Batley St. U31 96
Battenburg St. R32 95
Battery Clo. S36 113
Fulwood Dr.
Battle Way L16 20
Baucher Dr. Q25 55
Baxters La. HH29 82
Baycliff Rd. W29 76
Bayfield Rd. U37 130
Bayswater Gdns. J29 70
Bayswater Rd. J30 70
Baythorne Rd. S28 74
Baytree Clo. S 2 3
Baytree Rd., Birk. N35 111
Baytree Rd., W.Kirby D36 106
Beach Bnk. M24 38
Beach Gro. M30 71
Beach Lawn M24 38
Beach Priory Gdns. N 6 5
Beach Rd. S. N 6 5
Beach Rd., Lith. O25 54
Bridge Rd.
Beach Rd., Wirr. A34 105
Beach Wk., W.Kirby C37 122
Beacham Rd. Q 5 6
Beachcroft Rd. D32 88
Beacon Ct. Q30 73
Calder Rd.
Beacon Dr. C36 106
Beacon Gro. HH26 64
Billinge Cres.
Beacon La. H41 139
Beacon Rd. JJ22 49
Beacon St. O30 72
Beaconsfield Clo. N35 111
Brougham Av.
Beaconsfield Cres. GG35 120
Beaconsfield Gro. GG35 120
Beaconsfield Rd. Q 6 6
Beaconsfield Rd., Sefton N25 54
Beaconsfield Rd., Halton GG35 120
Beaconsfield Rd., St.H. EE26 62
Beaconsfield Rd., Wirr. O37 127
Beaconsfield Rd., Wool. W35 115
Beaconsfield St. R34 113
Beacontree Rd. V31 97
Beames Clo. S32 95
Crosfield Rd.
Beatrice Av. N37 127
Beatrice St., Boot. P28 73
Beatrice St., Wall. N31 93
Beatrice Wk. Q30 73
Beattie St. O26 54
Beattock Clo. V22 43
Beatty Clo., Caldy C38 122
Beatty Clo., Know. BB32 100
Beatty Rd. Q 6 6
Beatty Rd. U32 96
Oak Pk.
Beauclair Dr. U33 96
Beaufort L16 20
Beaufort Dr. K31 91
Beaufort Rd. K32 91
Beaufort St., Liver Q34 112
Beaufort St., P.Cross HH28 82
Beaumaris Dr. H38 124
Beaumaris Rd. J30 70
Beaumaris St. P29 73
Beaumont Av. EE27 62
Beaumont Av. EE27 62
Beaumont Dr. T24 42
Beaumont Gro. R33 95
Beaumont St. R33 95
Beauway Av. F35 107
Beauworth Av. F35 107
Hambledon Dr.
Beaver Gro. R26 56
Bebington Rd. M36 110
Bechers DD36 119
Beck Gro, Sefton O22 39
Beck Gro., St.H. GG25 63
Beck Rd. P26 55
Beckenham Av. T34 114
Beckenham Rd. L29 71
Becket St. P29 73
Beckett Gro. M38 126
Beckingham Cl. M33 92
Beckwith Clo. M33 92
Beckwith St., Liver. P33 94
Beckwith St., Wirr. L33 92
Becky St. R30 74
Bective St. S33 95
Bedale Wk. W23 43
Bedburn Dr. X31 98
Bedford Av., Sefton T22 42
Bedford Av., Wirr. N36 111
Bedford Clo. AA31 99
Bedford Clo., Liver. Q33 94
Bedford Ct. N36 111
Bedford Dr. M36 110
Bedford Pl. O36 111
Bedford Pl. NN22 51
Bedford Pl., Sea. N25 54
Ewart Rd.
Bedford Rd., Birk. N36 111
Bedford Rd., Liver. P28 73
Bedford Rd., Sefton O 8 9
Bedford Rd., Wirr. L30 71
Bedford St. HH28 82
Bedford St. N. Q32 94
Bedford St. S. Q33 94
Bedworth Rd. K34 109
Beech Av., Gt. Crosby O22 39
Beech Av., Hay. MM25 66
Beech Av., Pres. CC29 79
Beech Av., Sutt. HH31 103
Beech Av., Thing. H39 124
Beech Av., Upt. F34 107
Beech Av., Wadd. U23 42
Beech Av., Warr. LL35 152
Beech Clo. V23 43
Beech Court Mews V35 115
Beech Dr. J15 15
Beech Fld. T20 29
Beech Gdns., Rain. CC21 33
Beech Grn., Liver. U29 75
Beech Grn., Sefton N26 54
Beech Gro. S. Q 5 6
Beech Gro., Ain. R24 41
Beech Gro., Liver. R26 56
Beech Hey La. O44 147
Beech Lawn T37 130
Beech Pk. U30 75
Beech Rd., Beb. N37 127
Beech Rd., Birk. M35 110
Beech Rd., Hes. J41 140
Beech Rd., Know. Z32 99
Beech Rd., Liver. R28 74
Beech Rd., W.Lan. U17 153
Beech St., Liver. S32 95
Beech St., Sefton P27 55
Beech St., St.H. EE29 80
Beech Walks LL20 37
Beech Wk., The U31 96
Beechbank Rd. T34 114
Beechburn Cres. X31 98
Beechburn Rd. X31 98
Beechcroft Rd. M32 92
Beechdale Rd. U35 114
Beechdene Rd. R29 74
Beechfield Clo. G41 139
Beechfield Rd. V35 115
Beechill Clo. Y35 116
Beeching Clo. M33 92
Beechmouth Clo. Y32 98
Beechtree Rd. U33 96
Beechurst Clo. X34 116
Beechurst Rd. X34 116
Beechway U20 29
Beechways N39 127
Beechways Dr. J45 145
Beechwood Av., Know. Z37 133
Beechwood Av., Newt. OO27 67
Beechwood Av., Wigan NN24 51
Beechwood Av., Wirr. K30 70
Beechwood Clo. U37 130
Beechwood Ct., Sefton T20 29
Beechwood Ct., Wirr. H36 108
Beechwood Dr. J16 19

Beechwood Farm T37 130
Beechwood Gdns. T37 130
Beechwood Gro. CC31 100
Beechwood Rd., Liver. T38 130
Beechwood Rd., Sea. Q26 54
Beechwood Rd., Wirr. P41 143
Beeley Wk. R33 95
Beesley Rd. BB30 79
Beeston Clo. J34 109
Beeston Dr. G39 124
Beeston Dr., Ain. R23 41
Beeston Gro. U37 130
Beldon Cres. X31 98
Belfast Rd. U31 96
Belfield Cres. Z32 99
Belford Dr. E33 89
Belfort Clo. X34 116
Belfort Rd. X34 116
Belgrave Av. L31 92
Belgrave Clo. LL19 37
Belgrave Clo., C.Wood JJ35 121
Belgrave Pl. N 7 9
Belgrave Rd. S. N 7 9
Belgrave Rd., Lith. N25 54
Belgrave Rd., Liver. R35 113
Belgrave St., Liver. Q31 94
Belgrave St., Wirr. L31 92
Bell House Rd. HH36 121
Bell La. GG32 102
Bell Rd. M31 92
Bell St. U31 96
Bella Vista Rd. G31 90
Bellair Av. O23 39
Bellairs Rd. T29 75
Bellamy Rd. Q28 73
Belle Vale Rd. X35 116
Belle Vue T33 96
Belle Vue Rd., Gate. X35 116
Bellefield Av. U30 75
Bellefield Cres. L29 71
Bellevue Rd., Wall. M32 92
Bellew Rd. T29 75
Bellfield Dr. L35 110
Bellgreen Rd. U28 75
Bellhaven Rd. T34 114
Bellis Av. Q 4 6
Bellmore St. V37 131
Bells Clo. R19 28
Bells La. R19 28
Bellward Clo. N40 142
Finstall Rd.
Belmont Av., Wigan HH19 36
Belmont Av., Wirr. P40 143
Belmont Cres. M34 111
Derby St.
Belmont Dr., Liver. S30 74
Belmont Dr., Wirr. H39 124
Belmont Gro. S30 74
Belmont Rd., C.Wood HH36 121
Belmont Rd., Liver. R30 74
Belmont Rd., W.Kirby B35 105
Belmont Rd., Wall. L29 71
Belmont St., Sefton O 6 5
Belmont St., St.H. EE27 62
Gladstone St.
Belmont St., Wirr. M34 110
Belmont Vw. R30 74
Beloe St. Q35 112
Belper St. U38 130
Belston Rd. V33 97
Belton Rd. Y30 77
Belvedere Av. HH30 82
Belvedere Ct. H36 108
Belvedere Dr. K16 19
Belvedere Rd., Ains. M10 12
Belvedere Rd., St.H. NN27 66
Belvedere Rd., Wigan OO23 52
Belvidere Pk. N23 39
Belvidere Rd. R34 113
Belvidere Rd., Crosby M23 38
Belvidere Rd., Wirr. K30 70
Belvoir Av. GG36 120
Belvoir Rd. V37 131
Bembridge Clo. FF35 120
Ben La. Z20 32
Ben Nevis Rd. M36 110
Benbow St. O28 72
Bendee Av. L45 146
Bendee Rd. K45 145
Benedick St. P28 73
Bengarth Rd. Q 5 6
Benledi St. P30 73
Westmoreland Pl.
Benmore Rd. U36 114
Bennets La. D32 88
Bennett Clo. O45 147
Bennett St. V38 131
Bennett Wk. G39 124
Cheshire Way
Bennetts Hill L35 110
Bennetts La. JJ36 121
Bennison Dr. U37 130
Benson St. Q32 94
Bent Way H41 139
Heather Rd.
Bentfield Clo. M38 126
Bentfield Gdns. M37 126
Bentham Clo. K35 109
Bentham St. O 6 5
Bentinck Ct. M34 110
Bentinck Pl. M34 110
Bentinck St., Liver. O30 72
Bentinck St., St.H. HH28 82
Bentinck St., Wirr. M34 110
Bentley Clo. N39 127
Bentley Rd., Birk. L35 110
Bentley Rd., Liver. R34 113
Bentley Rd., Thing. G38 124
Bentley St. HH31 103
Benty Heath La. N43 147
Benwick Rd. U24 42
Berbice Rd. U34 114
Beresford Av. O38 127
Beresford Dr. Q 4 6
Beresford Rd., Birk. K35 109
Beresford Rd., Liver. Q35 112
Beresford Rd., Wirr. K30 70
Beresford St. FF29 81
Berkeley Av., Wigan LL20 37
Berkeley Av., Wirr. K36 109
Berkeley Ct. H36 108
Berkeley Dr. M29 71
Berkeley Rd. M22 38
Berkeswell Rd. U28 75
Berkley Av. V29 76
Berkley St. Q33 94
Bermuda Rd. F32 89
Bernard Av. L29 71
Berner St. M33 92
Berners Rd. U37 130
Berrington Av. W36 115
Berringtons La. DD24 47
Berry Hill Av. Y59 27
Berry Rd. EE36 119
Berry St., Edge H. Q33 94
Berry St., Sefton O27 54
Berrylands Rd. F32 89
Berrys La. JJ28 82
Bertha Gdns. K33 91
Bertha St.
Bertha St. K33 91
Bertram Dr. C33 88
Bertram Dr. N. C33 88
Bertram Rd. S35 113
Bertram St. NN27 66
Neville St.
Berwick Av., Hoy. C33 88
Berwick Av., Sefton M10 12
Berwick Av., Wirr. Q43 148
Berwick Clo. E33 89
Berwick Clo., Birk. J34 109
Berwick Dr. M22 38
Berwick St. R31 95
Berwyn Av. H38 124
Berwyn Boulevard N37 127
Berwyn Ct. P 7 10
Berwyn Dr. G40 139
Berwyn Gro. KK27 65
Berwyn Rd. S29 74
Berwyn Rd., Wall. L31 92
Beryl Rd., Wirr. J34 109
Beryl St. U32 96
Beryl Wk., Know. U25 57
Amanda Rd.
Besford Rd. X34 116
Bessborough Rd., Liver. T36 114
Bessborough Rd., Wirr. L35 110
Bessemer St. Q35 112
Beta Clo. O37 127
Beth Av. HH29 82
Bethany Cres. N38 127
Bettisfield Av. P42 143
Betula Clo. R27 56
Beulah Av, HH23 49
Bevans La. V29 76
Beverley Av. JJ20 36
Beverley Clo. S 2 3
Beverley Dr. H42 139
Beverley Gdns. H38 124
Beverley Rd., Beb. O37 127
Beverley Rd., Liver. U34 114
Beverley Rd., Wall. K30 70
Beverley Way R45 149
Beversbrook Rd. U28 75
Bevington Bush P31 94
Bevington St. P31 94
Bevington St. MM22 51
Bevyl Rd. H44 144
Bewley Dr., Know. W25 58
Bewley Dr., Sefton V24 43
Bewsey St. M31 92
Wittle St.
Bewsey St. EE28 80
Bex Clo. X39 132
Bianca St. P28 73
Bibby Rd. R 4 7
Bibby St. T31 96
Bibbys La. O26 54
Bickerstaffe St. GG27 63
Bickerton Av. M37 126
Bickerton Rd. N 7 9
Bickerton St. S35 113
Bideford Av. HH30 82
Bidston Av., Bids. K33 91
Bidston Av., Wall. J30 70
Bidston By-Pass H32 90
Bidston Clo., Birk. K34 109
Bidston Link Rd. J32 91
Bidston Moss J31 91
Bidston Rd. R29 74
Bidston Village Rd. J32 91
Bidston Way HH26 64
Big Meadow Rd. H35 108
Big Yard K30 70
Bigdale Dr. W23 43
Bigham Rd. S31 95
Billinge Cres. HH26 64
Billinge Rd., Asht. KK22 50
Billinge Rd., Wigan LL19 37
Billingham Rd. EE29 80
Billington Av. OO26 67
Bills La. K16 19
Bilston Rd. T37 130
Bilton Clo. JJ36 121
Kilsby Dr.
Bingley Rd. R29 74
Binns Rd. T32 96
Binsey Clo. F34 107
Biram St. HH28 82
Birbeck Rd. X23 44
Birbeck Wk. X23 44
Birch Av. FF26 63
Birch Av., Liver. R26 56
Birch Av., Wirr. F34 107
Birch Clo., Liver. T20 29
Birch Clo., Whist. CC31 100
Birch Clo., Wirr. L35 110
Birch Gdns., St.H. FF26 63
Birch Grn. J14 15
Birch Gro., Huy. CC31 100
Birch Gro., Oak.Pk. U32 96
Birch Gro., Roby Y32 98
Birch Gro., Wigan LL22 50
Birch Gro., Wirr. L29 71
Birch Heys E36 107
Birch Rd., Beb. O39 127
Birch Rd., Berk. L35 110
Birch Rd., Halton GG35 120
Birch Rd., Hoy. D33 88
Birch Rd., Know. Z32 99
Birch Rd., St.H. MM25 66
Birch St., Sefton O 7 9
Birch St., St.H. MM27 66
Birchall St. P29 73
Birchcliffe Rd. N36 111
Birchdale Rd., Liver. R27 56
Birchdale Rd., Sefton M24 38
Birchen Rd. AA37 133
Birches Clo. H40 139
Birches, The K44 145
Birchfield Av. GG36 120
Birchfield Clo. F33 89
Birchfield Gdns. GG34 120
Birchfield Rd., Anf. R28 74
Birchfield Rd., Edge H. T32 96
Birchfield Rd., Farn. GG34 120
Birchfield St. EE29 80
Birchfield Ter. Q31 94
Birchfield Way R18 23
Birchfield, Wirr. F33 89
Birchill Rd. Y24 44
Birchley Av. HH23 49
Birchley Rd. GG23 48
Birchley St. GG27 63
Birchley Vw. GG24 48

Birchmuir Hey, Know.	W24	43
Leighshey Cres.		
Birchover Wk.	R33	95
Angela St.		
Birchridge Clo.	P40	143
Birchtree Av.	FF25	63
Birchtree Rd.	T35	114
Birchway	J42	140
Bird St.	S33	95
Birdwood Rd.	T29	75
Birkdale Av.	L42	143
Brookhurst Av.		
Birkdale Cop	P 8	10
Birkdale Rd.	GG34	120
Birkenhead Rd., Hoy.	C33	88
Birkenhead Rd., Wall.	N32	93
Birkenhead Rd., Wirr.	M44	146
Birkenshaw Av.	L22	38
Birket Av.	G31	90
Birket Clo.	H31	90
Birket Rd.	G31	90
Birket Sq.	G31	90
Birket Av.		
Birkett Rd., Birk.	N36	111
Birkett Rd., W.Kirby	B35	105
Birkey La.	K16	19
Birkin Clo.	X25	59
Birkin Rd.	X25	59
Birkside Rd.	X34	116
Birkside Rd.	X34	116
Birnam Dr.	EE32	101
Birnam Rd.	M31	92
Birstall Av.	HH26	64
Markfield Cres.		
Birstall Rd.	R31	95
Birtle Croft	X29	77
Birtley St.	OO27	67
Bishop Dr.	BB32	100
Bishop Rd., Liver.	S30	74
Bishop Rd., St.H.	FF26	63
Bishop Rd., Wirr.	L32	92
Bishop Reeves Rd.	MM25	66
Elizabeth Rd.		
Bishopdale Dr.	EE32	101
Bishopgate St.	T33	96
Bishops Ct.	X36	116
Bishops Way	HH35	121
Bisley St.	L30	71
Bismarck St.	Q30	73
Bispham Av.	D33	88
Bispham Dr.	MM22	51
Bispham Rd.	Q 5	6
Bixteth St.	P32	94
Black Clo.	R27	56
Black Denton Pl.	HH36	121
Black Horse Clo.	C35	106
Black Horse Hill	C35	106
Black Horse La.	U31	96
Black Horse St.	HH27	64
Roper St.		
Black-a-Moor La.	Q16	22
Blackboards La.	R45	149
Blackbrook Rd.	JJ26	64
Blackburn Pl.	Q33	94
Blackburn St.	V39	131
Blackburne Av.	DD38	135
Blackburne Dr.	Y37	132
Blackcarr La.	O19	26
Blackdown Gro.	JJ28	82
Blacker St.	Q33	94
Blackeys La.	K45	145
Blackfield St.	P30	73
Stirling Way		
Blackheath Dr.	G31	90
Blackhurst Rd.	S18	23
Blackleyhurst Av.	JJ22	49
Royden Rd.		
Blacklock Hall Rd.	Y39	132
Blacklow Brow	Y32	98
Blackmoor Dr.	V30	76
Blackpool St.	N34	111
Blackrod Av.	Y39	136
Blackstock Ct.	P23	40
Granams Cft.		
Blackstock St.	P31	94
Blackstone Av.	HH26	64
Blackstone St.	O30	72
Blackthorn Clo.	G33	90
Blackthorne Rd.	R27	56
Blackwater Rd.	V27	58
Blackwood Av.	W35	115
Blacon La.	Q30	73
Blair Wk.	O27	54
Blair Wk., Speke	Z38	133
Blaisdon Clo.	U28	75
Blake Ct.	V38	131
Banks Rd.		
Blake Field Rd.	P22	40
Blakeacre Clo.	Z38	133
Blakeacre Rd.	Z38	133
Blakeley Brow	O42	142
Blakeley Ct.	O41	142
Blakeley Dene	O41	142
Blakeley Rd.	O41	142
Blakeney Clo.	H33	90
Blaking Dr.	Y27	59
Blandford Clo.	N 6	5
Blantyre Rd.	T34	114
Blaydon Clo.	Y37	132
Blaydon Clo., Ain.	R24	41
Blaydon Gro.	EE29	80
Bleak Hill Rd.	DD26	62
Bleasdale Av.	T24	42
Bleasdale Rd.	U35	114
Bleasdale Way	P23	40
Blenheim Av., Liver.	T34	114
Blenheim Av., Sefton	P25	55
Blenheim Rd., Sefton	L10	12
Blenheim Rd., Wigan	OO24	52
Blenheim Rd., Wirr.	M30	71
Blenheim St.	P31	94
Blessington Rd.	Q29	73
Bletchley Av.	K31	91
Bligh St.	T33	96
Blind Foot Rd.	BB25	61
Blomfield Rd.	V37	131
Blossom St.	P26	55
Blucher St	M24	38
Blue Acre	HH31	103
Blue Bell La.	Z31	90
Blue Stone La.	T20	29
Bluebell Av.	K33	91
Blundell Av., Formby	H15	15
Blundell Av., High.	K19	24
Blundell Av., S.Port	N 8	9
Blundell Dr.	K19	24
Blundell Gro.	K19	24
Blundell La.	S 3	3
Blundell Rd., Halton	EE37	135
Blundell Rd., Sefton	K19	24
Blundell St.	P33	94
Blundells Dr.	G32	90
Blundells La.	DD32	101
Blundellsands Rd. E.	M23	38
Blundellsands Rd. W.	L23	38
Blythe Rd.	P41	143
Blythe Way	Q31	94
Breck Rd.		
Blythe Way	GG35	120
Blythswood St.	R35	113
Boaler St.	R31	95
Boardmans La.	JJ27	64
Boathouse La.	H44	144
Bobbies La.	DD27	62
Bodden St.	HH31	103
Bodley St.	Q29	73
Bodmin Av.	R 2	3
Bodmin Gro.	HH25	64
Bodmin Rd.	R28	74
Bodmin Way	Z37	133
Bodnant Av.	Q30	73
Bodnant Clo.	X39	132
Bognor Clo.	X39	132
Dymchurch Rd.		
Bolan St.	T31	96
Bold La., St.H.	KK29	83
Bold La., W.Lan.	U17	153
Bold Pl.	Q33	94
Bold Rd.	JJ29	82
Bold St., Liver.	P32	94
Bold St., Sefton	O 5	5
Bold St., St.H.	FF27	63
Bolde Way	O40	142
Boleswith St.	S32	95
Bolton Av.	V24	43
Bolton Clo.	L16	20
Bolton Clo.	HH27	64
Bolton Clo.		
Bolton Clo.	HH27	64
Bolton Rd. E.	P38	128
Bolton Rd., Asht.	OO23	52
Bolton Rd., Sefton	O 7	9
Bolton Rd., Wirr.	O38	127
Bolton St.	HH27	64
Higher Parr St.		
Bolton St., Liver.	Q32	94
Bolton St., St.H.	HH27	64
Bolton St., Wigan	LL22	50
Bolyn, The	T19	29
Bond St., Know.	BB30	79
Kemble St.		
Bond St., Liver.	P31	94
Bonnington Av.	M22	38
Bonsall Rd.	U30	75
Boode Cft.	X28	77
Booker Av.	V36	115
Booth St., Liver.	U31	96
Booth St., Newton	NN27	66
Wellington St.		
Booth St., Pres.	EE29	80
Samuel St.		
Booth St., Sefton	O 5	5
Booths Brow Rd.	LL22	50
Borax St.	U32	96
Border Rd.	H41	139
Borella Rd.	T30	75
Borough Pavement	M34	110
Borough Pl.	N34	111
Grange Rd.E.		
Borough Rd., Birk.	M35	110
Borough Rd., St.H.	FF28	81
Borough Rd., Wall.	M31	92
Borron Rd.	NN26	66
Borrowdale Rd., Beb.	N39	127
Borrowdale Rd., Halton	EE37	135
Borrowdale Rd., Liver.	T34	114
Borrowdale Rd., Moreton	F33	89
Borrowdale Rd., St.H.	DD29	80
Boscow Cres.	HH29	82
Boskin St.	P29	73
Bostock St.	P30	73
Boswell Rd.	K37	125
Boswell St., Liver	S33	95
Boswell St., Sefton	O26	54
Bosworth Clo.	N40	142
Bosworth Dr.	L11	12
Bosworth Rd.	HH26	64
Botanic Gdns.	S32	95
Botanic Pl.	S32	95
Botanic Rd.	R 4	7
Botanic Rd.	S32	95
Botanic St.	S33	95
Botley Clo.	F34	107
Bough La.	N12	13
Boulevard, The	U29	75
Boulton Av.	B35	105
Boulton Rd.	O37	127
Bound St.	P30	73
Boundary Dr., Sefton	M22	38
Boundary Dr., Speke	Y37	132
Boundary Farm Rd.	Y38	132
Boundary La., Know.	Z24	45
Boundary La., Liver.	R31	95
Boundary La., Wirr.	H41	139
Boundary Rd., Beb.	O37	127
Boundary Rd., Bids.	J33	91
Boundary Rd., Know.	Z33	99
Boundary Rd., Lith.	P24	40
Boundary Rd., Sefton	P24	40
Boundary Rd., St.H.	FF27	63
Boundary Rd., W.Kirby	C37	122
Boundary St., Liver.	P30	73
Boundary St., Sefton	O 7	9
Boundary Wk.	Z33	99
Bourdmans La.	JJ27	64
Bourn Pk.	U20	29
Bourne Av.	RR25	68
Bourne St., Liver.	R31	95
Bourne St., St.H.	HH28	82
Bournville Dr.	N40	142
Finstall Rd.		
Bourton Rd.	X38	132
Bouverie St.	R34	113
Bowden Rd., Liver.	U38	130
Bowden Rd., Wirr.	K30	70
Bowden St.	O26	54
Bower Gro.	N25	54
Bower Rd., Know.	Z31	99
Bower Rd., Liver.	X35	116
Bower Rd., Wirr.	J41	140
Bower St.	HH36	121
Bowfell Clo.	P43	148
Bowfield Rd.	U37	130
Bowkers Green La.	W19	30
Bowland Av., Child.	V32	97
Bowland Av., St.H.	GG31	102
Bowland Av., Wigan	NN23	51
Bowland Clo.	P40	143
Hornby Rd.		
Bowland Dr.	P23	40
Bowles St.	O26	54
Bowley Rd.	T30	75
Bowling Green Clo.	Q 6	6
Bowness Av., Birk.	K36	109
Bowness Av., Brom.	P42	143
Bowness Av., Sefton	M11	12

Bowness Av., St.H.	GG25 63	Brandon St.	N34 111	Brickfields La.	Q35 112		
Bowood St.	Q35 112	Branker Av.	DD31 101	*Beresford Rd.*			
Bowring Clo.	R35 113	Bransford Clo.	OO24 52	Brickwall La.	Q22 40		
Bowring Dr.	H44 144	Branstree Av.	T28 75	Bride St.	Q28 73		
Bowring Park Av.	X32 98	Branthwaite Cres.	U28 75	Bridge Cft.	O23 39		
Bowring Park Rd.	W32 97	Brasenose Rd.	O28 72	Bridge Farm Clo.	H36 108		
Bowscales Rd.	U28 75	Brassey St., Liver.	Q34 112	Bridge Farm Dr.	T20 29		
Boxdale Rd.	U35 114	Brassey St., Wirr.	L33 92	Bridge Gro.	O 6 5		
Boxmoor Rd.	U36 114	Brattan Rd.	M35 110	Bridge La.	Q23 40		
Boyd Clo.	H31 90	Bratton Av.	LL20 37	Bridge Rd., Birk.	J35 109		
Boydell Clo.	X29 77	Braunton Rd.	T37 130	Bridge Rd., Crosby	M23 38		
Boyer Av.	S21 28	Brauton Rd.	L30 71	Bridge Rd., Edge H.	S33 95		
Boyess Brow	V23 43	*Kinnaird Rd.*		Bridge Rd., Hay.	S21 28		
Boysell Clo.	X29 77	Brauton Rd.	L30 71	Bridge Rd., Lith.	O25 54		
Boyton Ct.	S33 95	Bray Rd.	X39 132	Bridge Rd., Moss.H.	U35 114		
Brabant Rd.	T36 114	Bray St.	L33 92	Bridge Rd., Pres.	BB30 79		
Braby Rd.	P26 55	Braybrook Rd.	U27 57	Bridge Rd., Roby	Y32 98		
Bracebridge Dr.	Q 8 10	Braydon Clo.	Y38 132	Bridge Rd., St.H.	HH32 103		
Bracken Dr.	D36 106	Brayfield Rd.	S28 74	Bridge Rd., W.Kirby	B35 105		
Bracken La.	M38 126	Brechin Rd.	W24 43	Bridge St., Beb.	O38 127		
Brackend Av.	R25 56	Breck Clo.	R30 74	Bridge St., Boot.	O28 72		
Brackenhurst Dr.	M29 71	Breck Rd., Halton	GG36 120	Bridge St., Elles.	K45 145		
Brackenside	G40 139	Breck Rd., Liver.	R30 74	Bridge St., Newton	NN27 66		
Brackenway	L14 16	Breck Rd., Wirr.	K31 91	Bridge St., St.H.	GG27 63		
Brackenwood Rd.	M38 126	Breck Wk.	R31 95	Bridge St., S.Port	O 5 5		
Brackley Av.	O27 54	Breckfield Rd. N.	R30 74	Bridge St., Wall.	N33 93		
Brackley Clo.	K31 90	Breckfield Rd. S.	R30 74	Bridge St., Wigan	QQ25 68		
Brackley Clo., Sefton	O27 54	Breckside Av.	K31 91	Bridge Wills La.	S 2 3		
Brackley Clo., Wirr.	K31 91	Breckside Pk.	S30 74	*Preston New Rd.*			
Brackley Ct.	O27 54	Brecon Av.	Q24 40	Bridgecroft Rd.	L30 71		
Brackleyhurst Av.	JJ22 49	Brecon Rd.	M37 126	Bridgeman St.	EE27 62		
Bracknell Av.	V24 43	Breeze Clo.	O28 73	Bridgend Dr.	L11 12		
Bracknell Clo.	V24 43	Breeze Hill	P27 55	Bridgenorth Rd.	G39 124		
Bradbourne Clo.	W27 58	Breeze Hill	O28 73	Bridges La.	Q21 27		
Bradda Clo.	G34 108	Breeze La.	O27 55	Bridgewater Clo.	O24 39		
Braddan Av.	T30 75	Breeze Rd.	N 7 9	Bridgewater St.	P33 94		
Bradden Clo.	O40 142	Breezehill Clo.	K45 145	Bridle Av.	N32 93		
Braddocks, The	Q30 73	Breezehill Pk.	K45 145	Bridle Clo., Brom.	Q41 143		
Brade St.	S 3 3	Breezehill Rd.	K45 145	Bridle Clo., Upt.	H34 108		
Bradewell St.	Q29 73	Brelade Rd.	T31 96	Bridle Rd., Brom.	Q41 143		
Bradfield Av.	S23 41	Bremhill Rd.	T27 57	Bridle Rd., Sefton	Q25 55		
Bradford St.	S32 95	Bremner Clo.	S32 95	Bridle Rd., Wall.	N32 93		
Bradlegh Rd.	OO28 85	*Clint Rd.*		Bridle Way	Q25 55		
Bradley Cres., Huy.	AA33 99	Brenda Cres.	O21 26	Bridport St.	Q32 94		
Tarbock Rd.		Brendale Av.	S21 28	Brierley Clo.	R23 41		
Bradley La.	MM28 84	Brendans Way	Q23 40	Briery Hey	W24 43		
Bradley Pass.	HH36 121	Brendon Av.	O24 39	Briford Av.	U29 75		
Bradley Rd.	P24 40	Brendon Gro.	JJ27 64	Bright St., Birk.	M34 110		
Bradley Rd.	P25 55	*Malvern Rd.*		*Bentinck St.*			
Bradley St.	P 5 6	Brendor Rd.	X36 116	Bright St., Liver.	R31 95		
Bradman Clo.	F32 89	Brenig St.	K33 91	Bright St., Sefton	Q 5 6		
Bradman Rd., Know.	Y23 44	Brenka Av.	R24 41	Brighton Rd., Crosby	M24 38		
Bradman Rd., Wirr.	F32 89	Brent Way	Z38 133	Brighton Rd., Know.	AA31 99		
Bradmore Rd.	P41 143	*New Hutte La.*		*Lynton Rd.*			
Bradshaw St.	GG36 120	Brentfield	FF36 120	Brighton Rd., S.Port	O 7 9		
Bradshaw Wk.	O27 54	*Heath Rd.*		Brighton St., Birk.	M34 110		
Brackley Av.		Brenton St., Wirr.	K32 91	Brighton St., Wall.	M31 92		
Bradshaws La.	M10 12	Brentwood Av., Liver.	S35 113	Brighton Vale	L24 38		
Bradville Rd.	S25 56	Brentwood Av., Sefton	N22 39	Brill St.,	L33 92		
Bradway Clo.	C36 106	Brentwood Ct.	H36 108	Brimstage Av.	M37 126		
Brae St.	H32 95	Brentwood St.	M32 92	Brimstage Clo.	J41 140		
Braehaven Rd.	M29 71	Brereton Av.	O38 127	Brimstage Grn.	J41 140		
Braemar Av.	Q 4 6	Brereton Rd.	U34 114	*Brimstage Rd.*			
Braemar Clo.	CC31 100	Bretherton Pl.	DD31 101	Brimstage La.	L38 126		
Braemar St.	P28 73	*Warburton Hey*		Brimstage Rd., Beb.	N39 127		
Braemore Clo.	LL20 37	Bretherton Rd.	CC30 79	Brimstage Rd., Brim.	L40 141		
Braemore Rd.	K31 91	Bretlands Rd.	O22 39	Brimstage Rd., Hes.	H41 139		
Braeside Cres.	HH22 49	Breton Fld.	Q 6 6	Brimstage Rd., Liver.	O28 73		
Braeside Gdns.	G34 108	Brett St.	L33 92	Brimstage St.	M35 110		
Brahms Clo.	R34 113	Brewery La., Ain.	T23 42	Brindley Clo.	O24 39		
Braid St.	M33 92	Brewery La., Formby	K14 16	Brindley Rd., Kirkby	V24 43		
Brainerd St.	T30 75	Brewster St.	Q28 73	Brindley Rd., St.H.	JJ30 82		
Braithwaite Rd.	RR25 68	Brian Av.	G38 124	Brindley St.	P33 94		
Bramberton Pl.	S28 74	Briar Dr., Know.	Y32 98	Brinklow Clo.	L10 12		
Bramberton Rd.	S28 74	Briar Dr., Wirr.	H41 139	Brinley Clo.	P42 143		
Bramble Av.	K33 91	Briar Rd., Sefton	M11 12	Brinton Clo.	Y34 116		
Bramble Way	F32 89	Briar Rd., Wigan	QQ25 68	Brisbane Av.	K29 70		
Bramcote Av.	HH26 64	Briar St.	P29 73	Brisbane St.	EE29 80		
Bramcote Clo.	W23 43	Briar Wk.	QQ25 68	Briscoe Av.	G33 90		
Bramcote Rd.	W23 43	Briardale Rd., Beb.	N37 127	Briscoe Dr.	G33 90		
Bramcote Wk.	W23 43	Briardale Rd., Birk.	M35 110	Bristol Av.	M31 92		
Bramford Clo.	G34 108	Briardale Rd., Liver.	T35 114	Bristol Rd.	U34 114		
Bramhall Clo.	Z39 133	Briardale Rd., Wall.	N32 93	Britannia Av.	S33 95		
Bramhall Dr.	Q43 148	Briardale Rd., Will.	O44 147	Britannia Rd.	L31 92		
Bramhall Rd.	N25 54	Briarfield Av.	DD36 119	Britonside Av.	W25 58		
Bramley Av.	N37 127	Briarfield Rd., Liver.	T34 114	Brittage Brow	Z34 117		
Bramley Way	V23 43	Briarfield Rd., Wirr.	H41 139	Britton St.	O33 94		
Bramley Wk.	Y40 136	Briars Clo.	EE32 101	Broad Av.	KK26 65		
Brampton Ct.	KK27 65	Briars La.	T20 29	Broad Hey	O22 39		
Bramwell Av.	L36 110	Briarwood Rd.	T35 114	Broad La.	W25 58		
Bramwell St.	JJ27 64	Briary Cft.	K19 24	Broad La., Formby	L13 16		
Brancote Gdns.	P41 143	Brick St., Liver.	P33 94	Broad La., Hom.Grn.	P20 27		
Brancote Rd.	K34 109	Brick St., St.H.	MM27 66	Broad La., Liver.	T28 75		
Brandearth Hey	X29 77	Brickfield Rd.	AA32 99	Broad La., Lyd.	R16 23		
Brandon	DD36 119			Broad La., St.H.	GG24 48		

Street	Grid	Page
Broad La., W.Lan.	N16	21
Broad La., Warr.	LL29	83
Broad La., Wirr.	E40	138
Broad Oak Av.	KK26	65
Broad Oak Rd., Sefton	T20	29
Broad Oak Rd., St.H.	JJ27	64
Broad Pl.	T29	75
Broad Sq.	T29	75
Broadgate Av.	HH28	82
Broadgreen Rd.	U32	96
Broadheath Ter.	EE36	119
Broadlake	N45	147
Broadley Av.	RR25	68
Broadmead	J41	140
Broadmead, Liver.	W37	131
Broadoak Rd., Liver.	W31	97
Broadstone Dr.	N40	142
Broadway	DD26	62
Broadway Av., Liver.	Q27	55
Broadway Av., Wirr.	K30	70
Broadway Clo.	L10	12
Broadway, Beb.	M37	126
Broadway, Liver.	T28	75
Broadway, St.H.	EE29	80
Broadway, Upt.	G35	108
Broadwood Av.	S21	28
Broadwood St.	T33	96
Brock Av.	T20	29
Brock St.	Q29	73
Brockenhurst Rd.	R26	56
Brockholm Rd.	U36	114
Brocklebank La.	V37	131
Brocklebank Rd.	Q 4	6
Brocklebank St.	O28	72
Brockley Av.	L29	71
Brocstedes Av.	MM22	51
Brocstedes Rd.	LL22	50
Brodie Av.	U36	114
Bromborough Rd.	O38	127
Bromborough Village Rd.	Q40	143
Brome Way	O40	142
Bromilow Rd.	JJ28	82
Bromley Av., Liver.	T34	114
Bromley Av., Wigan	RR25	68
Bromley Av., Wirr.	G41	139
Bromley Rd.	L29	71
Brompton Av., Liver.	S34	113
Brompton Av., Sefton	M23	38
Brompton Av., Wirr.	M31	92
Brompton Rd., Liver.	T32	96
Brompton Rd., Sefton	Q 5	6
Bromsgrove Rd.	F35	107
Bronington Av.	P42	143
Bronte Clo.	L23	38
Bronte St., Liver.	Q32	94
Russell St.		
Bronte St., St.H.	EE27	62
Brook Bridge Rd.	T30	75
Brook Clo., Know.	EE34	119
Brook Clo., Wirr.	M30	71
Brook Hey	H44	144
Brook Hey Dr.	W23	43
Brook Hey Wk.	W23	43
Brook La., W.Lan.	FF21	35
Brook Meadow	G37	124
Brook Pl.	M33	92
Brook Rd., Kennessee Grn.	T21	29
Brook Rd., Boot.	O27	54
Brook Rd., Thornton	O22	39
Brook Rd., Walt.	R27	56
Brook St.	GG27	63
Brook St., Asht.	OO24	52
Brook St., Beb.	O38	127
Brook St., Birk.	M33	92
Brook St., Elles.	K45	145
Brook St., Gol.	QQ25	68
Brook St., Halton	GG36	120
Brook St., Liver.	O32	93
Brook St., Pres.	CC30	79
Brook St., Sefton	S 3	3
Brook St., Wall.	N33	93
Brook St., Whist.	CC31	100
Brook Ter.	B36	105
Brook Vale	N25	54
Brook Way	G34	108
Brook Way, Birk.	K37	125
Brook Wk.	F37	123
Brookdale	DD35	119
Brookdale Av. N.	G35	108
Brookdale Av. S.	G35	108
Brookdale Clo.	G35	108
Brookdale Rd.	T34	114
Brooke Rd. E.	M24	38
Brooke Rd. W.	M24	38
Brooke Wk.	Q27	54
Brookend	KK28	83
Brookeside Clo.	KK25	65
Brookfield Av., Crosby	M23	38
Brookfield Av., Lith.	N25	54
Brookfield Av., St.H.	EE30	80
Brookfield Dr.	S26	56
Brookfield Gdns.	B36	105
Brookfield La.	U17	153
Brookfield Rd.	B36	105
Brookfield St.	NN27	66
Brookhill Clo.	P27	55
Waterworks St.		
Brookhill Rd.	P27	55
Brookhouse Gro.	DD27	62
Brookhurst Clo.	P42	143
Brookhurst Rd.	P42	143
Brookland La.	KK28	83
Brookland Rd.	U31	96
Brookland Rd., Birk.	M34	110
Brooklands Av., Sefton	N25	54
Brooklands Av., Wigan	OO24	52
Brooklands Dr.	S21	28
Brooklands Gdns.	J44	145
Brooklands Rd., Elles.	J44	145
Brooklands Rd., St.H.	DD27	62
Brooklands, Know.	Z32	99
Brooklet Rd.	J40	140
Brooks Alley	P32	94
Brooks Rd.	J16	19
Brooks Sq.	OO27	67
Brooks Way	J16	19
Brookside	W29	76
Brookside, Crox.	W29	76
Brookside Av.	DD26	62
Brookside Av., Liver.	V31	97
Brookside Av., Sefton	N25	54
Brookside Clo.	KK25	65
Brookside Clo., Know.	CC31	100
Brookside Clo., St.H.	JJ22	49
Brookside Cres.	G34	108
Brookside Rd.	CC31	100
Brookside Clo.		
Brookside Vw.	KK25	65
Brookvale Clo.	MM30	84
Colne Rd.		
Brookway La.	JJ28	82
Brookway, Wall.	L30	71
Brookwood Rd.	Z31	99
Broom Clo.	CC30	79
Broom Hill	K33	91
Broom Rd.	DD29	80
Broom Way	Z37	133
Broome Rd.	O 7	9
Broomfield Clo.	F40	138
Broomfield Gdns.	Q26	55
Broomfield Rd.	Q26	55
Brooms Gro.	T24	42
Broseley Av.	P40	143
Broster Av.	F33	89
Broster Clo.	F33	89
Brosters La.	D32	88
School La.		
Brougham Av.	N35	111
Brougham Rd.	N31	93
Broughton Av., Sefton	P 7	10
Broughton Av., Wirr.	B35	105
Broughton Dr.	U37	130
Broughton Hall Rd.	W30	76
Grange Av.		
Broughton Rd.	L31	92
Brow La.	G41	139
Brow Rd., Bids.	J32	91
Brow Side	Q31	94
Brown St.	Q32	94
Brownbill Bnk.	Z34	117
Browne St.	O27	54
Brownheath Av.	HH23	49
Browning Av.	N36	111
Browning Clo.	Z32	99
Browning Rd., Liver.	T30	75
Browning Rd., Wirr.	J30	70
Browning St.	O27	54
Brownlow Arcade	GG27	63
Church St.		
Brownlow Hill	Q32	94
Brownlow La.	HH20	36
Brownlow Rd.	O37	127
Brownmoor Clo.	O23	39
Brownmoor La.	N23	39
Brownmoor Pk.	N23	39
Browns La.	Q23	40
Brownvale Rd.	S30	74
Brows La.	K16	19
Broxton Av., Birk.	K36	109
Broxton Av., W.Kirby	B35	105
Broxton Rd.	K30	70
Broxton St.	T33	96
Bruce Cres.	P42	143
Bruce St., St.H.	FF27	63
Bruce St., Wirr.	N32	93
Bruen Clo.	Y34	116
Brunel Clo.	R31	95
Brunel Dr.	O24	39
Brunel Mews	R31	95
Brunel Wk.	R30	74
Brunford Clo.	F33	89
Brunstath Clo.	J40	140
Brunswick Clo.	Q29	73
Humber Clo.		
Brunswick Ct.	N33	93
Brunswick Ms.	N25	54
Brunswick Par.	M25	53
Brunswick Pl.	O29	72
Brunswick Rd.	Q31	94
Brunswick Rd.	MM27	66
Brunswick St., Gars.	V39	131
Brunswick St., Liver.	P32	94
Brunswick St., Newt.	MM27	66
Brunswick St., St.H.	KK27	65
Bruton Rd.	Y30	77
Bryanston Rd., Liver.	R35	113
Bryanston Rd., Wirr.	L36	110
Bryant Rd.	O26	54
Bryce Way, The	V31	97
Brydges St.	R32	95
Bryer Rd.	BB31	100
Bryn Bnk.	M31	92
Bryn Rd.	NN22	51
Bryn Rd..S.	OO23	52
Bryn St.	NN23	51
Brynmore Rd.	U36	114
Brynmoss Av., Birk.	N36	111
Brynmoss Av., Wall.	K31	91
Brynn St.	GG27	63
Brythen St.	P32	94
Buccleuch Way	K32	92
Shannon St.		
Buccleugh St.	K32	91
Buchanan Rd., Liver.	Q27	55
Buchanan Rd., Wirr.	M31	92
Buckfast Av.	NN25	66
Buckfast Clo.	Q23	40
Buckfast Dr.	L16	20
Buckingham Av., Birk.	K34	109
Buckingham Av., Halton	GG35	120
Buckingham Av., Liver.	S34	113
Buckingham Av., Wirr.	N37	127
Buckingham Clo.	P23	40
Buckingham Gro.	K16	19
Buckingham Rd., Anf.	S30	74
Buckingham Rd., H.V.	R26	56
Buckingham Rd., Sefton	S20	28
Buckingham Rd., Wirr.	K31	91
Buckingham St.	Q30	73
Buckland Dr.	N40	142
Buckland St.	R35	113
Buckley Hill La.	P23	40
Buckley Wk.	Y40	136
Buckley Way	P22	40
Red Lomes		
Bude Av.	HH30	82
Bude Clo.	J34	109
Bude Rd.	FF36	120
Budworth Av.	GG31	102
Budworth Av., H.Green	EE36	119
Budworth Clo.	K35	109
Budworth Ct.	K34	109
Westwood		
Budworth Dr.	Y36	116
Buerton Clo.	J35	109
Buffs La.	H41	139
Buggen La.	J45	145
Bulford Rd.	T27	57
Bulkeley Rd.	M31	92
Bull Bridge La.	T24	42
Bull Cop	L15	16
Bull La.	Q26	55
Bullens Rd., Know.	W24	43
Bullens Rd., Liver.	Q29	73
Bulwer St., Birk.	N36	111
Bulwer St., Sea.	O26	54
Bundoran Rd.	T36	114
Bungalow Rd.	PP28	85
Bunns Pl.	O37	128
Victoria St.		
Bunter Rd.	W25	58
Burbo Bank Rd.	L23	38
Burbo Bank Rd. N.	L22	38
Burbo Bank Rd. S.	L23	38

Name	Ref	Pg
Burbo Cres.	L23	38
Burbo Mansions	L23	38
Burbown	J29	70
Burden Rd.	F33	89
Burdett Av.	N40	142
Burdett Clo.	N40	142
Burdett Av.		
Burdett Rd., Sefton	M24	38
Burdett Rd., Wirr.	J30	70
Burdett St.	S35	113
Burford Av.	L31	92
Burford Rd.	V32	97
Burgess Gdns.	S20	28
Burgess La.	N16	21
Burgess St.	Q32	94
Burkhardt Dr.	PP27	67
Burleigh Rd. N.	Q29	73
Burleigh Rd. S.	Q29	73
Burley Cres.	LL20	37
Burlingham Av.	C36	106
Burlington Av.	L15	16
Burlington Rd., Sefton	N 7	9
Burlington Rd., Wirr.	L29	71
Burlington St., Liver.	P31	94
Burlington St., Wirr.	N34	111
Burman Cres.	V37	131
Burman Rd.	V37	131
Burnage Av.	HH31	103
Burnage Clo.	Z40	137
Burnand St.	Q29	73
Burnard Clo.	W24	43
Burnard Cres.	W24	43
Burnard Wk.	W24	43
Burnell Clo.	FF27	63
Burnet St.	P30	73
Sumner St.		
Burnham Clo.	EE35	119
Burnham Rd.	V35	115
Burnie Av.	Q26	55
Burnley Av.	G33	90
Burnley Rd., Sefton	M10	12
Burnley Rd., Wirr.	G33	90
Burnley St.	R31	95
Burns Av.	L30	71
Burns Clo., Asht.	MM22	51
Burns Clo., Know.	CC31	100
Burns Clo., Wigan	HH20	36
Burns Gro.	AA32	99
Burns Rd.	GG31	102
Burns St.	O26	54
Burnsall St.	W38	131
Burnside Av.	L32	92
Burnside Rd.	L32	92
Burnthwaite Rd.	V31	97
Burnvale	LL20	37
Kirkstile Cres.		
Burr St.	KK26	65
Burrell Clo.	M36	110
Burrell Dr.	F33	89
Burrell Rd.	L37	126
Burrell St..	Q29	73
Burroughs Gdns.	P31	94
Burrows Av.	JJ26	64
Burrows La.	CC28	79
Burton Av., Rain.	DD31	100
Stoney La.		
Burton Av., Wirr.	J30	70
Burton Clo.	DD31	101
Burton Clo., Rain.	DD31	100
Stoney La.		
Burton Rd., Elles.	K45	145
Burtonhead Rd.	FF28	81
Burtons Way	V25	58
Burtree Rd.	X30	77
Burwell Av.	J16	19
Burwell Wk.	X23	44
Burwen Dr.	Q26	55
Bury Rd.	O 7	9
Bury St.	Q31	94
Busbys Cotts.	L29	71
Bushbys La.	J16	19
Bushbys Pk.	J16	19
Bushell Clo.	K45	145
Bushell Rd.		
Bushell Rd.	K45	145
Bushels Dr.	HH31	103
Bushey La.	BB20	33
Bushey Rd.	S28	74
Bushway	G41	139
Bushwell Wk.	X23	44
Butchers La.	T17	153
Butchers La.	NN24	51
Bute Pl.	O26	54
Seaforth Vale N.		
Bute St.	Q31	94
Butleigh Rd.	Y30	77
Butler Cres.	R31	95
Butler St.	R31	95
Buttercup Way	R27	56
Butterfield St.	Q29	73
Buttermere Av., St.H.	GG25	63
Buttermere Av., Wigan	NN22	51
Buttermere Av., Wirr.	J34	109
Buttermere Clo, Kirkby	V23	43
Buttermere Clo., Moss S.	T20	29
Buttermere Clo., Formby	J15	15
Buttermere Cres.	CC20	33
Buttermere Gdns.	N24	39
Buttermere Rd.	X32	98
Butterwick Dr.	W27	58
Wood Lea		
Button St.	P32	94
Butts La.	Q 6	6
Buxted Rd.	X25	59
Buxted Wk.	X25	59
Buxton La.	K30	70
Buxton Rd.	O36	111
Bye La.	S16	23
Byland Clo.	L16	20
Byles St.	R35	113
Byng Pl.	S29	74
Byng Rd.	S29	74
Byng St.	O28	72
Bypass, The	N23	39
Byrne Av.	N36	111
Byrom St., Liver.	P32	94
Byrom St., Sefton	Q 5	6
Byron Av.	CC31	100
Byron Clo., Formby	K15	16
Byron Clo., Know.	Z32	99
Byron Clo., Wirr.	K37	125
Byron Rd., Crosby	M23	38
Byron Rd., Lydiate	S19	28
Byron St., Liver.	V38	131
Byron St., Sefton	O26	54
Byton Wk.	X23	44
Byway, The	N22	39
C.H. Best Gro.	Q23	40
Cable Rd., Hoy.	B33	87
Cable Rd., Know.	CC30	79
Cable Rd., W.Kirby	B34	105
Charles Rd.		
Cable St. S.	O 5	5
Cable St., Formby	L15	16
Cable St., Liver.	P32	94
Cabot Grn.	W34	115
Caddick Rd.	X26	59
Cadman Rd.	Y34	116
Cadmus Wk.	Q31	94
Breck Rd.		
Cadnam Rd.	Y34	116
Cadogan Dr.	LL20	37
Kirkstile Cres.		
Cadwell Rd.	R18	23
Caernarvon Clo.	G34	108
Caerwys Gro.	M35	110
Caird St.	R31	95
Cairne St.	EE29	80
Cairnmore Rd.	U36	114
Cairns St.	R34	113
Cairo St., Liver.	Q28	73
Cairo St., St.H.	EE28	80
Caithness Dr., Sefton	N23	39
Caithness Dr., Wirr.	M30	71
Caithness Rd.	U36	114
Calcott Rake	Q23	40
Calday Grange Clo.	C36	106
Calday Gro.	KK25	65
Caldbeck Clo.	NN23	51
Caldbeck Gro.	HH24	49
Caldbeck Rd.	P40	143
Calder Av.	K36	109
Calder Clo.	X22	44
Calder Clo., C.Wood	JJ35	121
Calder Dr., Liver.	V35	115
Calder Dr., Sefton	T20	29
Calder Dr., St.H.	EE31	101
Calder Grange	W35	115
Calder Rd., Liver.	Q30	73
Calder Rd., Wirr.	M38	126
Calderfield Rd.	V34	115
Calderhurst Dr.	DD26	62
Calderstones Av.	V35	115
Calderstones Rd.	U35	114
Caldicott Av.	P41	143
Caldway Dr.	Y34	116
Caldwell Dr.	H36	108
Caldwell Rd.	V37	131
Caldwell St.	HH27	64
Caldy Gro.	HH26	64
Caldy Rd., H.V.	R25	56
Caldy Rd., W.Kirby	C37	122
Caldy Rd., Wall.	L30	71
Caledonia St.	Q33	94
Calgarth Rd.	Y30	77
California Rd.	S29	74
Callander Rd.	S31	95
Callestock Clo.	V26	58
Callon Av.	JJ26	64
Callow Rd.	S33	95
Calne Clo.	F37	123
Calthorpe St.	U37	130
Calton Av.	U34	114
Calveley Clo.	K35	109
Calver Wk.	R33	95
Calverhall Way	NN23	51
Calvin St.	P30	73
Cam Gro.	R33	95
Cam St.	W36	115
Camberley Clo.	N 6	5
Camberley Dr.	Y37	132
Camborne Av.	Y36	116
Cambourne Av., St.H.	HH25	64
Cambourne Rd., War.	MM30	84
Cambria St.	R31	95
Cambrian Clo.	F33	89
Cambrian Rd.		
Cambrian Cres.	LL20	37
Cambrian Rd.	F33	89
Cambrian Way	X35	116
Cambridge Av.	M22	38
Cambridge Av. S.	Q 4	6
Cambridge Av., Lith.	O25	54
Cambridge Dr.	M22	38
Cambridge Dr., Hale.	Z37	133
Cambridge Gdns.	Q 4	6
Cambridge Rd.	R 4	7
Cambridge Rd. S.	Q 4	6
Cambridge Rd., Birk.	L36	110
Cambridge Rd., Brom.	P41	143
Cambridge Rd., Crosby	M22	38
Cambridge Rd., Formby	J16	19
Cambridge Rd., Lith.	N25	54
Cambridge Rd., Liver.	P28	73
Cambridge Rd., Liver.	R25	56
Cambridge Rd., St.H.	FF27	63
Cambridge Rd., Wirr.	L29	71
Cambridge St., Edge H.	Q33	94
Cambridge St., Know.	BB30	79
Cambridge St., Know.	BB30	79
Station Rd.		
Camdale Clo.	X30	77
Chalfont Way.		
Camden St.	M34	110
Camden St.	Q32	94
Camelford Rd.	V26	58
Cameron Rd.	H31	90
Cameron St.	S32	95
Cammell Ct.	L34	110
Camp Gro.	MM23	51
Camp Rd., Know.	X36	116
Camp Rd., Wigan	MM23	51
Campania St.	V39	131
Campbell Dr.	W31	97
Campbell St., Boot.	O27	54
Campbell St., Liver.	P33	94
Campbell St., St.H.	FF27	63
Camperman St.	N34	111
Camphill Rd.	X37	132
Campion Clo.	GG25	63
Shireburn Av.		
Canal St., Liver.	O28	72
Canal St., St.H.	FF28	81
Canberra Av.	FF29	81
Canberra La.	V26	58
Candia Towers	Q30	73
Candlish Pl.	R31	95
Candy Gro.	T29	75
Canning Pl.	P32	94
Canning Rd.	R 5	7
Canning St., Liver.	Q33	94
Canning St., Sefton	M24	38
Canning St., Wirr.	N33	93
Cannington Rd.	GG28	81
Canniswood Rd.	KK26	65
Cannock Grn.	R20	28
Cannon St.	HH31	103
Canon Rd.	S29	74
Canon Wilson Clo.	LL26	65
Cansfield Gro.	NN23	51
Cansfield St.	GG27	63
Canterbury Av.	M23	38

Canterbury Clo. N 7 9
Canterbury Clo. T24 42
Canterbury Heights Q31 94
Canterbury Rd., Birk. O36 111
Canterbury Rd., Halton EE37 135
Canterbury Rd., Wall. M31 92
Canterbury St., Gars. V39 131
Canterbury St., Liver. Q31 94
Canterbury St., St.H. FF26 63
Canterbury Way Q23 40
Cantlow Fold L11 12
Canton Clo. Q 7 10
Cantsfield St. S33 95
Canvey Clo. U33 96
Cape Rd. S26 56
Captains Grn. P25 55
Captains La. P25 55
Captains La. OO23 52
Caradoc Rd. O26 54
Cardew Clo. Q29 73
Fountain Rd.
Cardigan Rd., Sefton N 8 9
Cardigan Rd., Wirr. L29 71
Cardigan St., Liver. S33 95
Cardigan St., Wirr. M34 110
Cardigan Way, Ain. R23 41
Corwen Dr.
Cardigan Way R31 95
Cardwell Rd. V38 131
Cardwell St. R33 95
Carey Av. M38 126
Carey Clo. LL20 37
Carey St. GG36 120
Carfax Rd. X23 44
Cargill Gro. O37 127
Carham Rd. C34 106
Carina St. O27 54
Carisbrooke Clo. C37 122
Carisbrooke Dr. Q 4 6
Carisbrooke Rd. Q28 73
Carkington Rd. Y36 116
Carlaw Rd. L36 110
Carlett Boul. Q42 143
Carley Wk. Z40 137
Carlingford Clo. R33 95
Carlis Rd. W25 58
Carlisle Av. Q24 40
Carlisle Clo. M34 110
Carlisle Mews M34 110
Carlisle Rd. O 8 9
Carlisle St. G13 25
Carlisle St. HH36 121
Carlisle St., Liver. R33 95
Carlow St. M31 80
West St.
Carlow St. EE28 80
Thompson St.
Carlton Clo. J44 145
Carlton Clo. NN23 51
Carlton La., Liver. T31 96
Carlton La., Wirr. C33 88
Carlton Rd., L.Beb. O39 127
Collingwood Rd.
Carlton Rd., New.B. L29 71
Carlton Rd., Sefton M10 12
Carlton Rd., Wirr. M35 110
Carlton St. FF27 63
Carlton St., Know. BB30 79
Grosvenor Rd.
Carlton St., Liver. O31 93
Carlton Ter. C33 88
Carlton Wk. O27 54
Carlyon Way Z36 117
Carmel Clo. L29 71
Carmelite Cres. DD26 62
Carmichael Av. F35 107
Carnarvon Rd., Liver. R27 56
Carnarvon Rd., Sefton N 8 9
Carnarvon St. EE29 80
Carnatic Rd. T35 114
Carnation Rd. R27 56
Carnegie Av. M23 38
Carnegie Cres. JJ29 82
Carnegie Rd., Oak.Pk. U32 96
Carnegie Rd., Stone. T31 96
Carnegie Wk. JJ29 82
Carnforth Clo., Liver. V28 76
Carnforth Clo., Wirr. M34 110
Carno St. T33 96
Carnoustie Gro. KK26 65
Gleneagles Dr.
Carnsdale Rd. G33 90
Carol Dr. J41 140
Carole Clo. JJ30 82
Caroline Pl. L34 110
Caronia St. V39 131
Luciana St.
Carpenters La. B36 105
Carpenters Row P33 94
Shaws Alley
Carr Bridge Rd. H35 108
Carr Cft. O23 39
Carr Clo. U28 75
Carr Gate E33 89
Carr Hey Clo. J36 109
Carr House La., Sefton N19 26
Carr House La., Wirr. E33 89
Carr La. C34 106
Carr La. AA30 78
Carr La. E. U28 75
Carr La. S. N 9 9
Carr La., Hale Bk. CC38 134
Carr La., Hoy. D32 88
Carr La., Liver. U28 75
Carr La., Roby Y32 98
Carr La., W.Kirby B34 105
Carr La., W.Lan. Q18 22
Carr Meadow Hey P24 40
Carr Mill Cres. JJ23 49
Carr Mill Rd. HH25 64
Carr Rd. P25 55
Carr Side La. O19 26
Carraway Rd. V26 58
Carrfield Av. O23 39
Carrfield Wk. U27 57
Carrhey E33 89
Carrhey Rd. E33 89
Carrick Ct. O23 39
Carrickmore Av. U36 114
Carrington Rd., Birk. L33 92
Carrington Rd., Wall. L30 71
Carrs Cres. J16 19
Carrs Cres. W. J16 19
Carrs Ter. BB31 100
Carruthers St. P31 94
Carsdale Rd. U34 114
Carsgoe Rd. C34 106
Carsington Rd. U28 75
Carstairs Rd. S31 95
Carsthorne Rd. C34 106
Cart Bridge La. Z36 117
Carter Av. DD22 47
Carter St. Q34 112
Carters, The F35 107
Harvester Way
Carterton Rd. C34 106
Cartmel Av., Sefton T20 29
Cartmel Clo., Know. Y31 98
Cartmel Clo., Wirr. M34 110
Cartmel Dr., Liver. V28 76
Cartmel Dr., More. G33 90
Cartmel Dr., Sefton L16 20
Cartmel Dr., St.H. DD31 101
Cartmel Rd. Y31 98
Cartmel Ter. U27 57
Cartmel Way, Know. Y31 98
Cartmell Av., St.H. FF25 63
Cartmell Clo., Sefton Q 7 10
Cartwright Clo. CC21 33
Carver St. Q31 94
Caryl Gdns. Q34 112
Caryl St. P34 112
Case Rd. LL26 65
Cases St. P32 94
Casino Rd. Y31 98
Cassia Clo. R27 56
Cassio St. Q28 73
Cassley Rd. AA39 133
Cassville Rd. U34 114
Castell Gro. FF27 63
Casterton St. S33 95
Castle Av. JJ27 64
Castle Clo. H31 90
Castle Dr., Sefton K16 19
Castle Dr., Wirr. G41 139
Castle Fields Estate G31 90
Castle Gate Gro. U29 75
Castle Hill PP27 67
Castle Rd. L30 71
Castle St., Halton HH36 121
Castle St., Liver. P32 94
Castle St., Sefton O 5 5
Castle St., Wirr. N34 111
Castle St., Wool. W36 115
Castle Wk. O 6 5
Castlefield Clo. U29 75
Castlefield Rd. U29 75
Castleford St. U33 96
Castlesite Rd. U29 75
Castleton Dr. R23 41
Castleton Way LL20 37
Castleview Rd. U29 75
Castleway CC31 100
Castleway N. G31 90
Castleway S. H31 90
Castlewell CC31 100
Hilton Av.
Castlewood Rd. R30 74
Castor St. R30 74
Catchdale Moss La. CC25 61
Caterall Av. HH30 82
Catford Grn. Z39 133
Cathcart St. M33 92
Cathedral Rd. S30 74
Cathedral Wk. Q32 94
Mount Pleasant
Catherine St., Birk. M34 110
Catherine St., Liver. Q33 94
Catherine St., Sefton O26 54
Catherine Way, Newt. NN28 84
Catherine Way, St.H. JJ26 64
Caton Clo. Q 3 2
Catonfield Rd. V34 115
Catrine Rd. M32 92
Catterall Av. HH30 82
Catterick Fold Q 7 10
Caulfield Dr. G35 108
Caunce Av. KK26 65
Fairclough Cres.
Caunce Av. NN29 84
Bradlegh Rd.
Caunce Av. QQ25 68
Caunce Av., Earls. OO28 85
Cause Way, The, Liver. V31 97
Causeway Clo. O38 128
The Causeway
Causeway La. O16 21
Causeway, The, Sefton S 2 3
Causeway, The, Wirr. O38 127
Cavan Rd. T29 75
Caveley Av. Q43 148
Cavell Clo. X37 132
Cavelley Av. Q43 148
Cavendish Av. L29 71
Cavendish Dr., Liver. R27 56
Cavendish Dr., Wigan LL20 37
Cavendish Dr., Wirr. M36 110
Cavendish Rd. S. N 7 9
Cavendish Rd., Wirr. L33 92
Cavendish St., Wirr. L33 92
Cavenidsh Rd., Crosby M23 38
Cavern Wks. P32 94
Matthew St.
Cawdor St. R34 113
Cawfield Av. FF36 120
Cawthorne Av. W25 58
Cawthorne Clo. W25 58
Caxton Clo. J34 109
Caxton Rd. FF32 102
Cazneau St. P31 94
Cearns Ct. L34 110
Cearns Rd. L34 110
Cecil Dr. DD26 62
Cecil Rd., Beb. O37 127
Cecil Rd., Birk. L36 110
Cecil Rd., Sefton N26 54
Cecil Rd., Wall. L31 92
Cecil St., Liver. S33 95
Cecil St., St.H. JJ29 82
Cedar Av. GG35 120
Cedar Clo. CC31 100
Cedar Cres. Y32 98
Cedar Ct. OO28 85
Cedar Dr. J16 19
Cedar Gro., Ain. S22 41
Cedar Gro., Crosby M24 38
Cedar Gro., Elles. L45 146
Cedar Gro., Liver. S34 113
Cedar Gro., St.H. MM25 66
Cedar Gro., Wigan LL22 50
Cedar Gro., Wirr. L32 92
Cedar Rd., H.Beb. N39 127
Cedar Rd., Know. BB31 100
Cedar Rd., Liver. R26 56
Cedar St. S. P 7 10
Cedar St., Lith. P27 55
Cedar St., Newt. OO28 85
Cedar St., St.H. EE28 80
Laurel Rd.
Cedar St., Wirr. M34 110
Cedar Tower W23 43
Cedardale Rd. R27 56
Cedars, The F33 89
Cedarway H42 139
Celan Way KK19 37

Celia St. P28 73
Celtic Rd. D32 88
Cement Av. N33 93
Cemetery Rd. O 7 9
Central Av. N 9 9
Central Av., Know. BB30 79
Central Av., Pres. CC29 79
Central Av., Speke Y39 132
Central Av., Wirr. P40 143
Central Dr., Rain. CC21 33
Central Dr., St.H. KK26 65
Central Dr., W.Derby U30 75
Central Park Av. M31 92
Central Rd. O38 127
Central Sq. S20 28
Central St. GG27 63
Central Way, St.H. PP28 85
Central Way, Wirr. K35 109
Centre Way, Know. Z32 99
Lathom Rd.
Centreville Rd. U34 114
Centurion Clo. D32 88
Centurion Dr. D32 88
Century Rd. M23 38
Certes St. P28 73
Cestrian Dr. H38 124
Chadlow Rd. W25 58
Chadwell Rd. W23 43
Chadwick Rd. HH25 64
Chadwick Sq. G33 90
Chadwick St., Liver. O31 93
Chadwick St., Wirr. G33 90
Chain La. HH25 64
Chain Wk. EE28 30
Chalfont Rd. V36 115
Chalfont Way X29 77
Chalkwell Dr. J41 140
Challis St. K31 91
Chalon Way GG27 63
Chaloner Gro. T38 130
Chaloner St. P33 94
Chamberlain St., Birk. N35 111
Chamberlain St., St.H. EE27 62
Chamberlain St., Wall. L32 92
Chambres Rd. P 6 6
Champion Way Z33 99
Chancel St. P29 73
Chancery La. JJ27 64
Chandley Clo. L10 12
Chandos St., Liver. R32 95
Chandos St., St.H. NN27 66
Change La. O45 147
Changford Grn. X23 44
Changford Rd. X23 44
Channel Rd., Sefton L23 38
Channel Reach L23 38
Channel, The J29 70
Channell Rd., Liver. S31 95
Chantrell Rd. D36 106
Chantry Clo. J34 109
Chantry Wk., Wigan MM22 51
Chantry Wk., Wirr. H42 139
Chapel Av. R26 56
Chapel Gdns. P30 73
Chapel La. DD27 62
Chapel La., Formby K15 16
Chapel La., Know. EE35 119
Chapel La., Neth. R22 41
Chapel La., St.H. FF32 102
Chapel La., Wadd. U23 42
Chapel La., Warr. MM30 84
Chapel Pl., Gars. V38 131
Chapel Rd., Gars. V38 131
Chapel Rd., Liver. S30 74
Chapel Rd., Wirr. C33 88
Chapel St. S. O 5 5
Chapel St., Asht. NN23 51
Chapel St., Lith. O27 54
Chapel St., Liver. O32 93
Chapel St., Newt. NN27 66
Chapel St., Pres. BB30 79
Eccleston St.
Chapel St., Rain. CC21 33
Victoria St.
Chapel St., St.H. FF26 63
Chapel Wk. QQ30 86
Chapelhill Rd. G33 90
Chapelhouse Wk. L15 16
Charing Cross M34 110
Charlcombe St. M35 110
Charlecote St. Q35 112
Charles Av. N10 13
Charles Berrington Rd. U34 114
Charles Rd. B34 105
Charles St., St.H. GG27 63
Charles St., Wirr. M33 92
Charlesville L34 110
Charlesworth Clo. R18 23
Manion Av.
Charley Wood Rd. X24 44
Charlotte Rd. M30 71
Charlottes Meadow O39 127
Charlton Pl. U32 96
Charlton Rd. U32 96
Charlwood Av. Y32 98
Charlwood Clo. J34 109
Charmalue Av. N23 39
Charnock Av. MM27 66
Charnock Rd. S27 56
Charnwood Rd. X31 98
Charnwood St. JJ27 64
Charterhouse Dr. T24 42
Charterhouse Rd. X36 116
Chartmount Way X35 116
Chartwell Rd. L10 12
Chase Heys R 4 7
Chase, The P42 143
Chase, The, Huy. Z33 99
Chatburn Wk. Q35 112
Chatham Clo. N25 54
Chatham Pl. R32 95
Chatham Rd. N36 111
Chatham St. Q33 94
Chatham St., App. GG36 120
Chatsworth Av., Liver. Q26 55
Chatsworth Av., Sefton L10 12
Chatsworth Av., Wirr. M31 92
Chatsworth Clo. MM23 51
Chatsworth Dr. EE35 119
Chatsworth Rd., Birk. O36 111
Chatsworth Rd., St.H. DD31 101
Chatsworth Rd., Wirr. G38 124
Chatsworth St. R33 95
Chatsworth Ter. O36 111
Chatterton Rd. V31 97
Chaucer Rd. EE26 62
Chaucer St., Liver. P31 94
Chaucer St., Sefton O27 54
Cheadle Av. T31 96
Cheapside, Liver. P32 94
Cheapside, Sefton L16 20
Cheddar Gro., Know. W25 58
Ribblers La.
Cheddar Rd. MM29 84
Chedder Clo. W36 115
Chedworth Dr. EE35 119
Chedworth Rd. W31 97
Chelford Av. RR25 68
Chellow Dene O22 39
Chelmarch Av. OO23 52
Chelsea Ct. W29 76
Chelsea Rd., H.V. R26 56
Chelsea Rd., Lith. O26 54
Cheltenham Av., Liver. S34 113
Cheltenham Av., Wirr. K30 70
Cheltenham Clo. T24 42
Cheltenham Dr. HH20 36
Cheltenham Way Q 7 10
Chelwood Av. W32 97
Chemical St. NN27 66
Queen St.
Chepstow Av. M31 92
Chepstow St. Q28 73
Chequers Gdns. T37 130
Cheriton Av. C36 106
Cheriton Clo., Know. Z36 117
Torcross Way
Chermside Rd. T36 114
Cherry Av. R28 74
Cherry Clo. R28 74
Cherry Grn. U15 153
Cherry La., Elles. L43 146
Cherry La., Liver. R28 74
Cherry Rd. M12 12
Cherry St. MM27 66
Cherry Sutton DD35 119
Cherry Tree Clo. KK26 65
Sycamore Av.
Cherry Tree Clo., Whist. BB31 100
Cherry Tree Dr. KK28 78
Cherry Tree Gro. KK26 65
Sycamore Av.
Cherry Tree La., St.H. GG24 48
Cherry Tree La., W.Lan. U15 153
Cherrydale Rd. U35 114
Cherryfield Cres. W24 43
Cherryfield Dr. V24 43
Cherrytree Rd., Know. Z33 99
Cherrytree Rd., Wirr. G33 90
Chervil Wk. LL19 37
Ribbesford Rd.
Cheryl Dr. HH36 121
Cheshire Acre H36 108
Cheshire Av., Lith. U26 57
Field La.
Cheshire Clo. PP27 67
Cheshire Gro. G33 90
Cheshire Way G39 124
Chester Av. S. Q 5 6
Chester Av., Liver. Q24 40
Chester Av., Wigan RR25 68
Chester Clo. O23 39
Chester Dr. OO24 52
Chester High Rd. L44 146
Chester La. GG30 81
Chester Rd., Elles. K45 145
Chester Rd., Know. AA31 99
Chester Rd., Liver. S30 74
Chester Rd., Sefton Q 5 6
Chester Rd., Wirr. N36 111
Chester Row OO29 85
Chester St., Birk. N34 111
Chester St., Egre. L32 92
Chester St., Halton GG36 120
Chester St., Know. BB30 79
Chester Wk. AA31 99
Chesterfield Clo. M11 12
Chesterfield Rd., Ains. M10 12
Chesterfield Rd., Cros. O22 39
Chesterfield Rd., Wirr. P43 148
Chesterton St. V39 131
Chestnut Av., Halton GG36 120
Chestnut Av., Know. Y33 98
Chestnut Av., Sefton N22 39
Chestnut Av., St.H. JJ26 64
Chestnut Clo. F36 107
Chestnut Clo. CC31 100
Chestnut Gro. M35 110
Chestnut Gro., Boot. O26 54
Chestnut Gro., Liver. T33 96
Chestnut Gro., St.H. HH25 64
Chestnut Gro., Wigan OO23 52
Chestnut Gro., Wirr. P41 143
Chestnut Rd. N25 54
Chestnut Rd. R27 56
Chestnut St. P 7 10
Chestnut Way J16 19
Cheswood Ct. H36 108
Chetwode Av. NN24 51
Chetwood Av. N22 39
Chetwood Dr. FF34 120
Chetwynd Clo. K35 109
Chetwynd Rd. L35 110
Chetwynd St. R35 113
Cheviot Av. JJ27 64
Cheviot Clo. LL20 37
Cheviot Rd., Liver. T32 96
Cheviot Rd., Wirr. M37 126
Cheviot Way, Know. W22 43
Saxon Way
Cheyne Clo. L23 38
Cheyne Gdns. T37 130
Cheyne Wk. FF30 81
Chidden Clo. F35 107
Beauworth Av.
Chilcott Rd. V31 97
Childer Cres. R45 149
Childer Gdns. R45 149
Childers St. T31 96
Childwall Abbey Rd. V34 115
Childwall Av. F33 89
Childwall Av., Edge H. S33 95
Childwall Bnk. V33 97
Childwall Clo. F33 89
Childwall Av.
Childwall Cres. V33 97
Childwall Grn. H36 108
Childwall Heights W33 97
Childwall La., Child. W34 115
Childwall La., Roby X32 98
Childwall Mount Rd. V33 97
Childwall Park Av. V34 115
Childwall Priory Rd. V33 97
Childwall Valley Rd. U33 96
Chillerton Rd. V29 76
Chillingham St. R35 113
Chillow Av. S33 95
Chiltern Clo. OO24 52
Chiltern Clo., Kirkby V23 43
Chiltern Dr., Know. V23 43
Chiltern Dr., Wigan LL19 37
Chiltern Rd., St.H. KK27 65
Chiltern Rd., Wirr. M36 110
Chimes Rd. MM22 51

Street	Grid	Page
China Farm La.	D35	106
Chindit Clo.	J16	19
Chippenham Av.	F35	107
Chipping Av.	L10	12
Chirk Way	G33	90
Chirkdale St.	Q28	73
Chisenhale St.	P31	94
Chislehurst Av.	X34	116
Chisnall Av.	EE27	62
Chiswell St.	S32	95
Cholmondeley Rd.	B36	105
Chorley Rd.	AA30	78
Chorley St.	FF27	63
Halefield St.		
Chorley Way	O40	142
Chorleys La.	HH35	121
Chorlton Clo.	W33	97
Chorlton Gro.	J30	70
Chrisleton Clo.	K36	109
Christchurch Rd.	L35	110
Christian St.	Q31	94
Christie Clo.	R44	149
Christie St.	HH36	121
Christopher Clo.	V33	97
Christopher Gdns.	HH29	82
Christopher Way	V33	97
Christophers Clo.	H39	124
Christow Wk.	V26	58
Chudleigh Clo.	Z36	117
Chudleigh Rd., Liver.	T31	96
Church All.	P32	94
Church Av., Liver.	R25	56
Church Cres.	N32	93
Church Dr.	O38	127
Church Field Rd.	Y34	116
Church Grn., Child.	W33	97
Well La.		
Church Grn., Know.	W23	43
Church Grn., Sefton	J16	19
Church Grn., Wirr.	M30	71
Church Hill	K31	91
Church La., Brom.	P40	143
The Rake		
Church La., Easth.	R43	149
Church La., Egre.	M31	92
Church La., Elles.	K45	145
Church La., Hes.	E38	123
Church La., Know.	Y27	59
Church La., Liver.	P32	94
Church La., Lyd.	R17	23
Church La., St.H.	DD27	62
Church La., W.Lan.	U16	153
Church La., Walt.	Q28	73
Church La., Wigan	RR25	68
Church La., Wood.	H36	108
Church Meadow La.	G41	139
Church Mt.	R32	95
Church Rd.	N25	54
Church Rd.	O25	54
Church Rd.	S21	28
Church Rd. W.	Q28	73
Church Rd., Birk.	M35	110
Church Rd., Crosby	N23	39
Church Rd., Formby	L15	16
Church Rd., Gars.	V38	131
Church Rd., Hale.	Z36	117
Church Rd., Hay.	MM25	66
Church Rd., L.Beb.	O39	127
Church Rd., Oak.Pk.	T32	96
Church Rd., Rain.	CC22	46
Church Rd., Roby	Y32	98
Church Rd., Sea.	N26	54
Church Rd., Thorn.	L42	141
Church Rd., Upt.	H34	108
Church Rd., Vic.Pk.	P26	55
Church Rd., W.Kirby	B36	105
Church Rd., Wall.	N32	93
Church Rd., Walt.	R28	74
Church Rd., Wav.	U33	96
Church Rd., Wool.	W35	115
Church Sq.	GG27	63
Market St.		
Church St., Birk.	N34	111
Church St., Lith.	O27	54
Church St., Liver.	P32	94
Church St., Marsh.	P 5	6
Church St., Newt.	PP27	67
Church St., Pres.	BB30	79
Church St., St.H.	GG27	63
Church St., Wall.	M31	92
Church Ter.	NN24	51
Church Vw., Lith.	O27	54
Church Vw., W.Lan.	U16	153
Church Way, Formby	J16	19
Church Way, Kirkby	W23	43
Church Way, Neth.	P23	40
Church Wk.	B36	105
St. Bridgets La.		
Churchdown Clo.	W31	97
Churchdown Rd.	W31	97
Churchfields	GG34	120
Churchgate	Q 5	6
Churchill Av.	Q 4	6
Churchill Av., Birk.	L33	92
Churchill Way	K45	145
Churchill Way N.	P32	94
Churchill Way S.	P32	94
Churchway Rd.	AA40	137
Churchwood Clo.	P40	143
Churn Way	F35	107
Churnet St.	Q29	73
Churston Rd.	W34	115
Churton Av.	K35	109
Churton Ct.	R31	95
Brunswick Rd.		
Cicely St.	R32	95
Cicero Ter.	Q30	73
Cinder La., Lith.	P25	55
Cinder La., Liver.	V34	115
Circular Dr., Beb.	O37	127
Circular Dr., Greas.	F35	107
Circular Dr., Hes.	G40	139
Circular Rd.	M34	110
Circular Rd. E.	T29	75
Circular Rd. W.	T28	75
Cirencester Av.	F35	107
City Gdns.	FF26	63
City Rd., Liver.	Q28	73
City Rd., St.H.	FF25	63
City Vw.	GG24	48
Civic Way	O38	127
Clairville Clo.	P27	55
Clairville Way	T30	75
Clamley Rd.	AA39	137
Clandon Rd.	V36	115
Clanfield Rd.	U28	75
Clanwood Clo.	LL20	37
Kirkstile Cres.		
Clapgate Cres.	DD38	135
Clapham Rd.	R30	74
Clare Clo.	FF29	81
Clare Cres.	K31	91
Clare Rd.	P28	73
Clare St.	Q31	94
Clare Ter.	Q30	73
Clare Way	K30	70
Clare Wk., Know.	U25	57
Amanda Rd.		
Claremont Av., Halton	HH35	121
Claremont Av., Sefton	R21	28
Claremont Av., St.H.	JJ22	49
Claremont Rd.		
Claremont Clo.	N25	54
Claremont Rd.		
Claremont Dr., App.	HH35	121
Claremont Rd. S.	O 7	9
Claremont Rd., Crosby	N23	39
Claremont Rd., Lith.	N25	54
Claremont Rd., St.H.	JJ22	49
Claremont Rd., W.Kirby	B35	105
Claremont Rd., Wav.	T34	114
Claremont Way	M37	126
Claremount Dr.	N39	127
Claremount Rd.	K30	70
Clarence Av.	GG35	120
Clarence Rd., Birk.	M35	110
Clarence Rd., Sefton	O 7	9
Clarence Rd., Wall.	M32	92
Clarence St., Liver.	Q32	94
Clarence St., St.H.	MM27	66
Clarence St., Wigan	MM23	51
Clarendon Clo.	M34	110
Clarendon Gro.	S18	23
Clarendon Rd., Ains.	M10	12
Clarendon Rd., Anf.	S30	74
Clarendon Rd., Gars.	V38	131
Clarendon Rd., Lith.	N26	54
Clarendon Rd., Wall.	M31	92
Clarendon Wk.	M34	110
Claribel St.	R34	113
Clarke Av.	N36	111
Clarkes Cres.	DD27	62
Classic Rd.	U31	96
Clatterbridge Rd.	M41	141
Claude Rd.	S30	74
Claudia St.	Q28	73
Claughton Clo.	S32	95
Ivatt Way		
Claughton Dr.	L31	92
Claughton Firs	L35	110
Claughton Pl.	M34	110
Claughton Rd.	M34	110
Claughton St.	GG27	63
Clavell Rd.	V37	131
Clay La., St.H.	CC27	61
Clay La., Warr.	MM30	84
Clay St.	O31	93
Clayfield Clo.	P28	55
Breeze Hill		
Clayford Cres.	U31	96
Clayford Rd.	U31	96
Clayford Way	V31	97
Clayhill Grn.	S45	149
Claypole Clo.	S33	95
Rokesmith Av.		
Clayton Cr.	GG36	120
Clayton La.	L32	92
Clayton Sq.	P32	94
Clayton St.	M34	110
Cleadon Clo.	X25	59
Cleadon Rd.	W25	58
Cleary St.	O27	54
Clee Hill Rd.	M36	110
Cleg St.	Q31	94
Clegg St.	O31	93
Clementina Rd.	L23	38
Clemmey Dr.	Q26	55
Clengers Brow	Q 3	2
Clent Av.	S19	28
Clent Gdns.	S19	28
Clent Rd.	S19	28
Cleopas St.	Q35	112
Beresford Rd.		
Cleve Way	L16	20
Clevedon Av.	LL19	37
Clevedon Bldgs.	R34	113
Clevedon Dr.	LL19	37
Clevedon St.	R34	113
Cleveland Clo.	V23	43
Cleveland Dr., Asht.	OO23	52
Cleveland Dr., Gol.	RR25	68
Cleveland Gdns.	M33	92
Cleveland Sq.	P33	94
Cleveland St.	L33	92
Cleveland St., St. H.	HH28	82
Cleveley Pk.	V36	115
Cleveley Rd., Liver.	V36	115
Cleveleys Av.	R 3	3
Cleveleys Av., App.	HH36	121
Cleveleys Rd.	R 3	3
Clevely Rd., Wirr.	D33	88
Cleves, The	T19	29
Clieves Hills La.	T15	153
Clieves Rd.	W24	43
Cliff Dr.	M30	71
Cliff Rd., Sefton	P 4	6
Cliff Rd., Wirr.	K31	91
Cliff St., Halton	HH36	121
Cliff St., Liver.	S32	95
Cliffe Rd.	DD31	101
Clifford Rd., Sefton	O 8	9
Clifford Rd., Wirr.	L31	92
Clifford St., Liver.	Q32	94
Clifford St., Wirr.	L33	92
Clifton Av.	Q43	148
Clifton Cres.	EE28	80
Clifton Ct.	V37	131
Clifton Dr.	S24	41
Clifton Gro.	M31	92
Clifton Gro.	Q31	94
Prince Edwin St.		
Clifton Rd.	HH33	49
Clifton Rd. E.	S30	74
Clifton Rd. S.	Q 6	6
Clifton Rd., Formby	L14	16
Clifton Rd., Liver.	S30	74
Clifton Rd., St.H.	HH23	49
Clifton Rd., Wigan	MM22	51
Clifton Rd., Wirr.	M34	110
Clifton St., Liver.	V38	131
Clifton St., St.H.	GG27	63
Clifton Ter.	EE28	80
Laurel Rd.		
Clifton Wk.	O27	54
Cliftonville Rd.	CC30	79
Maryville Rd.		
Clincton Clo.	DD37	135
Clincton Vw.	DD37	135
Clinning Rd.	O 8	9
Clint Rd.	S32	95
Clint Way	S32	95
Clint Rd.		
Clinton Pl.	T29	75
Clinton Rd.	T29	75
Clipsley Cres.	KK25	65

Clipsley La.	KK25 65
Clive Lodge	N 8 9
Clive Rd., Sefton	N 8 9
Clive Rd., Wirr.	L35 110
Clock Face Rd.	HH31 103
Clock La.	JJ35 121
Cloister, The	M23 38
Clominster Grn.	L16 20
Clorian Clo.	X23 44
Clorian Rd.	X23 44
Close St., Liver.	P30 73
Close St., St.H.	FF29 81
Close, The	Y30 77
Dannette Hey	
Close, The	DD26 62
Close, The, Beb.	M37 126
Close, The, Crosby	M23 38
Close, The, Greas.	F36 107
Close, The, Liver.	R27 56
Close, The, St.H.	JJ26 64
Close, The, Thing	F38 123
Closeburn Av.	G42 139
Clough Gro.	MM22 51
Clough Rd.	Y39 132
Clovelly Av.	HH30 82
Hawthorn Rd.	
Clovelly Dr.	N 9 9
Clovelly Rd.	R30 74
Clover Hey	GG25 63
Cloverfield Gdns.	S45 149
Club St.	GG24 48
Clwyd Gro.	U28 75
Clwyd St., Birk.	M34 110
Clwyd St., Wall.	L29 71
Clyde Rd.	T32 96
Clyde St.	N36 111
Clyde St., Boot.	O29 73
Clydesdale Rd., Hoy.	B33 87
Clydesdale Rd., Wall.	M31 92
Coach Rd.	Z20 32
Coachmans Dr.	W28 76
Coal Pit La.	BB19 33
Coalgate La.	BB32 100
Coalville Rd.	HH26 64
Coastal Dr.	J29 70
Coastal Rd.	L 8 8
Coastal Rd.	L11 12
Coastguard La.	H44 144
Cob Moor Av.	HH20 36
Cob Moor Rd.	HH20 36
Cobden Av.	N35 111
Cobden Clo.	W36 115
Cobden Ct.	N35 111
Cobden Av.	
Cobden Pl.	N35 111
Cobden Rd.	Q 6 6
Cobden St., Liver.	Q31 94
Cobden St., Newt.	PP27 67
Mercer St.	
Cobham Av.	Q26 55
Cobham Rd.	F33 89
Cobham Wk.	P23 40
Coburg St.	M34 110
Cockburn St.	Q35 112
Cockerell Clo.	Q29 73
Pugin St.	
Cockerham Way	U26 57
Cockle Dicks La.	Q 4 6
Cocks Head Rd.	X34 116
Cocks Head Way	X34 116
Cockspur St.	P32 94
Coerton Rd.	R25 56
Colbern Rd.	T21 29
Colchester Rd.	Q 7 10
Coldstone Dr.	LL23 50
Cole Av.	OO27 67
Cole St.	M34 110
Colebrook Rd.	R35 113
Colemere Dr.	H38 124
Coleridge Av.	EE27 62
Coleridge Rd.	HH20 36
Coleridge St.	O27 54
Coleridge St.	R31 95
Colerne Way	LL20 37
Coles Cres.	O22 39
Colesbourne Rd.	U28 75
Coleshill Rd., Liver.	T27 57
Coleshill Ri., Wigan	LL20 37
Coleus Clo.	R27 56
Freesia Av.	
Colin Clo., Know.	Y32 98
Lawton Rd.	
Colindale Rd.	W33 97
Colinton St.	T33 96
College Av., Crosby	M23 38
College Av., Formby	K14 16
College Clo.	H34 108
College Clo. S.	O 7 9
College Clo., Formby	J15 15
College Clo., Wirr.	K30 70
College Dr.	O37 127
College La.	P32 94
College Rd. N.	M22 38
College Rd., Crosby	M23 38
College Rd., Pres.	CC30 79
College St.	GG26 63
College St. N.	Q31 94
College St. S.	Q31 94
College Vw.	P28 73
College Way	Q31 94
College Wk.	Q31 94
Collin Rd.	K33 91
Collingwood Rd., St.H.	NN27 66
Collingwood Rd., Wirr.	O39 127
Collins Clo.	O26 54
Collins Green Rd.	MM28 84
Collins St.	O26 54
Colmore Av.	N40 142
Colmore Rd.	T28 75
Colne Rd.	MM30 84
Colombian Clo.	Q23 40
Colonels La.	QQ26 68
Coloquitt St.	Q33 94
Coltart St.	R34 113
Colton Rd.	X33 98
Columbia La.	L35 110
Columbia Rd.	R28 74
Columbia Rd., Ox.	L35 110
Columbine Clo.	DD35 119
Columbus Dr.	G39 124
Columbus St.	MM22 51
Column Rd.	C36 106
Colville Rd.	L31 92
Colville St.	T33 96
Colwall Clo.	X24 44
Colwall Rd.	X24 44
Colwall Wk.	X24 44
Colwell Clo.	X30 77
Colwell Rd.	X30 77
Colwyn Rd.	T32 96
Colwyn St.	K33 91
Colyton Av.	HH30 82
Axbridge Av.	
Comas St.	P31 94
Combermere St., Edge H.	S33 95
Comely Bank Av.	M31 92
Comely Bank Rd.	M31 92
Comer Gdns.	S19 28
Commercial Rd., Liver.	P30 73
Commercial Rd., Wirr.	Q39 128
Common Field Rd.	H36 108
Common Rd.	MM27 66
Common St.	EE20 80
Parliament St.	
Common St.	MM27 66
Compton Rd., Sefton	O 7 9
Compton Rd., Wirr.	J32 91
Compton Wk.	O27 54
Brackley Clo.	
Compton Way, Know.	Z38 133
Compton Way, Liver.	R31 95
Concert St.	P32 94
Concordia Av.	H34 108
Concourse Way	JJ28 82
Waterland La.	
Conder Gdns.	HH30 82
Eugene Av.	
Condor Clo.	V38 131
Condron Rd.	P24 40
Coney La.	Z33 99
Congress St.	R32 95
Conifer Clo.	R27 56
Coningsby Dr.	L31 92
Coningsby Par.	R29 74
Coniston Av., Brom.	P43 148
Coniston Av., Pres.	CC30 79
Coniston Av., Upt.	J34 109
Coniston Av., Wall.	K29 70
Coniston Av., Warr.	LL35 152
Coniston Av., Wigan	NN23 51
Coniston Clo., Know.	V23 43
Coniston Clo., Wirr.	R44 149
Coniston Gro.	GG25 63
Coniston Rd., Formby	J16 19
Coniston Rd., Irby	F38 123
Coniston Rd., Mag.	T20 29
Coniston Rd., St.	R30 74
Coniston Way	CC20 33
Windermere Dr.	
Conleach Rd.	Y40 136
Connaught Clo.	K33 91
Connaught Cio.	L33 92
Connaught Way	
Connaught Dr.	OO28 85
Connaught Rd.	R32 95
Connaught Way	L33 92
Connolly Av.	Q26 55
Conroy Way	OO28 85
Consett Rd.	EE30 80
Constance St., Liver.	Q32 94
Constance St., St.H.	EE28 80
Convent Clo.	M35 110
Rectory Clo.	
Conville Boul.	M37 126
Conway Clo.	M38 126
Conway Cres.	JJ22 49
Conway Dr., Newt.	PP27 67
Conway Dr., St.H.	JJ22 49
Conway Pl.	M34 110
Conway Rd.	PP22 52
Conway St., Birk.	M33 92
Conway St., Birk.	M34 110
Conway St., Liver.	Q30 73
Conway St., St.H.	EE28 80
Moxon St.	
Conway St., Wirr.	L31 92
Conyers Av.	N 7 9
Cook Rd.	H31 90
Cook St.	MM25 66
Cook St., Know.	CC31 100
Cook St., Liver.	P32 94
Cook St., Pres.	BB30 79
Cook St., Wirr.	M34 110
Cooks Rd.	M22 38
Cookson Rd.	O26 54
Cookson St.	Q33 94
Coombe Rd.	G38 124
Cooper Av.	MM27 66
Cooper Av. N.	U36 114
Cooper Av. S.	U36 114
Cooper Clo.	U37 130
Cooper St., Halton	GG36 120
Cooper St., St.H.	FF27 63
Coopers La., Know.	Y25 59
Coopers La., St.H.	LL26 65
Coopers Row	P32 94
Coopers Row, Sea.	N25 54
Copeland Clo.	G39 124
Copperas Hill	Q32 94
Copperas St.	FF27 63
Bold St.	
Coppice Clo.	H34 108
Coppice Cres.	Z31 99
Coppice Dr.	HH20 36
Coppice Gro.	F33 89
Coppice La.	AA33 99
Coppice Leys	K15 16
Coppice, The, Know.	Y27 59
Coppice, The, Wirr.	L29 71
Copple House La.	U25 57
Coppull Rd.	S19 28
Copse Gro.	G37 124
Copthorne Rd.	U24 42
Copthorne Wk.	U24 42
Copy La.	R23 41
Coral Av., Know.	Y31 98
Coral Av., St.H.	FF29 81
Kimberley Av.	
Coral Ridge	K34 109
Coral St.	U32 96
Corbet Clo.	V24 43
Corbet Wk.	V24 43
Corbridge Rd.,	V33 97
Corbyn St.	N32 93
Corfu La.	M34 110
Claughton Rd.	
Corinth St.	N36 111
Corinth Tower	Q30 73
Corinthian Av.	U31 96
Corinthian St.	N25 54
Corn Hill	P33 94
Corn St.	Q34 112
Corncroft Rd.	Y27 59
Corndale Rd.	U35 114
Cornelius Dr.	G38 124
Cornell Way	Z33 99
Corner Brook	W29 76
Cornett Rd.	R25 56
Corney St.	S33 95
Cornice Rd.	U31 96
Corniche Rd.	O38 127
Cornwall Dr.	L36 110
Cornwall Rd.	GG35 120
Cornwall St.	JJ28 82

Cornwall Way L11 12
Cornwallis St. P33 94
Cornwell Clo. O37 128
New Ferry Rd.
Corona Av. S18 23
Moss La.
Corona Rd., Liver. U31 96
Corona Rd., Sefton M24 38
Corona Rd., Wirr. P38 128
Corona St. LL22 50
Coronation Av., Know. W31 97
Coronation Av., Sefton L16 20
Coronation Av., Wirr. L29 71
Coronation Ct. T27 57
Coronation Dr., Halton DD37 135
Coronation Dr., Know. BB31 100
Coronation Dr., Roby W31 97
Coronation Dr., Sefton M23 38
Coronation Dr., St.H. NN25 66
Coronation Dr., Wirr. L39 128
Fairway North
Coronation Rd. M23 38
Coronation Rd., Newt. PP28 85
Coronation Rd., Sefton S19 28
Coronation Rd., St.H. EE26 62
Coronation Rd., Wirr. A34 105
Coronation Way HH23 49
Coronation Wk. O 5 5
Coroners La. GG34 120
Coronet Rd. V27 58
Coronet Way DD37 135
Corporation Rd. L33 92
Corporation St., Sefton O 5 5
Corporation St., St.H. GG27 63
Corrie Dr. N39 127
Corsewall St. S33 95
Corsham Rd. Z38 133
Cortsway G35 108
Cortsway Wk. F34 107
Corwen Clo. G33 90
Corwen Clo., Birk. H34 108
Corwen Cres. W32 97
Corwen Dr. R23 41
Corwen Rd., Liver. S29 74
Corwen Rd., Wirr. C33 88
Costain St. P29 73
Costessy Way LL19 37
Cotham St. GG27 63
Baldwin St.
Cotsford Clo. Y31 98
Cotsford Pl. Y31 98
Cotsford Rd. Y31 98
Cotsford Way Y31 98
Cotswold Gro. KK27 65
Cotswold Rd. M36 110
Cotswold St. R32 95
Cottage Clo., Brom. P42 143
Brookhurst Rd.
Cottage Clo., Elles. K45 145
Cottage Clo., Know. W25 58
Ribblers La.
Cottage Dr. G42 139
Cottage Dr. E. G42 139
Cottage La. G42 139
Cottage St. M33 92
Cottenham St. R32 95
Kensington St.
Cottesbrook Pl. U27 57
Cottesbrook Rd. U27 57
Cottesmore Dr. J41 140
Redmere Dr.
Cotton St. O31 93
Cotton Way V23 43
Cottrell Clo. V39 131
Coudray Rd. Q 4 6
Couldson St. R35 113
Coulthard Rd. O37 127
Coultshead Av. JJ22 49
Council Av. NN23 51
Council St. DD30 80
Countisbury Dr. W34 115
County Rd., Kirkby W23 43
County Rd., Liver. Q28 73
Court Av. AA36 117
Court Av. NN24 51
Court Cres. NN24 51
Court Hey Av. X32 98
Court Hey Dr. W32 97
Court Hey Rd. W32 97
Court Rd. P 5 6
Court St. NN24 51
Court, The Y30 77
Dannette Hey
Courtenay Rd. B34 105
Courtenay Rd., Wool. W35 115
Courteney Av. M24 38
Courteney Rd. M24 38
Courthope Rd. R28 74
Courtland Rd. U34 114
Courtney Av. K31 91
Courtney Rd. O37 127
Covent Gdn. P32 94
Coventry Av. Q24 40
Coventry Rd. U34 114
Coverdale Av. EE31 101
Coverside C36 106
Covertside D36 106
Cowan Way, Halton FF35 120
Cowan Way, Liver. R31 95
Cowdrey Av. J33 91
Cowley Clo. F34 107
Cowley Hill La. FF26 63
Cowley Rd. R28 74
Cowley St. GG26 63
Cowper Rd. U31 96
Cowper St., Sefton O26 54
Cowper St., St.H. HH28 82
Manville St.
Cowper Way AA32 99
Coyford Dr. R 3 3
Coylton Av. EE32 101
Crab St. FF27 63
Crabtree Clo. Y34 116
Cradley EE36 119
Crag Gro. GG24 48
Craigburn Rd. T30 75
Craighurst Rd. X33 98
Craigleigh Gro. Q43 148
Craigmore Rd. U36 114
Craigs Rd. T30 75
Craigside Av. U29 75
Craigwood Way, Know. X32 98
Woodlands Rd.
Craine Clo. R29 74
Cramond Av. U34 114
Cranbourne Av., Bids. K33 91
Cranbourne Av., Hoy. D32 88
Cranbourne Av., More. F33 89
Cranbourne Rd. S33 95
Cranbrook Av. NN23 51
Cranbrook St. HH28 82
Crane Av. HH30 82
Cranehurst Rd. R28 74
Cranfield Rd., Sefton O22 39
Cranford Clo. M43 148
Crosthwaite Av.
Cranford Dr. U32 96
Cranford Rd. U37 130
Cranford St. M32 92
Crank Hill FF23 48
Crank Rd., St.H. EE25 62
Crank Rd., Wigan FF21 35
Cranleigh Rd. X34 116
Cranmer St. P30 73
Cranmore Av. N24 39
Cranshaw Av. HH31 103
Cranshaw Ct. X31 98
Cranshaw La. GG34 120
Crantock Clo. V27 58
Crantock Clo., Hale. Z37 133
Crantock Gro. EE25 62
Cranwell Clo. S24 41
Cranwell Rd., Know. X33 98
Cranwell Rd., Wirr. E35 107
Crask Wk. W23 43
Craven Clo. M33 92
Craven St.
Craven Clo. M34 110
Craven Pl. M33 92
Craven Rd., St.H. EE31 101
Craven Rd., W.Derby V30 76
Craven St., Liver. Q32 94
Cravenwood Rd. Z37 133
Crawford Av., Halton DD36 119
Crawford Av., Liver. T34 114
Crawford Av., Sefton R19 28
Crawford Clo. HH31 103
Crawford Clo. JJ31 103
Crawford St.
Crawford Clo., W.Derby V29 76
Crawford Pk. T35 114
Crawford Rd. EE20 34
Crawford St. JJ31 103
Crawford Way T32 96
Pighue La.
Crawley Clo. Y37 132
Crediton Av. R 2 3
Crediton Clo. V26 58
Creek, The K29 70
Creekside M32 92
Cremorne Hey X29 77
Crescent Av., Sefton K16 19
Crescent Av., Wigan NN23 51
Crescent Gdn. M24 38
Crescent Gdns. M25 53
Crescent Grn. U15 153
Crescent Rd. S. N 7 9
Crescent Rd., Crosby L23 38
Crescent Rd., Lith. O26 54
Crescent Rd., Liver. R27 56
Crescent Rd., Wirr. M31 92
Crescent, The O22 39
Crescent, The, Beb. N38 127
Crescent, The, Cros. S 3 3
Crescent, The, Crosby N24 39
Crescent, The, Greas. F35 107
Crescent, The, Huy. AA32 99
Crescent, The, Mag. S21 28
Crescent, The, Speke Y39 136
Crescent, The, Thing. G38 124
Crescent, The, W.Kirby B36 105
Crescent, The, Wadd. S22 41
Crescent, The, Whist. CC31 100
Cressida Av. N37 127
Cressingham Rd. L29 71
Cressington Av. M36 110
Cressington Prom. U38 130
Crestor Rd. W35 115
Creswell Clo. Q24 40
Creswell St. FF27 63
Cretan Rd. S33 95
Crete Towers Q30 73
Crewe Grn. H36 108
Cricket Path K14 16
Cringles Dr. AA33 99
Crispin St. FF27 63
Critchley Rd. Z40 137
Crocketts Wk. DD26 62
Crockleford Av. Q 7 10
Crocus Av. K33 91
Crocus St. P29 73
Croft Av. E. P40 143
Croft Av., Wigan PP24 52
Croft Av., Wirr. P40 143
Croft Clo. K35 109
Croft Dr. G33 90
Croft Dr. E. C37 122
Croft Dr. W. C37 122
Croft Dr., Caldy C37 122
Croft Edge L35 110
Croft End JJ28 82
Croft Heys U15 153
Croft La., Liver. S25 56
Croft La., Wirr. P40 143
Croft, The, Liver. U29 75
Croft, The, Sefton R19 28
Croft, The, Wigan HH19 36
Croft, The, Wirr. F35 107
Crofters, The F35 107
Croftfield T20 29
Crofton Cres. U31 96
Crofton Rd., Liver. U31 96
Crofton Rd., Wirr. N35 111
Croftsway F41 138
Cromarty Rd., Liver. T32 96
Cromarty Rd., Wirr. K31 91
Cromdale Gro. JJ28 82
Cromer Dr. L30 71
Cromer Rd., Liver. T36 114
Cromer Rd., Sefton N 8 9
Cromer Rd., Wirr. B33 87
Cromer Way, Hale. Z38 133
Redbourn Av.
Cromford Rd. Z30 78
Crompton Dr. W27 58
Cromptons La. V34 115
Cromwell Rd. Q28 73
Crondall Gro. U33 96
Cronton Av. BB32 100
Cronton Av., Leas. G31 90
Cronton La. DD32 101
Cronton Park Clo. EE34 119
Cronton Rd., Know. BB34 118
Cronton Rd., Liver. U34 114
Crookhurst Av. HH22 49
Wells Av.
Cropper St. Q32 94
Cropton Rd. K15 16
Crosbie Heights Q31 94
Crosby Clo. G34 108
Crosby Grn. U29 75
Crosby Gro., Elles. O44 147
Crosby Gro., St.H. EE28 80
Formby Av.
Crosby Rd. N 7 9

Crosby Rd. N. N24 39
Crosby Rd. S. N26 54
Crosender Rd. M23 38
Crosfield Clo. S32 95
Crosfield Rd.
Crosfield Rd., Huy. CC31 100
Crosfield Rd., Liver. S32 95
Crosfield Rd., Wall. M32 92
Crosfield Wk. S32 95
Crosfield Rd.
Crosgrove Rd. S28 74
Crosland Rd., Know. X24 44
Crosland Rd., Sefton X24 42
Cross Barn La. N20 26
Cross Green Clo. L16 20
Cross Grn. L16 20
Cross Hey O24 39
Cross Hey Av. J34 109
Cross Hillocks La. CC35 118
Cross La., Beb. N39 127
Cross La., Know. BB31 100
Cross La., St.H. NN27 66
Cross La., Wall. J31 91
Cross La., Wigan HH19 36
Cross Pit La. CC22 46
Cross St. S. O 6 5
Cross St., Beb. O38 127
Cross St., Birk. N34 111
Cross St., Crosby M24 38
Cross St., Elles. K45 145
Cross St., Halton GG36 120
Cross St., Pres. BB29 79
Cross St., St.H. FF27 63
Waterloo St.
Cross St., Wigan QQ25 68
Cross, The, Elles. K45 145
Cross, The, Wirr. M40 143
High St.
Crossdale Rd. M23 38
Crossdale Rd. P42 143
Crossdale Way GG24 48
Crossfield St. GG27 63
Parr St.
Crosshall St. P32 94
Crossley Dr. F41 138
Crossley Rd. EE28 80
Crossvale Rd. Z32 99
Crossway K33 91
Crossway Clo. PP22 52
Crossway Clo. PP22 52
Linkway Av.
Crossways, Halton EE37 135
Crossways, Liver. W34 115
Crossways, Wirr. P39 128
Crosswood Cres. Y31 98
Crosthwaite Av. O43 148
Croston Av. DD30 80
Crouch St. HH29 82
Highfield St.
Crouch St. HH29 82
Robins La.
Crow La. E. OO27 67
Crow La. W. NN27 66
Crow Wood La. HH36 121
Crow Wood Pl. HH35 121
Crowland Clo. R 6 7
Crowland Way, Formby L16 20
Crown Av. DD37 135
Crown Clo. L16 20
Crown Rd. V29 76
Crown St., Liver. R33 95
Crown St., Newt. NN27 66
Crown St., Pres. EE29 80
Parliament St.
Crown Ter. PP27 67
Crown Way Y31 98
Crownacres Rd. Y37 132
Croxdale Rd. X30 77
Croxteth Av., Sefton O25 54
Croxteth Av., Wirr. L31 92
Croxteth Clo. T19 29
Croxteth Dr. CC21 33
Croxteth Dr., W.Derby U29 75
Croxteth Dr., Wind. S34 113
Croxteth Gate S34 113
Croxteth Gro. S34 113
Croxteth Hall La. V28 76
Croxteth La. Y28 77
Croxteth Rd. O26 54
Croxteth Rd. R34 113
Croxteth Vw., Know. W26 58
Croxteth Vw., W.Derby V29 76
Croyde Clo. R 2 3
Croyde Pl. HH31 103
Croyde Rd. AA39 133
Croydon Av. T34 114
Croylands St. Q29 73
Crucian Way V27 58
Crump St. Q33 94
Greenland St.
Crutchley Av. L33 92
Cubert Rd. V27 58
Cuckoo Clo. X35 116
Cuckoo La. X34 116
Cuckoo La., Nest. L45 146
Cuerdley Grn. KK36 152
Cuerdley Rd. LL35 152
Culcross Av. LL19 37
Cullen Av. P26 55
Cullen Clo. P43 148
Cullen St. S33 95
Culme Rd. T29 75
Cumber La. CC31 100
Cumberland Av., Liver. S34 113
Cumberland Av., Sefton P23 40
Cumberland Av., Wirr. K36 109
Cumberland Cres. KK26 65
Cumberland Gate R23 41
Cumberland Rd., St.H. DD29 80
Cumberland Rd., Wirr. L29 71
Cumberland St., Liver. P32 94
Cumberland St., Sefton P 6 6
Cumbria Way V28 76
Cummings St. P33 94
Wallis St.
Cummins Av. K14 16
Cumpsty Rd. P24 40
Cunard Av. M30 71
Cunard Clo. J34 109
Cunard Rd. O25 54
Cunliffe St. P32 94
Cunningham Clo. C38 122
Cunningham Dr. P40 143
Cunningham Rd., Halton EE37 135
Cunningham Rd., Liver. U32 96
Cunscough La. V20 30
Cupar Cres. Y31 98
Curate Rd. S29 74
Curbar Wk. R33 95
Curlender Clo. K32 91
Curlew Av. F34 107
Curlew Clo. F34 107
Curlew Way F32 89
Curtana Cres. V27 58
Curtis Rd. S28 74
Curzon Av., Birk. L33 92
Curzon Av., Wall. L29 71
Curzon Rd. S. P 6 6
Curzon Rd., Birk. L36 110
Curzon Rd., Crosby N24 39
Curzon Rd., Hoy. B33 87
Cusson Rd. X24 44
Custley Hey X29 77
Custom Ho. P32 94
Cut La. Z25 60
Cypress Av. GG35 120
Cypress Rd. Q 6 6
Cypress Rd. Y33 98
Cypress Rd., Sefton Q 6 6
Cyprians Way Q23 40
Cyprus St. BB30 79
Cyprus Ter. L29 71
Cyril Gro. T36 114

Dacre St., Boot. O28 72
Dacy Rd. R30 74
Daffodil Clo. JJ35 121
Daffodil Rd., Liver. U33 96
Daffodil Rd., Wirr. K33 91
Dagmar St. U32 96
Dagnall Rd. V24 43
Dahlia Clo. R27 56
Buttercup Way
Dairy Farm Rd. BB21 33
Daisey St. P29 73
Daisy Av. OO28 85
Daisy Mt. T21 29
Dakin Wk., Know. W23 43
Old Rough La.
Dale Acre Dr. P23 40
Dale Av., Brom. P41 143
Dale Av., Hes. G40 139
Dale Clo., Halton DD37 135
Dale Clo., Sefton S20 28
Dale Cres. HH30 82
Dale End Rd. J39 125
Dale Hey, Elles. Q44 148
Dale Hey, Wirr. L32 92
Dale La. X23 44
Dale Mews X35 116
Dale Rd., Know. V24 43
Dale Rd., Wigan QQ25 68
Dale Rd., Wirr. P42 143
Dale St. P32 94
Kingsway
Dale View Clo. H39 124
Dale Vw. OO27 67
Dalecrest HH20 36
Wordsworth Av.
Dalegarth Av. W28 76
Dalehead Pl. GG24 48
Dalemeadow Rd. V31 97
Dales Row AA32 99
Dales Wk. L14 16
Daleside Clo. G36 124
Daleside Rd. W23 43
Daleside Wk. W23 43
Dalesway G41 139
Dalewood W27 58
Daley Pl. Q25 55
Daley Rd. P24 40
Dallas Gro. R26 56
Dalmeny St. R35 113
Dalmorton Rd. L29 71
Dalry Cres. W25 58
Dalrymple St. P30 73
Dalston Dr. GG24 48
Dalston Gro. LL19 37
Dalton Clo. V28 76
Dalton Rd. M29 71
Daltry Clo. U29 75
Dam Row FF28 81
Dam Wood Rd. Y40 136
Damfield La. S21 28
Damhead La. N45 147
Damian Dr. NN26 66
Danby Clo. Q30 73
Hamilton Rd.
Dane Clo. G38 124
Dane Ct. EE31 101
Dane St. Q28 73
Danefield Rd., Liver. V37 131
Danefield Rd., Wirr. F36 107
Danehurst Rd. K29 70
Danesbury Clo. JJ23 49
Danescourt Rd., Liver. V30 76
Danescourt Rd., Wirr. L33 92
Danescroft DD35 119
Daneswell Dr. G32 90
Daneswell Rd. AA40 137
Daneville Rd. S28 74
Daneway L10 12
Danger La. G32 90
Daniel St. Q30 73
Dannette Hey Y30 77
Dans Rd. JJ36 121
Dansie St. Q32 94
Danube St. S33 95
Daphne Clo. U25 57
Darby Gro. U38 130
Darby Rd. U37 130
Dareham Way LL19 37
Darent Rd. KK25 65
Daresbury Av. L10 12
Daresbury Rd., St.H. DD27 62
Daresbury Rd., Wirr. L31 92
Darley Dr. V30 76
Darleydale Dr. Q42 143
Darling St. S33 95
Darlington St. M31 92
Darlton Gro. NN23 51
Darmond Rd. X23 44
Darmonds Grn. B35 105
Darrel Dr. S33 95
Dartington Rd. V33 97
Dartmouth Dr. P23 40
Dartmouth St. S24 41
Darvel Av. LL23 50
Darwall Rd. V37 131
Darwen St. O30 72
Darwick Dr. Z33 99
Darwin Gro. FF29 81
Daryl Rd. H40 139
Daulby St. Q32 94
Dauntsey Mews X33 98
Dauntsey Wk. X33 98
Davenham Av. K35 109
Davenham Clo. K36 109
Davenham Rd. K15 16
Davenhill Pk. S24 41
Davenport Clo. C38 122
Davenport Rd. G41 139
Daventree Rd. L30 71
Daventry Rd. T36 114

David St. Q35 112
Davidson Rd. T31 96
Davies Av. OO26 67
Davies St., Liver. P32 94
Davies St., Sefton P27 55
Davies St., St.H. HH27 64
Davis Rd. H31 90
Davy Clo. DD26 62
Davy St. R30 74
Dawber St., Wigan OO23 52
Dawley Clo. NN23 51
Dawlish Clo. Y37 132
Dawlish Dr. R 2 3
Dawlish Rd., Irby F38 123
Dawlish Rd., Wall. K31 91
Dawn Clo. FF29 81
Dawn Wk., Know. U25 57
  Amanda Rd.
Dawpool Dr., Brom. P41 143
Dawpool Dr., More. G33 90
Dawson Av., Cros. S 2 3
  The Causeway
Dawson Av., St.H. HH29 82
Dawson Av., Wirr. L33 92
Dawson Gdns. S20 28
Dawson St. P32 94
Dawstone Rd. G41 139
Day St. U31 96
Days Meadow F35 107
  Griffiths Clo.
De Grouchy St. B35 105
De Villiers Av, N22 39
Deacon Rd. GG36 120
Deacon St. R31 95
Deakin St. K33 93
Dean Av. K30 70
Dean Clo. HH23 49
Dean Ct. X36 116
Dean Rd. QQ25 68
Dean St. M25 53
Dean Way GG32 102
Deane Rd. S32 95
Deane St. P32 94
Deans Way, Halton EE37 135
Deans Way, Wirr. K33 91
Deansburn Rd. T30 75
Deanscales Rd. U28 75
Deansgate La. L14 16
Deansgate La. N. L14 16
Dearham Av. GG25 63
Dearnford Av. P42 143
Dearnley Av. JJ26 64
Deauville Rd. S25 56
Debra Clo. U23 42
Dee Clo. W22 43
Dee La. B36 105
Dee Park Clo. H42 139
Dee Rd. DD31 101
Dee View Rd. G41 139
Deeley Clo. S32 95
  Stanier Way
Deepdale EE35 119
Deepdale Av., St.H. HH24 49
  Dunmail Av.
Deepdale Av., Sea. O26 54
Deepdale Clo. J34 109
Deepdale Dr. EE31 101
Deepdale Rd. X33 98
Deepfield Dr. Z33 99
Deepfield Rd. T34 114
Deer Park Rd. H42 139
Deerbarn Dr. R23 41
Deerbolt Clo. V23 43
Deerbolt Cres. V23 43
Deerbolt Way V23 43
Deerwood Cres. S45 149
Deeside Clo. H34 108
Deirdre Av. GG36 120
Delabol Rd. V26 58
Delagoa Rd. T26 57
Delamain Rd. T30 75
Delamere Av., Halton EE36 119
Delamere Av., St.H. GG31 102
Delamere Av., Wirr. Q43 148
Delamere Clo. Q43 148
Delamere Clo., Birk. H34 108
Delamere Rd. L10 12
Delamore St. Q28 73
Delamores Acre O45 147
Delavor Clo. G41 139
Delavor Rd. G41 139
Delaware Cres. V24 43
Delf La. R16 23
Delf La., Speke X38 132
Delfby Cres. X24 44

Delfwood Dr. GG28 81
Dell Clo. O42 142
Dell Gro. O37 127
Dell La. H41 139
Dell St. S32 95
Dell, The, Liver. W28 76
Dell, The, Wirr. O36 111
Dellfield La. LL22 50
Dellside Clo. HH29 82
Dellside Gro. HH29 82
Delph Common Rd. U15 153
Delph La., Pres. CC30 79
Delph La., W.Lan. U16 153
Delph La., Warr. PP30 85
Delph La., Win. RR30 86
Delph Park Av. U16 153
Delph Rd. M21 25
Delph St. R28 74
Delta Dr. W28 76
Delta Rd. JJ27 64
Delta Rd., Sefton O25 54
Delta Rd., St.H. JJ27 64
Delta Rd., W. O36 111
Delta Rd., Wirr. O36 111
Delves Av. N39 127
Delyn Clo. N35 116
Delyn Gro. N36 111
Demesne St. N31 93
Denbigh Av. HH29 82
Denbigh Rd. R27 56
Denbigh Rd., Wall. M32 92
Denbigh St. O30 72
  Bentinck St.
Dencourt Rd. U28 75
Dene Av. MM27 66
Denebank Rd. R29 74
Denes Way X29 77
Deneshey Rd. C33 88
Denford Rd. W30 76
Denise Rd. U25 57
Denison Gro. FF29 81
Denman Dr. S31 95
Denman Rd. S31 95
Denman St. R32 95
  Kensington St.
Denmark Rd. R 4 7
Denmark St., Sefton M24 38
Dennett Clo. S21 28
Dennett Rd. BB31 100
Denning Dr. F37 123
Dennis Av. EE29 80
Denny Clo. G35 108
Denstone Av. S23 41
Denstone Clo. X31 98
Denstone Clo., Birk. H34 108
Denstone Cres. X30 77
Denton Dr. M30 71
Denton Gro. S30 74
Denton St., Halton HH36 121
Denton St., Liver. Q35 112
Dentons Green La. EE26 62
Dentwood St. R35 113
Denver Rd. V24 43
Depot Rd. Y23 44
Deptford Clo. Y34 116
  Stapleford Rd.
Derby Dr. DD22 47
Derby Gro., Liver. R31 95
Derby Gro., Sefton S22 41
Derby La. U31 96
Derby Pl. T32 96
Derby Rd. S. P 5 6
Derby Rd., Birk. M35 110
Derby Rd., Boot. O28 72
Derby Rd., Formby K14 16
Derby Rd., Gol. RR25 68
Derby Rd., Halton GG35 120
Derby Rd., Know. Z32 99
Derby Rd., Wall. L30 71
Derby Sq., Liver. P32 94
Derby Sq., Pres. CC30 79
Derby Sq., Wirr. M34 110
Derby St., Birk. M34 110
Derby St., Huy. AA32 99
Derby St., Liver. R32 95
Derby St., Newt. NN27 36
Derby St., Pres. BB30 79
Derbyshire Hill Rd. KK28 83
Dereham Av. H33 90
Dereham Cres. T25 57
Derna Rd. Y31 98
Derwent Av. J16 19
Derwent Av., Know. CC30 79
Derwent Av., Sefton Q 4 6

Derwent Clo., Know. V22 43
Derwent Clo., Sefton T20 29
Derwent Clo., St.H. DD31 101
Derwent Clo., Wirr. M38 126
Derwent Dr., Elles. R44 149
Derwent Dr., Sefton P25 55
Derwent Dr., Wall. L30 71
Derwent Dr., Wirr. G39 124
Derwent Rd., Beb. M38 126
Derwent Rd., Birk. L35 110
Derwent Rd., Halton EE36 119
Derwent Rd., Hoy. D33 88
Derwent Rd., Liver. T31 96
Derwent Rd., Sefton N24 39
Derwent Rd., St.H. GG25 63
Derwent Rd., Wigan PP22 52
Derwent Sq. T31 96
Derwent Way K45 145
Desborough Cres. U29 75
Desford Av. HH26 64
  Chain La.
Desford Av. HH26 64
  Chain La.
Desford Rd. T37 130
DeSilva St. AA32 99
Desmond Clo. J34 109
Desmond Gro. N23 39
Desoto Rd. EE38 135
Deva Clo. W22 43
Deva Rd. B36 105
Deveraux Dr. L31 92
Deverell Gro. U32 96
Deverell Rd. U32 96
Deverill Rd. N36 111
Devizes Clo. X33 98
Devizes Dr. F37 123
Devizes Mews X33 98
Devizes Wk. X33 98
Devoke Av. GG24 48
Devon Av. M30 71
Devon Clo. L23 38
Devon Ct. R30 74
  Tynemouth Clo.
Devon Dr. G39 124
Devon Farm Way L15 16
Devon Gdns., Liver. W34 115
Devon Gdns., Wirr. N36 111
  Chester Rd.
Devon Pl. GG35 120
Devon St., Liver. Q32 94
Devon St., St.H. EE27 62
Devon Way AA31 99
Devondale Rd. U34 114
Devonfield Rd. O26 55
Devonhall Gdns. R34 113
Devonport St. Q34 112
Devonshire Clo. L34 110
Devonshire Gdns. OO28 85
Devonshire Pl., Liver. Q30 73
Devonshire Pl., Wirr. L34 110
Devonshire Rd., Birk. L34 110
Devonshire Rd., Liver. R34 113
Devonshire Rd., Pen. G39 124
Devonshire Rd., Sefton M23 38
Devonshire Rd., Sefton R 5 7
Devonshire Rd., St.H. EE26 62
Devonshire Rd., Upt. G24 108
Devonshire Rd., W.Kirby C36 106
Devonshire Rd., Wall. L31 92
Dewey Av. R25 56
Dewlands Rd. N25 54
Dewsbury Rd. R29 74
Dexter St. Q34 112
Deycroft Av. W23 43
Deycroft Wk., Know. W23 43
  Deycroft Av.
Deyes End T20 29
Deyes La. S20 28
Deysbrook La. V30 76
Deysbrook Way V29 76
Deysbrookside V30 76
  Leyfield Rd.
Dial Rd. M35 110
Dial St. S32 95
Diana Rd. P25 55
Diana St. R29 74
Diane Rd. OO22 52
Dibb La. M21 25
Dibbins Hey O40 142
Dibbinsdale Rd. O41 142
Dicconson St. GG27 63
  College St.
Dickens Av. K36 109
Dickens Clo. K36 109
Dickens Rd. EE29 80

Dickens St. Q34 112
Dickinson Clo., Sefton K16 19
Dickinson Clo., St.H. KK26 65
Canniswood Rd.
Dickinson Rd. K16 19
Dickson St., Halton GG36 120
Dickson St., Liver. O31 93
Didcot Clo. Y37 132
Didsbury Clo. W24 43
Digby St. Q34 112
Digg La. F32 89
Digmoor Rd. W25 58
Dignum Mead Z34 117
Dilloway St. FF27 63
Dinas La. X31 98
Dineson Rd. V37 131
Dingle Av. MM28 84
Dingle Gro. R35 113
Dingle La. R35 113
Dingle Mt. R35 113
Dingle Rd., Liver. Q35 112
Dingle Rd., Wirr. M35 110
Dingle Vale R35 113
Dingley Av. Q26 55
Dingwall Dr. F35 107
Dinmore Rd. L31 92
Dinorben Av. HH29 82
Dinorwic Rd., Liver. R30 74
Dinorwic Rd., Sefton O 7 9
Dinsdale Rd. Q40 143
Ditchfield L16 20
Ditchfield Pl. DD37 135
Ditchfield Rd. DD37 135
Ditton La. F31 89
Ditton Rd. EE38 135
Dixon Av. OO26 67
Dixon Clo. NN25 66
Dixon Rd. X24 44
Dobbs Dr. L15 16
Dobbs Gutter L15 16
Dobsons La. FF29 81
Dock Rd. N. P38 128
Dock Rd. S. P39 128
Dock Rd., Liver. U38 130
Dock Rd., Wirr. L32 92
Doctors La. N16 21
Dodd Av., St.H. EE27 62
Dodd Av., Wirr. F35 107
Dodds La. S20 28
Dodleston Clo. J35 109
Dodman Rd. V26 58
Dodworth Av. Q 6 6
Doel St. R31 95
Does Meadow Rd. O41 142
Dollys La. S 5 7
Domar Clo. W24 43
Dombey St. Q34 112
Dominic Clo. W33 97
Dominic Rd. W33 97
Dominic Way HH29 82
Dominion St. S30 74
Domville CC32 100
Domville Dr. H35 108
Domville Rd. U32 96
Donalds Way T36 114
Donaldson St. R30 74
Doncaster Clo. Q 7 10
Doncaster Dr. G34 108
Donegal St. N36 111
Grove St.
Donhead Ms. X33 98
Donhead Wk. X33 98
Donne Av. N39 127
Donne Clo. N39 127
Donne Av.
Donsby Rd. R26 56
Dooley Dr. R23 41
Doon Clo. Q28 73
Dora St. R32 95
Dorbett Dr. N24 39
Dorchester Clo. X34 116
Dorchester Pk. X34 116
Dorchester Way MM30 84
Weymouth Rd.
Doreen Av. F33 89
Dorgan Clo. DD31 101
Doric Rd. U31 96
Doric St. N36 111
Doric St., Sea. N25 54
Dorien Rd. T32 96
Dorking Gro. U34 114
Dorothy St., Liver. R32 95
Dorothy St., St.H. FF29 81
Dorrington St. Q31 94
Dorrit St. Q34 112
Dorset Av., Liver. S33 95
Dorset Av., Sefton M12 12
Dorset Clo. P27 55
Waterworks St.
Dorset Dr. G39 124
Dorset Rd., Know. AA31 99
Dorset Rd., Liver. S30 74
Dorset Rd., St.H. EE28 80
Dorset Rd., W.Kirby C36 106
Dorset Rd., Wall. L29 71
Dorset St. HH27 64
Gloucester St.
Dorset St. HH27 64
Parr Stocks Rd.
Dosen Brow Z34 117
Douglas Av., Burt. KK30 83
Douglas Av., St.H. HH23 49
Douglas Clo. JJ35 121
Douglas Dr., Sefton T20 29
Douglas Dr., Wirr. F33 89
Douglas Pl. O28 72
Douglas Rd., Sefton S 3 3
Douglas Rd., Wirr. C35 106
Douglas Rd.,Liver. R30 74
Douglas Sq., Wirr. N34 111
Douglas St., St.H. EE27 62
Douglas Way W22 43
Doulton Clo. H34 108
Doulton Pl. BB31 100
Doulton St. EE27 62
Douro St. Q31 94
Dove Rd. Q26 55
Dove St. R33 95
Dovecot Av. W31 97
Dovecot Pl. W31 97
Dovedale Clo. K36 109
Dovedale Clo. S20 28
Dovedale Rd., Hoy. B33 87
Dovedale Rd., Liver. U35 114
Dovedale Rd., Wall. K29 70
Dovepoint Rd. D32 88
Dover Clo. M33 92
Dover Rd., Mag. S22 41
Dover Rd., S. N 8 9
Dovercliffe Rd. U31 96
Dovesmead Rd. J41 140
Stevens Rd.
Dovey St. R34 113
Doward St. HH36 121
Dowhills Dr. L22 38
Dowhills Rd. N. L22 38
Dowhills Rd. S. L22 38
Downall Green Rd. MM22 51
Downes Grn. O40 142
Downham Clo. W34 115
Downham Dr. H41 139
Downham Grn. W34 115
Downham Rd. M35 110
Downham Rd. N. H40 139
Downham Rd. S. H41 139
Downham Way W34 115
Downham Wk. HH20 36
Downhills Pk. L22 38
Downing Clo. L36 110
Downing Rd. P28 73
Downing St. R30 74
Downland Way JJ28 82
Downs Rd. FF28 81
Prescot Rd.
Downs, The L23 38
Downs, The LL19 37
Downside DD35 119
Downside Clo. Q23 40
Downside Dr. T24 42
Downway KK28 83
Dowsefield La. W35 115
Dragon Clo. V27 58
Dragon Cres. CC31 100
Dragon Dr. CC31 100
Dragon La. BB32 100
Dragon Yd. GG35 120
Drake Clo. U25 57
Drake Clo., Know. CC32 100
Neilson Av.
Drake Cres. U25 57
Drake Pl. T25 57
Drake Rd., Elles. K44 145
Drake Rd., Liver. T25 57
Drake Rd., Wirr. H31 90
Drake St. EE27 62
Drake Way U25 57
Drakefield Rd. T27 57
Draw Well Rd. Y24 44
Draycott St. Q35 112
Drayton Clo. F38 123
Drayton Cres. HH26 64
Drayton Rd., Liver. R28 74
Drayton Rd., Wirr. M32 92
Drayton St. KK27 65
Drennan Rd. W37 131
Drewell Rd. T35 114
Drewitt Cres. S 3 3
Driffield Rd. BB30 79
Drive, The, W.Derby U30 75
Driveway CC31 100
Droitwich Av. F35 107
Dromore Av. U35 114
Dronfield Way W33 97
Druid St. OO24 52
Druid Way H36 108
Druids Cross Gdns. V35 115
Druids Cross Rd. V35 115
Druids Pk. W35 115
Druidsville Rd. W35 115
Drummond Rd., Liver. S28 74
Drummond Rd., W.Green O22 39
Drummond Rd., Wirr. B34 105
Drury La. P32 94
Dryburgh St. Q29 73
Dryden Av. MM22 51
Dryden Clo. CC31 100
Dryden Clo., Birk. J34 109
Dryden Gro. Z32 99
Dryden Rd. T32 96
Dryden St., Liver. P31 94
Dryden St., Sefton O26 54
Dryfield Clo. F35 107
Drysdale St. R35 113
Dublin St. O31 93
Ducie St. R34 113
Duck Pond La. L36 110
Duckinfield St. Q32 94
Duddingston Av., Crosby N24 39
Duddingston Av., Liver. U34 114
Duddon Av. T20 29
Dudley Clo. L35 110
Dudley Cres. R43 149
Dudley Gro. N24 39
Dudley Pl. HH27 64
Baker St.
Dudley Rd., Liver. T34 114
Dudley Rd., Wirr. L29 71
Dudley St. NN22 51
Dudlow Ct. V34 115
Dudlow Dr. V34 115
Dudlow Gdns. V34 115
Dudlow La. V34 115
Dudlow Nook Rd. V34 115
Duke Av. P 7 10
Duke St. V38 131
Duke St. BB29 79
Grosvenor St.
Duke St. FF27 63
Duke St. S. O 6 5
Duke St., Asht. OO23 52
Duke St., Birk. M33 92
Duke St., Crosby M24 38
Duke St., Formby K16 19
Duke St., Liver. P33 94
Duke St., Newt. NN27 66
Duke St., Wall. L29 71
Dukes Pl. P33 94
Dukes Way K16 19
Dukes Wood La. EE19 34
Dulas Grn. X24 44
Dulas Rd., Know. X24 44
Dulas Rd., Liver. U34 114
Dulverton Rd. T37 130
Dumbarton St. Q28 73
Dumbrees Rd. W29 76
Dumfries Way V22 43
Dun Mail Av. HH24 49
Dunacre Way Z37 133
Dunacre Wk. Z37 133
Dunacre Wk. HH31 101
Four Acre La.
Dunbabin Rd. U34 114
Dunbar Cres. N 9 9
Dunbar Rd. N 8 9
Dunbar St. Q28 73
Dunbeath Av. EE32 101
Dunbeath Clo. EE32 101
Dunbeath Av.
Dunblane Clo. LL23 50
Duncan Av. OO26 67
Duncan Dr. F35 107
Duncan Pl. O28 72
Duncan St., Edge H. Q33 94
Duncan St., St.H. FF27 63
Duncan St., Wirr N34 111

Duncansby Dr.	P43 148	Earle Dr.	J45 145	Ebenezer St., St.H.	JJ26 64
Dunchurch Rd.	W30 76	Earle Rd.	S33 95	Ebenezer St., Wirr.	O36 111
Duncombe Rd. N.	U37 130	Earle St.	MM28 84	Eberle St.	P32 94
Duncombe Rd. S.	U37 130	Earle St., Birk.	O32 93	Ebor La.	Q31 94
Dundale Rd.	U31 96	Earls Clo.	M23 38	*Prince Edwin St.*	
Dundalk Rd.	EE37 135	Earlsfield Rd.	T34 114	Ebrington St.	V38 131
Dundee Gro.	L31 92	Earlston Rd.	L30 71	Eccles Gro.	JJ31 103
Dundee St.	O31 93	Earp St.	V38 131	Eccles Rd.	J16 19
Dundle Dr.	S23 41	Easby Clo.	L16 20	Ecclesall Av.	P25 55
Dundonald Rd.	T36 114	Easby Rd.	P29 73	Ecclesfield Rd.	DD26 62
Dundonald St.	L33 92	Easby Wk.	P29 73	Eccleshall Rd.	P38 128
Dunedin St.	FF29 81	*Easby Rd.*		Eccleshill Rd.	U30 75
Dunes Dr.	J15 15	Easdale Wk.	V22 43	Eccleston Av.	P40 143
Dunfold Clo.	W24 43	Easedale Dr.	L11 12	Eccleston Clo.	K35 109
Dungeon La.	Z40 137	Easington Rd.	EE30 80	Eccleston Gdns.	DD29 80
Dunham Av.	PP24 52	East Bank St.	O 5 5	Eccleston Rd.	Q26 55
Dunham Clo.	Q43 148	East Bnk.	L35 110	Eccleston St., Pres.	BB30 79
Dunham Rd.	U32 96	East Clo.	DD29 80	Eccleston St., St.H.	FF27 63
Dunkeld St.	R31 95	East Dam Wood Rd.	Z40 137	Echo La.	C36 106
Dunkirk Rd.	N 8 9	East Howard Rd.	P24 40	Edale Clo.	P42 143
Dunlop Dr.	U23 42	East La.	O20 26	Edale Rd.	U35 114
Dunlop Rd.	X40 136	East Lancashire Rd.,	T27 57	Eddisberry Rd.	L30 71
Dunluce St.	Q28 73	Liver.		Eddisbury Rd.	B35 105
Dunmore Rd.	T31 96	East Lunt Rd.	P20 27	Eddleston St.	MM22 51
Dunmow Way	Y37 132	East Mead	U15 153	Eden Av., Sefton	Q 3 2
Dunnerdale Rd.	U28 75	East Meade	S20 28	Eden Av., St.H.	CC21 33
Dunnet St.	O28 72	East Millwood Rd.,	Z39 133	Eden Av., Wirr.	M30 71
Dunning Clo.	G35 108	Hale.		Eden Clo., Know.	DD31 101
Dunnings Bridge Rd.	Q24 40	East Orchard La.	S25 56	Eden Clo., Sefton	W22 43
Dunnock Clo.	X34 116	East Park Ct.	N31 93	Eden Dr. N.	O23 39
Dunraven Rd., Elles.	L45 146	East Prescot Rd.	W31 97	Eden Dr. S.	O23 39
Dunraven Rd., Wirr.	B36 105	East St., App.	HH36 121	Eden Park Rd.	M35 110
Dunriding La.	EE27 62	East St., Crosby	M24 38	Edendale	DD36 119
Dunsdon Clo.	W35 115	East St., Know.	BB30 79	Edenfield Clo.	Q 7 10
Dunsdon Rd.	W34 115	*Warrington Rd.*		Edenfield Cres.	Z31 99
Dunsford	DD35 119	East St., Liver.	P32 94	Edenfield Rd.	T34 114
Dunsop Av.	HH31 103	East St., S.Port.	P 5 6	Edenhall Dr.	Y35 116
Dunstan La.	S33 95	East St., Wall.	N32 93	Edenhurst Av.	X33 98
Dunstan St.	T33 96	East St., Wigan	OO23 52	Edenhurst Clo.	J16 19
Dunster Gro., St.H.	HH31 103	East Way, More.	G32 90	Edenhurst Dr.	J15 15
Dunster Gro., Wirr.	H41 139	Eastbourne Rd., Ains.	O 7 9	Edenvale	Q23 40
Dunster Rd.	N 9 9	Eastbourne Rd., Crosby	L24 38	Edgar Ct.	M33 92
Dunston Gdns.	HH30 82	Eastbourne Rd., Liver.	R25 56	Edgar St.	GG28 81
Dunvegan Rd.	OO24 52	Eastbourne Rd., Wirr.	M34 110	*Emmett St.*	
Duoro Pl.	T32 96	Eastbourne Way	Q31 94	Edgar St., Liver.	P31 94
Durban Av.	N22 39	Eastcliffe Rd.	U31 96	Edgar St., Wall.	M33 92
Durban Rd., Liver.	U32 96	Eastcote Rd.	V37 131	Edge Green La.	PP24 52
Durban Rd., Wirr.	L30 71	Eastcott Clo.	F35 107	Edge Green Rd.	PP23 52
Durden St.	S33 95	Eastcroft	W22 43	Edge Grn.	PP24 52
Durham Av.	Q24 40	Eastcroft Rd.	M32 92	Edge Grn. Rd.	OO23 52
Durham Rd.	N25 54	Eastdale Rd.	T33 96	Edge Gro.	S32 95
Durham Rd., Farn.	GG35 120	Eastern Av., Liver.	Z40 137	Edge Hall Rd.	JJ19 36
Durham St.	V39 131	Eastern Av., Wirr.	P39 128	Edge La., Liver.	R32 95
Durham Way	AA31 99	Eastern Dr.	U37 130	Edge La., Sefton	O22 39
Durham Way, Ain.	R24 41	Eastfield Dr.	S35 113	Edge Lane Dr.	U32 96
Durley Dr.	K36 109	Eastfield Wk.	V24 43	Edge Moor Dr., Irby	F37 123
Durley Rd.	R26 56	Eastgate	O38 127	Edge St.	EE30 80
Durnford Hey	Y34 116	Eastham Clo.	W32 97	Edgefold Rd.	W24 43
Durning Rd.	S32 95	Eastham Cres.	HH31 103	Edgehill Rd.	F33 89
Durrant Rd.	T29 75	Eastham Rake	P43 148	Edgeley Gdns.	Q26 55
Durrington Bank	Y34 116	Eastham Village Rd.,	Q42 143	Edgemoor Clo.	H34 108
Dursley	CC32 100	Wirr.		Edgemoor Clo.	O23 39
Dursley Dr.	OO23 52	East Lake Av.	Q30 73	Edgemoor Dr., Liver.	U25 57
Durston Rd.	V33 97	Eastleigh Dr.	F37 123	Edgemoor Dr., Sefton	O22 39
Durweston Wk.	Y34 116	Eastmains Av., H.Cliff	AA39 137	Edgemoor Rd.	V30 76
Dutton Dr.	N40 142	Eastmnan Rd.	T29 75	Edgerley Pl.	NN23 51
Duxbury Clo., Sefton	T19 29	Easton Rd.	X31 98	Edgeware Gro.	LL19 37
Duxbury Clo., St.H.	DD21 34	Easton Rd., New F.	O37 127	Edgewood Dr.	P42 143
Dwerryhouse La.	P34 112	Eastside	HH28 82	Edgewood Rd., Wall.	G34 108
Stanhope St.		Eastway	S45 149	Edgewood Rd., Wirr.	C32 88
Dwerryhouse La.	U28 75	Eastway, Sefton	S20 28	Edgeworth Rd., Liver.	R30 74
Dyer St.	PP24 52	Eastway,, Birk.	G35 108	Edgeworth Rd., Wirr.	O39 128
Dyke St.	R31 95	Eastways	EE36 119	Edgeworth St.	JJ29 82
Dykin Clo.	JJ35 121	Eastwell Rd.	NN23 51	Edgmond St.	N32 93
Dykin Rd.	HH35 121	Eastwood Av.	PP27 67	Edgware Gro.	LL19 37
Dymchurch Rd.	X39 132	Eastwood Rd.	MM29 84	Edinburgh Clo.	R25 56
Dymoke Rd.	V27 58	Eaton Av., Orrell	P26 55	Edinburgh Dr., Know.	Z33 99
Dyson Hall Dr.	S26 56	*Aughton Rd.*		Edinburgh Dr., Wirr.	L36 110
Dyson St., Liver.	Q28 73	Eaton Av., Sefton	O25 54	Edinburgh Rd.	L30 71
Dyson St., St.H.	GG28 81	Eaton Av., Wirr.	M31 92	Edinburgh Rd., Liver.	R32 95
		Eaton Clo., Know.	Y32 98	Edinburgh Rd., Sefton	K16 19
		Eaton Clo., Liver.	U29 75	Edinburgh Rd., Widnes	DD37 135
Eager La.	R17 23	Eaton Gdns.	V31 97	Edington St.	T33 96
Eagle Cres.	DD22 47	Eaton Rd. N.	U29 75	Edith Rd.	M31 92
Eagle Dene	U26 57	Eaton Rd., Claugh.	L34 110	Edith Rd., Liver.	R30 74
Eagle Hall Rd.	T27 57	Eaton Rd., Hoy.	B36 105	Edith Rd., Sefton	P26 55
Eagle La.	S45 149	Eaton Rd., Liver.	U38 130	Edith St.	JJ29 82
Eaglehurst Rd.	X35 116	Eaton Rd., N.Green	U29 75	Edmonston St.	JJ27 64
Ealing Rd.	R25 56	Eaton Rd., Sefton	S22 41	*Fry St.*	
Eamont Av.	R 2 3	Eaton Rd., St.H.	EE26 62	Edmund St.	P32 94
Eardisley Rd.	U34 114	Eaton St.	BB30 79	Edmundson St.	JJ27 64
Earl Rd.	P27 55	Eaton St., Liver.	P31 94	*Broad Oak Rd.*	
Earl St., Beb.	O37 127	Eaton St., Wall.	L31 92	Edna Av.	U25 57
Earl St., Wigan	HH27 64	Eaves La., St.H.	GG30 81	Edrich Av.	J33 91
Earle Cres.	J44 145	Ebenezer Rd.	S33 95	Edward Dr.	NN23 51

Edward Jenner Av. Q23 40
Edward Rd., Know. CC30 79
Edward Rd., St.H. FF26 63
Edward Rd., Warr. LL34 152
Edward Rd., Wirr. C34 106
Edward St., Halton HH36 121
Edward St., Liver. Q32 94
Edward St., Newt. KK26 65
Edward St., P.Cross HH28 82
Edwards La. X38 132
Edwards Way EE37 135
Edwin St. HH36 121
Effingham St. O28 72
Egan Rd. K33 91
Egbert Rd. C33 88
Egdon Clo. JJ36 121
Kilsby Dr.
Egerton Br. N33 93
Egerton Dr., W.Kirby B36 105
Egerton Park Clo. N35 111
Egerton Rd., Beb. O37 127
Egerton Rd., Birk. L34 110
Egerton Rd., Know. BB30 79
Egerton Rd., Liver. S33 95
Egerton Rd., Wall. L30 71
Egerton St., Liver. Q33 94
Egerton St., St.H. HH28 82
Egerton St., Wirr. L29 71
Egeworth Rd. PP24 52
Eglington Av., Know. BB32 100
Dragon La.
Egremont Prom. M30 71
Egremont Rd. AA35 117
Egremount Clo. AA35 117
Egypt St. Q32 94
Eight Acre La. L14 16
Eighth Av. J32 91
Eilian Gro. V32 97
Elaine Clo. OO22 52
Elaine Clo., C.Wood HH36 121
Elaine St. Q34 112
Elbow La. K15 16
Elder Gdns. U37 130
Elder Gro. B36 105
Grange Rd.
Elderdale Rd. R29 74
Eldersfield Rd. U28 75
Elderwood Rd. N35 111
Eldon Gdns. NN22 51
Eldon Rd., Birk. N36 111
Eldon Rd., Wall. L31 92
Eldon St., Birk. M34 110
Eldon St., Liver. P31 94
Eldon St., St.H. FF28 81
Eldon Ter. K45 145
Eldred Rd. V34 115
Eleanor Rd., More. F32 89
Eleanor Rd., Sefton P26 55
Eleanor Rd., Wall. J33 91
Eleanor Rd., Wall. W33 91
Eleanor St. O28 72
Elenan St. L29 71
Elephant La. EE29 80
Elfet St. K33 91
Elgar Av. Q42 143
Elgar Rd. W30 76
Elgin Av. LL23 50
Elgin Ct. EE32 101
Coylton Av.
Elgin Dr. M30 71
Elgin St. N33 93
Eliot St. O26 54
Lionel St.
Eliza St. JJ29 82
Elizabeth Av. N10 13
Elizabeth Rd., Know. Z33 99
Elizabeth Rd., Liver. U26 57
Elizabeth Rd., Sefton P26 55
Elizabeth Rd., St.H. MM25 66
Elizabeth St., C.Face HH31 103
Balniel St.
Elizabeth St., Liver. Q32 94
Elizabeth St., Sutt. JJ29 82
Elizabeth Ter. EE36 119
Elkan Clo. JJ35 121
Elkan Rd. HH35 121
Elkstone Rd. U28 75
Ellaby Rd. EE31 101
Ellams Bridge Rd. JJ29 82
Ellel Gro. S30 74
Ellen Gdns. JJ29 82
Ellen St. JJ29 82
Ellens La. O38 127
Elleray Park Rd. L30 71
Ellergreen Rd. U28 75
Ellerslie Av. EE30 80
Ellerslie St. S30 74
Ellerton Way W27 58
Ellesmere Dr., Sefton S23 41
Ellesmere Dr., Wigan MM22 51
Ellesmere Gro. L30 71
Ellesmere Rd. MM23 51
Elliot St., Liver. P32 94
Elliot St., St.H. FF27 63
Ellis Ashton St. AA32 99
Ellis Rd. HH23 49
Ellison Dr. EE27 62
Elliston St. T31 96
Ellon Av. EE32 101
Elloway Rd., Boot. AA39 133
Elm Av., App. GG36 120
Elm Av., Ley.Green LL22 50
Elm Av., Sefton N22 38
Elm Av., Win. OO28 85
Elm Av., Wirr. F34 107
Elm Clo. G39 124
Elm Croft La. L19 25
Elm Dr., Formby J16 19
Elm Dr., Lith. N26 54
Elm Dr., St.H. HH22 49
Elm Dr., Wirr. F35 107
Elm Gdns. CC22 46
Elm Grn. N45 147
Elm Gro., App. GG36 120
Elm Gro., Hoy. C33 88
Elm Gro., Liver. R32 95
Elm Gro., Pres. CC29 79
Elm Gro., Vic.Pk. M35 100
Elm Hall Dr. U34 114
Elm House Mews X35 116
Elm Park Rd. L29 71
Elm Rd. N., Birk. L36 110
Elm Rd., Ains. o 7 9
Elm Rd., Birk. L36 110
Elm Rd., Boot. N26 54
Elm Rd., Hay. MM25 66
Elizabeth Rd.
Elm Rd., Higher T. M35 110
Elm Rd., Kirkby V23 43
Elm Rd., Liver. R28 74
Elm Rd., Pen. G38 124
Elm Rd., Thatto Heath EE29 80
Elm Rd., Will. N45 147
Elm Rd., Woodhey O38 127
Elm St., Boot. P27 55
Elm St., Know. AA32 99
Elm Ter. C33 88
Elm Vale S31 95
Elmar Rd. T36 114
Elmbank Rd. T34 114
Elmbank St. M31 92
Elmdale Clo. J16 19
Elmdale Rd. R27 56
Elmdene Ct. F36 107
Elmfield Clo. FF29 81
Elmfield Rd., Liver. R26 56
Elmham Cres. T25 57
Elmore Av. M38 126
Elmore Clo. Q30 73
Stanfield Av.
Elms Rd., Beb. O38 127
Elms Rd., Sefton S22 41
Elms, The, Liver. R35 113
Elms, The, Mag. S19 28
Alexander Rd.
Elmsby St. NN22 51
Elmsdale Rd. U34 114
Elmsfield Clo. X34 116
Elmsfield Pk. T18 153
Elmsfield Rd. O22 39
Elmshouse Rd. T31 96
Elmsley Rd. T35 114
Elmswood Av. EE32 101
Elmswood Ct. T35 114
Elmswood Gro. X31 98
Elmswood Rd., Liver. T36 114
Elmswood Rd., Wall. M31 92
Elmswood Rd., Wirr. M35 110
Elmtree Clo. V29 76
Elmure Av. M38 126
Elmwood Av., Liver. O22 39
Elmwood Av., Wigan NN24 51
Elmwood Dr. G40 139
Elphin Grn. R28 74
Elric Wk. W23 43
Elsie Rd. R30 74
Elsinore Hts. AA37 133
Elsmere Av. S35 113
Elson Rd. J16 19
Elstead Av. LL23 50
Elstead Rd., Kirkby V24 43
Elstead Rd., Liver. T27 57
Elstree Rd. S31 95
Elswick Rd. Q 3 2
Elswick St. Q35 112
Elsworth Clo. J17 19
Eltham Av. O24 39
Eltham Clo. H36 108
Eltham Clo. JJ35 121
Eltham Grn. H36 108
Eltham St. S32 95
Elton Av., Crosby M23 38
Elton Av., Neth. Q23 40
Elton Clo. M43 148
Ince Av.
Elton Dr. O40 142
Elton Head Rd. EE30 80
Elton St. Q28 73
Elvington Rd. L19 25
Elworth Av. GG34 120
Elworthy Av. Z36 117
Elwy St. R34 113
Elwyn Dr. Z37 133
Elwyn Rd. D32 88
Ely Av. F33 89
Ely Clo. Q24 40
Embledon St. R33 95
Emerald Clo. R23 41
Emery St. Q28 73
Emily St. EE29 80
Emley St., Liver. O28 72
Emlyn St., St.H. HH28 82
Emmanuel Rd. Q 4 6
Emmerson St. Q33 94
Vickers St.
Emmett St. GG28 81
Empire Rd. O26 54
Empire St. R31 95
Empress Rd., Anf. S30 74
Empress Rd., Birk. M31 92
Empress Rd., Pres. R32 95
Emstrey Wk. V24 43
Endbourne Rd. R26 56
Endbutt La. N23 39
Enderby Av. HH26 64
Endfield Pk. U37 130
Endmoor Rd. Y30 77
Endsleigh Rd., Liver. T31 96
Endsleigh Rd., Sefton L24 38
Eneaby Clo. J34 109
Enfield Av. N23 39
Enfield Rd. U32 96
Enfield St. FF28 81
Enfield Ter. L35 110
Engine La. M17 20
Enid St. Q34 112
Ennerdale Av., Lyd. T20 29
Ennerdale Av., St.H. GG25 63
Ennerdale Av., Wigan NN22 51
Ennerdale Av., Wirr. Q43 148
Ennerdale Clo., Formby J15 15
Ennerdale Clo., Kirkby V22 43
Ennerdale Dr., Lith. P25 55
Ennerdale Dr., Orm. U15 153
Ennerdale Rd., W. Kirby K36 109
Ennerdale Rd., Wall. K29 70
Ennerdale Rd., Formby J15 15
Ennerdale St. P31 94
Ennis Rd. W30 76
Ennisdale Dr. C35 106
Ennismore Rd., Liver. T31 96
Ennismore Rd., Sefton M22 38
Ensor St. O28 72
Enstone Av. O24 39
Enstone Rd. X38 132
Enswith Rd. U34 114
Epping Av. GG31 102
Epping Clo. EE32 101
Railton Av.
Epping Gro. U34 114
Epsom Clo. T24 42
Epsom St., Liver. P30 73
Latimer St.
Epsom St., St.H. JJ27 64
Epsom Way P30 73
Goodwood St.
Epstein Ct. R31 95
Coleridge St.
Epwith Clo. MM30 84
Epworth St. Q32 94
Erfurt Av. O39 127
Eric Gro. L31 92
Eric Rd. L31 92
Eric St. HH36 121
Eridge St. R35 113

Erl St. R26 56
Erradale Cres. LL20 37
Kirkstile Cres.
Errington St. O30 72
Errol St. R35 113
Erskine M34 110
Erskine Clo. JJ26 64
Erskine Rd. L31 92
Erskine St. Q32 94
Erylmore Rd. U36 114
Escolme Dr. F35 107
Escombe Dr. G35 108
Escor Rd. X34 116
Eshe Rd. M23 38
Eshe Rd. N. L22 38
Eshelby Clo. N24 39
Esher Clo. J34 109
Esher Ct. J34 109
Esher Rd., Liver. S31 95
Esher Rd., Wirr. O37 127
Esk St. O29 72
Eskburn Rd. T30 75
Eskdale Av., Beb. Q42 143
Eskdale Av., More. F32 89
Eskdale Av., St.H. GG25 63
Eskdale Dr., Formby J16 19
Eskdale Dr., Moss S. T20 29
Eskdale Rd., Liver. R26 56
Eskdale Rd., Wigan NN22 51
Eslington St. U37 130
Esmond St. R30 74
Esonwood Rd. BB31 100
Espin St. Q28 73
Esplanade, Sefton N 6 5
Esplanade, Wirr. O36 111
Esplen Av. N22 39
Essex Rd., Know. AA31 99
Essex Rd., Sefton O 9 9
Essex Rd., Wirr. C35 106
Essex St. GG28 81
Essex Way, Boot. P27 55
Esthwaite Av. HH25 64
Ethel Rd. M31 92
Ethelbert Rd. C33 88
Etna St. R31 95
Etna St. T31 96
Eton Dr., Sefton S24 41
Eton Dr., Wirr. K42 140
Eton St. Q28 73
Etruscan Rd. U31 96
Ettington Dr. L10 12
Ettington Rd. R29 74
Ettrick Clo. V22 43
Eugene Av. HH30 82
Euston Gro. L34 110
Euston St., Kirk. Q28 73
Evans Clo. MM25 66
Evans Rd. B33 87
Evans Rd. Y38 132
Evans St. BB29 79
Evelyn Av. JJ27 64
Evelyn Av., Pres. CC30 79
Evelyn Rd. M31 92
Evelyn St. JJ27 64
Evelyn Av.
Evenite Rd. DD37 135
Everard Rd. P 7 10
Evered Av. R27 56
Everest Rd., Sefton M23 38
Everest Rd., Wirr. M36 110
Evergreen Clo. F34 107
Eversleigh Clo. H34 108
Eversley DD36 135
Eversley Dr. O39 127
Eversley Pk. L35 110
Eversley St., Liver. R34 113
Eversley St., Wind. R33 95
Everton Brow Q31 94
Everton Gro. HH26 64
Everton Rd., Liver. Q31 94
Everton Rd., Sefton O 7 9
Everton St. LL22 50
Everton Ter. Q31 94
Everton Valley Q29 73
Everton Vw. Q28 72
Every St. R31 95
Evesham Clo. W36 115
Evesham Rd., Liver. S28 74
Evesham Rd., Wirr. K30 70
Ewart Rd., Know. X33 98
Ewart Rd., Sea. N25 54
Exchange Pl. EE31 101
Exchange S.E. O32 94
Exchange S.W. P32 94

Exchange St. GG27 63
Exe Gro. R33 95
Exeley CC32 100
Exeter Clo. T24 42
Exeter Rd. M30 71
Exeter Rd. P28 73
Exeter St. EE27 62
Exford Rd. V29 76
Exit Rd. AA38 133
Exmoor Clo., Sefton R 2 3
Exmoor Clo., Wirr. G38 124
Exmouth Gdns., Wirr. M34 110
Exmouth St. M34 110
Exmouth Way, St.H. MM30 84
Extension Vw. HH29 82
Eyes St. Q30 73

Factory La. HH35 120
Factory Row FF28 81
Fair Vw. N35 111
Fair Way, Know. AA31 99
Fairacre Rd. U37 130
Fairacres Rd., L.Beb. N39 127
Fairash Clo. J33 91
Fairbairn Rd. N24 39
Fairbank St. T33 96
Fairbeech Ct. J33 91
Fairbeech Ms. J33 91
Fairburn Clo. JJ35 121
Fairburn Rd. T30 75
Fairclough Cres. KK26 65
Fairclough La. L35 110
Fairclough Rd., Pres. DD31 101
Fairclough Rd., Roby Y30 77
Fairclough St., Earls. NN27 66
Fairclough St., Newt. MM30 84
Fairfax Pl. S28 74
Fairfax Rd., Beb. N35 111
Fairfax Rd., Liver. T28 75
Fairfax Rd., Wall. N32 93
Fairfield N23 39
Fairfield Av. X32 98
Fairfield Clo., Know. X32 98
Fairfield Clo., Liver. X34 116
Fairfield Cres. J33 89
Digg La.
Fairfield Cres. S31 95
Fairfield Dr., Know. X32 98
Fairfield Dr., Wirr. D35 106
Fairfield Rd., Halton GG26 120
Fairfield Rd., Sefton M10 12
Fairfield Rd., St.H. EE26 62
Fairfield Rd., Wirr. N36 111
Fairfield St. T31 96
Fairford Cres. U31 96
Fairford Rd. U31 96
Fairhaven Dr. P42 143
Fairhaven Rd., Sefton R 3 3
Fairhaven Rd., Widnes HH36 121
Fairhaven Rd., Wirr. N36 111
Fairhead Clo. U29 75
Fairholme Av., Elles. J44 145
Fairholme Av., Pres. CC30 79
Fairholme Av., Wigan NN23 51
Fairholme Rd. N23 39
Fairhurst Ter., Know. CC30 79
Scotchbarn La.
Fairlawn Clo. O42 142
Fairleaf Clo. J33 91
Fairleaf Way J33 91
Fairlie Cres. P25 55
Fairlie Dr. EE32 101
Fairmead Rd., Liver. T28 75
Fairmead Rd., Wirr. G32 90
Fairoak Clo. J34 109
Fairoak Ms. J34 109
Fairthorne Wk. X23 44
Fairtree Clo. J33 91
Fairview Av. HH22 49
Fairview
Fairview Clo., Wigan NN23 51
Fairview Clo., Wirr. L36 110
Fairview Rd. L35 110
Fairview Way G39 124
Fairview, Bill. HH22 49
Fairway Cres. P39 128
Fairway N. P39 128
Fairway S. P39 128
Fairway, S.Port P 4 6
Fairway, St.H. EE26 62
Fairway, The V31 97
Fairways M22 38
Fairways Clo. X37 132

Fairways Dr. S45 149
Fairways, The, Wool. Y37 132
Fairy St. Q30 73
Falcon Hey U26 57
Falcon Rd. M35 110
Falcondale Rd. QQ30 86
Falconer St. O26 54
Falconhall Rd. T27 57
Falkland Dr. LL23 50
Falkland Rd., Sefton P 7 10
Falkland Rd., Wirr. M31 92
Falkland St., More. K33 91
Falklands App. T28 75
Falkner Pl. R33 95
Falkner Sq. R33 95
Falkner St. S. R33 95
Falkner St., Edge H. R33 95
Falkner St., Liver. Q32 94
Fallow Clo. HH31 103
Fallow Field W23 43
Fallowfield Rd. T34 114
Falmouth St. V26 58
Falstaff St. P29 73
Falstone Clo. LL19 37
Melrose Dr.
Falstone Rd. X23 44
Far Meadow La. F38 123
Far Moss Rd. L22 38
Faraday Rd. X25 59
Faraday St. R30 74
Farefield Av. PP24 52
Fareham Rd. S33 95
Faringdon Clo. X38 132
Faringdon Rd. QQ30 86
Farley Av. P40 143
Farlow Rd. N36 111
Farm Clo. F35 107
Farm Clo., Sefton R 5 7
Farm Clo., St.H. HH31 103
Farm Rd., St.H. HH31 103
Farm Rd., Wirr. J36 109
Farm Vw. O24 39
Farm Way PP28 85
Farmdale Clo. U36 114
Farmdale Dr. T20 29
Farmer Pl. Q25 55
Farmers La. NN30 84
Farmside G31 90
Farmwood Av. J33 91
Farnborough Rd. N 9 9
Farndale GG34 120
Farndale Gro. OO24 52
Farndon Av., St.H. GG31 102
Farndon Av., Wirr. K30 70
Farndon Dr. D35 106
Farndon Way K35 109
Farnworth Av. G31 90
Farnworth Clo. GG35 120
Farnworth Rd., Warr. JJ35 121
Farnworth St. GG27 63
Pocket Nook St.
Farnworth St., Liver. R31 95
Farnworth St., Widnes GG35 120
Farr Hall Dr. G41 139
Farr Hall Rd. G41 139
Farrell Clo. U23 42
Farrier Rd. X24 44
Farriers Way Q25 55
Farringdon Clo. FF30 81
Fatherside Dr. P23 40
Faulkner Gdns. M10 12
Faulkners Clo. M10 12
Faversham Rd. T27 57
Fawcett Rd. S19 28
Fawley Rd., Liver. V36 115
Fawley Rd., St.H. FF32 102
Fazakerley Rd., Know. CC31 100
Fazakerley Rd., Liver. R27 56
Fazakerley St. O32 93
Fearney Way OO28 85
Fearnley Rd. M34 110
Fearnside St. S33 95
Feather La. G41 139
Fedora St. R31 95
Feeny St. GG32 102
Feilden Rd. O39 127
Feisted Av., Know. Y36 116
Mackets La.
Felbeech Clo. J33 91
Felicity Gro. F32 89
Fell Gro. GG25 63
Fell St. N32 93
Fell St. R32 95
Fell Vw. S 2 3
Felltor Clo. W35 115

Name	Ref	Pg	Name	Ref	Pg	Name	Ref	Pg
Felmersham Av.	T27	57	Fieldside Rd.	N36	111	Flawn Rd.	T29	75
Felspar Rd.	W25	58	Fieldton Rd.	U27	57	Flaxfield Rd.	L15	16
Felsted Dr.	T24	42	Fieldway Ct.	M33	92	Flaxhill	F32	89
Felton Clo.	E32	89	Fieldway, Beb.	M37	126	Fleck La.	C36	106
Felton Grn.	T31	96	Fieldway, C. Thornton	R45	149	Fleet La., Know.	KK28	78
Feltree Av.	J33	91	Fieldway, Know.	Z33	99	Fleet La., St.H.	HH27	64
Feltree Clo.	J33	91	Fieldway, Thorn.	J40	140	Fleet St.	P32	94
Feltwell Rd.	R30	74	Fieldway, Wall.	L30	71	Fleetcroft Rd.	H36	108
Feltwood Rd.	W29	26	Fifth Av., Liver.	S25	56	Fleetwood Rd.	P 4	6
Felwood Clo.	J33	91	Fifth Av., Wirr.	H34	108	Fleetwoods La.	P23	40
Fender Ct.	J36	109	Filbert Clo.	W22	43	Fleming Rd.	Y38	132
Fender La.	H32	90	Filton Rd.	X30	77	Flemington Av.	S28	74
Fender View Rd.	H33	90	Finborough Rd.	S28	74	Flemington Rd.	S28	74
Fender Way	H33	90	Finch Av.	DD22	47	Fletcher Av.	N36	111
Fender Way, Pen.	H39	124	Finch Clo.	HH31	103	Fletcher Dr.	U37	130
Fenneys La.	JJ29	82	Finch Dene	W30	76	Fletchers Gro.	T32	96
Peckers Hill Rd.			Finch La., Liver.	W30	76	Flint Clo.	K45	145
Fenton Clo., Speke	Y39	132	Finch La., Speke	AA38	133	Flint Dr.	K45	145
Fenton Clo., St.H.	FF27	63	Finch Lea Dr.	X30	77	Flint Meadow	K45	145
Fenton Grn.	Y40	136	Finch Pl.	Q32	94	Flint St.	P33	94
Fenwick St.	P32	94	Finch Rd.	X30	77	Flora St.	NN24	51
Ferguson Av.	F35	107	Finch Way	W30	76	Florence Av.	G40	139
Ferguson Rd., Liver.	T29	75	Fincham Clo.	X30	77	Florence Nightingale Clo.	Q23	40
Ferguson Rd., Sefton	P24	40	Fincham Grn.	X30	77	Florence Rd., Lith.	Q27	55
Fern Av.	OO28	85	Fincham Rd.	X30	77	Florence Rd., Wall.	M31	92
Fern Bnk.	CC21	33	Fincham Sq.	X30	77	Florence St., Liver.	Q29	73
Fern Gro.	S34	113	Finchdean Clo.	F35	107	Florence St., St.H.	EE29	80
Fern Hey	O22	39	*Beauworth Av.*			Florence St., Wirr.	M34	110
Fernbank Av.	Y32	98	Finchley Rd.	R29	74	Florentine Rd.	U31	96
Fernbank La.	G33	90	Findley Dr.	G31	90	Florida Ct.	U37	130
Fernbrook Clo.	J35	109	Findon Rd.	W25	58	Flowermead Clo.	D32	88
Ferndale Av.	L31	92	Fine Janes Way	R 5	7	Flukers Brook La.	X28	77
Ferndale Av., Frank.	E36	107	Fingall Rd.	U34	114	Folds La.	GG25	63
Ferndale Clo.	JJ33	103	Finger House La.	HH32	103	Folds Rd.	JJ26	64
Ferndale Rd., Liver.	T34	114	Finland Rd.	T33	96	Foley St.	Q29	73
Ferndale Rd., Sefton	M24	38	Finlay Clo.	NN28	84	Folkstone Rd.	Q 7	10
Ferndale Rd., Wirr.	B33	87	Finlay St.	S31	95	Folly La.	K31	91
Fernhill Av.	Q27	55	Finney Gro.	MM26	66	Fontenoy St.	P31	94
Harrison Dr.			Finstall Rd.	N40	142	Fonthill Clo.	P29	73
Fernhill Clo.	Q27	55	Finvoy Rd.	T29	75	Fonthill Rd.	P29	73
Fernhill Dr.	R34	113	Fiona Wk., Know.	U25	57	Forbes Pl.	Q26	55
Fernhill Gdns.	Q27	55	*Elizabeth Rd.*			Ford Access Rd.	AA39	133
Fernhill Rd.			Fir Av.	AA37	133	Ford By-Pass	CC22	46
Fernhill Mews E.	Q27	55	Fir Clo.	AA37	133	Ford Clo., Boot.	Q25	55
Fernhill Rd.			Fir Gro.	S25	56	Ford Clo., Lith.	O24	39
Fernhill Mews W.	Q27	55	Fir La.	U33	96	Ford Clo., Wirr.	H35	108
Fernhill Rd.			Fir Rd.	N24	39	Ford Dr.	H35	108
Fernhill Rd., Lith.	P26	55	Fir St.	M32	80	Ford La., Sefton	O24	39
Fernhill Rd., Wall.	L29	71	*Howard St.*			Ford La., Wirr.	H34	108
Fernhill Way	Q27	55	Fir St., C.Cross	HH36	121	Ford Lea Rd.	U29	75
Fernhill Rd.			Fir St., Pres.	EE29	80	Ford Lea Way	U29	75
Fernhurst Gate	U15	153	Fir St., Sefton	Q 6	6	Ford Precinct	H33	90
Fernhurst Rd.	V24	43	Fir Tree Clo.	FF21	35	Ford Rd., Pres.	CC30	79
Fernlea Clo.	EE29	80	Fir Tree Dr. N.	V27	58	Ford Rd., Upt.	H35	108
Fernlea Gro.	LL22	50	Fir Tree Dr. S.	V27	58	Ford St.	P31	94
Fernlea Rd.	H41	139	Fir Tree La., Newt.	NN29	84	Ford Vw.	O23	39
Fernley Rd.	O 6	5	Fir Tree La., Orm.	U15	153	Ford Way	H35	108
Ferns Clo.	F40	138	Fir Way	H42	139	Fordcombe Rd.	Y35	116
Ferns Rd.	M38	126	Firdale Rd.	R27	56	Fordham Clo.	Q 7	10
Fernwood Rd.	T35	114	Fire Station Rd.	CC30	79	Fordham St.	Q29	73
Ferny Brow Rd.	H35	108	Firs Av.	N39	127	Fordhill Vw.	G33	90
Ferny Knoll Rd.	CC19	33	Firs Clo.	J14	15	Fordsham Dr.	HH26	64
Fernybrow Gdns.	H35	108	Firs Cres.	J14	15	Fordsham St.	Q28	73
Fernyess La.	N45	147	Firs La.	T15	153	Forefield La.	N22	39
Ferrey Rd.	U25	57	Firs Link	J15	15	Forest Clo.	C32	88
Ferry By-Pass	O37	127	Firshaw Rd.	C32	88	Forest Ct.	K34	109
Ferry Rd.	R41	150	First Av., Birk.	J34	109	Forest Dr.	Y31	98
Ferry View Rd.	N32	93	First Av., Crosby	M23	38	Forest Grn.	U29	75
Ferryside La.	S 2	3	First Av., H.V.	S25	56	Forest Gro.	CC29	79
Festival Rd.	DD22	47	First Av., R.Hill	DD31	101	Forest Mead	DD28	80
Ffrancon Dr.	N37	127	Firthland Way	JJ28	82	Forest Rd., Gt.M.	C32	88
Fiddlers Ferry Rd.	HH36	121	Firwood Gro.	NN24	51	Forest Rd., Hes.	H40	139
Fidler St.	EE28	80	Fisher Av.	BB32	100	Forest Rd., Ox.	K34	109
Field Av.	O25	54	Fisher Dr.	Q 5	6	Forest Rd., Sefton	P 6	6
Field Clo., St.H.	HH31	103	Fisher Pl.	BB32	100	Forest Rd., St.H.	GG31	102
Field Clo., Wirr.	O37	127	Fisher St., Liver.	P34	112	Forfar Rd.	S30	74
Field Fare Clo.	X34	116	Fisher St., St.H.	JJ29	82	Forge St.	P29	73
Field Hey La.	O44	147	Fishermans Clo.	K14	16	Forlawn	U29	75
Field La., Faza.	U25	57	Fishers La.	G39	124	Formby Av.	EE28	80
Field La., Lith.	O25	54	Fishguard Clo.	Q31	94	Formby By-Pass	L17	20
Field Rd., St.H.	HH31	103	*Breck Rd.*			Formby Flds.	L16	20
Field Rd., Wall.	L29	71	Fishpond Rd.	DD31	101	Formby La., L.Alt.	L16	20
Field St., Asht.	MM22	51	Fiske Gdns.	HH30	82	Formby La., Orm.	T15	153
Field St., Liver.	Q31	94	Fistal Dr.	DD26	62	Formby St., Liver.	O31	93
Field Vw.	O24	39	Fitzclarence Way	Q31	94	Formby St., Sefton	K16	19
Field Way, Hoy.	D33	88	Fitzgerald Rd.	U31	96	Formosa Dr.	T25	57
Field Way, Pres.	EE30	80	Fitzroy Way	R31	95	Formosa Rd.	T25	57
Field Way, Roby	V33	97	Five Ways	DD27	62	Formosa Way	T25	57
Field Way, Sefton	T21	29	Flag La.	K45	145	Fornals Green La.	D33	88
Field Way, St.H.	HH36	121	Flail Clo.	F35	107	Forres Gro.	LL23	50
Field Wk.	O22	39	*The Scythes*			Forrest St.	P33	94
Fieldgate	DD37	135	Flat La.	K35	109	Forrester Av.	EE29	80
Fielding St.	R31	95	Flatfield Way	T20	29	Forshaw Av.	EE29	80
Fieldsend	Z33	99	Flatmans La.	Q16	22	Forshaws La.	MM29	84
			Flavian Gdns.	HH30	82			

Street	Grid	Page
Forsythia Clo.	S27	56
Fort Rd.	N26	54
Fort St.	M29	71
Forthlin Rd.	V36	115
Forwood Rd.	P41	143
Foscote Rd.	X23	44
Foster Rd., Sefton	J16	19
Foster St., Halton	GG36	120
Foster St., Liver.	P29	73
Fosters Gro.	JJ26	64
Fosters Rd., St.H.	JJ26	64
Foul La.	R 6	7
Foundry La., Widnes	DD38	135
Foundry La., Wigan	LL19	37
Foundry St., Newt.	NN27	66
Foundry St., St.H.	GG27	63
Salisbury St.		
Fountain Ct.	L22	38
Fountain Rd., Bower	Y27	59
Fountain Rd., New B.	L29	71
Fountain St.	M35	110
Fountain St.	EE30	80
Edge St.		
Fountains Av.	MM25	66
Fountains Clo.	Q29	73
Fountains Rd.	P29	73
Fountains Way	L16	20
Four Acre La.	GG31	102
Fouracre Dr.	O23	39
Fouracres	R21	28
Fourth Av., Ain.	S25	56
Fourth Av., Ford	H34	108
Fourways Clo.	Y33	98
Fowell Rd.	L29	71
Fowlor Clo.	S32	95
Stanier Way		
Fox Hey Rd.	K31	91
Fox House La.	T21	29
Fox Pl.	GG27	63
Fox St.	Q31	94
Fox St., Birk.	M34	110
Foxcote	DD36	119
Foxcover Rd.	J41	140
Foxcovers Clo.	O39	127
Foxcovers Rd.	O39	127
Foxdale Clo., Sefton	Q 7	10
Foxdale Clo., Wirr.	L34	110
Foxdale Rd.	T34	114
Foxfield Rd.	C33	88
Foxglove Rd.	K33	91
Foxhill Clo.	J15	15
Foxhill Clo., Liver.	R34	113
Foxhill La.	Z36	117
Foxs Bank Cotts.	CC34	118
Foxs Bank La.	CC32	100
Foxs Bnk.	CC34	118
Foxshaw Clo.	BB32	100
Foxwood	W29	76
Foxwood Clo.	D35	106
Foy St.	NN23	51
Frailey Clo.	M11	12
Frampton Rd.	S28	78
Francis Av., Birk.	L34	110
Francis Av., Moreton	F33	89
Francis Clo., Halton	EE37	135
Francis Clo., R.Hill	EE31	101
Francis St.	JJ29	82
Francis Way	V33	97
Frank St.	HH36	121
Frankby Av.	L31	92
Frankby Grn.	E36	107
Frankby Gro.	G35	108
Frankby Rd., Hoy.	C33	88
Frankby Rd., Liver.	R29	74
Frankby Rd., W.Kirby	C35	106
Frankey Clo.	E35	107
Franklin Rd.	H31	90
Franton Wk.	V24	43
Fraser Rd.	LL33	104
Fraser St.	Q32	94
Frawley Av.	OO26	67
Freckleton Rd., Sefton	Q 3	2
Freckleton Rd., St.H.	DD28	80
Freda Av.	HH30	82
Frederick Banting Clo.	O23	40
Frederick Gro.	U33	96
Frederick Lunt Av.	Y27	59
Frederick St., App.	GG36	120
Frederick St., Asht.	NN22	51
Frederick St., Liver.	P33	94
Frederick St., St.H.	JJ29	82
Freehold St.	S31	95
Freeland St.	Q29	73
Walton Rd.		
Freeman St., Edge H.	S33	95
Freeman St., Ham.	N33	93
Freemantle Av.	FF29	81
Freemasons Row	P31	94
Freesia Av.	R27	56
Freme Clo.	U27	57
French St., App.	HH36	121
French St., St.H.	EE28	80
Frenchfield St.	HH31	103
James St.		
Frensham Clo.	J39	125
Dutton Dr.		
Frensham Way	Y37	132
Freshfield Rd., Liver.	T34	114
Freshfield Rd., Sefton	K14	16
Friar St.	FF25	63
Friars Clo.	N39	127
Friars Gate	N34	111
Friars Wk.	L16	20
Friends La.	LL34	152
Frinsted Rd.	U28	75
Frobisher Rd., Elles.	K45	145
Frobisher Rd., Wirr.	H31	90
Frodsham St., Birk.	N35	111
Frogmore Rd.	T31	96
Frome Clo.	F37	123
Frome Way	Y37	132
Frost Dr.	F37	123
Frost St.	S32	95
Fry St.	JJ27	64
Fulbeck	EE36	119
Fulbrook Clo.	N40	142
Fulbrook Rd.	N40	142
Fulmar Gro.	W27	58
Fulshaw Clo.	Y34	116
Fulton Av.	C35	106
Fulton St.	O30	72
Fulwood Av.	P 7	10
Fulwood Dr.	S36	113
Fulwood Pk.	S36	113
Fulwood Rd.	S36	113
Fulwood Way	P23	40
Funchal Av.	J16	19
Furness Av.	K15	16
Furness Av., Formby	FF25	63
Furness Av., W.Derby	V28	76
Greenodd Av.		
Furness Clo.	L11	12
Furness St.	Q29	73
Walton Rd.		
Furze Clo.	F32	89
Furze Way	F32	89
Fylde Rd.	Q 3	2
Gable St.	NN27	66
Gabriel Clo.	G33	90
Gainborough Rd., Wall.	K31	91
Gainford Rd.	X30	77
Gainsborough Av.	R21	28
Gainsborough Rd., Sefton	N 7	9
Gainsborough Rd., Liver.	T33	96
Gainsborough Rd., Wirr.	G34	108
Gale Rd., Know.	Y25	59
Gale Rd., Sefton	P24	40
Gales Cft.	Z34	117
Gallopers La.	J38	125
Galloway Rd.	N24	39
Galloway St.	S33	95
Galston Av.	EE32	101
Galston Clo.	V22	43
Galsworthy Av.	P25	55
Galsworthy Pl.	Q25	55
Galtaes Pk.	N37	127
Galton St.	O31	93
Gambier Ter.	Q33	94
Gamble Av.	FF26	63
Gamlin St.	K33	91
Gamp Rd.	X36	116
Ganneys Meadow Rd.	H36	108
Gannock St.	S32	95
Gantley Av.	HH19	36
Gantley Cres.	HH19	36
Gantley Rd.	HH19	36
Ganton Clo.	GG35	120
Ganworth Clo.	Z40	137
Ganworth Rd.	Z39	133
Garden Ct.	M36	110
Garden Gro.	Y34	116
Garden Hey Rd., Hoy.	E33	89
Garden Hey Rd., More.	C32	88
Garden La., Liver.	S25	56
Garden La., Wirr.	G33	90
Garden Pl.	P27	55
Garden St.	X36	116
Garden Vw., Liver.	V30	76
Leyfield Rd.		
Garden Vw., Sefton	P27	55
Garden Way	P27	55
Garden Wk.	BB30	79
Gardeners Way	EE30	80
Gardens Rd.	O38	127
Gardenside	H31	90
Gardner Av.	P25	55
Gardner Rd., Liver.	T30	75
Gardner Rd., Sefton	L15	16
Gardners Dr.	S31	95
Gardners Row	P31	94
Gareth Av.	GG26	63
Lincoln Cres.		
Garfield Pl.	N33	93
Cleveland St.		
Garfield Ter.	H34	109
Salacre La.		
Garfourth Clo.	V37	131
Garfourth Rd.	V38	131
Garmoyle Rd.	T34	114
Garnet St., St.H.	HH29	82
Garnett Av.	Q29	73
Garnett St., Liver.	T32	96
Garnetts La.	DD39	135
Garrick Av.	E33	89
Garrick Rd.	K37	125
Garrick St.	S33	95
Garrowby Dr.	Y31	98
Garsdale Av.	EE31	101
Garsfield Rd.	S29	74
Garside Av.	RR25	68
Garstang Rd.	Q 3	2
Garston Old Rd.	U37	130
Garston Rd.	U37	130
Garston Way	U38	130
Garswood Av.	DD21	34
Garswood Clo.	G31	90
Garswood Clo.	T19	29
Garswood Clo., Mag.	T19	29
Garswood Cres.	JJ23	49
Garswood Old Rd.	HH24	49
Garswood Rd.	JJ23	49
Garswood Rd.	KK22	50
Garswood St.	NN23	51
Garswood St., Liver.	Q35	112
Garswood St., St.H.	GG27	63
College St.		
Garter Clo.	V27	58
Garth Av.	HH26	64
Markfield Cres.		
Garth Boul.	N37	127
Garth Dr.	U35	114
Garth Rd.	X25	59
Garth Wk., Know.	X25	59
Garth Rd.		
Garth, The	Z31	99
Garthdale Rd.	U35	114
Garthowen Rd.	S32	95
Edge La.		
Gartons La.	HH31	103
Garway	Y35	116
Gascoyne St.	P31	94
Gaskell Rake	Q22	40
Higher End Pk.		
Gaskell St.	HH28	82
Gaskells Brow	MM22	51
Gaskill Rd.	Y39	132
Gatclif Rd.	T29	75
Gateacre Brow	X35	116
Gateacre Park Dr.	W34	115
Gateacre Rise	X35	116
Gateacre Vale Rd.	X35	116
Gates La.	P20	27
Gatley Dr.	T21	29
Gatley Wk.	Z39	133
Gautby Rd.	K32	91
Gavin Rd.	DD37	135
Gawsworth Rd.	PP24	52
Gaybeech Clo.	H33	90
Gayhurst Cres.	U28	75
Gaynor Av.	MM25	66
Kenyons La.		
Gaypine Rd.	H33	90
Gayton Av., H.Beb.	M37	126
Gayton Av., New B.	L29	71
Gayton Clo.	LL19	37
Gayton Farm Rd.	H42	139
Gayton La.	H42	139
Gayton Parkway	J42	140
Gayton Rd.	G42	139
Gaytree Ct.	J33	91
Gaywood Av.	W25	58

Gaywood Clo., Bidston H33 90
Gaywood Clo., Know. W25 58
Gaywood Av.
Gaywood Grn. W25 58
Gellings Rd. X26 59
Geneva Rd., Liver. S31 95
Geneva Rd., Wirr. M32 92
Genista Clo. R27 56
Gentwood Rd. Y31 98
George Dr. N10 13
George Harrison Clo. R31 95
John Lennon Dr.
George Rd. C34 106
George St., Asht. OO23 52
George St., Earls. NN27 66
George St., Ham. N33 93
George St., Liver. P32 94
George St., St.H. GG27 63
Georges Av. EE26 62
Georges Par. O32 93
Georgian Clo., Hale. Z38 133
New Hutte La.
Geraint St. Q34 112
Gerald St. Q31 94
Gerard Av. K30 70
Gerard Gdns. Q32 94
Gerard Rd., W.Kirby B35 105
Gerard Rd., Wall. K30 70
Gerard St. NN23 51
Gerneth Clo. Y39 132
Gerneth Rd. X39 132
Gerosa Av. QQ29 86
Gerrard Rd. JJ22 49
Gerrards La., Know. Z36 117
Gertrude Rd. R30 74
Gertrude St. EE29 80
Geves Gdns. N24 39
Ghyll Gro. GG24 48
Gibbons Av. EE27 62
Gibbons Rd. LL24 50
Gibraltar Row O32 93
Gibson Clo. G39 124
Giddigate La. U22 42
Gidlow Rd. T32 96
Gidlow Rd. S. T32 96
Giffen St. S33 95
Gilbert Clo. N40 142
Dutton Dr.
Gilbert Rd. CC30 79
Gilbert St., Liver. P33 94
Gilead St. R32 95
Gilescroft Av. X23 44
Gilescroft Wk., Know. X23 44
Gilescroft Av.
Gill St. Q32 94
Gillars Grn. DD27 62
Gillars La. CC27 61
Gillmoss Clo. V27 58
Gillmoss La. V26 58
Gills La. H39 124
Gilmans St. R29 74
Gilmour Mt. L35 110
Gilpin Av. T20 29
Gilroy Rd., Liver. R31 95
Gilroy Rd., Wirr. C35 106
Gilwell Av. G33 90
Gilwell Clo. G33 90
Ginnel, The O38 127
Gipsy Gro. W34 115
Gipsy La. W34 115
Girton Av., Asht. MM23 51
Girton Av., Liver. Q28 73
Girtrell Clo. F34 107
Girtrell Rd. F34 107
Girvan Cres. LL23 50
Gisburn Av. PP24 52
Givenchy Clo. W33 97
Glade Rd. Z31 99
Glade, The C32 88
Gladeville Rd. T36 114
Gladstone Av. X33 98
Gladstone Av., Sea. O25 54
Gladstone Rd.
Gladstone Clo. M34 110
Gladstone Hall Rd. O39 127
Gladstone Rd. Q 6 6
Gladstone Rd., Birk. N35 111
Chester Rd.
Gladstone Rd., Elles. K45 145
Gladstone Rd., Gars. V38 131
Gladstone Rd., Sea. N25 54
Gladstone Rd., Som. M32 92
Gladstone Rd., Walt. R27 56
Gladstone St., Birk. M34 110
Craven St.
Gladstone St., Liver. P31 94
Vauxhall Rd.
Gladstone St., St.H. EE27 62
Gladstone St., Wind. R32 95
Gladstone St., Wool. W36 115
Glaidburn Cres. R 2 3
Glaisdale Dr. Q 8 10
Colchester Rd.
Glaisher St. R30 74
Glamis Dr. R 3 3
Glamis Gro. HH29 82
Glamis Rd. S30 74
Glanaber Pk. W29 76
Glasgow St. N36 111
Glasier Rd. F32 89
Glaslyn Way R27 56
Glassonby Cres. U28 75
Glasswood Gdns. H35 108
Glasven Rd. W23 43
Gleadlands LL20 37
Sandstone Rd.
Gleadmere EE36 119
Gleaston Clo. P40 143
Hornby Rd.
Gleave Clo. MM30 84
Gleave Sq. Q31 94
Gleave St. Q33 94
Gleave St. GG27 63
Glebe Av. OO24 52
Glebe Clo. S20 28
Glebe End Q21 27
Glebe Hey Z34 117
Glebe Hey Rd. H35 108
Glebe La. GG34 120
Glebe Rd. K30 70
Glebelands Rd. G33 90
Gleggside C36 106
Glegside Rd. X24 44
Glen Marsh Clo., Liver. V30 76
Glen Park Rd. L29 71
Glen Rd. U32 96
Glen Ronald Dr. F34 107
Glen Tree Clo. F34 107
Glen, The O39 127
Glen, The V35 115
Glenalmond Rd. M31 92
Glenathol Rd. V36 115
Glenavon Rd., Birk. L36 110
Glenavon Rd., Liver. V33 97
Glenbank Clo. R26 56
Glenborough Rd. M31 92
Glenburn Av. Q43 148
Glenby Av. N24 39
Glencairn Rd. T31 96
Glencoe Rd. L30 71
Glenconnor Rd. W32 97
Glencourse Rd. GG34 120
Glencoyne Dr. R 2 3
Glendale Av. OO23 52
Glendale Rd. GG25 63
Folds La.
Glendevon Rd., Huy. Z32 99
Glendevon Rd., Wav. V32 97
Glendower Rd. N24 39
Glendyke Rd. V36 115
Gleneagles Clo. G39 124
Gleneagles Dr., Farn. GG34 120
Gleneagles Dr., Sefton L11 12
Gleneagles Dr., St.H. KK26 65
Gleneagles Rd. V32 97
Glenfield Rd. U34 114
Glengariff St. T29 75
Glenhead Rd., U37 130
Glenholm Rd. S21 28
Glenluce Rd. U37 130
Glenlyon Rd. V33 97
Glenmarsh Clo., Beb. M38 126
Glenmarsh Way L15 16
Glenmore Av. U35 114
Glenmore Rd. L35 110
Glenn Bnk. M24 38
Glenn Pl. FF36 120
Glenpark Dr. R 3 3
Glenrose Rd. X35 116
Glenside V36 115
Glentrees Rd. U29 75
Glenvale Wk. Q31 94
Breck Rd.
Glenville Clo. X35 116
Glenwood Dr. G37 124
Glenwood Dr., Thing. G37 124
Glenwyllin Rd. N24 39
Glinda St. O37 127
Globe Rd. O27 54
Globe St. O29 73
Royal St.
Gloucester Av. QQ25 68
Gloucester Pl. R31 95
Gloucester Rd., Halton GG35 120
Gloucester Rd., Know. AA31 99
Gloucester Rd., Lith. P27 55
Gloucester Rd., Liver. S30 74
Gloucester Rd., S.Port N 6 5
Gloucester Rd., Wirr. K30 70
Gloucester St. HH28 82
Gloucester St., Liver. Q32 94
Glover Pl. O27 54
Glover St., Newt. OO27 67
Glover St., St.H. FF27 63
Glover St., Wirr. M35 110
Glovers Brow V23 43
Glovers La. Q23 40
Glyn Av. Q41 143
Glyn Rd. L31 92
Glynn St. T33 96
Glynne Gro. X33 98
Glynne St. P26 55
Goddison Av. Q29 73
Golborne Rd. OO23 52
Golborne Rd. RR25 68
Golborne Rd., Win. QQ29 86
Golbourne St. PP27 67
Golden Grn. R28 74
Goldfinch Farm Rd. Y39 132
Goldie St. Q29 73
Goldsmith Rd. K36 109
Goldsmith St., Lith. O27 54
Goldsmith Way K36 109
Golf Links Rd. L36 110
Golf Rd. J14 15
Gondover Av. Q26 55
Gonville Rd. P28 73
Gooch Dr. OO28 85
Goodacre Rd. R25 56
Goodacres Ct. H36 108
Goodakers Meadow H36 108
Childwall Grn.
Goodakers Meadow H36 108
Goodall Pl. Q29 73
Goodall St. Q28 73
Goodban St. JJ29 82
Goodison Rd. Q28 73
Goodlass Rd. X38 132
Goodleigh Pl. HH30 82
Woolacombe Av.
Goodwin Av. J32 91
Goodwood St. P30 73
Goose Grn., The C32 88
Goostrey Clo. O40 142
Gordon Av., Asht. MM23 51
Gordon Av., Crosby M24 38
Gordon Av., Hay. MM25 66
Kenyons La.
Gordon Av., Lyd. S19 28
Gordon Av., S.Port P 4 6
Gordon Av., Upt. G35 108
Gordon Av., Wirr. Q41 143
Gordon Ct. F35 107
Pickerill Rd.
Gordon Dr., Gars. U37 130
Gordon Dr., Pres. W31 97
Gordon Pl. U35 114
Gordon Rd., Lith. N26 54
Gordon Rd., Wall. L29 71
Gordon St., Birk. M34 110
Gordon St., Liver. T33 96
Gordon St., Sefton O 5 5
Gore St. Q34 112
Goree Piazza P32 94
Gores La., Sefton K14 16
Gores La., St.H. FF22 48
Gores Rd. Y24 44
Gorse Av. V28 76
Gorse Cres. M32 92
Gorse Fld. L14 16
Gorse La. D36 106
Gorse Rd. C33 88
Gorse Way J15 15
Gorsebank Rd. T34 114
Gorseburn Rd. T30 75
Gorsedale Rd., Liver. U35 114
Gorsedale Rd., Wirr. M32 92
Gorsefield EE29 80
Nursery Rd.
Gorsefield Av., Sefton O22 39
Gorsefield Av., Wirr. P42 143
Gorsefield Clo. P42 143
Gorsefield Rd. M35 110

Gorsefield, EE29 80
South St.
Gorsehill Rd., Wall. L29 71
Gorsehill Rd., Wirr. H40 139
Gorseville Rd. N38 127
Gorsewood Clo. Y34 116
Gorsewood Gro. X34 116
Gorsewood Rd.
Gorsewood Rd. X34 116
Gorsey Av. P23 40
Gorsey Brow HH22 49
Gorsey Brow Clo. HH22 49
Gorsey Cop Rd. X34 116
Gorsey Cop Way X34 116
Gorsey Croft CC29 79
Gorsey La. O24 39
Gorsey La., Burt. KK30 83
Gorsey La., C.Face JJ31 103
Gorsey La., C.Wood JJ36 121
Gorsey La., Sefton L20 25
Gorsey La., Som. M32 92
Gorseyville Cres. N38 127
Gorst St. Q29 73
Gort Rd. Z31 99
Gorton Rd. U32 96
Goschen St. T31 96
Goschen St., Anf. Q29 73
Goschen St., Bids. K33 91
Powel St.
Gosford St. Q35 112
Gosforth Rd. Q 5 6
Gossage St. GG36 120
Goswell St. T33 96
Gotham Rd. O40 142
Gothic St. N36 111
Gough Rd. T29 75
Gourley Rd. U32 96
Gourleys La. C36 106
Government Rd. B33 87
Govett Rd. EE29 80
Gower HH31 82
Gower St. HH28 82
Goyt Hey Av. JJ22 49
Graburn Rd. K15 16
Grace Av. U25 57
Grace Rd. R26 56
Grace St. HH29 82
Grace Ter. N33 93
Graces Sq. HH30 82
Gradwell St. P32 94
Grafton Dr., Sefton L10 12
Grafton Dr., Wirr. H35 108
Grafton Rd. L29 71
Grafton St., Clough. L34 110
Grafton St., Dingle P34 112
Grafton St., Newt. NN27 66
Grafton St., St.H. EE27 62
Grafton Wk. C36 106
Graham Clo. EE36 119
Graham Dr. AA37 133
Graham Rd., H.Green EE36 119
Graham Rd., Wirr. B35 105
Graham St. HH27 64
Grahams Rd. Z32 99
Grainger Av., Birk. K36 109
Grainger Av., Lith. Q26 55
Grainger Av., W.Kirby B35 105
Graley Clo. Z38 133
Grammar School La. C36 106
Grampian Av. G33 90
Grampian Rd. T32 96
Grampian Way, Easth. Q42 143
Grampian Way, More. G33 90
Granams Cft. P23 40
Granard Rd. U34 114
Granby Clo. Q 3 2
Granby Cres. O40 142
Granby St. R33 95
Grandison Rd. S28 74
Grange Av., Liver. Y37 132
Grange Av., Sefton Q 5 6
Grange Av., W.Derby W30 76
Grange Av., Wall. L30 71
Grange Clo., Wigan RR26 68
Grange Cr. R44 149
Grange Cross Clo. D36 106
Grange Cross La. D36 106
Grange Dr., H.Green EE36 119
Grange Dr., Hes. G40 139
Grange Dr., Pres. DD29 80
Grange Dr., Thorn. L41 141
Grange Farm Cres. D35 106
Grange La., Formby K14 16
Grange La., Gate. X34 116
Grange Meadow Rd. X34 116
Grange Mt., Birk. L34 110
Grange Mt., Hes. G40 139
Grange Mt., W.Kirby C36 106
Grange Park Rd. EE28 80
Grange Pavement N34 111
Grange Pavillion N34 111
Grange Pk. T21 29
Grange Pl. M34 110
Grange Rd. Q 5 6
Grange Rd. MM22 51
Grange Rd., Ain. R24 41
Grange Rd. E., Birk. M34 110
Grange Rd. E., Higher T. M34 110
Grange Rd. W., Ox. M34 110
Grange Rd., Clough. L34 110
Grange Rd., Hes. G40 139
Grange Rd., Sefton K18 19
Grange Rd., St.H. LL26 65
Grange Rd., W.Kirby B36 105
Grange St. S30 74
Grange Ter. T33 96
Grange Vale O36 111
Grange Valley LL26 65
Grange Way X34 116
Grange Weint X35 116
Grange, The, Hale. Z37 133
Grange, The, Wirr. M31 92
Grangeside X34 116
Granite Ter. AA32 99
Grant Av. T34 114
Grant Clo. X31 98
Grant Rd. H31 90
Grant Rd., Roby W31 97
Grant St., Liver. R32 95
Grant St., St.H. FF27 63
Grantham Clo. G39 124
Grantham Rd. O 8 9
Grantham St. R31 95
Grantham Way R23 41
Grantley Rd. U34 114
Grantley St. NN22 51
Granton Clo. K15 16
Granton Rd. R30 74
Granville Av. S20 28
Granville Clo., Orm. U16 153
Granville Clo., Wirr. K30 70
Granville Dr. R45 149
Granville Park W. U17 153
Granville Pk. U16 153
Granville Rd., Gars. V38 131
Granville Rd., Liver. S33 95
Granville Rd., Sefton M 7 8
Granville St. HH27 64
Granville Ter. J30 70
Grasmere Av., Pres. CC30 79
Grasmere Av., Sefton L19 25
Grasmere Av., St.H. GG25 63
Grasmere Av., Wirr. J34 109
Grasmere Clo. V23 43
Grasmere Clo., St.H. GG25 63
Grasmere Ct. GG25 63
Grasmere Dr., Asht. NN22 51
Grasmere Dr., Sefton Q24 40
Grasmere Dr., Wall. L30 71
Grasmere Fold GG25 63
Grasmere Gdns. N23 39
Grasmere Rd., Formby J15 15
Grasmere Rd., Mag. S20 28
Grasmere St. R30 74
Grass La. F32 89
Grass Wood Rd. H36 108
Grassendale Prom. T38 130
Grassendale Rd. U37 130
Grassington Cres. Y36 116
Grassville Rd. N35 111
Grasswood Gdns. H35 108
Gratrix Rd. P41 143
Gray Av. LL26 65
Gray Gro. Z33 99
Gray St. P26 54
Graylands P38 128
Graylands Pl. S28 74
Graylands Rd. S28 74
Grayling Dr. V27 58
Grays Av. CC30 79
Grayson St. P33 94
Shaws Alley
Graysons Rd. CC21 33
Grayston Av. HH30 82
Greasby Rd., Greas. F35 107
Greasby Rd., Upt. G35 108
Greasby Rd., Wall. L31 92
Greasbyhill Rd. C36 106
Great Crosshall St. P32 94
Great George Pl. Q33 94
Great George Sq. Q33 94
Great George St. Q33 94
Great Georges Rd. M25 53
Great Hey P22 40
Great Homer St. Q30 73
Great Mersey St. P30 73
Great Newton St. Q32 94
Great Richmond St. Q31 94
Greaves St. Q35 112
Grebe Av. DD29 80
Grebe Clo. KK19 37
Grecian St. N25 54
Grecian Ter. Q30 73
Gredington St. R35 113
Greek St. Q32 94
Green Acre Clo., HH31 103
St.H.
Green Acres M24 38
Green Av. L29 71
Green Back L40 141
Green Bank Cres. FF27 63
Green Bnk., Sefton T20 29
Green Croft O22 39
Green Dr. O41 142
Green End Pk. U29 75
Green Hall St. EE27 62
Green Hey Dr. P24 40
Green Heys Dr. T20 29
Green La., Brom. Q41 143
Green La., Child. V34 115
Green La., Crosby M24 38
Green La., Ditton FF36 120
Green La., Eccl. CC26 61
Green La., Ford O24 39
Green La., Formby K14 16
Green La., L.Beb. N38 127
Green La., L.Tran. N35 111
Green La., Leas. H30 69
Green La., Lith. O25 54
Green La., Liver. Q32 94
Green La., N. V34 115
Green La., N.Derby T30 75
Green La., Newt. MM29 84
Green La., Sefton R20 28
Green La., St.H. DD22 47
Green La., W.Green O22 39
Green La., Wall. J30 70
Green La., Wigan HH19 36
Green La., Win. QQ29 86
Green Lane Clo. QQ29 86
Green Lawn N36 111
Green Lawn Gro. N36 111
Green Link R20 28
Green Mt. H34 108
Green Oaks Path HH36 121
Green Park Dr. R20 28
Green Pk. Q22 40
Green Rd., Pres. BB30 79
Green Slate Ct. HH19 36
Green Slate Rd. JJ19 36
Green St. P31 94
Green Way Clo. X31 98
Green Way Sq. X31 98
Green Way, Know. X31 98
Green Way, Pen. G39 124
Green Way, The, Liver. W31 97
Green, The M22 38
Green, The, Beb. P38 128
Green, The, Caldy C37 122
Green, The, Claugh. L35 110
Green, The, Nest. M43 146
Green, The, Wav. V32 97
Green, The, Will. N45 147
Greenacre Clo., H.Cross Y37 132
Greenacre Dr. K41 142
Greenacre Rd., H.Cross Y37 132
Greenback Rd. M35 110
Greenbank Av., Elles. S45 149
Greenbank Av., Sefton S19 28
Greenbank Av., Wigan HH19 36
Greenbank Av., Wirr. L29 71
Greenbank Dr., Liver. T34 114
Greenbank Dr., Pen. G39 124
Greenbank Dr., Sefton N 8 9
Greenbank Dr., Wirr. G39 124
Greenbank La. T35 114
Greenbank Rd., Liver. T34 114
Greenbank Rd., Wirr. B35 105
Greenbank, Lith. N25 54
Greenburn Av. HH24 49
Greencroft Rd. M32 92
Greendale Rd., L.Beb. O38 127
Greendale Rd., Wool. W35 115
Greenend La. HH29 82
Greenfield EE26 62

Greenfield Clo. R 3 2
Marshside Rd.
Greenfield Dr. Z33 99
Greenfield Gro. Z32 99
Greenfield La., Sefton O24 39
Greenfield La., Wirr. F40 138
Greenfield Rd., Elles. S45 149
Greenfield Rd., Liver. U31 96
Greenfield Vw. HH23 49
Greenfield Way L31 92
Greenfield Way, Liver. V36 115
Greenfield Wk., Know. Z32 99
Sandiway
Greenfields Av. P41 143
Greenfields Cres. L41 143
Greenfields Av.
Greenfields Cres. NN23 51
Greenford Rd. M11 12
Greenhall St. FF27 63
Dilloway St.
Greenheath Way G31 90
Greenhey Rd. L31 92
Greenheys Rd., Liver. R34 113
Greenheys Rd., Wirr. F38 123
Greenhill Av. V35 115
Greenhill Clo. U36 114
Greenhill Cres. JJ22 49
Greenhill Rd., Bill. JJ22 49
Greenhill Rd., Liver. U36 114
Greenhill Rd., Liver. V37 131
Greenhow Av. B35 105
Greenlake Rd. U36 114
Greenland St., Know. Z32 99
Greenland St., Liver. P33 94
Greenlea Clo. N38 127
Greenleach Av. GG25 63
Greenleach Ct. HH25 64
Greenleach La. GG25 63
Greenleaf St. S33 95
Greenleigh Rd. U36 114
Greenleas Rd. J30 70
Greenloons Dr. J15 15
Greenloons Wk. J16 19
Greenock St. O31 93
Greenough Av. EE30 80
Brookfield Av.
Greens Bridge La. AA36 117
Greens La., Lyd. S16 23
Greens La., Wigan JJ20 36
Greens Rd. BB32 100
Greenside Q31 94
Greenside Av., Liver. U33 96
Greenside Av., Sefton T24 42
Greenville Clo. N38 127
Greenville Dr. S20 28
Greenville Rd. N38 127
Greenway Rd., App. GG36 120
Greenway Rd., H.Cliff AA39 137
Greenway Rd., Higher T. M35 110
Greenway, Asht. NN23 51
Greenway, Sefton O22 39
Greenway, The, Beb. P39 128
Eastern Av.
Greenway, Upt. G35 108
Greenways HH19 36
Greenwell Rd. LL26 65
Greenwich Rd. R25 56
Greenwood Clo., Know. CC30 79
St. James Rd.
Greenwood Gdns. O 6 5
Greenwood La. M30 71
Greenwood Rd. OO28 85
Greenwood Rd., All. U36 114
Greenwood Rd., Gt.M. D32 88
Greenwood Rd., Wood. H36 108
Gregory Clo. W33 97
Gregory Way W33 97
Gregson Ct. M29 71
Gregson Rd., Gr.Wood HH36 121
Gregson Rd., Pres. BB30 79
Gregson St. Q31 94
Gregson Way Q31 94
Gregsons Av. K14 16
Greig Way Q34 112
Grenfell Rd. T29 75
Grenloe Clo. Z34 117
Grenville Cres. P40 143
Grenville Dr. G39 124
Grenville Rd., Elles. K44 145
Grenville Rd., Wirr. N35 111
Grenville St. S. P33 94
Gresford Av., Liver. T34 114
Gresford Av., Pren. L36 110
Gresford Av., W.Kirby C35 106

Gresford Clo. CC31 100
Gresford Pl. M31 92
Gresham Rd. S32 95
Gresley Clo. S32 95
Crosfield Rd.
Gressingham Rd. V35 115
Greta St. R34 113
Gretton Rd. X30 77
Grey Friars MM23 51
Grey Rd., Asht. NN23 51
Grey Rd., Liver. Q27 55
Grey Rock Wk. R31 95
Grey St. Q33 94
Greyfriars Rd. L10 12
Greyhound Farm Rd. Y39 136
Greystoke Clo. G35 108
Greystone Cres. W31 97
Greystone Rd. T25 57
Greystone Rd., Roby W32 97
Gribble Rd. U25 57
Grice Wk. X23 44
Grierson St. R33 95
Grieve Rd. U25 57
Griffin Av. G33 90
Griffin Clo., Burt. MM30 84
Mitchell Av.
Griffin Clo., Liver. V27 58
Griffin Clo., St.H. CC27 61
Griffin Mews GG35 120
Griffin St. JJ29 82
Peckers Hill Rd.
Griffiths Clo. F35 107
Griffiths Dr. Q 5 6
Griffiths Rd. Z32 99
Griffiths St. Q33 94
Grimley Av. O27 54
Grimshaw St., Boot. O28 72
Grimshaw St., St.H. HH30 82
Grinfield St. R32 95
Grinshall Clo. R34 113
Grinstead Clo. N 8 9
Grinton Cres. Y32 98
Grisedale Rd. Q41 143
Grist St. Q28 73
'Grizedale Av., St.H. GG25 63
Grizedale Rd. Q30 73
Grizedale, H.Green EE36 119
Groes Rd. U37 130
Grogan Sq. P26 55
Gronow Pl. Q26 55
Groome Dr. C36 106
Grosmont Rd. W25 58
Grosvenor Av., Sefton N24 39
Grosvenor Av., Wigan RR25 68
Grosvenor Av., Wirr. B36 105
Grosvenor Clo. N 7 9
Grosvenor Dr. L29 71
Grosvenor Gdns. OO28 85
Grosvenor Pl. L34 110
Grosvenor Rd. KK25 65
Grosvenor Rd., Claugh. L34 110
Grosvenor Rd., Fam. GG35 120
Grosvenor Rd., Hoy. B34 105
Grosvenor Rd., Liver. U38 130
Grosvenor Rd., Mag. S22 41
Grosvenor Rd., Pres. BB30 79
Grosvenor Rd., Sefton M 7 8
Grosvenor Rd., W.Park EE28 80
Grosvenor Rd., Wall. L29 71
Grosvenor Rd., Wav. S33 95
Grosvenor St., Liver. P31 94
Grosvenor St., Wirr. L31 92
Grove Av., Hes. G40 139
Grove Clo. R33 95
Falkner St.
Grove Lands Q33 94
Falkner St.
Grove Mead T20 29
Grove Mount N35 111
Grove Park Av. U27 75
Grove Pk. S34 113
Grove Pk., Sefton Q 5 6
Grove Pl., St.H. FF28 81
Grove Pl., Wirr. B33 87
Grove Rd., Hoy. B33 87
Grove Rd., L.Tran. N36 111
Grove Rd., Liver. S31 95
Grove Rd., Wall. K30 70
Grove Side Q33 94
Falkner St.
Grove Sq. O37 127
Grove St., Asht. NN23 51
Grove St., Beb. O37 127
Grove St., Edge H. R33 95
Grove St., Lith. O27 54

Grove St., S.Port O 6 5
Grove St., St.H. FF27 63
Grove St., Wav. T33 96
Grove Way R33 95
Vine St.
Grove, The Y30 77
Water Park Dr.
Grove, The, Birk. L35 110
Grove, The, L.Beb. O38 127
Grove, The, Liver. T30 75
Grove, The, St.H. EE26 62
Grove, The, Wirr. M32 92
Grove, The, Woodhey N37 127
Grovedale Rd. T34 114
Grovehurst Rd. W31 97
Grovel Av. B33 87
Groveland Av. J30 70
Groveland Rd. J30 70
Groveside B36 105
Grundy St. QQ25 68
Grundy St., Boot. O30 72
Guelph St. R32 95
Guernsey Rd. T31 96
Guernsey Rd., C.Wood JJ35 121
Guest St. Q34 112
Guffitts Clo. D32 88
Guffitts Rake D32 88
Guild Hey Y27 59
Guildford Av. Q24 40
Guildford Rd. O 9 9
Guildford St. M31 92
Guildhall Rd. R26 56
Guilsted Rd. U28 75
Guinea Gdns. N31 93
Guion Gdns. O25 54
Guion Rd. R31 95
Gulls Way F41 138
Gun Site La. FF23 48
Gunn Gro. K45 145
Gunning Av. DD26 62
Gunning Clo. DD26 62
Gurnall St. Q29 73
Guthrie Way R31 95
Gutticar Rd. DD36 119
Gwendoline Clo. H38 124
Gwendoline St. Q34 112
Gwenfern Rd. R31 95
Gwent Clo. R30 74
Gwent St. R34 113
Gwladys St. Q28 73
Gwydir St. R34 113
Gwydrin Rd. V34 115

H.H. Hickman Clo. Q23 40
Hackett Av. P26 55
Hackett Pl. P26 55
Hackins Hey P32 94
Hadassah Gro. S35 113
Hadden Clo., Know. DD31 101
Long View Rd.
Haddon Av. Q26 55
Haddon Dr. G39 124
Haddon Dr., H.Green EE35 119
Haddon Rd. O36 111
Haddon St. MM22 51
Haddon Wk. W27 58
Hadfield Av. C33 88
Hadfield Clo. JJ36 121
Cheryl Dr.
Hadfield Gro. Y35 116
Hadleigh Rd. W24 43
Hadley Av. P41 143
Hadlow La. N45 147
Hadlow Rd. N45 147
Hadstock Av. J16 19
Hadyn Rd. W30 76
Haggerston Rd. R28 74
Hahnemann Rd. Q28 73
Haig Av., Sefton Q 6 6
Haig Av., Wirr. G33 90
Haig Rd. GG36 120
Haigh Cres. S19 28
Haigh Rd. N24 39
Haigh St. Q31 94
Hailbury Av. S23 41
Haileybury Rd. X37 132
Hailsham Rd. T37 130
Halby Rd. R26 56
Halcombe Rd. V29 76
Halcyon Rd. M35 110
Haldane Av. K33 91
Haldane Rd. R28 74
Hale Bank Rd. CC38 134
Hale Dr. Y40 136

Hale Gate Rd. DD39 135
Hale Gro. MM22 51
Hale Rd., Liver. Q28 73
Hale Rd., Speke X39 136
Hale Rd., Wall. M30 71
Hale Rd., Widnes DD39 135
Hale View Rd. AA32 99
Halefield St. FF27 63
Halewood Av. PP24 52
Halewood Clo. X35 116
Halewood Dr. X36 116
Halewood Pl. Y35 116
Halewood Rd. X35 116
Halewood Way Y36 116
Haley Rd. N. LL30 83
Haley Rd. S. LL30 83
Halidon Ct. O27 54
Chaucer St.
Halifax Cres. O22 39
Halifax Rd. M10 12
Halkirk Rd. V37 131
Halkyn Av. S34 113
Halkyn Dr. R30 74
Hall Av. DD36 119
Hall Dr., Kirkby W23 43
Hall Dr., Wirr. F35 107
Hall La. V24 43
Hall La. JJ19 36
Hall La., Bick. Z19 32
Hall La., Carr Ho. N19 26
Hall La., Know. Z32 99
Hall La., Know. EE33 101
Hall La., Lith. R25 56
Hall La., Liver. R32 95
Hall La., Lyd. R17 23
Hall La., Mag. S21 28
Hall La., Newt. NN29 84
Hall La., Pres. BB30 79
Hall La., Sefton W21 30
Hall Rd. E. L22 38
Hall Rd. W. L22 38
Hall Rd., Speke X39 132
Hall Rd., St.H. MM25 66
Hall Rd., Wirr. L37 126
Hall St. GG27 63
Hall St., Sefton P 5 6
Hall St., St.H. GG27 63
Hall St., St.H. HH31 103
Hallam St. S32 95
Hallam Wk. S32 95
Crosfield Rd.
Hallside Clo. U37 130
Halltine Clo. L22 38
Hall Rd. W.
Halltine Clo. L22 38
Hallville Rd. M31 92
Hallville Rd. U34 114
Halsall Clo. N22 39
Halsall Grn. O40 142
Halsall La. K15 16
Halsall Rd., Boot. P26 55
Halsall Rd., Sefton N 9 9
Halsall St. BB29 79
Halsbury Rd. L30 71
Halsey Av. T29 75
Halsey Cres. T29 75
Halsned Av. BB32 100
Halstead Ct. H33 90
Halstead Rd. M32 92
Halstead Rd. Q26 55
Halstead Wk. V24 43
Halton Cres. E35 107
Halton Hey BB32 100
Halton Rd., Sefton S19 28
Halton Rd., Wirr. K30 70
Halton St. MM26 66
Church Rd.
Halton View Rd. HH36 121
Hambledon Dr. F35 107
Hambleton Clo. U27 57
Hambleton Clo., H.Green EE35 119
Hamblett Cres. GG26 63
Hamer St. FF27 63
Hamil Clo. D32 88
Hamilton Clo. H44 144
Hamilton La. N33 93
Hamilton Rd., Liver. Q30 73
Hamilton Rd., St.H. EE26 62
Hamilton Rd., Wigan LL23 50
Hamilton Rd., Wirr. L29 71
Hamilton Sq. N33 93
Hamilton St. N34 111
Hamlet Rd. K30 70
Hamlin Rd. V38 131
Hammersley Av. HH31 103
Hammersley St. HH31 103
Hammill Av. FF26 63
Hammill St. EE26 62
Hammond Rd. Y23 44
Hammond St. HH28 82
Hampden Gro. M35 110
Hampden Rd. M35 110
Hampden St. Q28 73
Hampshire Av. P23 40
Hampson Clo. NN24 51
Hampson St. S30 74
Hampstead Rd. S31 95
Hampstead St. M31 92
Hampton Clo. JJ35 121
Hampton Court Rd. V30 76
Hampton Dr. EE34 119
Hampton Rd., Formby K16 19
Hampton Rd., Sefton P 6 6
Hampton St. Q33 94
Hanbury Rd. S29 74
Handel Clo. R34 113
Handfield Rd. M24 38
Handfield St. R30 74
Handford Av. Q42 143
Hands St. O26 54
Hanford Av. Q26 55
Hankey Dr. Q26 55
Hankin St. P30 73
Hankinson St. U32 96
Hanley Clo. EE36 119
Hanley Rd. EE36 119
Hanmer Rd. U24 42
Hannan Rd. S31 95
Hanns Hall Rd. M45 146
Hanover Clo. K34 109
Hanover St. P32 94
Hans Rd. R28 74
Hanson Pk. K35 109
Hanson Rd. S26 56
Hanwell St. R30 74
Hanworth Clo. W27 58
Hapsford Rd. O26 54
Hapton Mews H33 90
Harbern Clo. V29 76
Winterburn Gro.
Harbord Rd. M24 38
Harbord St. R32 95
Harbord Ter. M24 38
Harborne Dr. N40 142
Harbury Clo. L11 12
Harcourt Av. N31 93
Harcourt St., Liver. P29 73
Harcourt St., Wirr. M33 92
Hard La. EE26 62
Hardie Av. F32 89
Hardie Rd. AA31 99
Harding Av., Beb. N39 127
Harding Av., Wirr. J32 91
Harding St. R33 95
Hardinge Rd. V37 131
Hardman St. Q33 94
Hardnott Rd. Q40 143
Hardshaw St. GG27 63
Hardwick Rd. NN22 51
Hardy St., Gars. V39 131
Hardy St., Liver. Q33 94
Hare Croft W29 76
Harebell St. P29 73
Harefield Grn. Y39 132
Harefield Rd., Speke Y40 136
Haresfinch Rd. GG26 63
Haresfinch Vw. GG26 63
Harewell Rd., N.Green U28 75
Harewood Av. L10 12
Harewood Rd. L29 71
Sudworth Rd.
Hargate Rd. W24 43
Hargrave Av. K35 109
Hargrave Clo. K35 109
Hargrave La. N42 142
Hargreaves Clo. HH36 121
Hargreaves Rd. S35 113
Hargreaves St., Sefton P 6 6
Hargreaves St., St.H. JJ27 64
Harington Grn. J15 15
Harke St. R33 95
Harker St. Q31 94
Harland Grn. Z39 133
Harland Rd. M35 110
Harlech Rd. M23 38
Harlech St. MM22 51
Harlech St., Kirk. Q28 73
Harlech St., Wall. N32 93
Harleston Rd. X23 44
Harleston Wk. X23 44
Harley Av. M37 126
Harley St. R26 56
Harlian Av. F33 89
Harlow Clo. FF29 81
Harlow St. Q35 112
Harlyn Clo. Y38 132
Harold Av. NN22 51
Harold Rd. MM25 66
Harper Rd. R27 56
Harps Cft. P23 40
Harradon Rd. R25 56
Harringay Av., Liver. T34 114
Harrington Av., Wirr. C33 88
Harrington Clo. J15 15
Harrington Rd., Crosby M23 38
Harrington Rd., Formby J14 15
Harrington Rd., Lith. P24 40
Harrington St., Liver. P32 94
Harrington St., St.H. HH29 82
Harris Clo. N40 142
Harris Dr. P26 55
Harris St., Gr.Wood. HH36 121
Harris St., St.H. FF27 63
Harrismith Rd. T26 57
Harrison Dr., Lith. Q27 55
Harrison Dr., Rain. CC21 33
Harrison Dr., St.H. KK26 65
Harrison Dr., Wirr. K29 70
Harrison St. HH29 82
Waterdale Cres.
Harrison St., Widnes DD38 135
Harrock Wood Clo. G38 124
Harrocks Clo. P22 40
Great Hey
Harrod Dr. N 7 9
Harrogate Clo. L43 148
Harrogate Rd.
Harrogate Clo. O37 127
Harrogate Dr. Q30 73
Harrogate Rd., Beb. O37 127
Harrogate Rd., Elles. P43 148
Harrogate Way S 2 3
Harrogate Wk. O37 127
Harrops Cft. Q23 40
Harrow Dr. S24 41
Harrow Gro. P41 143
Harrow Rd., Liver. R30 74
Harrow Rd., Wirr. K31 91
Harrowby Clo. R33 95
Harrowby Rd. S. M35 111
Harrowby Rd.
Harrowby Rd., Birk. M35 110
Harrowby Rd., Lith. N25 54
Harrowby Rd., Som. M31 92
Harrowby St. R33 95
Hart St., Liver. Q32 94
Hart St., Sefton P 6 6
Hartdale Rd., Liver. U35 114
Hartdale Rd., Sefton O22 39
Hartford Clo. K35 109
Harthill Av. U35 114
Harthill Rd. V35 115
Harting Av. L33 92
Hartington Rd., Gars. V38 131
Hartington Rd., Sefton S34 113
Hartington Rd., St.H. EE26 62
Hartington Rd., W.Derby U30 75
Hartington Rd., Wirr. L31 92
Hartismere Rd. M31 92
Hartland Av., Sefton R 2 3
Hartland Rd., Liver. T28 75
Hartley Av. R26 56
Hartley Clo. Q29 73
Hartley Cres. N 8 9
Hartley Gro. EE29 80
Hartley Rd. N 8 9
Hartnup St. Q30 73
Hartopp Rd. X34 116
Hartsbourne Av. X33 98
Hartsbourne Clo. W33 97
Hartsbourne Rd.
Hartsbourne Heights W33 97
Hartsbourne Wk. X33 98
Hartwell St. O26 54
Hartwood Clo. W25 58
Hartwood Rd. S.Dene W25 58
Hartwood Rd., Sefton P 5 6
Hartwood Sq. W25 58
Harty Rd. KK26 65
Harvest La. F32 89
Harvester Way F35 107
Thresher Av.
Harvey Av. F35 107
Harvey Av. MM27 66
Sefton St.

Harvey La. PP24 52
Harvey Rd. L30 71
Harvington Dr. L10 12
Harwood Rd. V38 131
Haselbeech Clo. T27 57
Haselbeech Cres. T27 57
Hasfield Rd. U28 75
Haslemere CC32 100
Haslemere Dr. LL35 152
Haslemere Rd. X34 116
Haslingden Clo. U32 96
Oakhill Pk.
Hassal Rd. O37 127
Hassop Wk. R33 95
Hastie Clo. Z34 117
Hastings Rd., Crosby L24 38
Hastings Rd., Sefton N 8 9
Haswell Dr. X29 77
Haswell St. FF27 63
Volunteer St.
Hatchmere Clo. K35 109
Hatfield Clo. FF29 81
Hatfield Rd., Ains. M10 12
Hatfield Rd., Lith. O27 55
Hathaway R21 28
Hathaway Clo., Gate. X34 116
Hathaway Clo., Wind. R33 95
Hathaway Dr. X34 116
Hathaway Rd. X34 116
Hathaway St. R33 95
Hatherley Av. N24 39
Hatherley St. M32 92
Hatherley St. N35 111
Sidney Gdns.
Hathersage Clo. Z30 78
Hathersage Rd. Z30 78
Hatton Av. Q43 148
Hatton Clo. F40 138
Hatton Gdn. P32 94
Hatton Hill Rd. O24 39
Hattons La. V34 115
Hauxwell Gro. GG26 63
Havannah La. KK27 65
Havelock Clo. FF27 63
Haven Rd. T25 57
Haven Wk. S19 28
Haverston Rd. S31 95
Haverton Precinct NN29 84
Bradlegh Rd.
Haverton Wk. W27 58
Wood Lea
Hawarden Av. M31 92
Hawarden Av., Liver. T34 114
Hawarden Av., Wirr. L34 110
Hawarden Cres. O26 54
Hawdon Ct. S33 95
Hawes Av. HH25 64
Hawes Cres. NN22 51
Hawes Water Clo. V22 43
Haweside St. P 5 6
Haweswater Av. KK26 65
Leigh Rd.
Haweswater Gro. T20 29
Hawgreen Rd. U24 42
Hawick Clo. V22 43
Hawke Grn., Huy. AA33 99
Bradley Cres.
Hawke St. Q32 94
Hawkes Rd. Q27 55
Hawkesworth St. R30 74
Hawkins Rd. K44 145
Hawkins St. R31 95
Hawks Way G41 139
Hawkshead Av. V28 76
Hawkshead Clo. T20 29
Hawkshead Dr. P25 55
Hawkshead Rd. MM30 84
Hawkshead St. P 5 6
Hawksmoor Rd. U25 57
Hawkstone St. R35 113
Hawksworth Clo. L14 16
Hawksworth Dr. L14 16
Haworth Dr. P25 55
Hawthorn Av., LL22 50
Downhill G.
Hawthorn Av., App. GG36 120
Hawthorn Av., War. OO27 67
Hawthorn Clo., Bill. HH22 49
Hawthorn Clo., St.H. KK26 65
Hawthorn Dr. DD27 62
Hawthorn Dr., Newt. D36 106
Hawthorn Gro., Edge H. R32 95
Hawthorn Gro., W.Derby U30 75
Hawthorn Gro., Wall N32 93
Hawthorn La. P41 143
Hawthorn Rd., Pres. CC30 79
Hawthorn Rd., Roby Y32 98
Hawthorn Rd., Will. H44 144
Hawthorn Rd., Will. O44 147
Hawthorne Av. Z38 133
Hawthorne Cres. L16 20
Hawthorne Dr., Pen. G39 124
Hawthorne Gro., Sefton Q 5 6
Hawthorne Rd. P28 73
Hawthorne Rd. HH30 82
Hawthorne Rd., Lith. O25 54
Hawthorne Rd., Wirr. M35 110
Hawthornes, The Y34 116
Haxted Gdns. V38 131
Hay Clo. X34 116
Haydock La. LL26 65
Haydock Park Gdns. NN24 51
Haydock Park Rd. S23 41
Haydock Pl. NN27 66
Wellington St.
Haydock Rd. M30 71
Haydock St., Asht. NN24 51
Haydock St., Earls. NN27 66
Haydock St., St.H. GG27 63
Hayes Av. CC30 79
Hayes Dr. U23 42
Hayes St. EE29 80
Hayfield Pl. H33 90
Hayles Grn. X34 116
Haymans Clo. U29 75
Haymans Grn., Liver. U29 75
Haymans Grn., Sefton T20 29
Haymans Gro. U29 75
Haymans Grn., Liver.
Hazel Av., Kirkby V23 43
Hazel Av., Know. CC31 100
Hazel Gro., Beb. N38 127
Hazel Gro., Crosby N23 39
Hazel Gro., Liver. R26 56
Hazel Gro., Sefton Q 5 6
Hazel Gro., St.H. EE27 62
Hazel Gro., W.Kirby F37 123
Hazel Mews U23 42
Hazel Rd., Hoy. B33 87
Hazel Rd., Know. Z30 78
Hazel Rd., Wigan QQ25 68
Hazel Rd., Wirr. M34 110
Hazeldale Rd. R27 56
Hazeldene Av. L31 92
Hazeldene Av., Thing. H38 124
Hazeldene Way H38 124
Hazeldine MM21 51
Hazelhurst Clo. J16 19
Hazelhurst Gro. OO23 52
Hazelhurst Rd. R29 74
Hazelslack Rd. U28 75
Hazelwood F34 107
Hazleton Rd. V31 97
Head St. Q34 112
Headbolt La. N12 13
Headbolt La., Ains. O11 13
Headbolt La., Kirkby W23 43
Headbourne Clo. W33 97
Headington Rd. F34 107
Headland Clo. C37 122
Headley Clo. FF27 63
Heald St., Gars. V38 131
Healey Clo. Z35 117
Healt St., St.H. MM27 66
Heanor Dr. Q 7 10
Folkstone Rd.
Hearne Rd. EE27 62
Heath Clo., H.Cross W34 115
Heath Clo., Pres. CC29 79
Heath Clo., W.Kirby C37 122
Heath Dr., Hes. G40 139
Heath Dr., Upt. H34 108
Heath Field W23 43
Heath Gate Av. Z40 137
Heath Gro. R45 149
Heath Hay W34 115
Heath La., C.Thornton P44 148
Heath La., Wigan RR26 68
Heath Rd. NN24 51
Heath Rd., Halton FF36 120
Heath Rd., Know. X30 77
Heath Rd., Liver. V37 131
Heath Rd., Wigan OO24 52
Heath Rd., Wirr. N38 127
Heath St., St.H. EE29 80
Heath St., Wigan QQ25 68
Heath Vw. O23 39
Heathbank Av., Egre. K31 91
Heathbank Av., Pen. F37 123
Heathbank Rd. M35 110
Heathcote Clo. S33 95
Timpson St.
Heathcote Rd. Q28 73
Heathcott St. S33 95
Heathdale N39 127
Heather Bnk. M38 126
Heather Brae NN27 66
Heather Brow K33 91
Heather Clo. M12 12
Heather Dene P39 128
Heather Gro. PP23 52
Heather Rd. H40 139
Heather Rd., H.Beb. M38 126
Heather St. Q29 73
Heatherdale Clo. L35 110
Heatherdale Rd., Liver. U35 114
Heatherdale Rd., Wirr. B35 105
Heatherways L14 16
Heathfield Av. FF29 81
Heathfield Clo., Formby L14 16
Heathfield Clo., Orrell P26 55
Heathfield Rd., Ains. N10 13
Heathfield Rd., Beb. N38 127
Heathfield Rd., Crosby M24 38
Heathfield Rd., Liver. U34 114
Heathfield Rd., Sefton T21 29
Heathfield Rd., Wirr. L35 110
Heathfield St. Q32 94
Heathland Rd. R45 149
Heathmoor Av. RR26 68
Heathmoor Rd. F32 89
Heathside F40 138
Heathview Clo. DD38 135
Heathview Rd. DD38 135
Heathwaite Cres. U28 75
Heathway H41 139
Heaton Clo. Z39 133
Hebden Clo. NN22 51
Hebden Rd. U27 57
Hector Pl. P28 73
Hedge Cft. P22 40
Hedgecote, Know. W25 58
Ribblers La.
Hedgefield Rd. X34 116
Hedges La. T29 75
Hedley St. P30 73
Heisby St. HH31 82
Helen Bank Dr. CC21 33
Helen St. NN23 51
Helen St. PP24 52
Helena Rd. JJ29 82
Helena St. N34 111
Helena St., Liver. R32 95
Helena St., Sefton Q27 55
Helford Rd. V26 58
Heliers Rd. U32 96
Hell Nook PP24 52
Helmingham Gro. N35 111
Helmingham Rd. N35 111
Helsby Av. Q43 148
Helsby Rd. R25 56
Helsby St. R32 95
Helsby St., St.H. HH28 82
Helsby Way LL20 37
Helston Av., Know. Z36 117
Helston Av., St.H. HH25 64
Helston Clo. R 2 3
Helston Grn. Know. AA31 99
Lynton Rd.
Helston Rd. V26 58
Helton Clo. K35 109
Hemans St. O27 54
Hemer Ter. O26 54
Hemingford St. M34 110
Hemlock Clo. V27 58
Hempstead Clo. FF29 81
Henderson Clo. F34 107
Henderson Clo., Orm. LL34 152
Henderson Dr. DD21 34
Henderson Rd. AA31 99
Hendon Rd. S31 95
Hendon Wk. F35 107
Haldon Cres.
Henley Av. O25 54
Henley Clo. O40 142
Henley Dr. Q 4 6
Henley Rd. U34 114
Henlow Av. W25 58
Henny St., Liver. P33 94
Henry St., B.Green T32 96
Henry St., C.Wood HH36 121
Henry St., St.H. FF27 63
Henry St., Wirr. N34 111
Henthorn Rd. O37 127
Henthorne St. M34 110

Street	Grid	Page
Herald Clo.	V27	58
Heralds Clo., Widnes.	EE37	135
Herbarth Clo.	Q27	55
Herbert Pl.	N34	111
Henry St.		
Herbert St., Sefton	Q27	55
Herbert St., St.H.	JJ29	82
Herbert St., Warr.	MM30	84
Hawkshead Rd.		
Herberts La.	G41	139
Farr Hall Rd.		
Herculaneum Rd.	Q35	112
Hereford Av., Wigan	QQ25	68
Hereford Av., Wirr.	G34	108
Hereford Clo.	OO24	52
Lincoln Dr.		
Hereford Dr.	Q24	40
Hereford Rd., Liver.	U34	114
Hereford Rd., Sea.	N25	54
Hereford Rd., Sefton	Q 5	6
Heriot Pl.	P30	73
Heriot St.	P30	73
Herman Dr.	FF32	102
Hermes Clo.	Q25	55
Atlantic Way		
Hermes Rd.	U26	57
Hermitage Grn., Newt.	PP28	85
Hermitage Gro.	P25	55
Hermitage Gro., Newt.	PP28	85
Hero St.	P28	73
Heron Ct.	J45	145
Heron Gro.	DD22	47
Heron Rd.	D33	88
Herondale Av.	J33	91
Herondale Ct.	J33	91
Herondale Gdns.	J33	91
Herondale Rd.	U35	114
Heronhall Rd.	T27	57
Herrick St.	T31	96
Herschell St.	Q30	73
Hertford Dr.	M30	71
Hertford Rd.	P28	73
Hertford St.	HH31	82
Hesketh Av.	M36	110
Hesketh Dr.	Q 4	6
Hesketh Dr., Moss S.	T20	29
Hesketh Dr., Wirr.	H40	139
Hesketh Rd.	P 4	6
Hesketh St.	S35	113
Heskin Clo., Know.	DD31	101
Old La.		
Heskin Clo., S.Dene	W25	58
Heskin Clo., Sefton	S19	28
Heskin Rd.	W25	58
Heskin Wk.	W25	58
Hessle Dr.	G41	139
Hester Clo.	K19	24
Heswall Av., St.H.	GG31	102
Heswall Av., Wirr.	M37	126
Heswall Mt.	H38	124
Heswall Rd.	R25	56
Heward Av.	HH30	82
Hewitson Pl.	T30	75
Hewitson Rd.	T30	75
Hewitt Av.	EE27	62
Hewitts La.	Y26	59
Hexham Clo.	EE30	80
Consett Rd.		
Hey Green Rd.	T33	96
Hey Park	Z32	99
Hey Rd., Gate.	Z34	117
Hey Rd., Huy.	Z32	99
Heyburn Rd.	T30	75
Heydale Rd.	U35	114
Heydean Rd.	V36	115
Heydon Clo.	J16	19
Heyes Av.	DD22	47
Heyes Av., Rain.	DD21	34
Heyes Av., Wall.	LL26	65
Heyes Gro.	DD22	47
Heyes Rd.	EE37	135
Heyes St.	R30	74
Heyes, The	X36	116
Heyesmount	EE32	101
Heyfield Park Rd.	R45	149
Heygar Dr.	F35	107
Heygarth Rd.	Q42	143
Heys Av.	P41	143
Heyscroft Rd.	X36	116
Heysham Rd.	Q 5	6
Heysham Rd., Know.	AA35	117
Heysham Rd., Sefton	R24	41
Heysmoor Heights	R34	113
Heysome Clo.	FF23	48
Heythrop Dr.	J41	140
Heyville Rd.	N38	127
Heywood Boul.	H38	124
Heywood Clo.	K15	16
Heywood Rd.	V33	97
Heywoods Clo.	H38	124
Heyworth St.	Q30	73
Hicks Rd., Crosby	N24	39
Hicks Rd., Lith.	O25	54
Hickson Av.	S19	28
High Bank Clo.	J34	109
Cross Hey Av.		
High Oaks Rd.	X36	116
High Park Rd.	R 5	7
High Park St.	Q34	112
High St., Elles.	K45	145
High St., Know.	BB30	79
High St., Liver.	P32	94
High St., Newt.	OO27	67
High St., Wav.	T33	96
High St., Wigan	QQ25	68
High St., Wirr.	Q40	143
High St., Wool.	X36	116
Highacre Rd.	L29	71
Sudworth Rd.		
Higham Sq.	Q31	94
Prince Edwin St.		
Highbank Dr.	V38	131
Highcroft Av.	N38	127
Higher Bebington Rd.	N38	127
Higher Carr La.	P17	22
Higher End Pk.	Q22	40
Higher La.	S25	56
Higher La.	DD21	34
Higher Moss La.	N15	17
Higher Parr St.	GG27	63
Higher Rd.	AA38	133
Highfield	W22	43
Highfield Av.	PP25	67
Highfield Cres., Halton	GG36	120
Highfield Cres., Wirr.	N36	111
Highfield Dr., St.H.	FF23	48
Highfield Dr., Wirr.	F35	107
Highfield Grange Av.	LL20	37
Highfield Gro., Sefton	N22	39
Highfield Gro., Wirr.	N36	111
Highfield La., Warr.	RR29	86
Highfield La., Wigan	RR26	68
Highfield Pk.	T20	29
Highfield Pl., Know.	BB30	79
High St.		
Highfield Rd.	R 3	3
Highfield Rd., Elles.	K45	145
Highfield Rd., Halton	FF36	120
Highfield Rd., Lith.	O25	54
Highfield Rd., Liver.	U31	96
Highfield Rd., Vic.Pk.	Q27	55
Highfield Rd., Wirr.	N36	111
Highfield S.	N37	127
Highfield St., Liver.	P31	94
Highfield St., St.H.	HH29	82
Highfield Vw.	T31	96
Highfields	G41	139
Highfields	BB30	79
West St.		
Highgate Clo.	G40	139
Highgate Rd.	S19	28
Highgate St.	R32	95
Highgreen Rd.	M35	110
Hightor Rd.	W35	115
Highville Rd.	V34	115
Hignett Av.	KK28	83
Hilary Av.	W32	97
Hilary Clo., Halton	JJ35	121
Hilary Clo., Know.	CC29	79
Hilary Clo., Warr.	LL34	152
Hilary Dr.	H34	108
Hilberry Av.	T30	75
Hilbre Av., Hes.	G42	139
Hilbre Av., Wall.	L31	92
Hilbre Clo.	Q 4	6
Hilbre Ct.	B36	105
Hilbre Dr.	Q 4	6
Hilbre Rd.	B36	105
Hilbre St., Liver.	Q32	94
Hilbre St., Wirr.	M33	92
Hilda Rd.	W30	76
Hildebrand Rd.	S29	74
Hilgay Clo.	LL19	37
Hill Bark Rd.	E36	107
Hill Cres.	Q28	73
Hill Crest	T20	29
Hill Crest Av.	AA32	99
Hill Gro.	F33	89
Hill Pl.	FF27	63
Bath St.		
Hill Rd., Liver.	T35	114
Hill Rd., Wirr.	K34	109
Hill School Rd.	DD29	80
Hill St., Gt.Crosby	N23	39
Hill St., Know.	BB30	79
High St.		
Hill St., Liver.	P34	112
Hill St., S.Port	O 5	5
Hill St., St.H.	GG26	63
Hill Top La.	H41	139
Hill Top Rd., St.H.	DD24	47
Hill View Rd.	F37	123
Hill Vw., Halton	FF34	120
Hillam Rd.	J30	70
Hillary Cres.	S20	28
Hillary Dr.	O23	39
Hillary Rd., Liver.	S29	74
Hillary Rd., Wirr.	Q42	143
Hillary Wk.	O23	39
Hillbeck Cres.	LL23	50
Hillbrae Av.	GG25	63
Hillcrest Dr.	F35	107
Hillcrest Rd., Liver.	S28	74
Hillcrest Rd., Sefton	O23	39
Hillcroft Rd., Liver.	W35	115
Hillcroft Rd., Wirr.	M32	92
Hilldale Gro.	B35	105
Hillfield Dr.	G39	124
Hillfield Rd., Wirr.	S45	149
Hillfoot Av.	X38	132
Hillfoot Grn.	X37	132
Hillfoot Rd.	W36	115
Hillhead Rd.	Q28	73
Hillingden Av.	Z37	133
Hillingdon Av.	G40	139
Hillingdon Rd.	U34	114
Hills Moss Rd.	JJ29	82
Hillside Av., Know.	Y30	77
Hillside Av., St.H.	FF26	63
Hillside Av., Warr.	MM28	84
Hillside Clo., Liver.	Q28	73
Hillside Clo., St.H.	HH22	49
Hillside Cres.	Y30	77
Hillside Dr.	X35	116
Hillside Rd., Bids.	J33	91
Hillside Rd., Hes.	H41	139
Hillside Rd., Know.	Z30	78
Hillside Rd., L.Tran.	N35	111
Hillside Rd., Liver.	U34	114
Hillside Rd., Sefton	N 8	9
Hillside Rd., W.Kirby	C36	106
Hillside Rd., Wall.	K31	91
Hillsview Rd.	M11	12
Hilltop Rd., Liver.	V33	97
Hillview Av.	B35	105
Hillview Dr.	H34	108
Hillview Gdns.	W35	115
Hillview, Liver.	T36	114
Hillwood Clo.	N40	142
Hilton Clo.	M34	110
Hilton Ct.	P23	40
Hilton Pav.	M34	110
Hilton St.	OO23	52
Hinchley Grn.	R20	28
Hinckley Rd.	HH26	64
Hind St.	N34	111
Hindburn Av.	T20	29
Hinderton Dr., Hes.	G42	139
Hinderton Dr., Wirr.	D36	106
Hinderton La.	L44	146
Hinderton Rd.	K45	145
Hinderton Rd., Birk.	N34	111
Hindley Beech	R20	28
Hinson St.	N34	111
Hinton St., Liver.	S31	95
Hinton St., Sefton	O26	54
Hobart St., Liver.	Q30	73
Hobart St., St.H.	FF29	81
Hobb La.	U24	42
Hobbs Hey	P22	40
Hoblyn Rd.	K33	91
Hockenhall St.	P32	94
Hockenhull Clo.	O40	142
Inley Clo.		
Hodder Av.	T20	29
Hodder Clo.	GG25	63
Folds La.		
Hodder Pl.	Q30	73
Hodder Rd.	Q30	73
Hodnet Dr.	OO23	52
Hodson Pl.	R31	95
Hodson St.	P31	94
Hogarth St.	O26	54
Seaforth Vale N.		
Hogarth Wk.	P29	73

Hoghton Clo. JJ29 82
Hoghton Rd. JJ29 82
Hoghton St. O 5 5
Hogshill La. K17 19
Holbeck St. R30 74
Holborn Hill N35 111
Holborn Sq. N35 111
Queen St.
Holborn St. R32 95
Holcombe Av. RR25 68
Holcombe Clo. F35 107
Stapleton Rd.
Holden Gro., Liver. R33 95
Holden Rd. E. M24 38
Holden Rd., Know. BB31 100
Holden Ter. M24 38
Holden Rd. E.
Holdsworth St. R32 95
Kensington St.
Holford St. R31 95
Holford Way PP27 67
Holgate O21 26
Holgate Clo. J33 91
Holgate Gdns. J33 91
Holgate Pk. O21 26
Holland Gro. G40 139
Holland Pl. R32 95
Holland Rd., Know. Z38 133
Holland Rd., Liver. Z40 137
Holland Rd., Wirr. M30 71
Holland St. S31 95
Holland Way Z38 133
Holleytree Rd. X35 116
Holliers Clo. S20 28
Hollies Rd. Z37 133
Hollin Hey Clo. HH23 49
Hollingbourne Clo. U27 57
Hollingbourne Rd. U27 57
Hollins Clo. LL23 50
Hillbeck Cres.
Hollins Dr. QQ30 86
Hollins La. PP30 85
Hollins Way DD38 135
Hollow Croft X28 77
Holly Av. N39 127
Holly Av., Newt. OO27 67
Holly Bank Gro. HH27 64
Holly Bank St. HH27 64
Holly Clo., Liver. R27 56
Holly Clo., St.H. DD27 62
Holly Cres. DD22 47
Holly Fold La. CC19 33
Holly Gro., Know. X32 98
Holly Gro., Sefton N26 54
Holly Gro., Wirr. N35 111
Sidney Gdns.
Holly Hey BB32 100
Holly La. BB19 33
Holly Mt. U30 75
Holly Pl. G33 90
Holly Rd., Liver. S32 95
Holly Rd., St.H. JJ26 64
Holly Rd., Wigan RR25 68
Holly St., Liver. Q31 94
Holly St., Sefton P27 55
Hollybank Rd., Liver. T34 114
Hollybank Rd., Wirr. M34 110
Hollydale Rd. U34 114
Hollyfield Rd. Q26 55
Hollymead Clo. X35 116
Hollywood Rd. T35 114
Holm Hey Rd. K36 109
Holm La. K36 109
Holm Rd. DD28 80
Holm View Clo. L35 110
Holman Rd. V38 131
Holmdale Av. R 3 3
Holme Clo. DD29 80
Holme Field Gro., Sefton S20 28
Holme Rd. EE27 62
Holme St. O30 73
Holmefield Av. U37 130
Holmefield Rd. T37 130
Holmes House Av. LL19 37
Holmes St. S33 95
Holmlands Cres. K36 109
Holmlands Dr. K36 109
Holmlands Way K36 109
Holmleigh Rd. X34 116
Holmside Clo. G33 90
Holmside La. K36 109
Holmsway G39 124
Holmville Rd. N38 127
Holmway, L.Beb. N38 127
Holmwood Av. J38 125
Holmwood Clo. J15 15
Holmwood Dr., Sefton J15 15
Holmwood Dr., Wirr. J38 125
Holmwood Gdns. J15 15
Holt Av., St.H. HH23 49
Holt Av., Wirr. G33 90
Holt Coppice U16 153
Holt Cres. HH23 49
Holt Hill N35 111
Holt La., Know. DD31 101
Holt La., Liver. Y34 116
Holt La., St.H. DD30 80
Holt Rd., Liver. S32 95
Holt Rd., Wirr. N35 111
Holt Way V24 43
Holybrook Rd. O 6 5
Holyrood Av. GG35 120
Holywell Clo. H44 144
Home Farm Clo. J36 109
Home Farm La. Y28 77
Home Farm Rd. H36 108
Homefield Gro., Know. Z33 99
Homer Rd. Y27 59
Homerton Rd. S31 95
Homestall Rd. U28 75
Homestead Av. MM26 66
Homestead Av., Sefton R23 41
Homestead Av., St.H. NN26 66
Homestead Ms. B35 105
Homister Clo. AA35 117
Honey Hall Rd. Z38 133
Honey St. EE29 80
Florence St.
Honey St. EE29 80
Emily St.
Honeys Green Clo. V30 76
Honeys Green La. V30 76
Honeysuckle Dr. R27 56
Honister Av. HH25 64
Honiston Av. DD31 101
Honiton Rd. T36 114
Hood Rd. FF36 120
Hood Rd., Wall. M31 92
Hood St., Liver. P32 94
Hood St., Sefton O26 54
Hook St. P30 73
Sumner St.
Hoole Rd. H35 108
Hooton Grn. R44 149
Hooton La. R44 149
Hooton Rd., Liver. R25 56
Hooton Rd., Wirr. O45 147
Hooton Way R44 149
Hope Av. NN27 66
Hope Pl. Q33 94
Hope St., Know. BB30 79
Hope St., Liver. Q33 94
Hope St., Sefton P 5 6
Hope St., St.H. FF27 63
Hope St., Wirr. L29 71
Hope Way Q33 94
Hopfield Rd. G33 90
Hopwood Cres. DD22 47
Hopwood St. P30 73
Horace St. FF27 63
Horatio St. M34 110
Horby St. N34 111
Horn Gro. LL19 37
Horn House La. X25 59
Hornbeam Rd. AA37 133
Hornbeam Rd., Lith. S27 56
Hornby Av. P40 143
Hornby Boulevard O26 54
Hornby Clo. Q27 55
Hornby Cres. HH31 103
Hornby La., Warr. QQ30 86
Hornby Pk. V34 115
Hornby Pl. R26 56
Hornby Rd. O26 54
Hornby Rd. P27 55
Hornby Rd., Liver. Q27 55
Hornby Rd., Sefton R 3 3
Hornby Rd., Wirr. P40 143
Hornby St. N23 39
Hornby St., Lith. O26 54
Seaforth Vale N.
Horne St. R31 95
Hornsey Rd. R29 74
Hornspit La. U29 75
Horny La., Liver. V34 115
Horridge Av. OO26 67
Horringford Rd. T37 130
Horrocks Av. V38 131
Horrocks Clo. Y31 98
Horrocks Rd. Y31 98
Horwood Av. DD31 101
Hoscote Pk. B36 105
Hose Side Rd. K29 70
Hoseside Rd. K30 70
Hoskisson St. M34 110
Hospital Rd. O38 127
Hospital St. GG27 63
Hotel St. NN27 66
Hotham St. Q32 94
Hothfield Rd. M31 92
Hotstock Clo., Know. BB32 100
Greens Rd.
Hough Green Rd. DD36 119
Houghton Cft. EE34 119
Houghton Ct. H35 108
Houghton Rd. H35 108
Houghton St. NN27 66
Houghton St., Halton HH36 121
Houghton St., Know. EE31 101
Victoria St.
Houghton St., Liver. P32 94
Houghton St., Pres. BB30 79
Houghtons La. CC25 61
Houghwood Gra. MM23 51
Hougoumont Av. N24 39
Hougoumont Gro. N24 39
Houlding St. R30 74
Houlston Rd. U24 42
Houlston Wk. U24 42
Howard Av. P41 143
Howard Clo. T20 29
Howard Dr. U37 130
Howard Florey Av. Q23 40
Howard St., St.H. EE29 80
Howard St., Wirr. O31 93
Howards La. CC27 61
Howards Rd. H38 124
Howbeck Clo. K34 109
Howbeck Dr. K34 109
Howbeck Rd. K34 109
Howden Rd. X31 98
Howe St. O28 72
Howell Dr. F35 107
Howells Clo. S20 28
Howson St. N36 111
Hoylake Gro. HH31 103
Hoylake Prom. B33 87
Hoylake Rd., More. F33 89
Hoylake Road Bldgs. J32 91
Hoyle Rd. C33 88
Hubert St. U32 96
Huddlestone Rd. U32 96
Hudson Rd., Sefton S21 28
Hudson Rd., Wirr. H31 90
Hudson St. GG27 63
Higher Parr St.
Hughenden Rd. T30 75
Hughes Av. BB31 100
Hughes Clo. S32 95
Stanier Way
Hughes Dr. Q26 55
Hughes La. L35 110
Hughes La. Q25 55
Hughes St., St.H. HH29 82
Hughestead Gro. U38 130
Hughson St. Q34 112
Hulme St. O 5 5
Hulton Av. CC31 100
Humber Clo. Q29 73
Humber Clo., C.Wood JJ35 121
Humber Cres. HH30 82
Humber St. L32 91
Humphrey St. P26 55
Humphreys Hey O22 39
Huncote Av. HH26 64
Hunslet Rd. R26 56
Hunstanton Clo. H33 90
Hunt Rd. S20 28
Hunt Rd. MM26 66
Hunter St. HH28 82
Alma St.
Hunter St. P32 94
Hunters La. U33 96
Huntingdon Gro. S19 28
Huntley Gro. HH29 82
Huntley Rd. S31 95
Hunts Cross Av. X36 116
Huntsman Wood W29 76
Hurlingham Rd. S28 74
Hurrell Rd. J32 91
Hursley Rd. T27 57
Hurst Bank N37 127
Hurst Park Clo. AA31 99
Hurst Park Dr. AA31 99

Hurst Rd. T21 29
Hurst St. Oak.Pk. U32 96
Hurst St., Edge H. P33 94
Hurstlyn Rd. V36 115
Hursts La. X20 31
Huskisson St. Q33 94
Hutchinson St. R31 95
Hutchinson Wk. R31 95
Hutton St. P30 73
Huxley St. S29 74
Huyton Av. FF26 63
Huyton Church Rd. Z32 99
Huyton Hey Rd. Z32 99
Huyton House Clo. X31 98
Huyton House Rd. X31 98
Huyton La. Z31 99
Hyacinth Clo. MM26 66
Hyde St. M24 38
Hydes Brow DD21 34
Hydro Av. B36 105
Hygeia St. R31 95
Hylton Av. L31 92
Hylton Rd. V37 131
Hyslop St. Q34 112
Hythe Av. P25 55
Hythe Clo. Q 7 10

Ibbotsons La. T35 114
Ibstock Rd. O26 54
Iffley Clo. F34 107
Ikin Clo. J33 91
Ilchester Rd., Egre. M31 92
Ilchester Rd., Liver. W32 97
Ilchester Rd., Wall. K32 91
Ilex Av. QQ30 86
Ilford Av., Crosby M22 38
Ilford Av., Vic.Pk. Q26 55
Ilford Av., Wirr. L32 92
Ilfracombe Rd. HH30 82
Iliad St. Q31 94
Ilkley Av. S 2 3
Ilkley Wk., Know. Y39 132
Ilston Rd. K30 70
Imber Rd. W25 58
Imison St. Q27 55
Imison Way Q27 55
Imperial Av. L30 71
Imrie St. Q28 73
Ince Av., Crosby M22 38
Ince Av., Elles. Q43 148
Ince Av., Lith. O25 54
Ince Av., Liver. R29 74
Ince Clo. K35 109
Ince Cres. J15 15
Ince La. O21 26
Ince Rd. O21 26
Incemore Rd. U36 114
Inchcape Rd., Liver. W32 97
Inchcape Rd., Wirr. J30 70
Index St. Q28 73
Ingestre Av. U37 130
Ingestre Rd. L35 110
Ingham Av. OO28 85
Bradlegh Rd.
Ingham Rd. FF35 120
Ingle Gro. L22 38
Ingleborough Rd. M36 110
Ingleby Rd., Egre. L31 92
Ingleby Rd., L.Beb. O37 127
Ingledene Rd. V34 115
Inglegreen H41 139
Ingleholm Rd. U36 114
Inglemere Rd. N36 111
Inglemoss Dr. DD24 47
Ingleside Ct. M23 38
Ingleton Av. T34 114
Ingleton Clo. F35 107
Ingleton Dr. GG24 48
Dalston Dr.
Ingleton Rd., S.Dene W25 58
Ingleton Rd., Sefton Q 7 10
Inglewood Av. F33 89
Inglewood Rd. DD24 47
Inglis Rd. R25 56
Ingoe Clo. U24 42
Ingoe La. U24 42
Ingrave Rd. S28 ·74
Ingrow Rd. R31 95
Inigo Rd. U31 96
Inley Clo. N40 142
Inman Av. KK28 83
Inman Rd., Sefton O25 54
Inman Rd., Wirr. G34 108
Inner Central Rd. Z38 133
Inner Forum T27 57
Inner South Rd. Z39 133
Inner West Rd. Z38 133
Insall Rd. U32 96
Inskip Rd. R 3 3
Intake La., Bick. Z19 32
Intake La., Sefton Q17 22
Inver Clo. EE34 119
Invincible Clo. Q25 55
Invincible Way V26 58
Inwood Rd. V37 131
Iona Clo. R24 41
Ionic Rd. U31 96
Ionic St. N36 111
Ionic St., Sea. N25 54
Irby Av. L31 92
Irby Rd. R29 74
Irby Rd., Pen. G40 139
Irbymill Hill Rd. F37 123
Irbyside Rd. E36 107
Ireland Rd. LL26 65
Ireland St. HH36 121
Irene Av. HH25 64
Irene Rd. V34 115
Ireton St. Q28 78
Iris Av. K33 91
Irlam Dr. W24 43
Irlam Pl. Q27 54
Irlam Rd. O27 54
Ironside Rd. Y31 98
Irton Rd. Q 5 6
Irvin Av. S 2 3
The Causeway
Irvine Rd. M36 110
Irvine St. R32 95
Irvine Ter. P37 128
Seafield Rd.
Irving St. O 4 5
Irwell Clo. T35 114
Irwell La. T35 114
Irwell St. P32 94
Irwin Av. S 2 3
Irwin Rd. HH29 82
Isaac St. Q35 112
Isabel Gro. T29 75
Island Rd. V38 131
Island Rd. S. V38 131
Islands Brow HH26 64
Islington M23 38
Islington Q32 94
Islington Rd. M22 38
Islington Sq. Q32 94
Islip Clo. F37 123
Ismay Dr. M30 71
Ismay Rd. O25 54
Ismay St. Q28 73
Ivanhoe Rd., Liver. S35 113
Ivanhoe Rd., Sefton M23 38
Ivatt Way S32 95
Ivernia Rd. R28 74
Ivor Rd. M30 71
Ivy Av., Liver. U37 130
Ivy Av., Rain. DD31 100
Ivy Av., Warr. OO28 85
Ivy Av., Wirr. N39 127
Ivy Farm Rd. DD31 101
Ivy La. G32 90
Ivy Leigh T30 75
Ivy Rd. QQ25 68
Ivy St. NN23 51
Ivy St., Sefton P 6 6
Ivy St., Wirr. N34 111
Ivydale Rd., Moss.H. U35 114
Ivydale Rd., Walt. R27 56
Ivydale Rd., Wirr. N35 111
Ivyhurst Clo. T37 130

Jacksfield Way T37 130
Jackson Clo. N37 127
Jackson St., Hay. KK25 65
Sumner St.
Jackson St., Liver. V38 131
Jackson St., St.H. HH27 64
Jackson St., Warr. MM30 84
Jackson St., Wirr. N34 111
Jackson Way EE32 101
Jacob St. Q35 112
Jacqueline Dr. AA31 99
Jamaica St. P33 94
James Clo. X36 116
James Gro. FF28 81
James Holt Av. V24 43
James Pl. Q34 112
James Rd., Liver. X36 116
James Rd., St.H. MM25 66
James Simpson Way Q23 40
James St., Liver. P32 94
James St., Ox. L35 110
James St., St.H. HH31 103
James St., Wall. N32 93
Jamesbrook Clo. L33 92
Jamieson Av. O23 39
Jamieson Rd. T33 96
Jane St. JJ29 82
Janes Brook Rd. P 7 10
Janet St. R32 95
Jarrett Rd. X23 44
Jarrett Wk. X23 44
Jarrow Clo. L35 110
Jasmine Clo. F33 89
Jasmine Clo. Q30 73
Wentworth Dr.
Jasmine Gro. EE37 135
Jason St. Q30 73
Jean Wk., Know. U25 57
Elizabeth Rd.
Jedburgh Dr. V22 43
Jeffreys Cres. X32 98
Jeffreys Dr., Roby X32 98
Jeffreys Dr., Wirr. F34 107
Jellicoe Clo. C38 122
Jenkinson St. Q31 94
Jennet Hey MM22 51
Jericho Clo. S36 113
Jericho Farm Wk. S36 113
Jericho La. S36 113
Jerichoe Farm Clo. S36 113
Jermyn St. R34 113
Jerningham Rd. S27 56
Jerome Gdns. HH29 82
Flavian Gdns.
Jeromes Way Q23 40
Jersey Av. O24 39
Jersey Clo. P27 55
Jersey St., St.H. HH31 103
Jersey St., Wirr. N32 93
Jesmond St. S33 95
Jessamine Rd. N35 111
Jeudwine Clo. X37 132
Joan Av., More. F33 89
Joan Av., Upt. G35 108
Jocelyn Clo. O39 127
Jockey La. K29 70
John Bagot Clo. Q30 73
John Hunter Way Q23 40
John Lennon Dr. R31 95
John St., Wigan QQ25 68
John St., Wirr. N33 93
Johns Av. MM25 66
Johns Rd. K30 70
Johnson Av., Know. BB31 100
Johnson Av., St.H. NN26 66
Johnson Gro. W30 76
Elgar Rd.
Johnson La. JJ36 121
Johnson Rd. K36 109
Johnson St., Liver. P32 94
Johnson St., Sefton O 5 5
Johnson St., St.H. HH27 64
Johnson Wk. S32 95
Stanier Way
Johnston Av. Q26 55
Jones Farm Rd. Y35 116
Jonson Rd. K44 145
Jonville Rd. S25 56
Jordan St. P33 94
Jordon Pl. Q34 112
Joseph Lister Clo. Q23 40
Joseph St., Halton HH36 121
Joseph St., St.H. JJ29 82
Joshua St. Q30 73
Joy La., St.H. JJ32 103
Joy La., Warr. LL31 104
Joy Wk. JJ31 103
Eccles Gro.
Joyce Wk. U25 57
Elizabeth Rd.
Jubilee Av. HH19 36
Jubilee Av., Oak.Pk. V32 97
Jubilee Cres. MM25 66
Jubilee Cres., Beb. O38 127
Jubilee Dr., Liver. R32 95
Jubilee Dr., Sefton R24 41
Jubilee Dr., Wirr. B35 105
Jubilee Rd., Crosby M23 38
Jubilee Rd., Formby J16 19
Jubilee Rd., Lith. O25 54
Tattersall Rd.
Jubilee Way FF36 120

Street	Ref		Street	Ref		Street	Ref
Jubilee Dr., Know.	BB32 100		Kempton Park Rd.	T23 42		Keswick Clo., Ains.	M11 12
Jubits La.	GG33 102		Kempton Rd., Liver.	S33 95		Keswick Clo., Know.	EE36 119
Juddfield St.	KK26 65		Kempton Rd., Wirr.	O37 127		Keswick Clo., Moss S.	T20 29
Judges Dr.	S31 95		Kemsley Rd.	W31 97		Keswick Dr.	P25 55
Judges Way	S31 95		Ken St.	O25 54		Keswick Pl.	J33 91
Judges Dr.			Ken Wright Cres.	HH29 82		Keswick Rd., Liver.	V36 115
Julian Way	FF35 120		Kenbury Clo.	X23 44		Keswick Rd., St.H.	FF26 63
Julie Gro.	W30 76		Kenbury Rd.	X23 44		Keswick Rd., Wirr.	K30 70
Elgar Rd.			Kendal Clo., St.H.	CC20 33		Keswick Way	CC20 33
Juliet Av.	N37 127		Kendal Clo., Wirr.	N38 127		Kettering Rd.	L10 12
Juliet Gdns.	N37 127		Kendal Dr., Know.	DD31 101		Kevbank Rd.	U29 75
Juliet Av.			Kendal Dr., Rain.	CC20 33		Kevelioc Clo.	J39 125
July Rd.	S30 74		Kendal Dr., Sefton	S20 28		*Dutton Dr.*	
July St.	P26 55		Kendal Dr., Wall.	GG25 63		Kew Rd., Birk.	O 7 9
Junction La., St.H.	JJ29 82		Kendal Gro.	NN23 51		Kew Rd., Formby	J16 19
Junction La., Warr.	NN28 84		Kendal Rd., Halton	EE37 135		Kiddman St., Sefton	Q27 55
Junction Rd.	CC21 33		Kendal Rd., Liver.	W33 97		Kilbuck La.	MM2566
June Av.	P41 143		Kendal Rd., Wirr.	L32 92		Kilburn Av., Wigan	002352
June Rd.	S30 74		Kendal St.	N34 111		Kilburn Av., Wirr.	OQ42 143
June St.	P27 55		Kendal Way	L11 12		Kilburn Gro.	FF29 81
Juniper Clo.	F36 107		Kenilworth Clo.	W35 115		Kilburn St.	O26 54
Thorns Dr.			Kenilworth Dr.	G39 124		Kildale Cres.	S20 28
Jupiter Clo.	R30 74		Kenilworth Gdns., Warr.	OO28 85		Kildonan Rd.	T36 114
Jupiter St.	P29 73		Kenilworth Gdns., Wirr.	G34 108		Kilgraston Gdns.	T36 114
Justan Way	DD30 80		Kenilworth Rd.	M23 38		Killarney Gro.	L31 92
Amanda Rd.			Kenilworth Rd., Ains.	L10 12		Killarney Rd.	U31 96
Juvenal St.	P31 94		Kenilworth Rd., Wirr.	M31 92		Killester Rd.	X35 116
			Kenilworth St.	O27 54		Killington Way	Q29 73
			Kenilworth Way	W35 115		*Mercer dr.*	
			Kenilwroth Rd., Liver.	V33 97		Kilmalcolm Clo.	K35 109
Kaigh Av.	M22 38		Kenley Av.	EE34 119		Kilmory Av.	Y36 116
Kale Clo.	B36 105		Kenley Clo.	S31 95		Kiln Clo.	EE26 62
Karan Way	U23 42		Kenmare Rd.	T34 114		Kiln La.	EE26 62
Karen Clo.	MM30 84		Kenmay Wk.	W23 43		Kiln Rd.	H35 108
Karonga Rd.	T25 57		Kenmore Gro.	LL23 50		Kilnyard Rd.	M23 38
Karonga Way	T25 57		*Coldstone Dr.*			Kilrea Rd.	T29 75
Karren Rd.	G31 90		Kenmore Rd.	K36 109		Kilsail Rd.	X25 59
Karslake Rd., Liver.	T34 114		Kennelwood Av.	W23 43		Kilsby Dr.	JJ36 121
Karslake Rd., Wirr.	M32 92		Kennessee Clo.	T21 29		Kilshaw Rd.	MM30 84
Katherine Wk., Know.	U25 57		Kennessee Grn.	T21 29		Kilshaw St.	R31 95
Elizabeth Rd.			Kennet Rd., St.H.	LL26 65		Kimberley Av., Sefton	M23 38
Kear St.	R31 95		Kennet Rd., Wirr.	M38 126		Kimberley Av., St.H.	FF29 81
Kearsley Clo.	Q29 73		Kenneth Clo.	Q23 40		Kimberley Clo.	R33 95
Kearsley St.	Q29 73		Kenneth Rd.	EE37 135		Kimberley Dr.	M23 38
Keates St.	JJ29 82		Kennford Rd.	V26 58		Kimberley Rd.	L30 71
Keats Av., Know.	CC31 100		Kensington	R32 95		Kindale Rd.	K36 109
Keats Av., Wigan	HH20 36		Kensington Av.	HH29 82		Kinder Gro.	MM2251
Keats Grn.	Z32 99		Kensington Gdns.	G33 90		Kinder St.	Q31 94
Keats St.	O26 54		Kensington Rd., Formby	K16 19		King Av.	Q26 55
Keble Dr., Sefton	S23 41		Kensington Rd., S.Port	P 5 6		King Edward Clo.	DD31 101
Keble Dr., Wirr.	J30 70		Kensington St.	R32 95		King Edward Rd.	EE26 62
Keble Rd.	P28 73		Kent Av., Hogshill	L16 20		King Edward St., Wirr.	O32 93
Keble St.	R32 95		Kent Av., Orrell	P25 55		King Edwards Dr.	O38 127
Marvin St.			Kent Bnk.	V28 76		King Gdns.	Q34 112
Kedleston St.	R35 113		Kent Clo.	O41 142		King George Dr.	M30 71
Keele Clo.	J32 91		Kent Clo., Boot.	P27 55		King Georges Dr.	O38 127
Keenan Dr.	Q26 55		Kent Pl.	M34 110		King Georges Rd.	NN25 66
Keepers La.	L38 126		Kent Rd., Birk.	O 7 9		King Georges Way	K33 91
Keig St.	M33 92		Kent Rd., Formby	K16 19		King St., Crosby	M24 38
Keighley Av.	K30 71		Kent Rd., St.H.	HH29 82		King St., Earls.	NN27 66
Mosslands Dr.			Kent Rd., Wirr.	L31 92		King St., Eccl.	FF27 63
Keighley Wk.	Z39 133		Kent St., Halton	GG36 120		King St., Egre.	M31 92
Keir Hardie Av.	Q26 55		Kent St., Liver.	P33 94		King St., Know.	BB30 79
Keith Av.	R28 74		Kent St., Wirr.	L35 110		King St., Liver.	V39 131
Keith Dr.	P42 143		Kent Way	OO28 85		King St., Rock Ferry	O36 111
Kelday Clo.	W24 43		*Bradlegh Rd.*			King St., S.Port	O 5 5
Kelk Beck Clo.	T20 29		Kentmere Av.	HH25 64		King St., Wall.	M30 71
Kellets Pl.	N35 111		Kentmere Dr.	G39 124		Kingcroft Rd.	U31 96
Kellett Rd.	H31 90		Kenton Clo.	K14 16		Kingfield Rd.	Q26 55
Kellit Rd.	T33 96		Kenton Rd.	Z37 133		Kingfisher Clo.	W22 43
Kelly Dr.	Q26 55		Kenview Clo.	DD39 135		Kingfisher Way	F34 107
Kelly St.	CC30 79		Kenway	DD22 47		Kingham Clo., C.Wood	HH36 121
Kelmscott Dr.	K31 92		Kenwyn Rd.	L30 71		Kingham Clo., Liver.	Y36 116
Kelsall Av., Elles.	Q43 148		Kenyon La.	S19 28		Kinglake Rd.	M31 92
Kelsall Av., St.H.	GG31 102		Kenyon Rd.	U34 114		Kinglake St.	R32 95
Kelsall Clo., Elles.	Q43 148		Kenyons La., Sefton	L15 16		Kinglass Rd.	O39 127
Kelsall Clo., Halton	FF36 120		Kenyons La., St.H.	MM25 66		Kings Av.	C33 88
Kelsall Clo., Wirr.	K35 109		Kepler St., Liver.	Q31 94		Kings Brow	M38 126
Kelso Clo.	V22 43		Kepler St., Sefton	O26 54		Kings Clo., Liver.	S36 113
Kelso Rd.	S31 95		Kerr Gro.	JJ27 64		Kings Clo., Sefton	K16 19
Kelton Gro.	T36 114		Kerr St.	R31 95		Kings Clo., Wirr.	M37 126
Kelvin Gro., Liver.	R34 113		Kersey Rd.	W25 58		Kings Ct.	L35 110
Kelvin Gro., Wigan	LL22 50		Kersey Wk.	W25 58		Kings Ct., Sefton	N25 54
Stirling Dr.			Kershaw Av.	N23 39		Kings Ct., Wirr.	B33 87
Kelvin Rd., L.Tran.	N35 111		Kershaw St.	EE36 119		Kings Dock St.	P33 94
Kelvin Rd., Wall.	M32 92		Kershaw Way	OO26 67		Kings Dr. N.	C36 106
Kelvin Rd., Wall.	N32 93		Kerslake Way	K19 24		Kings Dr., Caldy	C37 122
Kelvinside	N24 39		Keston Wk.	Z38 133		Kings Dr., Gate.	Y35 116
Kemble St.	BB30 79		*New Hutte La.*			Kings Dr., Thing.	G38 124
Kemlyn Rd.	R29 74		Kestral Rd., Beb.	J41 140		Kings Dr., Wool.	X36 116
Kempsell Way	AA38 133		Kestral Av.	F34 107		Kings Gap, The	B34 105
Kempsell Wk.	AA37 133		Kestrel Clo.	F34 107		Kings Gdns.	O 6 5
Kempson Ter.	N39 127		Kestrel Dr.	U26 57		Kings Hey Dr.	Q 4 6
Kempston St.	Q32 94		Kestrel Rd., More.	F33 89		Kings La.	M37 126
Kempton Park Fold	Q 7 10		Keswick Av.	P43 148		Kings Moss La.	FF21 35

Kings Mt.	L35 110	
Kings Par.	J29 70	
Kings Rd.	M37 126	
Kings Rd., C. Thornton	S45 149	
Kings Rd., Crosby	M23 38	
Kings Rd., Formby	K16 19	
Kings Rd., Gol.	QQ25 68	
Kings Rd., Liver.	P28 73	
Kings Rd., St.H.	EE28 80	
Kings Sq.	N34 111	
Kings St.	LL26 65	
Kings Way, H.Beb.	M37 126	
Kings Wk., Rock Ferry	O36 111	
Kings Wk., W.Kirby	C36 106	
Kingsbury	C36 106	
Kingsbury Clo.	L11 12	
Kingscourt Rd.	V30 76	
Kingsdale Av., Know.	EE31 101	
Mossdale Av.		
Kingsdale Av., Wirr.	M36 110	
Kingsdale Rd.	U34 114	
Kingsdown Rd.	U28 75	
Kingsdown St.	N35 111	
Kingsfield Rd.	S21 28	
Kingsheath Av., Know.	X30 77	
Kingsheath Av., Liver.	W30 76	
Kingsland Cres.	T27 57	
Kingsland Rd., Liver.	S27 56	
Kingsland Rd., Wirr.	M35 110	
Kingsley Av.	Q43 148	
Kingsley Clo.	H39 124	
Kingsley Rd., Liver.	R33 95	
Kingsley Rd., St.H.	EE26 62	
Kingsley Rd., Wirr.	L31 92	
Kingsley St.	L33 92	
Kingsmead Dr.	X37 132	
Kingsmead Rd. N.	K34 109	
Kingsmead Rd. S.	K34 109	
Kingsmead Rd., More.	G32 90	
Kingsmead Rd., Ox.	K34 109	
Kingsnorth	CC32 100	
Kingsthorne Rd.	Y38 132	
Kingston Clo.	G33 90	
Kingston Cres.	S 2 3	
Kingsville Rd.	N38 127	
Kingsway	GG25 63	
Kingsway Tunnel	J31 91	
Kingsway, App.	GG36 120	
Kingsway, Crosby	N24 39	
Kingsway, Hes.	J42 140	
Kingsway, Roby	Y31 98	
Kingsway, S.Port	O 5 5	
Kingsway, Wall.	K30 70	
Kingsway, Warr.	OO28 85	
Kingsway, Whist.	CC31 100	
Kingswood Av.	N24 39	
Kingswood Av.	R25 56	
Kingswood Boul.	N37 127	
Kingswood Dr.	M23 38	
Kingswood Rd.	L30 71	
Kington Rd.	B35 105	
Kinlet Rd.	LL19 37	
Kinley Gdns.	Q26 55	
Kinloss Rd.	F35 107	
Kinmel St., Liver.	R34 113	
Kinmel St., St.H.	HH29 82	
Kinnaird Rd., Wirr.	L30 71	
Kinnaird St., Liver.	R35 113	
Kinross Av.	LL23 50	
Kinross Rd., Liver.	T25 57	
Kinross Rd., Sefton	N25 54	
Kinross Rd., Wirr.	J30 70	
Kintore Clo.	L43 148	
Duncansby Dr.		
Kintore Dr.	LL34 152	
Kintore Rd.	U37 130	
Kinver Clo.	Z38 133	
Kipling Av., Know.	AA32 99	
Kipling Av., Wirr.	N36 111	
Kipling Cres.	FF36 120	
Kipling Gro.	GG31 102	
Burns Rd.		
Kipling St.	O26 54	
Kirby Bank La.	Z24 45	
Kirby Clo.	C36 106	
Kirby Mt.	C37 122	
Kirby Pk.	B36 105	
Kirby Rd.	P26 55	
Kirk Rd.	P26 55	
Kirk St.	Q30 73	
Kirkbridge Clo.	AA35 117	
Kirkby Bank Rd.	X24 44	
Kirkby Row	V23 43	
Kirkdale Av.	Q29 73	
Kirkdale Rd.	P30 73	
Kirkett Clo.	O39 127	
Kirkett La.	N39 127	
Kirkham Rd., Halton	HH36 121	
Kirkham Rd., Sefton	R 3 3	
Kirklake Bnk.	J16 19	
Kirklake Rd.	J16 19	
Kirkland Av.	M36 110	
Kirkland Rd.	M29 71	
Kirkland St.	FF27 63	
Kirklands, The	C36 106	
Kirklees Rd.	N 8 9	
Kirkmaiden Rd.	U37 130	
Kirkmore Rd.	U36 114	
Kirkstall Dr.	L16 20	
Kirkstall Rd.	N 8 9	
Kirkstall St.	Q29 73	
Kirkstone Av.	HH25 64	
Kirkstone Rd. N.	P24 40	
Kirkstone Rd. S.	P25 55	
Kirkstone Rd. W.	O24 39	
Kirkway	G35 108	
Kirkway Rd.	L30 71	
Kirkway, H.Beb.	M37 126	
Kirkways	G34 108	
Kitchen St.	P33 94	
Kitchener Dr.	O26 55	
Kitchener St.	EE2762	
Kitling Rd.	X26 59	
Kiveton Dr.	OO24 52	
Knaresborough Rd.	K31 91	
Knight Rd.	MM30 84	
Knight St.	Q33 94	
Knighton Rd.	S28 74	
Knob Hall La.	Q 3 2	
Knoclaid Rd.	T29 75	
Knoll, The	L35 110	
Knowe, The	O45 147	
Knowle Av.	M10 12	
Knowle Hey Rd.	AA38 133	
Knowles House Av.	CC27 61	
Knowles St., Halton	HH36 121	
Knowles St., Wirr.	M34 110	
Knowsley Av.	QQ25 68	
Knowsley Clo.	O36 111	
Knowsley Ct.	O37 127	
Knowsley Heights	Z31 99	
Knowsley La.	Y27 59	
Knowsley Park La.	BB30 79	
Knowsley Rd.,	O36 111	
Rock Ferry		
Knowsley Rd., Know.	Y26 59	
Knowsley Rd., Lith.	O26 54	
Knowsley Rd., Liver.	U38 130	
Knowsley Rd., R.Hill	EE31 101	
Knowsley Rd., S.Port	P 4 6	
Knowsley Rd., St.H.	EE27 62	
Knowsley Rd., Wall.	K30 70	
Knowsley Vw.	CC21 33	
Knox Clo.	O38 127	
Knox St.	N34 111	
Knutsford Grn.	G33 90	
Knutsford Rd.	G33 90	
Knutsford Wk.	S19 28	
Kramar Wk.	W23 43	
Old Rough La.		
Kremlin Dr.	T30 75	
Kronsbec Av.	S45 149	
Kylemore Av.	U36 114	
Kylemore Dr.	G39 124	
Kylemore Rd.	L35 110	
Kylemore Way, Know.	Y37 132	
Kylemore Way, Wirr.	G39 124	
Kylmore Clo.	G39 124	
Kynance Rd.	V26 58	
Laburnam St.	NN24 51	
Laburnum Av., Know.	Z33 99	
Laburnum Av., St.H.	HH25 64	
Laburnum Cres.	V23 43	
Laburnum Gro.	F38 123	
Laburnum Gro.	Q 5 6	
Laburnum Gro., Mag.	T20 29	
Laburnum Pl.	P27 55	
Laburnum Rd., Liver.	S31 95	
Laburnum Rd., Ox.	L35 110	
Laburnum Rd., Wall.	L29 71	
Laburnum Rd., Warr.	LL34 152	
Lace St.	P32 94	
Lacey Rd.	CC30 79	
Lacey St.	EE29 80	
Ladies Wk.	PP29 85	
Lady Green La.	M19 25	
Ladyewood St.	M31 92	
Ladyfields	U30 75	
Ladysmith Av.	NN23 51	
Ladysmith Rd.	T26 57	
Laffack Rd.	HH25 64	
Lagrange Arc.	GG27 63	
Laird Clo.	K33 92	
Laird St.		
Lake Pl.	B33 87	
Lake Rd., Liver.	U33 96	
Lake Rd., Wirr.	B33 87	
Lake St.	R29 74	
Lakeland Av.	NN23 51	
Lakenheath Rd.	Z38 133	
Lakeside Av.	JJ19 36	
Lakeside Clo.	DD37 135	
Lakeside Ct.	L29 71	
Lambert St.	Q32 94	
Lambeth Rd.	P29 73	
Lambeth St.	P30 73	
Lambeth Wk.	P29 73	
Lambourn Av.	EE34 119	
Lambourne Gro.	KK27 65	
Lambourne Rd.	S28 74	
Lambshear La.	S19 28	
Lambton Rd.	R35 113	
Lammermore Rd.	U36 114	
Lampeter Rd.	S30 74	
Lancaster Av., H.Green	DD36 119	
Lancaster Av., Liver.	S34 113	
Lancaster Av., Sefton	M23 38	
Lancaster Av., Whist.	BB31 100	
Lancaster Av., Wigan	RR25 68	
Lancaster Av., Wirr.	L30 71	
Lancaster Clo., Hay.	MM27 66	
Lancaster Clo., Sefton	T20 29	
Lancaster Clo., Wirr.	O37 128	
Primrose Hill		
Lancaster Rd., Formby	K16 19	
Lancaster Rd., Halton	GG35 120	
Lancaster Rd., Know.	AA31 99	
Lancaster Rd., S.Port	M 7 8	
Lancaster St., Liver.	P30 73	
Lancaster St., Sefton	Q27 55	
Lancaster Wk.	AA31 99	
Lance Clo.	Q30 73	
Lance Gro.	U33 96	
Lance La.	U33 96	
Lancefield Rd.	O26 55	
Lancelyn Clo.	N39 127	
Lancelyn Ct.	K40 127	
Mobberly Way		
Lancing Av.	Y36 116	
Lancing Dr.	S24 41	
Lancing Rd.	Y37 132	
Lancing Way	Y37 132	
Lancots La.	HH29 82	
Land End	V20 30	
Land La.	S 3 3	
Landford Av.	T27 57	
Landford Clo.	T27 57	
Landford Way	T27 57	
Landican La.	J37 125	
Landown Pl., Liver.	Q30 73	
Landseer Av.	K45 145	
Landseer Rd.	Q30 73	
Lanfranc Rd.	W33 97	
Lang La.	B35 105	
Langbar Clo.	CC32 100	
Langdale Av., Sefton	J16 19	
Langdale Av., Wirr.	G39 124	
Langdale Clo.	EE37 135	
Langdale Clo., Formby	J16 19	
Langdale Dr.	T20 29	
Langdale Gdns.	N 8 9	
Langdale Rd., L.Beb.	N39 127	
Langdale Rd., Liver.	T34 114	
Langdale Rd., Wall.	K29 70	
Langdale St.	P27 55	
Langdsale Gro.	GG25 63	
Langfield Gro.	P42 143	
Langham Av.	S35 113	
Langham St.	Q29 73	
Langholm Clo.	LL19 37	
Melrose Dr.		
Langholm Rd.	LL23 50	
Langley Av.	OO28 85	
Langley Rd.	O40 142	
Langrove St.	Q30 73	
Langsdale St.	Q31 94	
Langshaw Ley	Z35 117	
Langton Rd.	S33 95	
Langton St.	O28 72	
Langtree St.	HH27 64	
Langtrey Clo.	P29 73	
Langtrey Rd.	P29 73	
Langwood La.	EE20 34	

Lanley Clo. K40 142
Lanley Rd.
Lansbury Av. JJ28 82
Lansbury Rd. AA31 99
Lansdown Pl., Wirr. K33 91
Lansdowne Clo. L33 92
Lincoln St.
Lansdowne Rd., Bids. K33 91
Lansdowne Rd., Sefton Q 6 6
Lansdowne Rd., Wall. K29 70
Lansdowne Way Z32 99
Derby Rd.
Lanville Rd. U36 114
Lanyork Rd. O31 93
Lapford Cres. X23 44
Lapford Wk. W23 43
Lapworth St. P30 73
Larch Av., Halton GG36 120
Larch Av., Warr. OO28 85
Larch Clo. HH22 49
Larch Lea R30 74
Larch Rd., Roby Y32 98
Larch Rd., St.H. MM25 66
Elizabeth Rd.
Larch Rd., Wirr. M35 110
Larch St. Q 6 6
Larch Tower W23 43
Larch Way J15 15
Larchdale Gro. R27 56
Larchdale Rd., R27 56
Larchfield Rd. O22 39
Larchwood Av. S21 28
Larchwood Clo., Liver. X34 116
Larchwood Clo., Wirr. G39 124
Larchwood Dr. N37 127
Larcombe Av, G34 108
Lark Hill La., Liver. T29 75
Lark Hill Pl. T29 75
Lark Hill Vw. T29 75
Lark La. S35 113
Larkfield Clo. S36 113
Larkfield Gro. S36 113
Larkfield La. R 3 3
Larkfield Rd. S36 113
Larkfield Vw. T33 96
Larkhill Av. H33 90
Larkhill Clo. K19 24
Larkhill La., Sefton J15 15
Larkhill Way G33 90
Larksway H41 139
Larton Rd. D35 106
Lascelles Rd. V37 131
Lascelles St. HH27 64
Latchford Rd. H42 139
Latham Av. OO27 67
Latham Clo. CC30 79
Latham Rd. P26 55
Latham St., Halton HH36 121
Latham St., Liver. P30 73
Latham Way O40 142
Lathbury La. T34 114
Lathom Av., Sea. N26 54
Chatham Clo.
Lathom Av., Wirr. L31 92
Lathom Clo., Sea. N26 54
Lathom Dr., Sefton T19 29
Lathom Dr., St.H. CC21 33
Lathom Rd., Huy. Z32 99
Lathom Rd., Sefton O 4 5
Lathom St. HH27 64
Roper St.
Lathwaite Clo. GG31 102
Latimer St. P30 73
Latrigg Rd. T36 114
Lauder Clo. V22 43
Laund, The K30 70
Laurel Av., H.Beb. M39 126
Laurel Av., Warr. OO28 85
Laurel Av., Wirr. G40 139
Laurel Bnk. GG35 120
Laurel Dr., Know. CC27 61
Laurel Dr., Wirr. O44 147
Laurel Gro., Asht. NN23 51
Laurel Gro., Crosby M24 38
Laurel Gro., Gol. RR25 68
Laurel Gro., Know. Z33 99
Laurel Gro., S.Port Q 5 6
Laurel Rd., Eccl. EE28 80
Laurel Rd., Hay. JJ26 64
Laurel Rd., Liver. S32 95
Laurel Rd., Pres. CC30 79
Laurel Rd., Wirr. M35 110
Laurelhurst Av. G39 124
Lauriston Rd. S28 74
Lavan St. EE29 80
Parliament St.
Lavender Way R27 56
Lawford Dr. J41 140
Lawler St. O26 54
Lawns Av. O42 142
Lawns, The Q 4 6
Lawrence Gro. T33 96
Lawrence Rd. T33 96
Lawrence Rd. EE26 62
Lawrence St. NN27 66
Wellington St.
Lawrenson St. FF27 63
Lawson Rd. NN25 66
Lawson St. R 5 7
Lawson Wk. V27 58
Grayling Dr.
Lawton Av. Q26 55
Lawton Rd., Know. EE32 101
Lawton Rd., Roby Y32 98
Lawton Rd., Sefton M24 38
Lawton St., Liver. Q32 94
Lawton St., Sefton P 5 6
Laxey St. Q34 112
Laxton Rd. Y38 132
Laybourne Clo. X34 116
Layford Clo. Y30 77
Layford Rd. Y30 77
Layton Av. K36 109
Layton Clo. Y36 116
Layton Rd. Y36 116
Lazenby Gro. MM2351
Lazonby Cres. MM23 51
Lea Clo. K35 109
Lea Green Rd. GG30 81
Lea Rd. M31 92
Lea St. N33 93
Leach Cft. X29 77
Leach La. HH30 82
Leach St. FF27 63
Volunteer St.
Leach Way F38 123
Leacroft MM22 51
Leafield Clo. G38 124
Leafield Rd. X38 132
LeamingtonGdns. H35 108
Leamington Av., Warr. OO28 85
Leamington Gdns. H35 108
Leamington Rd., Liver. S28 74
Leamington Rd., Sefton M10 12
Leander Rd. L31 92
Lear Rd. T32 96
Leas, The, Thing. H38 124
Leas, The, Wall. K30 70
Leasowe Av. K30 70
Leasowe Rd., Liver. R25 56
Leasowe Rd., More. G31 90
Leasowe Rd., Wall. J30 70
Leasoweside H31 90
Leather La. P32 94
Leatherbarrows La. T21 29
Leatherbarrows La. U22 42
Leathers La. Z38 133
Leathwood T20 29
Leaway La. F35 107
Leawood Gro. G33 90
Leckwith Rd. R24 41
Ledbury Clo. K36 109
Ledger Rd. KK26 65
Ledmore Gro. LL23 50
Coldstone Dr.
Ledsham Clo. K35 109
Ledsham Rd. V24 43
Ledsham Wk. V24 43
Ledson Gro. U16 153
Lee Clo. EE32 101
Lincoln Way
Lee Hall Rd. Y34 116
Lee Park Av. Y34 116
Lee Rd. C33 88
Lee St. JJ29 82
Lee Vale Rd. Y35 116
Leece St. Q33 94
Leecourt Clo. V30 76
Vineside Rd.
Leeds St., Liver. P31 94
Leeds St., Wirr. O31 93
Leeming Clo. V38 121
Banks Rd.
Lees Av. N35 111
Lees La. L45 146
Lees Rd. X24 44
Leeside Av. W25 58
Leeside Clo. W24 43
Leeswood Rd. H35 108
Legh Rd., St.H. KK26 65
Legh Rd., Wirr. O37 127
Legh St., St.H. NN27 66
Legh St., Wigan NN24 51
Legion La. L40 143
Allports Av.
Legion Rd. EE29 80
Leicester Av. M24 38
Leicester Rd. P27 55
Leicester St., Sefton O 5 5
Leicester St., St.H. EE29 80
Leigh Av. GG36 120
Leigh Rd., Liver. S32 95
Leigh Rd., Wirr. B35 105
Leigh St. QQ25 68
Leighs Hey Cres. W24 43
Leighton Av., Sefton S20 28
Leighton Av., Wirr. D33 88
Leighton Rd., Elles. J43 145
Leighton Rd., Wirr. N35 111
Leighton St. Q28 73
Leighton Vw. Q34 112
Leightons, The J45 145
Leinster Rd. U31 96
Leiston Clo. G37 124
Leith St. P29 73
Lemon Clo. S32 95
Stanier Way
Lemon St. P30 73
Lendel Clo. K15 16
Lenfield Dr. KK26 65
Lenham Way X39 132
Lennox Av. L29 71
Lennox La. J32 91
Lenthall St. Q28 73
Lenton Av. J15 15
Vicarage Rd.
Lenton Rd. Y34 116
Leominster Rd. L31 92
Leonard Cheshire Dr. Q23 40
Leonard St. JJ29 82
Leopold Gro. HH30 82
Leopold Rd., Liver. R32 95
Leopold Rd., Sefton M24 38
Leopold St. N31 93
Lesley Rd. Q 5 6
Leslie Av. F35 107
Leslie Rd. EE29 80
Lesseps Rd. S33 95
Lester Clo. Q29 73
Fountain Rd.
Lester Dr. F37 123
Lester Dr., St.H. DD26 62
Lestock St. Q33 94
Leta St., Liver. Q28 73
Leta St., Wirr. N34 111
Lethbridge Rd. P 6 6
Letita St. Q34 112
Letterson Clo. Q31 94
Breck Rd.
Letterson Wk. Q31 94
Breck Rd.
Leven St. Q29 73
Levens Hey F33 89
Levens Way EE37 135
Lever Av. N32 93
Lever Causeway L38 126
Lever St. HH31 103
Leveret Rd., Know. AA39 133
Leveret Rd., Liver. AA39 137
Leveson Rd. U32 96
Lewis Gro. EE36 119
Lewis St. FF27 63
Lewisham Rd., Liver. T28 75
Lewisham Rd., Wirr. P38 128
Lewlithia Pk. O25 54
Lexham Rd. V31 97
Lexton Dr. R 3 3
Ley Clo. HH31 103
Leybourne Av. N 9 9
Leybourne Grn. X34 116
Leybourne Gro. X34 116
Leybourne Rd. X34 116
Leyburn Clo. W25 58
Leyburn Rd. K30 70
Leyfield Clo. V30 76
Leyfield Rd.
Leyfield Ct. V30 76
Leyfield Rd.
Leyfield Rd. V30 76
Leyfield Wk. V30 76
Leyfield Rd.
Leyland Green La. LL22 50
Leyland Gro. KK26 65
Leyland Rd., Sefton P 4 6

Leyland Rd., St.H.	CC22 46	Linden Dr., Know.	Z33 99	Little Canning St.	Q33 94
Leyland St.	BB30 79	Linden Dri.	K36 109	Little Croft	BB32 100
Eccleston St.		Linden Gro., St.H.	HH23 49	*Dragon La.*	
Liberty St.	T33 96	Linden Gro., Wirr.	L30 71	Little Crosby Rd.	M21 25
Librex Rd.	P26 55	Linden Way	DD27 62	Little Heath Rd.	Z40 137
Lichfield Av., Sefton	M23 38	Linden Way, Farn.	FF35 120	Little Hey La.	M14 17
Lichfield Av., Wigan	RR25 68	Lindens, The	S21 28	Little Howler St.	O31 93
Lichfield Clo.	R24 41	Lindeth Av.	L32 92	Little La.	J44 145
Lichfield Gro.	OO24 52	Lindley Clo.	S33 95	Little La.	R 4 7
Lichfield Rd., Know.	Z38 133	*Dunstan La.*		Little Moss Hey	X29 77
Lichfield Rd., Liver.	U34 114	Lindrick Clo.	DD31 101	Little Parkfield Rd.	R35 113
Lichfield St.	M29 71	Lindsa Clo.	S31 95	Little St.	JJ28 82
Lickers La.	BB32 100	*Pendine Clo.*		Little St. Bride St.	Q33 94
Liddell Av.	U23 42	Lindsay Rd.	S29 74	Little Storeton La.	L38 126
Liddell Rd.	T29 75	Lindsay St.	HH31 103	Littledale	V31 97
Lidderdale Rd.	T34 114	*James St.*		Littledale Rd.	M31 92
Lidgate Clo.	LL19 37	Lindwall Clo.	J33 91	Littlemore Clo.	F34 107
Lifeboat Rd.	G16 18	Linear Vw.	OO28 85	Littler Rd.	KK26 65
Lifton Rd.	W24 43	Lineside Clo.	X34 116	Littleton Clo.	J35 109
Lightbody St.	O30 72	Linford Gro.	HH26 64	Littondale Av.	EE31 101
Lightfoot Clo.	H41 139	*Markfield Cres.*		Liver St.	P33 94
Lightfoot La.		Ling St.	R32 95	Liverpool Av.	M10 12
Lightfoot La.	H41 139	Lingdale Av.	K34 109	Liverpool Pl.	EE36 119
Lighthorn Dr.	L11 12	Lingdale Rd., Birk.	K33 91	Liverpool Rd.	M12 12
Lighthouse Rd.	B34 105	Lingdale Rd., N.	K33 91	Liverpool Rd.	S19 28
Lightwood Dr.	S33 95	Lingdale Rd., Ox.	K34 109	Liverpool Rd.	FF27 63
Rokesmith Av.		Lingdale Rd., W.Kirby	B35 105	Liverpool Rd. S.	S21 28
Lilac Av, Halton	GG36 120	Lingdales	L14 16	Liverpool Rd., Birk.	O 7 9
Lilac Av., Sefton	M12 12	Lingfield Gro.	V32 97	Liverpool Rd., Crosby	N23 39
Lilac Av., Wigan	LL22 50	Lingfield Rd.	V32 97	Liverpool Rd., Elles.	K45 145
Lilac Gro., Know.	Y33 98	Lingham La.	F32 89	Liverpool Rd., Formby	L16 20
Lilac Gro., St.H.	HH23 49	Lingholme Rd.	FF27 63	Liverpool Rd., H.Green	DD36 119
Lilac Gro., Wall.	JJ26 64	Lingley Rd.	LL34 152	Liverpool Rd., Know.	Y31 98
Lilian Rd.	R30 74	Lingmell Av.	GG24 48	Liverpool Rd., N.	S20 28
Lilley Rd.	S32 95	Lingmell Rd.	U29 75	Liverpool Rd., Orm.	U16 153
Lilley Vale	S31 95	Lingtree Rd.	U24 42	Liverpool Rd., St.H.	KK25 65
Lilly Gro.	R28 74	Link Av., Sefton	O22 39	Liverpool Rd., W.Lan.	W19 30
Lilly St.	O36 111	Link Av., St.H.	JJ26 64	Liverpool Rd., Warr.	KK33 104
Lillyfield	G42 139	Link Rd., Halton	DD37 135	Liverpool Rd., Wigan	LL24 50
Lily Av.	OO28 85	Link Rd., Know.	AA32 99	Liverpool Row	OO29 85
Lily Gro., Wirr.	N32 93	Links Av.	Q 4 6	Liverpool St.	FF27 63
Lily Pl.	OO24 52	Links Av.,	S45 149	Liversidge Rd.	M35 110
Lily Rd.	O26 54	*Little Sutton*		Livesleys La.	N16 21
Lily St.	PP22 52	Links Clo., Brom.	O42 142	Livingston Av.	S35 113
Limbo La.	F37 123	Links Clo., Wall.	K29 70	Livingston Dr.	S35 113
Lime Av., Halton	GG36 120	Links Hey Rd.	D38 122	Livingston Dr. N.	S35 113
Lime Av., Wirr.	M39 126	Links Rd.	W24 43	Livingston Dr. S.	S35 113
Lime Gro., Liver.	S34 113	*Mosslawn Rd.*		Livingstone Rd.	H31 90
Lime Gro., Sefton	O26 54	Links Vw., Ox.	K34 109	Livingstone Rd., Birk.	N35 111
Lime Gro., St.H.	CC22 46	Links Vw., Wall.	K29 70	Livingstone St., Wigan	NN22 51
Lime St., Liver.	P32 94	Linkside	M37 126	Livingstone St., Wirr.	M33 92
Lime St., Sefton	Q 6 6	Linkside Av.	QQ30 86	Llandaff Clo.	R24 41
Lime Tree Clo.	R27 56	Linkside Ct.	L22 38	Llewellyn St.	P30 73
Buttercup Way		Linkside Rd.	Y36 116	Lloyd Av.	L33 92
Lime Tree Gro.	J41 140	Linkstor Rd.	W35 115	Lloyd Clo.	Q31 94
Lime Tree Way	J16 19	Linksview Clo.	W36 115	Lloyd Cres.	MM27 66
Lime Vale Rd.	HH23 49	Linksway	K29 70	Lloyd Dr.	F35 107
Limedale Rd.	U34 114	Linkway	DD26 62	Lloyd St.	JJ26 64
Limekiln La., Liver.	P31 94	*Caldhurst Dr.*		Lobelia Av.	R27 56
Limekiln La., Wirr.	L32 92	Linkway Av.	PP22 52	Lobelia Rd.	X30 77
Limont Rd.	M10 12	Linner Rd.	Y40 136	Lochinvar St., Liver.	Q28 73
Linacre La., Sefton	P26 55	Linnet La.	S35 113	Lochinvar St., Sefton	Q27 55
Linacre La., W.Lan.	O17 21	Linnet Way	W22 43	Lochmore Rd.	U36 114
Linacre Rd.	O25 54	Linnets Way	G41 139	Lock Rd.	R41 150
Linaker St.	O 6 5	Linslade Clo.	W23 43	Lock Ryan Rd.	U37 130
Linbridge Rd.	W30 76	Linslade Cres.	W23 43	Lock St.	HH26 64
Linby Clo.	X25 59	Linton Av.	PP24 52	Locke St.	V39 131
Linby Rd.	X25 59	Lintons St.	Q28 73	Locker Pk.	F35 107
Lincoln Clo.	R31 95	Linville Av.	L23 38	Lockerby Rd.	S31 95
Lincoln Clo.	AA31 99	Linwood Rd.	M35 110	Locket Rd.	GG35 120
Lincoln Cres.	GG26 63	Lionel St.	JJ29 82	Locket Rd., Hay.	OO22 52
Lincoln Dr., Sefton	S23 41	Lions Clo.	K34 109	Loddon Clo.	H33 90
Lincoln Dr., Wigan	OO24 52	Lisburn La.	T29 75	Lodge La.	NN24 51
Lincoln Dr., Wirr.	M30 71	Lisburn Rd.	T36 114	Lodge La., Know.	DD35 119
Lincoln Gdns.	L33 92	Liscard Cres.	L31 92	Lodge La., Liver.	R33 95
Lincoln Grn.	R21 28	Liscard Gro.	L31 92	Lodge La., St.H.	BB20 33
Lincoln Rd., Sefton	O 8 9	Liscard Rd., Liver.	S33 95	Lodge La., Wirr.	O38 127
Lincoln Rd., St.H.	EE28 80	Liscard Rd., Wirr.	M31 92	Lodge Rd., Halton	DD37 135
Lincoln Sq.	GG36 120	Liscard Vill.	L31 92	Lodge Rd., Wigan	JJ19 36
Lincoln St., Boot.	O28 72	Liscard Way	L31 92	Lodore Rd.	U32 96
Lincoln St., Gars.	V39 131	Lisleholme Clo.	V30 76	Lodwick St.	O28 72
Lincoln St., Wirr.	K33 91	Lisleholme Cres.	V30 76	Log Wood Rd.	AA33 99
Lincoln Way, Huy.	AA31 99	Lisleholme Rd.	V30 76	Logan Height	P30 73
York Way		Lismore Rd.	U36 114	Lognor Rd.	V24 43
Lincoln Way, R.Hill	EE32 101	Lister Dr.	T31 96	Lognor Wk.	V24 43
Lincombe Rd.	X31 98	Lister Rd.	S33 95	Lombard Rd.	G32 90
Lind St.	O28 73	Liston St.	Q28 73	*Saxon Rd.*	
Lindale Av.	HH31 103	Litcham Clo.	H33 90	Lombardy Av.	E36 107
Lindale Rd.	T31 96	Litherland Av.	F33 89	Lomond Gro.	G33 90
Lindby Clo.	X25 59	Litherland Cres.	HH25 64	Lomond Rd.	T32 96
Lindby Rd.	X25 59	Litherland Pk.	O25 54	London Flds.	JJ22 49
Linden Av.	MM22 51	Litherland Rd.	P26 55	London La.	P 9 10
Linden Av., Crosby	M23 38	Little Acre	T21 29	London Rd.	Q32 94
Linden Av., Lith.	Q24 40	Little Barn Hey	P22 40	London St.	O 5 5
Linden Ct.	FF35 120	Little Brook La.	V24 43	Londonderry Rd.	S29 74

Long Acre Wk.	HH31 103	
Pasture Clo.		
Long Av.	R26 56	
Long Hey	BB32 100	
Long Hey Rd.	D37 122	
Long La., Formby	K15 16	
Long La., Gars.	V37 131	
Long La., Thorn.	O21 26	
Long La., Vic.Pk.	R26 56	
Long La., Wav.	T33 96	
Long La., Wigan	FF19 35	
Long Meadow	G42 139	
Long Moss	P24 40	
Musker Dr.		
Long Row	EE37 135	
Long View La.	Z31 99	
Longacre	Q 3 2	
Longacre Clo.	J30 70	
Longborough Rd.	Y28 77	
Longcliffe Dr.	L11 12	
Longcroft Av.	V37 131	
Longcroft Clo.	V37 131	
Longdale La.	P21 27	
Longden Rd.	NN23 51	
Longfellow St., Liver.	S33 95	
Longfellow St., Sefton	O26 54	
Longfield Av.	N22 39	
Longfield Clo., Sefton	L14 16	
Longfield Clo., Wirr.	F35 107	
Longfield Rd.	O26 54	
Longfield Wk.	N22 39	
Longfold	T20 29	
Longford Rd.	O 8 9	
Longford St.	R35 113	
Longland Rd.	L30 71	
Longmead Av.	OO23 52	
Longmeadow Rd.	Y27 59	
Longmoor Clo.	T25 57	
Longmoor Gro.	S25 56	
Longmoor La.	R26 56	
Longreach Rd.	W31 97	
Longridge Av.	HH26 64	
Longridge Wk.	Q29 73	
Mercer Dr.		
Longshaw Av.	JJ20 36	
Longshaw Dr.	JJ20 36	
Longshaw Common	JJ21 36	
Longshaw Old Rd.	JJ20 36	
Longstone Wk.	R33 95	
Longton Av.	RR25 68	
Longton Dr.	L14 16	
Longton La.	DD30 80	
Longview Av., Know.	DD31 101	
Longview Av., St.H.	DD30 80	
Longview Av., Wirr.	L30 71	
Longview Cres.	Z31 99	
Longview Dr.	Z31 99	
Longview Rd., Huy.	Z31 99	
Longview Rd., R.Hill	DD31 101	
Longview Rd., St.H.	DD30 80	
Longwood Clo.	DD24 47	
Longworth Way	X35 116	
Lonie Gro.	EE29 80	
Lonsboro Rd.	M31 92	
Lonsdale Av.	DD29 80	
Lonsdale Clo, Halton	EE37 135	
Lonsdale Clo., Sefton	O24 39	
Lonsdale Rd., Birk.	P 7 10	
Lonsdale Rd., Crosby	O24 39	
Lonsdale Rd., Formby	K15 16	
Looe Clo.	FF36 120	
Looe Rd.	V26 58	
Looms, The	H44 144	
Loomsway	F38 123	
Loraine St.	Q30 73	
Lord Nelson St.	Q32 94	
Lord Sefton Way	N16 21	
Lord St. W.	O 6 5	
Lord St., Gars.	V39 131	
Lord St., Liver.	P32 94	
Lord St., Newt.	NN27 66	
Lord St., Sefton	O 5 5	
Lord St., St.H.	GG26 63	
Lord St., Wirr.	N33 93	
Lordens Clo.	X30 77	
Lordens Rd.	X30 77	
Lords Fold	CC21 33	
Loreburn Rd.	U34 114	
Lorenzo Dr.	T28 75	
Loretto Dr.	H34 108	
Loretto Rd.	K31 91	
Lorn St.	N34 111	
Lorne Rd., Sefton	M34 38	
Lorne Rd., Wirr.	L35 110	
Lorne St.	T31 96	
Lorton Av.	GG25 63	
Lorton St.	R33 95	
Lostock Clo.	JJ22 49	
Lothair Rd.	R29 74	
Lothian St.	R34 113	
Loudon Gro.	R34 113	
Lough Grn.	O40 142	
Loughrigg Av.	GG24 48	
Louis Bratle Clo.	Q23 40	
Louis Pasteur Av.	Q23 40	
Lovat St.	R32 95	
Love La., Liver.	P31 94	
Love La., Wirr.	L31 92	
Lovelace Rd.	U37 130	
Lovell Rd., Liver.	Y40 136	
Lovell Ter.	DD38 135	
Lovell Way	Y39 136	
Low Bank Rd.	MM23 51	
Low Hill	R31 95	
Low Wood St.	R32 95	
Lowden Av.	O24 39	
Lowe St., St.H.	FF27 63	
Lowe St., Wigan	QQ25 68	
Lowell St.	Q28 73	
Lower Alt Rd.	K19 24	
Lower Appleton Rd.	GG36 120	
Lower Arkwright St.	Q30 73	
Lower Bank Vw.	O28 72	
Lower Breck Rd.	S30 74	
Lower Carr La.	P18 22	
Lower Castle St.	P32 94	
Lower Clo.	AA37 133	
Lower Farm Rd.	X33 98	
Lower Flaybrick Rd.	K33 91	
Lower Grn.	H35 108	
Lower Hey	O22 39	
Lower La.	T25 57	
Lower Mersey Vw.	O28 72	
Lower Rd., Know.	AA37 133	
Lower Rd., Wirr.	O38 127	
Lower Thingwall La.	J38 125	
Lowerson Cres.	T29 75	
Lowerson Rd.	T29 75	
Lowes Grn.	L15 16	
Loweswater Cres.	KK26 65	
Loweswater Way	V23 43	
Lowfield La.	FF30 81	
Lowfield Rd.	V31 97	
Lowfields Av.	P43 148	
Lowfields Clo.	Q43 148	
Lowndes Rd.	S30 74	
Lowry Bnk.	N31 93	
Lowther Av., Ain.	S24 41	
Lowther Av., Moss S.	T20 29	
Lowther Cres.	DD29 80	
Lowther Dr.	DD31 101	
Lowther St.	R33 95	
Lowton Gdns.	QQ26 68	
Lowwood Gro.	M34 110	
Lowwood Rd.	M34 110	
Loxley Rd.	P 7 10	
Loyola Hey	FF33 102	
Norlands La.		
Lucan Rd.	T36 114	
Lucania St.	V39 131	
Lucerne Gdns.	H35 108	
Lucerne Rd.	M32 92	
Lucerne St.	S35 113	
Ludford Rd.	U31 96	
Ludlow Dr.	B36 105	
Ludlow Gro.	P40 143	
Ludlow St.	Q28 73	
Ludwig Rd.	R30 74	
Lugard Rd.	T36 114	
Lugsmore La.	EE28 80	
Luke St.	N32 93	
Luke St., Liver.	Q34 112	
Lully St.	R33 95	
Lulworth Av.	M24 38	
Lulworth Rd., Liver.	Y34 116	
Lulworth Rd., Sefton	N 7 9	
Lumber La.	MM29 84	
Lumby Av.	Z31 99	
Lumley Rd.	M31 92	
Lumley St.	U38 130	
Lunar Dr.	Q23 40	
Lunar Rd.	R26 56	
Lundie Pl.	R30 74	
Lune Av.	T20 29	
Lune St.	N23 39	
Lune Way	EE37 135	
Lunesdend Av.	R25 56	
Lunsford Rd.	W31 97	
Lunt Av., Know.	CC31 100	
Lunt Av., Sefton	R24 41	
Lunt La.	P21 27	
Lunt Rd., Hom.Grn.	P21 27	
Lunt Rd., Linacre	P26 55	
Lunts Heath Rd.	GG34 120	
Lunts La.	L16 20	
Lupin Dr.	MM26 66	
Lupin Way	X30 77	
Lupton Dr.	O23 39	
Luscombe Clo.	AA37 133	
Lusitania Rd.	R28 74	
Luther Gro.	KK28 83	
Luton Gro.	Q29 73	
Luton St.	P30 73	
Lutyens Clo.	Q29 73	
Pugin St.		
Luxmore Rd.	R28 74	
Lycett Rd., Liver.	S29 74	
Lycett Rd., Wirr.	K30 70	
Lydbrook Clo.	N35 111	
Lydbury Cres.	W24 43	
Lydd Clo.	X39 132	
Lydford Rd.	U29 75	
Lydia Ann St.	P33 94	
Lydia Wk.	U25 57	
Amanda Rd.		
Lydiate La., Liver.	Y36 116	
Lydiate La., Sefton	O22 39	
Lydiate Rd.	P26 55	
Lydiate Rd., Wirr.	N45 147	
Lydiate Station Rd.	P18 22	
Lydiate, The	G41 139	
Lydieth Lea	Z34 117	
Lydney Rd.	Y31 98	
Lyelake Clo.	W24 43	
Lyelake Rd.	W24 43	
Lyfield Ct.	V30 76	
Lyme Clo.	Z30 78	
Lyme Cross Rd.	Z30 78	
Lyme Gro.	Z30 78	
Lyme St.	MM27 66	
Lymington Rd.	K31 91	
Lynas Gdns.	U37 130	
Lynas St.	M33 92	
Lyncot Rd.	R25 56	
Lyncroft Rd.	M32 92	
Lyndale Av.	Q43 148	
Lyndene Rd.	X34 116	
Lyndhurst	S20 28	
Lyndhurst Av., Liver.	T35 114	
Lyndhurst Av., Wirr.	H39 124	
Lyndhurst Clo.	H38 124	
Lyndhurst Rd., Gt.Crosby	O23 39	
Lyndhurst Rd., Birk.	O 8 9	
Lyndhurst Rd., Hoy.	D32 88	
Lyndhurst Rd., Irby	F38 123	
Lyndhurst Rd., Liver.	T35 114	
Lyndhurst Rd., Wall.	K30 70	
Lyndon Dr.	U35 114	
Lyndor Clo.	X36 116	
Lynedoch St.	R31 95	
Lyneham Clo.	CC32 100	
Lynholme Rd.	R29 74	
Lynmouth Gdns.	H35 108	
New Hey Rd.		
Lynmouth Gdns.	H35 108	
Lynmouth Rd.	T37 130	
Lynn Clo.	EE26 62	
Lynnbank	L35 110	
Lynnbank Rd.	V34 115	
Lynndene	S45 149	
Lynscott Pl.	V33 97	
Lynsted Rd.	W31 97	
Lynton Clo., Liver.	U37 130	
Lynton Clo., Wirr.	H42 139	
Lynton Cres.	FF36 120	
Lynton Dr., Sefton	N 8 9	
Lynton Dr., Wirr.	O39 127	
Lynton Grn.	W35 115	
Lynton Gro.	HH33 82	
Lynton Rd., Huy.	AA31 99	
Lynton Rd., Sefton	N 9 9	
Lynton Rd., Wirr.	K30 70	
Lynton Way	DD26 62	
Lynwood Av.	L31 92	
Lynwood Dr.	G38 124	
Lynwood Gdns.	Q26 55	
Lynwood Rd., Liver.	R26 56	
Lynwood Rd., Sefton	Q26 55	
Lynx Way, The	V31 97	
Lyon Clo.	FF27 63	
Lyon Rd.	R30 74	
Lyon St., Liver.	V39 131	
Lyon St., St.H.	FF27 63	
Lyons Clo.	G32 90	

Lyons Rd., Sefton O 6 5
Lyons Rd., Wirr. G32 90
Lyra Rd. M24 38
Lyster Rd. O27 54
Lytham Clo., Liver. T25 57
Lytham Clo., Sefton T24 42
Lytham Rd., Halton HH36 121
Lytham Rd., Sefton Q 3 2
Lytham Rd., Wigan MM22 51
Lytles Clo. L16 20
Lyttleton Rd. T36 114
Lytton Av. N36 111
Lytton St. Q31 94

Mab La. W28 76
Mab St. S33 95
MacAlpine Clo. H34 108
Macaulay St. G13 25
Macbeth St. P28 73
Macdona Dr. C37 122
Macdonald Av. JJ26 64
Macdonald Dr. F34 107
MacDonald Rd. F33 89
Macdonald St. T33 96
Macfarren St. U31 96
Mack Gro. P24 40
Mackenzie Rd. H31 90
Mackets Clo. Y36 116
Mackets Close Rd. Y36 116
Macqueen St. U32 96
Macrae Rd. U30 75
Madam Curie Av. Q23 40
Maddock Rd. M30 71
Maddock St. M33 92
Maddox Rd. U32 96
Maddrell St. O31 93
Madelaine St. R34 113
Madeley Clo. B36 105
Madeley Dr. B36 105
Madeley St. S31 95
Madryn Av. X24 44
Madryn St. R24 113
Maelor Clo. O42 142
Mafeking Pl. OO23 52
Magazine Av. L29 71
Magazine Brow M29 71
Magazine La. L29 71
Magazine Rd. P39 128
Magazines Prom. M29 71
Magdalene Dr. MM23 51
Magdalene Sq. Q23 40
Maghull Hey Cop P18 22
Magnolia Wk. F36 107
Maguire Av. Q27 55
Mahon Av. P26 55
Maiden La. S29 74
Maidens Gro. P32 94
Maidford Rd. W30 76
Main Av. EE29 80
Main Clo. KK26 65
Main Rd. O39 127
Main St. JJ22 49
Mainside Rd. W24 43
Maintree Cres., Speke AA39 133
Mainwaring Rd., Brom. P41 143
Mainwaring Rd., Wall. M31 92
Mairscough La. R16 23
Maitland Clo. R33 95
Maitland Rd. M29 71
Major St. P30 73
Makin St. Q28 73
Malcern Clo., Wirr. F35 107
Malcolm Cres. P42 143
Malcolm Gro. P28 73
Malden Rd. S31 95
Maldon Clo. Z38 133
Maldwyn Rd. L31 92
Maleson Rd. T29 75
Malham Clo. Q 7 10
Malhamdale Av. EE32 101
Mallaby St. L33 92
Mallard Way F32 89
Mallee Cres. R 3 3
Mallory Av. R19 28
Mallory Gro. HH26 64
Mallory Rd. M36 110
Mallow Rd. S31 95
Mallow Way Z33 99
Mallowdale Clo. P42 143
Malmesbury Clo. F35 107
Cirencester Av.
Malmesbury Rd. T28 75
Malpas Av. L36 110
Pulford Av.
Malpas Gro. K30 70
Malpas Rd., Beb. N37 127
Malpas Rd., Liver. V26 58
Malpas Rd., Wall. K30 70
Maltby Clo. Z38 133
Malton Clo. EE34 119
Malton Rd. X36 116
Malvern Av. W32 97
Malvern Clo. V23 43
Malvern Clo., Asht. NN23 51
Malvern Clo., Wigan LL19 37
Malvern Cres. W32 97
Malvern Gro. S24 41
Malvern Gro., Birk. M36 110
Malvern Rd., Liver. S31 95
Malvern Rd., Sefton P26 55
Malvern Rd., St.H. JJ27 64
Malvern Rd., Wall. J30 70
Malverns, The L35 110
Malwood St. Q35 112
Manchester Rd. Q 6 6
Manchester Rd., Know. BB30 79
Manchester Rd., S.Port P 5 6
Manchester Row OO29 85
Liverpool Row
Manchester St. P32 94
Manderville Clo. LL20 37
Mandeville St. Q28 73
Manesty La. P32 94
Manfred Rd. R31 95
Erskine St.
Manica Cres. T26 57
Manion Av. R18 23
Manion Clo. R18 23
Manion Av.
Manley Av. PP24 52
Manley Rd., Know. AA33 99
Manley Rd., Liver. AA40 137
Manley Rd., Sefton M24 38
Mann Island P32 94
Mann St., Liver. Q34 112
Mannering Rd. S35 113
Manners La. G42 139
Manning St. FF27 63
Borough Rd.
Manningham Rd. R30 74
Manor Av., Know. EE32 101
Manor Av., Sefton M22 38
Manor Av., St.H. MM27 66
Manor Av., Wigan RR25 68
Manor Clo., Elles. J45 145
Manor Clo., Liver. Q28 73
Manor Clo., Wigan LL23 50
Manor Cres. X36 116
Manor Ct. RR25 68
Manor Dr., Sefton R23 41
Manor Dr., Wirr. H34 108
Manor Farm Rd. Z32 99
Manor Hill L34 110
Manor House Clo., Sefton S20 28
Manor House Clo., St.H. GG24 48
Manor La., Wall. L30 71
Manor La.,. Birk. O36 111
Manor Pl. P38 128
Manor Rd. R 4 7
Manor Rd., Brom. P42 143
Manor Rd., Halton DD37 135
Manor Rd., Hay. MM25 66
Manor Rd., Hes. K40 140
Manor Rd., Hoy. C33 88
Manor Rd., Liver. X36 116
Manor Rd., Sefton M22 38
Manor Rd., W.Kirby F38 123
Manor Rd., Wall. L30 71
Manor Side Clo. G34 108
Manor St. HH28 82
Manor Way X36 116
Manorbier Cres. R27 56
Manorial Rd. J45 145
Manse Gdns. OO27 67
Mansell Dr. Z38 133
Mansell Rd. R31 95
Mansfield Dr. M11 12
Mansfield St., Liver. Q31 94
Mansfield St., Wigan PP24 52
Helen St.
Manton Rd. S31 95
Manvers Rd. W33 97
Manville Rd. L29 71
Manville St. HH28 82
Manx Janes La. R 3 3
Maple Av., App. GG36 120
Maple Av., Newt. OO28 85
Maple Av., St.H. KK25 65
Maple Av., Win. QQ30 86
Maple Clo., Formby J16 19
Maple Clo., Know. CC31 100
Maple Clo., Lith. O26 54
Maple Clo., St.H. HH22 49
Maple Cres. Y32 98
Maple Gro., Know. CC30 79
Maple Gro., St.H. EE27 62
Maple Gro., Wirr. P41 143
Maple Sq. V27 58
Grayling Dr.
Maple St., Sefton P 6 6
Maple St., Wirr. M34 110
Maple Tower W23 43
Mapledale Rd. U34 114
Mapleton Clo. K36 109
Mapletree Gro. J41 140
Marathon Clo. Q31 94
Spencer St.
Marbury Rd. V24 43
Marc Av. U23 42
March Rd. S30 74
Marcham Way U28 75
Marchfield Rd. Q26 55
Marchwood Way X33 98
Marcus St. M33 92
Mardale Av. GG25 63
Mardale Clo. AA35 117
Mardale Gro. B35 105
Mardale Rd. Y30 77
Mardale Rd., Liver. AA35 117
Mardale Wk. Y30 77
Marehall La. L45 146
Mareth Clo. U36 114
Marford Rd. U29 75
Marfords Av. P41 143
Margaret Av., Sefton P26 55
Margaret Av., St.H. HH29 82
Kent Rd.
Margaret Clo. R31 95
Margaret Rd. L22 38
Margaret Rd. Q28 73
Margaret St., Liver. R31 95
Margaret St., St.H. JJ31 103
Lindsay St.
Margarets La. Q45 148
Margery Rd. EE28 80
Freckleton Rd.
Margery St. M31 80
Freckleton St.
Maria Rd. Q27 55
Marian Av. MM27 66
Marian Clo. EE32 101
Marian Dr., Know. DD32 101
Marian Dr., Wirr. G33 90
Marian Rd. MM25 66
Marian Sq. Q23 40
Marian Way, The Q23 40
Marina Av., Sefton O25 54
Marina Av., St.H. HH29 82
Marina Cres., Know. Y32 98
Marina Cres., Sefton R24 41
Marina Rd. K16 19
Marine Cres. M24 38
Marine Dr., S.Port O 4 5
Marine Dr., S.Port Q 2 2
Marine Dr., Wirr. F41 138
Marine Gdns. M25 53
Marine Par., Sefton O 5 5
Marine Pk. B35 105
Marine Prom. L28 71
Marine Rd. B33 87
Marine Ter. M25 53
Mariners Par. P32 94
Mariners Rd., Sefton L24 38
Mariners Rd., Wirr. M29 71
Marion Gr. U36 114
Marion Rd. P26 55
Marion St. N34 111
Maritime Pk. M34 110
Oxton Rd.
Marius Clo. Q29 73
Mark Rake P40 143
Mark Rd. K19 24
Mark St., Liver. Q29 73
Market Pl., Know. BB30 79
Market Pl., Liver. V38 131
Market Place St. N34 111
Hamilton St.
Market Sq. N34 111
Market St. W. N34 111
Market St., Hoy. B33 87
Market St., Liver. P32 94
Market St., Newt. NN27 66
Market St., Sefton O 5 5

Market St., St.H.	GG27 63	Marton Clo., Know.	Y39 132	McCormack Av.	JJ27 64
Market St., Wall.	N33 93	Marton Clo., Liver.	Y39 136	McCulloch St.	HH27 64
Markfield Cres., Liver.	Y36 116	Marton Grn.	Y40 136	McFarlane Av.	EE27 62
Markfield Cres., St.H.	HH26 64	Marton Rd.	Z30 78	McMinnis Av.	KK28 83
Markham Dr.	Q 8 10	Marvin St.	R31 95	McVinnie Rd.	CC30 79
Marksway	G39 124	Marwood Towers	P30 73	Mead Av.	P25 55
Marl Gro.	HH19 36	Mary Av.	N10 13	Mead Way, Mag.	R21 28
Marl Rd., Know.	Y23 44	Mary Rd.	P26 55	Meade Clo.	EE32 101
Marl Rd., Sefton	R23 41	Mary St.	HH31 103	Meade Rd.	T30 75
Marlborough Av., Ain.	R24 41	*Balniel St.*		Meadfoot Rd.	F32 89
Marlborough Av., Mag.	S19 28	Marybone	P31 94	Meadow Av., Sefton	P 7 10
Marlborough Cres.	GG34 120	Maryland La.	F32 89	Meadow Av., St.H.	HH31 103
Marlborough Gro.	L35 110	Maryland Rd.	Y35 116	Meadow Bnk.	R20 28
Marlborough Rd., Crosby	M23 38	Maryland St.	Q33 94	Meadow Cft.	HH30 82
Marlborough Rd., Elles.	K45 145	Marylebone Av.	FF30 81	Meadow Cft., Nest.	N45 147
Marlborough Rd., Lith.	N25 54	Maryville Rd.	CC30 79	Meadow Cft., Sefton	K16 19
Marlborough Rd., Liver.	S30 74	Masefield Cres.	P25 55	Meadow Clo., Nest.	J45 145
Marlborough Rd., S.Port	P 5 6	Masefield Gro.	EE26 62	Meadow Clo., St.H.	MM27 66
Marlborough Rd., Wirr.	L30 71	Masefield Pl.	Q25 55	Meadow Clo., Wirr.	N45 147
Marlborough St.	P31 94	Masefield Rd.	P22 40	Meadow Cres.	H36 108
Marldon Av.	N24 39	Maskell Rd.	T31 96	Meadow Croft	HH30 82
Marldon Rd.	U29 75	Mason Av., Halton	GG35 120	Meadow Dr.	Z33 99
Marled Hey	X29 77	Mason Av., Wirr.	J32 91	Meadow La., Ains.	M11 12
Marley Clo.	FF32 102	Mason Clo.	OO23 52	Meadow La., Birk.	N36 111
Fawley Rd.		Mason St., Birk.	N34 111	Meadow La., Liver.	U29 75
Marlfield La.	H39 124	Mason St., Edge H.	R32 95	Meadow La., Mag.	T20 29
Marlfield Rd.	U30 75	Mason St., Sefton	M24 38	Meadow La., Nest.	N45 147
Marline Av.	P42 143	Mason St., Wall.	L29 71	Meadow La., St.H.	JJ28 82
Marlowe Rd.	K31 91	Mason St., Wool.	X36 116	Meadow Rd., Brom.	P41 143
Marlsfield St.	S31 95	Massams La.	K14 16	Meadow Rd., W.Kirby	D36 106
Marlsham Cres.	E35 107	Massey Pk.	L30 71	Meadow St.	L29 71
Marlston Av.	G38 124	Massey St., St.H.	HH29 82	Meadow Vw.	O23 39
Marlwood Av.	K30 70	Massey St., Wirr.	M33 92	Meadow Vw., C.Face	HH31 103
Marmaduke St.	R32 95	Massie Rd.	E34 107	*Farm Rd.*	
Marmion Av.	Q25 55	Mather Av.	JJ27 64	Meadow Way	U28 75
Marmion Rd., Liver.	S35 113	Mather Av., Moss.H.	U35 114	Meadow Wk.	G39 124
Marmion Rd., Wirr.	B33 87	Mather Rd.	L34 110	Meadow, The	H35 108
Marnwood Rd.	V24 43	Mather St.	R35 113	Meadowbrook Rd.	F33 89
Marnwood Wk.	V24 43	Matherley St.	M32 92	Meadowcroft Pk.	V31 96
Marple Clo.	K35 109	Mathers Av.	JJ27 64	Meadowcroft Rd.	D32 88
Marquis Rd.	O37 127	Mathison Rd.	EE38 135	Meadowcroft, Hes.	J40 140
Marquis St.	M35 110	Matlock Av.	O 7 9	Meadowcroft, Wigan	MM22 51
Marquis St.	Q32 94	Matlock Cres.	O 7 9	Meadowfield Clo.	N36 111
Mars Way	R31 95	Matlock Rd., Liver.	R26 56	Meadows, The	EE31 101
Marsden Av.	EE27 62	Matlock Rd., Sefton	O 7 9	Meadowside	H31 90
Marsden Clo., Wall.	M30 71	Matthew St., Liver.	P32 94	Meadway Av.	Q24 40
Poole Rd.		Matthew St., Wirr.	N32 93	Meadway Clo.	RR25 68
Marsden Rd.	Q 5 6	Matthews Gro.	EE29 80	Meadway, Brom.	P40 143
Marsden Rd., Know.	Z38 133	Maud St.	R34 113	Meadway, H.Green	DD36 119
Marsden Rd., Wall.	M30 71	Maureen Wk., Know.	U25 57	Meadway, Hes.	G42 139
Poole Rd.		*Amanda Rd.*		Meadway, Roby	V33 97
Marsden St.	R31 95	Mauretania Rd.	R28 74	Meadway, Upt.	H34 108
Marsh Av.	Q26 55	Mavis Dr.	H35 108	Meadway, Wall.	L30 71
Marsh Hall Rd.	GG35 120	Mawdesley St.	P29 73	Meadway, Whist.	CC31 100
Marsh La., Formby	M18 20	Mawdsley Clo.	L15 16	Meadway, Will.	R45 149
Marsh La., H.Beb.	M37 126	Max Rd.	W30 76	Mealors Weint	H44 144
Marsh La., Lith.	O27 54	Maxton Rd.	S31 95	Meander, The	W28 76
Marsh La., Warr.	LL36 152	Maxwell Clo.	H34 108	Measham Clo.	HH26 64
Marsh St.	P28 73	Maxwell Pl.	T30 75	*Mowbray Av.*	
Marshall Av.	HH29 82	Maxwell Rd.	T30 75	Medbourne Cres.	W25 58
Marshall Pl.	P31 94	Maxwell St.	FF27 63	Meddowcroft Rd.	K30 70
Summer Seat		*Carlton St.*		Medeas	Q30 73
Marshall St.	M33 92	May Av.	M32 92	Medlock St.	Q39 73
Marshalls Clo.	S19 28	May Clo.	O26 54	Medway Clo.	MM22 51
Marshalls Cross Rd.	GG29 81	May Dr.	R42 150	Medway Rd.	N36 111
Marshallsay	L16 20	May Rd.	G41 139	Melbourne St., St.H.	FF29 81
Marsham Clo.	G33 90	May St.	P27 55	Melbourne St., Wirr.	K29 70
Marsham Rd.	Y35 116	Maybank Clo.	R 4 7	Melbreck Rd.	U36 114
Marshfield Rd.	U28 75	Maybank Rd.	M35 110	Melbury Rd.	X30 77
Marshgate	DD37 135	Maybury Way	S36 113	Meldreth Clo.	J16 19
Marshland Gro.	JJ29 82	*Fulwood Dr.*		Meldrum Rd.	U34 114
Marshlands Rd.	J30 70	Mayer Av.	N39 127	Melford Dr., Asht.	NN23 51
Marshside Rd.	Q 3 2	Mayers St.	Q29 73	Melford Dr., Orrell	HH19 36
Marsland Wk.	JJ29 82	Mayew Rd.	G38 124	Melford Dr., Pren.	K36 109
Marsland Gro.		Mayfair Av., Liver.	W32 97	Melksham Dr.	F37 123
Marston clo., Elles.	Q43 148	Mayfair Av., Sefton	N22 39	Melling Av.	R25 56
Marston Clo., Wirr.	K36 109	Mayfair Clo.	R31 95	Melling Dr.	W23 43
Marston Cres.	L20 25	*Conway Dr.*		Melling La.	T21 29
Marten Av.	P40 143	Mayfair Gro.	EE36 119	Melling Rd., Ain.	R25 56
Martensen St.	R32 95	Mayfare Av.	S18 23	Melling Rd., Lith.	P26 55
Martin Av.	FF26 63	Mayfield Av., Know.	DD36 119	Melling Rd., S.Port	Q 5 6
Martin Clo., Know.	DD31 101	Mayfield Av., St.H.	FF29 81	Melling Rd., Wirr.	L29 71
Martin Clo., Liver.	U36 114	Mayfield Clo., Gars.	U37 130	Melling Way	W23 43
Martin Clo., Wirr.	F38 123	Mayfield Clo., W.Derby	V30 76	Mellings Av.	JJ20 36
Martin Rd.	U36 114	Mayfield Gdns.	K44 145	Mellock Clo.	K45 145
Martindale Rd., Liver.	V34 115	Mayfield Rd., Beb.	O39 127	Mellock La.	K45 145
Troutbeck Rd.		Mayfield Rd., Liver.	U37 130	Melloncroft Dr.	C37 122
Martindale Rd., St.H.	GG24 48	Mayfield Rd., Wall.	K30 70	Melloncroft Dr. W.	C37 122
Martine Clo.	U23 42	Mayfields	Q29 73	Mellor Clo., Huy.	AA33 99
Martinhall Rd.	T27 57	*Whitefield Av.*		*Tarbock Rd.*	
Martins La.	M31 92	Mayfields, New F.	P37 128	Mellor Rd.	L36 110
Martland Av.	T23 42	Maynard St.	R33 95	Melly Rd.	R36 113
Martland Rd.	Y35 116	Mayville Rd.	U34 114	Melmerby Clo.	MM23 51
Martlet Rd.	V30 76	McBride St.	V38 131	*Lazonby Cres.*	
Martock	CC32 100	McClellan Pl.	GG36 120	Melrose Av., Cros.	R 2 3

Melrose Av., Crosby N23 39
Melrose Av., St.H. DD26 62
Melrose Av., Warr. MM29 84
Melrose Av., Wirr. C33 88
Melrose Cres. LL23 50
Melrose Dr. LL19 37
Melrose Gdns. K37 125
Melrose Rd., Kirkby V22 43
Melrose Rd., Liver. P29 73
Melrose Rd., Sefton N25 54
Melside Rd. V29 76
Melton Clo. G34 108
Melton Dr. H35 108
Melverley Rd. U24 42
Melville Av. O36 111
Melville Pl. R33 95
Melville Pl., C.Wood HH36 121
Melville Rd., Sefton P25 55
Melville Rd., Wirr. N38 127
Melville St. Q35 112
Melwood Dr. V29 76
Menai Rd. P26 55
Mendell Clo. M41 143
New Chester Rd.
Mendip Av. LL19 37
Mendip Gro. JJ27 64
Mendip Rd., Liver. U34 114
Mendip Rd., Wirr. M36 110
Menivale Clo. R 2 3
Menlo Av. G38 124
Menlo Clo. K35 109
Menlove Av. U34 114
Menlove Gdns. N. U34 114
Menlove Gdns. S. U34 114
Menlove Gdns. W. U34 114
Menstone Rd. T31 96
Mentmore Cres. U28 75
Mentmore Rd. U36 114
Menzies St. R35 113
Meols Clo. K16 19
Meols Cop Rd. Q 6 6
Meols Dr. B35 105
Meols Par. C32 88
Mercer Av. V24 43
Mercer Ct. W30 76
Alun Dale Rd.
Mercer Rd., St.H. LL26 65
Mercer Rd., Wirr. K33 91
Mercer St., Asht. PP27 67
Mercer St., Liver. V38 131
Mercer St., Warr. MM30 84
Mercers La. X19 31
Mere Av. O42 142
Mere Bnk. T34 114
Mere Farm Gro. K35 109
Mere Farm Rd. K35 109
Mere Grn. R28 74
Mere Gro. GG24 48
Mere La., Hes. G40 139
Mere La., Liver. Q30 73
Mere La., Wall. K30 70
Mere Park Rd. F35 107
Mere Rd., Asht. OO23 52
Mere Rd., Newt. PP27 67
Mere Rd., Sefton J16 19
Mere View Cres. V27 58
Merecroft Av. M32 92
Meredale Rd. U35 114
Meredith St. W38 131
Merehey DD28 80
Mereland Way JJ28 82
Merepark Dr. R 3 3
Meribel Clo. O22 39
Meridan Av. N40 142
Meriden Clo., Sefton L10 12
Meriden Clo., St.H. HH26 64
Merlewood Av. R 3 3
Merlin Av. F34 107
Merlin Clo. F34 107
Merlin St. Q34 112
Merrills La. H34 108
Merrilocks Grn. L22 38
Merrilocks Rd. L22 38
Merrilox Av. S19 28
Merrion Clo. W35 115
Merritt Av. L33 92
Merrivale Rd. Y36 116
Mersey Av., Formby K14 16
Mersey Av., Liver. T37 130
Mersey Av., Mag. T20 29
Mersey Bank Rd. O37 127
Mersey La. S. O36 111
Mersey Mt. N35 111
Mersey Rd., Liver. T37 130
Mersey Rd., Sefton M23 38
Mersey Rd., Wirr. O36 111
Mersey St., St.H. KK27 65
Mersey St., Wall. N32 93
Mersey View Rd. DD39 135
Mersey Vw., Liver. V38 131
Mersey Vw., Sefton M24 38
Mersey Vw., Wirr. M38 127
Village Rd.
Merthyr Gro. W32 97
Merton Bank Rd. HH26 64
Merton Clo. X32 98
Merton Cres. X32 98
Merton Dr. X32 98
Merton Gro., Crosby M23 38
Merton Gro., Lith. P27 55
Merton Pl. M34 110
Merton Rd., Sefton P27 55
Merton Rd., Wall. L31 92
Merton Rd., Wigan KK19 37
Merton Rd., Will R43 149
Merton St. HH26 64
Mesham Clo. G35 108
Methuen St., Liver. T33 96
Methuen St., Wirr. L33 92
Mews Ct. N45 147
Mews, The Y30 77
Dannette Hey
Meyrick Rd. T28 75
Michaels Clo. K15 16
Michaels La. O11 13
Mickering La. U18 153
Micklefield Rd. T34 114
Mickleton Clo. L10 12
Middle Hey Rd. Y27 59
Middle Moss La. N15 17
Middle Rd. O38 127
Middle St. P30 73
Middle Way V26 58
Middle Withins La. N17 21
Middlefield Rd. W35 115
Middlehurst Av. FF27 63
Halefield St.
Middlehurst Clo. DD29 80
Middlemass Hey Z34 117
Middlesex Rd. P27 55
Middleton Rd., Liver. T32 96
Middleton Rd., Sefton N24 39
Midghall St. P31 94
Midland St., Halton GG36 120
Midland St., Wirr. M34 110
Midland Ter. M24 38
Midlothian Dr. M23 38
Midway Rd. Z31 99
Mild End P31 94
Mildenhall Rd. X34 116
Mildmay Rd., Liver. T28 75
Mildmay Rd., Sefton O26 54
Miles Clo. F35 107
Miles La. F36 107
Miles St. R35 113
Milford St. P30 73
Milk St. GG27 63
Mill Bnk. T30 75
Mill Brow, C.Face HH30 82
Mill Brow, H.Beb. M38 126
Mill Brow, St.H. DD27 62
Mill Clo. N22 39
Mill Ct. P22 40
Mill Green La. HH34 121
Mill Grn. V28 76
Mill Grn., Will. N45 147
Mill Gro. O25 54
Mill Hey FF32 102
Mill La.
Mill Hey Rd. C38 122
Mill Hill L35 110
Mill Hill Rd. F38 123
Mill La. R 4 7
Mill La. DD24 47
Mill La. PP27 67
Mill La. Cres. R 4 7
Mill La., Augh. T16 153
Mill La., Boot. P27 55
Mill La., Cron. EE34 119
Mill La., Farn. HH34 121
Mill La., Gol. QQ25 68
Mill La., Greas. F36 107
Mill La., Hes. H41 139
Mill La., Kirkby V23 43
Mill La., Know. Y26 59
Mill La., Olive. U33 96
Mill La., R.Hill EE32 101
Mill La., S.Port P 6 6
Mill La., St.H. HH30 82
Mill La., W.Derby U30 75
Mill La., Wall. L31 92
Mill La., Will. N44 147
Mill Park Dr. Q43 148
Mill Rd., Beb. P39 128
Mill Rd., Liver. R31 95
Mill Rd., Sefton M10 12
Mill Rd., Thing. H38 124
Mill Rd., Woodhey M37 126
Mill St. OO24 52
Mill St., Birk. M35 110
Mill St., Gol. QQ25 68
Mill St., Liver. Q34 112
Mill St., Nest. J45 145
Mill St., Pres. BB30 79
High St.
Mill St., St.H. FF27 63
Mill Ter. M38 126
Mill View Dr. M38 126
Millars Pl. R 2 3
Millbank La. T19 29
Millbank Rd. L31 92
Millbeck Gro. GG24 48
Millbrook Cres. W23 43
Millbrook Dr. W23 43
Millbrook La. DD27 62
Millbrook Wk. W23 43
Millbrow Clo. HH30 82
Mill Brow
Millbrow, Widnes. HH36 121
Millbut Clo. M38 126
Millcroft O22 39
Millcroft Rd. Y36 116
Miller Av. M22 38
Miller Clo. Q35 112
Miller Rd., Wirr. H41 139
Millers Bridge O28 72
Millers Way E33 89
Millersdale Clo. Q42 143
Millersdale Rd. U35 114
Millersend Av. R25 56
Millfield Clo. U30 75
Millfield Clo., H.Beb. M38 126
Millfield la. MM24 51
Millfield Rd. HH36 121
Millfields DD27 62
Millford Dr. W27 58
Millgreen Clo. W27 58
Millhouse La. E33 89
Millingford Av. PP24 52
Millingford Gro. NN23 51
Millington Clo. K36 109
Millom Av. DD31 101
Millom Gro. EE29 80
Millstead Rd. U33 96
Millthwaithe Rd. K31 91
Millvale St. S31 95
Millway Rd. AA39 133
Millwood M38 126
Millwood Av. DD27 62
Millwood Rd. Z39 137
Milman Clo. G35 108
Arrowe Park Rd.
Milman Rd. R28 74
Milne Clo. MM25 66
Milne Rd. T29 75
Milner Cop H41 139
Milner Rd., Liver. T36 114
Milner St. L33 92
Milnthorpe MM30 84
Milnthorpe Clo. Q29 73
Mercer Dr.
Milroy St. R32 95
Milton Av., R.Hill CC31 100
Milton Av., Roby W32 97
Milton Av., St.H. NN27 66
Milton Clo. CC31 100
Milton Cres. H40 139
Milton Gro. HH20 36
Milton Rd. E. M35 110
Milton Rd., Birk. M35 110
Milton Rd., Liver. T32 96
Milton Rd., Sefton N24 39
Milton Rd., W.Kirby B35 105
Milton Rd., Wall. M32 92
Milton Rd., Wigan RR25 68
Milton St., Lith. O27 54
Milton St., S.Port Q 5 6
Milton St., St.H. GG32 102
Milverton St. S31 95
Mimosa Rd. U33 96
Mindale Rd. T33 96
Minehead Gro. HH30 82
Minehead Rd. T37 130
Mines Av., Know. CC30 79
Mines Av., Liver. T37 130

Minshull St.	R32	95
Minstead Av.	W24	43
Minto Clo.	S32	95
Minto St.	R32	95
Kensington St.		
Minton Way	GG34	120
Mintor Rd.	X24	44
Minver Rd.	V29	76
Miranda Av.	N37	127
Miranda Pl.	P28	73
Miranda Rd.	P28	73
Mirfield Clo., Know	Z38	133
Mirfield Clo., Wigan	RR25	68
Mirfield St.	S31	95
Miriam Pl.	K33	91
Miriam Rd.	R30	74
Miskelly St.	P29	73
Missouri Rd.	S29	74
Miston St.	P29	73
Mitchell Av.	LL30	83
Mitchell Cres.	O24	39
Mitchell Rd., Bill.	JJ22	49
Mitchell Rd., Pres.	BB30	79
Mitchell Rd., St.H.	EE28	80
Mitchell St., Asht.	OO24	52
Mitchell St., Gol.	QQ25	68
Mitford Clo.	Q30	73
Mitford St.	Q30	73
Mitford Way	Q30	73
Mitre Clo.	BB32	100
Mittens La.	L15	16
Mitylene St.	Q30	73
Mobberley Way	O39	127
Mockbeggar Rd.	J29	70
Modred St.	Q34	112
Moffatdale Rd.	S29	74
Moffatt Rd.	R25	56
Moffatt Rd. W.	R25	56
Molesworth Gro.	W32	97
Moll Clo.	V29	76
Mollington Av.	T28	75
Mollington Rd.	M31	92
Mollington St.	N34	111
Mollys La.	Y25	59
Molton Rd.	V33	97
Molyneux Av.	V32	97
Molyneux Clo., Huy.	Z32	99
Molyneux Clo., R.Hill	BB31	100
Molyneux Clo., Upton	G35	108
Molyneux Dr., Know.	BB31	100
Molyneux Dr., Wirr.	L29	71
Molyneux La.	BB31	100
Molyneux Rd., Crosby	N24	39
Molyneux Rd., Liver.	R31	95
Molyneux Rd., Mag.	T21	29
Molyneux Rd., Moss.H.	T35	114
Molyneux Way	S23	41
Mona St., Sefton	P26	55
Mona St., St.H.	EE28	80
St. Georges Rd.		
Mona St., Wirr.	K33	91
Monash Rd.	T29	75
Monastery La.	JJ29	82
Monastery Rd., Liver.	S30	74
Monastery Rd., St.H.	JJ29	82
Mond Rd.	T25	57
Monfa Rd.	P26	55
Monica Dr.	GG34	120
Monica Rd.	X36	116
Monica Ter.	NN24	51
Monk Rd.	L31	92
Monk St., Birk.	N34	111
Cross St.		
Monk St., Liver.	Q30	73
Mere La.		
Monkfield Way	V39	131
Monks Carr La.	O18	21
Monks Clo.	L16	20
Monks Dr.	L16	20
Monks Ferry Brow	N34	111
Monks Way, Beb.	N39	131
Monks Way, Wool.	X36	116
Monksdown Rd.	U28	75
Monksferry Wk.	T37	130
Monksway, W.Kirby	C36	106
Monkswell Dr.	U33	96
Monkswell St.	R35	113
Monmouth Cres.	OO24	52
Monmouth Dr.	T24	42
Monmouth Gro.	HH28	82
Monmouth Rd.	K31	91
Montagu Rd., Sefton	K14	16
Montague Rd., Liver.	U32	96
Montclair Dr.	U34	114
Monterey Rd.	U32	96
Montgomery Av.	R 6	7
Montgomery Hill	D37	122
Montgomery Rd., Halton	EE37	135
Montgomery Rd., Know.	Y31	98
Montgomery Rd., Liver.	R26	56
Montpellier Cres.	K29	70
Montrey Cres.	LL23	50
Montrey Clo.		
Montrose Av.	N32	93
Montrose Dr.	Q 4	6
Montrose Pl., Hale.	X38	133
Redbourn Av		
Montrose Rd.	S30	74
Montrovia Cres.	T25	57
Monument Pl.	Q32	94
Monville St.	S25	56
Moon St.	GG36	120
Moor Clo.	N22	39
Moor La.		
Moor Clo.	HH36	121
Moor Coppice	N22	39
Moor Dr., Sefton	N22	39
Moor Hey Rd.	S22	41
Moor La., Ains.	M12	12
Moor La., Crosby	N22	39
Moor La., Faza.	U25	57
Moor La., Hom.Grn.	P21	27
Moor La., Ince.	N20	26
Moor La., Kirk.	R28	74
Moor La., Wirr.	G41	139
Moor Pl.	Q32	94
Moor St.	O26	54
Moor St.	P32	94
Moorcroft Rd., All.	V36	115
Moorcroft Rd., Know.	Z30	78
Moorcroft Rd., Wall.	J30	70
Moore Av., St.H.	KK27	65
Moore Av., Wirr.	N36	111
Moore Dr.	MM26	66
Moorfield	W22	43
Moorfield Dr.	J44	145
Moorfield Rd., Farn.	HH35	121
Moorfield Rd., Sefton	O22	39
Moorfield Rd., St.H.	EE26	62
Moorfields	P32	94
Moorfoot Rd.	JJ27	64
Moorfoot Way	V22	43
Moorgate Av.	N23	39
Moorgate Rd.	W26	58
Moorhouses	K19	24
Moorings, The	F41	138
Moorland Av.	N22	39
Moorland Clo.	H41	139
Moorland Pk.	H41	139
Moorland Rd., Sefton	S22	41
Moorland Rd., Wigan	PP23	52
Moorland Rd., Wirr.	N25	111
Moorlands Rd.	O22	39
Moorside Av.	J45	145
Moorside Clo.	N23	39
Moorside La.	J45	145
Moorside Rd.	N23	39
Moorway, St.H.	FF32	102
Moorway, Wirr.	H41	139
Morbreck Av.	W32	97
Morden Av.	NN23	51
Morden St.	S31	95
Morecambe St.	S30	74
Morecroft Rd.	O36	111
Morella Rd.	S29	74
Morello Dr.	O40	142
Moret Clo.	O22	39
Moreton Av.	HH31	103
Four Acre La.		
Moreton Clo.	PP24	52
Moreton Gro.	J30	70
Moreton Rd.	G34	108
Moreton Spur Rd.	G33	90
Morgan St.	HH28	82
Morland Av., Brom.	P41	143
Morland Av., Nest.	K45	145
Morley Av.	L33	92
Morley Rd., Sefton	P 4	6
Morley Rd., Wirr.	L32	92
Morley St.	FF26	63
Morningside	N23	39
Morningside Pl.	T28	75
Morningside Rd.	T29	75
Morningside Vw.	T29	75
Morningside Way	T29	75
Mornington Av.	N24	39
Mornington Grn. Rd.	L30	71
Mornington Rd.	P 5	6
Mornington St.	Q34	112
Morpeth Clo.	E32	89
Morpeth Rd.	B34	105
Morpeth St.	Q33	94
Morris Clo., St.H.	KK26	65
Morris Clo., Wirr.	J35	109
Morris St.	JJ28	82
Morston Av.	W25	58
Morston Cres.	W25	58
Morston Wk., Know.	W25	58
Morston Av.		
Mortimer St.	N34	111
Morton St.	Q34	112
Mortuary Rd.	L30	71
Morval Cres.	O28	73
Morven Rd.	Q 5	6
Moscow Dr.	T30	75
Mosedale Av.	GG24	48
Mosedale Rd.	R26	56
Moseley Av.	L31	92
Moseley Rd.	O40	142
Moses St.	Q35	112
Mosley St.	O 7	9
Moss Av.	HH19	36
Moss Bank Rd.	FF25	63
Moss Bnk.	X31	98
Moss Brow	CC21	33
Moss Close Rd.	O45	147
Moss Delph La.	U15	153
Moss End Way	Y23	44
Moss Gate Gro.	X31	98
Moss Gate Rd.	X31	98
Moss Green Way	KK28	83
Moss Grn.	L15	16
Moss Gro., Liver.	S34	113
Moss Gro., Wirr.	L36	110
Moss La., Barrow Nook	Z20	32
Moss La., Basford Farm	W21	30
Moss La., Birk.	L36	110
Moss La., Formby	M15	17
Moss La., Gol.	QQ26	68
Moss La., High.	L18	20
Moss La., Lith.	O25	54
Moss La., Lith.	O26	55
Moss La., Lyd.	R18	23
Moss La., Mag.	T20	29
Moss La., Northwood	X23	44
Moss La., S.Port	R 5	7
Moss La., St.H.	KK28	83
Moss La., W.Lan.	X19	31
Moss La., Wall.	DD25	62
East Lancs. Rd.		
Moss La., Wall.	EE22	47
Moss Nook La., Sefton	U21	29
Moss Nook La., St.H.	CC22	46
Moss Pits Clo.	T25	57
Moss Pits La., Faza.	T25	57
Moss Pitts La., Liver.	U33	96
Moss Rd., Sefton	P 8	10
Moss Rd., Wigan	HH19	36
Moss Side, Know.	X31	98
Moss Side, Sefton	L15	16
Moss St., Gars.	V38	131
Moss St., Know.	BB29	79
Moss St., Liver.	Q32	94
Moss Vale	S45	149
Moss Vw., Lith.	P25	55
Moss Vw., Mag.	T20	29
Moss Way	V27	58
Mossborough Hall La.	BB24	46
Mossborough Rd.	BB24	46
Mossbrow Rd.	Z31	99
Mosscroft	X22	44
Mosscroft Clo., Know.	AA31	99
Whiston La.		
Mossdale Dr.	EE31	101
Mossdene Rd.	K31	91
Mossfield Rd.	O26	55
Mossgiel Av.	L11	12
Mosshill Clo.	S19	28
Mosside	O25	54
Mosslands	DD27	62
Mosslands Dr.	K30	70
Mosslawn Rd.	X24	44
Mosslea Pk.	T35	114
Mossley Av., Liver.	T34	114
Mossley Av., Wirr.	P41	143
Mossley Bank Rd.	M31	92
Mossley Hill Dr.	T35	114
Mossley Hill Rd.	T36	114
Mossley Rd.	N35	111
Mossville Clo.	U36	114
Mossville Rd.	U36	114
Mostyn Av., Hes.	F41	138
Mostyn Av., Liver.	V37	131
Mostyn Av., Sefton	S23	41
Mostyn Av., W.Kirby	B36	105

Mostyn Clo. Q29 73
Mercer Dr.
Mostyn Gdns. H44 144
Mostyn St. L32 92
Motherwell Cres. Q 7 10
Folkstone Rd.
Mottershead Rd. GG36 120
Mottram Clo. W24 43
Mould St. P30 73
Mounsey Rd. M34 110
Mount Av., Beb. M37 126
Mount Av., Hes. G41 139
Mount Av., Sefton P25 55
Mount Clo. V23 43
Mount Cres. U23 42
Mount Dr. M37 126
Mount Gro. M34 110
Mount House Clo. L14 16
Mount House Rd. L15 16
Mount Olive L35 110
Mount Park Ct. X35 116
Mount Park Gate X35 116
Mount Park, Beb. M37 126
Kings Clo.
Mount Pleasant Av. KK27 65
Mount Pleasant Rd. L30 71
Mount Pleasant, App. GG36 120
Mount Pleasant, Liver. Q32 94
Mount Pleasant, Sefton M24 38
Mount Pleasant, Wirr. L35 110
Mount Rd. U23 42
Mount Rd. N. U23 42
Mount Rd., Beb. M39 126
Mount Rd., Birk. M36 110
Mount Rd., Upt. H34 108
Mount Rd., W.Kirby C36 106
Mount Rd., Wall. K29 70
Mount Rd., Wirr. N40 142
Mount St., Crosby M24 38
Mount St., Liver. Q33 94
Mount St., S.Port P 5 6
Mount Vernon Grn. R32 95
Mount Vernon R32 95
North Vw.
Mount Vernon Rd. R32 95
Mount Way M37 126
Mount Wood Rd. M37 126
Mount, The, Hes. G41 139
Mount, The, Wall. M31 92
Mounthaven Clo. H34 108
Moville St. Q35 112
Mowbray Av. HH26 64
Mowbray Gro. U32 96
Mowcroft La. KK35 152
Moxen Dale Z35 117
Moxon St. EE28 80
Mozart Clo. R34 113
Muirhead Av. T29 75
Muirhead Av. E. U28 75
Mulberry Av. EE27 62
Mulberry Clo. W22 43
Mulberry Gro. M31 92
Mulberry Rd. N36 111
Mulberry St. Q33 94
Mulcrow Clo. HH27 64
Mulgrave St. R33 95
Mulliner St. S33 95
Mullins Av. OO26 67
Mullion Clo., Know. Z36 117
Mullion Clo., Sefton R 2 3
Mullion Rd. V26 58
Mulveton Rd. N39 127
Donne Av.
Mumfords La. D32 88
Muncaster Clo. P40 143
Hornby Rd.
Muncaster Dr. DD21 34
Munro St. Q35 112
Mill St.
Munster Rd. U31 96
Murat Gro. M24 38
Murat St. M24 38
Murcote Rd. W30 76
Murdoch St. S33 95
Muriel Clo. LL33 104
Muriel St. R29 74
Murphy Gro. JJ27 64
Murray Gro. B35 105
Murrayfield Dr. G31 90
Murrayfield Rd. X34 116
Musker Dr. P23 40
Musker Gdns. N23 39
Musker St.
Musker St. N23 39
Muspratt Rd. O26 54

Muttocks Rake P22 40
Great Hey
Myddleton La. QQ30 86
Myers Gdns. HH30 82
Myers Rd. E. N23 39
Myers Rd. W. M23 38
Myerscough Av. O26 55
Mynsule Rd. N39 127
Delves Av.
Myrtle Av., Newt. OO28 85
Myrtle Av., Wall. KK25 65
Myrtle Av., Wigan MM22 51
Myrtle Gdns. R33 95
Myrtle Gro., Crosby M24 38
Myrtle Gro., Halton EE37 135
Myrtle Gro., S.Port Q 5 6
Myrtle Gro., St.H. HH23 49
Coronation Way
Myrtle Gro., Wirr. M31 92
Myrtle Parade Q33 94
Myrtle St.
Myrtle St. Q33 94
Myrtle St., Wirr. L33 92
Upper Beckwith St.

Nairn Clo. L43 148
Dancanby Dr.
Nansen Gro. R28 74
Nansen Rd. U32 96
Nant Park Ct. L29 71
Nantwich Clo. H36 108
Napier Clo. FF27 63
Napier Dr. G33 90
Napier Rd. O37 127
Napier St. Q31 94
Napier St. FF27 63
Naples Rd. M32 92
Napps Way, Liver. W33 97
Napps Way, Wirr. H40 139
Narrow La. U15 153
Naseby Clo. J35 109
Naseby St. Q28 73
Nasty Av. U20 29
Natal Rd. R26 56
Naylor Av. QQ25 68
Naylor Rd., App. HH36 121
Naylor Rd., Wirr. KK33 91
Naylor St. P31 94
Naylorsfield Dr., Y34 116
 Liver.
Naylorsfield Dr., Know. Y33 98
Nazeby Av. O23 39
Neale Dr. G36 108
Nedens Gro. S19 28
Nedens La. S19 28
Needham Cres. J35 109
Needham Rd. S32 95
Needwood Dr. N39 127
Neil St., Halton HH36 121
Neil St., Liver. Q30 73
Neills Rd. KK30 83
Neilson Av. CC32 100
Neilson Pl. BB32 100
Neilson Rd. R35 113
Nells La. T17 153
Nelson Dr. G39 124
Nelson Rd. O36 111
Nelson Rd., Lith. O25 54
Bridge Rd.
Nelson Rd., Liver. R32 95
Nelson St. O 6 5
Nelson St., Boot. O28 72
Nelson St., C.Face HH32 82
Waterdale Cres.
Nelson St., Liver. P33 94
Nelson St., Newt. NN27 66
Nelson St., Wirr. M29 71
Nelsons Cft. O39 127
Neptune St., Liver. O31 93
Neptune St., Wall. M33 92
Ness Acres La. N45 147
Neston Av. HH31 103
Eastham Cres.
Neston Gdns. L33 92
Neston Rd. N45 147
Neston Rd., Thorn. L42 141
Neston St. Q28 73
Netherby St. Q35 112
Netherfield EE37 135
Netherfield Clo. J35 109
Netherfield Rd. N. Q30 73
Netherfield Rd. S. Q31 94
Netherley Rd. AA34 117
Netherton Gra. R23 41

Netherton La. Q22 40
Netherton Park Rd. P25 55
Netherton Rd., Liver. U36 114
Netherton Rd., More. F33 89
Netherton Rd., Sefton P26 55
Netherwood Rd. T28 75
Netley St. Q29 73
Nettlestead Rd. U28 75
Neva Av. F33 89
Nevill St., Sefton O 5 5
Neville Av. KK28 83
Neville Clo. J35 109
Neville Rd., Brom. Q41 143
Neville Rd., Liver. S25 56
Neville Rd., Sefton M24 38
Neville Rd., Wall. L31 92
Neville St., St.H. NN27 66
Nevison St. R32 95
Nevitte Clo. X29 77
New Bank Rd. DD36 119
New Bird St. P33 94
New Boston MM25 66
New Bridge Clo. H35 108
New Carr La. P18 22
New Causeway L17 20
New Chester Rd. Q40 143
New Chester Rd., Beb. P38 128
New Cross St., Know. BB29 79
Rowson St.
New Cut AA25 60
New Cut La., Sefton O 9 9
New Cut La., St.H. BB24 46
New Ferry Pier App. O36 111
New Ferry Rd. O37 127
New Ferry Ter. O37 127
New Field Clo. P22 40
New Glade Hill JJ26 64
New Hall La., Liver. T28 75
New Haven Rd. M29 71
New Henderson St. Q34 112
New Hey U30 75
New Hey Clo. H35 108
New Hey La. N45 147
New Hey Rd. H35 108
New Hutte La. Z38 133
New Islington Q32 94
New La. O10 13
New La. S 3 3
New Meadow La. N17 21
New Mill Stile X35 116
New Quay O32 93
New Rd., Know. CC29 79
New Rd., Liver. T30 75
New Rd., Sefton L15 16
New Rd., Wirr. R45 149
New School La. R45 149
New St. N32 93
New St., St.H. OO23 52
New Tower Ct. HH30 82
New Way M29 71
Newark Clo. X20 31
Newark St. R23 41
Newbold Cres. Q28 73
Newborough Av., Liver. D35 106
Newborough Av., Sefton T34 114
Newbridge Clo. O23 39
Coldstone Dr. LL23 50
Newburn St. R28 74
Newburns La. L35 110
Newby Av. DD31 101
Burton Av.
Newby Clo. L11 12
Newby Dr. Y31 98
Newby Grn. V28 76
Newby Pl. GG25 63
Newby Rd. Y31 98
Newby St. Q29 73
Newcastle Rd. U34 114
Newcombe St. R30 74
Newcroft Rd. W35 115
Newcross St. FF27 63
Newcross St., St.H. F27 63
Newdown Rd. V26 58
Newell Rd. L31 92
Newenham Cres. W31 97
Newgate St. Q29 73
Newglade Hill HH26 64
Newhall La., W.Kirby B34 105
Newhall St. P33 94
Newholme Clo. W27 58
Newhouse Rd. S33 95
Newick Rd. V24 43
Newington Q32 94
Newland Dr. L31 92

Street	Grid	Page
Newland St.	S35	113
Newlands Dr.	RR25	68
Newlands Rd., St.H.	HH25	64
Newlands Rd., Wirr.	O39	127
Newling St.	M33	92
Newlyn Av., Lith.	O24	39
Newlyn Av., Mag.	T20	29
Newlyn Clo., Hoy.	D32	88
Newlyn Dr.	NN24	51
Newlyn Gro.	HH25	64
Newlyn Rd., Know.	V26	58
Newlyn Rd., Wirr.	D32	88
Newman St.	P29	73
Newmark Clo.	J35	109
Newport Av.	J30	70
Newport Clo.	J35	109
Newport St.	O30	72
News La.	CC20	33
Newsham Dr.	S30	74
Newstead Av.	L23	38
Nicholas Rd.		
Newstead Clo.	L23	38
Newstead St.	S33	95
Newstead Way	J35	109
Newstet Rd.	X24	44
Newton Clo.	U28	75
Newton Cross La.	D36	106
Newton Dr.	D36	106
Newton La.	PP26	67
Newton Park Dr.	PP27	67
Newton Park Rd.	D36	106
Newton Rd., Bill.	JJ22	49
Newton Rd., Hoy.	C33	88
Newton Rd., Newt.	KK27	65
Newton Rd., Wall.	L31	92
Newton Rd., Warr.	PP29	85
Newton Rd., Wigan	QQ27	68
Newton St.	Q 5	6
Newton Ter.	NN27	66
Rathbone St.		
Newton Way	G35	108
Newton Wk.	O27	54
Brackley Clo.		
Newtown	K45	145
Nicander Rd.	T34	114
Nicholas Rd.	L23	38
Nicholas Rd.	EE37	135
Nicholl Rd.	DD26	62
Nicholls Dr.	G39	124
Nicholson St.	JJ27	64
Nicks La.	J15	15
Nicol Rd.	NN22	51
Nicolmere Dr.	NN22	51
Nidderdale Av.	EE31	101
Nigel Rd.	J41	140
Nimrod St.	Q23	73
Nithsdale Rd.	T34	114
Nixon St.	Q28	73
Nixons La.	N 9	9
Noctorum Av.	J35	109
Noctorum Dell	J35	109
Noctorum Rd.	J34	109
Noctorum Way	J35	109
Noel Gte.	U15	153
Noel St.	S33	95
Nolan St.	P 6	6
Nook La., St.H.	JJ28	82
Nook La., Wigan	QQ25	68
Nook Rise	U33	96
Nook, The, Birk.	L34	110
Nook, The, Greas.	E36	107
Nook, The, Liver.	X35	116
Nook, The, St.H.	DD26	62
Noon Ct.	NN28	85
Norburn Cres.	K16	19
Norbury Av., Liver.	T34	114
Norbury Av., St.H.	HH22	49
Wells Av.		
Norbury Av., Wirr.	N38	127
Norbury Clo.	JJ36	121
Cheryl Dr.		
Norbury Clo.	JJ36	121
Norbury Clo., Sefton	S 2	3
Norbury Clo., Wirr.	N38	127
Norbury Fold	FF32	102
Fawley Rd.		
Norbury Rd.	V24	43
Norbury Wk.	V24	43
Norcliffe Rd.	DD31	101
Norcott Dr.	MM30	84
Kilshaw Rd.		
Norfolk Clo.	J35	109
Norfolk Clo., Boot.	P27	55
Norfolk Dr.	C36	106
Norfolk Gro.	N 8	9
Norfolk Pl.	EE37	135
Norfolk Pl., Sea.	O26	54
Seaforth Vale N.		
Norfolk Rd.	S21	28
Norfolk Rd.	JJ20	36
Norfolk Rd., Sefton	N 8	9
Norfolk Rd., St.H.	EE28	80
Norfolk St.	P33	94
Norgate St.	Q29	73
Norland St.	HH36	121
Norlands La.	F33	102
Norley Av.	Q43	148
Norley Dr.	DD28	80
Norley Pl.	Z38	133
Norma Av.	NN25	66
Norma Rd.	N24	39
Norman Av.	PP27	67
Norman Rd., Bids.	K33	91
Norman Rd., Crosby	M23	38
Norman Rd., Lith.	P25	55
Norman Rd., Wall.	M32	92
Normandale Rd.	S28	74
Normandy Rd.	Y31	98
Normans Rd.	JJ29	82
Normanston Rd.	L35	110
Normanton Av.	S35	113
Normington Clo.	S19	28
Norris Green Cres.	T28	75
Norris Green Rd.	U30	75
Norris Green Way	U28	75
Norris Rd.	BB30	79
Norris Way	L15	16
North Av.	X38	132
North Barcombe Rd.	W33	97
North Breeze Hill	Q28	73
North Cantril Av.	W29	76
North Clo.	P40	143
North Dingle	P29	73
North Dr., Hes.	H41	139
North Dr., Sefton	T24	42
North Dr., W.Derby	U30	75
North Dr., Wall.	K29	70
North Dr., Wav.	U33	96
North End La., Know.	Z35	117
North End La., Sefton	L18	20
North Florida Rd.	LL25	65
North Gro.	V36	115
North Gro., St.H.	EE29	80
North Hill St.	Q34	112
North John St., Liver.	P32	94
North John St., St.H.	FF27	63
North Linkside Rd.	Y36	116
North Manor Way	Y36	116
North Mayfields	O37	127
North Meade	R20	28
North Moss La.	M14	17
North Mossley Hill Rd.	T35	114
North Par., Elles.	H44	144
North Par., Know.	Y39	132
North Par., Liver.	Y39	136
North Par., Sefton	W24	43
North Par., Wirr.	B33	87
North Park Ct.	N31	93
North Park Rd.	U23	42
North Perimeter Rd.	Y23	44
North Rd., Birk.	M35	110
North Rd., Cros.	R 3	3
North Rd., Lith.	Q27	55
North Rd., Liver.	T38	130
North Rd., Speke	Z38	133
North Rd., W.Kirby	B36	105
North Rd., Will.	S43	149
North Sefton St.	MM27	66
Albion St.		
North St.	FF26	63
North St.	OO23	52
North St., Hay.	MM26	66
Church Rd.		
North St., Liver.	P32	94
North St., Newt.	MM27	66
North St., Sefton	P 5	6
North Sudley Rd.	T36	114
North Vw.	AA32	99
North Wallasey App. Rd.	J31	91
North Way, Liver.	U32	96
North Wood	K36	109
Northam Clo.	R 2	3
Northbrook Clo.	R33	95
Northbrook Rd.	M31	92
Northbrook St.	R33	95
Northbrooke Way	H35	108
Northcote Rd., Wirr.	J30	70
Northdale Rd.	T33	96
Northdunes	K19	24
Northern La.	DD35	119
Northern Perimeter Rd.	Q22	40
Northern Rd.	Z39	137
Northern Rd., The	N22	39
Northfield Clo.	HH31	103
Farm Rd.		
Northfield Rd.	Q26	55
Northgate Rd.	T30	75
Northleach Dr.	L10	12
Northmead Rd.	W37	131
Northop Rd.	K30	70
Northridge Rd.	H38	124
Northumberland St.	Q34	112
Northumberland Ter.	Q30	73
Northumberland Way	P23	40
Northway, Mag.	S20	28
Northway, W.Lan.	T17	153
Northway, Wirr.	J41	140
Northways, Halton	EE37	135
Northways, Wirr.	L39	128
Western Av.		
Northwich Clo.	O22	39
Northwood Av.	PP27	67
Northwood Clo.	LL19	37
Northwood Rd.	Z31	99
Norton Dr.	F37	123
Norton Gro.,	EE29	80
Thatto Heath		
Norton Gro., Sefton	S22	41
Norton Rd.	B35	105
Norton St., Liver.	Q32	94
Norton St., Sefton	O26	54
Norville	S45	149
Norville Rd.	V32	97
Norway St.	M24	38
Norwich Av., Asht.	OO23	52
Norwich Av., Gol.	RR25	68
Norwich Dr.	H33	90
Norwich Rd.	U34	114
Norwood Av.	MM22	51
Norwood Av., Lith.	Q24	39
Norwood Av., S.Port	Q 5	6
Norwood Av., Wigan	MM22	51
Norwood Clo.	R31	95
White Rock St.		
Norwood Cres.	Q 5	6
Norwood Ct.	F35	107
Pickerill Rd.		
Norwood Gro., Liver.	R31	95
West Derby Rd.		
Norwood Gro., St.H.	DD22	47
Norwood Rd., Greas.	F35	107
Norwood Rd., Sefton	Q 5	6
Norwood Rd., Wall.	L32	92
Norwood Way	R31	95
Norwyn Rd.	T28	75
Nostell Rd.	NN22	51
Nowshera Av.	G38	124
Nun Clo.	L35	110
Nunn St.	HH27	64
Nunsford Clo.	P24	40
Nurse Rd., Thing.	H38	124
Nurseries, The	L16	20
Formby Flds.		
Nursery Clo.	L35	110
Nursery Clo.	HH35	121
Nursery La.	V37	131
Nursery Rd.	EE29	80
Nursery Rd., W.Lan.	S18	23
Nut Clo.	EE29	80
Nut St.	EE29	80
Heath St.		
Nutgrove Av.	EE29	80
Nutgrove Hall Dr.	EE29	80
Nutgrove Rd.	EE30	80
Nuthall Rd.	Q 7	10
Redhill Dr.		
Nuttall St., Liver.	S32	95
Nuttall St., St.H.	FF28	81
Nylands Rd.	Y30	77
O'Brien Gro.	JJ27	64
O'Keefe Rd.	HH27	64
O'Neill St.	O27	54
O'Sullivan Cres.	JJ26	64
Oak Av., Liver.	R26	56
Oak Av., Newt.	OO27	67
Oak Av., St.H.	MM25	66
Oak Av., Wigan	QQ25	68
Oak Av., Wirr.	F34	107
Oak Bnk.	M34	110
Oak Clo., Know.	CC31	100
Oak Clo., Upt.	F33	89
Oak Clo., Wirr.	K36	109
Oak La.	V28	76

Oak La., Crox. V28 76
Oak Leigh T30 75
Oak Rd., Beb. N37 127
Oak Rd., Elles. Q44 148
Oak Rd., R.Hill CC31 100
Oak Rd., Roby Y33 98
Oak St., Lith. P27 55
Oak St., S.Port Q 6 6
Oak St., St.H. JJ29 82
Oak St., Wigan NN22 51
Oak Tower W23 43
Oak Vale U32 96
Oak Vw. AA39 133
Oakbank Rd. T34 114
Oakbank St. M31 92
Oakdale Av. M32 92
Oakdale Dr. F35 107
Oakdale Rd., Liver. U34 114
Oakdale Rd., Sefton M24 38
Oakdale Rd., Wirr. M32 92
Oakdene Clo. P42 143
Oakdene Rd., Liver. R29 74
Oakdene Rd., Wirr. M35 110
Oakenholt Rd. G33 90
Oakes St. Q32 94
Oakfield R30 74
Oakfield Av., Wigan PP24 52
Oakfield Av., Wool. X35 116
Oakfield Clo. EE29 80
Oakfield Dr., Halton DD37 135
Oakfield Dr., Know. Z33 99
Oakfield Dr., Sefton J15 15
Oakfield Gro. Z32 99
Oakfield Rd., Brom. P41 143
Oakfield Rd., Elles. Q45 148
Oakfield Rd., Kirk. R30 74
Oakfield Vw. M34 110
Oakham Dr. T24 42
Oakhill Clo. S20 28
Oakhill Cottage La. S19 28
Oakhill Dr. S19 28
Oakhill Pk. U32 96
Oakhill Rd., Liver. U32 96
Oakhill Rd., Sefton S20 28
Oakhurst Clo. X34 116
Oakland Clo. P26 55
Oakland Dr. H34 108
Oakland Rd. T37 130
Oaklands EE31 101
St. James Rd.
Oaklands Av. N22 39
Oaklands Dr., Beb. N38 127
Oaklands Dr., Hes. H40 139
Oaklands Ter. H40 139
Oaklands Dr.
Oakleigh Gro. N38 127
Oakley Av. JJ22 49
Oakley Clo. W27 58
Oakley Rd. G38 124
Oakmere Dr. F35 107
Oakridge Clo. P40 143
Oakridge Rd. P40 143
Oaks Clo. HH31 103
Oaks La. G39 124
Oaks Way H42 139
Oaks, The P41 143
Oakston Av. EE32 101
Ashton Av.
Oaktree Pl. N35 111
Oaktree Rd. DD26 62
Oakwood M10 12
Oakwood Av. NN24 51
Oakwood Dr. Z32 99
Oakwood Rd. Z37 133
Oakworth Dr., Huy. AA33 99
Bradley Cres.
Oakworth Dr., New F. P37 128
Oamsbey Gro. O42 142
Oarside Dr. L30 71
Oatfield La. O24 39
Oatlands Rd. U24 42
Oatlands, The C36 106
Oban Dr., Wigan LL23 50
Oban Dr., Wirr. H41 139
Milner Rd.
Oban Rd. R30 74
Oberon St. P28 73
Observatory Rd. J33 91
Ocean Rd. O25 54
Oceanic Rd. T32 96
Octavia Hill Rd. P24 40
Odsey St. S32 95
Oglet La., H.Cliff Y40 136
Oglet La., Speke Z41 137
Oil St. O31 93

Okehampton Rd. V33 97
Okell Dr. Z36 117
Old Acre K19 24
Old Barn Rd. L32 92
Old Barn Rd., Liver. R30 74
Old Bidston Rd. L33 92
Old Chester Rd. N35 111
Old Chester Rd., N37 127
Woodhey
Old Church Yd. O32 93
Old Colliery Rd. BB31 100
Old Colliery Yd. LL23 50
Old Eccleston La. EE27 62
Old Farm Clo. O45 147
Hooton Rd.
Old Farm Rd., Crosby N22 39
Old Farm Rd., Liver. W26 58
Old Garswood Rd. HH25 64
Old Hall Clo. S21 28
Old Hall Dr. NN24 51
Old Hall Gdns. DD21 34
Old Hall La. V24 43
Old Hall Rd., Sefton S21 28
Old Hall Rd., Wirr. Q40 143
Old Hall St. O32 93
Old Higher Rd. BB38 134
Old House La. T21 29
Old Hutte La. AA38 133
Old La., Hes. J41 140
Old La., Pres. CC30 79
Old La., R.Hill DD31 101
Old La., Rain. CC21 33
Old La., Widnes. EE37 135
Old Leeds St. O32 93
Old Maryland La. G32 90
Old Meadow Rd. G39 124
Old Mill Av. HH30 82
Old Mill Clo. H41 139
Old Mill La., Know. Z27 60
Old Mill La., Sefton K15 16
Old Nook La. JJ26 64
Old Park La. R 5 7
Old Penny La. NN25 66
Old Quay La. J45 145
Old Racecourse Rd. R21 28
Old Rd. NN23 51
Old Rectory Gro., Q21 27
Sefton
Old Rectory Grn. U16 153
Old Riding W30 76
Max Rd.
Old Rough La. W24 43
Old School House La. QQ29 86
Old Thomas Rd. V32 97
Old Town La. K15 16
Old Vicarage O45 147
Old War Grave Rd. OO28 85
Old Whint Rd. KK26 65
Old Wood Gro. J39 125
Old Wood Rd. G39 124
Oldbridge Rd. Z40 137
Oldfield CC31 100
Hilton Av.
Oldfield Clo. G40 139
Oldfield Dr. F40 138
Oldfield Farm La. F40 138
Oldfield La. E34 107
Oldfield Rd., Hes. F40 138
Oldfield Rd., Liver. U37 130
Oldfield Rd., Wall. K30 70
Oldfield St. FF26 63
Oldfield Way F40 138
Oldgate EE37 135
Oldham Pl. Q32 94
Oldham St. Q33 94
Olf Gorsey La. L32 92
Olga Rd. HH29 82
Olive Cres., Sefton R24 41
Olive Cres., Wirr. N35 111
Olive Dr. K45 145
Olive Gro., Know. Y32 98
Olive Gro., Sefton Q 5 6
Olive Gro., Wav. U32 96
Olive La. U32 96
Olive Mount Heights U33 96
Olive Mount Rd. U33 96
Olive Mount Vill. U32 96
Olive Mount Wk. U33 96
Olive Mt. N33 111
Olive Rd., Elles. K45 145
Olive Rd., Sefton N25 54
Olive St. R33 95
Olive Tree Rd. U32 96
Olive Vale T33 96
Olivedale Rd. T34 114

Oliver Gro. R33 95
Oliver La. N34 111
Oliver Lyme Rd. CC30 79
Oliver Rd. EE29 80
Oliver St. E. N34 111
Olivia Clo. J35 109
Olivia Ms. J35 109
Olivia St. P28 73
Ollerton Clo. J35 109
Ollery Grn. R23 41
Olney St. Q28 73
Olton St. T33 96
Onslow Cres. O 8 9
Onslow Rd., Liver. S31 95
Onslow Rd., Wall. L29 71
Onslow Rd., Wirr. O37 127
Oppenheim Av. EE29 80
Oran Rd. Y3198
Orb Clo. V27 58
Orchard Clo., Pres. DD29 80
Orchard Clo., St.H. HH25 64
Orchard Ct., Sefton T20 29
Orchard Ct., Wirr. N35 111
Orchard Dale N23 39
Orchard Dean EE31 101
Craven Rd.
Orchard Gro. F33 89
Orchard Hey, Ain. R23 41
Orchard Hey, Mag. T21 29
Orchard Hey, St.H. DD27 62
Orchard La., Sefton M11 12
Orchard La., Wirr. R45 149
Orchard Rd. G33 90
Orchard St. OO23 52
Orchard Way, Know. DD35 119
Orchard Way, Wirr. M38 126
Orchard, The, Know. Z32 99
Orchard, The, St.H. DD30 80
Stapleton Rd.
Orchard, The, Wirr. L29 71
Orford St. T33 96
Oriel Clo. S23 41
Oriel Cres. P28 73
Oriel Dr. S23 41
Oriel Rd., Liver. P28 73
Oriel Rd., Wigan MM23 51
Oriel Rd., Wirr. N35 111
Oriel St. P31 94
Orient Dr. X35 116
Origen Rd. V33 97
Oriole Clo. DD29 80
Grebe Av.
Orkney Clo. HH25 64
Orkney Rd. JJ35 121
Guernsey Rd.
Orlando Clo. J35 109
Orlando St. P28 73
Orleans Rd. U31 96
Ormande St. GG28 81
Ormerod Ct. O38 127
Ormiston Rd. L29 71
Ormond Ms. J35 109
Ormond St., Liver. P32 94
Ormond St., Wirr. L30 71
Ormond Way J35 109
Ormonde Av. S21 28
Ormonde Cres. X24 44
Ormonde Dr, S21 28
Orms Way K15 16
Ormskirk Rd., Know. Y26 59
Ormskirk Rd., Liver. R25 56
Ormskirk Rd., Wigan CC21 33
Ormskirk St. FF27 63
Orphan Dr. T31 96
Orphan St. R33 95
Orrell Hey P25 55
Orrell Hill La. M19 25
Orrell La. Q26 55
Orrell Mt. P25 55
Orrell Rd., Sefton P25 55
Orrell Rd., Wirr. M29 71
Orrell St. HH27 64
Orrets Meadow Rd. H35 108
Orrysdale Rd. B35 105
Orsett Rd. W25 58
Orston Cres. O40 142
Ortega Rd. P37 128
Orton Rd. V33 97
Orton Way MM23 51
Lazonby Cres.
Orton Way MM23 51
Orville St. JJ29 82
Orwell Clo. J16 19
Orwell Rd. P29 73
Osbert Rd. L23 38

Street	Grid	Page
Osborne Av.	L30	71
Osborne Grn.	L30	71
Osborne Rd., Ains.	L10	12
Osborne Rd., Birk.	L34	110
Osborne Rd., Formby	K16	19
Osborne Rd., Lith.	P24	40
Osborne Rd., Liver.	T30	75
Osborne Rd., St.H.	DD26	62
Osborne Rd., Wall.	L30	71
Osborne Rd., Wigan	NN23	51
Osborne Vale	L30	71
Osmaston Rd.	L36	110
Ospreys, The *Ribbesford Rd.*	LL19	37
Ossett Clo.	J35	109
Osterley Gdns.	O26	55
Oswald Clo.	QQ30	86
Oswald St.	P30	73
Oteley Av.	P41	143
Othello Clo.	P28	73
Otterburn Clo.	E33	89
Otterspool Dr.	S37	129
Otterspool Rd.	S36	113
Otterspool Riverside Prom.	S37	129
Otterton Rd.	V26	58
Ottery Clo.	R 2	3
Ottley Rd.	S31	95
Oulton Clo.	R19	28
Oulton Clo., Birk.	K35	109
Oulton Rd.	V34	115
Oulton Way	K36	109
Oundle Rd.	G32	90
Ouse St.	R34	113
Out La.	X36	116
Outer Central Rd.	Z38	133
Outer Forum	T27	57
Outlet La.	W20	30
Oval, The	K30	70
Overbury St.	R33	95
Overchurch Rd.	G34	108
Overdale Av.	J38	125
Overdale Rd.	O44	147
Overdene Wk.	W24	43
Overgreen Gro.	F32	89
Overhill Way	LL19	37
Overton Av.	O24	39
Overton Clo., Sefton	V24	43
Overton Clo., Wirr.	K35	109
Overton Grn., Know. *Overton Clo.*	V24	43
Overton St.	R32	95
Overton Way	K35	109
Ovington Dr.	Q 7	10
Ovolo Rd.	U31	96
Owen Rd., Know.	Y25	59
Owen Rd., Liver.	P29	73
Owen Rd., R.Hill	EE32	101
Owen St., St.H.	EE28	80
Owen St., Wirr.	O38	127
Owens La.	Q16	22
Ox La.	BB34	118
Oxbow Gro.	W29	76
Oxenholme Cres.	U28	75
Oxford Av., Boot.	Q27	55
Oxford Av., Sea.	O25	54
Oxford Clo. *Fulwood Dr.*	S36	113
Oxford Dr., Sefton	M24	38
Oxford Dr., Wirr.	K42	140
Oxford Rd., Boot.	P27	55
Oxford Rd., Crosby	M24	38
Oxford Rd., Faza.	R25	56
Oxford Rd., Know.	AA31	99
Oxford Rd., S.Port	N 7	9
Oxford Rd., Wirr.	M31	92
Oxford St., Liver.	Q32	94
Oxford St., Newt. *Haydock St.*	NN27	66
Oxford St., St.H.	FF26	63
Oxhouse Rd.	HH19	36
Oxley Av.	H31	90
Oxley St.	HH29	82
Oxton Clo., Faza.	V25	58
Oxton Clo., H.Green	EE35	119
Oxton Clo., Liver.	S36	113
Oxton Ct.	L35	110
Oxton Rd., Birk.	M34	110
Oxton Rd., Wall.	L31	92
Oxton St.	Q29	73
Pacefield Rd.	U34	114
Pacific Rd.	O27	54
Pacific Rd., Birk.	N33	93
Packing Rd.	T30	75
Paddington St.	R32	95
Paddock Clo.	L22	38
Paddock Dr.	J44	145
Paddock Gro.	HH31	103
Paddock Hey	Y34	116
Paddock Rd.	EE19	34
Paddock St.	O28	72
Paddock, The	W25	58
Paddock, The, Ains.	L11	12
Paddock, The, Asht.	MM22	51
Paddock, The, Formby	K14	16
Paddock, The, Gate.	X35	116
Paddock, The, Hes.	J41	140
Paddock, The, More.	F33	89
Paddock, The, St.H.	DD29	80
Paddock, The, Upt.	H34	108
Padstow Clo., Know. *Torcross Way*	Z36	117
Padstow Clo., Sefton	R 2	3
Padstow Dr.	DD26	62
Padstow Rd.	V33	97
Page Ct.	K15	16
Page Grn., Know. *Garrowby Dr.*	Y31	98
Page La.	HH36	121
Page Moss Av.	X31	98
Page Moss La.	X31	98
Pagebank Rd.	X31	98
Pagett Clo.	J35	109
Pagewood Clo.	J35	109
Paignton Clo., Wigan	JJ20	36
Paignton Rd., Know.	V33	97
Paignton Rd., Wirr.	K30	70
Paington Clo., Know.	AA31	99
Paisley Av., St.H.	HH25	64
Paisley Av., Wirr.	Q43	148
Paisley St.	O31	93
Palace Rd., Liver.	R26	56
Palace Rd., Sefton	N 6	5
Palatine Rd., Egre.	M32	92
Palatine Rd., Sefton	N 6	5
Palatine Rd., Wirr.	P40	143
Palermo St.	M32	92
Paley St.	Q29	73
Pall Mall, Liver.	P31	94
Palladian Rd.	U31	96
Palm Av., Wigan	LL22	50
Palm Clo.	S27	56
Palm Grn.	X36	116
Palm Gro.	P 6	6
Palm Hill	L35	110
Palm Vw.	L35	110
Palmer Clo.	FF27	63
Palmerston Av.	O25	54
Palmerston Dr.	O25	54
Palmerston Rd.	Q 6	6
Palmerston Rd., Gars.	V38	131
Palmerston Rd., Moss.H.	T35	114
Palmerston Rd., Wirr.	K31	91
Palmerston St., Birk.	N36	111
Palmwood	EE32	101
Palmwood Clo.	K36	109
Pamela Clo.	U25	57
Pamela Wk., Know. *Elizabeth Rd.*	U25	57
Pampas Gro. *Lavender Way*	R27	56
Pankhurst Rd.	P24	40
Pansy St.	P29	73
Parade Cres.	Z39	137
Parade St.	GG27	63
Parade, The	H44	144
Paradise Gdns.	T33	96
Paradise La., Formby	K14	16
Paradise La., Know.	BB32	100
Paradise St.	P33	94
Paragon Clo. *Wenger Rd.*	GG34	120
Parbold Av.	HH26	64
Parbrook Clo.	Y30	77
Parbrook Rd.	Y30	77
Park Av. N.	OO28	85
Park Av. S.	OO28	85
Park Av., App.	GG36	120
Park Av., Black.	KK26	65
Park Av., Crosby	N22	39
Park Av., Formby	K16	19
Park Av., H.V.	S25	56
Park Av., Know.	EE31	101
Park Av., Mag.	S19	28
Park Av., Moss.H.	T35	114
Park Av., Orrell	JJ20	36
Park Av., Sefton	Q 4	6
Park Av., St.H.	DD29	80
Park Av., Wigan	PP24	52
Park Av., Wirr.	M31	92
Park Bourn	U19	29
Park Brow Dr.	W24	43
Park Clo.	M34	110
Park Clo., Wadd.	U23	42
Park Cres.	P 4	6
Park Ct.	N24	39
Park Dr., Crosby	L22	38
Park Dr., Sefton	O21	26
Park Dr., Wirr.	L33	92
Park Gro., Sefton	P27	55
Park Gro., Wirr.	M34	110
Park Hill Rd., Liver.	Q35	112
Park La. W.	Q23	40
Park La., Hoy.	D32	88
Park La., Liver.	P33	94
Park La., Mag.	T20	29
Park La., Neth.	Q24	40
Park La., Vic.Pk.	P25	55
Park Link	U15	153
Park Pl., Dingle	Q34	112
Park Pl., Linacre	P27	55
Park Rd.	P 4	6
Park Rd. E.	M34	110
Park Rd. N.	L33	92
Park Rd. N.	PP27	67
Park Rd. S.	L34	110
Park Rd. S., Newt.	OO28	85
Park Rd., App.	GG36	120
Park Rd., Claugh.	L33	92
Park Rd., Crosby	N24	39
Park Rd., Easth.	Q42	143
Park Rd., Egre.	M31	92
Park Rd., Formby	K16	19
Park Rd., Gol.	PP25	67
Park Rd., Gt.M.	D32	88
Park Rd., Hes.	H40	139
Park Rd., Higher T.	M36	110
Park Rd., L.Beb.	O38	127
Park Rd., L.Tran.	N35	111
Park Rd., Liver.	Q34	112
Park Rd., Pres.	BB30	79
Park Rd., Som.	K33	91
Park Rd., St.H.	HH27	64
Park Rd., St.H.	LL33	104
Park Rd., Wadd.	U23	42
Park Rd., Warr.	OO28	85
Park Rd., Wigan	JJ20	36
Park Rd., Will.	O45	147
Park Rd., Wirr.	B36	105
Park St.	MM22	51
Park St. W.	K45	145
Park St., Birk.	M33	92
Park St., Broad Oak	KK26	65
Park St., Egre.	L31	92
Park St., Higher T.	M34	110
Park St., Liver.	Q34	112
Park St., Sefton	P27	55
Park St., St.H.	HH27	64
Park Vw., Crosby	M24	38
Park Vw., Formby	K16	19
Park Vw., Know.	Y31	98
Park Vw., St.H.	PP27	67
Park Vw., Wigan	NN24	51
Park Vw., Wirr.	P41	143
Park Wall Rd.	N19	26
Park Way Clo.	G38	124
Park Way E.	U23	42
Park Way W.	U23	42
Park Way, Gt.M.	D32	88
Park Way, Know.	Y29	77
Park Way, Liver.	Q33	94
Park West	F41	138
Park, The	LL35	152
Park, The, Huy.	Z32	99
Parkbridge Rd.	M35	110
Parkbury Ct.	L35	110
Parkend Rd.	M35	110
Parker Av.	N25	54
Parker St.	P32	94
Parkfield Av., Sefton	R24	41
Parkfield Av., Wirr.	M34	110
Parkfield Dr.	L31	92
Parkfield Gro.	S20	28
Parkfield Pl.	M34	110
Parkfield Rd., Liver.	R33	113
Parkfield Rd., Sefton	N24	39
Parkfield Rd., Wirr.	O39	127
Parkgate La.	K42	140
Parkgate Rd.	J45	145
Parkhill Rd., Wirr.	M35	110
Parkhouse St.	HH27	64
Parkhurst Rd., Liver.	T28	75
Parkhurst Rd., Wirr.	M36	110

Parkinson Rd. R27 56
Parkland Ct. H36 108
Parklands Q 5 6
Parklands Dr. H42 139
Parklands, H.Green EE35 119
Parkside M31 92
Parkside Av. GG31 102
Parkside Clo., Wirr. O38 127
Parkside Dr. U29 75
Parkside Rd., L.Beb. O38 127
Parkside Rd., L.Tran. N35 111
Parkside Rd., St.H. QQ27 68
Parkstile La. V27 58
Parkstone Rd. M35 110
Parkvale Av. J37 125
Parkvale Rd. R26 56
Parkview Rd. V26 58
Parkway, Crosby N24 39
Parkway, Neth. Q22 40
Parkway, Wall. K30 70
Parkway, Wirr. G38 124
Parkwood Clo. Q41 143
Bromborough Village Rd.
Parkwood Rd. X35 116
Parlane St. HH27 64
O'Keefe Rd.
Parlane St. HH27 64
Parley Gro. U36 114
Parliament Pl. Q33 94
Parliament St. P33 94
Parliament St., Thatto Heath EE29 80
Parlow Rd. T29 75
Parnell Rd. O40 142
Parr Gro. F35 107
Parr Gro. KK26 65
Parr Mill Rd. HH27 64
Parr Mount Ct. HH27 64
John St.
Parr Mount St. HH27 64
Parr St., App. HH36 121
Parr St., Liver. P33 94
Parr St., St.H. GG27 63
Parr Stocks Rd. HH27 64
Parren Av. BB32 100
Parrs Rd. L35 110
Part St. O 6 5
Partheneon Dr. S27 56
Partheneon Dr. T28 75
Partington Av. Q27 55
Parton St. S31 95
Partridge Rd. L23 38
Partridge Way G39 124
Passway HH25 64
Honister Av.
Pasture Av. G32 90
Pasture Clo., Liver. X36 116
Pasture Clo., St.H. HH31 103
Pasture Clo., Wigan MM22 51
Pasture Cres. G32 90
Pasture La., Sefton M14 17
Pasture La., St.H. DD23 47
Pasture Rd. F31 89
Pastures, The D36 106
Pastures, The, Cros. S 2 3
Paterson St. M34 110
Patmos St. Q30 73
Paton Clo. C35 106
Patricia Av. K32 91
Patricia Gro. P26 55
Patrick Av. P25 55
Patten St. L33 92
Pattens Clo. P23 40
Pattens La. Y26 59
Patterdale Clo. L11 12
Patterdale Cres. T20 29
Patterdale Dr. DD29 80
Patterdale Rd., Liver. T34 114
Patterdale Rd., Wirr. N39 127
Patterson St. NN27 66
Paul Clo. LL34 152
Paul McCartney Way R31 95
John Lennon Dr.
Paul St. P31 94
Pauldings La. O25 54
Pauls La. Q 3 2
Paulsfield Dr. G33 90
Paveley Bk. Y34 116
Paxton Pl. EE19 34
Paxton Rd. Z31 99
Paxton Way J35 109
Peach Gro. U23 42
Pear Gro. R31 95
Pear Tree Av. W28 76
Dalegarth Av.
Pear Tree Gro. L31 92
Pear Tree Rd. Z33 99
Pearce Clo. W34 115
Pearson Dr. Q25 55
Pearson St. T33 96
Peartree Clo. J40 140
Peasefield Rd. X31 98
Peasley Cross La. HH28 82
Peasley Cross La., St. H. GG27 63
Peasley Vw. HH28 82
Peatwood Av. W25 58
Peckers Hill Rd. JJ29 82
Peckmill Grn. Z34 117
Peebles Av. HH25 64
Peebles Clo. LL23 50
Peebles Clo., Kirkby V22 43
Peel Av. N35 111
Peel House GG35 120
Peel La. R20 28
Peel Rd., Sefton O26 54
Peel Rd., Wigan FF19 35
Peel St., Liver. R35 113
Peel St., Sefton Q 6 6
Peel St., St.H. NN27 66
Market St.
Peet Av. EE27 62
Peet St. R32 95
Peets La. R 4 7
Pelham Gro. S35 113
Pelham Rd. L31 92
Pemberton Clo. O45 147
Pemberton Dr. KK20 37
Pemberton Rd., Liver. U31 96
Pemberton Rd., Wigan KK20 37
Pemberton Rd., Wirr. H35 108
Pemberton St. FF28 81
Eldon St.
Pembrey Way Y37 132
Pembroke Av. G33 90
Pembroke Ct. N35 111
Pembroke Pl. W. Q32 94
Pembroke Rd. P28 73
Pembroke St. Q32 94
Pen Gallow Z34 117
Pencombe Rd. X31 98
Pendennis Rd. M31 92
Pendennis St. R30 74
Pendine Clo. S31 95
Pendle Av. HH26 64
Pendle Dr. P23 40
Pendle Pl. EE19 34
Pendlebury St. HH31 103
Pendleton Gr. Z37 133
Pendleton Rd. R28 74
Penfold T20 29
Pengwern St. R34 113
Pengwern Ter. M29 72
Holland Rd.
Pengwin Gro. S33 95
Penkett Gro. M30 71
Penkett Rd. L30 71
Penkford La. LL28 83
Penkford St. MM27 66
Penlake La. JJ29 82
Penley Cres. U23 42
Penman Clo. Z37 133
Penman Cres. Z37 133
Penmon Dr. G39 124
Pennant Av. V28 76
Pennard Av. Y30 77
Pennie Av. LL19 37
Pennine Av. LL19 37
Pennine Dr. JJ27 64
Pennine Rd., H.Beb. M37 126
Pennine Rd., Wall. K31 91
Pennine Way V23 43
Pennington Av. Q25 55
Pennington La. LL28 83
Pennington Pl. Y32 98
Pennington Rd. P26 55
Penny La., Know. DD34 119
Penny La., Liver. T34 114
Penny La., St.H. MM25 66
Penny La., Warr. LL29 83
Pennystone Clo. F34 107
Pennysylvania Rd. S29 74
Penrhos Rd. B34 105
Penrhyd Rd. F38 123
Penrhyn Av. H38 124
Penrhyn Av. O25 54
Penrhyn St. P30 73
Penrith Cres., Sefton T20 29
Penrith Cres., Wigan NN23 51
Penrith Rd. DD29 80
Penrith St. M34 110
Penrith St. Q34 112
Penrose Av. W32 97
Penrose Pl. FF19 35
Penrose St. Q30 73
Penryn Av. HH25 64
Penryn Rd. X26 59
Pensall Dr. G40 139
Pensarn Rd. T32 96
Pensby Clo. H38 124
Pensby Hall La. G40 139
Pensby Rd., Hes. G41 139
Pensby Rd., Thing. H38 124
Penstone Clo. X31 98
Pentire Av. DD26 62
Pentland Av. JJ27 64
Pentland Rd. X23 44
Pentlo Av. R28 74
Penuel Rd. R28 74
Penwick Sq. MM23 51
Peover St. P31 94
Peploe Rd. S28 74
Peplow Rd. U24 42
Percival St. U31 96
Percy Rd., Wirr. M32 92
Percy St., Liver. Q33 94
Percy St., Sefton O26 54
Percy St., St.H. JJ29 82
Percy St., Wirr. L29 71
Perimeter Rd. Y25 59
Perrian Rd. V37 131
Perrin Rd. K30 70
Perrins Rd. MM30 84
Pershore Gro. L11 12
Pershore Rd. W25 58
Perth Av. FF29 81
Perth Clo. V22 43
Perth St. R31 95
Peter La. P32 94
Peter Mahon Way O27 54
Peter Prices La. N39 127
Peter Rd. Q28 73
Peter St. FF27 63
Peter St., Gol. QQ25 68
Peter St., Liver. P32 94
Peter St., Wigan OO23 52
Peter St., Wirr. N32 93
Peterborough Dr. Q23 40
Peterborough Rd. U34 114
Peterlee Clo. FF29 81
Peterlee Way R24 41
Petersfield Clo. R24 41
Petherwick Rd. V26 58
Petunia Rd. X30 77
Petworth Av. LL20 37
Petworth Clo. X39 132
Petworth Rd. L10 12
Peveril St., Liver. Q28 73
Peveril St., Sefton Q27 55
Philbeach Rd. S28 74
Philharmonic Ct. Q33 94
Caledonia St.
Philip Gro., Liver. W30 76
Philip Gro., St.H. HH29 82
Philip Rd. EE37 135
Phillimore Rd. S31 95
Phillips Clo., Formby K16 19
Phillips Clo., Sefton O22 39
Phillips La. K16 19
Phillips St. P31 94
Phillips Way G41 139
Phipps La. MM29 84
Phythia Clo. R31 95
Phythian St., Liver. R31 95
Phythian St., St.H. JJ26 64
Park St.
Piccadilly JJ22 49
Pickerill Rd. F35 107
Pickering Rake P22 40
Red Loames
Pickering Rd. L29 71
Pickering St. R30 74
Pickerings Rd. DD38 135
Pickmere Dr. Q43 148
Pickop St. P32 94
Pickwick St. Q34 112
Picton Clo., Easth. P43 148
Picton Clo., Ox. K35 109
Picton Gro. S33 95
Picton Rd., Liver. S32 95
Picton Rd., Sefton M24 38
Piele Rd. MM25 66
Piercefield Rd. K15 16
Pierpoint St. QQ25 68
Pighue La. T32 96

Pigot St. FF27 63
Pigotts Rake Q22 40
Higher End Pk.
Pike House Rd. DD26 62
Pike Pl. DD27 62
Pikes Hey Rd. D37 122
Pilch Bank Rd. W31 97
Pilch La. W31 97
Pilch La. E. X32 98
Pilgrim Clo. QQ30 86
Pilgrim St., Liver. Q33 94
Pilgrim St., Wirr. N34 111
Pilkington Rd. P 6 6
Pilkington St., HH27 64
Pocket Nook
Park Rd.
Pilkington St., St.H. CC22 46
Pilling Clo. Q 2 2
Pilling La. R18 23
Pilot Gro. S33 95
Pimblett Rd. MM25 66
Pimbley Gro. E. S22 41
Pimbley Gro. W. S22 41
Pimbo La. FF19 35
Pimbo Rd., W.Pimbo EE19 34
Pimbo Rd., Wigan FF21 35
Pimhill Clo. R34 113
Pine Av., App. GG36 120
Pine Av., Beb. N39 127
Firs Av.
Pine Av., St.H. FF26 63
Pine Av., Warr. OO28 85
Pine Clo., Roby Y31 98
Pine Clo., Sefton V23 43
Pine Clo., St.H. LL26 65
Pine Clo., Whist. CC31 100
Pine Dale CC21 33
Pine Gro., Crosby M24 38
Pine Gro., Liver. R33 95
Pine Gro., S.Port P 5 6
Pine Gro., Vic.Pk. P27 55
Pine Gro., Wigan RR25 68
Pine Rd. H40 139
Pine Tree Av. J34 109
Pine View Dr. G40 139
Pine Vw. KK20 37
Pine Walks L36 110
Pine Way G40 139
Pinehey J44 145
Pinehurst Av., Liver. S29 74
Pinehurst Av., Sefton M24 38
Pinehurst Rd. R29 74
Pinemore Rd. U36 114
Pineridge Clo. P40 143
Pinetree Clo., Wirr. G33 90
Pinetree Dr. C36 106
Pinetree Gro. G33 90
Pinetree Rd. Y33 98
Pinewood Av., Crox. V27 58
Pinewood Av., Sefton J16 19
Pinewood Av., Wigan NN24 51
Pinewood Clo. J16 19
Pinewood Dr. H41 139
Pinewood Rd. MM29 84
Pinfold Clo. L11 12
Pinfold Cres. X25 59
Pinfold Dr. DD27 62
Pinfold La., Know. X27 59
Pinfold La., Sefton L11 12
Pinfold La., Wirr. B35 105
Pinfold Pl. EE19 34
Pinfold Rd. Y37 132
Pingot Rd. JJ22 49
Pingwood La. X22 44
Pipers Clo. F41 138
Pipers La. F40 138
Pirrie Rd. S27 56
Pit La. GG35 120
Pit Pl. X36 116
Pit St. X36 116
Pitch Clo. F35 107
The Scythes
Pitsmead Rd. W24 43
Pitt St. Q 6 6
Pitt St. HH27 64
Pitts House La. R 5 7
Pittville Ter. EE37 135
Pitville Av. U35 114
Pitville Clo. U36 114
Pitville Gro. U35 114
Pitville Rd. U35 114
Plane Clo. R27 56
Chestnut Rd.
Plane Tree Av. N39 127
Plane Tree Rd., St.H. NN25 66
Planetree Rd., Liver. W29 76
Plantation Rd. Q40 143
Planters, The F35 107
Platt Gro. O37 127
Platt St. N31 93
Platts St. KK26 65
West End Rd.
Plattsville Rd. U34 114
Playfield Rd. W29 76
Playfield Wk. W29 76
Pleasance Way OO27 67
Pleasant Hill St. P34 112
Pleasant St., Boot. O28 72
Pleasant St., Liver. Q32 94
Pleasant St., Wirr. L29 71
Pleasant Vw., Boot. O28 72
Pleasant Vw., Liver. T32 96
Pleasington Clo. K35 109
Pleasington Dr. K35 109
Plemont Rd. U30 75
Plex Moss La. N12 13
Plimsole Gro. R32 95
Pluckington Rd. AA31 99
Plum Tree Clo. DD30 80
Plumer St., Liver. T33 96
Plumer St., Wirr. L33 92
Plump St. Q31 94
Plymyard Av. P42 143
Plymyard Clo. P42 143
Plymyard Copse L42 143
Gorsefield Av.
Pocket Nook St. HH27 64
Podium Rd. U31 96
Poets Cor. P38 128
Poets Grn. CC31 100
Poll Hill Rd. G40 139
Pollard Rd. U32 96
Pollitt Cres. HH31 103
Pollitt Sq. O37 128
Shorefields
Pomfret St. Q34 113
Pomona St. Q32 94
Pond Green Way JJ28 82
Pond View Clo. J41 140
Pond Wk. KK28 83
Ponsonby Rd. K30 70
Ponsonby St. R34 113
Pool Bk. O38 127
Pool End JJ28 82
Pool Hey X29 77
Pool La., Wirr. P38 128
Pool La., Wood. H36 108
Pool Rd. O39 127
Pool St. Sefton S 2 3
Pool St., Wirr. M33 92
Poolbank Rd. O38 127
Poole Rd. M30 71
Poole Wk. R35 113
Threlfall St.
Poolside Wk. S 3 3
Poolwood Rd. H35 108
Pop Weint K45 145
Pope St., Liver. P31 94
Pope St., Sefton O26 54
Poplar Av. LL22 50
Poplar Av., Newt. OO27 67
Poplar Av., Sefton N22 38
Poplar Av., St.H. DD27 62
Poplar Av., Wirr. G34 108
Poplar Bk. Z32 99
Poplar Dr., Liver. R30 74
Poplar Dr., Sefton V23 43
Poplar Dr., Wirr. O39 127
Poplar Farm Clo. F34 107
Poplar Gro., Hay. LL26 65
Poplar Gro., Know. CC30 79
Poplar Gro., Sefton N26 54
Poplar Gro., St.H. EE27 62
Poplar Rd., St.H. LL26 65
Poplar Rd., Wirr. L35 110
Poplar St., Liver. Q30 73
Poplar St., Sefton Q 6 6
Poplar Ter. L29 71
Porchester Rd. T28 75
Porlock Av., Liver. W34 115
Porlock Av., St.H. HH30 82
Porlock Clo. H42 139
Port Causeway P39 128
Port Loe Dr. Z36 117
Port Way Y37 132
Portal Rd. G39 124
Portelet Rd. T31 96
Porter Av. OO26 67
Porter Clo. FF32 102
Porter St. O31 93
Portia Av. N37 127
Portia St. P28 73
Portico Av. DD30 80
Portico Ct. DD30 80
Portico La. DD30 80
Portland Av. M24 38
Portland Pl. Q31 94
Portland St. MM27 66
Portland St., New B. L29 71
Portland St., Sefton O 5 5
Portland St., Wirr. L33 92
Portland Way JJ28 82
Portlemouth Rd. V26 58
Portman Rd. S33 95
Porto Hey Rd. F38 123
Porton Rd. V24 43
Portreath Way DD26 62
Portree Av. L42 143
Banff Av.
Portree Clo. R26 56
Portrush St. T30 75
Post Office Av. O 6 5
Potter Pl. EE19 34
Potters La. DD39 135
Pottery Clo. BB31 100
Pottery Fields, Know. BB30 79
Warrington Rd.
Pottery La., Know. BB31 100
Pottery La., Liver. Q35 112
Beresford Rd.
Pottery St. CC30 79
Poulsom Dr. P23 40
Poulter Rd. R25 56
Poulton Br. L32 92
Poulton Clo. Y38 132
Poulton Dr. MM22 51
Poulton Hall Av. L31 92
Poulton Hall Rd. O41 142
Poulton Rd., Sefton Q 5 6
Poulton Rd., Wirr. L31 92
Poulton Royd Dr. N40 142
Pound Rd. S45 149
Poverty La. T21 29
Powder Works Yd. JJ29 82
Powderworks La. V19 30
Powell Dr. HH23 49
Powell St., St.H. JJ29 82
Powell St., Wirr. K33 91
Power Rd., Brom. Q40 143
Power Rd., Wirr. O37 127
Powerhouse Rd. R42 150
Powis St. R34 113
Pownall Sq. P32 94
Pownall St. P33 94
Poynter St. FF29 81
Pratt Rd. BB30 79
Precincts, The N23 39
Preesall Clo. Q 3 2
Preesall Way V26 58
Premier St. Q30 73
Prentice Rd. N36 111
Prenton Av. GG31 102
Prenton Dell Av. L37 126
Prenton Dell Rd. K36 109
Prenton Farm Rd. L37 126
Prenton Grn. Z39 133
Prenton Hall Rd. K36 109
Prenton La. L36 110
Prenton Park Rd. M35 110
Prenton Rd. E. M36 110
Prenton Rd. W. M36 110
Prenton Village Rd. K36 109
Prenton Way J37 125
Prescot By Pass AA30 78
Prescot Dr. S31 95
Prescot Rd., H.Green EE35 119
Prescot Rd., Know. CC34 118
Prescot Rd., Liver. W31 97
Prescot Rd., Sefton V20 30
Prescot Rd., St.H. DD29 80
Prescot St. L29 71
Prescot St., Liver. Q32 94
Prescott Av. PP24 52
Prescott Rd., Wigan FF19 35
Preseland Rd. N23 39
Prestbury Av., Sefton L10 12
Prestbury Av., Wirr. K36 109
Prestbury Clo. K36 109
Prestbury Rd. T27 57
Preston Av. BB30 79
Preston Gro. S30 74
Preston New Rd. R 3 3
Preston Rd., Know. BB30 79
Preston Rd., Sefton P 5 6
Preston St., Liver. P32 94

Preston St., St.H. GG32 102
Preston Way O23 39
Prestwick Dr. M22 38
Prestwood Cres. W31 97
Prestwood Pl. FF19 35
Pretoria Rd., Liver. R26 56
Pretoria Rd., Wigan NN23 51
Price Gro. KK28 78
Price St., Liver. P33 94
Price St., Wirr. L33 92
Prices La. L35 110
Priest St. R33 95
Priesthouse Clo. L15 16
Priesthouse La. L15 16
Primrose Clo., Cros. S 2 3
Primrose Clo., Formby L14 16
Primrose Clo., Halton FF36 120
Primrose Dr. Z30 78
Primrose Hill O38 127
Primrose Rd., Liver. V34 115
Primrose Rd., Wirr. K33 91
Primrose St. P29 73
Primula Dr. R27 56
Prince Alfred Rd. U33 96
Prince Andrews Gro. EE26 62
St. Georges Av.
Prince Charles Gdns. N 6 5
Prince Edward St. M33 92
Prince Edwin St. Q31 94
Prince St. M25 53
Prince William St. Q34 112
Princes Av., Brom. Q42 143
Princes Av., Hoy. B36 105
Princes Av., Liver. R34 113
Princes Av., Sefton M23 38
Princes Av., St.H. NN25 66
Princes Boulevard M37 126
Princes Par. O32 93
Princes Pl. N35 111
Quigley St.
Princes Pl. FF36 120
Princes Rd., Liver. Q33 94
Princes Rd., St.H. EE28 80
Princes St., Boot. O28 72
Princes St., Liver. P32 94
Princes St., Sefton O 6 5
Princes St., St.H. NN27 66
Princes Way GG25 63
Princes Way, Wall. L30 71
Princess Av., St.H. FF26 63
Princess Av., Wigan OO23 52
Princess Dr. W29 76
Princess Pavement N34 111
Grange Pavement
Princess Rd., Wigan OO23 52
Princess Rd., Wirr. L29 71
Princess Ter. M34 110
Princess Way, Sefton N26 54
Prior Ct. X36 116
Prior Rd. X36 116
Prior St. O26 54
Priorsfield G33 90
Priorsfield Ct. X36 116
Priorsfield Rd. X36 116
Priorswood Pl. FF19 35
Priory Clo., Know. BB32 100
Priory Clo., L.Beb. O39 127
Priory Clo., Sefton L16 20
Priory Gdns. N 7 9
Priory Gdns. FF25 63
Priory Rd., Liver. R29 74
Priory Rd., Wall. N31 93
Priory Rd., Wigan MM22 51
Priory Rd., Wirr. C36 106
Priory St. N34 111
Priory, The J44 145
Prison Weint O32 93
Pritchard Av. N25 54
Private Dr. J38 125
Private Rd. Z25 60
Prizett Rd. U37 130
Probyn Way J30 70
Procter Rd., L.Tran. O36 111
Proctor Rd., Hoy. C34 106
Proctor Rd., Sefton J15 15
Promenade, Ains. K10 11
Promenade, Hoy. C33 88
Promenade, Lwr.Sefton O 5 5
Promenade, Sefton O 5 5
Promenade, The, Formby H17 18
Prophet Q34 112
Prophet Wk. Q34 112
Prospect Pl. FF19 35
Prospect Rd., St.H. HH27 64
Prospect Rd., Wirr. L36 110
Prospect St. Q32 94
Prospect Vale, Liver. S31 95
Prospect Vale, Wirr. K30 70
Prospect Way R23 41
Provident St. KK27 65
Province Pl. P26 55
Province Rd. P26 55
Prussia St. P32 94
Pudsey St. Q32 94
Pugin St. Q29 73
Pulford Av. L36 110
Pulford Rd. N38 127
Pulford St. Q29 73
Pump La. E34 107
Pump Rd. N33 93
Pumpfields P31 94
Punnells La. Q18 22
Purbeck Dr. F37 123
Purley Rd. M24 38
Pye Clo. NN25 66
Pye Gdns. GG25 63
Pye Rd. H41 139
Pye St. U33 96
Pye St. JJ29 82
Pyecroft Rd. LL34 152
Pyes La. Y30 77
Pygons Hill La. S17 23
Pym St. Q28 73

Quaker La. G40 139
Quakers Meadow Y27 59
Quantock Clo. LL19 37
Quarry Av. N39 127
Quarry Bank Pl. M34 110
Quarry Bnk., Know. W23 43
Daleside Rd.
Quarry Bnk., Wirr. M34 110
Quarry Clo. W23 43
Quarry Clo., Hes. G40 139
Quarry Dale W23 43
Quarry Grn. W23 43
Quarry Hey W23 43
Quarry La. H38 124
Quarry Rd. E. G40 139
Quarry Rd. W. G40 139
Quarry Rd., Anf. T30 75
Quarry Rd., Beb. O39 127
Quarry Rd., Elles. L44 146
Quarry Rd., Kirkdale Q28 73
Quarry Rd., Sefton O22 39
Quarry St. W35 115
Quarry St. S. X36 116
Quarryside Dr. X23 44
Queen Anne St. Q31 94
Queen Av., Liver. P32 94
Queen Marys O38 127
Queen St., Gol. QQ25 68
Queen St., Hay. NN27 66
Queen St., L.Tran. N35 111
Queen St., St.H. FF26 63
Queen St., Waterloo M25 53
Queens Av. K14 16
Queens Av., Brom. Q40 143
Queens Av., Halton EE37 135
Queens Av., Hoy. C33 88
Queens Av., Wigan NN23 51
Queens Ct. V32 97
Queens Dr., Anf. T29 75
Queens Dr., Child. V33 97
Queens Dr., Hes. G41 139
Queens Dr., Moss.H. T35 114
Queens Dr., Newt. OO27 67
Queens Dr., Pren. L36 110
Queens Dr., St.H. EE26 62
Queens Dr., Walt. R28 74
Queens Dr., Wigan RR25 68
Queens Rd., C.Thornton S45 149
Queens Rd., Formby J16 19
Queens Rd., Gt.Crosby N23 39
Queens Rd., Hay. NN25 66
Queens Rd., Hoy. B33 87
Queens Rd., Know. CC30 79
Queens Rd., L.Tran. N36 111
Queens Rd., Liver. R31 95
Queens Rd., S.Port P 5 6
Queens Rd., Seacombe N31 93
Queens Rd., St.H. EE28 80
Queens Rd., Wigan NN23 51
Queens St., New.B. L30 71
Queensbury C35 106
Queenscourt Rd. V30 76
Queensdale Rd. U34 114
Queensland Av. FF29 81
Queensland St. R33 95
Queensway GG25 63
Queensway, Hes. J42 140
Queensway, Sefton N24 39
Queensway, St.H. DD22 47
Queensway, Wall. K30 70
Queenswood Av. N37 127
Quernmore Rd. X23 44
Quernmore Wk. X23 44
Quickswood Clo. W34 115
Quickswood Dr. W34 115
Quickswood Grn. W34 115
Quigley Av. R25 56
Quigley St. N35 111
Quillet, The K45 145
Quinesway H34 108
Quinton Clo. L11 12
Quorn St. R32 95

Raby Clo. HH36 121
Cheryl Dr.
Raby Clo., Elles. K45 145
Raby Clo., Hes. G41 139
Raby Clo., Wirr. O41 142
Raby Dr. Wirr. O41 142
Raby Dr., More. F33 89
Raby Gro. M37 126
Raby Hall Rd. N42 142
Raby Mere Rd. M42 141
Raby Park Rd. K45 145
Raby Rd., Nest. K45 145
Raby Rd., Nest. L43 146
Raby Rd., Wirr. L42 141
Rachel St. P31 94
Radburn Clo. O22 39
Radburn Rd. O22 39
Radcliffe Wk. Q31 94
Radford Av. O40 142
Radley Dr. S23 41
Radley Rd. K31 91
Radley St. FF29 81
Radmore Rd. V31 97
Rudyard Rd.
Radmore Rd. V31 97
Radnor Av. G40 139
Radnor Clo. Y38 132
Radnor Dr., Know. EE36 119
Radnor Dr., Marsh. Q 3 2
Radnor Dr., Sefton Q27 55
Radnor Dr., Wirr. M30 71
Radnor Pl., Liver. S30 74
Radnor Pl., Wirr. M34 110
Radstock Gro. HH30 82
Axbridge Av.
Radstock Rd., Liver. S31 95
Radstock Rd., Wirr. K30 70
Radstock Wk., Hale. Z38 133
Redbourn Av.
Radway Rd. Z30 78
Raeburn Av., Brom. P42 143
Raeburn Av., Elles. K45 145
Raeburn Av., W.Kirby C35 106
Raffer Av. Q25 55
Raffin Clo. H31 90
Raffles Rd. M34 110
Raffles St. Q33 94
Rafter Av. Q26 55
Raglan St. V38 131
Window La.
Raglan Wk. V38 131
King St.
Rail Clo. CC20 33
Railton Av. EE32 101
Railton Clo. EE32 101
Railton Av.
Railton Rd. T28 75
Railway JJ29 82
Railway Pl. NN27 66
Junction La.
Railway Rd., Wigan QQ25 68
Railway Rd., Wirr. N36 111
Railway St., Liver. V38 131
Railway St., Newt. NN27 66
Railway St., Sefton O 6 5
Railway St., St.H. GG27 63
Railway Ter., Sefton O 6 5
Railway Ter., St.H. JJ29 82
Railway Ter., Wigan NN22 51
Rainbow Dr. U23 42
Rainbow Dr., Hale. Z37 133
Raines Clo. G35 108
Rainfield Av. Q26 55
Rainford Rd. GG22 48
Rainford Rd., Rain. BB19 33
Rainford Rd., St.H. EE25 62

Rainford Sq.	P32	94
Rainham Clo.	V37	131
Rainhill Rd., Rain.	EE31	101
Rainhill Rd., St.H.	EE30	80
Rake Clo., Upt.	H35	108
Rake Hey	E33	89
Rake Hey Clo.	E33	89
Rake La., Wall.	L30	71
Rake La., Wirr.	H35	108
Rake, The	P41	143
Rakersfield Ct.	M29	71
Rakersfield Rd.	L29	71
Rakes La.	P22	40
Raleigh Av.	BB32	100
Raleigh Rd.	H31	90
Raleigh Rd., Nest.	K44	145
Raleigh St.	O28	72
Ralphs Wifes La.	S 2	3
Ramford St.	HH28	82
Ramilies Rd.	T34	114
Rampit Clo.	MM25	66
Ramsbrook Clo.	Y39	136
Ramsbrook Glass.	BB38	134
Ramsbrook Rd.	Y39	136
Ramsey Clo., C.Wood	JJ35	121
Ramsey Clo., Liver.	V37	131
Ramsey Clo., Wigan	NN24	51
Ramsey Rd.	V37	131
Ramsfield Rd.	AA39	137
Randall Dr.	P24	40
Randle Av.	CC21	33
Randle Clo.	J40	142
Inley Clo.		
Randles Rd.	X26	59
Randolph St.	Q29	73
Lowe St.		
Randon Cres.	FF27	63
Randon Gro.	FF27	63
Ranelagh Av.	O25	54
Ranelagh Dr.	N 9	9
Ranelagh Dr. N.	U37	130
Ranelagh Dr. S.	U37	130
Ranelagh Pk.	U37	130
Ranelagh Pl.	Q32	94
Ranelagh St.	P32	94
Ranfurly Rd.	U37	130
Range La.	J17	19
Rangemore Rd.	U36	114
Rankin St., Liver.	Q35	112
Rankin St., Wirr.	L32	92
Ranmore Av.	LL23	50
Ranworth Pl.	T27	57
Ranworth Sq.	T27	57
Ranworth Way	T27	57
Rappart Rd.	M31	92
Ratcliffe Pl.	DD31	101
Rathbone Rd., Liver.	T32	96
Rathbone Rd., Sefton	K19	24
Rathbone St., St.H.	NN27	66
Rathlin Clo.	JJ35	121
Rathmore Av.	U35	114
Rathmore Clo.	L35	110
Rathmore Cres.	R 3	3
Rathmore Dr.	L35	110
Rathmore Rd.	L35	110
Raven Meols La.	K16	19
Ravenglass Av.	S20	28
Ravenhead Av.	W25	58
Ravenhead Rd.	FF28	81
Ravenhill Cres.	G31	90
Ravenhurst Way	BB32	100
Ravenna Rd.	V37	131
Ravens Ct., Hale.	Z38	133
Leathers La.		
Ravenscroft	W22	43
Ravenscroft Rd.	M34	110
Ravensfield Clo.	Z37	133
Rainbow Dr.		
Ravensfield Dr.	EE35	119
Ravensthorpe Grn.	T27	57
Ravenstone Rd.	U37	130
Ravenswood Av., Wigan	LL19	37
Ravenswood Av., Wirr.	N37	127
Ravenswood Rd., Liver.	U31	96
Ravenswood Rd., Wirr.	H40	139
Rawcliffe Rd., Liver.	R27	56
Rawcliffe Rd., Wirr.	M34	110
Rawlins St.	S31	95
Rawlinson Cres.	AA37	133
Rawlinson Gro.	Q 4	6
Rawlinson Rd., Liver.	U32	96
Rawlinson Rd., S.Port	P 5	6
Rawson Clo.	N25	54
Rawson Rd.	N25	54
Ray Clo.	R27	56
Raymond Av.	R24	41
Raymond St.	M31	92
Raymond Way, Elles.	L45	146
Raymond Way, Wirr.	J35	109
Reade Clo.	K40	142
Chorley Way		
Reading St.	P29	73
Reay St.	HH36	121
Recreation Av.	OO23	52
Recreation Dr.	JJ22	49
Recreation St.	HH27	64
Rector Rd.	S29	74
Rectory Av.	RR25	68
Rectory Clo.	QQ30	86
Rectory Clo., Birk.	M35	110
Rectory La., Warr.	QQ30	86
Rectory La., Wirr.	G41	139
Rectory Rd.	Q 4	6
Rectory Rd., Wigan	LL22	50
Rectory Rd., Wirr.	B36	105
Red Acre	HH31	103
Red Bank Av.	PP28	85
Red Banks	C38	122
Red Barn Rd.	HH22	49
Red Cat La.	FF23	48
Red Cut La.	Z25	60
Red Gate	L16	20
Red Hill Rd.	L38	126
Red House Bnk.	B35	105
Red House La.		
Red House Clo.	B35	105
Red Lion Clo.	S20	28
Red Lion La.	S45	149
Red Lomes	P22	40
Red Pike	S45	149
Redbourn Av.	Z38	133
Redbourn St.	S30	74
Redbourne Dr.	EE35	119
Redbrook Clo.	L42	143
Dearnford Av.		
Redbrook St.	S30	74
Redbrook Rd.	Q 7	10
Redcar Clo., Sefton	Q 7	10
Redcar Clo., Wirr.	J35	109
Redcar Dr.	P42	143
Redcar Rd.	J30	70
Redcar St.	S30	74
Redcross St.	P32	94
Redditch Clo.	F35	107
Chippenham Av.		
Redfern St.	P29	73
Redfield St.	S30	74
Redford Clo.	F35	107
Redgate Av.	O23	39
Redgate Dr., Sefton	L16	20
Redgate Dr., St. H.	HH27	64
Redgrave Dr.	LL19	37
Redgrove St.	S32	95
Redhill Av.	W25	58
Redhill Dr.	Q 7	10
Redington Rd.	V37	131
Redland Rd.	R25	56
Redmayne Clo.	NN27	66
Redmere Dr.	J41	140
Redmond St.	N35	111
Redrock Clo.	R31	95
Redruth Av.	HH25	64
Redruth Rd.	V26	58
Redstone Clo.	C33	88
Redstone Dr.	F40	138
Redvers Av.	R44	149
Redvers Dr.	Q26	55
Redwing Clo.	X34	116
Redwing La.	X34	116
Redwood Av.	S19	28
Redwood Clo.	X34	116
Redwood Rd.	X34	116
Redwood Way	W22	43
Reedale Rd.	U35	114
Reeds Av. E.	G31	90
Reeds Av. S.	G31	90
Reeds Av. W.	G31	90
Reeds Brow	DD21	34
Reeds La., Know.	CC23	46
Reeds La., Wirr.	G31	90
Reeds Rd.	Z31	99
Reedville	L34	110
Reedville Gro.	G32	90
Reedville Rd.	N38	127
Reepham Clo.	LL19	37
Reeves Av.	O26	55
Reeves St.	JJ27	64
Fry St.		
Reform St.	T32	96
Regal Cres.	DD37	135
Regal Dr.	EE26	62
Regal Rd.	V27	58
Regal Wk.	Q29	73
Regent Av., Liver.	W32	97
Regent Av., Wigan	MM22	51
Regent Clo.	N 7	9
Regent Rd., App.	GG36	120
Regent Rd., Crosby	M23	38
Regent Rd., Lith.	O27	54
Regent Rd., Liver.	O28	72
Regent Rd., Sefton	N 7	9
Regent Rd., Wirr.	J30	70
Regent St., St.H.	NN27	66
Regent St., Wirr.	O31	93
Regents Clo.	H38	124
Regents Rd.	EE28	80
Regents Way	M37	126
Regina Av.	M24	38
Regina Rd.	R26	56
Reginald Rd.	JJ30	82
Reid Ct.	S45	149
Reigate Clo.	Y35	116
Rendal Clo.	R30	74
Rendcombe Grn.	T27	57
Rendel St.	M33	92
Rendell Clo.	OO28	85
Rendelsham Clo.	G34	108
Renfrew Av., St.H.	HH25	64
Renfrew Av., Wirr.	Q42	143
Renfrew St.	R32	95
Rennell Clo.	V31	97
Rennie Av.	EE27	62
Renshaw St.	Q32	94
Renville Rd.	V32	97
Renwick Av.	DD31	101
Renwick Clo.	J35	109
Renwick Rd.	R26	56
Renwick Sq.	MM23	51
Lazonby Cres.		
Repton Clo.	J35	109
Repton Gro.	S24	41
Repton Rd.	V33	97
Reservoir Rd.	W35	115
Reservoir Rd., Birk.	L36	110
Reservoir Rd., N.	L36	110
Reservoir St., Liver.	R31	95
Reservoir St., St.H.	EE29	80
Reservoir St., Wigan	OO23	52
Rest Hill Rd.	L38	126
Retford Rd.	W24	43
Retford Wk.	W24	43
Reva Rd.	W31	97
Rexmore Rd.	U36	114
Rexmore Way	T33	96
Reynolds Av.	KK28	83
Rhiwlas St.	R34	113
Rhodesia Rd.	R26	56
Rhodesway	H41	139
Rhona Clo.	L43	148
Turiff Dr.		
Rhosesmor Clo.	W25	58
Rhosesmor Rd.	W26	58
Rhyl St., Liver.	Q34	112
Rib, The	N14	17
Ribbesford Rd.	LL19	37
Ribble Av., Know.	EE31	101
Ribble Av., Mag.	T20	29
Ribble Av., Sefton	S 3	3
Ribble Clo.	JJ35	121
Ribble Cres.	HH23	49
Ribble Rd.	Y35	116
Ribble St.	K32	91
Ribblers La.	V25	58
Ribblesdale Clo.	Q42	143
Ribblesdale Rd.	U35	114
Ribblesend Av.	R25	56
Ribchester Way	AA33	99
Rice La., Sefton	Q27	55
Rice La., Wirr.	M31	92
Rice St.	Q33	94
Ricehey Rd.	M31	92
Rich Vw.	L35	110
Richard Allen Way	Q31	94
Bute St.		
Richard Allen Way	Q31	94
Richard Chubb Dr.	M30	71
Richard Dr.	W30	76
Elgar Rd.		
Richard Hesketh Dr.	V24	43
Richard Kelly Clo.	S29	74
Richard Kelly Dr.	S28	74
Richard Kelly Pl.	S29	74
Richard Martin Rd.	P24	40
Pankhurst Rd.		
Richard Rd.	L22	38
Richards Gro.	JJ27	64

Street	Grid	Page
Richardson Rd.	N37	127
Richardson St.	S33	95
Richlard Rd.	T30	75
Richmond Av., Sefton	O25	54
Richmond Av., St.H.	KK25	65
Richmond Clo., Know.	CC27	61
Richmond Clo., Wirr.	N38	127
Richmond Gdns.	OO29	85
Connaught Dr.		
Richmond Gro.	T19	29
Richmond Pk.	R30	74
Richmond Rd., Birk.	N 8	9
Richmond Rd., Sefton	N22	39
Richmond Rd., Wigan	MM22	51
Richmond Rd., Wirr.	N38	127
Richmond Row	Q31	94
Richmond St., Liver.	P32	94
Richmond St., Wirr.	L29	71
Richmond Ter.	R30	74
Richmond Way, Know.	AA33	99
Richmond Way, Pen.	G40	139
Richmond Way, Thing.	H38	124
Rickaby Clo.	P40	143
Rickman St.	P29	73
Ridale Gro.	B35	105
Riddock Rd.	O26	54
Ridge Clo.	S 2	3
Ridge Well Av.	RR25	68
Ridge, The	F40	138
Ridgefield Rd.	G38	124
Ridgemere Rd.	G38	124
Ridgemont Av.	T28	75
Ridgetor Rd.	W35	115
Ridgeway Dr.	S19	28
Ridgeway, The, Hes.	H41	139
Ridgeway, The, Hoy.	D33	88
Ridgeway, The, Know.	EE34	119
Ridgeway, The, Liver.	X35	116
Ridgeway, The, Wirr.	M37	126
Ridgewood Dr.	G39	124
Riding Hill Rd.	Y28	77
Riding La.	PP22	52
Riding St.	O 6	5
Ridings, The	J34	109
Ridley La.	S20	28
Ridley Rd.	S31	95
Ridley St.	M34	110
Rigby Dr.	F36	107
Rigby Rd.	R19	28
Rigby St.	NN23	51
Rigby St., St.H.	FF27	63
Rigby St., Wigan	QQ25	68
Rigbys La.	OO23	52
Riley Av.	P26	55
Rimmer Av.	X32	98
Rimmer Clo.	O25	54
Rimmer Gro.	JJ27	64
Rimmers Av.	K14	16
Rimmers Av.	O 6	5
Rimmington Rd.	T36	114
Rimrose Rd.	O26	54
Rimrose Valley Rd.	O23	39
Rindlebrook La.	BB30	79
South Av.		
Ringley Av.	PP24	52
Ringo Starr Dr.	R31	95
John Lennon Dr.		
Ringsfield Rd.	AA39	133
Ringsfield Wk.	AA39	137
Ringway	K44	145
Ringway Rd.	Y35	116
Ringway S.	FF27	63
Ringways	P39	128
Ringwood	L35	110
Ringwood Av.	W32	97
Ringwood Ct.	L35	110
Ripley Av.	O24	39
Ripley Clo.	T20	29
Croftfield		
Ripley Dr.	LL19	37
Ripon Av.	RR25	68
Ripon Clo., Birk.	Q 7	10
Ripon Clo., Sefton	Q24	40
Ripon Dr.	OO23	52
Ripon Rd.	K30	70
Ripon St.	Q28	73
Ripon St., Birk.	N35	111
Risbury Rd.	T28	75
Rishton Clo. S.	R30	74
Poplar Dr.		
Ritchie Av.	S25	56
Ritherup La.	EE31	101
Ritson St.	R34	113
Rivacre Rd.	R43	149
River Clo.	L16	20
River Gro.	O37	127
River View Rd.	N31	93
River Vw.	M24	38
River Way	Y35	116
Riverbank Clo.	G42	139
Riverbank Rd.	U37	130
Riverbank Rd., Hes.	G42	139
Riversdale Rd., Liver.	T37	130
Riversdale Rd., Wirr.	B36	105
Riverside	O38	127
Riverside Rd., Sefton	N25	54
Riverside Rd., Wirr.	M31	92
Riverside, Liver.	W28	76
Riverside, Sefton	K19	24
Riverslea Rd.	L24	38
Riverview Wk.	Q35	112
Riviera Dr.	M36	110
Rivington	EE27	62
Rivington Av.	FF26	63
Rivington Clo., Sefton	O 7	9
Rivington Clo., Wirr.	K35	109
Rivington Rd.	M31	92
Rivington St.	EE28	80
Roade St.	O26	54
Roadside Ct.	RR25	68
Rob La.	PP27	67
Robarts Rd.	R30	74
Robeck Rd.	U32	96
Robert Dr.	G35	108
Robert Gro.	W30	76
Elgar Rd.		
Roberts Av.	KK26	65
Roberts Dr.	Q25	55
Roberts St.	O31	93
Robertson St.	Q34	112
Robin Way	H36	108
Robina Rd.	HH29	82
Robins La.	HH29	82
Robinson Pl.	HH27	64
Baker St.		
Robinson Rd.	P24	40
Robinson St.	HH27	64
Robsart St.	Q30	73
Robson St., Kirk.	Q30	73
Robson St., Oak.Pk.	U32	96
Roby Clo.	EE31	101
Roby Rd.	Y32	98
Roby St., Sefton	P27	55
Roby St., St.H.	EE28	80
Roby Well Way	HH22	49
Robymount Av.	Y32	98
Rochester Av.	Q24	40
Rochester Rd., Liver.	R30	74
Rochester Rd., Wirr.	N36	111
Rock Av.	G40	139
Rock Bnk.	H34	108
Rock Ct.	U31	96
Rock St.		
Rock Ferry By-Pass	N35	111
Rock Gro.	U31	96
Rock St.		
Rock La. E.	O36	111
Rock La. W.	N36	111
Rock La., Halton	FF35	120
Rock La., Sefton	T22	42
Rock La., Wirr.	N37	127
Rock Mount Clo.	W35	115
Rock Park Rd.	O36	111
Rock Pk.	O36	111
Rock Rd.	V29	76
Rock St., Liver.	U31	96
Rock St., St.H.	EE29	80
Rock Way	R31	95
Rockbank Rd.	T30	75
Rockbourne Av.	W34	115
Rockbourne Grn.	W34	115
Rockbourne Way	W34	115
Rockfield Gdns.	S20	28
Rockfield Rd.	R29	74
Rockford Av.	W25	58
Rockford Clo.	W25	58
Rockford Wk.	W25	58
Rockhill Rd.	X36	116
Rockhouse St.	S30	74
Rockland Rd., Crosby	N24	39
Rockland Rd., Wirr.	K29	70
Rocklands Av.	N37	127
Rocklands La.	M41	141
Rockley St.	Q29	73
Rockmay St.	Q32	94
Rockmount Rd.	T36	114
Rockpoint Av.	L29	71
Rockside Rd.	U36	114
Rockville Rd.	V32	97
Rockville St.	N36	111
Rockwell Rd.	V29	76
Rockwood Clo.	V29	76
Rocky La. S.	H41	139
Rocky La. W.	S30	74
Rocky La., Liver.	V33	97
Rocky La., Wirr.	G41	139
Rockybank Rd.	M35	110
Roderick Rd.	R28	74
Rodick St.	W36	115
Rodmell Rd.	R26	56
Rodney St., Birk.	M34	110
Rodney St., Boot.	O28	72
Rodney St., Liver.	Q33	94
Rodney St., St.H.	FF27	63
Roe All.	P32	94
Roe La.	P 5	6
Roe St., Liver.	P32	94
Roe St., Wirr.	L33	92
Roeburn Way	LL35	152
Roedean Clo., Know.	X37	132
Roedean Clo., Sefton	S20	28
Roehampton Dr.	M22	38
Rogers Av.	Q26	55
Rokeby St.	Q31	94
Rokeden	OO27	67
Roker Av.	L31	92
Rokesmith Av.	S33	95
Roland Av., St.H.	HH25	64
Roland Av., Wirr.	M38	126
Roleton Clo.	R23	41
Corwen Dr.		
Rolleston Dr., Beb.	N39	127
Rolleston Dr., Wall.	K30	70
Rolling Mill La.	JJ29	82
Rollo St.	P29	73
Roman Ct.	K45	145
Roman Rd., Beb.	L37	126
Roman Rd., Wigan	NN22	51
Roman Rd., Wirr.	C32	88
Romer Rd.	S31	95
Romford St.	S32	95
Romford Way, Hale.	Z38	133
Redbourn Av.		
Romilly St., Liver.	R31	95
Romilly St., Wirr.	M34	110
Romley St.	Q28	73
Romney Clo.	K45	145
Romney Clo., C.Wood	JJ36	121
Romney Way	K45	145
Romsey Av.	L16	20
Romsey Gro.	LL20	37
Ronald Clo.	N24	39
Ronald Rd.	N24	39
Ronald Ross Av.	Q23	40
Ronald St.	T31	96
Ronalds Way, Sefton	O22	39
Ronaldshay	JJ36	121
Ronaldsway, Know.	AA37	133
Ronaldsway, Liver.	U25	57
Ronaldsway, Wirr.	G34	108
Ronan Clo.	O27	54
Rone Clo.	F33	89
Rookery Av.	NN24	51
Rookery Dr.	DD22	47
Rookery La.	DD22	47
Rookery Rd.	Q 4	6
Rookley Clo.	J35	109
Rooks Way	G41	139
Rooley, The	Y32	98
Roosevelt Dr.	R25	56
Roper St.	HH27	64
Ropers Bridge Clo., Know.	BB32	100
Dragon La.		
Ropewalk, The	J44	145
Rosalind Av.	N37	127
Rosalind St.	P28	73
Rosclare Clo.	J35	109
Rosclare Dr.	K30	70
Roscoe Av.	PP27	67
Roscoe Clo., Huy.	AA33	99
Ribchester Way		
Roscoe La.	Q33	94
Roscoe St., Liver.	Q33	94
Roscoe St., St.H.	EE27	62
Roscommon St.	Q31	94
Roscote Clo.	G41	139
Roscote, The	G41	139
Rose Av., Sefton	P25	55
Rose Av., St.H.	MM26	66
Rose Av., Sutton Leach	HH29	82
Rose Av., Sutton Leach	HH29	82
Rose Bank Way	Y30	77
Rose Brae	U35	114
Rose Brae, Birk.	N33	93

Rose Dr. DD22 47
Rose Hill St. MM22 51
Rose Hill, Liver. P31 94
Rose Hill, Sefton P 6 6
Rose La. U35 114
Rose Lea Clo. GG34 120
Rose Mt. L35 110
Rose Pl. N35 111
Union St.
Rose Pl., Liver. Q31 94
Rose Pl., St.H. DD22 47
Rose St. W36 115
Rose Vale Q30 73
Rose Vill. T33 96
Rose Vw. GG36 120
Rosebank Rd., Know. Y30 77
Rosebank Rd., Liver. V33 97
Rosebay Clo. L15 16
Roseberry Av. M31 92
Roseberry Gro. L36 110
Roseberry Rd., St.H. EE26 62
Roseberry Rd., Wigan NN22 51
Roseberry St., Liver. R33 95
Roseberry St., Sefton R 6 7
Rosebery Wk. R33 95
Rosebury Av. M24 38
Rosedale Av., Sefton N23 39
Rosedale Av., Wigan RR25 68
Rosedale Rd., Liver. U34 114
Rosedale Rd., Wirr. N35 111
Rosefield Av. N37 127
Rosefield Rd. Y36 116
Roseheath Dr. Z37 133
Rosehill Av. KK30 83
Rosehill Ct. X35 116
Roseland Clo. R19 28
Roselea Dr. S 3 3
Rosemary La. K15 16
Rosemead Av. G39 124
Rosemont Rd. T36 114
Rosemoor Dr. O22 39
Rosemount Clo. L35 110
Rosemount Dr. L29 71
Rake La.
Rosemount Pk. L35 110
Rosewell Ct. X30 77
Chalfont Way
Rosewood Gdns. U28 75
Wingrave Way
Roskell Rd. Y37 132
Roslin Ct. L35 110
Roslin Rd., Irby F38 123
Roslin Rd., Wirr. L35 110
Roslyn St. N35 111
Union St.
Ross Av. H31 90
Ross Clo. Y27 59
Ross Clo. HH22 49
Ross St. HH27 64
Ross St., App. GG36 120
Ross Tower Ct. M29 71
Rossal Rd., Wirr. G32 90
Rossall Av. S23 41
Rossall Gro. S45 149
Rossall Rd., Liver. U32 96
Rossall Rd., St.H. HH36 121
Rossendale Clo. J35 109
Rossett Av. T34 114
Rossett Rd. M23 38
Rossett St. S30 74
Rossini St. O26 54
Rosslyn Av. R21 28
Rosslyn Cres. G33 90
Rosslyn Dr. N.
Rosslyn Dr. G33 90
Rosslyn Pk. G33 90
Rosslyn Dr. N.
Rosslyn St. R35 113
Rossmore Gdns. S29 74
Rossmore Rd. S45 149
Rostherne Av. L31 92
Rostherne Av., Gol. RR25 68
Rostherne Cres. EE36 119
Rosthwaite Gro. GG24 48
Dalston Dr.
Rosthwaite Rd. V30 76
Rostron Cres. K16 19
Rothay Dr. LL35 152
Rothbury Clo. E32 89
Rothbury Rd. W30 76
Rotherwood Clo. M38 126
Rothesay Clo. JJ26 64
Rothesay Dr. N23 39
Rothesay Gdns. K36 109
Rothley Av. L11 12
Rothsay Dr. P43 148
Rothsay Sq. Q31 94
Prince Edwin St.
Rothwell Dr., Orm. U15 153
Rothwell Dr., Sefton L10 12
Rothwells La. O22 39
Rotten Row N 6 5
Rotunda St. P30 73
Rough Dale Clo. W25 58
Roughdale Av., Know. W25 58
Roughdale Av., St.H. GG31 102
Budworth Av.
Roughsedge Hey X29 77
Roughwood Dr. X23 44
Round Hey X29 77
Round Meade, The R20 28
Roundabout, The EE34 119
Roundway, The K19 24
Roundwood Dr. GG28 81
Routledge Rd. GG36 120
Rowan Av. W28 76
Rowan Clo. HH25 64
Rowan Clo. JJ26 64
Rowan Ct. E36 107
Rowan Dr. V23 43
Rowan Gro., Know. Y33 98
Rowan Gro., Wirr. N39 127
Rowan Tree Clo. E35 107
Rowans, The U16 153
Rowena Clo. N23 39
Rowland St. N34 111
Rowson St., Know. BB29 79
Rowson St., Wirr. L28 71
Roxborough Clo. NN30 84
Roxburgh Av., Liver. S33 113
Roxburgh Av., Wirr. M36 110
Roxburgh St. Q28 73
Royal Av. DD37 135
Royal Clo. L16 20
Royal Cres. L16 20
Royal Gro. EE28 80
Royal Mail St. Q32 94
Royal Pl. DD37 135
Royal St. Q29 73
Royal Ter. O 5 5
Royal, The A34 105
Royden Av. M30 71
Royden Cres. JJ22 49
Royden Rd. G34 108
Royden Rd. JJ22 49
Royden St. Q35 112
Royle St. JJ29 82
Taylor St.
Royston Av. M31 92
Royston St. R32 95
Royton Clo. Z38 133
Royton Rd. N24 39
Rudd Av. KK28 83
Rudd St. B33 87
Ruddington Rd. Q 7 10
Rudgate CC32 100
Rudgrave Clo. J35 109
Rudgrave Mews M30 72
Rudgrave Sq.
Rudgrave Pl. M31 92
Rudgrave Sq. M30 71
Rudley Wk. Z40 137
Rudston Rd. V33 97
Rudyard Clo. V31 97
Rudyard Rd.
Rudyard Rd. V31 97
Rufford Av. T19 29
Rufford Clo. T25 57
Rufford Rd., Lith. P26 55
Rufford Rd., Liver. S31 95
Rufford Rd., Rain. CC21 33
Rufford Rd., Sefton S 3 3
Rufford Rd., Wirr. L32 92
Rufford St. MM22 51
Rufford Wk. JJ26 64
Chain La.
Rugby Dr. T24 42
Rugby Rd., Liver. R25 56
Rugby Rd., Wirr. K31 91
Rugby St. O32 93
Earle St.
Ruislip Clo. Y36 116
Rullerton Rd. L31 92
Rumford Pl. P32 94
Rumford St. P32 94
Rumney Pl. P29 73
Rumney Rd. Q29 73
Rumney Rd. W. P29 73
Rundle Rd. T36 114
Rundle St. L33 92
Runic St. T32 96
Runnel, The J43 145
Runnells La. P22 40
Runnymeade Clo. X35 116
Runnymede Dr. KK25 65
West Side Av.
Runton Rd. Y34 116
Rupert La. Q31 94
Rupert Rd. Y31 98
Rupert St. R31 95
Rupert Ter. Q31 94
Ruscolm Clo. LL33 104
Ruscombe Rd. W30 76
Rushden Rd. X24 44
Rushey Hey Rd. W24 43
Rushmere Rd. T28 75
Rushmoor Av. PP23 52
Rusholme Clo. Z38 133
Rushton Av. NN27 66
Rushton Pl. X36 116
Ruskin Av., L.Tran. N36 111
Ruskin Av., St.H. OO27 67
Ruskin Av., Wirr. L31 92
Ruskin Dr. EE26 62
Ruskin St. Q28 73
Ruskin Way Y32 98
Rusland Av. G39 124
Rusland Rd. W25 58
Russell Pl. Q32 94
Russell Rd., Gars. V38 131
Russell Rd., Know. AA32 99
Russell Rd., L.Tran. N35 111
Russell Rd., Liver. T34 114
Russell Rd., Sefton R 5 7
Russell Rd., Wirr. K30 70
Russell St., Halton GG35 120
Russell St., Liver. Q32 94
Russell St., Wirr. N33 93
Russian Av. T30 75
Russian Dr. T30 75
Rutherford Rd., Liver. U34 114
Rutherford Rd., Sefton T21 29
Rutherford Rd., St.H. EE26 62
Rutherglen Av. N24 39
Ruthin Wk. R31 95
Ruthven Rd., Liver. U32 96
Ruthven Rd., Sefton O25 54
Bridge Rd.
Rutland Av., Liver. S34 113
Rutland Av., Wigan RR25 68
Rutland Clo., Liver. R30 74
Hamilton Rd.
Rutland Dr. OO23 52
Rutland Rd. P 6 6
Rutland St., Sefton P27 55
Rutland St., St.H. FF26 63
Rutland Way AA31 99
Rutter St. Q34 112
Rycot Rd., Know. X39 132
Rydal Av N24 39
Rydal Av., Pres. CC30 79
Rydal Av., Sefton J16 19
Rydal Av., Wirr. J34 109
Rydal Bnk. L31 92
Rydal Bnk. O37 127
Rydal Clo., Ain. V23 43
Rydal Clo., Sefton T24 42
Rydal Clo., Wigan OO23 52
Rydal Clo., Wirr. G39 124
Rydal Gro. GG25 63
Rydal Rd. Z32 99
Rydal St., Liver. R30 74
Rydal St., St.H. OO27 67
Rydal Way EE36 119
Ryder Clo. DD31 101
Lindrick Clo.
Ryder Cres. N 9 9
Rydinge, The L14 16
Rye Hey Rd. W24 43
Rye Moss La. O17 21
Ryecote W25 58
Ryecroft O23 39
Ryecroft Rd., Hes. J41 140
Ryecroft Rd., Liver. T25 57
Ryecroft Rd., Wirr. D33 88
Ryecroft Rd., Wirr. M32 92
Ryefield La. O23 39
Ryegate Rd. U37 130
Ryeground La. L14 16
Ryland Pk. H38 124
Rylands Hey F35 107
Rymer Grn. R28 74
Rymers Grn. K15 16
Ryton Rd. V24 43

Sackville Rd. EE26 62
Saddlers La. CC25 61
Sadler St., Halton HH36 121
St. Agnes Rd. P29 73
St. Agnes Rd., Huy. Z32 99
St. Aidans Clo. JJ22 49
St. Aidans Ter. K34 109
St. Aidans Way P23 40
St. Albans Clo. MM25 66
St. Albans Rd., Claugh. L34 110
St. Albans Rd., Sefton P27 55
St. Albans Rd., Wirr. L31 92
St. Albans Sq. P28 73
St. Albans St. R30 74
St. Ambrose Cft. Q23 40
St. Ambrose Gro. R30 74
St. Ambrose Way Q31 94
Everton Brow
St. Andrew Gdns. Q32 94
St. Andrew Rd. R30 74
St. Andrew St. Q32 94
St. Andrews Dr. M22 38
St. Andrews Gro. St.H. GG26 63
St. Andrews Gro., Sefton P23 40
St. Andrews Rd., Claugh. L34 110
St. Andrews Rd., Beb. Q39 127
St. Andrews Rd., Boot. P26 55
St. Andrews Rd., Sefton L22 38
St. Ann Pl. EE31 101
St. Anne Gro. M33 92
St. Anne Pl., Wirr. M33 92
St. Anne St., Liver. Q31 94
St. Anne St., Wirr. M33 92
St. Anne Ter. M33 92
St. Annes Clo. M33 92
St. Annes Cres. T36 114
St. Annes Ct. K14 16
St. Annes Gdns. T36 114
St. Annes Gro. T36 114
St. Annes Path K14 16
St. Annes Rd., Formby K14 16
St. Annes Rd., Halton HH36 121
St. Annes Rd., Know. Z32 99
St. Annes Rd., Liver. T36 114
St. Annes Rd., Marsh. Q 3 2
St. Annes Way M33 92
St. Anns Rd. EE28 80
St. Anthonys Gro. P23 40
St. Anthonys Rd. L22 38
St. Asaph Gro. Q24 40
St. Augustine St. P30 73
St. Augustines Way Q23 40
St. Austells Rd. Q28 73
St. Benets Way Q23 40
St. Bernards Clo. P23 40
St. Bernards Clo. S33 95
Timpson St.
St. Bernards Dr. P23 40
St. Bride St. Q33 94
St. Brides Rd. M30 71
St. Bridgets Gro. P23 40
St. Bridgets La. B36 105
St. Catherines Rd., Sefton P27 55
St. Catherines Rd., Liver. P28 73
St. Catherines Way JJ26 64
Ebenezar St.
St. Chads Dr. W24 43
St. Chads Par. W24 43
St. Christopher Av. P23 40
St. Chrysostoms Way R31 95
St. Clair Dr. R 4 7
St. Cuthberts Rd. R 4 7
St. Damians Cft. Q23 40
St. David Rd. R42 150
St. Davids Clo. J34 109
St. Davids Clo. EE31 101
Victoria St.
St. Davids Gro. P24 40
St. Davids La. J34 109
St. Davids Rd., Liver. R30 74
St. Davids Rd., Wool.H. X30 77
St. Davids Rd., Wirr. L34 110
St. Domingo Gro. R30 74
St. Domingo Rd. Q30 73
St. Domingo Vale R30 74
St. Dunstans Gro. P24 40
St. Edmunds Rd, P28 73
St. Elmo Rd. M30 71
St. Gabriels Av. AA32 99
St. George Gro. F33 89
St. Georges Av., St.H. EE26 62
St. Georges Av., Wirr. M36 110
St. Georges Gro. P24 40
St. Georges Heights Q30 73
St. Georges Hill Q30 73
St. Georges Mt. L29 71
St. Georges Pk. L29 71
St. Georges Pl. P32 94
St. Georges Rd., High Sefton L19 25
St. Georges Rd., Formby K15 16
St. Georges Rd., Know. Z30 78
St, Georges Rd., Sefton K18 19
St. Georges Rd., St.H. EE28 80
St. Georges Rd., Wirr. K30 70
St. Georges Way L41 141
Manor Rd.
St. Gregorys Cft. Q23 40
St. Helens Rd., Know. EE31 101
St. Helens Rd., Pres. CC29 79
St. Helens Rd., St.H. DD24 47
St. Hilary Brow K31 91
St. Hilary Dr. K31 91
St. Hilda St. Q29 73
St. Ives Gro. T31 96
St. Ives Rd., Claugh. L34 110
St. Ives Way Z36 117
St. James Clo. U30 75
St. James Dr. O27 54
St. James Pl. Q33 94
St. James Rd., Know. Z32 99
St. James Rd., Liver. Q33 94
St. James Rd., Pres. CC30 79
St. James St., Liver. P33 94
St. James St., Sefton O 6 5
St. James St., Wirr. L29 71
St. James Way P23 40
St. Jamess Mt. EE32 101
St. Jamess Rd., R.Hill EE32 101
St. Jamess Rd., Wigan HH19 36
St. Jamess Rd., Wirr. K33 91
St. Jeromes Way Q23 40
St. John St., Hay. NN27 66
St. John St., Pres. EE28 80
St. Johns Av. R26 56
St. Johns Clo. C33 88
St. Johns La. P32 94
St. Johns Pav. M34 110
St. Johns Pl. M24 38
St. Johns Rd., Crosby M24 38
St. Johns Rd., Know. Z32 99
St. Johns Rd., Liver. P29 73
St. Johns Rd., Sefton N 8 9
St. Johns Rd., Wirr. R42 150
St. Johns Sq. M34 111
Milton Pavement
St. Johns St., St.H. HH27 64
St. Johns St., Wirr. M34 110
St. Johns Ter. O28 72
St. Kildas Gro. F33 89
St. Leonards Clo. P23 40
St. Lucia Rd. M30 71
St. Lucid Rd. M30 71
St. Lukes Av. RR25 68
St. Lukes Church Rd. J16 19
St. Lukes Cres. GG35 120
St. Lukes Dr., Sefton J16 19
St. Lukes Dr., Wigan HH19 36
St. Lukes Gro., Neth. P23 40
St. Lukes Gro., Sefton P 5 6
St. Lukes Pl. Q33 94
St. Lukes Rd. EE27 62
St. Lukes Rd., Crosby M23 38
St. Lukes Rd., Sefton P 5 6
St. Margarets Gro. P24 40
Almond Av.
St. Margarets Rd. B34 105
St. Marks Av. L31 92
St. Marks Gro. P23 40
St. Marks Rd. Z32 99
St. Marks St. L31 92
St. Marks St. KK26 65
Juddfield St.
St. Mary Av. R28 74
St. Mary Gro. P24 40
St. Mary La. R28 74
St. Mary Pl. R28 74
St. Mary St., Wirr. L33 92
St. Marys Arc. GG27 63
St. Marys Av. HH23 49
St. Marys Gro. N34 111
St. Marys Rd., Know. Z32 99
St. Marys Rd., Liver. U38 130
St. Marys Rd., Sefton N24 39
St. Marys St., Wool. X36 116
St. Matthews Av. P25 55
St. Matthews Clo. LL19 37
St. Mawes Clo. FF36 120
St. Mawes Way DD26 62
St. Michael Gro. F33 89
St. Michael Rd. U16 153
St. Michaels Church Rd. R35 113
St. Michaels Clo., Sefton Q 3 2
St. Michaels Clo., Liver. S36 113
Fulwood Dr.
St. Michaels Gro. P23 40
St. Michaels Pk. U16 153
St. Michaels Rd., Crosby L22 38
St. Michaels Rd., Liver. R35 113
St. Michaels Rd., Halton EE37 135
St. Monicas Dr. P23 40
St. Nathaniel St. R33 95
St. Nicholas Dr. P23 40
St. Nicholas Gro. HH29 82
St. Nicholas Pl. O32 93
St. Nicholas Rd., Know. BB32 100
St. Nicholas Rd., Wirr. J30 70
St. Oswalds La. Q23 40
St. Oswalds Rd. NN24 51
St. Oswalds St. U31 96
St. Patricks Dr. P23 40
St. Paul St., St.H. FF27 63
St. Pauls Av. N32 93
St. Pauls Clo. N36 111
St. Pauls Gdns. R45 149
St. Pauls Rd., Rock. N36 111
St. Pauls Rd., Wirr. N32 93
St. Pauls Sq. P32 94
St. Pauls St., Sefton O 6 5
St. Pauls Vw. N36 111
St. Peters Av. J14 15
St. Peters Clo., Sefton J15 15
St. Peters Clo., Wirr. G41 139
St. Peters Mews O36 111
St. Peters Rd., Sefton O 7 9
St. Peters Rd., Wirr. O36 111
St. Philips Av. P25 55
St. Saviour Sq. R33 95
St. Seiriol Gro. L34 110
St. Stephens Clo., Wirr. J42 140
St. Stephens Clo., Liver. Y34 116
St. Stephens Ct. L36 110
St. Stephens Gro. P23 40
St. Stephens Rd., Sefton K19 24
St. Stephens Rd., Wirr. L36 110
St. Teresas Rd. EE27 62
St. Thomas Dr. P23 40
St. Thomas Sq. FF27 63
Liverpool Rd.
St. Vincent Rd. L34 110
St. Vincent St., Liver. Q32 94
London Rd.
St. Vincent St., Wirr. M31 92
St. Vincent Way Q32 94
St. Werberghs Sq. N34 111
Grange Pavement
St. William Rd. O22 39
St. Winefrides Av. O27 54
St. Winifred Rd., St.H. DD30 80
St. Winifreds Rd. L30 71
Sakers St. Q29 73
Salacre Clo. H35 108
Salacre Cres. H35 108
Salacre La. H35 108
Salcombe Dr., Liver. X37 132
Salcombe Dr., Sefton R 2 3
Salem Vw. L35 110
Salerno Dr. Y31 98
Saleswood Av. DD27 62
Salford Rd. M10 12
Salisbury Av., Sefton Q24 40
Salisbury Av., Wirr. B36 105
Salisbury Dr. O37 128
New Ferry Rd.
Salisbury Rd., Grassendale U38 130
Salisbury Rd., Liver. Q30 73
Salisbury Rd., Sefton O27 54
Salisbury Rd., St.H. MM25 66
Salisbury Rd., Walt. R27 56
Salisbury Rd., Wav. S33 95
Salisbury Rd., Wirr. L29 71

Salisbury St., Know.	BB30	79	Sandra Dr.	PP27	67	Saxon Way La.	W22	43
Grosvenor Rd.			Sandridge Rd., Thing.	G38	124	Saxonia Rd.	R28	74
Salisbury St., Liver.	Q31	94	Sandridge Rd., Wall.	L29	71	Saxony Rd.	R32	95
Salisbury St., Sefton	R 6	7	Sandringham Av., Sefton	N25	54	Saxthorpe Clo.	LL19	37
Salisbury St., Wigan	QQ25	68	Sandringham Av., Wirr.	C33	88	Sayce St.	GG36	120
Salisbury St., Wirr.	M34	110	Sandringham Clo., Beb.	O37	127	Scafell Clo.	P43	148
Salisbury Ter.	T33	96	Sandringham Clo., Wirr.	C33	88	Scafell Clo., Liver.	AA35	117
Salkeld Av.	MM23	51	Sandringham Dr., Liver.	R35	113	Scafell Rd., St.H.	GG25	63
Salop St.	Q29	73	Sandringham Dr., St.H.	HH29	82	Scaffold La.	L18	20
Salt Pit La.	T20	29	Sandringham Dr., St.H.	HH32	82	Scargreen Av.	T27	57
Saltash Clo., Know.	Z36	117	Sandringham Dr., Wirr.	L29	71	Scarisbrick Av., Lith.	O25	54
Carlyon Way			Sandringham Rd., Ains.	M10	12	Scarisbrick Av., S.Port	O 5	5
Saltburn Rd.	J30	70	Sandringham Rd., Bir.	N 7	9	Scarisbrick Clo.	T19	29
Saltney St.	O31	93	Sandringham Rd., Halton	GG35	120	Scarisbrick Cres.	S27	56
Saltram Rd.	LL19	37	Sandringham Rd., Formby	K16	19	Scarisbrick Dr.	S27	56
Salwick Clo.	Q 3	2	Sandringham Rd., Liver.	T29	75	Scarisbrick Dr.	S28	74
Samaria Av.	P37	128	Sandringham Rd., Mag.	S21	28	Scarisbrick New Rd.	P 6	6
Sambourn Clo.	L10	12	Sandringham Rd., Sea.	N25	54	Scarisbrick Pl.	S28	74
Samuel St.	EE29	80	Sandrock Rd.	L29	71	Scarisbrick Rd., Liver.	S28	74
Sand Dune Rd.	G31	90	Sands Rd., Liver.	W25	58	Scarisbrick Rd., St.H.	CC21	33
Sandbeck St.	Q35	112	Sands Rd., Moss.H.	T35	114	Scarisbrick St.	O 5	5
Sandbrook La.	G33	90	Sandstone Clo.	EE32	101	Scarsbrick Pl.	S27	56
Sandbrook Rd.	M11	12	Sandstone Dr.	D36	106	Scarsdale Rd.	T28	75
Sandbrook Rd., Child.	X33	98	Sandstone Dr., Rain.	EE32	101	Sceptre Clo.	NN27	66
Sandbrook Way	M11	12	Sandstone La.	Q35	112	*Crown St.*		
Sandcliffe Rd.	K29	70	*Beresford Rd.*			Sceptre Rd.	V27	58
Sandeman Rd.	S29	74	Sandstone Rd.	T31	96	Scholar St.	S33	95
Sanderling Rd.	X23	44	Sandstone Rd., Rain.	LL20	37	Scholes La.	DD29	80
Sandfield	Y32	98	Sandstone Wk.	H41	139	Scholes Pk.	DD29	80
Sandfield Av.	C32	88	Sandwash Clo.	EE23	47	Schombing St.	R31	95
Sandfield Clo., H.Beb.	M38	126	Sandway Cres.	U28	75	School Av.	K15	16
Sandfield Rd.			Sandy Brow La.	Z25	60	School Brow	JJ22	49
Sandfield Cres.	FF27	63	Sandy Grn.	S26	56	School Clo.	G32	90
Liverpool Rd.			Sandy Gro., Liver.	T30	75	School Dr.	JJ22	49
Sandfield Pk. E.	V30	76	Sandy La.	R26	56	School Hill	G41	139
Sandfield Pk., Wirr.	F41	138	Sandy La., Cron.	EE34	119	School La., Ain.	S24	41
Sandfield Pl.	O27	54	Sandy La., Hes.	H40	139	School La., Beb.	O37	127
Sandfield Rd., H.Beb.	M38	126	Sandy La., Irby	F38	123	School La., Bids.	J32	91
Village Rd.			Sandy La., Liver.	T30	75	School La., Birk.	D32	88
Sandfield Rd., H.Beb.	M38	126	Sandy La., Lyd.	R18	23	School La., Burt.	MM30	84
Sandfield Rd., Liver.	X35	116	Sandy La., Melling	U22	42	School La., Elles.	H44	144
Sandfield Rd., St.H.	DD26	62	Sandy La., Moss B.	FF24	48	School La., H.Beb.	M38	126
Sandfield Rd., Wall.	L29	71	Sandy La., Newt.	PP25	67	School La., Hoot.	Q44	148
Sandfield Rd., Wirr.	H36	108	Sandy La., Sefton	L19	25	School La., Hoy.	B33	87
Sandfield Ter.	L29	71	Sandy La., St.H.	FF25	63	School La., Know.	Z32	99
Sandfield Wk.	U30	75	Sandy La., W.Lan.	U17	153	School La., Lith.	O25	54
Sandford Dr.	S20	28	Sandy La., Wall.	K30	70	School La., Liver.	P32	94
Sandford St.	N33	93	Sandy La., Warr.	KK34	152	School La., Mell.	U22	42
Sandforth Clo.	U30	75	Sandy La., Wigan	HH19	36	School La., Nest.	L44	146
Sandforth Rd.	U30	75	Sandy La., Wirr.	B36	105	School La., S.Dene	W26	58
Sandgate Clo.	X39	132	Sandy Mount Dr., Beb.	N39	127	School La., Sefton	K15	16
Sandham Gro.	J41	140	Sandy Rd.	N25	54	School La., St.H.	FF32	102
Sandham Rd.	AA39	133	Sandymount Dr., Wirr.	K29	70	School La., St.H.	JJ33	103
Sandhead St.	S33	95	Sandyville Gro.	T29	75	School La., Thur.	E38	123
Sandhey Rd.	C33	88	Sandyville Rd.	S29	74	School La., Wigan	LL23	50
Sandheys Av.	M24	38	Sandyway	L34	110	School La., Wirr.	K31	91
Sandheys Clo.	Q29	73	Sanfield Rd.	P27	55	School Rd.	M33	92
Walton La.			*Breeze Hill*			School Rd.	K19	24
Sandheys Dr.	Q 4	6	Sangness Dr.	Q 7	10	School St.	OO22	52
Sandheys Gro.	M24	38	Sankey Rd., Sefton	S21	28	School St., Newt.	NN27	66
Sandheys Rd.	L29	71	Sankey Rd., St.H.	JJ26	64	School St., St.H.	JJ26	64
Sandheys Ter.	M24	38	Sankey St., Gol.	QQ25	68	*Park St.*		
Sandhills	K19	24	Sankey St., Liver.	Q33	94	School St., Wigan	QQ25	68
Sandhills La.	O29	72	Sankey St., Newt.	NN27	66	School Way, Halt.	HH35	121
Sandhurst Dr.	T24	42	Sankey St., St.H.	HH28	82	School Way, Know.	X39	132
Sandhurst Rd.	DD30	80	Sankey Ter.	NN27	66	School Way., Liver.	X39	136
Sandhurst St.	R35	113	*Rathbone St.*			School Wk.	O22	39
Sandhurst Way	R18	23	Santon Av.	T30	75	Schoolfield Clo.	H36	108
Sandilands Gro.	L19	25	Sapphire St.	T32	96	Schoolfield Rd.	H36	108
Sandiway	P42	143	Sarah St.	Q31	94	Scone Clo.	V27	58
Sandiway Av.	DD36	119	Sarahs Cft.	Q23	40	Score Bentham Dr.	V33	97
Sandiway Dr.	P42	143	Sark Rd.	T31	96	Score, The	GG29	81
Sandiway, Hoy.	C32	88	Sarsfield Av.	RR25	68	Scoresby Rd.	H31	90
Sandiway, Huy.	Z32	99	Sarum Rd.	X33	98	Scorton St.	S30	74
Sandiway, Whist.	BB31	100	Saughall Massie Rd.	F34	107	Scotchbarn La.	CC30	79
Sandiways Av.	Q24	40	Saughall Massie Rd.	G34	108	Scoter Rd.	W24	43
Sandiways Rd.	K30	70	Saughall Massie Rd., Wirr.	C35	106	Scotia Av.	P37	128
Sandlea Pk.	B36	105	Saughall Rd.	F33	89	Scotia Rd.	U31	96
Sandon Clo.	EE31	101	Saunby St.	V39	131	Scotland Pl.	P31	94
Sandon Gro.	DD22	47	Saunders Av.	BB31	100	Scotland Rd.	P31	94
Sandon Pl.	HH36	121	Saunders St.	O 4	5	Scott Av.	AA32	99
Cheryl Dr.			Savil Rd.	S19	28	Scott Av.	CC31	100
Sandon Prom.	M31	92	Saville Rd.	U32	96	Scott Clo., Mag.	S20	28
Sandon Rd., Egre.	M31	92	Savon Hook	L16	20	Scott Clo., Kirk.	Q29	73
Sandon Rd., Sefton	N 8	9	Sawdon Av.	Q 7	10	*Pugin St.*		
Sandon St., Liver.	Q33	94	Sawpit La.	Z32	99	Scott Pl.	K33	91
Sandon St., Sefton	M24	38	Saxby Rd.	X30	77	Scott St.	L30	71
Sandon St., St.H.	EE29	80	Saxon Clo.	R30	74	Scott St., Lith.	O26	54
Sandon Way	O30	72	Saxon Rd., Birk.	C33	88	Scott St., Sefton	R 5	7
Sandown La.	T33	96	Saxon Rd., Crosby	M23	38	Scott Wk.	OO28	85
Sandown Park Rd.	T23	42	Saxon Rd., More.	G32	90	*Bradlegh Rd.*		
Sandown Rd., Liver.	T32	96	Saxon Rd., Sefton	N 6	5	Scotts Av., St.H.	GG31	102
Sandown Rd., Sefton	N25	54	Saxon St.	R31	95	Scotts Clo.	F35	107
Sandpiper Clo.	F34	107	Saxon Ter.	GG36	120	Scythes, The	F35	107
Sandpiper Clo.	KK19	37				Scythia Clo.	P37	128
						Sea Rd.	K29	70

Street	Grid	Page
Sea View Av., Wirr.	F38	123
Sea View La.	F38	123
Sea View Rd., Sefton	O27	54
Sea Vw.	B33	87
Seabank Av.	M30	71
Seabank Rd., Sefton	O 5	5
Seabank Rd., Wall.	L29	71
Seabank Rd., Wirr.	G42	139
Seabrow	P32	94
Seacombe Prom.	N31	93
Seacroft Clo.	X30	77
Seacroft Cres.	R 2	3
Seacroft Rd.	X30	77
Seafield	L16	20
Seafield Av., Sefton	N23	39
Seafield Av., Wirr.	G42	139
Seafield Rd., Ains.	M10	12
Seafield Rd., Beb.	O37	127
Seafield Rd., Boot.	O27	54
Seafield Rd., Sefton	Q26	55
Seafield Rd., Wirr.	G31	90
Seaford Dr.	G33	90
Seafore Clo.	R19	28
Seaforth Dr.	G33	90
Seaforth La.	O25	54
Seaforth Rd.	O26	54
Seaforth Vw.	O26	54
Sealand Av.	J16	19
Sealand Clo	J16	19
Sealy Clo.	O40	142
Seaman Rd.	T33	96
Seascale La.	DD29	80
Seath Av.	JJ27	64
Seathwaite Clo.	L23	38
Seathwaite Cres.	V23	43
Seaton Gro.	EE30	80
Seaton Rd., Wall.	L30	71
Seaton Rd., Wirr.	M35	110
Seaton Way	R 2	3
Seaview Av., Brom.	R42	150
Seaview Av., Wall.	L30	71
Seaview Rd., Wirr.	L30	71
Seaview Ter.	M24	38
Seawood Gro.	F33	89
Second Av., Know.	DD31	101
Second Av., Liver.	S25	56
Second Av., Sefton	M23	38
Second Av., Wirr.	H34	108
Sedbergh Av.	S23	41
Sedbergh Gro.	X31	98
Sedbergh Rd.	K30	70
Sedburn Rd.	X25	59
Seddon Clo.	CC27	61
Seddon Rd., Liver.	V38	131
Seddon Rd., St.H.	DD29	80
Seddon St.	FF25	63
Sedge Cres.	MM3084	
Sedgefield Clo.	H31	90
Sedgefield Rd.	H33	90
Sedgelley Wk.	Z30	78
Sedgemoor Rd.	T27	57
Sedgewick Rd.	MM30	84
Sedley St.	R30	74
Seeds La.	S25	56
Seel Rd.	Z32	99
Seel St.	P32	94
Seeley Av.	L33	92
Sefton Av., Halt.	GG35	120
Sefton Av., Sefton	O25	54
Sefton Clo., Sefton	U23	42
Sefton Clo., Sefton	V23	43
Sefton Dr., Liver.	S34	113
Sefton Dr., Lt. Cros.	O21	26
Sefton Dr., Mag.	R21	28
Sefton Dr., Sefton	T24	42
Sefton Fold	HH22	49
Sefton Gro.	S35	113
Sefton La.	R21	28
Sefton Mill La.	Q21	27
Sefton Moss La.	P23	40
Sefton Moss Vill.	O25	54
Sefton Park Rd.	R34	113
Sefton Rd.	R27	56
Sefton Rd., Asht.	MM22	51
Sefton Rd., Beb.	O37	127
Sefton Rd., Boot.	P26	55
Sefton Rd., Lith.	O25	54
Sefton Rd., Sefton	K16	19
Sefton Rd., Wirr.	L29	71
Sefton Rd., Wirr.	O36	111
Sefton St., Lith.	O25	54
Sefton St., Liver.	P34	112
Sefton St., S.Port	P 6	6
Sefton St., Sefton	O 7	9
Sefton St., St.H.	MM27	66
Sefton Vw.	O23	39
Segars La.	M10	12
Selborne	CC32	100
Selborne Clo.	R33	95
Selborne St., Edge H.	R33	95
Selborne St., Liver.	Q33	94
Selby Dr., Sefton	L16	20
Selby Dr., Wigan	LL19	37
Selby Rd.	R26	56
Selby St., Wirr.	L30	71
Selkirk Av., Wigan	LL23	50
Selkirk Av., Wirr.	Q43	148
Selkirk Dr.	DD26	62
Selkirk Rd.	T32	96
Sellar St.	Q29	73
Selley Rd.	GG36	120
Selsdon Rd.	M24	38
Selside Rd.	Z35	117
Selston Clo.	O40	142
Selwin St.	Q28	73
Selworthy Grn.	V34	115
Selworthy Rd.	M 7	8
Selwyn Clo.	JJ35	121
Selwyn St.	Q28	73
Sennen Rd.	W25	58
September Rd.	S30	74
Sergim Rd.	Y31	98
Serpentine N., The	L22	38
Serpentine Rd.	M31	92
Serpentine S., The	L23	38
Serpentine, The, Liver.	U37	130
Serpentine, The, Sefton	L22	38
Servia Rd.	O25	54
Servite Clo.	M24	38
Manley Rd.		
Sessions Rd.	Q29	73
Settrington Rd.	T28	75
Seven Acre Rd.	O22	39
Seven Acres La.	H38	124
Sevenoaks Av.	L10	12
Seventh Av., Liver.	S25	56
Seventh Av., Wirr.	H33	90
SevernRd., Know.	DD31	101
Severn Clo.	HH23	49
Avon Rd.		
Severn Clo., C.Wood	JJ35	121
Severn Clo., St.H.	HH30	82
Severn Rd., Asht.	PP22	52
Severn Rd., Know.	W22	43
Severn St.	L32	92
Severs St.	R31	95
Sewell St.	BB30	79
Sexton Av.	KK28	83
Sexton Way	W32	97
Seymour Dr.	T19	29
Seymour Pl.	L29	71
Seymour St.		
Seymour Place W.	L29	71
Seymour Rd.	V32	97
Seymour Rd., Lith.	O25	54
Bridge Rd.		
Seymour St.	HH29	82
Robins La.		
Seymour St.	HH29	82
Waterdale Cres.		
Seymour St., Birk.	M35	110
Seymour St., Boot.	O28	72
Seymour St., Liver.	Q32	94
Seymour St., Wirr.	L29	71
Shacklady Rd.	X23	44
Shackleton Rd.	H31	90
Shadwell Clo.	O30	72
Shaftesbury Av.	O 9	9
Shaftesbury Rd., Sefton	O 9	9
Shaftesbury Ter.	U31	96
Shaftesbury Way	MM29	84
Shaftsbury Rd., Crosby	M23	38
Shaftway Clo.	MM25	66
Shakespeare Av.	N36	111
Shakespeare Clo.	R31	95
Shakespeare Rd., Elles.	K44	145
Shakespeare Rd., Halton	GG36	120
Shakespeare Rd., St.H.	GG31	102
Shakespeare Rd., Wirr.	M32	92
Shakespeare St.	V38	131
King St.		
Shakespeare St., Lith.	O26	54
Shakespeare St., S.Port	O 6	5
Shaldon Clo.	X25	59
Shaldon Rd.	X25	59
Shaldon Wk.	X25	59
Shalford Dr.	C36	106
Shallmarsh Clo.	M38	126
Shallmarsh Ct.	M38	126
Shallmarsh Rd.	M38	126
Shallot St.	R34	113
Shammon St.	K32	91
Shamrock Rd.	K33	91
Shanklin Rd.	T32	96
Shap Way, Halton	EE37	135
Shap Way, Know.	EE36	119
Shard Clo.	U26	57
Shard St.	JJ29	82
Peckers Hill Rd.		
Sharples Cres.	O23	39
Shavington Av.	K35	109
Shaw Cres.	L15	16
Shaw Entry	CC33	100
Shaw La., Know.	BB31	100
Shaw La., Wirr.	F35	107
Shaw Rd.	Y38	132
Shaw St., Asht.	NN22	51
Shaw St., Hoy.	B33	87
Shaw St., Liver.	Q31	94
Shaw St., Newt.	MM26	66
Shaw St., St.H.	GG27	63
Shaw St., Wirr.	M34	110
Shawbury Av.	M37	126
Shawell Ct.	JJ36	121
Swinford Av.		
Shaws All.	P33	94
Shaws Av.	O 8	9
Shaws Dr.	C32	88
Shaws La.	O 9	9
Shaws Rd.	O 8	9
Shawton Rd.	V33	97
Shearman Clo.	G39	124
Shearman Rd.	G39	124
Sheen Rd.	L30	71
Sheepfield Clo.	S45	149
Sheffield Row	OO29	85
Shefford Rise	LL20	37
Sheil Rd.	S31	95
Sheila Wk., Know.	U25	57
Elizabeth Rd.		
Shelagh Av.	GG36	120
Sheldon Clo.	N40	142
Sheldon Rd.	V29	76
Shelley Clo.	Z32	99
Shelley Gro., Liver.	V38	131
Shelley Gro., Sefton	Q 6	6
Shelley Pl.	CC31	100
Shelley Pl., Huy.	CC31	100
Byron Av.		
Shelley Rd.	GG36	120
Shelley St., Sefton	O27	54
Shelley St., St.H.	GG32	102
Shelley Way	C37	122
Shellfield Rd.	R 3	3
Shellingford Rd.	X31	98
Shelton Dr.	L11	12
Shelton Rd.	K30	70
Shenley Clo.	N38	127
Shenley Clo.	S 2	3
Baytree Clo.		
Shenley Rd.	V33	97
Shenstone St.	R32	95
Shenton Av.	HH26	64
Shepherd Clo.	F35	107
Thresher Av.		
Sheppard Av.	X33	98
Shepston Av.	R28	74
Shepton Rd.	Y30	77
Sherborne Av., Liver.	Y37	132
Sherborne Av., Sefton	Q23	40
Sherborne Rd.	K30	70
Sherborne Sq.	Z32	99
Sherbourne Clo.	S25	56
Sherbourne Way	MM30	84
Weymouth Way		
Sherdley Park Dr.	GG29	81
Sherdley Rd.	FF29	81
Sheridan Pl.	O28	72
Sheridan St.	Q31	94
Iliad St.		
Sheriff Clo.	Q31	94
Prince Edwin St.		
Sherlock Rd.,	MM25	66
Sherlock St.	L32	92
Sherlock St.	Q29	73
Sherman Dr.	EE32	101
Shern Av.	RR25	68
Sherri Dr.	OO28	85
Sherringham Rd.	N 8	9
Sherry La.	H36	108
Sherwood Av., Crosby	M22	38
Sherwood Av., Wirr.	F37	123
Sherwood Clo.	EE36	119
Sherwood Dr.	N37	127

Sherwood Gdns.	MM30 84	
Milnethorpe Rd.		
Sherwood Rd.,	M31 92	
Sherwood Rd., Sefton	M22 38	
Sherwood Rd., Wirr.	D33 88	
Sherwood St., Wall.	O31 93	
Sherwoods La.	T25 57	
Sherwyn Rd.	S29 74	
Shetland Clo.	JJ35 121	
Shevington Clo.	JJ35 121	
Shevingtons La.	V22 43	
Shewell Clo.	M35 110	
Shiel Rd.	L29 71	
Shimmin Gdns.	HH29 82	
Shimmin St.	R32 95	
Shipley Wk.	Y39 136	
Shirburne Rd.	J14 15	
Shirdley Av.	W25 58	
Shirdley Cres.	M11 12	
Shirdley Wk.	W25 58	
Shire La.	L18 20	
Shireburn Av.	GG25 63	
Shirley Rd.	V37 131	
Shirley St.	N31 93	
Shirwell Gro.	HH31 103	
Shop La.	S20 28	
Shop Rd.	Y27 59	
Shore Dr.	P38 128	
Shore La.	C37 122	
Shore Rd.	C37 122	
Shore Rd., Birk.	N33 93	
Shore Rd., Lith.	N26 54	
Shore Rd., Sefton	K10 11	
Shorebank	P38 128	
Shorefields	P37 128	
Short Croft La.	M16 20	
Short St.	MM26 66	
Church Rd.		
Short St.	MM27 66	
Shortfield Rd.	H35 108	
Shortwood Rd.	W31 97	
Shottesbrook Grn.	T27 57	
Shotwalk St.	T32 96	
Shrewsbury Av.	M23 38	
Shrewsbury Clo.	K34 109	
Shrewsbury Ct.	L35 110	
Shrewsbury Dr., Sefton	S23 41	
Shrewsbury Dr., Wirr.	H34 108	
Shrewsbury Rd.	V38 131	
Shrewsbury Rd. N., Ox.	K34 109	
Shrewsbury Rd., Bids.	K33 91	
Shrewsbury Rd., Ox.	L35 110	
Shrewsbury Rd., W.Kirby	B36 105	
Shrewsbury Rd., Wall.	K30 70	
Shrewton Rd.	X33 98	
Shuttleworth Clo.	G34 108	
Overchurch Rd.		
Sibford Rd.	V30 76	
Sibley Av.	OO23 52	
Siddal St.	FF25 63	
Siddeley Dr.	MM27 66	
Siddeley St.	S35 113	
Sidgreave St.	FF27 63	
Siding La.	Y21 31	
Siding La.	BB20 33	
Sidlaw Av.	JJ27 64	
Sidney Av.	L29 71	
Sidney Clo.	K44 145	
Sidney Rd.		
Sidney Pl.	R32 95	
Sidney Powell Av.	V24 43	
Sidney Rd.	N35 111	
Sidney Rd., Elles.	K44 145	
Sidney Rd., Liver.	P28 73	
Sidney Rd., Sefton	Q 5 6	
Sidney St.	N33 93	
Sidney St., St.H.	EE27 62	
Sidney Ter.	N35 111	
Sidwell St.	V38 131	
Signal Works Rd.	T25 57	
Silcock St.	QQ25 68	
Silcroft Rd.	W25 58	
Silkstone St.	EE27 62	
Silver Av.	KK26 65	
Silver Birch Way	R18 23	
Silverbeech Av.	U35 114	
Silverbeech Rd.	M31 92	
Silverburn Av.	G33 90	
Silverdale Av.	T30 75	
Silverdale Clo., Know.	Z33 99	
Fieldsend		
Silverdale Dr., Sefton	P25 55	
Silverdale Gro.	GG25 63	
Silverdale Rd., Beb.	N37 127	
Silverdale Rd., St.H.	NN27 66	

Silverdale Rd., Wirr.	L35 110	
Silverlea Av.	L31 92	
Silverstone Dr., Mag.	R19 28	
Silverthorne Dr.	Q 4 6	
Silverton Rd.	T37 130	
Silverwell Rd.	V26 58	
Silverwell Wk.	V26 58	
Silvester St.	P30 73	
Simms Av.	JJ27 64	
Simms Rd.	S30 74	
Simons Cft.	P23 40	
Simons Clo.	BB33 100	
Simonsbridge	C38 122	
Simonside	EE36 119	
Simonswood La., Kirkby	X24 44	
Simonswood La., Sefton	W19 30	
Simonswood Wk.	X24 44	
Simpson Av.	P33 94	
Simpson St., Liver.	P33 94	
Simpson St., Wirr.	M34 110	
Sinclair Av.	CC30 79	
Sinclair Clo.	CC30 79	
Sinclair Dr.	U34 114	
Sineacre La.	Z21 32	
Singleton Av., Birk.	M35 110	
Singleton Av., St.H.	HH26 64	
Singleton Dr.	Y27 59	
Sir Howard Way	Q33 94	
Sir Thomas St.	P32 94	
Sir Thomas White Gdns.	Q30 73	
Siskin Grn.	X34 116	
Sixpenny Brook	N13 17	
Sixteen Acre La.	L14 16	
Sixth Av.	S25 56	
Sixth Av., Bids.	H33 90	
Skeffington	CC32 100	
Skelhorne St.	Q32 94	
Skellington Fold	Z34 117	
Skelton Clo.	GG25 63	
Skelton St.	MM22 51	
Skerries Rd.	R30 74	
Skipton Av.	S 2 3	
Skipton Rd.	R29 74	
Skipton Rd., Know.	AA31 99	
Lynton Rd.		
Skirving St.	P30 73	
Skye Clo.	JJ35 121	
Sladeburn Cres.	PP24 52	
Edge Green La.		
Slag La.	KK25 65	
Slag La., Gol.	RR25 68	
Slater St.	P33 94	
Slatey Rd.	L34 110	
Sleaford Rd.	X30 77	
Sleepers Hill	Q29 73	
Slessor Av.	C35 106	
Slim Rd.	Z31 99	
Slingsby Dr.	H35 108	
Smeaton St.	Q28 73	
Smethurst Hall Pk.	HH20 36	
Smethurst Rd.		
Smethurst Rd.	HH20 36	
Smilie Av.	F32 89	
Smith Av.	L33 92	
Smith Dr.	Q26 55	
Smith Pl.	P30 73	
Smith St., Know.	BB30 79	
Warrington Rd.		
Smith St., Know.	CC30 79	
Smith St., Liver.	Q30 73	
Smith St., St.H.	JJ29 82	
Smith-down Rd.	S33 95	
Smithdown La.	R32 95	
Smithdown Rd.	T34 114	
Smithfield St.	HH28 82	
Smithfield St., Liver.	P32 94	
Smithy Clo., Cron.	EE34 119	
Smithy Clo., Sefton	L15 16	
Smithy Grn.	L15 16	
Smithy Hey	C35 106	
Smithy Hill	L42 141	
Smithy La., Know.	EE34 119	
Smithy La., Liver.	Q28 73	
Smithy La., W.Lan.	T17 153	
Smithy La., Wirr.	O45 147	
Smock La.	LL23 50	
Smollett St.	O26 54	
Smyth Rd.	HH36 121	
Snaefell Av.	T30 75	
Snaefell Gro.	T30 75	
Snowberry Clo.	JJ35 121	
Snowden Gro., St.H.	HH29 82	
Snowdon Rd.	M36 110	
Snowdrop Av.	K33 91	
Snowdrop Rd.	F33 89	
Snowdrop St.	P29 73	

Snowshill Dr.	LL19 37	
Soho Sq.	Q31 94	
Soho St.	Q31 94	
Solar Rd.	R26 56	
Solly Av.	N36 111	
Solomon St.	R32 95	
Solva Clo.	Q31 94	
Solway St., Liver.	R33 95	
Solway St., Wirr.	K33 91	
Soma Av.	P25 55	
Somerford Rd., Know.	X31 98	
Somerford Rd., Liver.	W31 97	
Somerset Dr.	M12 12	
Somerset Pl.	S30 74	
Somerset Rd., Crosby	M24 38	
Somerset Rd., Pen.	G39 124	
Somerset Rd., Sefton	P27 55	
Somerset Rd., Wall.	K31 91	
Somerset Rd., Wirr.	C35 106	
Somerset St.	HH28 82	
Somerton St.	T33 96	
Somerville Clo.	O42 142	
Somerville Gro.	M24 38	
Somerville Rd., Crosby	M24 38	
Somerville Rd., Halton	EE37 135	
Somerville St.	N33 93	
Somery St.	Q30 73	
Sonning Av.	O24 39	
Sonning Rd.	S28 74	
Sorany Clo.	O22 39	
Sorogold St.	HH27 64	
Soughers La.	MM22 51	
Soughers St.	MM22 51	
Soulsby Gdns.	HH29 82	
South Albert Rd.	S35 113	
South Av.	BB30 79	
South Bank Rd., Gars.	U37 130	
South Bank Rd., Liver.	S32 95	
South Barcombe Rd.	W33 97	
South Bidston Rd.	K34 109	
South Bnk.	L35 110	
South Boundary Rd.	X25 59	
South Brook Rd.	Y33 98	
South Cantril Av.	W28 76	
South Castle St.	P32 94	
South Dr., Hes.	H41 139	
South Dr., Irby	F38 123	
South Dr., Liver.	U33 96	
South Dr., W.Derby	U30 75	
South Gro., All.	V36 115	
South Gro., Dingle	R35 113	
South Hey Rd.	F38 123	
South Highville Rd.	V34 115	
South Hill Gro.	R35 113	
South Hill Rd.	L35 110	
South Hill Rd., Liver.	Q35 112	
South Hunter St.	Q32 94	
South John St.	P32 94	
South La.	JJ34 121	
South Lane Entry	JJ34 121	
South Manor Way	Y36 116	
South Marine Gdns.	O 6 5	
South Mayfields	O37 127	
South Meade	R20 28	
South Moor Dr.	N23 39	
South Mossley Hill Rd.	U36 114	
South Par., Kirk.	W24 43	
South Par., Sefton	N23 39	
South Par., Speke	Y39 132	
South Par., W.Kirby	B36 105	
South Park Ct.	N31 93	
South Park Ct.	V23 43	
South Park Rd.	U23 42	
South Park Way	P28 73	
South Parkside	U29 75	
South Parkside Dr.	V30 76	
South Rd., Crosby	M24 38	
South Rd., Gras.	T38 130	
South Rd., Higher T.	M36 110	
South Rd., Sefton	Q27 55	
South Rd., Speke	Z39 133	
South Rd., Upt.	H34 108	
South Rd., W.Kirby	B36 105	
South St., Liver.	R34 113	
South St., Liver.	R35 113	
South St., St.H.	EE29 80	
South Station Rd.	X35 116	
South Sudley Rd.	U37 130	
South View	N25 54	
South Villas	L30 71	
South Vw., Wirr.	P38 128	
Southbank Rd., Sefton	P 6 6	
Southbank Way	Y34 116	
Southbourne Rd.	J30 70	
Southcroft	W42 43	

Southcroft Rd., Wirr. J30 70
Southdale Rd., Liver. T33 96
Southdale Rd., Wirr. N36 111
Southdean Rd. X30 77
Southern Cres. Q34 112
Southern Rd. Z40 137
Southerns La. DD22 47
Southery Av. LL19 37
Southey Gro. S22 41
Southey Rd. EE29 80
Southey St. O27 54
Southfield Rd. Q26 55
Southfield Rd. S45 149
Station Rd.
Southgate Clo. W27 58
Southgate Rd. U31 96
Southmead Gdns. W37 131
Southmead Rd. W37 131
Southport Old Rd. L13 16
Southport Rd., Boot. Q26 55
Southport Rd., Formby L14 16
Southport Rd., Lith. P23 40
Southport Rd., Lyd. R17 23
Southport Rd., Thor. O21 26
Southport St. KK27 65
Southridge Rd. H38 124
Southview, Know. AA32 99
Southward Rd. NN25 66
Southwark Gro. Q24 40
Southway U33 96
Southways EE37 135
Southwell Pl. Q34 112
Southwell St. Q34 112
Southwood Rd. R36 113
Southworth La. RR29 86
Southworth Rd. PP27 67
Sovereign Rd. V27 58
Sovereign Way V27 58
Sparks La. C38 124
Sparling St. P33 94
Sparrowhall Clo. T27 57
Sparrowhall Rd. T27 57
Speakman Av. OO26 67
Speakman Rd. EE26 62
Speedwell Clo. J41 140
Speedwell Dr. J41 140
Speedwell Rd. K33 91
Speke Boul. X39 132
Speke Church Rd. X39 132
Speke Hall Av. X39 132
Speke Hall Rd. X38 132
Speke Rd., Gars. V38 131
Speke Rd., Liver. X36 116
Speke Town La. X39 132
Spekeland Rd. S33 95
Spekeland St. R33 95
Spellow La. Q29 73
Spence Av. P26 55
Spencer Av. H33 90
Spencer Gdns. HH29 82
Spencer Gdns. HH29 82
Robina Rd.
Spencer Pl. P25 55
Spencer Rd. K44 145
Spencer St. Q31 94
Spencers La., Sefton T23 42
Spencers La., W.Lan. N11 13
Spenser Av. N36 111
Spenser St. O27 54
Spike Rd. N33 93
Spindle Hillock MM23 51
Spindus Rd. X39 132
Spinney Av. DD36 119
Spinney Clo., Know. Y25 59
Spinney Clo., St.H. HH31 103
Spinney Cres. L22 38
Spinney Grn. DD28 80
Spinney Rd. Y25 59
Spinney Vw. Y25 59
Spinney Way Y31 98
Spinney, The BB29 79
Spinney, The, Beb. O39 127
Spinney, The, Elles. J45 145
Spinney, The, Hes. J42 140
Spinney, The, Liver. X29 77
Spinney, The, Sefton L14 16
Spinney, The, St.H. CC22 46
Spinney, The, Wirr. D36 106
Spion Kop NN23 51
Spital Heyes O39 127
Spital Rd. P39 128
Spofforth Rd. S33 95
Spooner Av. P25 55
Sprainger St. O31 93
Sprakeling Pl. Q25 55
Spray St. FF27 63
Spring Av. P42 143
Spring Clo. O 6 5
Spring Fld. CC20 33
Spring Gdns. T21 29
Spring Gro. P27 55
Spring Gro., W.Derby V30 76
Spring Meadow Rd. X34 116
Spring Pool KK20 37
Spring St. N35 111
Spring Vale K30 70
Spring Villas L35 110
Spring Way W29 76
Springbank Rd. R30 74
Springbourne Rd. R36 113
Springbrook Clo. DD27 62
Springby Rd. R30 74
Springcroft J44 145
Springdale Clo. V29 76
Springe Clo. J16 19
Springfield Av. PP24 52
Springfield Av., Gol. PP25 67
Springfield Av., Sefton P25 55
Springfield Av., Wirr. D36 106
Springfield Clo., St.H. EE29 80
Springfield Rd.
Springfield Clo., Wirr. J36 109
Springfield La. DD26 62
Springfield Rd., Halt. DD37 135
Springfield Rd., St.H. EE29 80
Springfield Rd., W.Lan. T17 153
Springfield St. Q31 94
Springhill Av. L42 143
Springville Rd. S25 56
Springwell Rd. P25 55
Springwood Av. V37 131
Spruce Way J15 15
Spur Rd. V27 58
Spur, The M23 38
Spurgeon Clo. Q30 73
Hamilton Rd.
Spurling Rd. MM30 84
Spurriers La. V21 30
Spurston Clo. K35 109
Spymers Cft. L14 16
Squires Av. GG36 120
Squires St. R33 95
Squirrel Grn. J15 15
Stable Clo. F35 107
The Crofters
Stackfield, The D35 106
Stadium Rd. Q39 128
Stafford Clo. AA31 99
Stafford Dr., Sefton Q27 55
Stafford Rd., Bir. O 8 9
Stafford Rd., St.H. EE28 80
Stafford St. Q32 94
Stag La. R24 41
Stainburn Av. T27 57
Stainer Clo. W30 76
Stainton Clo. GG25 63
Stainton Clo., Hale. Z37 133
Rainbow Dr.
Stairhaven Rd. U36 114
Stalbridge Av. T34 114
Staley Av. N23 39
Staley St. P26 55
Stalisfield Av. U28 75
Stalisfield Gro. U28 75
Stalisfield Pl. U28 75
Stalmine Rd. R27 56
Stamford Rd. O 7 9
Stamford St. S32 95
Stamfordham Dr. V37 131
Stamfordham Gro. V37 131
Stamfordham Pl. V37 131
Stanbury Av. O38 127
Stand Park Av. Q24 40
Stand Park Clo. Q24 40
Stand Park Rd. V34 115
Stand Park Way Q23 40
Standale Rd. T33 96
Standard Pl. N35 111
Standard Rd. V27 58
Standen Clo. FF27 63
Standish Cres. JJ22 49
Standish Dr. DD21 34
Standish St., Liver. P32 94
Standish St., St.H. GG27 63
Standring Gdns. DD29 80
Stanfield Av. Q30 73
Stanfield Av. T20 29
Stanfield Dr. N39 127
Stanford Av. L29 71
Stanford Cres. Y36 116
Stangate R20 28
Stanhope Dr., Roby Y31 98
Stanhope Dr., Wirr. P40 143
Stanhope St., Liver. P34 112
Stanhope St., St.H. FF26 63
Stanier Way S32 95
Stanlawe Rd. K14 16
Stanley Av., Sefton N 7 9
Stanley Av., St.H. CC21 33
Stanley Av., Wall. J30 70
Stanley Av., Warr. LL33 104
Stanley Av., Wirr. L37 126
Stanley Bank Rd. KK25 65
Stanley Clo. M43 148
Mill Park Dr.
Stanley Clo. HH36 121
Stanley Cres. BB30 79
Stanley Ct. N35 111
Cobden Av.
Stanley Gdns. Q26 55
Stanley La. Q43 148
Stanley Park Av. N. R28 74
Stanley Park Av. S. R29 74
Stanley Pk. O25 54
Stanley Rd. P26 55
Stanley Rd., Beb. O37 127
Stanley Rd., Formby K14 16
Stanley Rd., Know. Z31 99
Stanley Rd., Lith. N25 54
Stanley Rd., Liver. P29 73
Stanley Rd., Sefton S22 41
Stanley Rd., W.Kirby A34 105
Stanley Rd., Wirr. K32 91
Stanley St., Gars. V39 131
Stanley St., Liver. P32 94
Stanley St., Liver. T31 96
Stanley St., S.Port O 5 5
Stanley St., St.H. NN27 66
Market St.
Stanley St., Wirr. N32 93
Stanley Ter., Liver. U35 114
Stanley Ter., Wall. L29 71
Stanley Yd. R27 56
Stanlowe Vw. T38 130
Back La.
Stanmore Pk. E35 107
Stanmore Rd. U34 114
Stanny Field Dr. O22 39
Stanton Av. O24 39
Stanton Clo. LL26 65
Stanton Clo., Neth. P22 40
Great Hey
Stanton Cres. V24 43
Stanton Ct. K45 145
Stanton Rd. N39 127
Stapland Rd. V32 97
Stapleford Rd. Y34 116
Stapleton Av., Know. EE31 101
Stapleton Av., Liver. Y39 132
Stapleton Av., Wirr. F35 107
Stapleton Clo. EE30 80
Stapleton Rd.
Stapleton Rd., Sefton J16 19
Stapleton Rd., St.H. DD30 80
Stapleton Way DD38 135
Starkie St. Q31 94
Starr Inn Cotts. DD23 47
Church Rd.
Start Av. HH23 49
Startham Av. HH23 49
Starworth Dr. P37 128
Statham Rd. J33 91
Station App. D33 88
Station Av. S45 149
Station Gro. S45 149
Station Rd., S45 149
Little Sutton
Station Rd., Ain. M10 12
Station Rd., Bids. K32 91
Station Rd., C.Wood HH35 121
Station Rd., Hes. G42 139
Station Rd., Liver. X34 116
Station Rd., Lyd. R18 23
Station Rd., Nest. J45 145
Station Rd., Nest. K45 145
Station Rd., Orm. LL35 152
Station Rd., Pres. BB30 79
Station Rd., R.Hill EE31 101
Victoria St.
Station Rd., Roby Y32 98
Station Rd., Sefton T21 29
Station Rd., St.H. JJ29 82
Station Rd., St.H. LL26 65
Station Rd., W.Kirby B34 105
Station Rd., Wadd. U23 42

210

Station Rd., Wigan	LL23 50	Stopgate La., Walt.	S27 56	Summer Seat	O27 54
Station Rd., Wirr.	E38 123	Storeton Clo.	L35 110	Summer Seat	P31 94
Station Rd., Wirr.	K38 125	Storeton La., Wirr.	J39 125	Summerfield	P40 143
Station St.	EE31 101	Storeton Rd.	L35 110	Summerhill Dr.	T21 29
Station Rd.		Stormont Rd.	U38 130	Summertree Av.	F35 107
Statton Rd.	U32 96	Storrington Av.	U27 57	Summerwood	F37 123
Staveley Rd., Ains.	M11 12	Storrsdale Rd.	U35 114	Summit Way	W35 115
Staveley Rd., Gars.	U37 130	Stour Av.	DD31 101	Summit, The	L31 92
Stavert Clo.	U27 57	*Weaver Av.*		Sumner Rd.	K33 91
Stavordale Rd., More.	G32 90	Stour Av.	EE31 101	Sumner St., Liver.	P30 73
Steble St.	Q34 112	*Weaver Av.*		Sumner St., St.H.	KK26 65
Steel Av.	L30 71	Stourcliffe Rd.	L31 92	Sunbeam Rd.	U31 96
Steel St.	P30 73	Stourport Clo.	F35 107	Sunbeam St.	OO27 67
Steers Cft.	X29 77	*Droitwich Av.*		Sunbourne Rd.	R36 113
Steers St.	Q31 94	Stourton Rd., Ains.	M11 12	Sunbury Dr.	L11 12
Stephen Way	DD30 80	Stourton Rd., Liver.	W25 58	Sunbury Rd., Liver.	R29 74
Amanda Rd.		Stourton St.	M32 92	Sunbury Rd., Wirr.	M31 92
Stephenson Rd.	U32 96	Stourvale Rd.	Z37 133	Sunbury St.	EE29 80
Rathbone Rd.		Stowe Av.	T24 42	Suncroft St.	J41 140
Stephensons Way	L16 20	Stowell St.	Q33 94	Sundale Av.	CC30 79
Stepney Grn.	R28 74	Stradbank Rd.	U34 114	Sunfield Rd.	G32 90
Sterrix Av.	P24 40	Straight Up La.	S 5 7	Sunlight St.	S30 74
Sterrix Grn.	P24 40	Strand Av.	NN23 51	Sunningdale Av.	EE36 119
Sterrix La.	P24 40	Strand Rd., Boot.	P27 55	Sunningdale Clo.	MM29 84
Stevenage Clo.	FF29 81	Strand Rd., Hoy.	B33 87	Sunningdale Dr., Crosby	M22 38
Stevens Rd.	J41 140	Strand Rd., Lith.	O27 54	Sunningdale Dr., Wirr.	H38 124
Stevens St.	EE29 80	Strand St.	P32 94	Sunningdale Dr., Wirr.	O42 142
Stevenson Cres.	EE27 62	Strand, The, Ash.	NN23 51	Sunningdale Rd., Liver.	T33 96
Stevenson Dr.	N39 127	Strand, The, Liver.	P32 94	Sunningdale Rd., Wirr.	K29 70
Stevenson Rd., Liver.	U32 96	Strange Rd.	LL23 50	Sunny Bank	M38 126
Stevenson Rd., Warr.	OO28 85	Stratford Clo.	L10 12	Sunny Bank Rd.	V33 97
Stevenson St.	T33 96	Stratford Rd.	T37 130	Sunny Rd.	R 4 7
Stewart Av.	Q27 55	Stratford Way	J35 109	Sunnybank, Upton	G34 108
Stewart Clo.	G39 124	Strathallan Clo.	G40 139	Sunnyfields	LL20 37
Stile Hey	O22 39	Strathcona Rd., Liver.	T33 96	Sunnygate Rd.	U37 130
Stirling Av.	N23 39	Strathcona Rd., Wall.	L30 71	Sunnymead Dr.	S19 28
Stirling Cres., St.H.	GG30 81	Strathearn Rd.	G41 139	Sunnyside Rd., Asht.	MM22 51
Stirling Dr.	LL23 50	Strathmore Av.	NN22 51	Sunnyside Rd.,	M23 38
Stirling St.	L32 92	Strathmore Dr.	N23 39	Crosby
Stirling Way	P30 73	Strathmore Gro.	HH30 82	Sunnyside, Liver.	R34 113
Stitt St.	Q31 94	Strathmore Rd.	S31 95	Sunnyside, Wirr.	F32 89
Stockbridge La.	Y30 77	Stratton Dr.	V24 43	Sunsdale Rd.	U34 114
Stockbridge St.	S30 74	Stratton Rd.	V24 43	Surrey Av.	G34 108
Stockmoor Rd.	T27 57	Stratton Wk.	V24 43	Surrey Clo.	S 2 3
Stockpit Rd.	Y24 44	Strauss Clo.	R34 113	Surrey Dr., Wirr.	C36 106
Stocks Av.	JJ27 64	Strawberry Rd.	T28 75	Surrey St., St.H.	HH27 64
Stocks La.	LL34 152	Streatham Av.	T34 114	Surrey St., Wirr.	L32 92
Stockswell Rd.	CC35 118	Street Hey La.	O44 147	Susan Clo.	HH36 121
Stockton Gro.	EE30 80	Stretton Av.	JJ27 64	*William St.*	
Stockton Wood Rd.	Y39 136	Stretton Av., St.H.	JJ22 49	Susan Gro.	F33 89
Stockville Rd.	W35 115	*Standish Av.*		Susan Wk., Huy.	CC30 79
Stoddart Rd.	R28 74	Stretton Av., Wirr.	L31 92	*Gilbert Rd.*	
Stoke Clo.	Q43 148	Stretton Clo.	Q43 148	Sussex Clo.	G39 124
Stokesay	J34 109	Stretton Clo., Birk.	K35 109	Sussex Clo., Boot.	P27 55
Stone Cross La.	RR26 68	Stretton Dr.	Q 5 6	Sussex Gro.	HH28 82
Stone Hey, Know.	BB32 100	Strickland St.	GG27 63	Sussex Rd.	S21 28
Banner Hey		Stringhey Rd.	M30 71	Sussex Rd., Sefton	P 5 6
Stone Sq., Sefton	Q26 55	Stroma Rd.	U36 114	Sussex Rd., Wirr.	C35 106
Stone St., Know.	BB30 79	Stroud Clo.	F35 107	Sussex Rd., Boot.	P27 55
High St.		Stuart Av., Liver.	Y37 132	*Gloucester Rd.*	
Stone St., Liver.	P31 94	Stuart Av., Wirr.	G32 90	Sussex St., Cros.	M24 38
Stone St., Wirr.	O31 93	Stuart Clo.	G33 90	Sussex St., Halton	HH36 121
Stonebarn Dr.	S19 28	Stuart Cres.	HH22 49	Sutcliffe St.	R31 95
Stonebridge La.	U26 57	Stuart Dr.	W31 97	Sutherland Dr.	P43 148
Stoneby Dr.	K29 70	Stuart Rd., Crosby	N24 39	Sutherland Rd.	CC30 79
Stonecroft Ter.	NN23 51	Stuart Rd., Liver.	Q28 73	Sutton Clo.	Q43 148
Stonedale Cres.	U27 57	Stuart Rd., Sefton	Q27 55	Sutton Heath Rd.	FF30 81
Stonefield Rd.	W31 97	Stuart Rd., Sefton	U23 42	Sutton Lodge Rd.	GG28 81
Stonehaven	LL20 37	Stuart Rd., St.H.	EE26 62	Sutton Moss Rd.	JJ29 82
Kirkstile Cres.		Stuart Rd., Wirr.	M35 110	Sutton Oak St.	HH28 82
Stonehey Dr.	C36 106	Studholme St.	P29 73	Sutton Park Dr.	HH29 82
Stonehey Dr., Wirr.	C37 122	Studland Rd.	T27 57	Sutton Rd., Sefton	K16 19
Stonehey Rd.	W25 58	Studley Rd.	K30 70	Sutton Rd., St.H.	HH28 82
Stonehey Wk.	W25 58	Sturdee Rd.	U32 96	Sutton Rd., Wirr.	L29 71
Stonehill Av.	O38 127	Sturgess St.	MM27 66	Sutton St.	T30 75
Stonehill St.	R30 74	Suburban Rd.	S30 74	Sutton Wood Rd.	Y39 136
Stonehouse Rd.	K30 70	Sudbury Clo.	Y36 116	Suttons La.	N16 21
Stoneleigh Clo.	M11 12	Sudbury Rd.	L24 38	Swainson Rd.	T25 57
Stoneville Rd.	U31 96	Sudell Av.	T20 29	Swale Av.	EE31 101
Stoney Hey Rd.	L29 71	Sudell La.	S18 23	Swale Clo.	P42 143
Stoney La.	DD31 101	Sudworth Rd.	L29 71	Swaledale Av.	EE31 101
Stoney Vw.	DD31 101	Suez St.	NN27 66	Swalegate	S20 28
Fishpond Rd.		Suffield Rd.	P29 73	Swallow Clo.	W22 43
Stoneycroft	U31 96	Suffolk Pl.	EE37 135	Swallowhurst Cres.	U28 75
Stoneycroft Clo.	U30 75	Suffolk Rd.	O 9 9	Swan Av.	KK28 83
Stoneycroft Cres.	U30 75	Suffolk St.	P27 55	Swan La.	T17 153
Stoneyfield	Q22 40	Suffolk St., Liver.	P33 94	Swan Rd.	LL27 65
Stoneyhurst Av.	S23 41	Sugar La.	Y27 59	Swan St.	T31 94
Stoneyhurst Clo.	GG25 63	Sulby Av.	T30 75	Swan Wk.	T21 29
Folds La.		Sulby Clo.	N 7 9	*Station Rd.*	
Stoneyhurst Rd.	X36 116	Sulgrave Clo.	V32 97	Swanhey	T21 29
Stonham Clo.	G34 108	Sullivan Av.	G35 108	*Station Rd.*	
Stopford St.	Q35 112	Summer Av.	Q27 55	Swanside Av.	W31 97
Stopgate La.	X22 44	Summer Clo.	EE32 101	Swanside Rd.	W31 97
Stopgate La., Lith.	S27 56	Summer Fld.	V22 43	Swanston Av.	R28 74

Sweden Gro.	M24	38
Denmark St.		
Sweet Rd.	S45	149
Sweetfield Gdns.	S45	149
Sweeting St.	P32	94
Swift St., St.H.	GG26	63
Swifts Clo., Sefton	P23	40
Swifts La.	P23	40
Swinbrook Grn.	T28	75
Swinburn Gro.	HH20	36
Wordsworth Av.		
Swinburne Rd.	EE26	62
Swindon Clo.	F35	107
Chippenham Av.		
Swindon St.	P29	73
Swinford Av.	JJ36	121
Swiss Rd.	S31	95
Sword Clo.	V27	58
Swynnerton Way	GG34	120
Sybil Rd.	R29	74
Sycamore Av., Crosby	N22	39
Sycamore Av., Halton	GG36	120
Sycamore Av., Know.	Z38	133
Sycamore Av., More.	F33	89
Sycamore Av., Newt.	OO27	67
Sycamore Av., St.H.	KK26	65
Sycamore Av., Wirr.	F34	107
Sycamore Clo., Lith.	S27	56
Hornbeam Rd.		
Sycamore Clo., More.	F33	89
Sycamore Clo., St.H.	DD27	62
Hawthorn Dr.		
Sycamore Dr., Wigan	KK20	37
Sycamore Dr., Wirr.	F35	107
Sycamore Gdns.	FF26	63
Sycamore Gro.	J16	19
Sycamore Rd., Know.	Z33	99
Sycamore Rd., Sefton	N24	39
Sycamore Rd., Wirr.	M35	110
Sycamore Vill.	HH34	113
Sydall St.	FF25	62
Friar St.		
Sydenham Av.	S34	113
Syders Gro.	Y27	59
Sydney St.	R26	56
Sykes St.	R31	95
Sylvia Clo.	U26	57
Sylvia St.	P28	73
Syren St.	P29	73
Syston Av.	HH26	64
Sytch Cft.	K45	145
Tabley Av.	EE36	119
Tabley Clo.	K36	109
Tabley Rd.	S33	95
Tabley St.	P33	94
Tadlow Clo.	J16	19
Tagart Av.	V34	115
Tage Rd.	Q28	73
Tailors La.	T21	29
Talaton Clo.	R 2	3
Talbot Av.	L40	141
Talbot Ct.	L35	110
Talbot Rd.	L35	110
Talbot St., Sefton	O 6	5
Talbot St., Wigan	QQ25	68
Talbotville Rd.	V32	97
Talgarth Way	X33	98
Taliesin St.	P30	73
Talisman Way	O27	54
Talland Clo.	Z36	117
Tallarn Rd.	U24	42
Talton Rd., Liver.	S33	95
Tamar Rd.	LL26	65
Tamworth St.	EE27	62
Sidney St.		
Tamworth St., Liver.	Q34	112
Tamworth St., St.H.	NN27	66
Tamworth Way	J34	109
Tan House Dr.	LL20	37
Tan House La., Warr.	NN30	84
Tan House La., Wigan	LL20	37
Tanar Clo.	O39	127
Tanat Dr.	U35	114
Tancred Rd., Liver.	R29	74
Tancred Rd., Wirr.	L30	71
Tanhouse Rd.	O22	39
Tanners La.	QQ25	68
Tannery La., Elles.	K45	145
Tannery La., Warr.	LL35	152
Tansley Clo.	D36	106
Tapley Pl.	T32	96
Taplow St.	R30	74
Tarbock Rd., Huy.	Y32	98
Tarbock Rd., Speke	Y39	132
Tarbot Hey	F33	89
Tarbrock Ct.	P22	40
Great Hey		
Target Rd.	E41	138
Tariff St.	P30	73
Tarleton Rd.	R 5	7
Tarleton St.	P32	94
Tarlton Clo.	DD30	80
Croston Av.		
Tarn Clo., Liver.	Y34	116
Tarn Clo., Wigan	NN22	51
Tarn Gro.	GG25	63
Tarn Rd.	J15	15
Tarporley Clo.	K36	109
Tarran Dr.	F32	89
Tarran Way E.	F32	89
Tarran Way N.	F32	89
Tarran Way S.	F32	89
Tarran Way W.	F32	89
Tarves Wk., Know.	W24	43
Hargate Rd.		
Tarvin Clo.	GG31	102
Tarvin Rd.	Q43	148
Tasker Ter.	EE31	101
Rainhill Rd.		
Tasman Gro.	FF29	81
Tate St.	Q29	73
Tatlock Clo.	JJ22	49
Mitchell Rd.		
Tatlock St.	P31	94
Tattersall Pl.	O28	72
Everton Vw.		
Tattersall Rd.	O25	54
Tatton Dr.	MM23	51
Tatton Rd.	Q26	55
Tatton Rd., Birk.	M34	110
Taunton Av.	HH30	82
Taunton Clo.	J34	109
Taunton Dr.	T24	42
Taunton Rd., Know.	AA32	99
Taunton Rd., Wirr.	K30	70
Taunton St.	T33	96
Taverner Clo.	L42	143
Alistair Dr.		
Tavistock Clo.	J35	109
Tavistock Dr.	L10	12
Tavistock Rd.	K30	70
Tavistock Wk.	Q35	112
Tawd St.	Q29	73
Tay St.	P30	73
Taylor Rd.	MM26	66
Taylor St., C.Wood	HH36	121
Taylor St., St.H.	JJ29	82
Taylor St., Wirr.	N33	93
Taylors Clo.	Q27	55
Taylors La.	KK36	152
Taylors La., Walt.	Q27	55
Teal Clo.	KK19	37
Teals Way	F41	138
Teasville Rd.	W35	115
Tebay Rd.	Q41	143
Teck St.	R32	95
Tedbury Clo.	W25	58
Tedbury Wk., Know.	W25	58
Cawthorne Av.		
Tedder Av.	R 5	7
Tedder Sq.	EE37	135
Teehey Clo.	M38	126
Teehey Gdns.	M38	126
Teehey La.	M38	126
Tees Clo.	P28	73
Tees St.		
Tees Pl.	Q28	73
Tees St., Liver.	P28	73
Tees St., Wirr.	K32	91
Teesdale Rd., St.H.	LL25	65
Teesdale Rd., Wirr.	N39	127
Teesdaleway	EE30	80
Teesside Park Dr.	Q 7	10
Teilo St.	R34	113
Telegraph La.	H30	69
Telegraph Rd.	G40	139
Telegraph Rd., Wirr.	D37	122
Telford Clo.	L35	110
Tempest Hey	P32	94
Temple Ct.	P32	94
Temple La.	P32	94
Temple Rd.	M36	110
Temple St.	P32	94
Templemore Av.	U35	114
Templemore Rd.	L35	110
Tenbury Dr.	NN23	51
Tenby Av.	O24	39
Tenby Dr.	G33	90
Tenby Dr.	MM23	51
Tenby St.	R30	74
Tennis St.	FF26	63
Tennyson Av.	N36	111
Tennyson Dr.	HH20	36
Tennyson Rd., Halton	GG36	120
Tennyson Rd., St.H.	AA33	99
Tennyson St., Sefton	O26	54
Tennyson St., St.H.	GG32	102
Tennyson Wk.	Q34	112
Tensing Av.	S20	28
Tent St.	P31	94
Teray Clo.	T20	29
Terence Rd.	V34	115
Terminus Rd., Know.	X30	77
Terminus Rd., Wirr.	P39	128
Tern Clo., Kirk.	W22	43
Tern Clo., Warr.	GG35	120
Tern Way	E32	89
Tern Way	DD29	80
Ternhall Rd.	T27	57
Terret Cft.	X29	77
Tetbury St.	M34	110
Tetlow St.	Q29	73
Teulon St.	Q29	73
Pugin St.		
Tewit Hall Clo.	Y39	132
Tewit Hall Rd.	Y39	132
Tewkesbury Av.	QQ25	68
Tewkesbury Clo.	Y36	116
Teynham Av.	Y27	59
Teynham Cres.	T28	75
Thackeray Gdns.	P25	55
Thackeray Rd.	EE29	80
Thackeray Sq.	Q34	112
Thackeray St.	Q34	112
Thames Rd.	HH30	82
Thatchers Mt.	LL28	83
Penkford La.		
Thatto Heath Rd.	EE29	80
Thermal Rd.	P39	128
Thermopylae Ct.	J34	109
Thermopylae Pass.	J34	109
Thickwood Moss La.	CC22	46
Thingwall Av.	V32	97
Thingwall Dr.	H38	124
Thingwall Hall Rd.	V32	97
Thingwall La.	V31	97
Thingwall Rd.	F38	123
Thingwall Rd. E.	H38	124
Thingwall Rd., Olive.	U33	96
Third Av., Faza.	S25	56
Third Av., Liver.	M23	38
Third Av., Sefton	H34	108
Thirlmere Av., Formby	L16	20
Thirlmere Av., Lith.	P25	55
Thirlmere Av., St.H.	GG25	63
Thirlmere Av., Wigan	OO23	52
Thirlmere Av., Wirr.	J34	109
Thirlmere Clo.	T20	29
Thirlmere Dr., Sefton	L11	12
Thirlmere Dr., Wirr.	L30	71
Thirlmere Grn.	R30	74
Thirlmere Rd., Liver.	R30	74
Thirlmere Rd., Sefton	L19	25
Thirlmere Way	EE37	135
Thirlmere Wk.	V23	43
Thirlstane St.	R35	113
Thirsk Rd.	Q 7	10
Thirty Acre La.	M14	17
Thistleton Av.	K33	91
Thistlewood Rd.	T32	96
Thistley Hey	W24	43
Thomas Dr., Know.	BB31	100
Thomas Dr., Roby	V32	97
Thomas La.	V31	97
Thomas St.	N34	111
Thomaston St.	Q30	73
Thompson Clo.	OO28	85
Thompson St., Asht.	OO23	52
Thompson St., Birk.	M35	110
Thompson St., Liver.	R31	95
Thompson St., St.H.	EE28	80
Thomson Rd.	O25	54
Thor Grn.	Y31	98
Thorburn Rd.	O37	127
Thorburn St.	R32	95
Thorn Rd.	EE27	62
Thornaby Gro.	EE30	80
Thornbeck Av.	K19	24
Thornbridge Av.	P25	55
Thornburn Clo.	O37	128
Chester Rd.		
Thornburn Cres.	O37	128
Thornburn Rd.		

212

Thornbury Rd.	S29 74
Thorncliffe Rd.	L31 92
Thorncroft Dr.	H39 124
Thorndale Rd.	M24 38
Thorndeck Av.	K20 25
Thorndyke Clo.	FF32 102
Fawley Rd.	
Thorne Clo.	Z38 133
Thorneycroft St.	L33 92
Thornfield Clo.	RR25 68
Thornfield Hey	O40 142
Thornfield Rd., Vic.Pk.	Q26 55
Thornfield Rd., W.Green	O22 39
Thornham Av.	HH29 82
Thornham Clo.	H33 90
Thornhead La.	V30 76
Thornhill Rd.	LL23 50
Thornhill, Liver.	U33 96
Thornhill, Orm.	U16 153
Thornholme Cres.	U28 75
Thornhurst, Know.	W25 58
Ribblers La.	
Thornleigh Av.	Q43 148
Thornley Rd.	F33 89
Thorns Dr.	F36 107
Thorns, The	R20 28
Thornside Wk.	X35 116
Thornton Av., Sefton	P25 55
Thornton Av., Wirr.	M37 126
Thornton Clo.	MM23 51
Thornton Common Rd.	L41 141
Thornton Cres.	H42 139
Thornton Gro.	M37 126
Thornton Rd., Lith.	P26 55
Thornton Rd., Roby	W32 97
Thornton Rd., Sefton	Q 5 6
Thornton Rd., Wall.	K30 70
Allerton Rd.	
Thornton Rd., Wirr.	M37 126
Thornton St., Dingle	Q35 112
Thornton St., Wirr.	L33 92
Thornycroft Rd.	S33 95
Thorpe Br.	N37 127
Thorstone Dr.	F37 123
Thorsway	C37 122
Thorsway	N36 111
Three But La.	T30 75
Three Tuns La.	K15 16
Threlfall St.	R35 113
Threlfalls La.	Q 4 6
Thresher Av.	F35 107
Throne Rd.	V27 58
Throstles Nest	R27 56
Thurlby Clo.	OO23 52
Thurlstone	K15 16
Thurne Way	X34 116
Thurnhams St.	S30 74
Thursby Clo., Ains.	L11 12
Thursby Clo., Know.	W24 43
Thursby Cres.	
Thursby Cres.	W24 43
Thursby Rd.	Q40 143
Thursby Wk.	W25 58
Thurstaston Rd.	E38 123
Thurstaston Rd., Hes.	G40 139
Thurston Rd.	R30 74
Tibbs Cross La.	HH33 103
Tiber St.	R34 113
Tickle Av.	HH27 64
Tickle St.	HH27 64
Tide Way	K29 70
Tilney St.	R26 56
Tilstock Av.	O37 127
Tilstock Cres.	K36 109
Tilston Clo.	S27 56
Tilston Rd., Kirkby	V24 43
Tilston Rd., Liver.	S27 56
Timmis Cres.	GG36 120
Timms Clo.	K14 16
Timms La.	
Timms La.	K14 16
Timon Av.	Q27 55
Timor Av.	FF29 81
Dorothy St.	
Timpson St.	S33 95
Timway Dr.	W29 76
Tinsley Av.	Q 7 10
Tinsley St.	R29 74
Tinsleys La.	Q 8 10
Tintagel Rd.	V26 58
Tintern Av.	OO23 52
Tintern Dr., Sefton	L16 20
Tintern Dr., Wirr.	G33 90
Titchfield St.	P31 94
Tithe Barn La.	U22 42

Tithe Barn Rd.	N23 39
Tithe Barn Rd.	Y27 59
Tithebarn Dr.	H44 144
Tithebarn La.	V24 43
Tithebarn Rd., Asht.	LL24 50
Tithebarn Rd., Sefton	P 6 6
Tithebarn St.	P32 94
Tiverton Av.	L31 92
Tiverton Clo., H.Green	EE35 119
Tiverton Clo., Hale.	Y38 132
Tiverton Clo., Know.	AA31 99
Tiverton St.	T33 96
Tobermory Clo.	KK26 65
Tobin St.	M31 92
Tobruk Rd.	Y31 98
Todd Rd.	GG27 63
Warrington Old Rd.	
Toft St.	S32 95
Toleman Av.	O38 127
Tollemache Rd.	K33 91
Tollemache St.	L29 71
Tollerton Rd.	T30 75
Tolver Rd.	NN22 51
Tolver St.	GG27 63
Tomlin St.	P31 94
Tonbridge Clo.	X39 132
Tonbridge Dr.	S23 41
Tontine Mkt.	GG27 63
Lagrange Arc.	
Toothill St.	NN22 51
Topgate Clo.	H40 139
Buffs La.	
Torcross Clo.	R 2 3
Torcross Way	Z36 117
Toronto Clo., Know.	Y30 77
Hillside Cres.	
Toronto St., Boot.	O28 72
Toronto St., Egre.	N31 93
Torquay Dr.	JJ21 36
Torr St.	Q30 73
Torrington	L31 92
Torrington Dr.	Y38 132
Torrington Dr., Thing.	H38 124
Torrington Gdns.	H37 124
Torrington Dr.	
Torrington Rd.	U37 130
Torrisholme Rd.	S27 56
Torus Rd.	U31 96
Torwood	K34 109
Tothale Turn	Z35 117
Totnes Av.	Z36 117
Totnes Dr.	R 2 3
Totnes Rd.	V26 58
Towcester St.	O26 54
Tower Gdns.	O32 93
Tower Mt.	M35 110
Tower Prom.	M29 71
Tower Rd. N.	G40 139
Tower Rd. S.	G40 139
Tower Rd., Higher T.	M35 110
Tower Rd., Vic.Pk.	L36 110
Tower Rd., Wall.	N33 93
Tower Way	X35 116
Towerland St.	R32 95
Towers Av.	S20 28
Towers Rd.	V34 115
Town Field Av.	NN24 51
Town La.	Q 7 10
Town La., H.Beb.	N38 127
Town Meadow La.	F32 89
Town Rd.	M35 110
Town Row	U29 75
Townfield Clo.	K35 109
Townfield La.	K35 109
Townfield La.	N37 127
Townfield La., Ox.	K35 109
Townfield Rd.	B36 105
Townfields	NN23 51
Townsend Av., Irby	F38 123
Townsend Av., Liver.	T28 75
Townsend La.	S29 74
Townsend St., Wall.	K31 91
Townsend St., Liver.	O30 72
Townsend View Av.	T27 57
Townsend Vw.	O24 39
Townsfield Rd.	QQ30 86
Townshends Yd.	HH19 36
Towson St.	Q30 73
Toxteth Gro.	R35 113
Toxteth St.	Q34 112
Tracks La.	HH19 36
Tracy Dr.	PP27 67
Trafalgar Av.	M30 71
Trafalgar Dr.	O39 127

Trafalgar Pl.	O38 128
Gardens Rd.	
Trafalgar Rd., Bir.	N 8 9
Trafalgar Rd., Egre.	M30 71
Trafalgar St.	FF27 63
Dilloway St.	
Trafalgar Way	Q31 94
Tragan Dr.	LL35 152
Tramway Rd.	S35 113
Trap Hill	J16 19
Trapwood Clo.	DD27 62
Travers Entry	KK29 83
Traverse St.	HH27 64
Trawden Way	P23 40
Treborth St.	R34 113
Trecastle Rd.	X23 44
Treen Clo.	R 2 3
Treesdale Clo.	N 7 9
Treforris Rd.	K30 70
Trendeal Rd.	V26 58
Trent Av., Liver.	W32 97
Trent Av., Mag.	T20 29
Trent Clo., Crox.	V27 58
Trent Clo., Farn.	GG35 120
Trent Clo., Rain.	DD31 101
Trent Clo., St.H.	HH30 82
Trent Rd., Asht.	PP22 52
Trent Rd., Rain.	DD31 101
Trent Rd., St.H.	HH23 49
Trent St., Lith.	O26 54
Trent St., Wall.	K32 91
Trent Way	H42 139
Trentham Av.	T34 114
Trentham Clo.	GG35 120
Trentham Rd., Egre.	M32 92
Trentham Rd., Kirk.	V24 43
Tressell St.	Q27 55
Trevelyan Dr.	HH20 36
Wordsworth Av.	
Trevelyan St., Liver.	Q28 73
Trevelyan St., Sefton	Q27 55
Treviot Clo.	V22 43
Trevor Dr.	N23 39
Trevor Rd., Ains.	M11 12
Trevor Rd., H.V.	R26 56
Trimley Clo.	G34 109
Trinity Gdns.	O 6 5
Trinity Gro.	L23 38
Trinity La.	N33 93
Trinity Pl., Sefton	P27 55
Trinity Rd., Hoy.	B33 87
Trinity Rd., Kirk.	P28 73
Trinity Rd., Wall.	L30 71
Trinity St., Birk.	M33 92
Trinity St., St.H.	GG27 63
Higher Parr St.	
Trinity Ter.	N33 93
Trispen Clo.	Z37 133
Trispen Rd.	V26 58
Tristams Cft.	P23 40
Troon Clo.	L42 143
Wentworth Dr.	
Troon Clo., St.H.	KK26 65
Troughton St.	R33 95
Troutbeck Av.	MM27 66
Troutbeck Av., Mag.	T20 29
Troutbeck Clo.	H36 108
Troutbeck Gro.	GG24 48
Troutbeck Rd.	OO22 52
Troutbeck Rd., Liver.	V34 115
Trouville Rd.	S29 74
Trowbridge St.	O32 94
Trueman St.	P32 94
Trumans La.	S45 149
Truro Av., Cros.	R 2 3
Truro Av., Neth.	Q23 40
Truro Clo.	HH25 64
Truro Clo., Birk.	J35 109
Truro Rd.	U34 114
Tudor Av., L.Beb.	O39 127
Tudor Av., Sea.	N32 93
Tudor Av., Ains.	L10 12
Tudor Rd., Crosby	M23 38
Tudor Rd., Know.	Y37 132
Tudor Rd., L.Tran.	N35 111
Tudor St.	R31 95
Tudorville Rd.	N38 127
Tudorway	H41 139
Tue La.	DD34 119
Tuffins Cor.	Y34 116
Tulip Av.	K33 91
Tulip Gro.	N32 93
Tulip Rd., Hay.	MM26 66
Tulip Rd., Liver.	U33 96
Tulketh St.	O 5 5

Street	Grid	Page
Tullimore Rd.	U36	114
Tullis St.	FF28	81
Tullock St.	R31	95
Tully Av.	MM27	66
Tumilty Av.	Q27	55
Tunnel Rd.	R33	95
Tunnel Rd., Birk.	N34	111
Kings Sq.		
Tunstall Clo.	G34	108
Tunstall St.	S33	95
Tunstalls Way	HH31	103
Turiff Dr.	P43	148
Turmar Av.	H38	124
Turnacre, Formby	L14	16
Turnacre, Know.	W31	79
Coronation Rd.		
Turnall Rd.	DD37	135
Turnbridge Rd.	S19	28
Turner Av.	Q25	55
Turner St.	M34	110
Turney Rd.	K31	91
Turnpike Rd.	U15	153
Turnstone Clo.	W27	58
Turret Rd.	L30	71
Turton St.	QQ25	68
Tuscan Clo.	GG35	120
Tuson Dr.	FF35	120
Tweed St., Bids.	K32	91
Twickenham Dr.	G31	90
Twig La.	T20	29
Twig La., Roby	Y31	98
Twiss St.	R34	113
Twist Av.	RR25	68
Twistfield Clo.	N 6	5
Two Butt La.	DD30	80
Twyford Av.	O24	39
Twyford Clo., Farn.	GG34	120
Twyford Clo., Sefton	T20	29
Twyford La.	HH33	103
Twyford Pl.	HH27	64
Twywood St.	R30	74
Tyburn Clo.	N40	142
Tyburn Rd.		
Tyburn Rd.	N40	142
Tyndal Av.	N25	54
Tyne Clo.	Q29	73
Tynemouth Clo.	R30	74
Tynville Rd.	S25	56
Tynwald Cres.	FF34	120
Tynwald Hill	T31	96
Tynwald Rd.	B36	105
North Rd.		
Tyrer Rd.	OO28	85
Tyrer St.	K32	91
Tyrers Clo.	K16	19
Tyron St.	P32	94
Ulldale Clo.	U28	75
Ulldale Way	U28	75
Ullet Rd.	S34	113
Ullswater Av., Asht.	NN23	51
Ullswater Av., St.H.	GG25	63
Ullswater Av., Wirr.	J34	109
Ullswater Clo.	V23	43
Ullswater St.	R30	74
Ulster Rd.	U31	96
Ulverston Clo.	KK26	65
Leigh Rd.		
Ulverston Clo., Hale.	Z35	117
Ulverston Clo., Sefton	T20	29
Undercliffe Rd.	U31	96
Underhill Rd.	EE28	80
Underley St.	S33	95
Underley Ter.	O37	128
Bebington Rd.		
Unicorn Rd.	V27	58
Union Ct.	P32	94
Union La.	GG32	102
Union St., Egre.	M31	92
Union St., L.Tran.	N35	111
Union St., S.Port	P 5	6
Union St., St.H.	GG27	63
Unit Rd.	M10	12
University Rd.	P28	73
Upavon Av.	E35	107
Upholland Rd.	HH19	36
Upland Dr.	OO23	52
Upland Rd., Pres.	DD29	80
Upland Rd., Upt.	G34	108
Uplands Rd.	P40	143
Upper Aughton Rd., S.Port	O 7	9
Upper Baker St.	R31	95
Upper Beau St.	Q31	94
Douro St.		
Upper Beckwith St.	L33	92
Upper Brassey St., Bids.	K33	91
Upper Bute St.	Q31	94
Bute St.		
Upper Duke St.	Q33	94
Upper Essex St.	Q34	112
Upper Flaybrick Rd.	K33	91
Upper Frederick St.	P33	94
Upper Hampton St.	Q33	94
Upper Harrington St.	Q34	112
Upper Hill St.	Q34	112
Upper Mann St.	Q34	112
Upper Milk St.	P31	94
Upper Newington	Q32	94
Upper Park St.	Q34	112
Upper Parliament St.	Q33	94
Upper Pitt St.	Q33	94
Upper Pownall St.	P33	94
Upper Raby Rd.	L44	146
Upper Rice La.	M30	71
Upper Stanhope St.	Q33	94
Upper Warwick St.	Q34	112
Uppingham Av.	T24	42
Uppingham Rd., Liver.	T30	75
Uppingham Rd., Wall.	K30	70
Upton Av.	L10	12
Upton Barn	R20	28
Upton Bridle Path	FF35	120
Upton Clo., Asht.	RR25	68
Upton Clo., Speke	Z39	137
Upton Clo., Upt.	G34	108
Upton Ct.	G34	108
Upton Grn., Speke	Z39	133
Upton La.	FF35	120
Upton Park Dr.	H34	108
Upton Rd.	G33	90
Upton Rd., Birk.	J34	109
Upwood Rd.	RR25	68
Urmson Rd.	L30	71
Urmston Av., Hay.	NN26	66
Queens Dr.		
Ursula St.	P28	73
Usher Clo.	O37	128
Easton Rd.		
Utting Av.	R29	74
Utting Av. E.	T28	75
Uxbridge St.	R32	95
Harbord St.		
Valance Rd.	S29	74
Vale Clo.	W36	115
Vale Cres.	M12	12
Vale Dr.	L29	71
Vale Rd., Crosby	M23	38
Vale Rd., Wool.	W35	115
Valencia Gro.	DD29	80
St. Helens Rd.		
Valencia Rd.	U33	96
Valentia Rd.	B33	87
Valentine Gro.	T24	42
Valentine Rd.	MM27	66
Valerian Rd.	K33	91
Valerie Clo.	U26	57
Valescourt Rd.	V30	76
Valkyrie Rd.	L30	71
Valley Clo., Gt.Crosby	O23	39
Valley Clo., Wadd.	T24	42
Valley Rd.	V24	43
Valley Rd., Anf.	R30	74
Valley Rd., Bids.	K32	91
Valley Rd., Brom.	P41	143
Valley Rd., Gate.	Y34	116
Valley Rd., Liver.	U25	57
Valley Views	X34	116
Vanbrugh Cres.	S29	74
Vanbrugh Rd.	S29	74
Vanderbilt Av.	R25	56
Vanderbyl Av.	P40	143
Vandries St.	O31	93
Vandyke St.	S33	95
Vang St.	Q30	73
Vardon St.	M33	92
Varley Rd., Liver.	U36	114
Varley Rd., St.H.	HH27	64
Varthen St., Liver.	R29	74
Vaughan Clo.	J15	15
Vicarage Rd.		
Vaughan Rd., Sefton	O 7	9
Vaughan Rd., Wirr.	L29	71
Vaughan St.	K33	91
Vaux Cres.	P26	55
Vaux Pl.	P26	55
Vauxhall Rd.	P31	94
Venables Clo.	O40	142
Venables Dr.	O40	142
Venice St.	Q30	73
Venmore St.	Q30	73
Ventnor Rd.	T33	96
Verdala Towers	V36	115
Verdi Av.	O26	54
Verdi St.	N26	54
Verdi Ter.	N26	54
Vermont Av.	M23	38
Vermont Rd.	M23	38
Verney Cres.	V37	131
Verney Cres. S.	V37	131
Vernon Av., Egre.	M32	92
Vernon Av., Hoot.	R44	149
Vernon Rd.	R 5	7
Vernon St., Liver.	P32	94
Vernon St., St.H.	HH27	64
Verona St.	Q30	73
Verulam Clo.	R33	95
Verulam Rd.	R 3	3
Verwood Clo.	F37	123
Veryan Clo.	Z36	117
Vescocks St.	P31	94
Vesuvius St.	P30	73
Vetch Hey	Z34	117
Viaduct St.	NN27	66
Vicar Rd.	S29	74
Vicarage Clo.	J15	15
Vicarage Rd.		
Vicarage Dr.	KK25	65
Vicarage Gro.	M31	92
Vicarage Pl.	BB30	79
Vicarage Rd.	KK25	65
Vicarage Rd., Formby	J15	15
Vicarage Rd., Orrell	HH19	36
Vicarage Rd., Wigan	NN24	51
Victor St.	S33	95
Victoria Av., Halton	GG35	120
Victoria Av., Liver.	T33	96
Victoria Av., Sefton	M23	38
Victoria Av., St.H.	GG25	63
Victoria Av., Wirr.	G42	139
Victoria Bridge Rd.	P 6	6
Victoria Clo.	T36	114
Victoria Ct.	U33	96
Victoria Dr., Beb.	O38	127
King Edward Dr.		
Victoria Dr., Rock.	O36	111
Victoria Dr., Sefton	Q26	55
Victoria Dr., W.Kirby	B36	105
Victoria Gdns., Birk.	L35	110
Victoria Gro., Halton	GG35	120
Victoria Gro., Wirr.	N31	93
Victoria La.	L35	110
Victoria Mt.	L35	110
Victoria Pk.	T33	96
Victoria Pl.	U31	96
Rock St.		
Victoria Pl., B.Green	V32	97
Victoria Pl., Know.	EE31	101
Victoria Pl., Roby	V32	97
Victoria Pl., Wirr.	N32	93
Victoria Rd.	M23	38
Victoria Rd., Higher T.	M36	110
Victoria Rd., Formby	J14	15
Victoria Rd., H.Beb.	M38	126
Victoria Rd., Ince	N19	26
Victoria Rd., Know.	Z32	99
Victoria Rd., Moss.H.	T35	114
Victoria Rd., Newt.	OO27	67
Victoria Rd., Sea.	N25	54
Victoria Rd., St.H.	LL23	50
Victoria Rd., W.Derby	T30	75
Victoria Rd., W.Kirby	B36	105
Victoria Rd., Wall.	L29	71
Victoria Sq.	GG27	63
Bickerstaffe St.		
Victoria St.	O 5	5
Victoria St., Liver.	P32	94
Victoria St., R.Hill	EE31	101
Victoria St., Rain.	CC21	33
Victoria St., St.H.	GG26	63
Victoria St., Wirr.	O37	128
Grove St.		
Victoria Ter.	EE31	101
Victoria Way	J14	15
Victory Av.	R 5	7
Victory Clo.	Q25	55
Vien St.	N31	93
Vienna St.	Q30	73
View Rd.	EE31	101

Village Clo. J30 70
Village Rd., H.Beb. M38 126
Village Rd., Hes. G41 139
Village Rd., Ox. L35 110
Village Rd., W.Kirby B36 105
Village St. Q31 94
Village Way, Sefton K19 24
Village Way, Wirr. K30 70
Village, The O38 127
Village, The, Upton H34 108
Villars St. Q32 94
Villiers Cres. CC27 61
Vincent Av. M34 110
Vincent Rd., Know. DD31 101
Vincent Rd., Sefton P24 40
Vincent St. GG27 63
Vine St. R33 95
Vineries, The W35 115
Vineside Rd. V30 76
Vineyard St. W38 131
Vining Rd. CC30 79
Vining St. Q34 112
Viola St. P28 73
Violet Rd., Sefton O26 54
Violet Rd., Wirr. K33 91
Violet St. NN24 51
Virga St. O32 93
Virgil St. Q31 94
Great Homer St.
Virgil St. FF27 63
Virginia Av. S19 28
Virginia Gro. S19 28
Virginia Rd. L28 71
Virginia St. P 6 6
Virgins La. N21 26
Vista Av. NN27 66
Vista Rd. NN25 66
Vittoria Ct. M33 92
Vittoria St. M33 92
Vivian Av. N32 93
Voces La. X19 31
Voelas St. R34 113
Vogan Av. O23 39
Volunteer St. FF27 63
Vronhill Clo. R34 113
Vulcan Clo., Warr. OO28 85
Vulcan Clo., Wirr. K33 91
Vulcan Ct. P 5 6
Vulcan St., Boot. O27 54
Vulcan St., Liver. O31 93
Vulcan St., S.Port P 5 6
Vulcan St., Speke V39 131
Vyner Clo., Upt. J34 109
Vyner Rd. N., Bids. J33 91
Vyner Rd. N., Liver. X34 116
Vyner Rd. S., Liver. X34 116
Vyner Rd. S., Upt. J34 109
Vyner Rd., Wall. K30 70
Vyrnwy St., Liver. Q30 73

Waddicar La. U23 42
Wadeson Rd. S28 74
Wadham Rd. P28 73
Wagon La. KK26 65
Waine St. JJ26 64
Park St.
Waine St., St.H. HH27 64
Wainfleet Clo. LL19 37
Dunscore Rd.
Wainwright Clo. S33 95
Timpson St.
Wainwright Gro. U38 130
Wakefield Dr. G31 90
Wakefield Rd. R24 41
Wakefield St., Liver. Q31 94
Wakefield St., Wigan QQ25 68
Walbert Rd. R35 113
Walby Clo. J36 109
Walcroft O45 147
Walden Rd. V31 97
Waldgrave Pl. U32 96
Waldgrave Rd. U32 96
Waldorf Clo. LL20 37
Walford Clo. N40 142
Walford Rd. OO23 52
Walk O Way Z36 117
Walk, The Y30 77
Dannette Hey
Walker Av. GG31 102
Walker Dr. P25 55
Walker Ms. M35 110
Walker Pl. M35 110
Walker Rd. O25 54
Walker St., Birk. M35 110
Walker St., Hoy. B33 87
Walker St., Liver. R31 95
Walker St., Wirr. O38 127
Walkers Cft. K30 70
Walkers Clo. K16 19
Walkers La. GG31 102
Wallace Av. AA31 99
Wallace Dr., Know. AA31 99
Wallace St., Liver. R26 56
Wallace St., Wirr. N32 93
Wallacre Rd. K31 91
Wallasey Bridge Rd. K32 91
Wallasey Rd. K31 91
Wallasey Village K30 70
Wallbrook HH20 36
Wordsworth Av.
Wallen St. O26 54
Wallgarth Clo. LL20 37
Kirkstile Cres.
Wallgate Rd. W34 115
Wallgate Way W34 115
Wallrake G41 139
Walmer Rd., Bir. O 7 9
Walmer Rd., Sea. N25 54
Walmesley Dr. DD22 47
Walmesley Rd. DD26 62
Walmesley St., St.H. OO27 67
Walmesley St., Wirr. M30 71
Walmsley St. P30 73
Walney Rd. U29 75
Walney Rd., Rain. LL20 37
Kirkstile Cres.
Walnut Av. S27 56
Walnut St. P 7 10
Walpole Av. CC31 100
Walsingham Clo. R24 41
Walsingham Rd., Liver. W33 97
Walsingham Rd., Wirr. M31 92
Walter St., Halton HH26 121
Walter St., Liver. O30 72
Waltham Rd. S30 74
Waltho Av. T20 29
Walton Breck Rd. R30 74
Walton Hall Av. R28 74
Walton La. Q29 73
Walton Pk. R27 56
Walton Rd., Liver. Q29 73
Walton Rd., Liver. R29 74
Walton Rd., St.H. EE26 62
Walton St. N34 111
Oliver St.
Walton St. P 5 6
Walton Vale R26 56
Walton Village R28 74
Wandsworth Rd. T28 75
Wango La. T24 42
Wapping P33 94
Wapshire Rd. T29 75
Warbeck Moor R25 56
Warbreck Av. R25 56
Warbreck Rd. R26 56
Warburton Hey DD31 101
Ward Av. J16 19
Ward Gro. N37 127
Ward Rd., Sefton L22 38
Ward Rd., Wirr. O37 127
Ward St., Pres. BB29 79
Ward St., St.H. GG27 63
Warden St. Q29 73
Wardgate Av. W27 58
Wardlow Wk. R33 95
Chatsworth St.
Wareing Rd. S26 56
Waresley Cres. T27 57
Wargrave Rd. OO28 85
Warham Rd. S29 74
Waring Av., Warr. KK28 83
Waring Av., Wirr. M36 110
Warison Rd. W31 97
Warmington Rd. V31 97
Warminster Gro. LL20 37
Warner Ville Rd. U32 96
Warren Ct. N 6 5
Warren Dr., Newt. PP27 67
Warren Dr., Wirr. K29 70
Warren Grn. J15 15
Warren Hey O40 142
Warren Rd., Hoy. B33 87
Warren Rd., Sefton L22 38
Warren Rd., W.Lan. R 5 7
Warren Rd., Wirr. J29 70
Warren Wk. F40 138
Warren, The H34 108
Warrenhouse Rd., Know. X23 44
Warrenhouse Rd., Sefton L24 38
Warrington New Rd., St.H. GG27 63
Warrington Old Rd., St.H. GG27 63
Warrington Rd., App. HH36 121
Warrington Rd., Gol. QQ26 68
Warrington Rd., Know. EE32 101
Warrington Rd., Warr. LL35 152
Warrington Rd., Wigan NN24 51
Warton Clo. Y36 116
Warton St. O26 54
Warton Ter. O26 54
Warwick Av., Asht. OO24 52
Warwick Av., Newt. OO28 85
Warwick Av., Sefton M23 38
Warwick Av., Warr. LL33 104
Warwick Clo., Birk. M34 110
Westbourne Rd.
Warwick Clo., Know. AA31 99
Warwick Clo., Sefton O 7 9
Warwick Dr., Caldy C37 122
Warwick Dr., Wirr. M30 71
Warwick Rd., Know. AA31 99
Warwick Rd., Sefton P27 55
Warwick Rd., Upton G34 108
Warwick St., Liver. O34 112
Warwick St., Sefton O 7 9
Warwick St., St.H. EE27 62
Balfour St.
Wasdale Av. T20 29
Wasdale Av., Sefton T20 29
Wasdale Av., St.H. GG25 63
Wasdale Rd. R26 56
Washbrook Av. J33 91
Washington Par. P27 55
Washway La. GG25 63
Wastdale Dr. F32 89
Wastle Bridge Rd. Z30 78
Watchyard La. L15 16
Water Hey La. M14 17
Water La., Know. BB35 118
Water La., Sefton S 2 3
Water St. FF27 63
Water St., Egremont M31 92
Water St., L.Beb. O38 127
Water St., L.Tran. N34 111
Water St., Liver. P32 94
Water St., Sea. N25 54
Water St., Sefton O22 39
Waterdale Cres. HH29 82
Waterdale Pl. HH29 82
Waterdale Cres.
Waterfield Clo. M38 126
Waterford Dr. L45 146
Waterford Rd. K34 109
Watergate La. X36 116
Watergate Way X36 116
Waterland La. JJ28 82
Waterloo Pl. P32 94
Waterloo Pl., Birk. N34 111
Waterloo Pl., St.H. HH29 82
Waterloo Rd., Bir. N 7 9
Waterloo Rd., Liver. O31 93
Waterloo Rd., New.B. L28 71
Waterloo Rd., Sea. N25 54
Waterloo St., Liver. U33 96
Waterloo St., St.H. FF27 63
Watermede JJ19 36
Waterpark Clo. K36 109
Waterpark Dr. X29 77
Waterpark Rd. L36 110
Waterpark, Liver. W29 76
Waterside Q22 40
Waterway Av. R23 41
Waterworks Clo. P27 55
Waterworks La., Elles. Q44 148
Waterworks St. P27 55
Watery La. DD26 62
Watery La., St.H. JJ29 82
Watery Mill La. PP30 85
Watford Rd. R29 74
Watkins Av. MM27 66
Watkinson St. P33 94
Watling Av. O24 39
Watmough St. Q31 94
Everton Brow
Watson Av. PP24 52
Watson Av. OO23 52
Watson St. M33 92
Watson St., Pres. FF28 81
Wattonbeck Clo. T20 29
Watts Clo. X23 44
Watts La. P25 55
Wauchope St. T33 96
Wavell Av., Halton EE37 135

Wavell Av., Sefton	R 5 7	
Wavell Rd.	Z31 99	
Waverley Ct.	LL19 37	
Waverley Gro.	M36 110	
Waverley Rd., Liver.	S35 113	
Waverley Rd., Sefton	M23 38	
Waverley Rd., Wirr.	C33 88	
Waverley St.	D 2 15	
Hulme St.		
Waverley St., Sefton	O27 54	
Waverley St., Wirr.	N32 93	
Waverton Av.	K36 109	
Wavertree Av.	T32 96	
Wavertree Boul.	S32 95	
Wavertree Grn.	U33 96	
Wavertree Nook Rd.	V33 97	
Wavertree Rd.	R32 95	
Wavertree Vale	T33 96	
Wayfarers Arc.	O 5 5	
Waylands Dr.	X37 132	
Wayville Clo.	U36 114	
Weardale Rd.	T34 114	
Weates Clo.	JJ35 121	
Weaver Av., Kirk.	W22 43	
Weaver Av., Rain.	DD31 101	
Weaver Gro.	KK27 65	
Weaver La.	T22 42	
Weaver St.	Q27 55	
Webb Dr.	MM30 84	
Webb St., Liver.	S33 95	
Webb St., St.H.	HH28 82	
Webber Rd.	X24 44	
Webster Av., Sefton	Q27 55	
Webster Av., Wirr.	M30 71	
Webster Dr.	W24 43	
Webster Rd.	S33 95	
Webster St.	O26 54	
Webster St.	S33 95	
Wedge Av.	KK26 65	
Wedgewood Dr.	GG35 120	
Wedgewood St.	R32 95	
Weedon Av.	NN26 66	
Weightman Gro.	R26 56	
Welbeck Av., Liver.	T34 114	
Welbeck Av., Warr.	OO28 85	
Welbeck Rd.	N 7 9	
Welbeck Rd.	NN23 51	
Welbourne Rd.	V33 97	
Weld Blundell Av.	R18 23	
Weld Dr.	J15 15	
Weld Rd., Crosby	M23 38	
Weld Rd., S.Port	N 6 5	
Weldon St.	Q28 73	
Welford Av., Warr.	RR25 68	
Welford Av., Wirr.	K36 109	
Well Cotts.	L35 110	
Well La., Birk.	M36 110	
Well La., Child.	W33 97	
Well La., Greas.	F35 107	
Well La., H.Beb.	M38 126	
Well La., Hes.	H42 139	
Well La., Sefton	P27 55	
Well Lane Gdns.	C 3 43	
Mill La.		
Well Lane Gdns.	P27 55	
Well Rd.	DD35 119	
Welland Clo.	Y38 132	
Welland Rd., Asht.	PP22 52	
Welland Rd., Wirr.	M38 126	
Wellbrae Clo.	F34 107	
Wellbrook Clo., Liver.	Y39 132	
Wellbrook Grn., Liver.	Y39 132	
Wellbrow Rd.	R28 74	
Wellcroft Rd.	Z31 99	
Weller St.	Q34 112	
Weller Way	R35 113	
Wellesborne Pl.	U28 75	
Wellesbourne Rd.	U27 57	
Wellesley Rd., Liver.	R35 113	
Wellesley Rd., Wirr.	L31 92	
Wellfield	DD23 47	
Church Rd.		
Wellfield Av.	W24 43	
Wellfield Rd.	R27 56	
Wellfield, Farn.	GG35 120	
Wellgreen Rd., Liver.	W33 97	
Wellgreen Wk.	W33 97	
Wellington Av.	S33 95	
Wellington Clo.	O38 127	
Wellington Rd.		
Wellington Clo.	S23 41	
Wellington Ct.	L35 110	
Wellington Flds., Liver.	S34 113	
Wellington Gro.	T33 96	
Wellington Rd., Birk.	L35 110	
Wellington Rd., L.Beb.	O38 127	
Wellington Rd., Lith.	O25 54	
Wellington Rd., Liver.	Q35 112	
Wellington Rd., Wav.	T33 96	
Wellington Rd., Wirr.	K29 70	
Wellington St.	O 6 5	
Wellington St., Crosby	M24 38	
Wellington St., Gars.	V38 131	
Wellington St., Oakhill	U32 96	
Wellington St., St.H.	NN27 66	
Wellington Ter.	GG26 63	
Wellington Ter., Wirr.	M34 110	
Wells Av.	HH22 49	
Wells St.	T33 96	
Wellstead Clo.	U33 96	
Wellstead Wk.	U33 96	
Welsh Rd.	Q45 148	
Welton Av.	G34 108	
Welton Clo.	Y39 136	
Welton Gro.	Y39 136	
Welton Rd.	Q40 143	
Welwyn Av.	M10 12	
Welwyn Clo.	FF30 81	
Wembley Gdns.	Q26 55	
Wembley Rd.	N23 39	
Wembley Rd., Liver.	U35 114	
Wendell St.	S33 95	
Wendover Av.	S35 113	
Wendover Clo.	J35 109	
Wendron Rd.	V26 58	
Wenger Rd.	GG34 120	
Wenlock Rd.	R29 74	
Wenning Av.	T20 29	
Wennington Rd.	Q 5 6	
Wensley Rd.	R25 56	
Wensleydale Av., Brom.	Q42 143	
Wensleydale Av., Know.	EE31 101	
Wensleydale Clo.	R19 28	
Wensleydale Dale	R25 56	
Wentworth Av.	L29 71	
Wentworth Clo., Ains.	M11 12	
Wentworth Clo., Farn.	GG34 120	
Wentworth Clo., Wirr.	J35 109	
Wentworth Dr., Brom.	P42 143	
Wentworth Dr., Liver.	Q31 94	
Wentworth Gro.	X32 98	
Wentworth Rd.	NN22 51	
Wernbrook Rd.	S29 74	
Wervin Clo., Wirr.	K36 109	
Wervin Rd.		
Wervin Rd., Kirkby	V24 43	
Wervin Rd., Wirr.	K36 109	
Wervin Way	V24 43	
Wervin Rd.		
Wesley Av., St.H.	MM25 66	
Elizabeth Rd.		
Wesley Av., Wall.	M30 71	
Wesley Gro.	M31 92	
Wesley Pl.	T33 96	
Wesley St.	M25 53	
Wesley St.	O 6 5	
Wesleydale Clo.	R20 28	
West Clo., St.H.	DD29 80	
West Clo., Wirr.	J34 109	
West Derby Rd.	R31 95	
West Derby Village	U29 75	
West Dr., Hes.	H41 139	
West Dr., Upt.	H34 108	
West End	JJ26 64	
West End Gro.	KK26 65	
West End Rd.	JJ26 64	
West Gro.	G41 139	
West House Clo.	L42 143	
Brookhurst Rd.		
West Kirby Rd.	F34 107	
West La.	K14 16	
West Meade	R20 28	
West Moor Dr.	N22 39	
West Moorland Av., Halton	GG36 120	
West Morland Rd., S.Port	P 6 6	
West Oakhill Pk.	U32 96	
West Orchard La.	S25 56	
West Palm Gro.	L34 110	
West Park Rd.	EE28 80	
West Park St.	R33 95	
West Rd., Birk.	J34 109	
West Rd., Know.	Y38 132	
West Rd., Sefton	Q27 55	
West Side Av.	KK26 65	
West St., Liver.	R34 113	
West St., Pres.	BB30 79	
West St., S.Port	O 5 5	
West St., Thatto Heath	EE28 80	
West St., Wall.	L30 71	
West View Av.	AA32 99	
West Warison Rd.	W31 97	
Westbank Av.	L29 71	
Westbank Rd., Liver.	T32 96	
Westbank Rd., Wirr.	M35 110	
Westbourne Av., Thor.	O22 39	
Westbourne Av., W.Kirby	B36 105	
Westbourne Gro.		
Westbourne Gro.	B36 105	
Westbourne Rd., Birk.	M34 110	
Westbourne Rd., S.Port	M 7 8	
Westbourne Rd., W.Kirby	B36 105	
Westbourne Rd., Wall.	K31 91	
Westbourne St.	Q31 94	
Westbourne Way	Q31 94	
Westbourne Wk.	Q31 94	
Westbrook Av.	AA30 78	
Westbrook Rd., Liver.	Y34 116	
Westbrook Rd., Wirr.	LL20 37	
Westbury Av.	N35 111	
Westbury St.	U29 75	
Westcliffe Rd., Liver.	N 6 5	
Westcliffe Rd., S.Port	S29 74	
Westcombe Rd.	LL19 37	
Westcott Dr.	R30 74	
Westcott Rd.	W22 43	
Westcroft	T33 96	
Westdale Rd., Liver.	N36 111	
Westdale Rd., Wirr.	X31 98	
Western Av., Roby	Y40 136	
Western Av., Speke	P39 128	
Western Av., Wirr.	U37 130	
Western Dr.	R35 113	
Western St.	W30 76	
Westerton Rd.	W32 97	
Westfield Av., Liver.	NN23 51	
Westfield Av., Wigan	Q26 55	
Westfield Rd., Sefton	M32 92	
Westfield Rd., Wirr.	FF27 63	
Westfield St.	U24 42	
Westfield Wk., Know.		
Benwick Rd.		
Westgate Rd., Liver.	U34 114	
Westgate Rd., Wirr.	O39 127	
Westhead Av.	W24 43	
Westhead Wk.	W24 43	
Westleigh Pl.	HH30 82	
Woolacombe Av.		
Westmains Av.	AA39 133	
Westminster Av.	Q23 40	
Westminster Clo., Liver.	Q28 73	
Westminster Clo., Halton	DD37 135	
Westminster Dr., Ains.	L10 12	
Westminster Dr., St.H.	MM25 66	
Westminster Dr., Wirr.	P41 143	
Westminster Rd.	Q29 73	
Westminster Rd., Kirk.	P28 73	
Westminster Rd., Wirr.	L31 92	
Westmoreland Av., Sefton	P23 40	
Westmoreland Pl., Liver.	P30 73	
Westmoreland Rd., Wirr.	L29 71	
Westmorland Rd., Huy.	Z32 99	
Weston Ct.	L23 38	
Weston Gro.	S22 41	
Westone La.	C36 106	
Westover Clo.	S20 28	
Westover Rd.	S20 28	
Westside	HH28 82	
Westview	AA32 99	
Westward Ho!	C38 122	
Barton Hey Dr.		
Westward Vw.	L24 38	
Westway Sq.	G32 90	
Westway, Greas.	F35 107	
Westway, Hes.	G42 139	
Westway, Liver.	U33 96	
Westway, Mag.	S20 28	
Westway, More.	G32 90	
Westway, Noct.	J35 109	
Westway, Sefton	K19 24	
Westwood	K34 109	
Westwood Clo.	Q 7 10	
Westwood Gro.	L31 92	
Westwood Pl.	X31 98	
Westwood Rd., Liver.	V37 131	
Westwood Rd., Wirr.	J34 109	
Wetherby Av.	K30 71	
Mosslands Dr.		
Wethersfield Rd.	K35 109	
Wexford Clo.	K35 109	

Wexford Rd.	K35	109
Wey Clo.	N40	142
Weybourne Clo.	H33	90
Weyman Av.	CC31	100
Weymouth Av.	JJ28	82
Weymouth Rd.	MM30	84
Weymouth St.	JJ29	82
Whaley La.	G38	124
Whalley Av., Rain.	CC22	46
Whalley Av., St.H.	FF25	63
Whalley Ct.	P23	40
Granams Cft.		
Whalley Dr.	L16	20
Whalley Gro.	HH35	121
Whalley Rd.	M34	110
Whalley St.	Q35	112
Mill St.		
Wharf Rd., Warr.	MM28	84
Wharf Rd., Wirr.	K32	91
Wharf St., Wirr.	O38	127
Wharfdale St.	W38	131
Wharfdale Av.	L36	110
Wharfedale Dr., Know.	EE31	101
Wharfedale Dr., Wirr.	Q42	143
Wharfedale Rd.	K30	70
Wharmby Rd.	MM26	66
Wharncliffe Rd.	U31	96
Wharncliffe Rd. E.	U31	96
Wheat Hills	Z34	117
Wheat St.	Q28	73
Grist St.		
Wheatcroft Rd.	V36	115
Wheatfield Clo., Sefton	R23	41
Wheatfield Clo., Wirr.	G33	90
Wheatfield Rd.	EE34	119
Wheatfield Vw.	O24	39
Wheathill Rd.	Z33	99
Wheatland Clo.	HH31	103
Wheatland La., Wirr.	M32	92
Wheatland Rd.	J41	140
Wheatlands Clo.	Y34	116
Wheatley Av., Sefton	Q26	55
Wheatley Av., St.H.	OO26	67
Wheatsheaf Av.	HH30	82
Wheeler Dr.	U23	42
Whernside	EE35	119
Whetstone La.	M34	110
Whinfell Rd.	V30	76
Whinfield Rd., Thorn.	O22	39
Whinfield Rd., Walt.	Q26	55
Whinhowe Rd.	U28	75
Whinmoor Clo.	J34	109
Whinmoor Rd.	V30	76
Whinney Gro. E.	S22	41
Whinney Gro. W.	S22	41
Whiston La.	AA31	99
Whitburn Clo.	LL23	50
Abinger Rd.		
Whitburn Rd.	X23	44
Whitby Av.	K30	71
Mosslands Dr.		
Whitby Av.	S 2	3
Whitby St.	S30	74
Whitcroft Rd.	S31	95
White Acre	HH31	103
White Bailey St.	P33	94
White Beam Dr.	V27	58
Grayling Dr.		
White Haven Clo.	L11	12
White Lodge Av.	Y31	98
White Lodge Clo.	P42	143
White Meadow Dr.	O22	39
White Well Rd.	G34	108
Whitebeam Clo.	W22	43
Whitebeam Wk.	E36	107
Whitechapel	P32	94
Whitefield Av., Liver.	O29	73
Whitefield Av., Warr.	PP28	85
Whitefield Clo.	QQ25	68
Whitefield Dr.	U24	42
Whitefield Gro.	KK26	65
Harrison Dr.		
Whitefield Gro., St.H.	KK26	65
Harrison Dr.		
Whitefield La.	AA34	117
Whitefield Rd., Liver.	R30	74
Whitefield Rd., St.H.	EE26	62
Whitefield Sq., Know.	V24	43
Whitefield Dr.		
Whitefield Way	R31	95
Whitegate Clo.	Y27	59
Whitegates Clo.	N45	147
Whitegates Cres.	N44	147
Whitehall Clo.	Q28	73
Whitehart Clo.	R28	74
Whitehead Clo.	X24	44
Whiteheath Way	G31	90
Whitehedge Rd., Liver.	U37	130
Whitehouse Av.	L15	16
Whitehouse Clo.	KK26	65
Whitehouse La., Sefton	L15	16
Whitehouse La., Wirr.	J40	140
Whitehouse Rd.	U32	96
Whitelands Meadow	G35	108
Whiteledge	NN22	51
Whiteledge Grn.	NN22	51
Whitelodge Dr.	PP23	52
Whiterock Ct.	R31	95
Whiterock St.	R31	95
Whiteside Av.	JJ26	64
Whiteside Rd.	KK26	65
Whitestone Clo.	Y28	77
Whitfield La., Wirr.	H40	139
Whitfield Rd.	R26	56
Whitfield St.	M35	110
Whitfields Cross	JJ35	121
Whitford Rd.	M35	110
Whithorn St.	S33	95
Whitland Rd.	S31	95
Whitledge Rd.	NN22	51
Whitley Dr.	M30	71
Whitley St.	O31	93
Whitman St.	T33	96
Whitmoor Clo.	FF32	102
Whitney Rd.	Y36	116
Whittacker Clo.	T32	96
Whittaker St.	HH28	82
Whittier St.	S33	95
Whittle Av.	KK26	65
Whittle St., Liver.	O30	73
Whittle St., St.H.	EE28	80
Wickets Clo.	V26	58
Wickham Clo.	M32	92
Wicks Cres.	J15	15
Wicks Green La.	J15	15
Wicks Grn.	J15	15
Wicks La.	J15	15
Widdale Av.	EE31	101
Widemouth St.	P30	73
Widmore Rd.	Y35	116
Widnes Rd.	KK36	152
Wiend, The, L.Beb.	O38	127
Wiend, The, Wirr.	M36	110
Wigan Rd.	JJ21	36
Wigan Rd.	NN22	51
Wightman St.	R31	95
Wignalls Meadow	K19	24
Wigston Clo.	L11	12
Wilberforce Rd.	R28	74
Wilbraham Pl.	P30	73
Wilbraham St., Birk.	N34	111
Grange Rd. E.		
Wilbraham St., Liver.	P30	73
Wilbraham St., St.H.	JJ31	103
Wilbraham St., St.H.	JJ31	103
Wilbur St.	JJ29	82
Wilburn St.	Q28	73
Wilcox Rd.	NN25	66
Wild Pl.	Q25	55
Wilfer Clo.	S33	95
Rokesmith Av.		
Wilfred St.	FF27	63
Volunteer St.		
Wilkes Av.	H31	90
Wilkin St.	O29	73
Archer St.		
Wilkinson St.	M34	110
Will St.	HH27	64
Willan St.	L35	110
Willard Av.	HH19	36
Willard St.	P26	55
Willaston Rd., Elles.	M44	146
Willaston Rd., More.	F32	89
Willaston Rd., Raby	M42	141
Willeston Av.	N23	39
William Brown St.	P32	94
William Harvey Clo.	Q23	40
William Henry St.	O28	72
William Morris Av.	Q26	55
William Rd.	JJ26	64
William Roberts Av.	V24	43
William St., St.H.	HH36	121
William St., Wirr.	N32	93
William Wall Rd.	O24	39
Williams Av., Newt.	OO26	67
Williams Av., Sefton	O26	55
Williams St., Know.	BB30	79
Williams St., St.H.	HH27	64
Williamson Sq.	P32	94
Williamson St.	P32	94
Willingdon Rd.	W32	97
Willington Av.	Q43	148
Willink Rd.	HH25	64
Willis Clo.	BB32	100
Willis La.	BB32	100
Willmer Rd.	M34	110
Willoughby Dr.	DD29	80
Willoughby Rd., Liver.	W32	97
Willoughby Rd., Sefton	N24	39
Willoughby Rd., Wirr.	K31	91
Willow Av., Halton	GG36	120
Willow Av., Huy.	Z33	99
Willow Av., Kirkby	V23	43
Willow Av., St.H.	PP27	67
Willow Av., Whist.	BB31	100
Willow Bank Est.	PP27	67
Willow Bnk.	PP27	67
Willow Grn.	W35	115
Willow Gro., Oak.Pk.	U32	96
Willow Gro., Pres.	CC30	79
Willow Gro., Sefton	K15	15
Willow Gro., Sefton	Q 5	6
Willow Gro., Wigan	PP22	52
Willow Gro., Wirr.	F33	89
Willow Hey	T21	29
Willow La.	M43	146
Willow Pk.	F35	107
Mere Park Rd.		
Willow Rd., Hay.	MM25	66
Willow Rd., Newt.	PP27	67
Willow Rd., St.H.	EE27	62
Willow St.	M34	111
Greenfield St.		
Willow Tree Av.	HH31	103
Willow Way	N22	39
Willow Way	V26	58
Willow, The, Liver.	R30	74
Willowbank Rd.	M35	110
Willowbrow Rd.	M43	146
Willowcroft Rd.	M32	92
Willowdale Rd., Liver.	R27	56
Willowdale Rd., Moss H.	T34	114
Willowes Rd.	O38	127
Willows, The, Wall.	K29	70
Wills Av.	S20	28
Wills St.	M31	92
Willy St.	O36	111
Wilmcote Gro.	L11	12
Wilmer Rd.	R29	74
Wilmere La.	GG34	120
Wilmott Wk.	Q31	94
Wilne Rd.	L30	71
Wilson Clo., St.H.	FF27	63
Wilson Gro.	V38	131
Wilson Rd., Huy.	Z32	99
Wilson Rd., Know.	BB31	100
Wilson Rd., Wall.	M31	92
Wilson St.	R35	113
Wilsons La.	O25	54
Wilstan Rd.	M38	126
Wilton Gro.	U32	96
Alexandra Rd.		
Wilton Rd., Roby	Y32	98
Wilton Rd., Wirr.	O36	111
Wilton St.	Q32	94
Wilton St., Wall.	L31	92
Wiltons Dr.	Y27	59
Wiltshire Dr.	P23	40
Wimbledon St.	T33	96
Wimbledon St., Wall.	L30	71
Wimborne Av.	H38	124
Wimborne Clo.	X30	77
Wimborne Pl.	X30	77
Wimborne Rd.	X30	77
Wimborne Way	F37	123
Wimbrick Clo.	G33	90
Wimbrick Hey	G33	90
Wimpole St.	R32	95
Winchester Av., Asht.	NN23	51
Winchester Av., Crosby	M23	38
Winchester Av., Sefton	S23	41
Winchester Dr.	K31	91
Winchester Pl.	EE37	135
Winchester Rd., Asht.	MM24	51
Winchester Rd., Liver.	S30	74
Winchester Rd., Wigan	HH20	36
Winchfield Rd.	T34	114
Windbourne Rd.	S36	113
Windermere Av.	GG25	63
Windermere Av., Farn.	GG35	120
Windermere Clo.	K45	145
Windermere Cres.	M11	12
Windermere Dr., Kirkby	V23	43
Windermere Dr., Liver.	V28	76
Windermere Dr., Sefton	T20	29

Windermere Dr., St.H. CC20 33
Windermere Pl. GG25 63
Windermere Av.
Windermere Rd., Sefton L19 25
Windermere Rd., St.H. KK26 65
Windermere Rd., Wirr. J34 109
Windermere St., Halton GG35 120
Windermere St., Liver. R30 74
Windermere Ter. S34 113
Windfield Gdns. S45 149
Windfield Rd. V39 131
Windle Av. O23 39
Windle City FF26 63
Windle Gro. EE26 62
Windle Hall Dr. FF25 63
Windle St. FF26 63
Windle Vale FF26 63
Windleshaw Rd.
Windlebrook Cres. DD26 62
Windlehurst Av. FF26 63
Windleshaw Rd. EE26 62
Windley Ash S20 28
Windmill Av. N22 39
Window La. V39 131
Winds Clo. F35 107
Windsor Av. O25 54
Windsor Clo. O37 127
Windsor Dr. NN25 66
Windsor Gdns. R33 95
Windsor Park Rd. S23 41
Windsor Rd. OO24 52
Windsor Rd., Asht. NN24 51
Windsor Rd., Bill. JJ22 49
Windsor Rd., Crosby M22 38
Windsor Rd., Know. CC31 100
Windsor Rd., Liver. R26 56
Windsor Rd., Liver. S30 74
Windsor Rd., Mag. S21 28
Windsor Rd., Roby X31 98
Windsor Rd., S.Port P 6 6
Windsor Rd., Sefton K16 19
Windsor Rd., St.H. EE27 61
Windsor Rd., Walton Pk. Q26 55
Windsor Rd., Widnes GG35 120
Windsor Rd., Wigan RR25 68
Windsor St., Liver. Q34 112
Windsor St., Sefton M34 110
Windsor St., Wall. L29 71
Windsor Vw. R33 95
Windus St. FF27 63
Eccleston St.
Windways S45 149
Windy Arbor Clo. BB32 100
Windy Arbor Rd. BB32 100
Windy Arbour Brow BB33 100
Windy Bnk. O38 127
Windy Harbour Rd. N 9 9
Wineva Gdns. N23 39
Winfrith Clo. J40 140
Winfrith Dr.
Winfrith Dr., Wirr. N40 142
Winfrith Rd. Y35 116
Wingate Av. EE30 80
Consett Rd.
Wingate Clo. K35 109
Wingate Rd., Brom. P42 143
Wingate Rd., Kirkby W23 43
Wingate Rd., Liver. T36 114
Wingate Towers, Know. Z31 99
Blue Bell La.
Wingate Wk. W23 43
Wingrave Way U28 75
Winhill X35 116
Winifred La. U15 153
Winifred Rd. U25 57
Winifred St., Liver. R32 95
Winifred St., Wirr. M31 92
Winnington Rd. B34 105
Winser St. O38 127
Winsford Clo. MM25 66
Kenyons La.
Winsford Dr. MM29 84
Winsford Rd. T30 75
Winsham Clo. W25 58
Winsham Rd. W25 58
Winskill Rd. U29 75
Winslade Rd. R28 74
Winslow St. Q28 73
Winsor Av. OO28 85
Winstanley Rd. JJ19 36
Winstanley Rd., Sefton N24 39
Winstanley Rd., Wirr. O37 127
Winster Rd. AA35 117
Winston Av. KK28 83
Winston Cres. Q 7 10
Ruddington Rd.
Winston Dr. J34 109
Winston Gro. G33 90
Winstone Rd. X31 98
Winter Garden Ter. O 5 5
Winter Gro. KK27 65
Winter St. R31 95
Winter St., Liver. R31 95
Walker St.
Winterburn Cres. V29 76
Winterburn Heights V29 76
Winterney Av. L32 92
Winthrop Pk. K34 109
Winton Ct. K29 70
Winwick La. RR28 86
Winwick Link Rd. QQ30 86
Winwick Rd. PP28 85
Winwick Vw. LL29 83
Winwood Hall X36 116
Wirral Clo. N39 127
Wirral Gdns. N39 127
Wirral Mt., W.Kirby C35 106
Wirral Mt., Wall. K30 70
Wirral Village K30 70
Wirral Vw. T38 130
Back La.
Wirral Way, Upt. J34 109
Wirral Way, W.Kirby B36 105
Witham Av. N23 39
Withens La. L30 71
Withens Rd., Hay. MM25 66
Withens Rd., Mag. S19 28
Withens, The X29 77
Withensfield L30 71
Withers St. T32 96
Withert Av. M37 126
Withington Rd., Egre. M31 92
Withington Rd., Liver. Z39 133
Withins Fld. K19 24
Withins La. N17 21
Withnell Clo. U32 96
Withnell Rd. U32 96
Witley Av. G32 90
Witley Clo. G32 90
Witney Clo. F35 107
Chippenham Av.
Wittering La. F41 138
Witterings, The K44 145
Witton Rd. S30 74
Witton Way CC21 33
Woburn Av. OO28 85
Woburn Clo. T31 96
Woburn Clo. MM25 66
Woburn Hill T31 96
Woburn Rd. L30 71
Wolfe Rd. JJ28 82
Wolfenden Av. Q26 55
Wolfrick Dr. O40 142
Wolfson Dr. MM23 51
Wolfson Sq. MM23 51
Wollaton Dr. Q 8 10
Colchester Rd.
Wolmer St. NN23 51
Wolseley Rd., St.H. FF26 63
Wolsten Holme Sq. P32 94
Wolvert St. R30 74
Wood Av. Q26 55
Wood Clo., Kirkby V24 43
Wood Clo., Wirr. R44 149
Wood Grn. BB30 79
Wood Gro. T32 96
Wood La., Altcar P16 22
Wood La., Elles. J43 145
Wood La., Huy. AA32 99
Wood La., Know. Z34 117
Wood La., Pres. AA30 78
Wood La., Wirr. F34 107
Wood Lea W27 58
Wood Rd., Hale. Z37 133
Wood St. BB30 79
Wood St., Claugh. M33 92
Wood St., Gars. V38 131
Wood St., Gol. QQ25 68
Wood St., Halton HH36 121
Wood St., L.Beb. O39 127
Wood St., Lith. O25 54
Wood St., Liver. P32 94
Wood St., Newt. MM27 66
Wood St., St.H. HH27 64
Wood View Rd., Know. W35 115
Wood Vw. Y27 59
Woodbank Clo. W33 97
Woodbine St. P29 73
Woodbourne Rd. V31 97
Woodbrook Dr. LL19 37
Woodburn Boul. N37 127
Woodchurch La. L36 110
Woodchurch La., Thing. J37 125
Woodchurch Rd., Stoney. U31 96
Woodchurch Rd., Wood. K36 109
Woodcock St. JJ29 82
Woodcot La. G40 139
Woodcote Bnk. N37 127
Woodcroft Dr. G40 139
Woodcroft La. N37 127
Woodcroft Rd. S33 95
Woodedge NN23 51
Woodend G39 124
Woodend Av., Know. Y38 132
Woodend Av., Lith. N22 39
Woodend Av., Mag. S21 28
Woodend La, Know. Y39 132
Woodfarm Hey X29 77
Woodfield Av. N37 127
Woodfield Cres. NN24 51
Woodfield Rd., Beb. O39 127
Woodfield Rd., Pen. G39 124
Woodfield Rd., Roby Y32 98
Woodfield Rd., Sefton Q26 55
Woodford Rd., Beb. O37 127
Woodford Rd., Liver. W31 97
Woodford Rd., St.H. EE26 62
Woodgreen Rd. U31 96
Woodgrove St. V38 131
Woodhall Av. M31 92
Woodhall Rd. U31 96
Woodhead Rd. P38 128
Woodhead St. O37 127
Woodhey Rd., L.Beb. N37 127
Woodhey Rd., Liver. U37 130
Woodhouse Clo. Q29 73
Woodin Rd. O37 127
Woodkind Hey O40 142
Woodland Av., App. FF36 120
Woodland Av., Newt. PP27 67
Woodland Av., Wirr. C32 88
Woodland Dr. NN22 51
Woodland Dr., Wood. H35 108
Woodland Gro. N37 127
Woodland Rd., Hale. Z37 133
Woodland Rd., L.Beb. N37 127
Woodland Rd., Sea. N25 54
Woodland Rd., W.Kirby D36 106
Woodland Rd., Wadd. U23 42
Woodland Rd., Walt. S29 74
Woodland Vw., Crosby O21 26
Woodland Vw., Elles. R45 149
Woodland Wk. L41 143
Beechwood Rd.
Woodlands Clo., Formby J16 19
Woodlands Clo., Nest. J45 145
Woodlands Dr., New B. M29 71
Woodlands Dr., Thing. J39 125
Woodlands Pk. U30 75
Woodlands Rd., Aig. T36 114
Woodlands Rd., Formby J15 15
Woodlands Rd., Nest. J45 145
Woodlands Rd., Roby X32 98
Woodlands Rd., St.H. HH25 64
Woodlands Rd., Wirr. F38 123
Woodlands, The CC29 79
Central Av.
Woodlands, The, Claugh. M34 110
Claugh.
Woodlands, The, Upt. G34 108
Woodlea Clo. P42 143
Woodlea Clo., Cros. S 2 3
Baytree Clo.
Woodlee Rd. Y35 116
Woodley Rd. S22 41
Woodpecker Clo. F34 107
Woodrock Rd. X36 116
Woodruff St. Q35 112
Woodside Av., Ains. L11 12
Woodside Av., St.H. FF25 63
Woodside Av., Wirr. F33 89
Woodside Clo. U27 75
Woodside Rd., Hay. MM25 66
Woodside Rd., Wirr. G38 124
Woodside St. R32 95
Woodside Wk. X35 116
Woodsorrel Rd., Liver. U33 96
Woodsorrel Rd., Wirr. K33 91
Woodstock Av. OO28 85
Woodstock Dr. N 9 9
Woodstock Rd. L31 92
Woodstock St. P30 73
Woodvale Ct. H36 108
Woodvale Rd., Liver. X36 116

Woodvale Rd., Sefton M12 12
Woodview Av. M32 92
Woodview Cres. DD37 135
Woodview Rd., Hale Bk. DD37 135
Woodville Av. M23 38
Woodville Pl. EE36 119
Woodville Rd. M35 110
Woodville St. GG27 63
Woodville Ter. R30 74
Woodward Rd., Know. Y23 44
Woodward Rd., Wirr. O37 127
Woodway F35 107
Woodyear Rd. Q41 143
Woolacombe Av. HH30 82
Woolacombe Rd. W34 115
Wooler Clo. E33 89
Woolfall Clo. X31 98
Woolfall Cres. X31 98
Woolfall Heath Av. Y30 77
Woolfall Heights Y30 77
Woolfall Ter. O26 54
  Crescent Rd.
Woolfalls Br. Y31 98
Woolhope Rd. R28 74
Woollam Dr. S45 149
Woolton Clo. MM22 51
Woolton Hill Rd. W35 115
Woolton Mt. X35 116
Woolton Park Clo. X35 116
Woolton Pk. X35 116
Woolton Rd., Child. V34 115
Woolton Rd., Gars. V38 131
Woolton Rd., Moss.H. U34 114
Woolton Rd., Wav. U33 96
Woolton St. X36 116
Worcester Av., Cros. M24 38
Worcester Av., Gol. QQ25 68
Worcester Av., Liver. S29 74
Worcester Dr. N. S29 74
Worcester Rd., Sefton P27 55
Worcester Rd., Wirr. J33 91
Wordsworth Av., St.H. GG31 102
Wordsworth Av., Wigan HH20 36
Wordsworth Av., Wirr. N36 111
Wordsworth St., Liver. S33 95
Wordsworth St., Sefton O26 54
Wordsworth Way Z32 99
Wordsworth Wk. C37 122
Worrow Clo. U27 57
Worrow Rd. U27 57
Worsley Brow JJ29 82
Worsley St., St.H. JJ26 64
  Park St.
Worsley St., Wigan QQ25 68
Worthing Clo. N 7 9
Worthing St. M24 38
Wortley Rd. T25 57
Wray Av. HH31 103
Wrayburn Clo. S33 95
Wrekin Clo. X37 132
Wrekin Dr. T24 42
Wrenbury Clo. K36 109
Wrenby St. S32 95
Wrenfield Gro. S36 113
Wright St., Liver. P30 73

Wright St., Sefton O 5 5
Wright St., Wirr. M31 92
Wrightman Av. 0026 67
  Dixon Av.
Wrights La. JJ36 121
Wrights La. KK36 152
Wrights St. U33 96
Wrigley Rd. MM26 66
Wrigleys Clo. K14 16
Wrigleys La. K14 16
Wroxham Clo. H35 109
  Wroxham Dr.
Wroxham Dr. H35 108
Wroxham Way H34 109
  Salacre La.
Wryneck Clo. DD29 80
  Grebe Av.
Wrynose Q41 143
Wulstan St. P29 73
Wycherley Rd. M35 110
Wycherley St., Know. BB30 79
  Grosvenor Rd.
Wycliffe Rd., Liver. S29 74
Wycliffe Rd., St.H. MM25 66
Wycliffe St. N36 111
Wye Clo. N35 111
Wyedale Rd. LL25 65
Wyk Gro. HH26 64
Wyke Cop S 6 7
Wyke La. S 5 7
Wykeham Way P29 73
Wyken Gro. HH26 64
Wykham St. P29 73
Wyllin Rd. X24 44
Wylva Av. O23 39
Wylva Rd. R30 74
Wyncroft Clo. EE37 135
Wyncroft Rd. EE37 135
Wyncroft St. R35 113
Wyndale Clo. U35 114
Wyndcote Rd. U34 114
Wyndham Av. X32 98
Wyndham Rd. J30 70
Wynne Rd. FF26 63
Wynnstay Av. S19 28
Wynnstay Rd. C33 88
Wynnstay St. R34 113
Wyre Rd. Q29 73
Wyres Court Rd. V30 76
Wyresdale Av. P 7 10
Wyresdale Av., St.H. FF25 63
Wyresdale Rd., W.Lan. R25 56
Wythburn Cres. HH25 64
Wyvern Rd. G33 90

Yarcombe Clo., Know. Z36 117
  Walk Way
Yardley Dr. O40 142
Yardley Rd. Y24 44
Yarrow Av. T20 29
Yates Ct. BB30 79
Yates St. Q34 112
Yeadon Wk. X39 136
Yellow House La. O 6 5

Yelverton Clo. Z36 117
Yelverton Rd., Liver. S29 74
Yelverton Rd., Wirr. M35 110
Yeoman Cotts. C34 106
Yeoman Fold Y34 116
Yew Bnk. V33 97
Yew Tree Av., St.H. HH30 82
Yew Tree Clo., Liver. W30 76
Yew Tree Clo., Wirr. H36 108
Yew Tree La. T20 29
Yew Tree La. W30 76
Yew Tree La., Wirr. B36 105
  Grange Rd.
Yew Tree Rd., Huy. Y33 98
Yew Tree Rd., Know. Y37 132
Yew Tree Rd., Liver. V35 115
Yew Tree Rd., More. G32 90
Yew Tree Rd., Walt. R27 56
Yew Tree Rd., Wirr. N39 127
Yew Way G32 90
Yewdale Av. GG24 48
Yewdale Pk. L35 110
Yewdale Rd. R27 56
Yewtree Av., Newt. NN27 66
Yewtree Grn. U23 42
York Av., Cros. M23 38
York Av., Liver. S34 113
York Av., S.Port O 6 5
York Av., W.Kirby B36 105
York Av., Wirr. M32 92
York Clo. FF27 63
York Pl., Liver. Q30 73
York Pl., St.H. FF27 63
  Lowe St.
York Rd. S. OO24 52
York Rd., Crosby N23 39
York Rd., Formby K15 16
York Rd., Halton EE37 135
York Rd., Know. AA31 99
York Rd., Mag. S22 41
York Rd., S.Port N 7 9
York Rd., Wigan OO24 52
York Rd., Wirr. M32 92
York St. M25 53
York St., Beb. P38 128
York St., Birk. N34 111
York St., Gars. V39 131
York St., Liver. P33 94
York St., Sefton Q27 55
York Ter. Q30 73
York Way, Know. AA31 99
York Way, Liver. V39 131
Yorkaster Rd. V36 115
Youatt Av. CC31 100
Youens Way W31 97
Yvonne Clo. OO22 52

Zetland Av. T34 114
Zetland Rd., Birk. M34 110
Zetland Rd., Wall. K29 70
Zetland St. P 5 6
Zig Zag Rd., Liver. V30 76
Zig Zag Rd., Wirr. L30 71